PROSE AND POETRY FOR CANADIANS

ADVENTURES

Authorized for use in the schools of Alberta

*Approved by the Protestant Committee of the Council of Education
for the Province of Quebec*

PROSE AND POETRY

ADVENTURES

FOR CANADIANS

Edited by
J. W. CHALMERS
Inspector of High Schools,
Edmonton, Alberta

H. T. COUTTS
Faculty of Education,
Edmonton, Alberta

General Editors
J. KENNER AGNEW
FLOY WINKS DELANCEY
MARION T. GARRETSON
SUSAN B. RILEY

Designed and Illustrated by
GUY BROWN WISER
W. REDVERS STARK

J. M. DENT & SONS (CANADA) LIMITED

In This Series

PROSE AND POETRY FOR CANADIANS

Journeys (7th year)
Adventures (8th year)
Enjoyment (9th year)

The Prose and Poetry Series

Prose and Poetry for Appreciation (10th year)
Prose and Poetry of America (11th year)
Prose and Poetry of England (12th year)

This Canadian edition is made
possible by kind permission of,
and by a special arrangement with

THE L. W. SINGER COMPANY, INC.
Syracuse, N.Y.

Copyright 1951 in Canada,
by
J. M. Dent & Sons (Canada) Limited

Fifteenth Printing, March, 1967

•

PRODUCED AND MANUFACTURED IN CANADA
BY
THE HUNTER ROSE CO. LIMITED

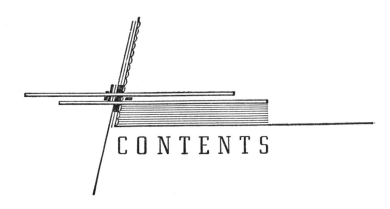

CONTENTS

UNIT I. ADVENTURES NEAR

1. People and Places

Art Appreciation

2. Animal Trails

The asterisks indicate poems and songs.

UNIT V. ADVENTURES IN NEW INTERESTS

1. Romance and Reality

Art Appreciation

2. Beholding the World with New Eyes

UNIT VI. ADVENTURES IN UNDERSTANDING

1. Understanding Other People

Art Appreciation

2. Learning to Know Ourselves

3. For Further Reading: Adventures in Understanding

APPENDIX

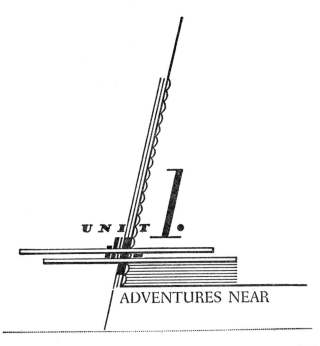

UNIT 1.

ADVENTURES NEAR

How big is the world you live in? Have you travelled widely in your own country, enjoying life in the towns and cities, finding new interests in the fields and forests, and making new friends everywhere? Or have you been a stay-at-home, doing the same things with the same people every day in the same old ways?

No matter which of these descriptions fits you, there are adventures ahead. You may not be free to travel, but that is no real handicap. In these pages you will find new and exciting companions and experiences, both, in this country and in lands across the sea. All you need' to do is to accept and enjoy them.

Let us begin then, our new adventures. For a while we will go here and there among the familiar scenes of our homeland. Then we will streak away through time and space, gathering thrills, friends, and understanding as we go.

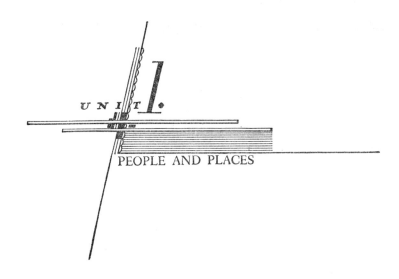

UNIT 1.

PEOPLE AND PLACES

STOLEN DAY* SHERWOOD ANDERSON

IT MUST be that all children are actors. The whole thing started with a boy on our street named Walter, who had inflammatory rheumatism. That's what they called it. He didn't have to go to school.

Still he could walk about. He could go fishing in the creek or the waterworks pond. There was a place up at the pond where in the spring the water came tumbling over the dam and formed a deep pool. It was a good place. Sometimes you could get some good big ones there.

I went down that way on my way to school one spring morning. It was out of my way but I wanted to see if Walter was there.

He was, inflammatory rheumatism and all. There he was, sitting with a fish pole in his hand. He had been able to walk down there all right.

It was then that my own legs began to hurt. My back too. I went on to school but, at the recess time, I began to cry, I did it

* Copyright 1941 by Eleanor Anderson. Reprinted by permission of Harold Ober Associates.

3

when the teacher, Sarah Suggett, had come out into the school-house yard.

She came right over to me.

"I ache all over," I said. I did, too.

I kept on crying and it worked all right.

"You'd better go on home," she said.

So I went.   I limped painfully away.   I kept on limping until I got out of the schoolhouse street.

Then I felt better. I still had inflammatory rheumatism pretty bad but I could get along better.

I must have done some thinking on the way home.

"I'd better not say I had inflammatory rheumatism," I decided. "Maybe if you've got that you swell up."

I thought I'd better go around to where Walter was and ask him about that, so I did—but he wasn't there.

"They must not be biting today," I thought.

I had a feeling that, if I said I had inflammatory rheumatism, Mother or my brothers and my sister Stella might laugh. They did laugh at me pretty often and I didn't like it at all.

"Just the same," I said to myself, "I have got it." I began to hurt and ache again.

I went home and sat on the front steps of our house. I sat there a long time. There wasn't anyone at home but Mother and the two little ones. Ray would have been four or five then and Earl might have been three.

It was Earl who saw me there. I had got tired sitting and was lying on the porch. Earl was always a quiet, solemn little fellow.

He must have said something to Mother for presently she came.

"What's the matter with you? Why aren't you in school?" she asked.

I came pretty near telling her right out that I had inflammatory rheumatism but I thought I'd better not. Mother and Father had been speaking of Walter's case at the table just the day before. "It affects the heart," Father had said. That frightened me when I thought of it. "I might die," I thought. "I might just suddenly die right here; my heart might stop beating."

On the day before I had been running a race with my brother Irve. We were up at the fairgrounds after school and there was a half-mile track.

"I'll bet you can't run a half mile," he said. "I bet you I could beat you running clear around the track."

And so we did it and I beat him, but afterwards my heart did seem to beat pretty hard. I remembered that lying there on the porch. "It's a wonder, with my inflammatory rheumatism and all, I didn't just drop down dead," I thought. The thought frightened me a lot. I ached worse than ever.

"I ache, Ma," I said. "I just ache."

She made me go in the house and upstairs and get into bed.

It wasn't so good. It was spring. I was up there for perhaps an hour, maybe two, and then I felt better.

I got up and went downstairs. "I feel better, Ma," I said.

Mother said she was glad. She was pretty busy that day and hadn't paid much attention to me. She had made me get into bed upstairs and then hadn't even come up to see how I was.

I didn't think much of that when I was up there, but when I got downstairs where she was, and when, after I had said I felt better and she only said she was glad and went right on with her work, I began to ache again.

I thought, "I bet I die of it. I bet I do."

I went out to the front porch and sat down. I was pretty sore at Mother.

"If she really knew the truth, that I have inflammatory rheumatism and I may just drop down dead any time, I'll bet she wouldn't care about that either," I thought.

I was getting more and more angry the more thinking I did.

"I know what I'm going to do," I thought; "I'm going to go fishing."

I thought that, feeling the way I did, I might be sitting on the high bank just above the deep pool where the water went over the dam, and suddenly my heart would stop beating.

And then, of course, I'd pitch forward, over the bank into the pool and, if I wasn't dead when I hit the water, I'd drown sure.

They would all come home to supper and they'd miss me.

"But where is he?"

Then Mother would remember that I'd come home from school aching.

She'd go upstairs and I wouldn't be there. One day during the year before, there was a child got drowned in a spring. It was one of the Wyatt children.

Right down at the end of the street there was a spring under a birch tree and there had been a barrel sunk in the ground.

Everyone had always been saying the spring ought to be kept covered, but it wasn't.

So the Wyatt child went down there, played around alone, and fell in and got drowned.

Mother was the one who had found the drowned child. She had gone to get a pail of water and there the child was, drowned and dead.

This had been in the evening when we were all at home, and Mother had come running up the street with the dead, dripping child in her arms. She was making for the Wyatt house as hard as she could run, and she was pale.

She had a terrible look on her face. I remembered that.

"So," I thought, "they'll miss me and there'll be a search made. Very likely there'll be someone who has seen me sitting by the pond fishing, and there'll be a big alarm and all the town will turn out and they'll drag the pond."

I was having a grand time, having died. Maybe, after they found me and had got me out of the deep pool, Mother would grab me up in her arms and run home with me as she had run with the Wyatt child.

I got up from the porch and went around the house. I got my fishing pole and lit out for the pool below the dam. Mother was busy—she always was—and didn't see me go. When I got there I thought I'd better not sit too near the edge of the high bank.

By this time I didn't ache hardly at all, but I thought.

"With inflammatory rheumatism you can't tell," I thought.

I had got my line into the pool and suddenly I got a bite. It was a regular whopper. I knew that. I'd never had a bite like that.

I knew what it was. It was one of Mr. Fenn's big carp.

Mr. Fenn was a man who had a big pond of his own. He sold ice in the summer and the pond was to make the ice. He had bought some big carp and put them into his pond and then, earlier in the spring when there was a freshet, his dam had gone out.

So the carp had got into our creek and one or two big ones had been caught—but none of them by a boy like me.

The carp was pulling and I was pulling and I was afraid he'd break my line, so I just tumbled down the high bank holding onto the line and got right into the pool. We had it out, there in the pool. We struggled. Then I got a hand under his gills and got him out.

He was a big one all right. He was nearly half as big as I was myself. I had him on the bank and I kept one hand under his gills and I ran.

I never ran so hard in my life. He was slippery, and now and then he wriggled out of my arms; once I stumbled and fell on him, but I got him home.

So there it was. I was a big hero that day. Mother got a wash-tub and filled it with water. She put the fish in it and all the neighbours came to look. I got into dry clothes and went down to supper—and then I made the break that spoiled my day.

There we were, all of us, at the table, and suddenly Father asked what had been the matter with me at school. He had met the teacher, Sarah Suggett, on the street and she had told him how I had become ill.

"What was the matter with you?" Father asked, and before I thought what I was saying I let it out.

"I had the inflammatory rheumatism," I said—and a shout went up. It made me sick to hear them, the way they all laughed.

It brought back all the aching again, and like a fool I began to cry.

"Well I *have* got it—I *have*, I have," I cried, and I got up from the table and ran upstairs.

I stayed there until Mother came up. I knew it would be a long time before I heard the last of the inflammatory rheumatism. I was sick all right, but the aching I now had wasn't in my legs or in my back.

DISCUSSING THE STORY

Can we not all remember the days when the sunshine, the rippling streams, or the playgrounds seemed so inviting that we were tempted to desert school and chores and spend the time playing? On such days our minds worked overtime inventing schemes to get outdoors. And our reasoning seemed so logical—at least it seemed logical until someone found one little error and we were brought back to reality with a bump. It is because we can see right through the boy's scheme to steal a day from school that this story is amusing. Maybe it wouldn't seem so funny if it were happening to us.

1. Why did having inflammatory rheumatism seem so inviting to the boy? Tell how his scheme developed as he went to school.

2. On the way home the boy's illness seemed to improve. What made it get worse at home? Did the scheme seem to be working out well at this point?

3. Doctors say that people often are ill because they think they are. Do you think the boy really became ill as he thought about his condi-

tion? Did lack of sympathy have anything to do with the way he felt?
Show how the story backs up your view on these questions.

4. What happened to cure the ailment? How did this incident lead
to a breakdown of the whole scheme?

5. As the story ends, the boy is ailing again. What was the cause this
time? Was this ailment a real or imagined one? Explain how you think
the boy felt. Was the stolen day worth the cost?

LITTLE BATEESE 🐝 WILLIAM HENRY DRUMMOND

You bad leetle boy, not moche you care
How busy you're kipin' your poor gran'pere
Tryin' to stop you ev'ry day
Chasin' de hen aroun' de hay—
5   W'y don't you geev' dem a chance to lay?
        Leetle Bateese!

Of on de fiel' you foller de plough
Den w'en you're tire you scare de cow
Sickin' de dog till dey jomp de wall
10   So de milk ain't good for not'ing at all—
An' you're only five an' a half dis fall,
        Leetle Bateese!

Too sleepy for sayin' de prayer tonight?
Never min' I s'pose it'll be all right
15   Say dem tomorrow—ah! dere he go!
Fas' asleep in a minute or so—
An' he'll stay lak dat till de rooster crow,
        Leetle Bateese!

Den wake us up right away toute suite
20   Lookin' for somet'ing more to eat,
Makin' me t'ink of dem long leg crane

2. GRANDPÉRE—Grandfather.
19. TOUTE SUITE—Immediately.

Soon as dey swaller, dey start again,
I wonder your stomach don't get no pain,
                              Leetle Bateese!

25 But see heem now lyin' dere in bed,
    Look at de arm onderneat' hees head;
    If he grow lak dat till he's twenty year
    I bet he'll be stronger dan Louis Cyr
    An' beat all de voyageurs leevin' here,
30   Leetle Bateese!

    Jus' feel de muscle along hees back,
    Won't geev' heem moche bodder for carry pack
    On de long portage, any size canoe,
    Dere's not many t'ing dat boy won't do
35 For he's got double-joint on hees body too,
                              Leetle Bateese!

    But leetle Bateese! please don't forget
    We rader you're stayin' de small boy yet,
    So chase de chicken an' mak' dem scare
40 An' do w'at you lak wit' your ole gran'pere
    For w'en you're beeg feller he won't be dere—
                              Leetle Bateese!

29. VOYAGEURS—French-Canadian boatmen.
33. PORTAGE—Stretch of land between two navigable bodies of water, over which canoes or boats and cargoes must be carried.

CLUES TO MEANING

If you have read other selections by William Henry Drummond, you will realize that the poet is not imitating a French-Canadian dialect, but rather the language which a French-Canadian with limited knowledge of English would use in speaking to a person with no understanding of French.

ENJOYING THE POEM

1. Humour is often most appreciated when it is contrasted with pathos, which is that quality which arouses feelings of pity or sadness. How is that contrast achieved in this poem?

2. What details in this poem reflect the French-Canadian culture, or way of life?

3. Do you think Little Bateese was a real boy, or just the poet's idea of a boy? Why?

OTTAWA BEFORE DAWN 💠 D. C. SCOTT

THE stars are stars of morn; a keen wind wakes
The birches on the slope; the distant hills
Rise in the vacant North; the Chaudière fills
The calm with its hushed roar; the river takes
5   An unquiet rest, and a bird stirs, and shakes
The morn with music; a snatch of singing thrills
From the river; and the air clings and chills.
Fair, in the South, fair as a shrine that makes
The wonder of a dream, imperious towers
10   Pierce and possess the sky, guarding the halls
Where our young strength is welded strenuously;
While in the East, the star of morning dowers
The land with a large tremulous light, that falls
A pledge and presage of our destiny.

KEYS TO ENJOYMENT

Pleasure unspoiled by the commotion of man's activity is the reward of those who arise before dawn and focus their attention on the sights, the sounds, and the odours of the world about them. We may all experience this thrill if we have the desire. Duncan Campbell Scott was sensitive to this pleasure as he observed Ottawa at this early morning hour.

1. What were the things Scott saw and heard as he observed Ottawa before dawn?

2. What does he mean in the lines:

> "imperious towers
> Pierce and possess the sky, guarding the halls
> Where our young strength is welded strenuously . . ."?

3. Discuss the form of this poem. In what ways does the form affect the way in which the poet's ideas are presented?

QUEBEC ✿ JEAN BLEWETT

Quebec, the grey old city on the hill,
Lies with a golden glory on her head,
Dreaming throughout this hour so fair, so still,
Of other days and her beloved dead.
5   The doves are nesting in the cannon grim,
The flowers bloom where once did run a tide
Of crimson when the moon rose pale and dim
Above a field of battle stretching wide.
Methinks within her wakes a mighty glow
10   Of pride in ancient times, her stirring past.
The strife, the valour of the long ago
Feels at her heart-strings. Strong and tall and vast
She lies, touched with the sunset's golden grace,
A wondrous softness on her grey old face.

KEYS TO ENJOYMENT

Quebec has an older history than has Ottawa. This poem pictures the city as if it were an older person looking back in memory upon the scenes of times long past.

1. How does the poet suggest the age of the city?

2. What events of the past does the poet associate with Quebec?

3. Compare the form of this poem with that of the poem "Ottawa Before Dawn."

4. Poetry sometimes uses personification to attribute to inanimate things the characteristics of human beings. Discuss the use which the poet makes of personification in this poem.

BETWEEN THE DARK AND THE DAYLIGHT 🦋 NANCY HALE

THIS was the bed where Sara had always been put when she was sick—not her own bed, narrow and tidy against the wall of her room, among her own books, her own furniture, so well known to her that she did not see them any more. This bed was different. This was the guest-room bed, a double bed with white-painted iron from head to foot. All her fifteen years she had been put here when she had a cold or tonsillitis or measles. It was higher, and broader, and softer than her own bed, and being here pulled her back to the books she had read when she had been sick, or that

had been read to her; to the long, unlaboured trains of fantasy that had swung in her mind like slow engrossing ocean swells.

Within the enchantment of the bed in the guest room her mind was released over centuries and into palaces and into the future, and she could alter her person from small to tall, from quiet to commanding. In this bed she had been by turns a queen, a Roman, a man during the Massacre of St. Bartholomew.[1] Here she had imagined herself grown up and having five children, had given them names and learned their separate faces and spoken to them and punished them. She had always dreamed in this bed of new things and new feelings. She had never reached backward for anything within her own experience.

She had not been sick in several months, but she had bronchitis now, and since she had been sick last something had dropped away from her. She had changed. Without questioning what was happening to her, or even being conscious of it, she had stopped playing in brooks and running fast in sneakers and wearing her hair in two pigtails. In these autumn months the girls she played with had changed too. They bought sodas in the drugstore. They walked slowly, eternally, along the tarred New England sidewalks, with their arms around each other's waists. Suddenly they would laugh together helplessly for a moment; at what, they did not know. They cut their hair and curled it, or brushed it out smooth and tied a hair ribbon around it. They watched themselves pass in the shop windows of the town. And all of it had come like a natural change and occupied her fully.

It was not that she turned her head away from one side and looked towards the other. The old things she had known so many years now stood still without a sound to call her as they used, and until she took sick she did not think of them. But as she lay in the guest-room bed she resented more and more what was happening to her. She did not want to go that way. It all began when she read the Indian book.

After three days her fever went down and she stopped coughing

[1] MASSACRE OF ST. BARTHOLOMEW—The massacre of many thousand Huguenots which began in Paris on St. Bartholomew's Day, August 24, 1572.

so much and was allowed to go from the guest room into her own room, in her nightgown and wrapper, and take books out of the shelves and bring them back to bed. The first day she brought a book of Poe's short stories that she loved, and two of the Little Colonel books and a book about English history, and an old book, that she had not read for years, about Indians and wood lore. Her Uncle Lyman had sent it to her one autumn after he had been at their house for a visit. That was when she was eleven.

He belonged to a mountain-climbing club and took long walks in the woods behind their house and she used to go with him. She felt something wonderful in the way he walked without noise along the smooth brown paths, and liked to walk behind, watching him. When it grew dark early in those fall afternoons he would still follow the path without hesitation.

One afternoon when it was cold and frosty and the sun was setting, they came out on a hillside that ran down to the road. There was a clump of birches at the top and he took a knife out of his pocket and showed her how to cut away a strip of birch bark and then to pare its delicate, pale-pink paper from within. That was Indian paper, he said. He took up a rock with big spots of mica and held it up into the shining of the late sun. "If there was someone over on that far hill, I could signal to him with this," he said, "if we were Indians."

What he had said about the Indians filled her mind after he was gone. Through the winter and through the spring she went to the woods. In the winter it was only in the afternoons that she could go, late, after she got home from school. But when the spring came there was more time; it didn't get dark so early. She found a pool beside a rock, covered with green slime, and at the edges the ice water was full of the blobs of transparent jelly that held a million black spots: frogs' eggs. She took them home with her in a tin lard pail and put them in a glass bowl, to watch the polliwogs hatch out. They turned from eggs to tadpoles, to strange creatures with a tail and two legs. And one morning they jumped out of the bowl and hopped about the dining-room floor and had to be thrown out in the garden.

When it was summer she could go all day. She asked for Indian clothes and was given them for her birthday: a fringed coat and skirt, and a leather band for her head, with a feather in it. The skirt had a pocket on the side, where she carried her lunch, done up in waxed paper. When she was alone, on the long paths that had been there for a hundred years and led, if you could follow them, to the other states, to other woods and meadows miles away, she was satisfied and at home. She lived within her own private world—this world with a pine-needle floor, peopled by the shadow shapes of men who moved without noise, surmounted by tall plumes. This world was beautiful and intricate and still. The ground pine ran along under the dead leaves in secret; the shallows of the little ponds were filled with minute and busy life, tiny fish and frogs and "rowboats" that skittered across the slimy surface into the shade. The grouse hid in the underbrush, and the small animals, the rabbits and the sudden moles, ran at intervals across the path, into the sunlight and out of it.

When she went home late in the afternoons it was walking out of one world into another. It required a readjustment of the hearing. From the minute sounds of the woods to which she was acute all day, she walked down along the road past the cultivated meadows, where the sounds were bolder—loud crickets and the long squeal of cicadas [2]—past the hunting dogs that were penned up behind the neighbour's house and barked at all passers, past the hired man putting his tools away in the barn.

Finally there was the house, and she would have supper with her mother and father. In a cotton dress and socks and sneakers, she would sit at the round table and talk and eat and watch the sun going down at last through the west window. The door stood open on the garden and the smell of early-evening grass, the sound of birds, came in as they finished supper. Much later, when she was going to bed, she would kneel down on the floor in her room and crane her head far out of the window to smell the smell that came across the fields, to see through the light summer night the dark,

[2] CICADAS (sǐ-kā'dáz)—Large insects, better known as locusts or harvest flies, which produce long shrill notes by vibrating certain sound organs on the underside of the abdomen.

irregular silhouette against the sky; that was the smell and shape of the woods.

But somehow it had sifted away, melted into the next year of her life, and become like a streak of old colour in the long stream of being alive. Now, as she read that book, which had been a Bible to her, everything she had been doing for months seemed dingy and dull and unbeautiful. The Indian book awoke in her the recollection of the woods and being in the woods. For the first time in her life, now in this bed, she thought longingly of something that she had already experienced. She felt her mind entering the woods and inhabiting them again. She had never finished with the woods, she decided. She had left them for no reason, and when she was well again she would go back to them. That was what she wanted. She did not know why she had penetrated that other world, the new, sharp, bright-lit life that she had begun lately, but it was not what she wanted. She did not want to grow up and be with people. It was not suited to her, and she rejected it now, lying free to choose in bed.

She lay with her legs spread comfortably beneath the smooth, cool sheet and stared sightless at the bare yellow-and-white buttonwood branches outside her window. Trays were brought to her and she ate thin soup with lemon in it, and hot buns, and scrambled eggs, and ice cream. The sunshine moved regularly across the floor of the guest room, from beside her bed in the morning to the farthest corner by the window at sunset. Then it disappeared and twilight filled the room. In the house across the road the lights went on for supper and the lights went out for sleep.

She was in bed six days and at the end of that time she got up. She saw things again vertically and shook herself like a dog and went outside on the side porch, where the November sunshine lay in pale, lemon-coloured stripes. The outdoors smelled sharp and sunny, and her muscles came to life and itched to move. She ran down through the garden to the apple tree and climbed it as she had always done for years, up through its round, rough, pinky-grey branches to a crotch high up, where she sat and surveyed the land. The swamp lay beyond, all still and golden. The apple trees round her were not as high as this one, and she could look down into them.

Across the fields the white farmhouse let a thin stream of smoke up through its chimney, where it wavered and turned blue and vanished into the chilly blue sky. The air smelled of late autumn; the air smelled of dead leaves; the air was sharp and lively and wishful. Sara sat in the tree and swung her legs and thought about nothing until somebody called her and she looked down. It was her friend Catherine, who lived in the farmhouse. She stood under the tree and squinted her eyes up at Sara.

"Hi!" Sara said.

"You all well?"

"Sure!"

"Let's go for a walk!"

"O. K."

She clambered down the tree and they left the orchard and started to walk down the road to the town, along the lumpy sidewalk made of tar and pebbles. The trees beside the road were bare and clean, and the sky was blue, and the cars drove by gaily. In this November day there was a feeling of activity and of happiness, the brisk, anticipatory feeling of winter coming. Sara and Catherine put their arms around each other's waists and strolled, smiling and talking about what had been happening in school, and about boys.

It was exciting to talk about school.

Talking about it, Sara smelled the smell of the classroom, of new, freshly sharpened lead pencils. The impetus of living took hold of her and she was eager and ready for it. She looked at Catherine's plaid wool skirt switching beside her own blue one, casting a thin, swaying shadow on the sidewalk. They strolled on into the town. All the plate-glass windows of the stores glittered in the sun and there was a busy air about the town, of things to be done, of putting on storm doors, of settling down to wait for the winter. They passed Tracey's newsstand, where the boys stood in a group looking around. Catherine waved and Sara looked over her shoulder.

"Ha ya?" the Tracey boy said.

"Ha ya doing?" Sara said. She and Catherine laughed lightly, meaningly, and walked on down the street to the drugstore. They went inside and sat at one of the black glass-topped tables with triangular seats. The store smelled of soda and drugs and candy. The soda clerk walked over to their table.

"What are you having?" he asked.

"Chocolate float," Catherine said.

"Chocolate float, too," Sara said.

It was somehow delightful in the drugstore, full of promise and undisclosed things. To sit, elbows on the damp black glass, and watch the solid glass door and the people who went in and out was somehow exciting. Sara looked at the other customers out of the corners of her eyes, wisely with poise, and drank her drink through a straw without looking down at it.

"Gee, I'm glad you're over that old bronchitis," Catherine said.

"Gee, so am I."

"I thought you'd never be out. You must have been in the house a whole week."

"Pretty near."

"Don't you just *hate* being sick?"

"I certainly do. Just lying there in bed."

"My mother's going to buy me four new dresses for school. She said I could pick them out myself."

"That's keen. My mother says. . ."

Sara went on talking, eagerly, with satisfaction. She was glad to be well and out and doing things. She felt new vistas opening up before her: school, the girls at school, boys, and beyond that unimaginable things, growing up. For an instant her thought trembled alone, apart from what she was saying.

She thought it was nice to be well and going on with living. It was horrid to be sick and just lie and think. Then her mind switched away from that, the inaction of it, and back into the occupying present, and was happy.

DISCUSSING THE STORY

1. If one is not too sick, a short illness is a mildly pleasant experience. There is time to read, or listen to the radio, or just daydream. What kind of daydreams had the girl in this story enjoyed during brief periods

of illness in her childhood? Tell how your own experience has been like hers—or different from it.

2. When we are well we are usually too busy to spend long hours thinking about things we have done in the past. What reminded Sara of the pleasant experiences she had had in the woods? Tell about the sights, and smells, and special things about the woods that she enjoyed. Why had she given up going to the woods?

3. Sara's resolve to resume her old interests faded away when she was well again. It was good to be back in the whirl of school, new clothes, romance, and all the happy activities of her world. Do you think her feeling was a natural part of the experience of growing up? Tell about some of the interests that absorbed you when you were eleven. What new interests have come into your life since then?

EL PONIENTE* ✮ RUTH COMFORT MITCHELL

BENEATH the train the miles are folded by;
High and still higher through the vibrant air
We mount and climb. Silence and brazen glare;
Desert and sagebrush; cactus, alkali,
5   Tiny, low-growing flowers brilliant, dry;
A vanishing coyote, lean and spare,
Lopes slowly homeward with a backward stare
To jig-saw hills cut sharp against the sky.
In the hard turquoise rides a copper sun.
10   Old hope comes thronging with an urge, a zest;
Beside the window gliding wires run,
Binding two oceans. Argosy and quest!
Old dreams remembered to be dreamed and *done!*
It is young air we breathe. This is the West!

* Reprinted from *Narratives in Verse* by Ruth Comfort Mitchell. Copyright, 1923, D. Appleton & Company. Reprinted by permission of the publishers, Appleton-Century-Crofts, Inc.

CLUES TO THE MEANING

There is much variety on our continent and there are many ways of describing each section. Ruth Comfort Mitchell has chosen to jot down the things she sees and the impressions she feels as she looks out the window from her seat on a west-bound train.

1. Do you think she has given you enough details to tell you what the West is like? What would you add to fill out a description? What details suggest colour? vastness? ruggedness? dryness? wildness?

2. If you wanted to write a poem about your own section of the country, what details would you include?

THE NAVAJO 𝒶 ELIZABETH COATSWORTH

B1   LEAN and tall and stringy are the Navajo,

B2   Workers in silver and turquoise, herders of flocks,

      Their sheep and goats cover the hills like scattered rocks.

B3   They wear velvet shirts, they are proud, they go

   5 Through the sage, upright on thin bright horses.

B1   Their speech is low.

B2   At their necks they gather the black smooth cataract of
      their locks.

      Quick are their eyes and bright as the eyes of a fox.

B1   You may pass close by their encampments and never
      know.

1. NAVAJO—Pronounced năv'á-hō.

CLUES TO THE MEANING

The Navajo Indians were once roving hunters and fierce fighters. Then they ranged north of the United States in what is now Canada. However, more than a hundred years ago they moved southward in their search for the buffaloes which then inhabited the south-western plains of America. Finally, after a series of tribal wars, chiefly with the Pueblo Indians of New Mexico and Arizona, they settled down to more peaceful pursuits.

What are the details of the poem that best help you picture the Navajo? How do you know that they are now a quiet and orderly people?

SKI HIGH* 𝒶 B. J. CHUTE

RUSTY MORRIS lay on his back and gazed sombrely at his skis, which were sticking up forlornly from a large bank of snow.

* Reprinted by permission of the author and *Boys' Life*, published by the Boy Scouts of America.

"The trouble," said Rusty in a plaintive voice, "is that *I'm* still attached to 'em. Pete, do something!"

Pete Lester, who was standing by and leaning comfortably on his ski poles, shook his head. "You have to learn how to fall down and get up," Pete pointed out. "It's very important."

Rusty said he had already learned how to fall down, in fact he had learned it so well that he might just as well stay down and be done with it. Pete said he was being defeatist.[1]

"It isn't de feet, it's de skis," said Rusty, and then rolled over hastily to get out of the way of Pete's poles, which were threatening him. "All right, all right," he said a moment later, taking his face out of the snow. "I'll be good. You just tell me how to get out of this mess."

"Get your skis downhill from you," Pete advised. "They're above your centre of gravity now, the way you're lying."

"I have no centre of gravity," Rusty told him sadly. "I lost it halfway down the hill, along with my balance. Boy!" he added, rearing up a little to gaze at the hill he had just come down. "I sure rolled a long way."

Pete grinned slightly. "I'll admit it was a handsome spill," he

---

[1] DEFEATIST—One who admits defeat because victory seems impossible.

said. "Come on, come on. Get your skis under you. You're going back and do that hill again."

Rusty groaned, and began to battle his way out, raising clouds of snow like a fountain. "Why I ever decided to learn to ski—" he grumbled, and then broke off, and sank back into his tunnel. "Oh, oh."

"Now what?"

"Here comes Van Parker," said Rusty. "The World's Greatest Skier—to hear him tell it. Hi, Van."

Van Parker's long legs brought him swiftly and gracefully across the powdery surface, and to Rusty's side. "Did you fall?" said Van.

"Oh, no." Rusty rewarded this remark with a slightly curdled look. "I came out here to play tennis, and I just sat down to rest between sets. What do *you* think?" He turned his head slightly and noted, without surprise, that his right ski had cuddled up to his ear. "I *thought* I was feeling rather double-jointed," he murmured, pleased to have his suspicions confirmed.

"You'll never get up that way, clumsy," Van said, extending an impatient hand. "Here."

Rusty shook his head grimly. "Nope. Thanks just the same. Pete says I should learn how to fall and get up again, and by golly I'm going to. Oopf—ugh!"

Van glanced at Pete with a superior smile. "Oh, Pete does, does he? Since when did you become a teacher, Pete?"

"Two days ago," Rusty answered for his friend. "And just now I almost came down a hill standing up—practically. I can't do a snowplow yet, but I think I've got the plot."

"You're doing very well," Pete said comfortingly.

"You should learn faster than that," Van disapproved. "Why, when I was in the Alps—"

"'Alp, 'alp," said Rusty, sinking backwards again. "Here we go on another personally conducted tour."

But Van had dropped the Alps, struck by another thought. "Suppose *I* teach you, Rusty? You'd learn much quicker and much better." He turned patronizingly to Pete. "No offense," he said. "But of course I *am* the better skier."

"Of course," said Pete dryly, "you are."

They then both looked at Rusty, who was lying flat on his back with his skis waving and his mouth making strange noises. "Well, of all the cast-iron conceit," Rusty began, loyally indignant at this insult to his friend, "you certainly take the gold-spangled chocolate bar. Why, I could learn more from Pete in a day than you could teach me in six months. And who says you're a better skier than Pete is, anyway?"

"Hush, infant," Pete soothed. "Maybe he is. Why don't you take him up, Rusty? You might learn faster, at that."

But Rusty was now quite carried away on a tide of mounting fury, somewhat hampered by his position. He had been hearing a good deal about Van's wonderful skiing the past month or more—from Van himself—and the cool offer to replace Pete paradoxically made him boil.

"Why, in another two weeks," Rusty seethed, "Pete'll practically have me doing high jumps. You certainly have a good opinion of yourself, Mr. High-and-Mighty Parker."

Van shrugged. "Of course, if you don't *want* to learn," he said, "far be it from me to interfere. Only when I was in Switzerland, I took lessons from—"

Indignation succeeded where honest effort had failed. Rusty regained his feet at a single bound. "We've heard *all* about it," Rusty assured him, "about eighty-nine thousand times. Personally, I don't think you're so hot."

"No?" said Van idly.

"No. And what's more I'll prove it to you. Three weeks from now I'll race you down the side of Lookout, and I'll beat you—that's what I'll do."

"Rusty!" Pete wailed, suddenly realizing that he had let this argument run on too long. He was always forgetting Rusty's red hair, which was odd, as it was certainly noticeable.

Van gave a loud laugh of pure derision. "Look at what thinks it can ski!" he chortled sarcastically.

"What I can do after three weeks of Pete's teaching is something else again!" Rusty snapped. "Are you scared to take me up?"

"You aren't serious," Van told him contemptuously. "You're not even a ski-baby yet, much less a racer."

"Laugh away," Rusty invited. "Is it a bet, or are you scared you'll get licked?"

Van made a slight gesture. "If you want to be shown up for an idiot," he murmured, "who am I to stand in your way?" He began to laugh heartily, throwing his blond head back and giving every indication of tremendous amusement.

Rusty, roused, started to express himself, but one of his skis was on an icy patch and, as he moved suddenly, it deserted him. The other stayed where it was, and Rusty, torn between them and wailing like a hoot owl, went over backwards.

"Look who's going to beat *me*," said Van. "The World Famous Teacher and Student—what a combination!" He put his weight suddenly on his poles, sprang into the air in a graceful geländesprung,[2] and, coming down lightly, glided away, his amused laughter floating back to them.

Rusty propped himself up with his elbows behind him and stared after Van's departing figure.

"What ever possessed you?" Pete groaned. "Of all the crazy idiotic, dim-witted, chuckle-headed—"

"I know, I know." Rusty struggled gamely for a moment, and finally sat upright. "Only he makes me so wild—" He gave a violent shudder. "Pete, did I actually say I'd race him down the side of Lookout?"

"You did."

"Holy smoke," said Rusty, awed. "The motto of the Morrises: Talk first and think afterwards. Boy, oh boy," and he sank back into the snow.

"You said it," Pete agreed with unkind readiness.

Rusty gave a low, wondering whistle. "When will I ever learn to keep my mouth shut?" he mourned. "Pete, ol' pal, something tells me we've got a busy three weeks ahead of us."

One bright afternoon a week later, Rusty crawled out from under

[2] GELÄNDESPRUNG (gĕ-lĕn'dĕ-shproŏng)—A jump, usually made over an obstacle.

a large bush, where he had spontaneously come to rest, and re-marked gloomily that stem-turning was his idea of first-degree insanity, and that if Pete would kindly have him incarcerated,[8] he, Rusty, would be very much obliged.

Pete brushed some snow off his friend and slapped him cheer-fully on his back. "If you'd get over that trick of weighting the wrong ski," he said mildly, "you'd get along much better. Natu-rally, you start going in the wrong direction, and that excites you, and then you—"

"Wrap myself around the nearest bush," Rusty agreed. "Listen, I have enough trouble just coming down a hill standing up, with-out trying to do squeegees at the same time. Do you realize I've hardly got a whole bone left?"

"Go up and do that lifted stem-turn," said Pete unsympatheti-cally.

Rusty turned pale. "That's the nasty one where you wind your-self around your pole, isn't it? Like a blooming grapevine. I don't like that one at all, I don't."

"You'll need it coming down Lookout," Pete assured him brightly. "It's the safest and most practical way of taking very steep slopes where there are obstacles—"

Rusty swallowed hard. "Very steep? Obstacles?"

"Certainly," said Pete. "You know what Lookout's like, don't you? I mean, you've seen the trail?"

Rusty shook his head. "Just in summer. It didn't look danger-ous then."

Pete clutched at his head. "No wonder you made that screwy bet with Van!" he yowled. "If you'd ever seen it—Look, Rusty, my idea is for you to take the whole trail just as carefully as you can, of course—I'm not expecting you to come in more than two hours behind Van—but, even if you take it slow—well, I mean, there *are* places where you *can't* go slow. Shambles Corner, for instance."

"Gluk," said Rusty. "*What* corner?"

"Shambles Corner," Pete said again. "It's—"

Rusty waved a feeble hand. "Don't tell me," he begged. "I can

[8] INCARCERATED (ĭn-kär'sẽr-ȧt-ĕd)—Put in prison.

guess." He looked up at the hill he had just come down and which he had thought quite steep enough, and shook his head. "Look," he managed finally, "if you ever see me making a bet like this again, will you hit me gently but firmly over the head with a hammer?"

"It'll be a pleasure," Pete told him politely. "Now get on up there and try that lifted stem-turn again."

Rusty turned and started up the hill, muttering, "Shambles Corner, huh?" in a fatalistic manner. When he got high enough up for practice purposes, he turned and waved to Pete.

Pete shouted, "Pretend that patch of icy snow there is an obstacle, and make your turn just before you reach it."

Rusty nodded and shoved off.

"Skis like a poker," said Pete to himself sadly, and yelled, "Relax!" in a constructive manner.

Rusty tried to obey and succeeded so well that he relaxed right down into the snow and had to start over again. This time Pete gave no advice, and Rusty arrived within striking distance of the ice patch, unweighted his inside ski, and stuck his pole into the snow, intending to use it as a pivot as he had been shown.

However, as usual, he timed it wrong, stuck the pole in too soon, got it caught between his legs, tried to turn anyhow, gave an outraged squawk, and, falling backwards onto his skis, rode the rest of the way downhill in restful splendour.

"That was very pleasant," said Rusty, getting up, "and it gives me an idea. Why can't I come down Lookout that way?"

Pete gave him a long look. "I should like to see you turn those corners sitting on your skis," he said finally. "You know something?"

Rusty ignored him, still pursuing his inspiration. "I could attach a little motor and a steering wheel," he said wistfully. "Pete, must I learn that nasty lifted stem-turn? It gives me the jitters."

"I think," said Pete slowly, also pursuing his own line of thought, "that it would be a very good thing for you to climb Lookout with me right now, and take a look at that trail. We won't ski—we'll walk."

When they came back, quite late. Rusty was inclined toward a thoughtful, not to say profound, silence. Finally, he drew a deep breath and said, "Which one was it that you called Suicide Curve, Pete?"

"The one with the outside bank," said Pete, feeling a certain sympathy for his pupil.

Rusty took another deep breath. "And Parachute Jump was the one that ended among the rocks that you said I'd have to miss, wasn't it?"

Pete nodded. "It's not much of a jump," he said, trying to be consoling. "Not more than six feet."

"Not more than six feet," Rusty repeated meditatively. "A mere nothing—a mere little twiddle through the air, and there you are. Look, Pete."

"Huh?"

"We never said anything in this bet about following the trail, did we? Why couldn't I come down some different way?" There was a long silence. "Aren't you listening?" Rusty demanded finally. "I said—"

"I was listening," said Pete. "Rusty, my poor fellow, I hate to break it to you, but when they cut the Lookout run they chose the easiest way of coming down, so as to make it a safe trail."

Rusty gave a gulp and shut his eyes. "Oh," he said. "How very, very cute." He was silent for a while, brooding, and then he said, "Safe trail, huh? Personally, I'd just as lief come down the side of a skyscraper."

"Ski-scraper," Pete suggested.

Rusty opened one eye and gave his friend a very pained look. "That isn't funny," he complained. "It's gruesome."

"Remember the motto of the Morrises," Pete encouraged him.

"The motto of the Morrises," said Rusty, "has been changed, by popular request. From now on it's: Look before you leap, and then take the elevator."

Word had got around of the stupendous skiing race to be held between Rusty Morris and Van Parker, and a considerable number of spectators stood in the snow at the bottom of Lookout and cheered impartially as Rusty and Van started the upward climb.

Pete had decided to wait for Rusty at the bottom, on the perfectly sound theory that he would certainly be needed if Rusty ever arrived, and Rusty had bid him a fond and touching farewell.

The two racers climbed Lookout in an unsociable silence, which was very hard on Rusty, because when he was nervous he was also inclined to be chatty, and on this occasion could have talked down three debating teams and a political convention with both hands tied behind him. As it was, his only comment—a dull one about the weather—elicited nothing more than a superior sort of grunt.

When they reached the top, however, Van condescended to speak.

"It's two minutes before the hour," he said, glancing at his wrist watch. "Check your watch by mine, and we'll both shove off on the hour exactly."

Rusty, whose knees were swaying in the wind, gulped and nodded.

"Sure you want to go through with this?" said Van, amusedly.

Rusty, who was perfectly sure he didn't want to do anything of the kind, drew himself up loftily. "Certainly," he said. "Why? You trying to back out?"

The only response to this effort at a retort was a short, sharp laugh full of self-confidence, and Rusty looked again at his watch. The second hand moved in little nervous jerks, and Rusty felt a brotherly sympathy toward it. What he knew about nervous jerks would have filled an encyclopaedia.

Van gave a shout. "See you in a couple of hours," he jeered, and, pushing off, whizzed over the brow of the first hill on the run, fine snow crystals fanning out behind him.

He vanished from sight almost at once, and Rusty remembered with a hollow feeling that the first hill was more or less of a drop-off. "Oh, my!" said Rusty miserably, and pushed one ski cautiously out ahead of him.

His original plan had been to close his eyes tight and shove off before he had too much time to think about it. Now, having made the initial mistake of approaching the question with his eyes wide open, he arrived at the brow of the hill with all the stately speed of a home-loving snail.

"Golly!" said Rusty, peering dismally over the edge, and backed up. Maybe there *was* an easier way down—maybe Pete was wrong —maybe . . .

He turned and went in the opposite direction in a paralyzed kind of way, with the idea of taking just one little look, but when he got to the only other possible take-off, he shuddered and turned pale.

There was a straight drop of some thirty feet, and beyond that an uninviting collection of trees. Rusty turned to leave.

What happened next was never quite clear in his mind. One moment, he was safely, if unhappily, leaving the edge of the hill. The next, the snow under his feet had crumbled and shelved, and he was flying through the air with his skis windmilling in all directions and his poles stabbing the sky in wild abandon.

Like a disorganized comet, he sped through space. Above him was the calm summit of Lookout, which seemed suddenly a very desirable place to be. Below him was a smooth, spotless blanket of deep snow.

It was not destined to remain so long. By good luck the snow had drifted heavily under the lee of the hill, and Rusty sailed in a thoroughly disorganized manner straight into the centre of a ten-foot pile, which broke his fall but effectively removed him from the landscape.

For a while there was nothing to be seen except a white expanse of snow with a large hole in it. After a while, a gloved hand appeared through the top of this hole, clutching a ski pole, and a moment later this was followed by a thatch of bright red hair.

The rest of Rusty appeared eventually like a conservative groundhog investigating rumours of sun. "Whoosh," said Rusty, making swimming motions to bring himself to the top. "Splush—foogle." He blew snow in all directions and struggled valiantly to get his skis under him again and himself on top of the snow, having a splendid opportunity to put all Pete's good advice about getting up after a fall into practice.

"Leaping hyenas!" he snorted, mastering his skis at last and beginning to dig snow out from up his sleeves and down his neck. "Some fun! What happens next?"

He gazed up at his starting place, and decided there was no getting back there again, even if he had wanted to. Then he looked below him, and gave a gratified exclamation. True, there were trees, but from here on, the hill apparently dropped in a gentle, humane slope. It had been avoided for the trail, of course, he assured himself, because of the bad beginning—here he permitted himself a shudder—but from now on it looked almost navigable.

With a light heart, if a slightly shaken collection of bones, Rusty pushed off.

One of the things he hadn't yet had time to learn about skiing was how quickly an innocent-looking slope can turn into a precipice, and with what horrifying speed a skier can gain momentum, once he is off to a good start.

At the beginning, Rusty had even had time to admire the scenery in a hurried sort of way. Within three short seconds, the scenery was flying by so fast that he had no way of proving there was any.

A tree popped up under his nose. He forgot everything Pete had taught him about making turns, gave a convulsive wiggle sideways and a desperate dig with his poles, and felt the tree zig past his left ear with about the hundredth part of a thin shadow to spare.

He would have yelled, but the wind of his flight stuffed the words back down his throat. He passed so close to a rock that the side of his ski actually screeched against it, but he was helpless to turn or stop and the hill kept falling away under his feet with increasing speed.

He had just time to think sadly of all the friends he had left behind him and to forgive Van his boasts, when another officious tree got in his way, and this time he had no time for his pole-digging contortions.

He sat backwards abruptly, then was thrown forward by the shock of landing and rolled head over heels down the decline like a wound-up hedgehog, with skis and poles protruding recklessly. Round and round, over and over, bump and bounce he went, until he rolled into a bush, clutched at its saving branches, and pulled himself dizzily erect.

"I think," said Rusty to himself in a weak, flat voice, "I'll sit this one out, thank you just the same."

The branch thought differently and divided in his hand. With a despairing shriek, Rusty felt his skis start downhill again on their mad course. Naturally, Rusty went with them. He had no choice.

The drop-off this time was, as Pete would have said, "only" about ten feet high, but it ended in a blackberry thicket, and the vines took a base advantage of Rusty's helpless condition on arrival and twined themselves around him and around his skis.

He got stiffly to his feet and rubbed the back of his neck, then bent down to unfasten his right ski. He had just kicked his boot loose from the binding when a rabbit shot suddenly across the track in front of him, startling him so that he loosed his hold on the ski, and it skittered down the slope ahead, basely deserting him at a critical moment.

Unconsciously, Rusty made a grab for it, forgetting that he was still on a steep incline, and the movement jerked him loose and started him on a teetering, crazy, one-skied flight. It would have ended in a moment because his dragging foot slowed him, but he fell anyhow, and made the interesting discovery that it is possible to ride a single ski as if it were an extremely narrow sled.

Cheering weakly, he caught up with his runaway ski at the next tree, and decided forthwith to slide the rest of the way on both of them, sitting down in dignity.

"Hold it!" said Rusty to himself, suddenly valiant as he looked ahead. "That doesn't look so bad in front of me." He shook himself gently, to see if any of his bones rattled, and, when nothing happened, he felt encouraged and began recklessly to strap his ski on again.

"All I want," he told himself, "is to get off this hill forever, and the quicker the better."

He gave himself a rash shove, thought better of it, too late as usual, and zoomed off down the hill.

In front of him, suddenly, was a tree. To the left of the tree was a rock. To the right of the tree was a clear open space. Rusty's mind remembered with wonderful clarity all that Pete had taught him about a stem-turn to the right. The unweighted ski swung to the . . .

You stuck your ski out to the . . .

Ah, but which ski?

"A good question," Rusty thought, and in a fleeting instant of intelligence he tried to rationalize the question in his head. Did you weight *toward* the object you wanted to miss, or away from it?

He remembered, desperately, something about an open Christiania. Surely, this was just the place for an open Christy—good, old, open Christy. He tried to get his left foot out, promptly decided it should have been his right foot, tried to get the left one back and the right one out, gave a wild hoot of utter disintegration, and finally, plunging, staggering, and fighting nobly to get his skis back in some sort of relation to each other, he surrendered and dived headfirst into another of his familiar, friendly snowbanks.

This time, when he reappeared looking like Santa Claus after a hard day's work, he got a shock.

It was such a pleasant shock that it took him a moment to believe that it was true. He was at the bottom of Lookout.

He was actually at the bottom of Lookout; so far as he could tell, most of his bones were still with him; and, across the white snow, people were running toward him, waving and shouting in a frantic and irrational manner.

"Rusty! For the love of mud!" Pete had him by the collar and was hauling him out of his cozy little nest. "Say something! Are you all right?"

"No," Rusty croaked crossly. "I'm dead."

"But how'd you get here?" Pete demanded excitedly. "How'd you—"

Rusty heaved a discontented sigh, remembering something. "How many hours ago did Van get in?" he inquired morosely, putting his hand around behind his back and making a cautious experiment with his spinal column.

"Van isn't down yet," said Pete in a bewildered voice as if he suspected everyone's sanity, including his own. "I don't know what became of him." He gave his friend an exasperated shake. "How'd *you* get here?"

Rusty jerked his head toward the hill he had just come down, and then wished he hadn't. His neck seemed to be tied in knots. "Straight down there," said Rusty. "Oh, my neck! Ouch!"

"Straight—down—there?" said several wondering voices at once.

Rusty started to nod, and then decided to forego all exercise involving his neck muscles. He said "Yes" instead, and leaned heavily against Pete.

"Over the drop-off?" said Pete wonderingly. "You can't have! You're crazy."

"Are you telling me?" Rusty retorted bitterly. "However, if you don't believe me, you can go and look at my tracks. I imagine," he added thoughtfully, "they're well worth looking at. Say—" He seized Pete suddenly, forgetting his soreness. "Did you say Van wasn't down yet?"

Pete shook his head, still looking as if he had been hit on it. "No. He's vanished somewhere. I guess you've won the race, but, Rusty, I can't believe—"

"Hi," said an assured voice behind them, and Van Parker skied lightly toward the group, not seeing Rusty, who was behind Pete. "What're all you fellows doing over here? I expected a welcoming committee at the foot of the trail."

"What on earth became of you?" someone demanded. "You took an awfully long time."

Van waved an airy hand and gave an amused laugh. "I waited for Rusty at the end of the first hill. Thought it'd be fun to let him get ahead and then zoom past him." He sounded aggrieved that this delightful pastime had failed to work out according to Hoyle. "In fact, I waited at quite a few different points, but he never turned up, so I finally came down anyhow." He shrugged his shoulders. "He's probably still sitting up on the top of Lookout, trying to warm his cold feet—"

At this moment, Pete moved aside, and Van saw Rusty. His mouth opened, and a strange croaking sound came forth.

After a long time, he managed something that sounded like, "Rusty! What—how—"

"Rusty," said Pete simply, "Rusty took a short cut."

Van goggled hopelessly. "You mean, he—he—came down *there?*"

It was Rusty's turn to wave an airy hand. "A mere nothing," said Rusty, seizing his opportunity. "An interesting little trip, but really a mere nothing."

"In three weeks!" Van was saying dimly. "You learned to ski like that in three weeks!"

"Well," said Rusty, "I had Pete for a teacher. That makes a difference." He couldn't resist the opening. "Of course," he went on solemnly, "if I'd had you, I could probably have learned to do that—" he gestured up at the hill, "in two weeks, or maybe even one and a half. What do you think?"

Van shook his head in awed wonder, then made a gigantic effort to recover himself. "It was a pretty good job," he admitted, "and I guess you won the race, all right. But, of course, it isn't like skiing in the Alps."

Rusty turned to him suddenly. "Tell us about the Alps," he urged enthusiastically. "We all want to hear about the Alps. Do tell us about the Alps."

"In the Alps—" Van began, and then Lookout caught his eye. "No. Never mind the Alps. How'd you take that first drop-off?"

"Well," said Rusty, "I'll tell you. I took it like a bird—just like a bird." He then added in an aside, for Pete's benefit only, "Just like a cuckoo."

Van registered sudden, honest admiration. "I would never have believed it possible," he said. "If you weren't actually here—"

"Skiing is believing," Rusty told him. "The motto of the Morrises—revised."

DISCUSSING THE STORY

1. Anyone who has had any experience in learning how to ski understands very well the difficulty Rusty Morris had in just keeping on his feet. Do you think skiing or any sport can be learned by watching someone else, or must one always learn the hard way? If you enjoy skiing, tell about some of your early experiences.

2. Both Pete and Van were expert skiers. Why did Van think he was a better skier than Pete? Do people like Van annoy you as much as he annoyed Pete and Rusty? Tell why.

3. Sometimes, without quite realizing how, we get ourselves into most uncomfortable situations. Tell how Rusty invited trouble for himself. Since he could not escape with honour from his rash bet, how did Rusty prepare himself for the race?

4. Rusty's wild ride down Lookout slope seems hilariously funny to us. Tell about the part you liked best. Do you think the outcome of the race is too impossible? What, besides the situation itself, makes this story so amusing?

5. Did you understand the skiing terms used in this story? A *snow-plow*, for example, is a term used to describe the double stem for slowing down or stopping. Find the terms *stem turn* and *open Christiania* in the "New Words" section of a dictionary and explain them.

CALGARY OF THE PLAINS 🌾 E. PAULINE JOHNSON

NOT of the seething cities with their swarming human hives,
Their fetid airs, their reeking streets, their dwarfed and
poisoned lives,
Not of the buried yesterdays, but of the days to be,
The glory and the gateway of the yellow West is she.

5   The Northern Lights dance down her plains with soft and
silvery feet,
The sunrise gilds her prairies when the dawn and daylight
meet;
Among her level lands the fitful southern breezes sweep,
And beyond her western windows the sublime old mountains
sleep.

The Redman haunts her portals, and the Paleface treads her
streets,
10   The Indian's stealthy footstep with the course of commerce
meets,
And hunters whisper vaguely of the half forgotten tales
Of phantom herds of bison lurking on her midnight trails.

Not hers the lore of olden lands, their laurels and their bays;
But what are these, compared to one of all her perfect days?
15 For naught can buy the jewel that upon her forehead lies—
The cloudless sapphire Heaven of her territorial skies.

DISCUSSING THE POEM

1. What are some of the attributes of Calgary that arouse Pauline Johnson's admiration? In what ways would you expect the following cities to be different: Vancouver? Winnipeg? Toronto? Montreal? Halifax? What characteristics does each share with Calgary?
2. The people of Alberta are proud to call their home a "next year's country." What does this expression mean? How does the poet indicate this idea in this poem?
3. Calgary of the Plains is evidently a city of rich hues. What colours does the writer mention?
4. The poet contrasts the "level lands" and the "sublime old mountains." What other contrasts can you find?

THE MAGIC CANE ⚑ MARK HAGER

EFFIE's pa's geese never did like me. I never did know why. I couldn't think of any reason why the geese shouldn't like me. But they didn't. From the time I was big enough to walk past Effie's pa's house until I was big enough to carry Effie's books, her pa's geese had nibbled my legs black and blue. And after I started carrying Effie's books, the geese got worse. They'd lay for me along the road and tackle me before I got near the house.

It was getting me into trouble because the geese didn't bother Otis Riley. And with me detouring around Effie's pa's place in order to get to school, it left the road wide open for Otis Riley to walk on by Effie's house and wait for her at the yard gate like I wanted to do. It made my heart ache just to think about Otis Riley having such advantage over me with my girl.

Once I asked Otis. "Does them geese of Effie's pa's ever tackle you?" I said.

"Why, shucks, no," Otis said, and then he looked at me like he was thinking I was some kind of a coward. He explained how you had to let girls and geese and things like that know you ain't afraid of them, and they won't bother you.

But still, I had the feeling Effie was really my girl if I could only get past this flock of geese of her pa's. I had that feeling because she would tag me at playtime at the schoolhouse, and then run around behind the schoolhouse with me after her. Then she'd lean her shoulders against the schoolhouse and put her hands first in front and then behind her and be all fidgety, and say, "You didn't come by to carry my books."

I'd say, "I was late this morning. I had to take the near cut across the ridge."

I didn't want to come right out and tell Effie how I was being bit by this flock of geese of her pa's.

One time she showed me a present she had bought for her pa because it was his birthday. It was a pipe with a crooked stem, and I said, "You know, Effie, I'd kind of like to buy your pa a birthday present."

"Why would you?" Effie asked.

"Oh, just because he's your pa, I reckon." Then I asked her what else besides a pipe did she think her pa would like. Of course Effie knew I did not have any money except nickels and dimes I could wheedle out of my mother the same as she wheedled her nickels and dimes. So she told me her pa had lost his walking cane, and had been searching the hills for another cane like it. She said he fell off the foot-log one day and the cane got loose from him and floated down the creek and he never did hear from it any more.

I said, "Why, honey, that's a small scimption to find your pa another walking cane."

"Not like the one he lost," Effie said. "You see my pa's a man who never did like to bend his back, and after years of searching he found a cane that was crooked in just the right places so that in case he dropped it, he could step on it, and one end would come back up to his hands without him stooping over. And since he lost it and had to use ordinary canes that you have to pick up, he's had no end of trouble with his back."

"Sorry to hear that," I said, "and I still say I can find your pa a cane he can step on and fetch it back up, 'cause I know where there is a ten-acre boundary of dogwood bushes crookeder'n a dog's hind leg. How long have I got to find this cane before your pa's birthday comes up?"

"This is Wednesday," Effie said, "and Pa's birthday comes up Sunday. You got Thursday, Friday, and Saturday—but you can't do it, Joe. No, sir, because Otis Riley's been hunting one for a month and he can't find none like my pa wants. I reckon Otis has fetched him a dozen, and Pa steps on them but they won't come up 'cause they ain't got the right crooks at the right places, so my pa says."

"You'll see me Sunday morning," I told Effie, "and I'll have your pa's cane with just the right crooks in it." The bell rang and we had to get back inside the schoolhouse.

On Thursday and Friday evenings and until late in the night I searched the dogwood thickets. When it got dark I searched with my flashlight, and chopped out canes with my hatchet. I'd trim them up good, and they'd look perfect—not straight anywhere, like a capital S. I'd take a shoulder load of canes home and step on them, but they wouldn't come back up just right. It was about midnight on Saturday night that I brought in the last shoulder load, and after trying them out, I came to one that would come back up from being stepped on at three different places.

I took it to bed with me that night and didn't sleep much for just feeling of the curves and crooks of this cane for Effie's pa. I had a feeling that her pa being a man who did not like to bend his back would appreciate this a lot, and that once I could devise some plan to get by the flock of geese, I would have no trouble in taking Effie away from Otis Riley. . . .

I thought my mother never was going to get up and get breakfast that Sunday morning. It wasn't that I was hungry and wanted to eat. I wanted to get started with Effie's pa's cane, and I did not want to stir up any nosiness by leaving before the rest of the folks got up.

Even as it was, my mother took notice. She wanted to know how I came to get up without her pulling me out of bed. I said just because, and she looked at me like she was wondering could I be losing my mind. She put her finger under my chin and lifted it and said:

"Joe, I have been aiming to ask you something."

I said, "What?"

She said, "Why on earth you been out so much at night lately—and why you carrying in shoulder loads of green dogwood sticks?"

I said, "I'm just hunting me a good cane. With all the bitin' dogs 'tween here and the schoolhouse, a person ought to have a cane."

I don't think she believed that. From the best I could tell, I'd puzzled my mother for the first time in my life, and as I walked down the river road with my cane, I glanced back and saw her standing in the door, watching me.

But I couldn't think about that any more. I had to start looking out for Effie's pa's flock of geese, and when I turned around a bunch of willow bushes, I saw them way down the river road.

They seemed at peace with all the world. They were resting on the ground under a wild-cherry tree, and they all had their heads tucked under their wings except this one old gander—and he had his head up and was looking up and down the river road.

I thought maybe a goose'd be smart enough to know this was Sunday and that I wouldn't be on my way to school.

But anyway, whether they knew it was Sunday or not, the old gander saw me at about the same time I saw him. He let go with a mean honk that echoed far up and down the river. It was enough to wake up every goose in ten miles.

Then the other geese took their heads from under their wings, got up, and huddled around the old gander. It looked like he was the leader of the flock and they took combat orders from him.

They didn't honk loud now, but only huddled and chuckled and muttered. The best I could tell from goose language, they were getting set, and each goose was being told where to bite me on the legs.

They began to whet their bills, and it sounded something like when you whet a mowing scythe with a flint rock. Then they'd try their bills on the grass under the wild-cherry tree.

They came out in the middle of the road where the hot sunshine beat down, and in single file they came to meet me. The old gander led the charge, but he was quiet. I wondered if they kind of dreaded me since I was growing up now, and maybe it wouldn't be so easy to take a billful of the calf of my leg as it used to be— or whether it was a solemn moment like when soldiers start to go over the top or take a machine-gun nest. But of course, I couldn't tell for sure what was passing through the minds of the geese. I only knew the battle was shaping up. They didn't move to the right nor the left, but pressed straight toward me. Once, I stopped and considered.

I decided that there was no reason why a person should keep on being run over by a flock of geese and driven out of the road. This was a public highway, and I had heard people say it was against the law even to shoot a gun across the public highway. I remembered in my history books about men and rulers of nations coming to the end of their patience.

*   *   *

With these thoughts boiling up, and the geese coming at me, I tried Effie's pa's dogwood cane for a swing and balance. My first thought was to stand in the middle of the road and crack the old gander on top of the head with the dogwood cane. But then other thoughts came that kind of upset that plan—thoughts of the hereafter, and turning the other cheek, and the sin of aggressors, and things eternal and in the heavens. I decided if there was to be any sin connected with this battle with this flock of geese, I would wash my hands and put all the blood on the geese.

So I turned and broke to run, and, naturally, that was to the advantage of the geese, 'cause that turns the calves of your legs to them, and that's their choice meat. Besides you can't outrun a goose—they can come up partly on wing, kind of half fly and half run. Pretty soon the old gander had his bill full of the calf of my leg. His reinforcements came up fast, and I half turned, and let him have one little crack on top of the head. He went down and started flopping and bouncing up and down there in the road, and the other geese seemed to quit me and started marching a circle around their dying leader. I stood back and watched.

But I couldn't stand long. No telling who might come in sight. I guessed that maybe that very day Effie's pa might take a notion to count his geese, and me being the only boy in the neighbourhood seen to be up this early of a Sunday morning, there was no telling what the hereafter of the thing might be. So I picked up the old gander and found a hollow stump and put him in it. Then I tried to throw the feathers out of the road where the old warrior had flopped. But you can't do any good throwing feathers, and they floated back at me, and I stuck them in my pocket.

The rest of the geese circled the black stump and quarreled a while and then went off to the river and started to float with the summer blossoms on the water. I started on down the road, but something made me stop and consider. I thought maybe this was not the honourable thing I was doing. Maybe I should go back to the stump and get the dead goose and take it to Effie's pa along with this magic cane. But before I got back to the stump, I remembered something in my history book about another boy who got into trouble on account of a book he had borrowed. It rained on the book and this boy had done the honourable thing and took the wet book back—and he was rewarded for his honesty by being allowed to pull fodder for three whole days for that one book— when there's nobody can help it raining.

*　　*　　*

So, I considered how to make the dead goose turn out to my advantage. I figured with the fighting goose dead in the stump and the others having retreated to swim on the river, the road was practically open for me to walk by Effie's house of mornings and carry her books to school.

But there was one thing that still bothered me. There was still this Otis Riley. It seemed to me that me and Otis both could not be happy with taking turns at carrying Effie's books. I just had to figure some plan out to break Otis Riley away. I remembered what Effie had said about Otis trying so hard to find her pa a back-savin' cane. So I took the cane I had cracked the goose in the head with and ran across the ridge and whistled Otis Riley out of bed. He got up and came out to the fence, stuffing his shirttail in his britches as he came.

The thought struck me not to let Otis see the magic cane until after I had felt him out, and so I hid the cane in the tall weeds.

"Otis," I said, "you know what today is?"

"Sunday," said Otis. "Why?"

"What else besides Sunday?" I asked.

Otis scratched his head. "I don't know," he said.

I said, "Ain't you been searchin' the woods for a birthday present?"

"Oh," said Otis, "it's Effie's pa's birthday. Yeah, her pa has miseries in his back when he stoops over to pick up things, but they ain't such a cane in these mountains as her pa wants."

"They is, too," I said. "I found one. How much'll you give me for it and you can take it to her pa?"

"Shucks, I ain't got no money," Otis said. "Let's see the cane."

Reaching over in the weeds, I got the cane and stepped on it and showed Otis how it was crooked in the right places so as to jump back up in your hand when you stepped on it, and Otis' eyes widened.

"I got my dog, old Bounce," Otis said, "and I got my .22 rifle."

"Aw, I don't aim to hold you up for the cane," I told him. "You can have it cheaper'n your dog or your .22 rifle, and you don't need a penny of money. There. Try it. Step on it."

Otis took the cane and stepped on it and it curled back up to his hands.

"That'd sure be a back-saver for her pa, wouldn't it?" he said.

"Best cane since Moses," I said.

"What I gotta do?" said Otis.

"Only carry a dead goose to Effie's pa," I said, "and give him his cane along with his dead goose. Effie's pa's old gander bit me and I hit him on top of the head with this magic cane. I hadn't any idea a goose was that easy killed. And I was just thinkin' that with you bein' in good standin' with Effie and her pa on account of you been searchin' the woods for a back-savin' cane for him, he wouldn't say a word if you took his dead goose to him."

"Sure," Otis said. "That's easy."

"But remember," I said, "you gotta tell him his gander bit you and you killed him, see?"

Otis scratched his head again. "I ain't sure about that part of it," Otis said. "Ever notice Effie's pa's arms? Big as fence posts and hairy as stumps in a bamboo patch."

"Yeah," I said, "but you're still a minor, Otis. You ain't in six years of bein' a man yet, and it's agin the law for a man to hit a boy, same as it's agin the law for you to shoot across the public highway with your .22 rifle."

Otis said, "Why didn't you take him the goose and the cane?"

"Because," I said. "The flock of geese was layin' for me by the road. You see I ain't liked around their house, not even by the geese, but you got a stand-in down there."

Otis acted a little cold to the idea, and said there was no telling what attitude her pa might take with respect to the dead goose.

"But it could make you great," I said. "Ain't ever been but one other cane like this. Moses had it. Remember? And remember that Pharaoh was Moses' stepgrandpa, and Pharaoh had great magicians who could turn their canes into snakes and make 'em crawl. But know what? Moses went out in the woods and found a cane that he could turn into a snake and it swallowed his grandpa's cane-snakes."

"Where's the dead goose?" said Otis, and I told him in a hollow stump by the road. He tore out back to the house to comb his hair and change his shirt and I waited.

Then we went to the stump and got the dead goose out, and Otis put it across his shoulder, holding it by the feet, and he took the magic cane in the other hand, and I stood and watched him go off down the river road toward Effie's pa's house. I turned and started walking slow back along the river road, thinking I had just done a smart piece of manoeuvring. I figured you had to be pretty crafty to shift a dead goose from your shoulder to the shoulder of somebody else. . . .

It all seemed so good. I just sat down on a mossy rock by the river and for a long time I watched the summertime blossom petals float slow on the still, deep water. I thought of my girl, Effie, and from where I sat, it looked like I had cleared the road. I couldn't imagine anything else but what her pa would blow up when Otis told him he had killed his goose, and that he would run Otis off the place, and tell him to stay off. Under the circumstances, Otis wouldn't be coming by of mornings to carry Effie's books and walk with her to school.

After a long time, I got up and moseyed[1] off slow toward home. It was up toward noon when I got back to the house. The door

---

[1] MOSEYED—Strolled or shuffled.

was locked and my mother was gone. I couldn't imagine what had happened, as she had said nothing about leaving that day.

I could not get in the house, and I was hungry now. I ate some sweet cherries from the tall sweet-cherry tree, and then got down and lay on the ground in the shade of the cherry-tree, and dreamed of my girl, Effie, and the great thing I had done for her pa in finding him a magic cane, with him not even knowing I had found it—and it could always be a secret feeling of a kind in my heart.

But as the day wore on, I got lonesome. I even wondered what had happened down at Effie's that day, and how she and Otis might be spending the day, or had Otis come home yet. I got up and meandered over to Otis' house to whistle him out again, and see if Effie's pa had hit him or run him off.

But when I whistled at Otis' house, nobody answered except Otis' dog, old Bounce. He came out and greeted me, and I played with him a while, and then came back home.

About dark, my mother came home.

"Effie's pa had a birthday today," she said, "and they had him a big birthday dinner, and they called up and wanted me to come have dinner with them, and Otis Riley's folks were all there, and we had the grandest time! They phoned for me to come."

"Did you see Otis and Effie? What were they doing?" I asked.

"Oh, Otis took Effie to church," my mother said. "Effie's pa sure is putting a lot of store by Otis Riley. Know what? Otis killed Effie's pa's old gander this morning, and it sure pleased the old man the way Otis acted about it. Instead of hiding the dead goose like some boys would do, why Otis upped with it on his shoulder and carried it to the old man, which the old man says shows the kind of stuff Otis Riley's got in him.

"And what's more," my mother went on, "Effie's pa had lost his cane, and that boy, Otis Riley, actually searched the woods—just like you did—until he had found the kind of a cane the old man wanted. It's a crooked cane, and the old man showed me how he could step on it and it would jump back up in his hands in case he dropped it, and it saves him the misery of bending his back."

"And didn't he blame Otis none for killing his goose?"

"Goodness no," my mother said. "He and Effie both said they had been expecting somebody would have to knock that old gander in the head, he was so bad to fight, and he said the cane Otis brought him was the most magical cane since the days of Moses. And oh, yes. Here," my mother said, "Here's a sandwich Effie sent you. I know you ain't had a bite to eat today!"

I took the sandwich, and I was hungry in the stomach and in the heart—but I could not swallow a bite of it, for it was roast goose.

DISCUSSING THE STORY

1. The problems of young suitors are sometimes quite serious. Why did the boy in this story have difficulty in making a good impression on his girl? How did he plan to win favour with Effie's father?

2. The best-laid plans often fail to work out right. Tell how the geese spoiled Joe's plan. Why do you think the geese never chased Otis Riley?

3. The boy had to choose between what he knew was the right thing to do and what he thought would work out to his advantage. How did he solve his problem? Tell how his new plan worked out. Have you ever had a similar experience of having a clever scheme backfire? Tell about it.

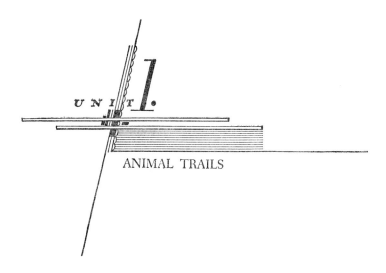

U N I T 1.

ANIMAL TRAILS

THIS IS JODY'S FAWN 🐾 MARJORIE KINNAN RAWLINGS

In the centre of a small pine island in the heart of the Florida scrub lived Penny Baxter and his family. Life was not easy, but the family was happy in its freedom. Then one day tragedy stalked close. Setting out with his son Jody to track some hogs which had been lured away by his neighbours, the Forresters, Penny was bitten by a rattler. Blindly he headed for home, and for once his luck held. In the path before him a doe leaped to her feet. Quickly Penny lifted his shotgun, ran to the stricken doe, and in a moment had slashed her body open and withdrawn the liver and heart. Applying them swiftly to the twin punctures on his arm, he drew out most of the poison. Jody went for Doc Wilson and throughout the long night Penny fought for his life. By dawn they knew he had won. But Jody, his father's safety assured, remembered the small spotted fawn that had gazed so bewilderingly at its dead mother.

JODY allowed his thoughts to drift back to the fawn. He could not keep it out of his mind. It stood in the back of it as close as he had held it, in his dreaming, in his arms. He slipped from the table and went to his father's bedside. Penny lay at rest. His eyes were open and clear, but the pupils were still dark and dilated.

Jody said, "How you comin', Pa?"

"Jest fine, son. Ol' Death gone thievin' elsewhere. But wa'n't it a close squeak!"

"I mean."

Penny said, "I'm proud of you, boy, the way you kept your head and done what was needed."

"Pa—"

"Yes, son."

"Pa, you recollect the doe and the fawn?"

"I cain't never forget 'em. The pore doe saved me, and that's certain."

"Pa, the fawn may be out there yit. Hit's hongry, and likely mighty skeert."

"I reckon so."

"Pa, I'm about growed and don't need no milk. How about me goin' out and seein' kin I find the fawn?"

"And tote it here?"

"And raise it."

Penny lay quiet, staring at the ceiling.

"Boy, you got me hemmed in."

"Hit won't take much to raise it, Pa. Hit'll soon git to where it kin make out on leaves and acorns."

"Dogged if you don't figger the farrest of ary young un I've ever knowed."

"We takened its mammy, and it wa'n't no-ways to blame."

"Shore don't seem grateful to leave it starve, do it? Son, I ain't got it in my heart to say 'No' to you. I never figgered I'd see day-light, come dawn to-day."

"Kin I ride back with Mill-wheel and see kin I find it?"

"Tell your Ma I said you're to go."

He sidled back to the table and sat down. His mother was pouring coffee for everyone.

He said, "Ma, Pa says I kin go bring back the fawn."

She held the coffeepot in mid-air. "What fawn?"

"The fawn belonged to the doe we kilt, to use the liver to draw out the pizen and save Pa."

She gasped.

"Well, for pity sake—"

"Pa says hit'd not be grateful, to leave it starve."

Doc Wilson said, "That's right, Ma'am. Nothing in the world don't ever come quite free. The boy's right and his daddy's right."

Mill-wheel said, "He kin ride back with me. I'll he'p him find it."

She set down the pot helplessly. "Well, if you'll give it your milk—we got nothin' else to feed it."

"That's what I aim to do. Hit'll be no time, and it not needin' nothin'."

The men rose from the table.

Doc said, "I don't look for nothing but progress, Ma'am, but if he takes a turn for the worse, you know where to find me."

She said, "Well. What do we owe you, Doc? We cain't pay right now, but time the crops is made—"

"Pay for what? I've done nothing. He was safe before I got here. I've had a night's lodging and a good breakfast. Send me some syrup when your cane's ground."

"You're mighty good, Doc. We been scramblin' so, I didn't know folks could be so good."

"Hush, woman. You got a good man there. Why wouldn't folks be good to him?"

Buck said, "You reckon that ol' horse o' Penny's kin keep ahead o' me at the plow? I'm like to run him down."

Doc said, "Get as much milk down Penny as he'll take. Then give him greens and fresh meat, if you can get it."

Buck said, "Me and Jody'll tend to that."

Mill-wheel said, "Come on, boy. We got to git ridin'."

Ma Baxter asked anxiously, "You'll not be gone long?"

Jody said, "I'll be back shore, before dinner."

"Reckon you'd not git home a-tall," she said, "if 'twasn't for dinnertime. . . . "

Doc's eyes caught the cream-coloured 'coonskin knapsack.

"Now ain't that a pretty something? Wouldn't I like such as that to tote my medicines?"

Jody had never before possessed a thing that was worth giving away. He took it from its nail and put it in Doc's hands.

"Hit's mine," he said. "Take it."

"Why, I'd not rob you, boy."

"I got no use for it," he said loftily. "I kin git me another."

"Now I thank you. Every trip I make, I'll think, 'Thank you, Jody Baxter.'"

He was proud with old Doc's pleasure. They went outside to water the horses and feed them from the scanty stock of hay in the Baxter barn.

Buck said to Jody, "You Baxters is makin' out and that's about all, ain't it?"

Doc said, "Baxter's had to carry the work alone. Time the boy here gets some size to him, they'll prosper."

Buck said, "Size don't seem to mean much to a Baxter."

Mill-wheel mounted his horse and pulled Jody up behind him. Doc mounted and turned away in the opposite direction. Jody waved after him. His heart was light.

He said to Mill-wheel, "You reckon the fawn's yit there? Will you he'p me find him?"

"We'll find him, do he be alive. How you know it's a he?"

"The spots was all in a line. On a doe-fawn, Pa says the spots is ever' which-a-way. . . ."

Jody gave himself over to thoughts of the fawn. They passed the abandoned clearing.

He said, "Cut to the north, Mill-wheel. Hit were up here Pa got snake-bit and kilt the doe and I seed the fawn."

"What was you and your daddy doin' up this road?"

Jody hesitated. "We was huntin' our hogs."

"Oh—huntin' your hogs, eh? Well, don't fret about them hogs. I jest got a idee they'll be home by sundown."

"Ma and Pa'll shore be proud to see 'em come in."

"I had no idee you-all was runnin' so tight."

"We ain't runnin' tight. We're all right."

"You Baxters has got guts, I'll say that."

"You reckon Pa'll not die?"

"Not him. His chitlins[1] is made o' iron."

Jody said, "Tell me about Fodder-wing.[2] Is he shore enough ailin'? Or didn't Lem want I should see him?"

---

[1] CHITLINS—Chitterlings, a term for the stomach and intestines.
[2] FODDER-WING—Mill-wheel's young brother and friend of Jody.

"He's purely ailin'. He ain't like the rest o' us. He ain't like nobody. Seems like he drinks air 'stead o' water, and feeds on what the wild creeturs feeds on, 'stead o' bacon."

"He sees things ain't so, don't he? Spaniards and sich."

"He do, but dogged if they ain't times he'll make you think he do see 'em."

"You reckon Lem'll leave me come see him?"

"I'd not risk it yit. I'll git word to you one day when mebbe Lem's gone off, see?"

"I shore crave to see Fodder-wing."

"You'll see him. Now whereabouts you want to go, huntin' that fawn? Hit's gittin' right thick up this trail."

Suddenly Jody was unwilling to have Mill-wheel with him. If the fawn was dead, or could not be found, he could not have his disappointment seen. And if the fawn was there, the meeting would be so lovely and so secret that he could not endure to share it.

He said, "Hit's not fur now, but hit's powerful thick for a horse. I kin make it a-foot."

"But I'm daresome to leave you, boy. Suppose you was to git lost or snake-bit, too?"

"I'll take keer. Hit'll take me likely a long time to find the fawn, if he's wandered. Leave me off right here."

"All right, but you go mighty easy now, pokin' in them pal-meeters.[8] This is a rattlesnake heaven in these parts. You know north here, and east?"

"There, and there. That fur tall pine makes a bearin'."

"That's right. Now do things go wrong again, you or Buck, one, ride back for me. So long."

"So long, Mill-wheel. I'm shore obliged."

He waved after him. He waited for the sound of the hoofs to end, then cut to the right. The scrub was still. Only his own crackling of twigs sounded across the silence. He was eager almost past caution, but he broke a bough and pushed it ahead of him where the growth was thick and the ground invisible. Rattlers got

[8] PALMEETERS—Dialect for palmettos or palm trees.

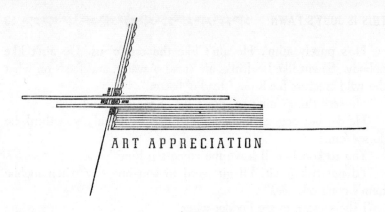

ART APPRECIATION

SPRING ICE ✥ TOM THOMSON

Tom Thomson's pictures are among the best examples of what might be termed the modern tradition in Canadian art. This tradition emphasizes the effect or impression that the artist is trying to produce, rather than the faithful portrayal of a particular scene. Consequently, the artist feels free to change the face of Nature to suit his purposes. Unimportant details are omitted and attention is paid to the over-all pattern, or design of the composition. To indicate the clear Canadian atmosphere, bright sunlight, and vivid hues of Nature, modern Canadian artists commonly use bright colours in large areas. The influence of our vast and empty distances is also evident in Canadian landscapes such as this.

SPRING ICE

Tom Thomson

TOM THOMSON

[1877-1917]

Perhaps more than any other one man, Tom Thomson was responsible for teaching Canadian artists that they should turn their attention to the rugged beauties of their own country rather than continue to imitate the soft, misty landscapes of European tradition. Largely self-taught, he worked for a while as a commercial artist in Toronto. But his real home was the Algonquin Park country of Northern Ontario, where for eight months each year he worked as a canoeman and guide, and made innumerable brilliant sketches which, during four winter months in Toronto, became the bases of his formal paintings. At the height of his artistic powers his life ended under tragic and mysterious circumstances at Canoe Lake, Algonquin Park.

out of the way when they had a chance. Penny had gone farther into the dark thicket than he remembered. He wondered for an instant if he had mistaken his direction. Then a buzzard rose in front of him and flapped into the air. He came into the clearing under the oaks. Buzzards sat in a circle around the carcass of the doe. They turned their heads on their long scrawny necks and hissed at him. He threw his bough at them and they flew into an adjacent tree. Their wings creaked and whistled like rusty pump-handles. The sand showed large cat-prints, he could not tell whether of wildcat or of panther. But the big cats killed fresh, and they had left the doe to the carrion birds. He asked himself whether the sweeter meat of the fawn had scented the air for the curled nostrils.

He skirted the carcass and parted the grass at the place where he had seen the fawn. It did not seem possible that it was only yesterday. The fawn was not there. He circled the clearing. There was no sound, no sign. The buzzards clacked their wings, impatient to return to their business. He returned to the spot where the fawn had emerged and dropped to all fours, studying the sand for the small hoofprints. The night's rain had washed away all tracks except those of cat and buzzards. The cat-sign had not been made in this direction. Under a scrub palmetto he was able to make out a track, pointed and dainty as the mark of a ground dove. He crawled past the palmetto.

Movement directly in front of him startled him so that he tumbled backward. The fawn lifted its face to his. It turned its head with a wide, wondering motion and shook him through with the stare of its liquid eyes. It was quivering. It made no effort to rise or run. Jody could not trust himself to move.

He whispered, "It's me."

The fawn lifted its nose, scenting him. He reached out one hand and laid it on the soft neck. The touch made him delirious. He moved forward on all fours until he was close beside it. He put his arms around its body. A light convulsion passed over it but it did not stir. He stroked its sides as gently as though the fawn were a china deer and he might break it. Its skin was softer than the white 'coonskin knapsack. It was sleek and clean and had a sweet scent of grass. He rose slowly and lifted the fawn from the ground. It was no heavier than old Julia. Its legs hung limply. They were surprisingly long and he had to hoist the fawn as high as possible under his arm.

He was afraid that it might kick and bleat at sight and smell of its mother. He skirted the clearing and pushed his way into the thicket. It was difficult to fight through with his burden. The fawn's legs caught in the bushes and he could not lift his own with freedom. He tried to shield its face from prickling vines. Its head bobbed with his stride. His heart thumped with the marvel of its acceptance of him. He reached the trail and walked as fast as he could until he came to the intersection with the road home. He stopped to rest and set the fawn down on its dangling legs. It wavered on them. It looked at him and bleated.

He said, enchanted, "I'll tote you time I git my breath."

He remembered his father's saying that a fawn would follow that had been first carried. He started away slowly. The fawn stared after him. He came back to it and stroked it and walked away again. It took a few wobbling steps toward him and cried piteously. It was willing to follow him. It belonged to him. It was his own. He was light-headed with his joy. He wanted to fondle it, to run and romp with it, to call to it to come to him. He dared not alarm it. He picked it up and carried it in front of him over his two arms. It seemed to him that he walked without effort. He had the strength of a Forrester.

His arms began to ache and he was forced to stop again. When he walked on, the fawn followed him at once. He allowed it to walk a little distance, then picked it up again. The distance home was nothing. He could have walked all day and into the night, carrying it and watching it follow. He was wet with sweat but a light breeze blew through the June morning, cooling him. The sky was as clear as spring water in a blue china cup. He came to the clearing. It was fresh and green after the night's rain. He could see Buck Forrester following old Caesar at the plow in the cornfield. He thought he heard him curse the horse's slowness. He fumbled with the gate latch and was finally obliged to set down the fawn to manage it. It came to him that he would walk into the house, into Penny's bedroom, with the fawn walking behind him. But at the steps, the fawn balked and refused to climb them. He picked it up and went to his father. Penny lay with closed eyes.

Jody called, "Pa! Lookit!"

Penny turned his head. Jody stood beside him, the fawn clutched hard against him. It seemed to Penny that the boy's eyes were as bright as the fawn's. His face lightened, seeing them together.

He said, "I'm proud you found him."

"Pa, he wa'n't skeert o' me. He were layin' right up where his mammy had made his bed."

"The does learns 'em that, time they're borned. You kin step on a fawn, times, they lay so still."

"Pa, I toted him, and when I set him down, right off he follered me. Like a dog, Pa."

"Ain't that fine? Let's see him better."

Jody lifted the fawn high. Penny reached out a hand and touched its nose. It bleated and reached hopefully for his fingers.

He said, "Well, leetle feller. I'm sorry I had to take away your mammy."

"You reckon he misses her?"

"No. He misses his rations and he knows that. He misses somethin' else but he don't know jest what."

Ma Baxter came into the room.

"Look, Ma, I found him."

"I see."

"Ain't he purty, Ma? Lookit them spots all in rows. Lookit them big eyes. Ain't he purty?"

"He's powerful young. Hit'll take milk for him a long whiles. I don't know as I'd give my consent, if I'd knowed he was so young."

Penny said, "Ory, I got one thing to say, and I'm sayin' it now, and then I'll have no more talk of it. The leetle fawn's as welcome in this house as Jody. It's hissen. We'll raise it without grudgment o' milk or meal. You got me to answer to, do I ever hear you quarrelin' about it. This is Jody's fawn jest like Julia's my dog."

Jody had never heard his father speak to her so sternly. The tone must hold familiarity for his mother, however, for she opened and shut her mouth and blinked her eyes.

She said, "I only said it was young."

"All right. So it is."

He closed his eyes.

He said, "If ever'body's satisfied now, I'd thank you to leave me rest. Hit puts my heart to jerkin', to talk."

Jody said, "I'll fix its milk, Ma. No need you should bother."

She was silent. He went to the kitchen. The fawn wobbled after him. A pan of morning's milk stood in the kitchen safe. The cream had risen on it. He skimmed the cream into a jug and used his shirt sleeve to wipe up the few drops he could not keep from spilling. If he could keep the fawn from being any trouble to his mother, she would mind it less. He poured milk into a small gourd. He held it out to the fawn. It butted it suddenly, smelling the milk. He saved it precariously from spilling over the floor. He led the fawn outside to the yard and began again. It could make nothing of the milk in the gourd.

He dipped his fingers in the milk and thrust them into the fawn's soft wet mouth. It sucked greedily. When he withdrew them, it bleated frantically and butted him. He dipped his fingers again and as the fawn sucked, he lowered them slowly into the milk. The fawn blew and sucked and snorted. It stamped its small hoofs impatiently. As long as he held his fingers below the level of the milk, the fawn was content. It closed its eyes dreamily. It was ecstasy to feel its tongue against his hand. Its small tail flicked back and forth. The last of the milk vanished in a swirl of foam and gurgling. The fawn bleated and butted but its frenzy was appeased. Jody was tempted to go for more milk, but even with his father's backing he was afraid to press his advantage too far. A doe's bag was as small as a yearling heifer's. Surely the fawn had had as much as its mother could have given it. It lay down suddenly, exhausted and replete.

He gave his attention to a bed for it. It would be too much to ask, to bring it into the house. He went to the shed behind the house and cleaned out a corner down to the sand. He went to the live oaks at the north end of the yard and pulled down armfuls of Spanish moss. He made a thick bed in the shed.

DISCUSSING THE STORY

1. All his life Jody had wanted a pet of his own, but the isolated farm where the Baxters lived had barely provided food for the family. After the accident to his father, however, Jody had some persuasive arguments in his favour. For what reasons did Penny consent to let him look for the fawn?

2. The Forresters certainly were not the best of neighbours, but they were not all bad. How did they make right the wrong they had done? How did the doctor help Penny?

3. Some experiences mean so much to us we cannot bear to share them with anyone else. Describe the delight Jody experienced in finding the fawn. Tell how he won its confidence and got it home.

4. Having a pet means having responsibilities too. How did Jody take care of the fawn? If you have ever had a young animal for a pet, tell how you cared for it.

THE HAWK 🌾 A. C. BENSON

THE hawk slipt out of the pine, and rose in the sunlit air:
Steady and still he poised; his shadow slept on the grass:
And the bird's song sickened and sank: she cowered with furtive stare
Dumb, till the quivering dimness should flicker and shift and pass.

5   Suddenly down he dropped: she heard the hiss of his wing,
Fled with a scream of terror: oh, would she had dared to rest!
For the hawk at eve was full, and there was no bird to sing
And over the heather drifted the down from a bleeding breast

UNDERSTANDING THE POEM

1. Tell in your own words the tragedy that is described in "The Hawk."

2. Find an example in this poem to show that the sound of a word sometimes suggests what it is describing.

3. What does the poet mean when he says of the hawk, "his shadow slept on the grass"?

4. Find other examples of effective images or figurative language in this poem.

THE LAST WORD OF A BLUEBIRD ✸

ROBERT FROST

As I WENT out, a Crow
In a low voice said "Oh,
I was looking for you
To tell Lesley (will you?)
5 That her little Bluebird
Wanted me to bring word
That the north wind last night,
That made the stars bright
And made ice on the trough,
10 Almost made him cough
His tail feathers off.
He just had to fly!
But he sent her good-by
And said to be good,
15 And wear her red hood,
And look for skunk tracks
In the snow with an ax—
And do everything!
And perhaps in the spring
20 He would come back and sing."

CLUES TO THE MEANING

Everyone should know about Robert Frost. He is one of the best of American poets, and through his poetry he has become a good friend of all who read. The littlest things in life are full of meaning to this man who has spent a long life observing everything. The people he meets, the birds and animals, each season—all are exciting and full of poetry. "The Last Word of a Bluebird" is a good example of how Mr. Frost can get us to thinking about whole seasons with a little poem.

1. What time of year is described in the poem? What does the crow have to say?

2. What pleasant experiences will come before the return of the little bird? Add some adventures to which you look forward at this time each year.

STRIPES 🦋 FREDERIC DOYLE

THE explosion was terrific—not the sharp, crackling report of gunfire, but a deep, rumbling roar which came from the very heart of the hills. Great slabs of white sandrock heaved, burst open, and settled back into a shattered mass. Even the tree roots trembled.

Stripes solemnly pulled his fuzzy tail tight between his legs and snuggled close to his mother's warm side. He was only a few hundred yards from the blast.

His mother, a narrow-stripe skunk, had selected an abandoned woodchuck den on the southern slope of Smoky Ridge as a base from which to feed the nine hungry little mouths which had recently come to her leaf-lined nest. She raised her head as a shower of pebbles from the outside world rattled down the narrow passageway of her burrow.

Stripes shuddered as another explosion shook the hillside.

A screech owl had settled itself on the branches of a pig-hickory tree nearby to send out its thin, quavering call before the skunk ventured into the open. It was a warm June evening, with the blended fragrance of early summer in the air. Clumsy May beetles clattered against the rough bark of the hickory, while ground crickets piped their high, shrill tunes from the fence corners.

The skunk had not trailed ten feet from the mouth of her den before she stopped short, and wheeled about. With all the solemnity of night itself marched her nine little skunklings in her wake.

The skunk surveyed the coming procession with a look of neither surprise nor annoyance. The time had come when they would be constantly at her heels. Eight weeks is a long babyhood for any wild thing. Red-capped sparrows of the same age had long since been making their own way. White-footed wood mice were almost ready to gather thistledown to line homes of their own.

Stripes lifted his nose and sniffed in the direction from which the afternoon blasts had come. A hundred strange odours were mingled in the night, but the acrid[1] tang of burned dynamite smoke and the muggy taint of exploded gasoline stung in his sensitive nostrils. The deadly combination had already scarred his delicate nervous system. Instinctively he cringed.

In single file, with the mother in the lead, the procession started toward the upheaval of rocks at the foot of the hill. Huge boulders lay strewn about; fresh-cut stumps shone white in the darkness. Brush piles littered the torn-up earth. Powerful steam shovels and tractors loomed clumsily in the midst of the destruction. A new cement road was in the making.

Beyond the swath of torn earth lay green pasture fields. Carefully the skunk led the way through ragged rocks until the black pads of her feet again bruised tender grass shoots in her familiar hunting grounds.

Stripes lifted his feet gingerly, waved his plume, and pricked up his round, tufted ears. Without warning he broke rank and started in the direction of an old, blighted chestnut tree which stood out boldly against the background of stars. Suddenly his nose went to the ground, as he let out a high-pitched squeak. In another instant he had pinned a large black ant under his paws. With bared teeth he snapped at the struggling insect several times before his sharp teeth broke the shell of the tough old warrior.

Then, like a family of romping kittens, every skunkling tracked down the ants which streamed from the old chestnut.

[1] ACRID—Bitter.

Softly a huge, black shadow flitted across the face of the full moon. It was only for a split second, but Stripes looked up to see his mother standing stiff-legged with her nose pointed toward the bare limbs of the tree. Stripes, too, braced himself—for what he did not know, but, as he crouched low in the dewy grass, he saw a sinister form hunched on a branch above him. Two large eyes, set deep in sockets of dark feathers, glared down at him.

Stripes froze to the ground. Only the small star of white with two spearheads pointing over his shoulder blades was visible in the low grass.

The huddled bundle of feathers silently unfolded, and the great yellow eyes shot toward him.

Stripes flattened his ears. He felt the rush of chill air stir the silky floss of his skin as the muffled wings of the great owl swept over him.

There was a soft thump as the powerful, needle-pointed talons of the night bird struck a more unwary member of the frolicking band. The luckless skunkling let out a long-drawn "squee-e-e-e" before the hooked beak of the owl quieted its startled cry.

Stripes remained motionless for a long time, and not until the startled family aroused themselves and started single file back across the pasture field did Stripes hustle to gain his position ahead of his brothers and sisters.

A grey fox, slinking among the dewberry briers in search of harvest mice, raised his pointed nose at the coming of the train of skunks. The skunk did not swerve in her course. Retaining her solemn dignity, she headed toward the burrow on the hill. She knew what every skunk knows. They demand and get the undisputed right-of-way on all the trails of the bush. The wolf, the bear, the falcon stand by when the white-tipped plume of the skunk is hoisted for action.

Insensible to the fiery spray of any skunk, the Great Horned Owl stands out as an exception to the rule. Even this winged tiger of the night strikes down a skunk only when his crop has been empty for some time.

Still another and more deadly killer of all wildlife, Stripes was soon to know. Even the blinding, liquid fire which had been handed down from the fittest of his distant ancestors as a most positive weapon of defense would prove futile against this new and terrible danger.

It was late in the summer before Stripes had his first actual encounter with an automobile. The blasting had long since ceased at the foot of the hill, and a wide ribbon of hard, grey cement crawled out through the valley and flattened itself in the hot summer sun. Day and night the huge beetlelike creatures hissed by on the new highway.

Contrary to the usual rule of waiting for the first dim stars to appear in the heavens, the skunk started out one mid-afternoon. Unhesitatingly she stepped forth on the hot pavement of the highway. The eight surviving kittens followed her. At the precise moment when the family was strung across the road, a glittering motor car swung into view.

The dull roar of the motor grew ominously louder as the mountain of polished steel bore down upon them. The skunk squatted, turned herself half over in a threatening position. Stripes stopped dead in his tracks. His head was up. He swished his tail as the brakes of the car squealed. Lurching crazily from side to side, the blue sedan careened toward him.

Stripes blinked at the strange and terrible beetle. Giving his tail another flick, he trotted out to meet the blue monster.

Perhaps it was this move that saved his life. In another instant this thundering bulk of steel and rubber roared over him. The searing blast of smoke stopped his breath. The flying whirlwind of pebbles and dust bruised the sensitive nerve ends of his nose.

Stripes shook himself violently, kicking one hind foot at the empty air, and smoothed back his whiskers with two quick laps of his long, pink tongue.

A quivering movement close by raised his hackles.[2] A second look, and he saw one of his own brothers lying in a heap. The black pads of the little fellow were twitching spasmodically;

[2] HACKLES—Bristles along an animal's neck and back.

red bubbles formed and broke on the tip of his nose. As Stripes watched he saw the toes go limp. The torn silky fur flattened. The even row of sharp teeth gleamed in the bright sunlight as the lower jaw sagged and grew still.

Stripes did not hesitate for the next move. An urge, an impulse —deep-seated, and as old as the world—gleamed from his jewel-like eyes. The elephant coming to the aid of a wounded comrade, or a common crow circling frantically over the shattered body of one of his flock is moved by the same flood of emotion which sent Stripes into action.

Gently but firmly he sank his teeth into the matted fur of his fallen brother. With all the power of his tender muscles he started to tug the limp and mangled form into the cool shade of an elderberry thicket beyond the road.

The red planet Mars was slanting its fiery beams from the western horizon when the assembled band of skunks headed back to the hillside burrow. To reach that safe retreat they had to re-cross the wide grey band of cement. Stripes approached it with some misgivings. While the rest struck out unhesitatingly to reach the gravel bank beyond the elderberry bushes, Stripes held back.

Some deep and ancient instinct awakened by the afternoon's tragedy guided his pattering feet far down along the sweeping curve of the road.

The rest of the family had long since wrapped their tails around themselves, and buried their noses deep in the soft blanket when Stripes shouldered the rasping teasel[3] stems near the den.

It was the beginning of the second spring of his life before Stripes began to lose interest in the well-worn burrow where he had spent his first days. A strange restlessness drove him to the surrounding hills.

He followed unfamiliar trails until the bright shafts of morning sunlight cut short his nightly wanderings. His silky, black coat became matted with cockleburs. Sharp shale and flint rock cut deep into the black pads of his feet.

The roaring March winds had died to a whisper before he came to the end of his quest. Rounding a steep ledge of rocks, overhung with sumac trees, he met a beautiful black skunk. Only a wisp of white on the tip of her tail, and a tuft of white on her forehead marked her as one of his clan. Padding softly behind her marched another skunk. His broad head, short, stalky legs, and superior size were a challenge to any four-footed prowler of the night. Stripes saw nothing but the trim body of the female.

A deep-throated growl stopped Stripes dead in his tracks. He threw up his head; braced himself.

Stealthily the broad skull, set with glittering eyes, moved toward him. Stripes raised his hackles; curled his lip. From his own throat came a guttural growl—a low vibrant rumble that matched the threatening challenge of the newcomer.

The female crouched. Her ears flattened as Stripes met the first snarling lunge of the larger skunk.

Stripes felt searing fangs tear into his flank. Hot blood spurted from the wound. Tearing himself free, he wheeled; raised himself

---

[3] TEASEL—A plant covered with stiff hooked leaves.

on his haunches. His first call to battle tapped deep wells of energy which he had never felt before.

Rage and pain tightened the sinews of every muscle. As the larger skunk lunged toward him, he ducked his head sidewise and caught the bristling fighter under the throat. His jaw bulged as he sank his teeth into the soft flesh. With grim tenacity Stripes held his grip.

Over and over they rolled. Quite suddenly he felt the muscles of his foe grow lax.

Loosening his grip, Stripes drew back. Cautiously he circled the limp form. No odour marked the torn-up battleground. Even unto death the broad-skulled fighter held to the gentlemen's agreement among all skunks to withhold his powerful weapon of defense against his own kind.

Although torn and bleeding and weak Stripes lashed his tail, arched his back, and marched proudly toward the crouching female. With feminine grace she drew herself back into her black muff, and watched him with affected terror and suspicion.

Yet it was not fear that sparkled from her round, black eyes.

They found an abandoned burrow under the sprawling ruins of an old lime kiln along the southern slope of Smoky Ridge. Together they roamed the old pasture fields, the rocky hillsides, and the sandy creek bottom. One morning in early May Stripes was surprised and annoyed to discover the warm leaf-lined nest taken up by a dozen mouse-sized bits of squirming life. The female bristled at his sulking manner. Thereafter he went his rounds alone.

It was early summer when the creamy blossoms of the black locust perfumed the warm nights, before the new family was ready to explore the outside world.

Stripes took the lead. Down the hill toward the formidable hard band of cement marched the ceremonial procession. With all the dignity of the king's court they arrived at the edge of the road. Here Stripes stopped, pricked up his ears, and looked askance at the waddling kittens.

Fearlessly they pranced out upon the hard surface of the highway. Stripes stiffened. The echoes again; thunderous earth tremors; roaring fantasies of the highway awakened him to action.

His tail flew up, and with amazing alacrity he headed off the eager balls of fur, and shouldered them back to the edge of the road.

The female stood back. A clanking truck rumbled down the highway. The blinding headlights clearly outlined the scrambled formation.

For half a mile Stripes led the puzzled followers down the curve of the road. Suddenly he dropped over the rim of the bank, rounded the end of a concrete culvert, and marched proudly *under* the road.

Food there was in abundance in the fields beyond. Mice overran the fence rows, salamanders wriggled contentedly in the spring gutters, and grasshoppers hung lazily in clusters on the timothy straw.

Now after many years, if you are very cautious, and creep to the edge of the young Scotch-pine wood on Smoky Ridge, and look across the open field to the scattered ruins of the old lime kiln you can see a black, furry ball curled on a flat rock above a well-worn den. From this point, Stripes, and you too, can see skunks and skunklings meander down the hill, march under the oil-soaked ribbon of cement, and disappear in the twilight dusk.

And when the dagger of Orion [4] begins to glitter in the heavens, Stripes will rise to his feet, stretch, yawn, and run over the ledge of rocks to begin anew his never-ending search of the mysteries of the night.

DISCUSSING THE STORY

All living things seem to have their place in the scheme of nature. One kind lives to provide food for a second, while the second is the mortal enemy of a third. And so it goes, with the environment providing the means of life and death for all. Man alone, with his machines of civilization, is the enemy of every kind of life, including his own.

[4] ORION (ō-rī'ŏn)—A constellation resembling the figure of a man, in which is a row of three stars sometimes called Orion's Sword.

1. What do you learn from the story about the family life of the skunk? How are young skunks trained to look for food? What do they eat? Describe their formation as they travel about together.

2. What woodland thing is the enemy of the skunk? Tell about the family's meeting with this enemy.

3. Explain how the building of a road creates danger for all wildlife. What other activities of man can you think of that endanger the living things of the woods? What are some of the things man can do to help conserve the things of nature?

4. How long did Stripes live with his family before he ventured into the world on his own? Tell about his encounter with the "broad skull."

5. In what ways do you think Stripes and his relatives live useful lives? Do you think they are the enemies or friends of the farmer? If you have seen a skunk, or a family of them, in the country or in a zoo, tell about your experience.

DILEMMAS OF THE WILD 🦋

ARCHIBALD RUTLEDGE

FEW aspects of nature are more fascinating than the amazing ability of wild creatures to escape peril. When their lives or those of their young are threatened they show not only high intelligence and wiliness, but sometimes display a spiritual quality comparable to human valour.

I once saw a female duck hawk defending her two fledglings against the depredations of a falconer [1] who was bent on stealing the young birds. This hawk had a nest halfway down the face of a precipitous cliff; to reach it the falconer had lowered himself by a rope. When I arrived on the scene he was dangling in mid-air just above the nest. The mother hawk was dashing at his eyes with beak and talons, and the man drew his pistol and fired blank cartridges at the bird. To protect her fledglings on the rocky shelf below, the mother bird courageously disregarded the pistol shots, and continued her furious attack. But finally she realized that the falconer was not to be frightened away, and that her young would be taken if they remained in their nest and within the reach of the intruder.

[1] FALCONER (fôl'kŭn-ẽr)—A person who breeds or trains hawks for taking birds or game.

Faced by this tragedy, the mother hawk made an instantaneous decision. She flew to the limb of a pine tree about thirty feet across the gorge and uttered a distress signal that evidently told her young ones that they must fly to her or be captured. One fledgling was too afraid or too weak to attempt the perilous flight, and consequently fell prey to the falconer, but the other responded at once to her call and, flapping precariously on its untested baby wings, flew across the chasm to his mother's side—and safety.

A wild creature in a tight spot always asks itself, "What's safest to do now?" And instinct answers with the lifesaving artifice that is most likely to succeed. A bird or animal caught flatfooted by an enemy, unable to hide, and unwilling to resort to combat until all other possibilities of escape have been exhausted, will often feign ferocity or madness, or simulate death. An assumption of ferocity or other antic behaviour perhaps suggests hydrophobia [2] which animals know and fear. At any rate, these frightening postures usually delay an enemy's attack, and may even frighten the foe away.

The more harmless a creature is, the more defenseless he is; therefore in a crisis he is likely to imitate one that is highly dangerous. Innocuous snakes will vibrate their tails like rattlers. The innocent puff adder inflates himself fearsomely until he is almost twice his natural size, and blows in a manner terrifying to the uninitiated. This serpent can put on the most convincing and appalling of all dying acts and appears to reach dissolution only after a gruesome pantomime of suffering. The opossum feigns death convincingly—his eyes even roll back and his mouth falls open.

While some animals and a good many birds will try to hiss like snakes, I believe the best imitation is given by the wild turkey hen when she is brooding eggs on her nest in the thick underbrush. On several occasions I have leaped away from that sound—only to find that I had almost stepped on a turkey nest. Young turkeys early develop the power to hiss.

All wild creatures, when wounded or disabled, resort to amazing stratagems in order to survive. Once when I was in the woods at twilight I saw a regal wild turkey in a pathetic dilemma. One of

[2] HYDROPHOBIA (hī-drŏ-fō'bĭ-à)—Madness.

his great wings, broken by a hunter, or by some accident in the woods, was dragging on the ground. Night was coming on, and it was high time for the gobbler to be in a roost far up in a moss-shrouded cypress or lofty pine, but he could not fly to a roost. Yet to stay on the ground would be fatal, for a fox or wildcat would surely catch him.

Even in his apparently hopeless plight, however, he was not at a complete loss. Nearby was a tree that had been broken twenty feet from the ground. The break had not been complete, and the upper half formed a long incline that reached from the ground to the summit of the part that was still standing. The old gobbler walked slowly up this incline and at length reached the top. While he had achieved elevation, he knew that he would not be safe there: a wildcat might follow him up that incline. Then, to escape all enemies of the night, the wary old tactician took a mighty leap and, beating his one good wing, made his way across a wide space, landing safely in an oak. Here he would be safe from the prowlers of the darkness—and that he really escaped them I know, because I saw him afterwards while his wing was healing, and finally I had the satisfaction of watching him beat his way, under his own wing-power, to a gnarled limb seventy feet up in a lordly yellow pine.

The fox's shrewdness is most acute when Reynard [3] is attempting to escape from pursuing hounds. One warm afternoon in early autumn I was sitting on a stump near a stream when a grey fox hove in sight. Not far behind him the dogs were baying, and I could see that the fox was tired out from a long run. Across the stream an old tree had fallen, making a natural bridge. I was not surprised to see the fox start across this log. To obtain superior elevation and vision, Sir Brushtail often runs along dead trees lying on the ground. But what the wily grey one did next was one of the most sagacious feats that I have ever observed.

When halfway across the log, he paused, turned sideways, and peered down. Below him in the stream was a tiny green island, only a few feet in area, where lush grasses grew. Down to this

[3] REYNARD (rā'nárd)—Proper name of the fox in a celebrated poem, "Reynard the Fox."

islet the fox gracefully leaped. I expected that he would then jump across the water to the farther bank; instead, he jumped back to the side of the stream that he had just left. Then he ran down the edge of the stream in the opposite direction from the yelping dogs.

When the hounds came up they followed the trail to the middle of the log, then crossed to the farther side of the stream. But no scent awaited them there and for many minutes they vainly cast about to pick up the trail. Finally, with the air of creatures who knew they had been outwitted, they gave up the chase and turned homeward.

I have seen a good many thousand white-tailed deer in their native wilds, and can testify to their alertness and resourcefulness. A most appealing performance occurred one day in the pineland wilds near the humble home of a backwoodsman. I had met him in a forest path, within distant sight of his house. He had been rounding up some hogs in the woods; and these, twenty or more in number, were in the pathway ahead of us, slowly making their way toward the barnyard. As we were talking we heard a solitary hound; we were almost certain that he was bringing a deer in our direction. We sat down together on a log, and did not have long to wait. Running perhaps a half mile ahead of the hound, a beautiful buck appeared. He was plainly tired. Both seeing and winding the hogs, he stopped—not so much to rest as to consider a situation. For at least three minutes he stood motionless and thoughtful; then he stole forward toward the path, where he deliberately fell in with the hogs and began to walk with them toward the barnyard. This strange behaviour had in it wild intelligence and the deep design of high strategy. By mingling with this drove of swine the buck knew that, for the pursuing hound, his scent would cease to be solitary and compelling.

Within thirty yards of the stable lot the buck left the path, stealing away through the woods. By this time the hound was within sight, and we watched to see whether the buck's ruse would outwit him. It did. Coming to the path, he fell in behind the hogs, ran them full cry, and chased them into the barnyard. After all, this was more exciting than following a deer he had never seen!

In Poe's famous story, "The Purloined Letter," the missive proves impossible to find because it is not really concealed at all; it had merely been put in such an obvious place that the searchers never thought of looking for it there. This principle—that the best hiding place is not always the most secret—is to be observed in nature. On my southern plantation lived a famous buck, so huge and superbly antlered that he had become a legend to local hunters. One winter I missed him from his accustomed haunts in the woods, nor did any hunter report having seen Old Roland, as he was called. He never appeared during the long hunting season, and I was afraid that he had been killed.

After the season had closed I was talking one day with an old Negro named Steve, whose tiny cabin stood in a field of broom sedge and fennel.

"How come nobody hunt Old Roland dis year?" he asked me.

"Everybody hunted for him," I said, "but nobody found him."

Steve doubled up with laughter. "Dat old buck been sleepin' close by my house all winter," he said. "I done see him 'most every day. Lemme show you."

In the fennel and broom grass, not more than fifty feet from his cabin, Steve pointed out to me where Roland had slept. While the hunters had ranged the distant woods in search of him, he had crouched here in safety, in the sanctuary afforded by the neglected field of the lonely and harmless old Negro. Instinct must have told the buck two things: first, that Steve was no hunter; secondly, that no one would dream of looking for a wary old stag living so close to an inhabited cabin.

In crises, the ability to remain perfectly motionless until danger has passed is a favourite—and usually successful—ruse of wild creatures. The knowledge that perfect quiescence will save them goes deeper than dependence on mere protective camouflage; it requires something very much like *character* to let an enemy come perilously close, and yet make no frightened burst for freedom. Oddly enough, the deer, almost the fleetest of animals, frequently takes refuge in utter immobility. I once saw what appeared to be a set of antlers protruding from behind a fallen pine. I froze into

immobility and watched for at least twenty minutes. They did not move, and I concluded that they were bare branches of the dead tree. But as soon as I moved they proved to be real antlers after all; the crafty buck had been watching me, and had at first decided that standing still was a better manoeuvre than running away.

Another time I saw a doe standing in a greenwood with her tiny fawn. Like a statue the mother stood looking and listening, but the baby wanted to play, and kept running around her on unsteady legs. At last, aware of the danger of this infant behaviour, the doe raised her forefoot, gently but firmly set it on his back, and pressed her baby down into the grass, thus hiding him and keeping him still.

One of the most ingenious acts of a wild creature I ever saw was that of a snowy egret that I spied while it was wading knee-deep in the shallows of a sea marsh. Every few minutes it would dart its javelinlike beak into the water. Fishing was good. Its appetite satisfied, the bird lifted its wings to fly away. But its efforts were unavailing—the egret seemed to be anchored where it stood. Plainly in distress, it struggled to free one leg. Just as I was about to go to its aid, the bird managed to lift itself into the air. Dangling from its left foot was a huge clam. The egret had stepped into the clam's open shell and the mollusk had closed on it like a vise. I watched, curious to see whether the bird could meet so perplexing a dilemma—one which might eventually result in the egret's starving to death because of the hampering weight.

Running out into the water was an old fence. Flying off-balance to it, the egret alighted on a fence post. For a moment he teetered on one foot; then, lifting his imprisoned foot high, he began to whack the clam against the side of the post. Soon the shell broke at the hinge, and the clever egret, freed once more, calmly preened its feathers as if such a misadventure were all in the day's work. And, indeed, such crises do make up no small part of the life of wild animals.

DISCUSSING THE SELECTION

1. In a lifelong study of creatures of the wild the author has observed courage, craftiness, and something that is much like the intelligence of human beings. How are these characteristics demonstrated by the mother hawk? by the turkeys?

2. Look up the meanings of the words *intelligence* and *instinct* in the dictionary, then tell whether you think the fox acted intelligently or instinctively.

3. How are shrewdness and cunning shown in the stories of the deer? To what extent were courage and self-control necessary?

4. Man and his trained animals are not the only enemies of wildlife. How does the story of the egret illustrate this fact? Give some other examples of your own of wild creatures and their natural enemies.

5. Explain what the word in italics means in each of the following phrases:

   a. the *depredations* of a falconer . . .
   b. . . . down the face of a *precipitous* cliff . . .
   c. A bird or animal . . . will often *feign ferocity* or madness, or *simulate* death.
   d. *Innocuous snakes* will vibrate their tails . . .
   e. All wild creatures . . . resort to amazing *stratagems* . . . perfect *quiescence* will save them . . .

THE SNAKE ✠ EMILY DICKINSON

G1   A NARROW fellow in the grass
         Occasionally rides;
B1   You may have met him—did you not?
G2   His notice sudden is.

G3 5 The grass divides as with a comb,
         A spotted shaft is seen;
B2   And then it closes at your feet
         And opens further on.

B3   He likes a boggy acre.
     10 A floor too cool for corn.
G   Yet when a child, and barefoot,
         I more than once, at morn,

         Have passed, I thought, a whiplash
         Unbraiding in the sun—
G1 15 When, stooping to secure it,
         It wrinkled, and was gone.

B   Several of nature's people
         I know, and they know me;
         I feel for them a transport
    20 Of cordiality;

All   But never met this fellow,
         Attended or alone,
         Without a tighter breathing,
         And zero at the bone.

CLUES TO THE MEANING

Emily Dickinson spent her entire life in Amherst, Massachusetts. She seemed just an ordinary girl who attended school, learned about housework, and wrote sentimental letters and poems for her own pleasure.

As she grew older she found peace and satisfaction in writing poetry, and more than one thousand poems were found in her home after her death. Her poems are short, and many are about the things in nature. Like "The Snake," each one is full of little pictures we can understand because they recall experiences we have had.

1. Describe each of the little pictures the poet uses to tell about the snake. If you have had experiences recalled by these scenes, tell about them.

2. Miss Dickinson is not talking about the dangerous poisonous snakes that inhabit parts of our country. Where she lived there are few, if any, snakes that are dangerous. Nevertheless, in the last stanza she describes a feeling many of us have had. In your own words tell what is meant by "zero at the bone."

THE SNAIL 🌟 CHARLES LAMB

THE frugal snail, with forecast of repose,
Carries his house with him where'er he goes;
Peeps out—and if there comes a shower of rain,
Retreats to his small domicile again.
5 Touch but a tip of him, a horn—'tis well—
He curls up in his sanctuary shell.
He's his own landlord, his own tenant; stay
Long as he will, he dreads no Quarter Day.
Himself he boards and lodges; both invites
10 And feasts himself; sleeps with himself o' nights.
He spares the upholsterer trouble to procure
Chattels; himself is his own furniture,
And his sole riches. Wheresoe'er he roam—
Knock when you will—he's sure to be at home.

8. QUARTER DAY—A day beginning a quarter of a year and on which a quar-
terly payment, as of rent, becomes due.
12. CHATTELS—Personal property, such as movable goods or money.

CLUES TO THE MEANING

1. What ways does the poet use to tell us that the snail needs no nest or shelter? In what sense is the snail "frugal"? What other word for "house" is used in the poem? In what way does the shell serve as a "sanctuary"?

2. Have you thought about why even the lowly snail is provided by nature with a protective covering? What other living things carry their houses with them? What would happen to all of them without this covering? What purpose does the snail serve in nature?

THE FISHERS OF THE AIR 🐟

CHARLES G. D. ROBERTS

THE lake lay in a deep and sun-soaked valley facing south, sheltered from the sea-winds by a high hog-back of dark green spruce and hemlock forest, broken sharply here and there by out-croppings of white granite.

Beyond the hog-back, some three or four miles away, the green seas creamed and thundered in sleepless turmoil against the towering black cliffs, clamorous with seagulls. But over the lake brooded a blue and glittering silence, broken only, at long intervals, by the long-drawn, wistful flute-cry of the Canada whitethroat from some solitary tree-top:

*Lean—lean—lean-to-me—lean-to-me—lean-to-me—*of all bird voices the one most poignant with loneliness and longing.

On the side of the lake nearest to the hog-back the dark green of the forest came down to within forty or fifty paces of the water's edge, and was fringed by a narrow ribbon of very light, tender green—a dense, low growth of Indian willow, elder shrub, and withe-wood, tangled with white clematis and starred with wild convolvulus. From the sharply-defined edge of this gracious tangle a beach of clean sand, dazzlingly white, sloped down to and slid beneath the transparent golden lip of the amber-tinted water. The sand, both below and above the water's edge, was of an amazing radiance. Being formed by the infinitely slow breaking down of the ancient granite, through ages of alternating suns and rains and heats and frosts, it consisted purely of the indestructible, coarse white crystals of the quartz, whose facets caught the sun like a drift of diamonds.

The opposite shores of the lake were low and swampy, studded here and there with tall, naked, weather-bleached "rampikes"—the trunks of ancient fir trees blasted and stripped by some long-past forest fire. These melancholy ghosts of trees rose from a riotously gold-green carpet of rank marsh-grasses, sweeping around in an interminable, unbroken curve to the foot of the lake, where, through the cool shadows of water-ash and balsam-poplar, the trout-haunted outlet stream rippled away musically to join the sea some seven or eight miles farther on. All along the gold-green sweep of the marsh-grass spread acre upon acre of the flat leaves of the water-lily, starred with broad, white, golden-hearted, exquisitely-perfumed blooms, the paradise of the wild bees and honey-loving summer flies.

Over this vast crystal bowl of green-and-amber solitude domed a sky of cloudless blue, and high in the blue hung a great bird, slowly wheeling. From his height he held in view the intense sparkling of the sea beyond the hog-back, the creaming of the surf about the outer rocks, and the sudden upspringing of the gulls, like a puff of blown petals, as some wave, higher and more impetuous than its predecessor, drove them from their perches. But the aerial watcher had heed only for the lake below him, lying windless and unshadowed in the sun. His piercing eyes, jewel-bright, and with an amazing range of vision, could penetrate to all the varying depths of the lake and detect the movements of its finny hordes. The great sluggish lake-trout, or "togue," usually lurking in the obscurest deeps, the shining, active, vermilion-spotted brook-trout, foraging voraciously nearer the shore and the surface, the fat, mud-loving "suckers," rooting the oozy bottom like pigs among the roots of the water-lilies, the silvery chub and the green-and-gold, fiercely spined perch haunting the weedy feeding-grounds down toward the outlet—all these he observed, and differentiated with an expert's eye, attempting to foresee which ones, in their feeding or their play, were likely soonest to approach the surface of their glimmering golden world.

Suddenly he paused in his slow wheeling, dipped forward, and dropped, with narrowed wings, down, down from his dizzy height to within something like fifty yards of the water. Here he stopped, with wings wide-spread, and hovered almost motionless, slowly sinking like a waft of thistledown when the breeze has died away. He had seen a fair-sized trout rise lightly and suck in a fly which had fallen on the bright surface. The ringed ripples of the rise had hardly smoothed away when the trout rose again. As it gulped its tiny, half-drowned prey, the poised bird shot downward again—urged by a powerful surge of his wings before he closed them—this time with terrific speed. He struck the water with a resounding splash, disappeared beneath it, and rose again two or three yards beyond with the trout securely gripped in his talons. Shaking the bright drops in a shower from his wings, he flapped hurriedly away with his captive to his nest on the steep slope of the hog-back. He flew with eager haste, as fast as his broad wings would carry him; for he feared lest his one dreaded foe, the great white-headed eagle, should swoop down out of space on hissing pinions and rob him of his prize.

*　　　*　　　*

The nest of the osprey was built in the crotch of an old, lightning-blasted pine which rose from a fissure in the granite about fifty feet above the lake. As the osprey had practically no foes to be dreaded except that tyrannical robber, the great white-headed eagle—which, indeed, only cared to rob him of his fish, and never dared drive him to extremities by appearing to threaten his precious nestlings—the nest was built without any pretence of concealment, or, indeed, any attempt at inaccessibility, save such as was afforded by the high, smooth, naked trunk which supported it. An immense grey, weather-beaten structure, conspicuous for miles, it looked like a loose carload of rubbish, but in reality the sticks and dried rushes and mud and strips of shredded bark of which it was built were so solidly and cunningly interwoven as to withstand the wildest of winter gales. It was his permanent summer home, to which he and his handsome, daring mate were wont to return each spring from their winter sojourn in the sun lands of the south. A little tidying-up, a little patching with sticks and mud, a relining with feathers and soft, winter-withered grasses, and the old nest was quickly ready to receive the eggs of his mate—beautiful and precious eggs, two, three, or four in number, and usually of the rich colour of old ivory very thickly splashed with a warm purplish brown.

This summer there were four nestlings in the great untidy nest; and they kept both their devoted parents busy, catching and tearing up into convenient morsels fish enough to satisfy their vigorous appetites. At the moment when the father osprey returned from the lake with the trout which he had just caught they were full-fed and fast asleep, their downy heads and half-feathered, scrawny necks comfortably resting across one another's pulsing bodies. The mother-bird, who had recently fed them, was away, fishing in the long green-grey seas beyond the hog-back. The father, seeing them thus satisfied, tore up the trout and swallowed it, with dignified deliberation, himself. Food was plentiful, and he was not over-hungry. Thus, having scrupulously wiped his beak and preened his feathers, he settled himself on the edge of the nest and became apparently lost in contemplation of the spacious and tranquil scene outspread beneath him. A pair of bustling little crow-blackbirds, who had made their own small home among the outer sticks of the gigantic nest, flew backwards and forwards diligently, bringing insects in their bills for their naked, newly-hatched brood. Their metallic black plumage shone iridescently, purple and green and radiant blue, in the unclouded sunlight, and from time to time the great osprey rolled his eyes upon them with a mild and casual interest. Neither he nor his mate had the slightest objection to their presence—being amicably disposed towards all living creatures except fish and possible assailants of the nest. And the blackbirds dwelt in security under that powerful, though involuntary, protection.

The osprey, the great fish-hawk or fish-eagle of Eastern North America, was the most attractive, in character, of all the predatory tribes of the hawks and eagles. Of dauntless courage without being quarrelsome or tyrannical, he strictly minded his own business, which was that of catching fish; and none of the wild folk of the forest, whether furred or feathered, had cause to fear him so long as they threatened no peril to his home or young. On account of this well-known good reputation he was highly respected by the hunters and lumbermen and scattered settlers of the back-woods, and it was held a gross breach of the etiquette of the wilder-ness to molest him or disturb his nest. Even the fish he took—and he was a most tireless and successful fisherman—were not greatly grudged to him; for his chief depredations were upon the coarse-fleshed and always superabundant chub and suckers, which no human fisherman would be at the trouble to catch.

With all this good character to his credit, he was at the same time one of the handsomest of the great hawks. About two feet in length, he was of sturdy build, with immensely powerful wings whose tips reached to the end of his tail. All his upper parts were of a soft dark brown, laced delicately and sparsely with white, and the crown of his broad-skulled, intelligent head was heavily splashed with white. All his underparts were pure white except the tail, which was crossed with five or six even bars of pale umber. His long and masterful beak, curved like a sickle and nearly as sharp, was black; while his formidable talons, able to pierce to the vitals of their prey at the first clutch, were of a clean grey-blue. His eyes, large and full-orbed, with a beautiful ruby-tinted iris encircling the intense black pupil, were gem-like in their brilliance, but lacked the implacable ferocity of the eyes of the eagle and the goshawk.

Presently, flying low over the crest of the hog-back with a gleam-ing mackerel in her talons, appeared his mate. Arriving swiftly at the nest, and finding the nestlings still asleep, she deposited the mackeral in a niche among the sticks, where it lay flashing back the sun from its blue-barred sides, and set herself to preening her feathers, still wet from her briny plunge. The male osprey, after a glance at the prize, seemed to think it was up to him to go her one better. With a high-pitched musical, staccato cry of *Pip-pip—pip-pip—pip-pip*—very small and childish to come from so formid-able a beak—he launched himself majestically from the edge of the nest and sailed off over the hot green tops of the spruce and fir to the lake.

Instead of soaring to his "watch-tower in the blue," he flew now quite low, not more than fifty feet or so above the water; for a swarm of small flies was over the lake, and the fish were rising to them freely. In every direction he saw the little widening rings of ripple, each of which meant a fish, large or small, feeding at the surface. His wide, all-discerning eyes could pick and choose. Whimsically ignoring a number of tempting quarry, he winnowed slowly to the farther side of the lake, and then, pausing to hover just above the line where the water-lilies ended, he dropped suddenly, struck the water with a heavy splash, half submerging himself, and rose at once, his wings beating the spray with a big silver chub in his claws. He had his prey gripped near the tail, so that it hung, twisting and writhing with inconvenient violence, head downwards. At about twenty-five or thirty feet above the water he let it go, and swooping after it caught it again dexterously in mid-air, close to the head, as he wanted it. In this position the inexorable clutch of his needle-tipped talons pierced the life out of the chub, and its troublesome squirming ceased.

Flying slowly with his solid burden, he had just about reached the centre of the lake when an ominous hissing in the air above warned him that his mighty foe, from far up in the blue dome, had marked his capture and was swooping down to rob him of the prize. He swerved sharply, and in the next instant the eagle, a wide-winged, silvery-headed bird of twice his size, shot downward past him with a strident scream and a rustle of stiff-set plumes, swept under him in a splendid curve, and came back at him with wide-open beak and huge talons outspread. He was too heavily laden either to fight or dodge, so he discreetly dropped the fish. With a lightning swoop his tormentor caught it before it could reach the water, and flew off with it to his eyrie in a high, inaccessible ravine at the farthest end of the hog-back, several miles down the outlet stream. The osprey, taking quite philosophically a discomfiture which he had suffered so many times before, stared after the magnificent pirate angrily for a few seconds, then circled away to seek another quarry. He knew that now he would be left in peace to enjoy what he might take.

But this time, in his exasperated anxiety more than to make good his loss, his ambition somewhat over-reached itself. To borrow the pithy phrase of the backwoodsmen, he "bit off more than he could chew."

One of these big grey lake-trout, or "togue," which, as a rule, lurk obstinately in the utmost depths, rose slowly to investigate the floating body of a dead swallow. Pausing a few inches below the surface, he considered as to whether he should gulp down the morsel or not. Deciding through some fishy caprice, to leave it alone—possibly he had once been hooked, and broken himself free with a painful gullet!—he was turning away to sink lazily back into the depths when something like a thunderbolt crashed down upon the water just above him, and fiery pincers of horn fixed themselves deep into his massive back.

With a convulsive surge of his broad-fluked, muscular tail he tried to dive, and for a second drew his assailant clean under. But in the next moment the osprey, with a mighty beating of wings which thrashed the water into foam, forced him to the surface and lifted him clear. But he was too heavy for his captor, and almost immediately he found himself partly back in his own element, sufficiently submerged to make mighty play with his lashing tail. For all his frantic struggles, however, he could not again get clear under, so as to make full use of his strength; and neither could his adversary, for all his tremendous flapping, succeed in holding him in the air for more than a second or two at a time.

And so the furious struggle, half upon and half above the surface, went on between these two so evenly-matched opponents, while the tormented water boiled and foamed and showers of bright spray leapt into the air. But the osprey was fighting with brains as well with wings and talons. He was slowly but surely urging his adversary over toward that white beach below the hog-back, where, in the shallows, he would have him at his mercy and be able to end the duel with a stroke or two of his rending beak. If his strength could hold out till he gained the beach, he would be sure of victory. But the strain, as unusual as it was tremendous, was already beginning to tell upon him, and he was yet some way from shore.

His mate, in the meantime, had been watching everything from her high perch on the edge of the nest. At sight of the robber eagle's attack and his theft of the chub her crest feathers had lifted angrily, but she had made no vain move to interfere. She knew that such an episode was all in the day's fishing, and might be counted a cheap way of purchasing immunity for the time. When her gallant partner first lifted the big lake-trout into the air, her bright eyes flamed with fierce approval. But when she saw that he was in difficulties her whole expression changed. Her eyes narrowed, and she leaned forward intently with half-raised wings. A moment more, and she was darting with swift, short wing-beats to his help.

By the time she arrived the desperate combatants were nearing the shore, though the big fish was still resisting with undiminished vigour, while his captor, though undaunted, was beginning to show signs of distress. With excited cries of *Pip-pip, pip-pip,* she hovered close above her mate, seeking to strike her eager talons into his opponent's head. But his threshing wings impeded her, and it was some moments before she could accomplish it without hampering his struggles. At last she saw her opportunity, and with a lightning pounce fixed her talons upon the fish's head. They bit deep, and through and through. On the instant his struggles grew feeble, then died away. The exhausted male let go his hold and rose a few yards into the air on heavy wings; while his victorious mate flapped inwards to the beach, half carrying her prey, half dragging it through the water. With a mighty effort she dropped it and alighted beside it, with one foot firmly clutching it in sign of victory. Her mate promptly landed beside it, whereupon she withdrew her grip, in acknowledgment that the kill was truly his.

After a few minutes' rest, during which the male bird shook and preened his ruffled plumage into order, the pair fell to at the feast, tearing off great fragments of their prey and devouring them hastily, lest the eagle should return, or the eagle's yet more savage mate, and snatch the booty from them. Their object was to reduce it to a size that could be carried home conveniently to the nest. In this they were making swift progress when the banquet was interrupted. A long-limbed woodsman in grey homespun, with a grizzled beard and twinkling grey-blue eyes, and a rifle over his shoulder, came suddenly into close view around a bend of the shore.

The two ospreys left their feast and flapped up into the top of a near-by pine tree. They knew the man, and knew him unoffending as far as they were concerned. He had been a near neighbour ever since their arrival from the south that spring, for his rough shack, roofed with sheets of whitish-yellow birch-bark, stood in full view of their nest and hardly two hundred paces from it. Furthermore, they were well accustomed to the sight of him in his canoe on the lake, where he was scarcely less assiduous a fisherman than themselves. But they were shy of him, nevertheless, and would not let him watch them at their feeding. They preferred to watch him instead, unafraid and quite unresentful, but mildly curious, as he strolled up to the mangled body of the fish and turned it over with the toe of his moccasined foot.

"Jee-hoshaphat!"[1] he muttered admiringly. "Who'd ever a' thought them there fish-hawks could a' handled a togue ez big ez that? Some birds!"

He waved a lean and hairy brown hand approvingly at the two ospreys in the pine-top, and then moved on with his loose-jointed stride up through the trees towards his shack. The birds sat watching him impassively, unwilling to resume their feast till he should be out of sight. And the big fish lay glittering in the sun, a staringly conspicuous object on the empty beach.

But other eyes meanwhile—shrewd, savage, greedy eyes—had marked and coveted the alluring prize. The moment the woodsman disappeared around the nearest clump of firs, an immense black bear burst out through the underbrush and came slouching down the beach towards the dead fish. He did not hurry—for who among the wild kindred would be so bold as to interfere with him, the monarch of the wild?

[1] It must be understood that this expression is a polite euphemism for the backwoodsman's too vigorous expletive.—C.G.D.R.

He was within five or six feet of the prey. Then there was a sudden rush of wind above his head—harsh, rigid wings brushed confusingly across his face—and the torn body of the fish, snatched from under his very nose, was swept into the air. With a squeal of disappointed fury he made a lunge for it, but he was too late. The female osprey, fresher than her mate, had again intervened in time to save the prize, and lifted it beyond his reach.

Now, under ordinary circumstances the bear had no grudge against the ospreys. But this was an insult not to be borne. The fish had been left upon the beach, and he regarded it as his. To be robbed of his prey was the most intolerable of affronts; and there is no beast more tenacious than the bear in avenging any wrong to his personal dignity.

The osprey, weighed down by her heavy burden, flew low and slowly toward the nest. Her mate flew just above her, encouraging her with soft cries of *Pip-pip-pip, pip-pip-pip, pip-pip-pip;* while the bear galloped lumberingly beneath, his heart swelling with vindictive wrath. Hasten as he would, however, he soon lost sight of them; but he knew very well where the nest was, having seen it many times in his prowlings, so he kept on, chewing his plans for vengeance. He would teach the presumptuous birds that his overlordship of the forest was not lightly to be flouted.

After four or five minutes of clambering over a tangle of rocks and windfalls he arrived at the foot of the naked pine trunk which bore the huge nest in its crotch, nearly fifty feet above the ground. He paused for a moment to glare up at it with wicked eyes. The two ospreys, apparently heedless of his presence and its dreadful menace, were busily tearing fragments of the fish into fine shreds and feeding their hungry nestlings — *his* fish, as the bear told himself, raging at their insolent self-confidence. He would claw the nest to pieces from beneath, and devour both the nestlings themselves and the prey which had been snatched from him. He reared himself against the trunk and began to climb—laboriously, because the trunk was too huge for a good grip, and with a loud rattling of claws upon the dry, resonant wood.

At that first ominous sound the ospreys took alarm. Peering both together over the edge of the nest, they realized at once the appalling peril—a peril beyond anything they had dreamed of. With sharp cries of rage and despair they swooped downwards and dashed madly upon their monstrous foe. First one and then the other, and sometimes both together, they struck him, buffeting him about the face with their wings, stabbing at him in a frenzy with beak and talons. He could not strike back at them but, on the other hand, they could make little impression upon his tough hide under

its dense mat of fur. The utmost they could do was to hamper and delay his progress a little. He shut his eyes and climbed on doggedly, intent upon his vengeance.

The woodsman, approaching his shack, was struck by that chorus of shrill cries, with a note in them which he had never heard before. From where he stood he could see the nest, but not the trunk below it. "Somethin' wrong there!" he muttered, and hurried forward to get a better view. Pushing through a curtain of fir trees he saw the huge black form of the bear, now half-way up the trunk, and the devoted ospreys fighting madly, but in vain, to drive him back. His eyes twinkled with appreciation, and for half a minute or so he stood watching, while that shaggy shape of doom crept slowly upwards. "Some birds, sure, them fish-hawks!" he muttered finally, and raised his rifle.

As the flat crash of the heavy Winchester .38 startled the forest, the bear gave a grunting squawl, hung clawing for a moment, slithered downward a few feet, then fell clear out from the trunk and dropped with a thud upon the rock below. The frantic birds darted down after him, heedless of the sound of the rifle, and struck at him again and again. But in a moment or two they perceived that he was no longer anything more than a harmless mass of dead flesh and fur. Alighting beside him, they examined him curiously, as if wondering how they had done it. Then, filled with exultation over their victory, they both flew back to the nest and went on feeding their young.

DISCUSSING THE STORY

1. In any hockey game in which we are interested, there is one team that enlists our sympathies, that we cheer for, and that we hope will win. The other team we regard as the enemy, whose utter defeat we long for, and for whom no fate can be too harsh. Similarly, in many stories there are the characters with whom we identify ourselves. These are called the protagonists. There may also be other characters who are the enemies of the protagonists. These are called the antagonists. Can you identify both protagonists and antagonists in this story?

2. An interesting story usually contains a struggle. The protagonists strive to reach some goal. They meet obstacles on the way, and we are not sure for a long time whether or not they will be successful. Or they may meet initial success or failure, and go on to a final crisis (called climax). Can you trace the struggle or conflict in this story? What crises are surmounted before the climax is reached? What is the climax?

3. What character intervenes at two critical points in the story? How does he both hinder and help the ospreys?

4. Roberts devotes considerable attention to the character of the osprey. Why does he admire it so much?

5. The setting of this story is very important and is carefully developed. What do we mean by "setting"? Why is it so important in the story? Which details are important?

✻ FOR FURTHER READING: ADVENTURES NEAR

EVERETT E. ALTON, *Gridiron Courage*
The story of a football coach who meets unusual courage.

JACK BECHDOLT, *Greg Sheridan, Reporter*
A present-day vocational story about the newspaper world.

FAIRFAX DOWNEY, *Dogs of Destiny*
An interesting account of famous dogs.

FREDERIC DOYLE, *Smoky Ridge*
More stories about woodland creatures by the author of "Stripes."

JOHN L. AND JEAN GEORGE, *Vulpes, the Red Fox*
The adventures of a clever fox who successfully outwits his enemies.

JACK HAMBLETON, *Young Bush Pilot*
The story of a young pilot employed by the Ontario Forestry Service
and of his ordeal by forest fire.

ELIZABETH HEADLEY, *She's My Girl*
A girl spends a wonderful summer managing a kennel for dogs.

STEPHEN HOLT, *The Phantom Roan*
An engaging story of an Alberta boy and his horse.

RUTH ADAMS KNIGHT, *Valiant Comrades*
The story of the testing and training of dogs for wartime service.

MARIE McSWIGAN, *Our Town Has a Circus*
An amusing story of community co-operation in a small United States
town.

E. F. O'BRIEN, *Clowns of the Forest*
An interesting account of bears.

MARJORIE K. RAWLINGS, *The Yearling*
The story of a fine friendship between a boy and an animal.

CHARLES G. D. ROBERTS, *Red Fox*
A vivid and unforgettable story, full of suspense and drama, of Red
Fox's career and his final triumph over his enemies.

SAMUEL SCOVILLE, JR., *Wild Folk*
Stories of forest creatures written with understanding and sympathy.

ERNEST THOMPSON SETON, *Wild Animals I Have Known*
Stories of Lobo, Raggylug, Bingo, Wully, and Redruff.

ARTHUR D. STAPP, *Escape on Skis*
Danger and suspense on a ski trip on Mt. Rainier.

EDITH TALLANT, *The Girl Who Was Marge*
The story of a volunteer worker with the Grenfell Mission in far-off Labrador.

INTERESTING COLLECTIONS OF POETRY

WILLIAM HENRY DRUMMOND, *Complete Poems*
ADOLPH GILLIS AND WILLIAM ROSE BENÉT, *Poems for Modern Youth*
E. PAULINE JOHNSON, *Flint and Feather*
A. M. STEPHEN, *The Rosary of Pan*
SARA TEASDALE, *Stars Tonight*

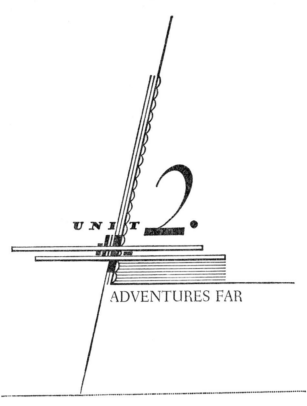

UNIT 2.

ADVENTURES FAR

For just a minute let us consider the advantages of
following the trail of adventure in books as compared with
seeking adventure in reality. First of all, we already
know that we can go almost anywhere we wish without
leaving home. With a flip of a few pages we are on our
way to China, Africa, the South Seas, or India. We can
experience the most violent dangers and, at the same
time, remain relatively secure by our fireside. And what
about time?—time is a small problem. In a little while
we shall be adventuring in legendary Italy. Then, in
the time necessary to turn just one page, we will find we
have been transported to Mexico. Let us not waste an
instant. Just ahead danger and excitement await us.

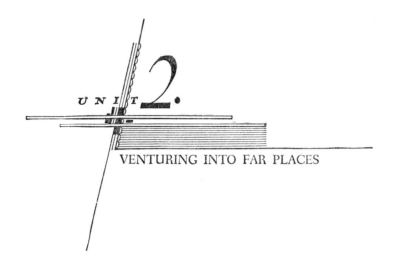

UNIT 2.

VENTURING INTO FAR PLACES

THE GOOD RIVER 🌿 PEARL BUCK

ALL her life Lan Ying had lived by the river with her father and her mother and her three younger brothers. The good river, they called it, because the river helped them in many ways—although its name was Yangtze,[1] or Son of the Sea. In the spring the river brought swelling tides down from the snow melting on the hundred mountains where was its source. Many an hour had Lan Ying wondered about that source as she sat watching the fish net for her father. The river ran so wide and deep and yellow here at her feet, below the great net spread out on bamboo poles, that it seemed impossible to believe that it was ever a small stream somewhere, tumbling down some rocky cliff, or running small and sluggish through some sandy desert. The only way she could realize it was to think of her baby brother, newly born three years ago, how small he was and how different from a man—and yet he, too, would grow out of that smallness, even as the river did, until it was so great it could be called truly a Son of the Sea.

Sitting by the fish net and waiting patiently until it was time to pull the rope that lifted it again, Lan Ying stared across the river. She could see the opposite shore only as a line of clear green. On

[1] YANGTZE (yăng′tsĕ)—The principal river in China.

misty mornings she could not see it at all, and she might have been sitting beside a muddy ocean. Nearly all her days did Lan Ying sit here beside the great river, and it had come now to mean something like a person to her. Her father was not a fisherman but a farmer, and he planted rice and wheat on his land that edged the river and ran back inland an acre or two to the hillock, where the hamlet was where they lived with half a dozen or so other families. They were all families of farmers like Lan Ying's father, but they all had nets, tended too, by children, or by old grandfathers who had grown too old to work any more in the fields. Fish brought them in the extra pennies they could spend for the various holidays and for incense to burn before the gods, and for new clothes sometimes, and besides all this, fish was good meat to eat as well.

Lan Ying rose suddenly from the low, little bamboo stool where she sat, and pulled with all her might at the rope. Up came the net slowly. Many a time there was nothing in it. Sometimes there were tiny fish that she had to scoop up with a long-handled dipper. Sometimes there was a big fish, once in several days or so. But there was none now, only a flash of tiny minnows. She stooped and dipped them up. Her mother would pin each one by a sliver of bamboo to a bit of matting on a board and dry them in the sun, and then they were salted and very good to eat with morning rice. She let the net down slowly and sat down once more.

Sometimes the days were very long, sitting here alone. She came just after her breakfast and sat until noon when she could go home again. But she liked it better than the other things the children must do on the river farms. She liked it better than herding the buffalo and sitting astride its hard and hairy back all day, as her second brother did. She liked it better than herding the ducks in the little inlets from the river as her eldest brother did. Yes, she liked it because there was something very companionable about the moving river, about the boats that passed by her there, and the coveys of wild ducks that floated down sometimes, great flocks of them carried askew by the currents and bobbing up and down on the water. There was always something to see. As for the boats, there was every kind, from small fishing sculls to the sailed junks

with their painted eyes staring out at her from their bows. Once in many days low-set foreign craft came by and sometimes smoking steamers. She hated these and the river hated them, too. It always swelled into angry waves and rocked back and forth as they passed. Sometimes waves grew so high that the little fishing boats almost capsized, and the fishermen shouted loud curses at these foreign ships. Seeing the river angry like this, Lan Ying was angry, too, and ran out to hold her net steady. Still, oftentimes after these steamers passed there would be fish in her net, frightened there into commotion, and Lan Ying, when she saw the big silver bodies flapping in the bottom of the net, gave thanks to the river in her heart for sending her the big fish. It was a good river. It brought them food from the land and meat from its waters, and it came to mean to Lan Ying, whose life was there beside it, something like a god, and staring out over it day after day, she could read its face and catch its mood for the day.

It was, indeed, the only book she could read, for she did not dream of going to school. In their hamlet there was no school, but she knew very well what a school was, because in the market town to which she and her mother went once a year there was a school. There were no pupils there on that day, for it was a fair day, and the school was out for the day, but she used to look curiously into the empty room as she passed, and see the empty seats and the tables and pictures hung on the wall. The first time she had asked her mother, "And what is it they do there?"

To this her mother said, "They learn the books there."

Now Lan Ying had never seen a book and so she asked with great curiosity, "Did you so learn when you were a child?"

"No, indeed!" said her mother loudly. "When did I ever have time for such stuff? I have had to work! It is only idle people who go to school—city people and such like. It is true my father talked of sending my eldest brother to school for the looks of the thing. He was a proud man and he thought it would look well to have one of the family who could read and write. But when my brother had gone three days he grew weary of so much sitting, and begged to be sent no more and wept and pouted so that my father did not make him."

Lan Ying pondered awhile longer on all this and she asked again, "And do all city people learn books, even the girls?"

"I have heard it is the new fashion," said her mother, shifting her load of cotton thread she had spun and now brought to the fair to sell. "But what use it can be to a girl I do not know. She has but the same things to do, to cook and sew and spin and tend the net, and when she is wed she does the same things over again and bears her children, too. Books cannot help a woman." She went along more quickly for the load on her back grew heavy, and Lan

Ying hurried a little, and then saw the dust on her new shoes and, stooping to brush them, forgot about books.

Nor did she think about them any more when she went back to the river. No, books had nothing to do with her life here by the good river. To lift the net and lower it again, to go home at evening and burn the grass fuel in the earthen oven upon which two iron cauldrons were set and in which the rice was heated for their supper, and when they had eaten it with a bit of fish, if the river had been kind that day, to run with the bowls to the river's edge and rinse them there, and back again before the night was too dark, to creep into bed and lie and listen to the soft rush of the river among its reeds—this was all her life of every day. Only on a feast day or a fair day did it differ, and then but for that one day.

It was a quiet life thus spent, but a very safe one. Sometimes Lan Ying heard her father say that in the market town where he went often to sell his cabbages and grain, he had heard of famine to to the north because there had been no rains, and he would always add:

"You see how fine it is to dwell beside a good river! Whether it rains or not is nothing to us, who have only to dip our buckets into the river and there is water for our fields. Why, this good river of ours brings us the water from a hundred valleys—and rains or none it is nothing to us."

And when she heard this Lan Ying thought that theirs was surely the best life in the world, and life in the best place, where fields were always fruitful and willows always green and the reeds were ever lush and deep for fuel, and everything came from this river. No, she would never move away from this river so long as she lived.

Yet there came a spring when the river changed. Who could have foreseen that the river would change? Year after year it had been the same until this year. Lan Ying, sitting beside the fish net, saw it change. It is true that every year it swelled with spring flood as it did now. The water ran high against the clay banks, but so it ever did in the spring. The yellow water curled in great wheels and tore at its banks, so that often a great clod would shudder and tear itself away from the land and sink, and the river licked it up triumphantly. Lan Ying's father came and moved the net away to an inlet's mouth, lest the bit of land upon which she sat might so sink and bear her away. For the first time in her life, Lan Ying felt a little afraid of the river.

The time came for the river to go down, but it did not subside. Surely by now those upper snows were melted, for it was summer and the winds were hot and the river ought to lie quiet and smooth beneath the bright skies. But it did not lie quiet. No, it tore on as though fed by some secret and inexhaustible ocean. Boatmen who came down from the upper gorges, their craft buffeted by high rapids, told of torrents of rain, days and weeks of rain when the times for rain were past. The mountain streams and the lesser rivers, thus fed, all poured into the great river and kept it high and furious.

Lan Ying's father moved the net still farther up the inlet, and Lan Ying, when she was left alone, did not look over the river any more. No, she turned her back on it and looked over the fields. She was actually afraid of the river now.

For it was a cruel river. All during the hot summer months it rose, each day a foot, two feet. It crept over the rice fields where the half-grown grain stood; it covered the grain and took away the hope of harvest. It swelled into the canals and streams and flooded their banks. Stories came everywhere of dikes falling, of great walls of water rushing over deep, rich valleys, of men and women and children engulfed and swept away.

Lan Ying's father moved the net far back now, for the inlet was flooding its banks, too. Again and again he moved it back, cursing the river and muttering, "This river of ours has gone mad!"

At last there came a day when he tied the handle that lifted the net to one of the many willow trees that grew at the edge of the threshing floor that was the dooryard to Lan Ying's home. Yes, the water had risen as high as this, and the little hamlet of half a dozen earthen houses, thatched with straw, was on an island now, surrounded by the yellow river water. They must all fish, for there could be no more farming.

Now it did not seem possible that the river could do more than this. At night Lan Ying could scarcely sleep, the water rushed so near the bed where she lay. At first she could not believe it would come nearer than this. But she saw the great fear in her father's eyes. It was true that the water was rising nearer. Was it not halfway across the threshing floor the day before yesterday? Yes, it was rising. In three days it would come into the house.

"We must go to the innermost dike," said Lan Ying's father. "Once before, in my father's father's time, I heard the river did this and they had to go to the innermost dike where the water does not come once in five generations. It is our curse that the time has fallen in our lifetime."

The youngest little boy began to howl in a loud voice for he was suddenly afraid. So long as the roof of the house was over them and its walls about them, it was only a strange thing to see the water everywhere and be like a ship perched above it thus. But when he heard they must go and live on a dike he could not bear it. Lan Ying's tears came in sympathy and she drew him to her and pressed his face against her breast.

"But may I take my black goat?" he sobbed.

He had a black goat that he had taken as a kid for his own from the two or three goats his father kept.

"We will take all the goats," answered his father loudly, and when his wife said, "But how can we get them across all the water?" he said simply, "We must, for we will have them as food."

On that very day, then, he took the door from its wooden hinge and lashed it together with the wooden beds and with the table, and he tied the rude raft to a little scull he owned, and upon the raft climbed Lan Ying and her mother and the little boys. The buffalo they tied to a rope and let it swim, and the ducks and four geese also. But the goats were put upon a raft. Just as they left the house, the yellow dog came swimming after them, and Lan Ying cried, "Oh, my father, look! Lobo wants to come, too!"

But her father shook his head and rowed on. "No," he said, "Lobo must look after himself and seek his own food now, if he lives."

It seemed a cruel thing to Lan Ying, and the eldest shouted, "I will give him half my bowl of rice!"

Then did the father shout as though he were angry, "Rice? What rice? Can a flood grow rice?"

The children were all silent then, not understanding but afraid. They had never been without rice. At least the river had given them rice every year. When at last Lobo grew weary and swam more and more slowly and was farther and farther behind, there came a time when they could not see his yellow head against the yellow water.

Across the miles of water they came at last to the inner dike. It stood like a ridge against the sky, and it seemed a heaven of safety. Land, good dry land! Lan Ying's father lashed his raft against a tree and they climbed ashore.

But there were many there before them. Along that ridge stood huts of mats and heaps of saved furniture, benches and tables and beds, and everywhere were people. For even this inner dike had not stood against the water. It had been a hundred years since it had been so attacked by the river, and in many places people had forgotten there could ever come such attack and they had not kept the dike sound and whole. The river crashed its way through these weak places and swept behind even into the good lands behind the dike. The dike stood then still an island, and upon it clung these people from everywhere.

Not people only, but the wild beasts and the field rats and the snakes came to seek this bit of land, too. Where trees stood up out of the water, the snakes crawled up into them and hung there. At first the men battled with them and killed them and threw their dead bodies into the flood. But the snakes kept coming and at last they let them be, unless there was one more dangerous than the others.

Through the summer and the autumn did Lan Ying live here with her family. The basket of rice they had brought was long since eaten. The buffalo, too, they killed at last and ate, and Lan Ying saw her father go and sit alone by the water when he had killed the beast; and when she went near him he shouted at her surlily, and her mother called her and said in a whisper, "Do not go near him now. He is thinking how will he ever plough the land again with the buffalo gone."

"And how will he?" asked Lan Ying.

"How, indeed!" said her mother grimly, hacking at the meat.

It did not seem possible that it was the good river that had done all this. They had eaten the goats before the buffalo, and the little boy had not dared even to complain when he saw his pet kid gone. No, there was the grim winter ahead of them.

There came the day they knew must come, when no food was left. What then? Well, they had their fishing net left. But the river sent no large fish here into these stagnant flood waters. There were only shrimps here and crabs crawling slowly up the muddy banks. Among all the people no food was left. Each family kept closely to itself, hoarding its last bit, telling no one what was left. A few families had a little left and they ate secretely in the darkness of the night lest they be forced to share. But even these slender stores were soon gone. There was nothing left then but the shrimps and the crabs. Nor was there fuel to burn that they could be cooked. They must be eaten raw. At first Lan Ying thought she could not—that she would rather starve. Her father said nothing, but he watched her and smiled a little grimly when, having starved a day, she picked from the heap of shrimps one that did not move.

"At least I will not eat them alive," she muttered.

Day passed after day. Winter drew near in chill winds and sudden frosty nights. When it rained they were all drenched to the skin and huddled together like sheep. But it did not often rain, and the next day they could dry their garments in the sun. Lan Ying grew very thin, so thin she was always cold. But she looked at them all, and the boys were thin, too, and very silent. They never played. Only the eldest would move slowly to the water's edge when his father called to him to come and help to catch the day's shrimps. Lan Ying saw her mother's round face grow pale and hollow, and her hands that had been red and plump and dimpled at the knuckles were like a skeleton's hands. Still she was cheerful and she said often, "How fortunate are we to have even shrimps, and how fortunate that we are all strong enough to live!"

It was true that many had died among those who had come to the dike, so there was no crowd as there had been. No, there was plenty of room now for those who were left.

No boats ever passed by in these days. Lan Ying, sitting by habit and looking over the water, used to think of all the boats that had been wont to pass by in a day's time of fishing. It seemed another life. Had there been a time once not like this? It seemed they were the only people left in the world, a little handful of people perched upon a bit of land in the midst of a flood.

Sometimes the men talked together in faint tones. Not one of them had his old strong voice now. Each man talked as though he had been ill a long time. They talked of when the flood would abate and what they would do to find new beasts to pull their ploughs, and always Lan Ying's father would say sombrely, "Well, I can harness myself to my plough, and my old woman will do it for once, I swear, but what is the good of ploughing when there is no seed to put into the ground? Where shall we get our seed, having no grain?"

Lan Ying began to dream of boats coming. Surely somewhere

there were people in the world left who had grain. Might not boats come? Every day she sat looking earnestly over the waters. If a boat would come, she thought, at least there would be a living man in it and they would call to him and say, "Save us who are here starving! We have eaten nothing but these raw shrimps for many days—"

Yes, even though he could do nothing he might go away and tell someone. A boat was the only hope. She began to pray to the river to send a boat. Every day she prayed, but no boat came. It is true that one day she saw on the horizon, where the yellow water was dark against the blue sky, the form of a small boat, but it passed into the sky and came no nearer.

Yet the sight heartened her. If there was this boat, might there not be others? She said timidly to her father, "If a boat should come—"

But he did not let her finish. He said sadly, "Child, and who knows we are here? No, we are at the mercy of the river."

She said no more, but she still looked steadfastly over the water.

Suddenly one day she saw, sharp and black against the sky, the shape of a boat. She watched it, saying nothing. She would wait lest it fade away again as that other boat had faded. But this boat did not fade. It grew larger, clearer, more near. She waited. At last it came near enough so that she could see in it two men. She went to her father then. He lay sleeping as all the men slept when they could, so that they might forget their gnawing bellies. She shook him, panting a little, plucking at his hand to waken him. She was very faint and too weak to cry aloud. He opened his eyes.

"There is a boat coming," she gasped.

Then he rose, fumbling and staggering in his feebleness, and peered out over the water. It was true there was a boat. It was true it came near. He pulled off his blue coat and waved it weakly, and his bare ribs stood forth like a skeleton's. The men in the boat shouted. But no one among those men on the land could answer, so feeble they were.

The boat came near. The men tied it to a tree and leaped up the bank. Lan Ying, staring at them, thought that she had never seen such men as these, so fat, so fed. They were talking boisterously —what were they saying?

"Yes, we have food—yes, food for all! We have been searching for such as you! How long have you been here? Four months— heaven have pity! Here, eat this rice we brought cooked! Yes, yes, there is more! Here is wheat flour, too—no, not too fast— remember to eat a little at first and then a little more!"

Lan Ying stared as they dashed into the boat and brought back the rice gruel and loaves of wheaten bread. She stretched out her hand without knowing what she did, and her breath came as fast as a spent animal's does. She did not know what she did except that she might have food at last—she must have food. One of the men gave her a piece of the loaf he tore off and she sank her teeth into it, sitting down suddenly on the ground, forgetting everything except this bit of bread she held. So did they all and so did they eat, and when all had something the two men stood and looked away as if they could not bear to see this famished eating. No one spoke.

No, not one voice spoke until suddenly one man said, having eaten a while and as much as he dared, "Look at this bread, how white it is! I have never seen this wheat to make such white bread!"

They all looked, and it was true; the bread was white as snow. One of the men from the boat spoke, then, and said, "It is bread made from wheat grown in a foreign country. They have heard what the river did and have sent us this flour."

Then they all looked at the bits of bread that were left and men murmured over it, how white and good it was, and it seemed the very best bread they had ever eaten. Lan Ying's father looked up and he said suddenly, "I should like to have a bit of this wheat to plant in my land when the flood goes down. I have no seed."

The other man answered heartily, "You shall have it—you shall all have it!"

He said it as easily as though he spoke to a child, for he did not know what it meant to these men who were farmers to be told they had seed to plant again. But Lan Ying was a farmer's daughter and she knew. She looked at her father secretly and saw he had turned his head away and was smiling fixedly, but his eyes were full of tears. She felt the tears knot together in her throat, too, and she rose and went to one of the men and plucked at his sleeve. He looked down at her and asked, "What is it, child?"

"The name—" she whispered, "what is the name of the country that has sent us this fair wheat?"

"America," he answered.

She crept away then and, unable to eat more, sat and held the precious bit of bread he had left and looked out over the water. She held it fast, although the men had promised them more. She felt suddenly faint and her head was swimming. She would eat more bread when she could—only a little at a time, though, this good bread! She looked out over the river, and feared it no more. Good or bad, they had bread again. She murmured to herself, "I must not forget the name—America!"

ABOUT THE AUTHOR

Although Pearl Buck was born in America, she went with her missionary parents to live in China while she was still very small. She did not return to the land of her birth to live for any long period until she was old enough to go to college. In the meantime she had learned to understand and to love the Chinese people. Inspired by her mother to write about the things she saw around her in China, Pearl's novels and stories became favourites among both old and young. Certainly many thousands have learned more about China from Pearl Buck's stories than from any other source.

DISCUSSING THE STORY

1. Flowing eastward through Central China for about 3200 miles, the Yangtze River feeds many fertile valleys and supports a vast population. Tell how, except in times of flood, it is a "good river" to families like Lan Ying's.

2. When the flood came upon them, the lives of the people were entirely changed. How did they try to save themselves? Tell about some of the hardships Lan Ying's family endured.

3. How did help finally reach the isolated people? In what ways has America helped other countries in time of need? How are disaster areas in our own country helped?

4. Tell some of the impressions about China that you have gained from this story. How does the Chinese farmer's way of life differ from an American farmer's? What opportunities for education do most Chinese children have? Do you think it is good for the people of one country to learn about those of another? Tell why you feel as you do.

OLD SHIPS ❧ DAVID MORTON

G1   There is a memory stays upon old ships,
       A weightless cargo in the musty hold,
    Of bright lagoons and prow-caressing lips,
       Of stormy midnights, and a tale untold.

B1   5 They have remembered islands in the dawn,
       And windy capes that tried their slender spars,
    And tortuous channels where their keels have gone,
       And calm blue nights of stillness and the stars.

All   Ah, never think that ships forget a shore,
  10   Or bitter seas, or winds that made them wise;
    There is a dream upon them, evermore;
G1   And there be some who say that sunk ships rise
    To seek familiar harbours in the night,
      Blowing in mists, their spectral sails like light.

CLUES TO THE MEANING

1. Have you ever watched a train go by and wondered where it was going, or where it had been? It is one way to travel to places we have never been, or may never go. What kind of places does the poet think an old ship may have visited? Can you point out where some of these places might be on a map of the world?

2. How do poems and stories in books provide us with adventures in other lands?

THE LADY AND THE ELEPHANTS* 🐘

OSA JOHNSON

For many years Martin and Osa Johnson spent their lives "a-going and a-seeing." Martin was a born adventurer and when Osa became his wife she literally "married adventure" as she states in the title of her fascinating book on their experiences. Together they travelled to far places—to the Solomon Islands, the South Seas, Borneo. Behind the love of adventure lay Martin's serious work—the making of complete film records of colonies of savages and of wild animals in their native state.

On April 12, 1924 they arrived at Lake Paradise, an uncharted region in northern Africa near the Abyssinian border. The lake, lying in the centre of an extinct volcano and surrounded by steep, wooded banks two hundred feet high, was a perfect haven for the animals which the Johnsons had so long wished to photograph in their natural, undisturbed state.

OUR many encounters with elephants during the four years we spent at Lake Paradise endeared the splendid creatures to us and helped us, I think, to understand Boculy's[1] reverence for them. Dignified, conservative, intelligent, with an apparent awareness of his place in life, this fine animal attends strictly to his own business and lets other creatures severely alone. Elephants fight among themselves, are intelligent parents, and have an instinct for tribal loyalty. They have their own leaders and follow and wait upon their decisions.

There were times when Martin and I were so interested in the animals themselves that we almost forgot our job of getting pictures of them. At the end of one very hot day spent in a blind (I remember we both had splitting headaches and were on the point of gathering up our things and going back to camp), we saw a herd of some twenty elephants ambling toward our water hole. We were to leeward, but the big fellow who obviously was the leader, sensed, if not our presence exactly, something that warned him all was not as usual. Perhaps at some time or other on one of his

* Reprinted from *I Married Adventure* by Osa Johnson. By permission of the publishers, J. B. Lippincott Company.

[1] BOCULY (bō-kū'lĭ)—The Johnsons' native guide.

migrations he had heard the explosions of guns, had seen a companion fall, had caught the scent of man. At any rate, he stopped abruptly; his troupe halted instantly in their tracks. His ears stood out, his trunk lifted and waved exploringly, and he advanced alone to the water hole to investigate. A little fellow, probably his son, started to follow, whereupon the father paused long enough to smack him sharply with his trunk and send him back into the herd. This second investigation proved no more satisfactory than the first —I could have sworn the big fellow sighed and shook his head— and returning to his family and companions, led them quietly but firmly away.

Martin and I loved baby animals of every kind, but baby elephants were simply irresistible. There was one little fellow—he couldn't have been over a few weeks old—who was being led for perhaps the first time down to a water hole. It was another of those very hot days and the baby lagged behind the herd and whined and complained bitterly. As a matter of fact I felt certain that if we could have been close enough, we would have seen big tears rolling down his face. His mother lost patience finally, seized him by the ear with her trunk, held him firmly with her huge foot and then proceeded to squirt water over him. The infant squawked and struggled in vain and wasn't released until his mother was satisfied he had had enough both to cool and discipline him.

My husband and I almost laughed aloud when the baby got to his feet still squawking—his pink mouth wide open—only to find that he felt refreshed and almost happy. He took hold of his mother's tail with his trunk, quite as one of our own babies would take his mother's hand, and stood complacently while she had her drink. Then he followed her quietly into the tall grass still holding her tail.

I suppose it would sound very silly for anyone to say that elephants conduct schools for their young ones and yet if it was not a school, or class, that we came upon in the forest about eight miles from our Lake Paradise home, I'm sure I don't know what it was. Four mothers with as many youngsters apparently had chosen this quiet retreat—a discreet distance, I assume, from the male members of the family—to go into the intricacies and art of trumpeting. Fortunately they were so busy and earnest about it all that we were able to watch them for quite a long time without being observed. The procedure seemed to be for each mother in turn to lift her trunk and let forth a mighty blast, and then for her young one to set himself also a mighty blast, only to emit a thin squeak somewhat resembling a tin whistle. The disappointment and despair of the mothers and the abashment of the babies over all this had us laughing out loud, finally, and school was dismissed promptly and in some alarm.

Thanks to Boculy, we were able to secure many fine pictures of elephants in herds, but I think we were equally interested in coming on single animals at close range. In these circumstances the big animal was without the guidance of leader or herd, and his reactions, if anything, were sharper. His great ears would push straight out from his head, his long trunk wave exploringly, and he would squint his small eyes in our direction in an effort at identifying us. After a long look then and a great sniff, he would usually decide that while we were nothing to fear, exactly, neither were we familiar to him, and backing off a few paces he would turn around and stroll dignifiedly away.

There was one mammoth old lady whom I should have liked to spank for her habit of breaking into my garden and systematically eating ten square feet of my sweet potatoes. We set up our cameras, one night, with wires and flashlights, and just as we were getting into bed heard the boom of the flashlight powder.

"Good," I said, as I heard her crashing into our stockade paling. "Perhaps this will teach her a lesson."

The photographs turned out sharp and clear and Martin was delighted. He liked sweet potatoes but he liked photography even better and hoped she would come back. She did, repeatedly, in spite of booming flashlights, and one night, to prove how completely unafraid she was, she proceeded to strip the thatching from one of our huts. A little tardily I decided that the best way to please the old lady, as well as to stop the destruction, would be to plant a bed of sweet potatoes for her outside of our stockade.

Martin and I have heard "big game hunters" boast of killing elephants, and there's no doubt but that to bring the animals down requires fine marksmanship or luck—or both. The need for either skill or luck is that the only vulnerable places in the creature's noble head—other than his tiny eyes, of course—are a spot no larger than a dollar in the centre of his forehead, a similar spot at the temple, and another behind the ear.

Our only boast with regard to killing elephants, is that in all our years of association with them, we have taken the life of only one. We were having lunch in camp on that occasion, and Boculy, much excited, came running.

"Big elephants," he cried, "all together very quiet."

Within half an hour our gunbearers and porters had carried our cameras to the place indicated by Boculy and there they were, a small but complete herd of six or seven big females, several young ones, and four big bulls. They were in the open ground, grouped closely together with the babies playing tag around the legs of the older ones, and the lighting, atmosphere, everything, were right for a perfect picture.

It was I who usually "stirred up" the game to get action, but this time Martin insisted that inasmuch as there was little or no cover to run to in case of a charge, he would take over my job and I would take his behind the camera.

My husband moved slowly toward the herd. They were unaware of us. I cranked steadily, admiring the magnificent creatures and wishing it were possible to photograph in colour the rich shades of their big grey bodies against the tawny yellows of the veldt.[2] With too great suddenness, perhaps, the largest bull saw Martin. Startled, he spread his ears, raised his trunk, shifted uneasily, snorted —and charged!

Martin ran. In similar circumstances my husband and I had often stopped a charge by simply yelling and waving our arms, but this animal, apparently angered at being taken by surprise, refused to be either swerved or halted.

Martin dodged, doubled, swung about, but the beast took every

[2] VELDT (fĕlt)—African grass country.

turn with him and was gaining fast. True to our pact I kept on grinding; I kept screaming too, and my gunbearer stood ready at my side with my rifle. Terror then was added to terror as the rest of the herd tore after their leader. One part of my brain told me that this would be a magnificent picture, the other told me that unless I brought the lead elephant down, Martin would be trampled. I snatched my gun and fired. I have no recollection whatever of even stopping to take aim—and the big animal faltered and fell not fifteen feet off to the side from where we stood. The rest of the herd, startled at seeing their leader pitch to the ground, swerved and lumbered off.

Released from the tension and excitement, I started involuntarily to run, fell into a pig hole and Martin came and fished me out—covered with mud!

DISCUSSING THE SELECTION

1. Mrs. Johnson describes the elephant as dignified and intelligent. What incidents in the article tell about the elephant's dignity and his ability to meet unexpected situations? What amusing incidents does Mrs. Johnson tell about the care and training of young elephants?

2. Most big game hunters boast about the fine specimens they kill or capture. What did the Johnsons boast of? Which kind of hunter would you prefer to be? Tell how Mrs. Johnson happened to kill an elephant.

3. Martin Johnson's work grew out of his interest in photography. Do you think his work was worth while or only an amusing hobby? Tell about hobbies you have had that might lead to an interesting life work.

THE FORBIDDEN ISLAND ✻ ARMSTRONG SPERRY

Long ago on a small island in the South Seas there lived a youth who who was known as the Boy who Was Afraid. This lad who had been christened Mafatu or Stout Heart, and whose father was the great chief of a seafaring people who worshipped courage, lived in daily terror of the sea. Perhaps his fear had been born on that dreadful day when, as a boy of three, he had been tossed into a churning, thunderous sea by a great hurricane. No matter how it had come about, it was true—he was the Boy Who Was Afraid. Taunted by his companions, feeling his father's silent sorrow, Mafatu suddenly understood what he must do— he must find a way to conquer his fear.

"WE'RE going away, Uri."[1] he whispered fiercely. "Off to the south there are other islands."

The outrigger canoes lay drawn up on the beach like long slim fish. Silent as a shadow, the boy crossed the sand. His heart was hammering in his throat. Into the nearest canoe he flung half a dozen green drinking nuts, his fish spear. He gave his *pareu*[2] a brave hitch. Then he picked up a paddle and called to Uri. The dog leaped into the bow. There was only Kivi[3]—Mafatu would miss his albatross. He scanned the dark sky for sight of the bird, then gave it up and turned away.

The lagoon was as untroubled as a mirror. Upon its black face

[1] URI (ōō'rē)—Mafatu's (mä'fä-tōō) dog.
[2] *Pareu* (pä'rä-ōō)—Waistcloth.
[3] KIVI (kē'vē)—Mafatu's pet albatross. An albatross is a sea bird,

the stars lay tracks of fire. The boy shoved off and climbed into the stern. Noiselessly he propelled the canoe forward, sending it half a length ahead with each thrust of his paddle. As he drew nearer to the barrier reef, the thunder of the surf increased. The old, familiar dread of it struck at his stomach's pit and made him falter in his paddling. The voices of the Old Ones were fainter and fainter now.

The reef thunder mounted—a long-drawn, hushed, yet mighty sound that seemed to have its being not in the air above but in the very sea beneath. Out beyond lurked a terrifying world of water and wind. Out there lay everything most to be feared. The boy's hands tightened on his paddle. Behind him lay safety, security from the sea. What matter if they jeered? For a second he almost turned back. Then he heard Kana's [4] voice once more saying: "Mafatu is a coward."

The canoe entered the race formed by the ebbing tide. It caught up the small craft in its churn, swept it forward like a chip on a millrace. No turning back now. . . .

There was a fan of light spreading in the east. Mafatu stirred and opened his eyes. For a moment he lay there motionless in the cool mosses, forgetful of the events which had cast him up on this strange shore. Then it all came crowding back upon him, and he scarcely dared to believe that there was earth, solid earth beneath him; that once more Moana, the Sea God, had been cheated. He struggled to sit upright, then fell back upon one elbow. Uri lay close at hand, holding a robber-crab in his forepaws, cracking the tough shell and extracting the meat with gusto. There was Kivi, too, with his beak tucked back under his wing in sleep. Kivi, who had led his friends to this island. . . .

Mafatu pulled himself to a sitting position. The action called

[4] The proper names and italicized words in this story are not difficult to pronounce: Kana (kä′nä); Moana (mō′ä-nä); Maui (mou′ē); Tahiti (tä-hē′tē); *purau* (pōō′rä-ōō); Hikueru (hē-kōō′ä-rōō); *mapé* (mä-pä′); Ruau (rōō′ou); *umu* (ōō′mōō); *puaa* (pōō′ä-ä); *aué* (ou-ä′); Tavana Nui (tä′vä-nä nōō′ē); *tamanu* (tä′mä-nōō); *cassi* (kä′sē); *aid* (ä-ē-ä′); *marae* (mä′rä-ä); *motu tabu* (mō′tū tä′bōō); Varua Ino (vä′rōō-ä ē′nō).

for more strength than he realized. He was giddy with thirst and
there was an odd weakness in his limbs. His right leg was swollen
and painful. He remembered then that he had banged it against
the coral [5] when the canoe struck. He discovered that there was a
gash on his calf; he must take care of it, for coral wounds were
poisonous.

The chuckle of the cascade reached his ears and made him aware
of a stabbing need of water. He plunged his face into the pool and
drank deeply. Then prompted more by instinct than by conscious
thought, he withdrew, to let the water run down his swollen throat
sparingly, with caution. Its cool magic stole through his tissues,
bringing with it new life and restoring force. He sighed and sank
back on the mossy bank, relishing the strength that quickened his
tired body. Soon he must find food. . . . There were thousands
of coconut trees on every hand, rich with green fruit; but Mafatu
was not yet strong enough to climb. Later he would try it. Then
he would make fire, too; and he must search the island to find out
if it were inhabited; and there was a shelter to build. Oh, there was
much to do! He hardly knew where to begin. But now it was
enough just to lie there and feel strength returning, to know that
he was safe from the sea. The sea. . . He shuddered. Maui,
God of the Fishermen, had carried him safely across the ocean
currents.

"Uri," the boy muttered thickly, "we're alive! It wasn't all a
bad dream. It really happened."

The answering wag of his dog's tail was further assurance of
reality. As Mafatu's brain cleared of cobwebs, a sudden thought
brought him up swiftly; this silent island was not Tahiti. What
island was it then? Did it . . . oh! did it belong to the black
eaters-of-men? Were they even now watching him from secret
places in the jungle, biding their time? He glanced about in apprehension. But the solitude was unbroken save for the soft cooing
of ghost-terns and the gentle splash of the cascade.

On his left hand, far offshore, the reef boomed to the charging

---

[5] CORAL—The hard skeleton of certain sea animals. It sometimes forms sharp
reefs or small islands.

surf; the curve of the beach reached out like two great arms to inclose the lagoon. Coconuts and pandanus [6] trooped in shining legions to the very edge of the sea. A flight of green and purple parakeets flashed across the sky and vanished. There was no other sign of life—no voices of men; no laughter of children; no footprint in the sand.

The volcanic peak that formed the background of the island rose perhaps three thousand feet straight up out of the sea. It was the cone of a volcano long extinct. From its base, ridges of congealed lava flowed down to the distant shore. Once in the dim beginnings of the world, this mountain had belched forth fire and brimstone, spreading destruction over the land. But the forgiving jungle through fertile centuries had crept back up the slopes, clothing them in green, green.

The boy rose and stood stretching his stiff limbs. The water had restored him and he felt much stronger. But he found that the

[6] PANDANUS—Slender tropical plants with swordlike leaves often used as a fibre for weaving.

earth heaved with the sea's own motion, and he swayed to keep his balance. His leg still pained, and he would need the juice of limes to cauterize [7] the coral wound, and *purau* leaves to make a healing bandage. Near by was a tree loaded with wild limes. He plucked half a dozen of the fruits, broke them on a bit of coral, and squeezed the juice into the wound. He winced as the caustic stung; but when he had bound on the leafy bandage with a twist of vine, it seemed that already his leg felt better. Soon the swelling would be gone.

Close at hand he discovered a rude trail made by wild pigs and goats in their wanderings across the mountain. The trail led up through the foothills to a high plateau which, the boy decided, would make a splendid lookout. From that point of vantage he would be able to survey his entire island and the sea for a distance of many miles.

He followed the path where it led back into the jungle, along the course of the swift-flowing stream. The trail sloped up sharply and Mafatu pulled himself up by roots and trailing lianas, [8] now climbing, now crawling on his stomach. He found that he had to stop every now and then to catch his breath. Uri ran beside him, dashing off on this scent and that; the dog's shrill, sharp bark shattered the morning stillness.

For a quarter of a mile the coconuts held, beautiful trees that were more luxuriant than any in Hikueru. It was always thus in the rich soil of the volcano islands. Then came a belt of breadfruit and wild bananas, of oranges and guavas and mangoes. The roots of the *mapé* trees—the island chestnut—twisted over the ground in strange, tormented shapes. Vines trailed like aerial ropes from the high branches where orchids bloomed, while little parakeets fled on swift wings and vanished in the green gloom. Mafatu had never before seen woods like these, for Hikueru was open and wind-swept. These endless legions of trees seemed to close in upon him, imprison him with reaching arms, with heady odours, with eerie

---

[7] CAUTERIZE (kô′tẽr-īz)—To burn tissue for the purpose of preventing infection.

[8] LIANAS (lẽ-ä′nảz)—Climbing vines.

light and shadow. Ferns grew higher than a tall man's head; the roof of leaves was powdered with starry blossoms.

By the time Mafatu reached the plateau he was exhausted and his leg throbbed with pain. He lay down full length upon the volcanic rock and watched wild goats leaping from peak to peak high above his head and heard their shrill bleating in the clear air. When he caught his breath he sat up again and looked about. The plateau appeared to divide the island into halves. From his vantage point the boy could see its whole circumference. He was hoping desperately for some sign of human habitation, yet fearing it too; for who knew whether humans might prove friends or enemies? He almost hoped that the island was uninhabited, but if it were— He shivered as he realized his isolation. Even at sea in his small canoe he had not felt so utterly alone as he did here on this strange, high island. Everything about it was alien and forbidding.

He stood there looking off to the southwest, and all at once his heart gave a jump, and he strained forward. A cone-shape, vague as a cloud upon the horizon, showed him the existence of another high island. It must have been fifty miles distant. As the boy watched eagerly, scarcely daring to believe the testimony of his eyes, he saw what might have been a column of smoke lifting high into the air from the peak of the cone. He had heard Grandfather Ruau tell of the Smoking Islands, the home of savage tribes. They were the dark islands of the eaters-of-men. Was that distant island one such? Perhaps this very island upon which he stood belonged to them, too! It was a terrible thought.

As he stood there surveying his world, the wind that swept up from the wide Pacific beat hard against him, whistling in his ears. Almost he had to lean against it to keep his balance. It was a southwest wind that blew straight from the Smoking Island, whipping the sea to anger. Inside the barrier reef the water deepened and shoaled in changing hues. Up here the whole world seemed consumed with light and colour. Far off a mist of gulls drifted above the breaking surf, their hoarse cries as unceasing as the hum within a shell. Towering above Mafatu's head, the basalt cone * of

* BASALT CONE—The dark, dense substance of a lava flow formed like a cone.

the island looked as soft in hue as an amethyst, broken and worn by a thousand years of wind and storm.

He observed that the barrier reef encircled the entire island. There were only two openings in the reef through which canoes might enter. One opening lay on the side of the island where Mafatu had been cast ashore; the other was here to the southwest, facing the distant Smoking Island. In each case the opening was caused by a river which flowed from the mountain down into the lagoon; for the tiny coral polyp [10] which builds up its ramparts from the floor of the sea cannot withstand fresh water. Wherever a river flows into the sea there will be a breach in the barrier reef.

Mafatu jumped in alarm as a wild boar crashed through the undergrowth. It was so close that the boy caught a glimpse of its dark hide. Uri leaped in pursuit, barking furiously. Mafatu relaxed, and a smile crossed his face. Pig roasted underground in the hot oven stones of the *umu—Aué!* His mouth watered at the golden prospect. He would make a spear and kill the *puaa*, that's what he would do! He was fired with excitement and set for the adventure. Then the thought of killing a wild boar in single-handed combat struck him dumb with wonder. Why, he would never have dreamed of such a thing in Hikueru! He was Mafatu, the Boy Who Was Afraid. . . . He set his jaw with fierce resolution. He had never known a man who killed a wild pig. But Grandfather Ruau, who had travelled as far as distant Tahiti, had told how the warriors of that island killed pigs in the mountains with naught but a knife for a weapon, bracing themselves so that the animal impaled itself upon the blade. It needed a strong arm, and a stouter heart. Could he, Mafatu, ever accomplish such a feat? Grandfather brought back with him a necklace made from the curling tusks of the boar, and Mafatu could remember to this day how the dark-blue scrolls of tattooing on the old man's copper flesh set off the handsome ivory teeth. That necklace was the envy of every man in Hikueru and its possession earned Grandfather much respect.

"I will make such a necklace for myself from the tusks," the boy promised bravely. "And when I return to Hikueru men will

[10] POLYP (pŏl'ĭp)—A form of animal life in the sea which has a long body with many tentacles or arms extending from it.

look up to me and say: 'There goes Mafatu. He killed the wild boar single-handed!' And Tavana Nui, my father, will be filled with pride."

The prospect of returning home set another train of thought in motion. "I must find a tree, a *tamanu*, for my canoe," the boy said aloud. "I will burn it out, then make an adze [11] of basalt to finish it. I'll plait a sail of pandanus. And oh, it will be a wonderful canoe!"

At that moment his eye fell upon a mango tree loaded with juicy fruit, and he plucked a fruit and sank his teeth into the rosy pulp. For a few seconds while he ate his fill and the juices ran down over his chin, he forgot all about his canoe; forgot that he needed shelter, food, fire, and weapons. Then, his hunger satisfied, his mind ran ahead again to the happy day when he would set sail for Hikueru, with all his demons put to rout and the bright flame of courage burning in his heart. Never again would he be called Mafatu, the Boy Who Was Afraid. He stood there taut with purpose, high above the demon sea.

"Maui, God of the Fishermen, hear me!" he pleaded. "I shall return home one day, I swear it. My father, Tavana Nui, will be filled with pride at my homecoming. It is a vow that I take now, O Maui. I have spoken."

The wind from the sea swept up around him, its voice warm and soft and reassuring in his ear. Maui, God of the Fishermen, had heard and answered.

Mafatu decided that before he retraced his steps to his own beach he would explore the opposite side of the island. The trail dropped from the plateau in a series of swift turns and spirals. The boy clambered down, slipping and sliding, catching hold of roots and vines to keep from falling. Far below, a cool dark stream wound its way through a sheltered valley. Perhaps in that valley he would find some people.

At the base of the ancient crater, long ridges of lava descended to the valley. Of a sudden Mafatu remembered an old tale out of his childhood: he had been told how the youths of Tahiti slid down the lava slide on sleds of giant leaves! The thought had scarcely

[11] ADZE (ădz)—A cutting tool with a thin curved blade set at right angles to the handle.

struck him before he was wrenching off half a dozen great leaves from a nearby banana tree. Even as he did so he stopped, suddenly alert. They were splendid trees, three times his own height, with broad leaves that waved to the wind like tattered banners. But what caught and held his attention were the stems where fruit had grown: they had been severed cleanly by a knife! His heart gave a great thump and hung fire.

He examined the stems with care. Tree after tree had been stripped of fruit, and within a week, too. Who had cut these bananas? Well—he would have to find out! His lips were grim as he set about making his "sled." He bound the leaves together with a fibrous rope of vines and soon had a toboggan as long as his body. When Mafatu reached the lava slide, he set his sled in place and flung himself down upon it. Wth a shout and a shove he was off.

Down the natural slide he sped at terrifying speed. Trees whizzed past. Wind drove the air from his nostrils. The valley rushed to meet him. He brought up with a bump in a thicket of *cassi*. As he extricated himself from the thorns he was still breathing with excitement. *Aué*, but that was fun! He did not stop to think how he would regain his plateau, for at that moment his eye fell upon a broad, well-defined path leading down through the jungle.

"*Aiá!*" he exclaimed. "This fine trail was never made by the feet of wild pigs!"

The boy stood there irresolute and uncertain. Some premonition of danger kept him poised, alert and wary. He was half-tempted to retrace his way and explore no farther. Then an overpowering desire to know who had made that path urged him onward. The trail led toward the sea, widening as it went. Soon it opened into a cleared circle some hundred feet in circumference. Involuntarily Mafatu started forward, then drew back with a sharp cry. What he beheld filled him with awe and it set him trembling.

He saw a series of wide stone terraces rising in a pyramid many feet high; on top of this pyramid a grotesque idol, hideously ugly, reared in the brilliant sunshine. It was an ancient idol, its contours softened with fungus and lichens,[12] corroded by the rains of ages.

[12] LICHENS (lī'kĕnz)—Plants which grow on flat rocks or bark.

The roots of convolvulus[13] writhed about its base. No wind reached this hidden circle, and insects hummed in the hot air. Mafatu felt that he was stifling. His heart pounded. A *marae*—a Sacred Place . . .

Scarcely daring to breathe, he advanced a step. Then he drew up short. Around the base of the idol he saw piles of bones, charred, but not old. The platform was strewn with them—bones too large for dogs, too large for pigs. And then Mafatu understood. His heart congealed. This was a *motu tabu*, a Forbidden Island. Here the eaters-of-men made their terrible sacrifices to the *Varua Ino*.

Mafatu stood rooted, unable to advance, powerless to flee. Uri slunk at his side growling low, the hair on his neck lifting stiffly. Involuntarily the boy looked up; through an opening in the trees the cloud-cone of Smoking Island floated on a wine-coloured sea. . . . Could that distant island be the home of the savages who used this *motu tabu* for the Place of Sacrifice? Was it here that they came in their black canoes to turn the night hideous with their drums and ceremonies and leaping fires? Mafatu shivered. He had believed that Maui, God of the Fishermen, had led him safe to this island. But perhaps after all it had been only a cruel prank of Moana, the Sea God, angry at having been cheated. The boy seemed to hear Moana saying: "Someday, someday, Mafatu, I will claim you."

It was evident that the savages had been here recently, for the piles of ashes rested undisturbed by wind and storm. The cleared circle seemed to hold its breath, locked in a supernatural silence.

As the boy paused, irresolute, looking up at the towering *marae*, his eye was caught and held by a gleam of light and his heart gave a mighty leap. For he saw that a spearhead lay on the sacred platform—finely ground, sharp-edged; a spear for food, a weapon against attack. Dare he take it? It might mean death. . . . His heart pounded. He moved one foot forward. His hands were damp and cold. The flashing spearhead winked back at him like an evil eye. The boy's limbs turned to water. For a second he was

13 CONVOLVULUS (kŏn-vŏl'vû-lŭs)—A large plant with twining stems.

powerless to move. In that moment had a score of black men leaped forth from the jungle he could not have stirred or cried. He fought himself for control. Taking a deep breath, he whispered: "It is you, Maui, who have led me to this island. I know it. Do not forsake me now!"

Almost it seemed as if he could see dark shadows moving among ferns and hear the phantom whisper of voices. But he edged forward, poised for instant flight. There—he was so close to the idol that he could have touched it. It took every ounce of will. The spearhead glistened brightly. . . . His fingers closed about it, tightened. The towering idol cast a shadow of darkness across the green earth. Quickly the boy drew the spearhead toward him. But in moving it he dislodged a bone. It fell at his feet. Its touch was deathly cold. Mafatu gasped. Then he whipped about and was running, running. But he still gripped the spearhead in his fist.

He scrambled back up the path whence he had come. His heart was hammering, his leg stiff and sore. The twisted roots of the *mapé* trees reached for him as he fled. Never had they seemed so much like grasping fingers. The giant tree-ferns turned the jungle to an eerie gloom. The boy was filled with unaccountable dread. His limbs seemed weighted. When at last he reached the base of the lava slide, he turned at right angles and fought his way upward, hauling, pulling himself by vines.

At last he gained the plateau—drew up breathless and panting. The spear flashed in his hand. He looked down at it in wonder. Nothing had happened to him! He had touched the *marae*, dislodged a bone on the place *tabu*, yet still he lived. The sun shone. The sky arched blue. Nothing was changed. And this spear, *aué!* But it was a beautiful one! It was worth all the risk. Those eaters-of-men had wrought well. Now he, Mafatu, could kill the wild pig! Now he could defend himself against attack.

But most important of all, he knew that he had won a great victory over himself. He had forced himself to do something that he dreaded, something that took every ounce of his will. The taste of victory salted his lips. He threw out his chest and cried: "It is you, Maui, who have helped me! My thanks, my thanks to you!" Uri leaped and pranced with excitement at his master's side.

DISCUSSING THE STORY

As a boy Armstrong Sperry listened to his great-grandfather's tales of the China Seas, and of islands rich with pearls and inhabited by cannibals. Eventually he visited the islands of the South Seas where he found people who were friendly and courageous. It is this courage that is the theme of his books, most of which are written for young people.

1. Mafatu had learned to be afraid but he did not yet know how to conquer his fear. What had caused his fear? What did he decide he must do to erase this blot on the family honour?

2. How can you tell that the journey to the strange island must have been a long and difficult one? What were his feelings as he awoke among strange surroundings?

3. What geographical features of the island did Mafatu observe? What foods were available? Tell about his plans for living alone.

4. What discoveries did Mafatu make as he explored the other side of the island? What part did superstition play in the boy's feelings? How did he know that the island was a "forbidden" one?

5. In spite of his fear, the boy took the spearhead. What feeling did he experience after he forced himself to take it? What was the great victory he had won over himself? What suggestions does this story offer for conquering fears we ourselves may have?

ROADWAYS ✤ JOHN MASEFIELD

B   ONE road leads to London,
        One road runs to Wales,
      My road leads me seawards
        To the white dipping sails.

G   5 One road leads to the river,
        As it goes singing slow;
      My road leads to shipping,
        Where the bronzed sailors go.

B   Leads me, lures me, calls me
   10   To salt green tossing sea;

A road without earth's road-dust
Is the right road for me.

G   A wet road heaving, shining,
        And wild with seagulls' cries,
15 A mad salt sea-wind blowing
        The salt spray in my eyes.

All   My road calls me, lures me
          West, east, south, and north;
        Most roads lead men homewards,
20   My road leads me forth

        To add more miles to the tally
        Of grey miles left behind,
        In quest of that one beauty
        God put me here to find.

CLUES TO THE MEANING

John Masefield says that there are roads going everywhere but just one that he wants to travel. Which road is it? Where do you think it will take him? What does he expect to find along his road?

LOCH LOMOND ❧ SCOTTISH FOLK SONG

No one seems to know how old this Scottish song is, or who its author was. What we do know is that English-speaking people everywhere still enjoy the sentimental words and the sprightly music. Read the lines as you would any other poem, then sing them.

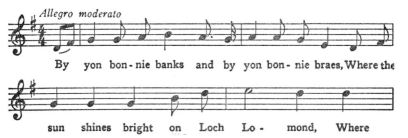

Allegro moderato

By yon bon-nie banks and by yon bon-nie braes, Where the
sun shines bright on Loch Lo - mond, Where

SCOTTISH FOLK SONG

me and my true love were ev - er wont to be, On the
bon - nie, bon - nie banks of Loch Lo - mond.

Chorus

Oh, ye'll take the high road and I'll take the low road, And
I'll be in Scot - land be - fore ye; But
me and my true love will nev - er meet a - gain On the
bon - nie, bon - nie banks of Loch Lo - mond.

By YON bonnie banks and by yon bonnie braes,
Where the sun shines bright on Loch Lomond,
Where me and my true love were ever wont to be,
On the bonnie, bonnie banks of Loch Lomond.

5 *Chorus: Oh, ye'll take the high road and I'll take the low road,
And I'll be in Scotland before ye;
But me and my true love will never meet again
On the bonnie, bonnie banks of Loch Lomond.*

'Twas there that we parted in yon shady glen,
10 On the steep, steep side of Ben Lomond,
Where purple in hue, the Highland hills we view,
And the moon coming out in the gloaming.

THE SOUTH 𝇈 WANG CHIEN

In the southern land many birds sing;
Of towns and cities half are unwalled.
The country markets are thronged by wild tribes;
The mountain-villages bear river-names.
5 Poisonous mists rise from the damp sands;
Strange fires gleam through the night-rain.
And none passes but the lonely fisher of pearls
Year by year on his way to the South Sea.

CLUES TO THE MEANING

1. This is an example of Chinese poetry after it has been translated for us. What do you learn from it about Chinese cities and the Chinese countryside?

2. Do you think this poem was written in recent years or many years ago? Tell why you think as you do.

MOTI GUJ—MUTINEER 𝇈 RUDYARD KIPLING

Once upon a time there was a coffee planter in India who wished to clear some forest land for coffee planting. When he had cut down all the trees and burned the underwood, the stumps still remained. Dynamite is expensive and slow fire slow. The happy medium for stump clearing is the lord of all beasts, who is the elephant. He will either push the stump out of the ground with his tusks, if he has any, or drag it out with ropes. The planter, therefore, hired elephants by ones and twos and threes, and fell to work. The very best of all the elephants belonged to the very worst of all the drivers or mahouts;[1] and this superior beast's name was Moti Guj. He was the absolute property of his mahout, which would never have been the case under native rule; for Moti Guj was a

---

Title—Moti Guj is pronounced mō'tē gōōzh.
[1] MAHOUT (må-hout')—An elephant driver and trainer.

creature to be desired by kings, and his name, being translated, meant the Pearl Elephant. Because the British government was in the land, Deesa, the mahout, enjoyed his property undisturbed. He was dissipated. When he had made much money through the strength of his elephant, he would get extremely drunk and give Moti Guj a beating with a tent peg over the tender nails of the forefeet. Moti Guj never trampled the life out of Deesa on these occasions, for he knew that after the beating was over, Deesa would embrace his trunk and weep and call him his love and his life and the lover of his soul, and give him some liquor. Moti Guj was very fond of liquor—arrack [2] for choice, though he would drink palm-tree toddy if nothing better offered. Then Deesa would go to sleep between Moti Guj's forefeet, and as Deesa generally chose the middle of the public road, and as Moti Guj mounted guard over him, and would not permit horse, foot, or cart to pass by, traffic was congested till Deesa saw fit to wake up.

There was no sleeping in the daytime on the planter's clearing;

[2] ARRACK (är'ăk)—A strong Oriental liquor distilled from the juice of the coco palm.

the wages were too high to risk. Deesa sat on Moti Guj's neck and gave him orders, while Moti Guj rooted up the stumps—for he owned a magnificent pair of tusks; or pulled at the end of a rope— for he had a magnificent pair of shoulders—while Deesa kicked him behind the ears and said he was the king of elephants. At evening time Moti Guj would wash down his three hundred pounds' weight of green food with a quart of arrack, and Deesa would take a share and sing songs between Moti Guj's legs till it was time to go to bed. Once a week Deesa led Moti Guj down to the river, and Moti Guj lay on his side luxuriously in the shallows, while Deesa went over him with a coir swab[3] and a brick. Moti Guj never mistook the pounding blow of the latter for the smack of the former that warned him to get up and turn over on the other side. Then Deesa would look at his feet and examine his eyes, and turn up the fringes of his mighty ears in case of sores or budding ophthalmia.[4] After inspection the two would "come up with a song from the sea," Moti Guj, all black and shining, waving a torn tree branch twelve feet long in his trunk, and Deesa knotting his own long wet hair.

It was a peaceful, well-paid life till Deesa felt the return of the desire to drink deep. He wished for an orgy. The little draughts that led nowhere were taking the manhood out of him.

He went to the planter, and "My mother's dead," said he, weeping.

"She died on the last plantation, two months ago, and she died once before that when you were working for me last year," said the planter, who knew something of the ways of nativedom.

"Then it's my aunt, and she was just the same as a mother to me," said Deesa, weeping more than ever. "She has left eighteen small children entirely without bread, and it is I who must fill their little stomachs," said Deesa, beating his head on the floor.

"Who brought you the news?" said the planter.

"The post," said Deesa.

---

[3] COIR SWAB—A coarse brush made of nut-husk fibre.
[4] OPHTHALMIA (ŏf-thăl'mĭ-à)—An inflammation of the membrane.

"There hasn't been a post here for the past week. Get back to your lines!"

"A devastating sickness has fallen on my village, and all my wives are dying," yelled Deesa, really in tears this time.

"Call Chihun,[5] who comes from Deesa's village," said the planter.

"Chihun, has this man got a wife?"

"He?" said Chihun. "No. Not a woman of our village would look at him. They'd sooner marry the elephant."

Chihun snorted. Deesa wept and bellowed.

"You will get into difficulty in a minute," said the planter. "Go back to your work!"

"Now I will speak Heaven's truth," gulped Deesa, with an inspiration. "I haven't been drunk for two months. I desire to depart in order to get properly drunk afar off and distant from this heavenly plantation. Thus I shall cause no trouble."

A flickering smile crossed the planter's face. "Deesa," said he, "you've spoken the truth, and I'd give you leave on the spot if anything could be done with Moti Guj while you're away. You know that he will only obey your orders."

"May the light of the heavens live forty thousand years. I shall be absent but ten little days. After that, upon my faith and honour and soul, I return. As to the inconsiderable interval, have I the gracious permission of the heaven-born to call up Moti Guj?"

Permission was granted, and in answer to Deesa's shrill yell, the mighty tusker swung out of the shade of a clump of trees where he had been squirting dust over himself till his master should return.

"Light of my heart, protector of the drunken, mountain of might, give ear!" said Deesa, standing in front of him.

Moti Guj gave ear and saluted with his trunk. "I am going away," said Deesa.

Moti Guj's eyes twinkled. He liked jaunts as well as his master. One could snatch all manner of nice things from the roadside then.

"But you, you fussy old pig, must stay behind and work."

The twinkle died out as Moti Guj tried to look delighted. He hated stump hauling on the plantation. It hurt his teeth.

---

[5] CHIHUN—Pronounced chi'hŭn.

"I shall be gone for ten days, oh, delectable one! Hold up your near forefoot and I'll impress the fact upon it, warty toad of a dried mud puddle." Deesa took a tent peg and banged Moti Guj ten times on the nails. Moti Guj grunted and shuffled from foot to foot.

"Ten days," said Deesa, "you will work and haul and root the trees as Chihun here shall order you. Take up Chihun and set him on your neck!" Moti Guj curled the tip of his trunk, Chihun put his foot there and was swung onto the neck. Deesa handed Chihun the heavy ankus, the iron elephant goad.

Chihun thumped Moti Guj's bald head as a paver thumps a curbstone.

Moti Guj trumpeted.

"Be still, hog of the backwoods! Chihun's your mahout for ten days. And now bid me good-bye, beast after mine own heart. Oh, my lord, my king! Jewel of all created elephants, lily of the herd, preserve your honoured health; be virtuous. Adieu!" [6]

Moti Guj lapped his trunk round Deesa and swung him into the air twice. That was his way of bidding him good-bye.

"He'll work now," said Deesa to the planter. " Have I leave to go?"

The planter nodded, and Deesa dived into the woods. Moti Guj went back to haul stumps.

Chihun was very kind to him, but he felt unhappy and forlorn for all that. Chihun gave him a ball of spices and tickled him under the chin, and Chihun's little baby cooed to him after work was over, and Chihun's wife called him a darling; but Moti Guj was a bachelor by instinct, as Deesa was. He did not understand the domestic emotions. He wanted the light of his universe back again—the drink and the drunken slumber, the savage beatings and the savage caresses.

None the less he worked well, and the planter wondered. Deesa had wandered along the roads till he met a marriage procession of his own caste, and, drinking, dancing, and tippling, had drifted with it past all knowledge of the lapse of time.

[6] ADIEU (à-dū')—Good-bye.

The morning of the eleventh day dawned, and there returned no Deesa. Moti Guj was loosed from his ropes for the daily stint. He swung clear, looked round, shrugged his shoulders, and began to walk away, as one having business elsewhere.

"Hi! ho! Come back, you!" shouted Chihun. "Come back and put me on your neck, misborn mountain! Return, splendour of the hillside! Adornment of all India, heave to, or I'll bang every toe off your fat forefoot!"

Moti Guj gurgled gently but did not obey. Chihun ran after him with a rope and caught him up. Moti Guj put his ears forward, and Chihun knew what that meant, though he tried to carry it off with high words.

"None of your nonsense with me," said he. "To your pickets, devil son!"

"Hrrump!" said Moti Guj, and that was all—that and the fore-bent ears.

Moti Guj put his hands in his pockets, chewed a branch for a toothpick, and strolled about the clearing, making fun of the other elephants who had just set to work.

Chihun reported the state of affairs to the planter, who came out with a dog whip and cracked it furiously. Moti Guj paid the white man the compliment of charging him nearly a quarter of a mile across the clearing and "Hrrumphing" him into his verandah. Then he stood outside the house, chuckling to himself and shaking all over with the fun of it, as an elephant will.

"We'll thrash him," said the planter. "He shall have the finest thrashing ever elephant received. Give Kala Nag and Nazim twelve feet of chain apiece, and tell them to lay on twenty."

Kala Nag—which means Black Snake—and Nazim were two of the biggest elephants in the lines, and one of their duties was to administer the graver punishment, since no man can beat an elephant properly.

They took the whipping chains and rattled them in their trunks as they sidled up to Moti Guj, meaning to hustle him between them. Moti Guj had never, in all his life of thirty-nine years, been whipped, and he did not intend to begin a new experience. So he waited, waving his head from right to left and measuring the precise spot in Kala Nag's fat side where a blunt tusk could sink deepest. Kala Nag had no tusks; the chain was the badge of his authority; but for all that, he swung wide of Moti Guj at the last minute and tried to appear as if he had brought the chain out for amusement. Nazim turned round and went home early. He did not feel in fighting trim that morning, and so Moti Guj was left standing alone with his ears cocked.

That decided the planter to argue no more, and Moti Guj rolled back to his amateur inspection of the clearing. An elephant who will not work and is not tied up is about as manageable as an eighty-one-ton gun loose in a heavy seaway. He slapped old friends on the back and asked them if the stumps were coming away easily; he talked nonsense concerning labour and the inalienable rights of elephants to a long "nooning;" and, wandering to and fro, he thoroughly demoralized the garden till sundown, when he returned to his picket for food.

"If you won't work, you shan't eat," said Chihun, angrily. "You're a wild elephant, and no educated animal at all. Go back to your jungle."

Chihun's little brown baby was rolling on the floor of the hut and stretching out its fat arms to the huge shadow in the doorway. Moti Guj knew well that it was the dearest thing on earth to Chihun. He swung out his trunk with a fascinating crook at the end, and the brown baby threw itself, shouting, upon it. Moti Guj made fast and pulled up till the brown baby was crowing in the air twelve feet above his father's head.

"Great Lord!" said Chihun. "Flour cakes of the best, twelve in number, two feet across and soaked in rum, shall be yours on the instant, and two hundred pounds' weight of fresh-cut young sugar cane therewith. Deign only to put down safely that insignificant brat who is my heart and my life to me!"

Moti Guj tucked the brown baby comfortably between his forefeet, that could have knocked into toothpicks all of Chihun's possessions, and waited for his food. He ate it, and the brown baby crawled away. Moti Guj dozed and thought of Deesa. One of many mysteries connected with the elephant is that his huge body needs less sleep than anything else that lives. Four or five hours in the night suffice—just two before midnight, lying down on one side; just two after one o'clock, lying down on the other. The rest of the silent hours are filled with eating and fidgeting, and long, grumbling soliloquies.[7]

At midnight, therefore, Moti Guj strode out of his pickets, for a thought had come to him that Deesa might be lying drunk somewhere in the dark forest with none to look after him. So all that night he chased through the undergrowth, blowing and trumpeting and shaking his ears. He went down to the river and blared across the shallows where Deesa used to wash him, but there was no answer. He could not find Deesa, but he disturbed all the other elephants in the lines, and nearly frightened to death some gypsies in the woods.

At dawn Deesa returned to the plantation. He had been very drunk indeed, and he expected to get into trouble for outstaying his leave. He drew a long breath when he saw that the bungalow and the plantation were still uninjured, for he knew something of Moti Guj's temper, and reported himself with many lies and salaams.[8] Moti Guj had gone to his pickets for breakfast. The night exercise had made him hungry.

"Call up your beast," said the planter; and Deesa shouted in the mysterious elephant language that some mahouts believe came from China at the birth of the world, when elephants and not men were masters. Moti Guj heard and came. Elephants do not gallop. They move from places at varying rates of speeed. If an elephant wished to catch an express train he could not gallop, but he could catch the train. So Moti Guj was at the planter's door almost before Chihun noticed that he had left the pickets. He fell into Deesa's arms trumpeting with joy, and the man and beast wept and slobbered over each other and handled each other from head to heel to see that no harm had befallen.

"Now we will get to work," said Deesa. "Lift me up, my son and my joy!"

---

[7] SOLILOQUIES (sŏ-lĭl'ō-kwĭz)—Talks to one's self.

[8] SALAAM (sȧ-läm')—An act of homage performed by bowing very low and placing the right palm on the forehead.

DISCUSSING THE STORY

1. Rudyard Kipling grew up in India where he absorbed much of material which he later used in stories and poems. In this story of Moti Guj, the elephant, he combines just enough fact and fancy to make an interesting tale. How much of this story is true or possible? What parts are added for interest?

2. Deesa and Moti Guj understood each other. Do you think Kipling exaggerated their relationship? Tell how Deesa made Moti Guj understand what he wanted him to do. What happened while Deesa was away. What happened when he did not return? Tell about an instance of friendship between an animal and a person that you yourself know about.

3. Part of the humour of the story is in the affectionate terms Deesa called his elephant. What were some of these names? Another source of humour is the way Kipling describes Moti Guj as if he were a person—for example, Moto Guj "shrugged his shoulders." What other such examples can you find?

THE RAT TRAP ✣ SELMA LAGERLOF

ONCE upon a time there was a man who went around selling small rat traps of wire. He made them himself at odd moments, from material he got by begging in the stores or at the big farms. But even so, the business was not especially profitable, so he had to resort to both begging and petty thievery to keep body and soul together. Even so, his clothes were in rags, his cheeks were sunken, and hunger gleamed in his eyes.

No one can imagine how sad and monotonous life can appear to such a vagabond, who plods along the road, left to his own meditations. But one day this man had fallen into a line of thought which really seemed to him entertaining. He had naturally been thinking of his rat traps when suddenly he was struck by the idea that the whole world about him—the whole world with its lands and seas, its cities and villages—was nothing but a big rat trap. It had never existed for any other purpose than to set baits for people. It offered riches and joys, shelter and food, heat and clothing, exactly as

the rat trap offered cheese and pork, and as soon as anyone let himself be tempted to touch the bait, it closed in on him, and then everything came to an end.

The world had, of course, never been very kind to him, so it gave him unwonted joy to think ill of it in this way. It became a cherished pastime of his, during many dreary ploddings, to think of people he knew who had let themselves be caught in the dangerous snare, and of others who were still circling around the bait.

One dark evening as he was trudging along the road he caught sight of a little grey cottage by the roadside, and he knocked on the door to ask shelter for the night. Nor was he refused. Instead of the sour faces which ordinarily met him, the owner, who was an old man without wife or child, was happy to get someone to talk to in his loneliness. Immediately he put the porridge pot on the fire and gave him supper; then he carved off such a big slice from his tobacco roll that it was enough for both of them.

The old man was just as generous with his confidence as with his porridge and tobacco. The guest was informed at once that in his days of prosperity his host had been a crofter [1] at Ramsjö Iron-

---

[1] CROFTER—One who rents and tills a very small piece of land.

works and had worked on the land. Now that he was no longer able to do day labour, it was his cow which supported him. She could give milk for the creamery every day, and last month he had received all of thirty kroner [2] in payment.

The stranger must have seemed incredulous, for the old man got up and went to the window, took down a leather pouch which hung on a nail in the very window frame, and picked out three wrinkled ten-kroner bills. These he held up before the eyes of his guest, nodding knowingly, and then stuffed them back into the pouch.

The next day both men got up in good season. The crofter was in a hurry to milk his cow, and the other man probably thought he should not stay in bed when the head of the house had gotten up. They left the cottage at the same time. The crofter locked the door and put the key in his pocket. The man with the rat traps said good-bye and thank you, and thereupon each went his own way.

But half an hour later the rat-trap peddler stood again before the door. He did not try to get in, however. He only went up to the window, smashed a pane, stuck in his hand, and got hold of the pouch with the thirty kroner. He took the money and thrust it into his own pocket. Then he hung the pouch back in its place and went away.

As he walked along with the money in his pocket he felt quite pleased with his smartness. He realized, of course, that at first he dared not continue on the public highway, but must turn off the road, into the woods. During the first few hours this caused him no difficulty. Later in the day it became worse, for it was a big and confusing forest which he had gotten into. He walked and walked, without coming to the end of the wood, and finally he realized that he had been walking around in the same part of the forest. All at once he recalled his thoughts about the world and the rat trap. Now his own turn had come. He had let himself be fooled by a bait and had been caught. The whole forest, with its trunks and branches, its thickets and fallen logs, closed

[2] KRONER (krō'nĕr)—A Scandinavian coin worth about twenty-five cents in Canadian money.

in upon him like an impenetrable prison from which he could never escape.

It was late in December. Darkness was already descending over the forest. This increased the danger, and increased his gloom and despair. Finally he saw no way out, and he sank down on the ground, tired to death, thinking that his last moment had come. But just as he laid his head on the ground, he heard a sound—a hard, regular thumping. There was no doubt as to what that was. He raised himself. "Those are the hammer strokes from an iron mill," he thought. "There must be people nearby." He summoned all his strength, got up, and staggered in the direction of the sound.

The Ramsjö Ironworks, which is now closed down, was, not so long ago, a large plant, with smelter, rolling mill, and forge. In the summertime long lines of heavily loaded barges and scows slid down the canal which led to a large inland lake, and in the wintertime the roads near the mill were black from all the coal dust which sifted down from the big charcoal crates.

During one of the long dark evenings just before Christmas, the master smith and his helper sat in the dark forge near the furnace waiting for the pig iron, which had been put in the fire, to be ready to put on the anvil. Every now and then one of them got up to stir the glowing mass with a long iron bar, returning in a few moments, dripping with perspiration.

All the time there were many sounds to be heard in the forge. The big bellows groaned and the burning coal cracked. The fire boy shoveled charcoal into the maw[s] of the furnace with a great deal of clatter. Outside roared the waterfall, and a sharp north wind whipped the rain against the brick-tiled roof.

It was probably on account of all this noise that the blacksmiths did not notice that a man had opened the gate and entered the forge, until he stood close up to the furnace.

Surely it was nothing unusual for poor vagabonds without any better shelter for the night to be attracted to the forge by the glow of light which escaped through the sooty panes, and to come in to

[s] MAW—Huge pit.

warm themselves in front of the fire. The blacksmiths glanced only casually and indifferently at the intruder. He looked the way people of his type usually did, with a long beard, dirty, ragged, and with a bunch of rat traps dangling on his chest.

He asked permission to stay, and the master blacksmith nodded a haughty consent without honouring him with a single word.

The tramp did not say anything, either. He had not come there to talk but only to warm himself and sleep.

In those days the Ramsjö iron mill was owned by a very prominent ironmaster whose greatest ambition was to ship out good iron to the market. He watched both night and day to see that the work was done as well as possible, and at this very moment he came into the forge on one of his nightly rounds of inspection.

Naturally the first thing he saw was the tall ragamuffin who had eased his way so close to the furnace that steam rose from his wet rags. The ironmaster did not follow the example of the blacksmiths, who had hardly deigned to look at the stranger. He walked close up to him, looked him over very carefully, then tore off his slouch hat to get a better view of his face.

"But of course it is you, Nils Olof!" he said. "How you do look!"

The man with the rat traps had never before seen the ironmaster of Ramsjö and did not even know what his name was. But it occurred to him that if the fine gentleman thought he was an old acquaintance, he might perhaps throw him a couple of kroner. Therefore he did not want to undeceive him all at once.

"Yes, God knows things have gone downhill with me," he said.

"You should not have resigned from the regiment," said the ironmaster. "That was a mistake. If only I had still been in the service at the time, it never would have happened. Well, now of course you will come home with me."

To go along up to the manor house and be received by the owner like an old regimental comrade—that, however, did not please the tramp.

"No, I couldn't think of it!" he said, looking quite alarmed.

He thought of the thirty kroner. To go up to the manor house would be like throwing himself voluntarily into the lions' den. He only wanted a chance to sleep here in the forge and then sneak away as inconspicuously as possible.

The ironmaster assumed that he felt embarrassed because of his miserable clothing.

"Please don't think that I have such a fine home that you cannot show yourself there," he said. "There is no one at home except my oldest daughter and myself. We were just saying that it was too bad we didn't have any company for Christmas. Now come along with me and help us make the Christmas food disappear a little faster."

But the stranger said no, and no, and again no, and the iron-master saw that he must give in.

"It looks as though Captain von Stahle prefers to stay with you tonight, Stjernstrom," he said to the master blacksmith, and turned on his heel.

But he laughed to himself as he went away, and the blacksmith, who knew him, understood very well that he had not said his last word.

It was not more than half an hour before they heard the sound of carriage wheels outside the forge, and a new guest came in, but this time it was not the ironmaster. He had sent his daughter, apparently hoping that she would have better powers of persuasion than he himself.

She entered, followed by a valet,[4] carrying on his arm a big fur coat. She was not at all pretty, but seemed modest and quite shy. The stranger had stretched himself out on the floor and lay with a piece of pig iron under his head and his hat pulled down over his eyes. As soon as the young girl caught sight of him she went up and lifted his hat. The man was evidently used to sleeping with one eye open. He jumped up abruptly and seemed to be quite frightened.

"My name is Edla Willmansson," said the young girl. "My father came home and said that you wanted to sleep here in the

[4] VALET (văl'ĕt)—A man who takes care of another's clothing and personal grooming.

forge tonight, and then I asked permission to come and bring you home to us. I am so sorry, Captain, that you are having such a hard time."

She looked at him compassionately with her heavy eyes, and she noticed that the man was afraid. "Either he has stolen something or else he has escaped from jail," she thought, and added quickly, "You may be sure, Captain, that you will be allowed to leave us just as freely as you came. Only please stay with us over Christmas Eve."

She said this in such a friendly manner that the rat-trap peddler must have felt confidence in her.

"It would never have occurred to me that you would bother with me yourself, miss," he said. "I will come."

He accepted the fur coat which the valet handed him with a deep bow, threw it over his rags, and followed the young lady out to the carriage, without granting the astonished blacksmiths so much as a glance.

But while he was riding up to the manor house he had evil forebodings.

"Why the devil did I take that fellow's money?" he thought. "Now I am sitting in the trap and will never get out of it."

The next day was Christmas Eve, and when the ironmaster came into the dining room for breakfast he probably thought with satisfaction of his old regimental comrade whom he had run across so unexpectedly.

"First of all we must see to it that he gets a little flesh on his bones," he said to his daughter, who was busy at the table. "And then we must see that he gets something else to do than to run around the country selling rat traps."

"It is queer that things have gone downhill with him as badly as that," said the daughter. "Last night I did not think there was anything about him to show that he had once been an educated man."

"You must have patience, my little girl," said the father. "As soon as he gets clean and dressed up, you will see something different. Last night he was naturally embarrassed. The tramp manners will fall away from him with the tramp clothes."

Just as he said this the door opened and the stranger entered. Yes, now he was truly clean and well shaved. The valet had bathed him, cut his hair, and shaved him. Moreover, he was dressed in a good-looking suit of clothes which belonged to the ironmaster.

But although his guest was now so well groomed, the ironmaster did not seem pleased. He looked at him with puckered brow, for now, when he stood there in broad daylight, it was impossible to mistake this strange fellow for an old acquaintance.

"What does this mean?" he thundered.

The stranger saw at once that all the splendour had come to an end.

"It is not my fault, sir," he said. "I never pretended to be anything but a poor trader, and I pleaded and begged to be allowed to stay in the forge. But no harm has been done. At worst I can put on my rags again and go away."

"Well," said the ironmaster, hesitating a little, "it was not quite honest, either. You must admit that, and I should not be surprised if the sheriff would like to have something to say in the matter."

The tramp took a step forward and struck the table with his fist.

"Now I am going to tell you, Mr. Ironmaster, how things are," he said. "This whole world is nothing but a big rat trap. All the good things that are offered you are nothing but cheese rinds and bits of pork, set out to drag a poor fellow into trouble. And if the sheriff comes now and locks me up for this, then you, Mr. Ironmaster, must remember that a day may come when you yourself may want a big piece of pork, and you will get caught in the trap."

The ironmaster began to laugh.

"That was not so badly said, my good fellow. Perhaps we should let the sheriff alone on Christmas Eve. But now get out of here as fast as you can."

But just as the man was opening the door, the daughter said, "I think he ought to stay with us today. I don't want him to go." And with that she went and closed the door.

"What in the world are you doing?" said the father.

The daughter stood there quite embarrassed and hardly knew what to answer. That morning she had felt so happy when she thought how homelike and Christmassy she was going to make things for the poor hungry wretch. She could not get away from the idea all at once, and that was why she had interceded for the vagabond.

"I am thinking of this stranger here," said the young girl. "He walks and walks the whole year long, and there is probably not a single place in the whole country where he is welcome and can feel at home. Wherever he turns he is chased away. Always he is afraid of being arrested and cross-examined. I should like to have him enjoy a day of peace with us here."

The ironmaster mumbled something in his beard. He could not bring himself to oppose her.

"It was all a mistake, of course," she continued. "But anyway I don't think we ought to chase away a human being whom we have asked to come here, and to whom we have promised Christmas cheer."

The young girl took the stranger by the hand and led him up to the table.

"Now sit down and eat," she said, for she could see that her father had given in.

The man with the rat traps said not a word; he only sat down and helped himself to the food. Time after time he looked at the young girl who had interceded for him. Why had she done it?

After that, Christmas Eve at Ramsjö passed just as it always had. The stranger did not cause any trouble because he did nothing but sleep. The whole forenoon he lay on the sofa in one of the guest rooms and slept at one stretch. At noon they woke him up so that he could have his share of the good Christmas fare, but after that he slept again. It seemed as though for many years he had not been able to sleep as quietly and safely as here at Ramsjö.

In the evening, when the Christmas tree was lighted, they woke him up again, and he stood for a while in the drawing room, blinking as though the candlelight hurt him, but after that he disappeared again. Two hours later he was aroused once more. He then had to go down into the dining room and eat the Christmas fish and porridge.

As soon as they got up from the table he went around to each one present and said thank you and good night, but when he came to the young girl she gave him to understand that it was her father's intention that the suit which he wore was to be a Christmas present —he did not have to return it; and if he wanted to spend next Christmas Eve in a place where he could rest in peace, and be sure that no evil would befall him, he would be welcomed back again.

The man with the rat traps only stared at the young girl in amazement.

The next morning the ironmaster and his daughter got up in good season to go to the early Christmas service. Their guest was still asleep, and they did not disturb him.

When, at about ten o'clock, they drove back from church, the young girl sat and hung her head even more dejectedly than usual. At church she had learned that one of the old crofters of the iron-works had been robbed by a man who went around selling rat traps.

"Yes, that was a fine fellow you let into the house," said her father. "I only wonder how many silver spoons are left in the cupboard by this time.

The wagon had hardly stopped at the front steps when the iron-master asked the valet whether the stranger was still there. He added that he had heard at church that the man was a thief. The valet answered that the fellow had gone and that he had not taken anything with him at all. On the contrary, he had left behind a little package which Miss Willmansson was to be kind enough to accept as a Christmas present.

The young girl opened the package, and gave a little cry of joy. She found a small rat trap, and in it lay three wrinkled ten-kroner notes. But that was not all. In the rat trap lay also a letter written in large, jagged characters:

"Honoured and Noble Miss:

"Since you have been so nice to me all day long, as if I was a captain, I want to be nice to you, in return, for I do not want you to be embarrassed at this Christmas season by a thief; but you can give back the money to the old man on the roadside, who has the money pouch hanging on the window frame as a bait for poor wanderers.

"The rat trap is a Christmas present from a rat who would have been caught in this world's rat trap if he had not been raised to captain, because in that way he got power to clear himself.

"Written with friendship and high regard,

CAPTAIN VON STAHLE"

DISCUSSING THE STORY

1. The rat-trap peddler had acquired little worldly goods, but he had developed a curious idea about life. What was it? Explain how the peddler forgot for a moment what he had observed and allowed himself to be caught in the world's trap.

2. One mistake often leads to another. How did the peddler get himself into further trouble? Describe his experience as a guest in the home of the ironmaster. Why do you think the girl was so kind to him?

3. More often than not, men respond in a like way to the kind of treatment they receive at the hands of other men. Anger kindles anger; kindness calls forth kindness. How does this idea apply to the behaviour of the man as he left the ironmaster's home? What might have happened if the ironmaster had called the sheriff? How many people have benefited because a girl has been kind?

4. As in many stories, there is a lesson suggested here. What forms of tempting bait do you think the world offers to-day? How can people avoid getting caught in the trap?

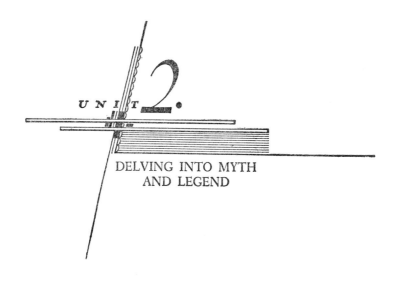

UNIT 2.

DELVING INTO MYTH
AND LEGEND

THE MAGIC BOX ✤ RUTH SAWYER

IN ONE of the fertile valleys of the Apennines—north in Emilia—
long ago there lived a rich farmer. He had much land. His vineyards were the best pruned and yielded the best vintage; his olive
grove was watched over with the utmost care and never suffered a
frost. His fields of grain harvested more than his neighbours'; his
cattle were sleeker and his sheep gave more wool at the spring
shearings. Yes, everything prospered with him. On market-and-
fair-days his neighbours would wag their thumbs at him and say:
"There goes Gino Tomba. His sons will be very rich men one of
these days."

He had two sons. The older was a daredevil who handled a
rapier better than a pruning knife and could swing a broadsword
with steadier aim than a mattock,[1] Tonio, the younger, was an easy-
going, pleasure-loving rascal who knew more about fiddling than
he did about winnowing grain. "If I had a third son, he might
have been a farmer," old Tomba used to say when he came bringing his skins of wine to the inn to sell. "But we must make the
most of what the good Virgin provides," and so he let his older

[1] MATTOCK—An instrument for digging.

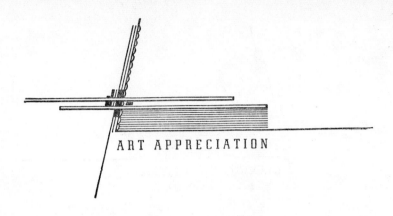

ZAPATISTAS ✦ JOSÉ CLEMENTE OROZCO

There was very little painting with native flavour in
Mexico during the nineteenth and early twentieth centuries. What few artists there were seemed satisfied to copy
the works of European masters. Then, after a series of revo-
lutions, the long oppressed Indians struggling for justice
became heroic figures to a new school of artists. The natives
who had taken part in the revolutionary fighting were celebrated in the sweeping murals that began to dominate the
walls of public buildings, and native themes of all kinds
were subjects for painters. The aim of artists like Orozco
was to paint the anguish and the aspirations of the Mexican
people, so that the humblest individual might read and
understand his history. "Zapatistas" is a picture that looks
back to the Revolution of 1910 and before. We see a band
of the rebellious men under arms, followed by the wives,
sisters, and cousins who will care for them as they march
and fight. The figures are somewhat severe and highly imaginative, but as a whole the painting is as vivid, dramatic,
and colourful as the Mexican landscape.

ZAPATISTAS
José Clemente Orozco

JOSE CLEMENTE OROZCO

[1883-1949]

*A descendant of early Spanish settlers, vitally inter-
ested in the well-being of the Mexican people, José
Clemente Orozco was a painter with roots deep in the
past, who saw great things in the future for his countrymen. He was trained as an architect, but he learned
to paint without formal training. Profoundly religious,
indigant at sinfulness, and filled with hope, his paintings reflect the kind of man he was.*

*Orozco lived and worked in the United States for
many years. For a time he painted in New York City.
Then he became a teacher of art at Dartmouth College
where he worked on a series of murals in the college
library. His Dartmouth murals, covering 3000 square
feet, depict a cultural history of the North American
continent. "Zapatistas," and some other works of the
artist, may be seen in The Museum of Modern Art in
New York City.*

son march off to the wars and set about making Tonio ready to look after his lands when he had gone.

"Hearken to me, boy; I am leaving you as fine an inheritance as any here in the north. See that you keep a sharp eye on it and render it back with increase to your brother. Some day he will grow tired of fighting Spain and the French and come marching home."

In less than a twelvemonth old Tomba was dead. Tonio came from the burying, turned himself once about the farm to make sure it was all there, and settled down to easy living. He made what you call good company. It was, Tonio, come to the fair; and Tonio, stay longer at the inn; and Tonio, drink with this one; and Tonio, dance with that. He could step the tarantella [2] as well as any man in the north, and he could fiddle as he danced. So it was here and there and anywhere that a feast was spread or a saint's day kept; and Tonio, the younger son of old Tomba, danced late and drank deep and was the last to stop when the dawn broke. Often he slept until the sun was already throwing late shadows on the foothills.

The time came when his thrifty neighbours took him soundly to task for idling away his days and wasting what his father had saved. Then he would laugh, braggadocio: [3] "Am I a sheep to graze in the pasture or a grain of wheat to get myself planted and stay in my fields all day and every day? The lands have grown rich for my father for fifty years; let them grow rich for me for fifty more. That is all I ask—that, and for my neighbours to prune their tongues when next they prune their vineyards."

But Tonio had asked too much. A place with a master is one thing, but without a master it is quite different. The banditti [4] came down from the mountains and stole his cattle while the herdsmen slept; wolves ravaged his sheep; the bad little oil-fly came in swarms and spoiled the olives as they ripened; the grapes hung too long, and the wine turned thin and sour. And so it went—a little here, a little there, each year. The labourers took to small thieving

[2] TARANTELLA (tä-rán-tĕl'ä)—A dance.
[3] BRAGGADOCIO (brăg-à-dō'shĭ-ō)—In boastful fashion.
[4] BANDITTI (băn-dĭt'ĭ)—Outlaws, brigands.

—a few lambs from the spring dropping before they were driven in from the pastures for counting, a measure of wheat, a skin of wine, that would never be missed. The barns were not fresh-thatched in time, and the fall rains mildewed much of the harvest; the rats got in and ate their share. So, after years of adding one misfortune to another misfortune, there was a mountain of misfortune—large enough for even Tonio to see.

Over one night he became like a crazy man, for over one night he had remembered his brother. Any day he might be returning. At the inn the day before there had been two soldiers fresh from the wars, drinking and bragging of their adventures. Another night and who might not come? Once home, the older brother would be master. First, he would ask for an accounting. And what then? As master he could have him, Tonio, flogged or flung into prison. More final than that, he could run him through with his clever rapier, and no one would question his right to do it. The more Tonio thought about it, the more his terror grew. He began running about the country like a man with fever in his brain. First he ran to the inn and asked the landlord what he should do, and the landlord laughed aloud. "Sit down, Tonio, and drink some of my good Chianti.⁵ Why worry about your brother now, when he may be lying in a strange country, stuck through the ribs like a pig?"

He ran to a neighbour, who laughed louder than the landlord. "Take up your fiddle and see if you cannot play your cattle back into the pasture and the good wine into its skins."

He ran on to his favourite, Lisetta. She cocked her pretty head at him like a saucy macaw. "Let me see," she laughed, "you have forgotten your brother for ten years, yes? Then come to the inn tonight and dance the tarantella with me, and I will make you forget him for another ten years."

After that he ran to the priest, and found him finishing mass. He did not laugh, the priest. Instead he shook his head sorrowfully and told him to burn candles for nine days before the shrine of Saint Anthony of Padua and pray for wisdom. On the way to the shrine he met the half-witted herdboy Zeppo, who laughed fool-

⁵ CHIANTI (kē-än'tē)—A kind of wine.

ishly when he saw his master's face and tapped his own forehead knowingly. "Mister, you are so frightened it has made you quite mad, like me." Then he put his lips to Tonio's ear. "Hearken, I will tell you what to do. Go to the old tsigane ⁶ woman of the grotto. She has much wisdom and she makes magic of all kinds—black and white. Go to her, master."

In the end it was the advice of the mad herdboy that Tonio took. He climbed the first spur of the mountain to a deep grotto that time

or magic had hollowed out of the rock, and there he found the tsigane woman. She was ages old and withered as a dried fig. She listened to all Tonio had to tell, and left him without a word to go deeper into the grotto, where she was swallowed up altogether in blackness. When she came back at last, she was carrying something in her hand—a small casket bound strongly with bands of brass, and in the top a hole so small it could hardly be seen in the pattern of the carving. She put the box into Tonio's hand and fixed him with eyes that were piercing as two rapier points. When she spoke, it was as if her voice rumbled out, not from her, but from deep in the rocks.

⁶ TSIGANE (tsĭ'găn-ĭ)—Gypsy.

"Every morning, while the dew still lies heaviest, shake one grain of dust from the box in every corner of your lands—barns, pastures, and vineyards. See to it that no spot is left forgotten. Do this, and you will prosper as your father prospered. But never let one morning pass, and never till the day you die break the bands or look inside. If you do, the magic will be gone."

That night Tonio did not fiddle or dance with Lisetta at the inn. He went to bed when the fowls went to roost and was up at the crowing of the first cock. With the magic box under his arm, he went first to his barns to sprinkle the precious grains; but he found the men still asleep and the cattle unfed. Out of their beds he drove them with angry words. And, still lashing them with his tongue, he watched while they stumbled sleepily about, beginning the day's work. From the barns he went to the fields, and found the grain half cut and none of it stacked. The scythes were left rusting on the ground and the men still asleep in their huts. Tonio scattered more dust, and then drove the reapers to their work.

And so it was in the olive grove, the vineyards, and the pastures. Everywhere he found men sleeping and the work half done. "Holy Mother, defend us!" the men said among themselves after Tonio had gone. "The master is up early and looking about for himself, even as the old master did. We shall have to keep a sharper watch out on things or he will be packing us off to starve."

After that, every morning Tonio was abroad before the sun, shaking the dust from his magic box into every corner of his lands. And every morning he was seeing something new that was needing care. In a little time the inn and the market place knew him no more; and Lisetta had to find a new dancing partner. A twelve-month passed, and the farm of old Gino Tomba was prospering again. When Tonio came to the market place to sell his grain and wine, his neighbours would wag their thumbs at him as they had wagged them at his father and they would say: "There goes Tonio Tomba. His sons—when he marries and they are born—will be very rich men."

And in the end what happened? The older brother never came home to claim his inheritance. He must have been killed in the wars; at any rate, all the lands were Tonio's for the keeping. He married the daughter of the richest neighbour and had two sons of his own, even as his father had had. And when the time came for him to die he called them both to his side and commanded young Gino to bring him the casket and break the bands, his hands being too weak for the breaking. Raising the lid he looked in, eager for all his dying, to discover the magic that the box had held all those years.

What did he find? Under the lid were written these words: "Look you—the master's eye is needed over all." In the bottom were a few grains of sand left, the common kind that any wayfarer can gather up for himself from the road that climbs to the Apennines.

DISCUSSING THE STORY

1. It is not by chance that most fortunes are made. How had Gino Tomba become prosperous? Describe the character of each of the sons. What qualities promised success or failure for each?

2. Tell what happened after old Tomba's death. Why did the same lands that had grown rich for Tomba now yield little for Tonio?

3. What thoughts finally drove Tonio to do something about his fortunes? Tell how the magic box changed Tonio's habits and character. Was it a magic charm or something else that restored the lands? Do you think the words in the box can be a magic charm for anyone?

THE TALE OF ANAHUAC 𝕏 CHARLES J. FINGER

ONE hot day I rode into the town of El Valle [1] in Mexico and tied my horses in the shade of the *adobe cuartel*,[2] or prison. Someone inside the prison was singing as he twanged a guitar, and this was the song:

> "Beautiful bloom guard me!
> Keep away evil!

---

[1] EL VALLE—Pronounced ĕl väl′yā.
[2] *Adobe cuartel*—Pronounced a-dō′bĕ kwär-tĕl′.

Grant I may grow old in peace!
Hikuli [3] Flower, guard me!
Much do I thank thee for being what thou art!"

The singer sang in the slow style of people of the open, with long spaces between the lines, and the tune was pleasant enough, though somewhat sad. After I had fed and watered my three horses, I walked about the town, which did not take long to do because it was only one street and that a short one. There was nothing to see except men asleep in the shade and dogs wandering about in the dusty road and children playing. When I got back to my horses, I saw the man in the prison (there was only one) looking sadly out of the window through the bars. I nodded to him for politeness' sake because he was looking at me; then came a surprise, for he said, "Good day, Don Carlos," in Mexican.

It was a surprise, because I had never been in that place before and did not know the man, but I lifted a hand and called in return, "Good day," though I thought it could not have been a very good day for him in that cell.

Then he called to my dog, "Good Jock," naming its name, and Jock looked up and wagged his tail, so I was sure that he knew the man's voice. Naturally, all that led to talk, and I found that the man knew me because he had herded sheep near a town called Knickerbocker in Texas. Although I did not know him I had friends in that town. Then it came out that he was in prison because he had quarrelled with someone, and he would be free on payment of a two dollar fine. I found the officer, who was also the barber, paid the fine, and Pedro [4] stepped outside a free man. As I was going nowhere, only seeing the places I stopped at, and as he had nowhere to go and was looking for work, I let him ride one of the horses, and we went to the west.

That evening we made camp in a pleasant place by a mountain stream when the western sky was rose and gold. Pedro did his share of the work—looking after the horses and building a fire— and I noticed that he seemed very much pleased when he found a

[3] HIKULI—Pronounced hē-kōō'lē.
[4] PEDRO—Pronounced pä'drō.

cactus in bloom, the kind called *peyote*.⁵ He touched the flower gently, as a child might, then remarked, "It is the best flower in the world."

I nodded, to please him, thinking that there were flowers that were grander, but that Pedro had not seen very much living in that desert country.

"It was 'Coatl's ⁶ flower," he said.

Then he began to push little twigs into the fire and watched them melt into flame, all the while humming the tune he had been singing in prison to the accompaniment of a guitar, perhaps the jailor's.

"You read books," he said presently. "Did you find anything about Anahuac ⁷ in them?"

"I remember the name, but no more," I told him.

"Did you read about the Smoking Mountain, Popocatepetl?" ⁸ he next asked.

"I have seen it," I said. "It is near the City of Mexico."

"You are the first man I ever saw who has seen it," he exclaimed, and looked at me as if I had done something wonderful.

"Does the fire come out of it?" was his next question.

"Only a little smoke and ashes," I told him. Then I asked, "What has the Smoking Mountain to do with the cactus flower; or the cactus flower with Anahuac?"

"I heard the tale told by my mother's mother; and it is very old and wonderful," he answered. "I thought of it when I was in prison, for if I had remembered the words of Anahuac, I would not have been there. I got there because of a quarrel, and Anahuac said, 'A wise man will as soon run into fire as into a quarrel.' If I had heeded that, I would not have been in the trouble you found me."

I knew that he was coming to the tale in his round-about-way, so I said nothing.

"As for the flower," remarked Pedro, "it means that we are happy only when we see beauty, not when we burn ourselves up trying to get money."

⁵ *Peyote*—Pronounced pā-yō'tĕ.
⁶ 'COATL (kō-ä'tl)—An Aztec god.
⁷ ANAHUAC—Pronounced ä-nä'wäk.
⁸ POPOCATEPETL (pō-pō-kä-tä'pĕtl)—A volcano in Mexico.

For a little while Pedro pushed twigs into the fire, then when the silver moon came sliding up the sky from behind the hills, he began.

Everyone in Mexico knows or has heard of Popocatepetl, and almost everyone knows that the name means "Smoking Mountain." Once it was like any other mountain, tree-covered and beautiful, rose-coloured when the sun touched it in the early morning and like a purple cloud in the evening. Then came a day when thunder rolled and lightning flashed, and there were deep rumblings in the earth—a day of storm so fearful that people ran into their houses and hid. When the storm passed, the top of the mountain had changed. It seemed to have blown off; and violet black smoke came from it. Some say the smoke took shape as a serpent, then as a bird, then as a fearful giant. A shadow that stilled the song of birds lay over the valley. Red lava ran down the mountainside, scorching growing things and killing trees. Then they say that 'Coatl came out of the smoke. He stalked down the mountainside, a mighty giant, and into the valley, and wherever he stepped, things died. No one talked to him and few saw him, for when word came that he was on the way to a place, people fled and hid. For days he went about spoiling things. Then one night, in the shape of a serpent, he flew away, leaving a trail of sparks in the sky. People were thankful that he had gone, and they hoped they would never see him again. They went on with their work, for the Toltecs were a gentle and kindly folk. That was the coming and the going of 'Coatl, or Xiuhcoatl,[9] as some called him.

'Coatl flew to a land called Texcatlipoca,[10] where he came to earth in a valley of great beauty and lay there in the form of a serpent, breathing out fire and smoke which scorched wherever it touched. Thereupon the king of that place called on his own people to come out with their bows and arrows to kill the creature, and they came. One group of men lined themselves on one side of the valley; another lined on the other side. Then they shot, the while a strange mist hung about the giant. But instead of the arrows killing 'Coatl, they killed men—their own friends and

---

[9] XIUHCOATL—Pronounced hē-ōō-kō-ä'tl.
[10] TEXCATLIPOCA—Pronounced tĕs-kät-lĕ-pō'kä.

brothers. Anger filled the people's hearts, not so much against the giant as against one another. In a short time, everyone was shooting and killing and hating, while 'Coatl roared his pleasure, for he had brought war into the land.

"Ho! Ho!" he bellowed. "Brave sport! Brave sport! Keep on."

After a time people came to see what folly they had been guilty of, because it was not only killing they had done, but destroying, too, burning houses and laying gardens waste.

The king of the land went to 'Coatl, who was looking down from the top of the mountain, and spoke hot words, for he was not cowardly, although sometimes very foolish.

"You have brought mischief here," the king said. "My people were happy until you came, and now there is all this trouble."

"You ought to be glad that I came," answered 'Coatl. "Look at all the work I have left for your people to do."

"Who is to pay them to do it?" cried the king angrily.

"The way is easy," replied 'Coatl. "Let those who have lost their houses and gardens and who have nothing work for those who have not lost. Those who have something can feed those who have nothing; and the feeding will be pay."

So the king ordered things to be that way, and thus slavery came into the land. Presently, the people who did the work and who had nothing of their own began to grumble, so the king again talked with 'Coatl.

"I shall show you how to brew a drink which will mend matters," said 'Coatl. "Those who drink it will forget their misery and dream dreams and be satisfied to be slaves."

With that he taught the king how to make a certain wild drink from the cactus. When the king tasted it he smiled foolishly and said, "It does seem now that everything is all right, no matter how wrong it is."

Thus strong drink came into the world, and 'Coatl had brought the three bad gifts.

"I have helped you, and some day you must help me," he said to the king. Then changing to a mighty, hideous bird, he flew away.

Back to the land of the Toltecs went 'Coatl, but no one there welcomed him. The people were busy and happy; happy because they were busy. Their fruits and grains were ripening fast. Men and women worked and sang, enjoyed the sunshine and flowers, and knew how to laugh. People were friendly, and although 'Coatl tried in many ways, he could not make them unfriendly with one another. Yet he did some mischief in calling winds from the north, with hail and sleet on the highlands, so that the fair harvests were spoiled. But 'Coatl could not set the people against one another in enmity.

Now there was a brave young lad named Anahuac who tended sheep. He and his dog knew every nook and cranny of the moun-tains, especially one place where few people went because it was stony and without grass and strewn with cactus. In that one place was a dark cave into which no man had ventured. Anahuac decided to make a trap there. Willing men helped him to roll a great rock above the opening of the cave, placing it so carefully that it would fall almost at a touch. By the side of and behind that great rock they set others, a hundred or more, all of which would fall when the first one fell. To the first great rock they tied a rope which went inside the cave, and to that rope they tied another near its mouth, and passed the ropes from one side of the cave to the other. Thus, if any creature of size wandered in, it must needs stumble against the cross ropes and, so stumbling, bring down all the rocks, thus sealing up the mouth of the cave. At the mouth and inside as well, they laid dainty fruits and meats, hoping that 'Coatl would go that way. Days became weeks, and weeks grew into months, but still 'Coatl was not trapped.

Then brave Anahuac had another thought. He knew that 'Coatl was never happier than when he saw people miserable, nor more miserable than when he saw people happy. So, day after day, he passed by the mountain where 'Coatl hid, always singing, or whistling, always with his dog, playing with it, racing with it, glad to hear its joyous barking. When 'Coatl put sharp stones in Anahuac's way, the lad only laughed and made sandals for himself to save his feet. Whatever mischief 'Coatl did, Anahuac laughed at. Then came a day when 'Coatl made up his mind to catch Anahuac and his dog and drop them into the hole at the top of Popocatepetl. The giant hid in a valley where Anahuac would pass in the evening after he had left the sheep he tended.

When the sun was low and Anahuac had done his day's work, he walked near the valley where 'Coatl was hiding, whistling as he went, his dog at his heel. What 'Coatl forgot was that the sun made shadows and that his own long shadow lay across the valley where Anahuac would pass. It was a great shadow of a man that reached to the farther hill and halfway to its top. When Anahuac first saw the shadow, he thought it might be the shadow of a tree, for one of the arms was crooked like a dead branch. But as he looked, the shadow moved a little, and the twigs became claws. Then Anahuac knew, but he gave no sign. He went on, his dog with him, the lad whistling a merry tune; but he was thinking hard what was to be done. Soon he saw the shadow move again but pretended he had noticed nothing strange, and he went on whistling though his heart beat fast. The shadow showed two arms now with spread fingers, and Anahuac knew that 'Coatl was moving nearer to him. Then he saw the shadow crouching.

In spite of his fear, Anahuac was glad. If he could get 'Coatl into the trap, he would do a great deed, even if he lost his own life for his people and their well-being. Knowing that 'Coatl had crouched to leap on him, Anahuac turned, as quick as a lizard, and went running as fast as he could to a narrow part of the valley, a part too narrow for the giant who had to keep to wide places.

On went Anahuac and his dog, keeping to narrow valleys, dodging among great rocks, bending low under branches, leaping over fallen tree trunks, darting this way and that into canyons. On came the giant, all the while roaring and bellowing in anger, the more because he had to keep to the hills, dislodging rocks, sometimes stumbling or getting his feet into narrow places, growing more furious at every step. He bent and broke trees as he went, and at places his feet made marks in the solid rock which are to be seen to this day. Sometimes he bent to try to catch Anahuac; but he only lost time, because to bend he had to slacken his pace. Anahuac kept to the narrow valley which he knew so well, and his good dog followed him closely.

Some of the Toltecs saw part of that race from hilltops, and they shouted to Anahuac and to his dog, cheering them. Other dogs ran at the giant, barking, biting his feet, getting between his legs, bothering him in fifty ways. It was a roaring, bellowing, shouting, barking, clattering world. A thousand wild animals and birds took up the noise, even the coyotes in the hills and the lobos [11] in the forest.

Then of a sudden it became a silent world. People who were watching saw that brave Anahuac and his dog were running away to lead the giant into the trap. They were giving their lives for others and would soon vanish into the dark cave to be seen no more. Then some people shouted to Anahuac begging him to turn another way, and some who were bold ran down toward the giant. But all the good wishes and all the shouting was useless. Down the wide valley leading to the cave went Anahuac and his dog, and close behind

---

[11] LOBOS—Timber wolves.

ran the giant 'Coatl. The giant had almost caught Anahuac when the lad vanished into the dark of the cave, his faithful dog with him. For a moment or two the giant stood outside and people wondered whether he would go in; then bellowing like a bull he plunged in, his head bent low.

But still some of the people hoped that it would be well with Anahuac. They hoped that in the dark he might be able to turn and dodge out again into the light of day, leaving the giant inside. But it was not to be so. The sound of thunder was heard; down came the rocks which blocked the opening; then other rocks, and others by the hundred, so that it seemed as if the whole mountain were sliding. A great dust arose, a dust so thick that for a time those who looked could see nothing. When it cleared away, nothing could be seen of the cave, and people knew that 'Coatl was sealed up in it, and with him Anahuac and the faithful dog. People turned away sadly. They were full of grief because everyone loved the lighthearted Anahuac who went about with a smile and a song.

Now this is what happened inside the cave.

In the gloom of the cave Anahuac saw the giant outside, eyes gleaming and teeth showing. Anahuac also saw the rope. He stepped over it, being careful not to touch it, and he made his dog go underneath; for had either as much as touched the rope with a hand or a paw, the cave would have been sealed with the giant outside and Anahuac and his dog lost inside. In that moment, as the giant waited, Anahuac laughed aloud to annoy the fearful fellow, and it was then that the terrible creature bent his head and plunged in. Anahuac and his dog stepped farther back and hid in a corner. With a noise louder than thunder, the rocks came down, and after that, the dark. Anahuac could hear the giant grumbling and groping about, and once a great hand touched Anahuac's foot, but the lad drew himself together and made himself small, hardly daring to breathe.

It was a great comfort for Anahuac that his dog was with him, and that faithful creature crawled close to his master's hand. Then the dog went away a little but soon came back and licked Anahuac's hand. Again he went away, Anahuac could not know where, and again he came back, and again the sign of friendliness. That happened three times. Then Anahuac decided that the dog knew something about the cave, which was true, for the dog had been there before unknown to his master, when chasing a rabbit. So Anahuac followed the dog the next time.

Crawling along a low narrow passage where the giant could not follow, they went, the lad's hand touching the dog, for it was so pitchy dark nothing could be seen. They crawled a long way until Anahuac, looking up, saw a blue-white spot that was light, but no bigger than his hand. On went the dog, Anahuac following close. The spot of light grew larger, although how far away it was the lad could not tell. Yet his heart jumped with joy, because he knew the giant could never follow now. Soon he saw the sky, then the sweet green of trees and grass. By wriggling after the dog by a crooked way, he came out under the blue sky on the mountainside and was in the good world again, his dog by his side, looking up to be patted. To make sure, Anahuac rolled a stone over the little opening by which he had come out (which was a long way from the entrance) so that no ray of light, even one as small as a needle, could shine in.

As for the Toltec people who were waiting and wondering, they knew nothing other than the noises made by 'Coatl in the cave. They feared that the worst had befallen Anahuac. But there was a shepherd boy, who on the evening after the cave was blocked, went to look for a lost sheep. When the setting sun turned the great cloud of dust that hung in the air to a fiery red, the shepherd boy saw Anahuac. He went running to him calling out, "Anahuac! Anahuac!" and he was the happiest boy alive.

So it was that Anahuac saved his people and 'Coatl was sealed in the cave.

DISCUSSING THE STORY

Popocatepetl is one of the most colourful sights in Mexico. Rising to a height of 17,520 feet, the volcano has been in a somewhat quiet state for several centuries, but it still throws out the smoke and ashes which give it its name—"Smoking Mountain." Reasoning like other primitive peoples, early Mexicans believed that the roars and mutterings of the volcano were the cries of an evil god who inhabited it. Many stories have been told about 'Coatl, the terrible Aztec god. The one told here is often heard by visitors to Mexico.

1. Summarize briefly the story that Pedro tells of the coming of 'Coatl to the land of the Toltecs. Why did he go to Texcatlipoca? Tell how he brought three great evils to the people there.

LADY ISABEL AND THE ELF-KNIGHT 🌸 SCOTTISH BALLAD

B   THERE came a bird out of a bush,
              On water for to dine,
            And sighing sore, says the king's daughter,
G1   "O woe's this heart of mine!"

G   5 He's taken a harp into his hand,
              He's harped them all asleep,
            Except it was the king's daughter,
            Who one wink could not get.

B   He's leaped upon his berry-brown steed,
    10   Taken her on behind himsel',
            Then both rode down to that water
            That they call Wearie's Well.

B1   "Wade in, wade in, my lady fair,
              No harm shall thee befall;
    15 Oft times have I watered my steed,
              With the water of Wearie's Well.' '

G   The first step that she steppéd in,
              She steppéd to the knee;

And sighing says this lady fair,
G1 20   "This water's not for me."

B1   "Wade in, wade in, my lady fair,
             No harm shall thee befall;
         Oft times have I watered my steed
             With the water of Wearie's Well."

G   25   The next step that she steppéd in,
             She steppéd to the middle;
G1   "O," sighing says this lady fair,
             "I've wet my golden girdle."

B1   "Wade in, wade in, my lady fair,
    30   No harm shall thee befall;
         Oft times have I watered my steed
             With the water of Wearie's Well."

G   The next step that she steppéd in,
             She steppéd to the chin;
G1 35   "O," sighing says this lady fair,
             "I'll wade no farther in."

B1   "Seven king's daughters I've drownéd there,
             In the water of Wearie's Well,
         And I'll make you the eighth of them,
    40   And ring the common bell."

G1   "Since I am standing here," she says,
             "This dreadful death to die,
         One kiss of your comely mouth
             I'm sure would comfort me."

B   45   He leanéd over his saddle bow,
             To kiss her cheek and chin;
G   She's taken him in her arms two,
             And thrown him headlong in.

G 1   "Since seven king's daughters ye've drownéd there,
50   In the water of Wearie's Well,
      I'll make you bridegroom to them all,
      And ring the bell mysel'."

DISCUSSING THE POEM

More than five hundred years ago when the story of Lady Isabel was first heard somewhere in Scotland, few people could read or write. How then, were stories preserved? They were handed down by word of mouth. For example, a story was told, possibly in some wayside inn. A passing minstrel heard the tale, and with his talent for making verses he fashioned it into a ballad to be sung in the next town he visited. The listeners enjoyed the song and sang it themselves, adding whatever details came from their imaginations from time to time. In some such way "Lady Isabel and the Elf-Knight" was begun, and after being sung for many generations, was finally written down.

1. As you read the poem you will notice that each stanza adds something to the development of the story. In what mood do we find the lady?

2. Because of the lack of learning there were many superstitions, with unusual happenings explained as the work of elves, fairies, witches, and the like. What kind of magic is suggested in the second stanza?

3. Where does the knight take the lady? What does he ask her to do?

4. Lady Isabel must have been a stronger character than the seven before her because she finally decides things have gone far enough. Tell about the trick she plays on the knight.

THE HIGHWAYMAN* 🦋 ALFRED NOYES

I

G   The wind was a torrent of darkness among the gusty trees,
      The moon was a ghostly galleon tossed upon cloudy seas,

* Reprinted from *Collected Poems in One Volume*, copyright 1906, 1934 by Alfred Noyes. By permission of J. B. Lippincott Company.

The road was a ribbon of moonlight over the purple
    moor,
All   And the highwayman came riding—
   5   Riding—riding—
The highwayman came riding, up to the old inn door.

B   He'd a French cocked hat on his forehead, a bunch of
    lace at his chin,
A coat of the claret velvet, and breeches of brown doe-
    skin;
They fitted with never a wrinkle: his boots were up to
    the thigh!
All 10 And he rode with a jewelled twinkle,
    His pistol butts a-twinkle,
His rapier hilt a-twinkle, under the jewelled sky.

G   Over the cobbles he clattered and clashed in the dark
    innyard,
And he tapped with his whip on the shutters, but all
    was locked and barred;
  15 He whistled a tune to the window, and who should be
    waiting there
All   But the landlord's black-eyed daughter,
    Bess, the landlord's daughter,
Plaiting a dark red love knot into her long black hair.

B   And dark in the dark old innyard a stable-wicket
    creaked
  20 Where Tim the ostler listened; his face was white and
    peaked;
His eyes were hollows of madness, his hair like mouldy
    hay,
All   But he loved the landlord's daughter,
    The landlord's red-lipped daughter,
Dumb as a dog he listened, and he heard the robber say:

B1   **25**   "One kiss, my bonny sweetheart, I'm after a prize tonight,

But I shall be back with the yellow gold before the morning light;

Yet, if they press me sharply, and harry me through the day,

Then look for me by moonlight,

    Watch for me by moonlight,

30   I'll come to thee by moonlight, though hell should bar the way."

G   He rose upright in the stirrups; he scarce could reach her hand,

But she loosened her hair i' the casement! His face burned like a brand

As the black cascade of perfume came tumbling over his breast;

All   And he kissed its waves in the moonlight,

35   (Oh, sweet black waves in the moonlight!)

Then he tugged at his rein in the moonlight, and galloped away to the West.

II

B   He did not come in the dawning; he did not come at
      noon;
    And out o' the tawny sunset, before the rise o' the moon,
    When the road was a gypsy's ribbon, looping the purple
      moor,

All 40 A redcoat troop came marching—
      Marching—marching—
    King George's men came marching, up to the old inn
      door.

G   They said no word to the landlord, they drank his ale
      instead,
    But they gagged his daughter and bound her to the foot
      of her narrow bed;

  45 Two of them knelt at her casement, with muskets at
      their side!

All   There was death at every window;
      And hell at one dark window;
    For Bess could see, through her casement, the road that
      he would ride.

B   They had tied her up to attention, with many a snig-
      gering jest,

  50 They had bound a musket beside her, with the barrel
      beneath her breast!
    "Now keep good watch!" and they kissed her. She
      heard the dead man say—

B1   *Look for me by moonlight;*
      Watch for me by moonlight;
    I'll come to thee by moonlight, though hell should bar
      the way!

G 55 She twisted her hands behind her; but all the knots held
      good!

She writhed her hands till her fingers were wet with
    sweat or blood!
They stretched and strained in the darkness, and the
    hours crawled by like years,

All Till, now, on the stroke of midnight,
    Cold, on the stroke of midnight,
60 The tip of one finger touched it! The trigger at least
    was hers!

G The tip of one finger touched it; she strove no more for
    the rest!
Up, she stood up to attention, with the barrel beneath
    her breast,
She would not risk their hearing; she would not strive
    again;

All For the road lay bare in the moonlight;
65   Blank and bare in the moonlight;
And the blood of her veins in the moonlight throbbed to
    her love's refrain.

G1 *Tlot-tlot; tlot-tlot!* Had they heard it? The horse
    hoofs ringing clear;
Tlot-tlot, tlot-tlot, in the distance! Were they deaf
    that they did not hear?

All Down the ribbon of moonlight, over the brow of the hill,
70 The highwayman came riding,
    Riding—riding—
The redcoats looked to their priming! She stood up,
    straight and still!

G1 *Tlot-tlot,* in the frosty silence! *Tlot-tlot,* in the echoing
    night!
Nearer he came and nearer! Her face was like a light!
75 Her eyes grew wide for a moment; she drew one last
    deep breath,

All Then her finger moved in the moonlight,

Her musket shattered the moonlight,
Shattered her breast in the moonlight and warned him
—with her death.

B   He turned; he spurred to the Westward; he did not
know who stood
80 Bowed, with her head o'er the musket, drenched with
her own red blood!
Not till the dawn he heard it, and slowly blanched to
hear
All   How Bess, the landlord's daughter,
The landlord's black-eyed daughter,
Had watched for her love in the moonlight, and died in
the darkness there.

B   85 Back he spurred like a madman, shrieking a curse to the
sky,
With the white road smoking behind him, and his rapier
brandished high.
Blood-red were his spurs i' the golden noon; wine-red
was his velvet coat,
All   When they shot him down on the highway,
Down like a dog on the highway,
90 And he lay in his blood on the highway, with the bunch
of lace at his throat.

G   *And still of a winter's night, they say, when the wind is*
in the trees,
When the moon is a ghostly galleon tossed upon cloudy
seas,
When the road is a ribbon of moonlight over the purple
moor,
All   *A highwayman comes riding—*
95   *Riding—riding—*
A highwayman comes riding, up to the old inn door.

B   *Over the cobbles he clatters and clangs in the dark*
             innyard;
     And he taps with his whip on the shutters, but all is
             locked and barred;
     He whistles a tune to the window, and who should be
             waiting there

All 100   *But the landlord's black-eyed daughter,*
        Bess, the landlord's daughter,
     Plaiting a dark red love knot into her long black hair.

DISCUSSING THE POEM

1. "The Highwayman" is a legend told in modern poetry. The story itself is located in time at least one hundred and fifty years ago. See if you can find the clues that tell us the approximate date of the story.

2. Briefly tell the tragic tale of the lovers. Are your sympathies with them or with the soldiers? Why? Do you think it is possible for such a story to end in some other way?

3. Explain what each of the following passages means to you:
   a. "The moon was a ghostly galleon tossed upon cloudy seas"
   b. "Yet if they press me sharply, and harry me through the day"
   c. "When the road was a gypsy's ribbon, looping the purple moor"
   d. "With the white road smoking behind him, and his rapier brandished high"

4. Find several lines that suggest sounds, and see if you can explain how the sound effects are made in a poem like this one.

THE WOMAN FROM LALO-HANA ✹

PADRAIC COLUM

Long, long ago, my younger brothers, there lived in Hawaii a King whose name was Koni-konia. He sent his fishermen out to catch deep-sea fish for him, and they, without knowing it, let down their lines and fishhooks at a place where, before this, strange things had happened.

In a while after they had let them down, the hooks were taken off the lines. The fishermen wondered at this, for they knew that

no fish had bitten at their baits. They went back to the King, and they told him what had happened. There had come no quiver on their lines, they said, as there would have come if fish had touched their baits, and their hooks had been cut off the lines as if someone with a knife had done it.

Now the King had heard before of strange things happening at the place in the sea where the fishermen had been; and after they had shown him the lines with the hooks cut off, he sent for a wizard, that he might learn from him how these strange things had come to be.

The wizard (he was called a Kahuna) came before the King, and after he had been told of what had happened to the fishermen's lines he said: "Your fishermen let their lines down over Lalo-hana, a country that is at the bottom of the sea, just under the place where they let their canoes rest. A woman lives there, a very beautiful woman of the sea whose name is Hina; all alone she lives there, for her brothers, who were given charge of her, have gone to a place far off." When the King heard of this beautiful woman of the sea, he longed to see her and to have her for his wife.

The Kahuna told him how she might be brought out of the sea to him. The King was to have a great many images made—images of a man, each image to be as large as a man, with pearl-shell eyes and dark hair, and with a malo or dress around it. Some of the images were to be brought out to sea, and some of them were to be left on the beach and along a path that went up to the King's house; and one of them was to be left standing by the door of the house.

The Kahuna went with the men who had taken the images in their canoes. When they came to that part of the sea that the country of Lalo-hana was under, the Kahuna told the men to let down one of the images. Down, down, the image went, a rope around it. It rested on the bottom of the sea. Then another image was let down. But this image was not let as far as the bottom of the sea: it was held about the height of a house above the bottom. Then another image was let down and held above that, and then another image, and another image, all held one above another, while other images were left standing in canoes that went in a line back to the beach. And when all the images were in their places, a loud trumpet was blown.

The woman of Lalo-hana, Hina, came out of her house, that was built of white and red coral, and she saw the image of a man of dark colour, with dark hair and eyes of pearl-shell, standing before her. She was pleased, for she had never seen even the likeness of a man since her brothers had gone away from her; and she went to the image, and she touched it. As she did so she saw an image above her; and she went and she touched this image too. And all the way up to the top of the sea there were images; and Hina went upward, touching them all.

When she came up to the surface of the sea she saw canoes, and in each canoe there was an image standing. Each one seemed to be more beautiful than the others; and Hina swam on and on, gazing on each with delight and touching this one and that one.

And so, Hina, the Woman of the Sea, came to the beach. And on the beach there were other images; and she went on, touching each of them. And so she went through the grove of coconut trees and came before the King's house. Outside the house there was a very tall image with very large pearl-shell eyes and with a red malo around it. Hina went to that image. The wreath of sea flowers that she had in her hair was now withered with the sun; the Woman of Lalo-hana was wearied now, and she lay down beside the image and fell asleep.

When she wakened it was not the image, but the King, who was beside her. She saw him move his hands, and she was frightened because of the movements she saw him make and the sounds that were around her after the quiet of the sea. Her wreath of sea flowers was all shrivelled up in the sunlight. The man kissed her, and they went together into the house.

And so the Woman of Lalo-hana, the Country under the Sea, came to Hawaii and lived there as the wife of Koni-konia, the King.

After a while, when she had learned to speak to him, Hina told Koni-konia about precious things that she had in her house in Lalo-hana, the Country under the Sea, and she begged the King to send a diver to get these things and bring them to her. They were in a calabash [1] within her house, she said. And she told the King that the diver who brought it up was not to open the calabash.

So Koni-konia the King sent the best of his divers to go down to Lalo-hana, the Country under the Sea, and bring up the calabash that had Hina's precious things in it. The diver went down, and found the house of red and white coral, and went within and took the calabash that was there. He brought it back without opening it and gave it to Hina.

After some days Hina opened the calabash. Within it was the moon. It flew up to the heavens, and there it shone clear and bright. When it shone in the heavens it was called *Kena*. But it shone down on the sea too, and shining on the sea it was called *Ana*.

And then, seeing *Ana* in the sea, the Woman of Lalo-hana was frightened. "My brothers will come searching for me," she said. And the next day she said, "My brothers will bring a great flood of waters upon this land when they come searching for me." And after that she said, "My brothers will seek me in the forms of

[1] CALABASH—A basket made from the dry shell of a gourd.

pa-o'o² fishes, and the Ocean will lift them up so that they can go seeking me." When the King heard her say this he said, "We will go far from where the Ocean is, and we will seek refuge on the tops of the mountains."

So the King with Hina, with all his people, went to the mountains. As they went they saw the Ocean lifting up. Hina's brothers in the forms of pa-o'o fishes were there, and the Ocean lifted them up that they might go seeking her.

Over the land and up to the mountains the Ocean went, bearing the pa-o'o fishes along. Koni-konia and his people climbed to the tops of the mountains. To the tops of the mountains the Ocean went, bearing the pa-o'o fishes that were Hina's brothers. Koni-konia and Hina and all the people climbed to the tops of the trees that were on the tops of the mountains. And then the Ocean, having covered the tops of the mountains, went back again, drawing back the pa-o'o fishes that were Hina's brothers. And it was in this way that the Great Flood came to Hawaii.

And after the waters of the Ocean had gone back to their own place, Koni-konia the King, with Hina and his people, went back to the place where their houses had been. All was washed away; there were mud and sand where the houses and fields had been. Soon the sun dried up the puddles and the wetness in the ground; growth came again; they built their houses and cultivated their fields; and Koni-konia, with Hina and with his people, lived once again in a wide land beside the Great Ocean.

² PA-O'O—Pronounced pā-ŏ'ŏ.

DISCUSSING THE STORY

1. Long before the white man came to the islands of Hawaii, the native peoples were telling stories that grew out of their environment, their imagination, and their strange beliefs. Unable to explain the causes of natural events, they often devised mythological characters and elements of superhuman powers. Tell how the wizard explained why the fishermen lost their baits. Do you think there might have been some reasonable explanation for this?

2. How was the Woman of Lalo-hana lured to the earth? Tell the

legend that has developed as an explanation of a great flood. Show how it is likely that many different stories might arise from the same incident.

3. Tell an Indian legend or some other story you have read which is an imaginative explanation of something in nature, or if you prefer, make up an original story of this kind. Perhaps you have read stories about the Big Dipper, the moon, the change of seasons, an eclipse of the sun, or some other natural occurrence.

ONE CANDLE POWER 🌿 ALICE GEER KELSEY

PERHAPS Nasr-ed-Din Hodja[1] had been sitting too long in the warm coffee house, swapping yarns with his friends. The boasts were growing bigger and bigger. None was bigger than the Hodja's.

"I could stand all night in the snow without any fire to warm me." The Hodja noisily gulped down one more hot cup of sweet black coffee.

"No one could do that!" One of the men shivered as he looked through the window at the falling snow.

"I could!" The Hodja spread his hands over the open pan of burning coals. "I'll do it this very night."

"You can't!"

"I will! If I have so much as a glow of fire to warm myself, I'll —I'll—I'll give a feast for you all at my house tomorrow!"

The wager was on.

The friends of Nasr-ed-Din Hodja went home to their warm beds, while he stood alone in the snow-draped market square. He had never realized how much longer the hours were at night than in the daytime. He had never realized how many hours there were in the night. Once in a while a prowling dog or an adventuring cat would sniff at him and then slink off to a snugger spot. The cold snow swathing his feet and tickling his neck was hard enough to bear. Harder still was the sleepiness that plagued him. It would never do to fall asleep in the snow. He must keep awake to stamp

---

[1] NASR-ED-DIN HODJA—Pronounced năzr-ĕd-dĭn hŏj'à.

his cold feet and beat his cold arms. He found that it was easier to fight off sleep if he fastened his eyes on the flickering candle in Mehmet Ali's house across the market square. There was something cheering about the wavering of that tiny flame, which helped his tired eyes stay open.

Morning came at last. Curious men met the shivering and yawning Hodja on his way home to a cup of hot coffee. They asked about his night and marvelled at what he had done.

"How did you keep awake all night?" they asked.

"I fixed my eyes on a flickering candle in Mehmet Ali's house," he answered.

"A candle?"

"A burning candle?"

"Did you say a candle?"

"Of course!" The Hodja saw no harm in watching a candle.

"A lighted candle gives flame. Flame gives heat. You were warming yourself by the heat of that candle. You have lost your wager."

At first the Hodja tried to laugh at their joke, but he soon found that they were not joking. For once, the Hodja was too tired to argue successfully. Try as he would, he could not convince his friends that a candle in a distant house could give no warmth to a cold man standing in a snowy market square.

"What time shall we come for the feast at your house tonight?" The laughing men gathered about the Hodja, insisting that they had won the wager.

"Come at sunset," said the Hodja. He plodded drearily toward home. He was cold and very tired, but he was thinking—and thinking hard.

Just after the muezzin's[2] musical voice sent the sunset call to prayer trilling over Ak Shehir,[3], a group of men knocked at Nasr-ed-Din Hodja's street gate. It creaked open for them. They walked across the courtyard and left their shoes in a row beside the house door. They entered the Hodja's house and sat crosslegged on the floor.

"Dinner is not quite ready." It was the Hodja's voice from the kitchen.

"Oh, that's all right," called the men. "We are in no hurry."

They waited. There was an occasional footstep in the kitchen, but no sound of clattering dishes. They sniffed the air to guess what the feast might be, but they could smell no cooking food. They waited—and waited—and waited.

"I hope you are not hungry," called the Hodja from the kitchen. "Dinner is not quite ready yet."

"Perhaps we could help," suggested a hungry guest.

"Fine," called the Hodja. "You might all come out in the kitchen to help."

The men, glad of anything to do, stretched their cramped legs. As each man entered the kitchen, there passed over his face a look of surprise and then a sheepish grin.

There stood the Hodja earnestly stirring the contents of a big copper kettle which was suspended high in the air. Far below it burned one flickering candle.

[2] MUEZZIN (mù-ĕz'ĭn)—A Mohammedan crier of the hour of prayer.
[3] AK SHEHIR—Pronounced ăk shĕ'hĭr.

"Just a few minutes!" The Hodja, standing a-tiptoe, peered into the cold kettle. "It should boil before long. A candle gives so much heat, you know!"

DISCUSSING THE STORY

Among the most amusing folk tales from other countries are those told about Nasr-ed-Din, the cunning schemer from Turkey known as "the Hodja." He is the kind of person who is adept at getting into trouble, but equally skilful at getting out. Those who match wits with the Hodja usually regret it.

1. What was the wager Nasr-ed-Din Hodja made with his friends? Why did the friends think they had won the wager? Tell how the Hodja turned the situation to his own advantage.

2. If your library has a copy of Mrs. Kelsey's *Once the Hodja*, find another story to read or tell to the class.

✿ FOR FURTHER READING: ADVENTURES FAR

FLORENCE AYSCOUGH, *Firecracker Land*
A sympathetic account of the Chinese people and their customs.

NINA B. BAKER, *He Wouldn't Be King*
The life story of Simon Bolivar, the hero of South America.

OLIVIA E. COOLIDGE, *Greek Myths*
A collection of favourite myths retold in an unusual style.

MARIBELLE CORMACK, *Road to Down Under*
The history of the settlement of Australia—plus an interesting romance.

ROBERT DAVIS, *That Girl of Pierre's*
A modern French girl meets some of the problems of growing up.

CHARLES FINGER, *Tales from Silver Lands*
South American legends retold in vivid, dramatic style.

DELIA GOETZ, *Other Young Americans*
Sketches of young Latin Americans—their dress, home life, recreation, and work.

ALBERTA HANNUM. *Spin a Silver Dollar*
A vivid picture of Navajo Indian life.

FRU MARIE ANDERSEN HAMSUN, *A Norwegian Farm*
A story of family life and experiences on a farm.

MARTIN HYDE, *The Singing Sword: The Story of Sir Ogier the Dane*
A thrilling story of the adventures of a boy at the court of Charlemagne.

CLAYTON KNIGHT, *Quest of the Golden Condor*
Adventures in South America.

ELIZABETH FOREMAN LEWIS, *Young Fu of the Upper Yangtze*
A vivid story of a modern young Chinese.

MARIE McSWIGAN, *Juan of Manila*
History and adventure combined in a story of a spy.

FREDERICK C. NANO, *Land and People of Sweden*
Interesting pictures of the customs, crafts, and special qualities of the Swedish people.

VANYA OAKES, *By Sun and Star*
A story of young people in present-day China and of their efforts to escape persecution during the war.

GEORGE AND HELEN PAPASHVILY, *Yes and No Stories*
Folk tales told in Georgia, province of Russia.

BERTRAND L. SHURTLEFF, *Two Against the North*
Two dogs and their owners make an exciting journey across Alaska.

ARMSTRONG SPERRY, *Call it Courage*
In the South Sea Islands a lone boy and his dog set out in a canoe to meet and conquer his fear of the sea.

DORIS S. STILL, *Sue in Tibet*
An interesting story of a summer spent in the remote region of Tibet.

THEODORE J. WALDECK, *On Safari*
A semi-biographical account of the high spots of the author's three journeys to Africa as a scientist and photographer.

YOSHIKO UCHIDO, *The Dancing Kettle and Other Japanese Folk Tales*
Japanese folklore retold in humorous and sprightly style.

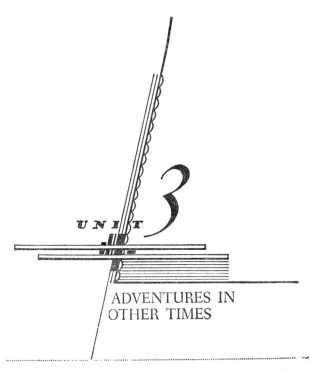

UNIT 3

ADVENTURES IN
OTHER TIMES

More than three centuries ago explorers and adven-
turers began to leave their homes in Europe. They
crowded into tiny ships which they pointed westward
across the terrifying seas. Some of the most courageous
hoped to find freedom—freedom from debts, freedom
for worship, freedom from the power of cruel rulers.
Others hoped to make quick fortunes from the promised
riches of a new land. And there were those who joined
the voyagers for the joy of adventuring in strange and
unknown lands. In the years between then and now
people continued to come to North America in increasing streams. They settled the land and made homes.
They built cities and created machines. A whole new
civilization arose about them. And they left records of
their glorious adventures for us to sample as we will.

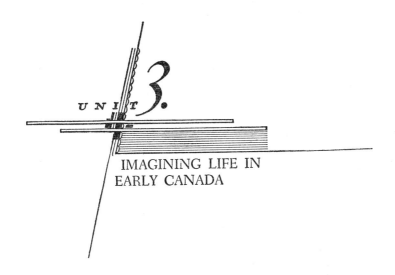

UNIT 3.

IMAGINING LIFE IN EARLY CANADA

HERE WILL I NEST ⚑ HILDA MARY HOOKE

CHARACTERS

COLONEL THOMAS TALBOT.

GEORGE CRANE.

MAHLON BURWELL, *surveyor to the Provincial Government of Upper Canada.*

JOHN PEARCE.

FANNY PEARCE.

ISABELLA PEARCE.

SCENE: *The living-room of "Castle Malahide," Talbot's log house on the shores of Lake Erie, in Upper Canada, on a Sunday morning in June, 1809.*

In one wall of the room is built a capacious stone fireplace, with an iron crane for hanging pots over the fire. A window at the back looks out on the cliffs and the lake below; at right is a door leading to the outer entrance; another door leads to the kitchen, and at left is a door opening into a bedroom. There is a rush-bottomed chair by the fireplace, with one of Talbot's shirts hanging over it

*to dry; a pair of woollen socks hangs from the mantel for the same
purpose. Under the window is a "bunk" bed, covered with a homespun blanket, a sturdy wooden table stands in the middle of the
room, with a wooden chair at each end. Across one corner of the
room are built rough shelves for crockery, etc.*

*At the rise of the curtain George Crane, spare, wiry, with the
trimness of the British soldier about him in spite of his rough
home-made clothes, is putting the requirements of a meal on the
table. Presently, failing to find something that he needs, he goes
toward the kitchen door and shouts.*

George.   Colonel!

Talbot (from the kitchen).   Ay?

George.   Any more salt?

Talbot.   Salt?—Isn't there some in the tin?

George.   Not a grain, sir.   Bare as me hand.

Talbot.   Have to do without then. There'll be no more till Jim
goes up to Buffalo, some time next month.

George.   Right, sir. (*Going on with his work*).

Talbot.   George!

George.   Yes, sir?

Talbot.   One of these tubs is leaking. Do you know anything
about it?

George.   Tubs, sir? (*Virtuously*). Oh no, sir.

*Talbot (appearing at the door with a wet garment dripping in
his hands, his arms covered with soapsuds).* How was it I found
this one out in the middle of the yard?   Didn't I tell you not to
leave 'em out in the sun?

George.   Oh, I didn't, sir! You see, I thought it was going to
rain, so I put it out there to catch some rain-water—for laundry
day, sir—

Talbot.   And then it didn't rain, and the sun came out.

George.   Yes, sir.

Talbot.   Well, next time you catch rain-water, do it in the
shade.

George.   Yes, sir.

Talbot (*throwing the wet garment at him and coming into the room*). Put this with the rest of the wash, and then bring in the food, there's a good fellow. I'll finish after dinner. Gad, I could eat an ox.

[GEORGE *goes out to the kitchen.* TALBOT *dries his hands by the simple expedient of wiping them on his trousers, and drops into a chair by the table. He wears a rough linen shirt and homespun trousers tucked into heavy boots; he is about thirty-eight years old, bronzed and sturdy.*]

George (*coming in with platters of cold meat and corn bread*). Provisions are running a little short, Colonel.

Talbot. Yes—losing those young cattle was a blow. If old Molly hadn't been tied in the barn she'd have gone too, and all our milk and butter with her. I'm going to wait up for those wolves some night.

George. That's just the night they won't come.

Talbot. Every night until they do. (*George goes out and comes back with a coffee-pot*). I don't think we're in any danger of running short of provisions. It'll be back to salt pork for a bit, that's all.

George. Not much of that, either. That troupe of Indians that slept in the kitchen last week took away half the barrel with them.

Talbot. And left us two feather head-dresses and a pair of worn-out moccasins!

George. Heathen varmints.

Talbot. Oh, well, they meant kindly. They'll probably be along soon with some game or a brace of birds—they usually pay for what they take sooner or later.

George.—I don't trust 'em—slipping in after decent folk have gone to bed, and out again before you know what they're up to. I'd keep the house shut up, then they'd have to sleep in the woods, as we've done before now.

Talbot. I shouldn't like to lock the door against them. They're friendly enough, and they'd be bad enemies to make. Cheer up, George, we shan't starve. We've got corn and potatoes, and the garden is yielding some crops already for my trouble—why, we live like princes.

George (*shaking his head*). You can never tell, sir.

Talbot (*laughing*). How cheerful I'd feel if I listened to you, George! Pour me some coffee, there's a good fellow, and come and sit down. (*George pours coffee and then sits at the other end of the table*). Who'd have thought, George, when we were fighting Frenchmen in Flanders twelve years ago, that to-day we'd be sitting opposite one another in this beautiful wilderness, at a table made by our own hands, in a house every log of which we've set ourselves—drinking coffee made from dried peas and toasted bread! (*He takes a long drink, emptying his cup*). Good coffee, too; you're a genius at it, George. (GEORGE *refills* TALBOT's *cup*). Ever sorry you came?

George. That's a question you ought to be able to answer, Colonel.

Talbot. You've never complained, even at the worst of times; but I've sometimes wondered. Six years, George! It hardly seems possible.

George. Six years last May. We've turned over some soil since then.

Talbot. Yes . . . I wonder how my English friends would feel if they could see me sometimes—baking bread, milking my cows, making butter and cheese, coming in from the woods black as any chimney sweep—they'd probably say, "What a blockhead you've been, Tom!"

George. Do you think you have been, sir?

Talbot. George, I'd rather be eating this homely fare than the best dinner in London. I regret nothing. It's been a glorious struggle; and we've won, so far.

George. So far, sir.

Talbot. I know what that careful tone means, George. Six years—and no settlers yet.

George. It *is* a long time, sir.

Talbot. I know—and the Provincial Government sitting in its swivel chair and shaking its wise head over mad Tom Talbot and his mythical settlers. If it hadn't been for my good friend Simcoe they would have never let me have the land in the first place. But we'll fool them yet—when our pioneer farmers arrive.

George (buttering corn bread attentively). Where will they come from, Colonel?

Talbot (snapping a little). How should I know?—Scotland, perhaps, like Selkirk's unfortunates. More likely from among the loyalists stranded in the northern states—mark my words, George, in a few years, people will be streaming up these cliffs so fast that we'll be put to it to deal with 'em all.

George (pausing on his way back to his chair after again filling Talbot's cup, to look hopefully out of the window). That'll be nice, sir . . . Sounds like a boat landing down there now.

Talbot. It may be Burwell. This is about the date he expected to be back; flying his flags high, no doubt, if the Government sided with him in the road question, as they probably would. Obstinate young blockhead! he wouldn't take my word for it, but must go bleating to the Administration. Anyone coming up, George?

George. I think it's Colonel Burwell, sir.

Talbot (looking out of the window). Yes . . . those are his long legs. Well, we'll see what the latest headwagging at York has accomplished. Clear off the table, George.

George (beginning to take the plates and dishes off the table). Do you want your maps, sir? They're underneath the bunk.

Talbot. That's no place for them to be. They'll get smothered in dust.

George. Yes, sir. You put them there yourself, sir, if you'll remember. You said you wouldn't have the shelf cluttered with papers.

[TALBOT *stares at him and then begins to laugh.*]

Talbot. George, you always put me in the wrong. And so nicely, too. I apologize about the maps. I shall be very crotchety when I'm old . . . it's the result of being a bachelor, I expect.

George. You may remedy that, Colonel.

Talbot. Not I. I've been unlucky, George. Those I would have, wouldn't have me; and those that would have me—faith, the devil himself wouldn't have them!

George (with a reminiscent grin). The lady on the boat, sir?

Talbot. Yes! That was a narrow escape; and the good-hearted lass who came with her father from Delaware and thought we needed a woman's hand . . . No, George, you may marry, but I never shall.

George (outraged). I, sir!

Talbot. Yes. You'd be soft enough, if some woman got hold of you.—Here's Burwell. (*Knock at the outer door*). Let him in, George.

[*George goes out. Burwell's voice is heard outside.*]

Burwell. Is Colonel Talbot in?

George. Yes, sir. Come in. The Colonel is expecting you.

[*Mahlon Burwell enters, a handsome, solemn-faced young man some twelve years younger than Talbot. He takes himself and his work very seriously.*]

Talbot. Hello, Burwell. You made good time. I hardly expected to see you so soon.

Burwell. Good morning, Colonel. I hope you don't object to my intruding on you on Sunday!

Talbot. Not a bit. Sit down. Did you have good weather?

Burwell. Yes; the lake's like a mill-pond to-day.

Talbot. I hope your discussions at headquarters were as calm. Was the Governor there?

Burwell. Yes; I had a chat with him. He was very pleasant.

Talbot. Oh, I've nothing against Gore; he's a good fellow, and does his best with a shrewish council. Some of them should be boiled in oil—'twould be the only way of sweetening them. But how did you fare at the capital? Did you arrange the little matter we spoke of?

Burwell. Well, yes—we arranged it, more or less.

Talbot. What's the decision of headquarters regarding the new road?

Burwell. They made no definite decision. I think they're curious to see what you're going to do. They simply asked me to lay before you the recommendations as to the policy of settlement they would wish you to follow in the event of the road being opened up.

Talbot.   Hm. They approve of the plans for the road then?

Burwell.   Oh, entirely. The Governor said that you were an enterprising fellow, and that he heartily wished you success in your undertakings.

Talbot.   The old boy must have been in a good mood—or else your famous diplomacy worked on his feelings. But what are these recommendations regarding settlements?

Burwell.   Well—you remember we discussed the question of placing grants in the block system—beginning in the township of Dunwich?

Talbot.   Do I not! If my memory serves me right we sat up an entire night arguing over it!

Burwell (*smiling*).   I believe we did. Well, the Council's ruling was that the settlement should be known as the Talbot Settlement, and that it should be kept as compact as possible, under the terms originally agreed upon by you, namely—

Talbot.   You needn't go over all that again. I know the original terms backwards.

Burwell.   But one or two of the Council members were quite insistent about them. You know, Talbot, you can't go on deliberately ignoring their wishes—after all, the roads will be Government property—

Talbot.   My dear chap, I don't want to interfere with their precious property! I merely stand on my rights to settle my own land as I choose—and apparently they are still determined that I shall be wedged into my castle like a sardine in a tin, with all the other little sardines neartly packed around me.

Burwell (*laughing*).   I don't really think the Executive considered you as a sardine, Talbot.

Talbot.   They don't consider me at all; that's the trouble.

Burwell.   If you'd defer a little to their opinions—

Talbot.   What's the use of doing that, when I don't agree with em. I haven't got your patience, Burwell. I can't use tact to gain my ends.

Burwell (*shaking his head*).   You'll never make a politician.

Talbot (*cheerfully*). Never. So let's get down to work. Let's see your map. (BURWELL *unrolls his map and they both bend over it*). Here's the route to be laid out. Port Talbot—here. Now the present road runs through Dunwich to this point. . . My plan is to extend the new road through Southwold, Yarmouth, across Houghton and up to the east line of Middleton townships.

Burwell. Yes—that should open up a good line for settlement.

Talbot. "The Talbot Settlement," eh? Think, Burwell! ten, twenty years from now—thriving farms branching out from this highway like leaves along a stem; villages springing up, towns, schools, churches—a truly British colony, self-contained and self-supporting—doesn't that thrill you?

Burwell. I hope your optimism will be justified.

Talbot (*looking at him, half amused, half angry*). You're a cold fish, Burwell! Here am I on fire with the new project, seeing this country opening like a great flower in the sun—and you say, "I hope your optimism will be justified!"

Burwell. Sorry! I didn't mean to throw cold water. I admire your enthusiasm enormously. (*Gathering up his papers*). With any luck I can begin surveying the eastern territory next week. I'll go back to York [1] tomorrow, get my equipment together, and come back prepared to make a long stay.

Talbot. Can't be too soon for me. I can scarce wait to hear the sound of pick and shovel ringing on the trail. What a life it is, Burwell! Who would trade civilization for the glorious freedom of these woods, for the feel of open spaces—above all, for the knowledge that this corner is mine, my nest, my castle—my kingdom of Malahide, that I dreamed of so long!

Burwell. When did you first think about settling here, Talbot?

Talbot. Ever since I can remember, it seems to me. When I was a lad in Ireland I used to read the Journals of old Pierre Charlevoix, written during his voyages down the Mississippi—and I used to talk to my friend Arthur Wellesley about them.

Burwell. Wellesley! I heard that he has been created Viscount lately. He is well thought of in military circles, I believe.

Talbot. Yes, he'll be great soldier some day. Once when I was

[1] Now Toronto.

pouring out my ambitions to him—as I often did, poor fellow—he said, "You're a throw-back to feudal days, Tom—wanting to be a little king in your own right!"

Burwell. Well—you've acquired the castle. That's a step in the right direction!

Talbot. Ay—and the lands too. But where are the subjects?

[GEORGE *enters hurriedly, unusual excitement on his well-trained features.*]

George. Excuse me for interrupting you, sir—but Jim Fleming's here—

Talbot. Fleming! I thought he was on his way to Long Point. What does he want?

George. He was, sir—but he was delayed, and when he went down to the landing he saw them coming—and—they're here, Colonel, asking for you!

Talbot. Who are here? What are you talking about?

George (*in a burst*). The settlers, sir!

Talbot. Settlers!

George. Yes—from Pennsylvania, just as you said, sir—they're at the landing now—

[*In two strides Talbot pushes him aside and makes for the door.*]

Talbot (*shouting*). Fleming! What's all this about?

[*He is outside. Fleming's voice is heard explaining.*]

Burwell.—Who are these people, Crane?

George. I don't know, sir—Jim ran on ahead to tell the Colonel, and left them coming ashore; they'll be here in a moment . . .

Talbot (*coming in*). George!

George. Yes, sir!

Talbot. Put this stuff away. Clear up the room . . . get a meal ready, everything you can find . . . heat some water, make tea, coffee, soup, anything . . . if I'm not back when you've finished come down to the landing . . (*Shouting*) How many are there, Fleming?

Fleming (*outside*). Three, Colonel, and more coming; you see—

Talbot. Great Saints! George, there are more coming . . .(*He is outside again*). Get on, man, for heaven's sake get on—what are

you staring at? Let's get down to 'em! (*He is heard hustling
Fleming off*).

Burwell (*uncertainly*). Perhaps I'd better—

[*Talbot rushes back and grabs Burwell by the arm.*]

Talbot. Come on, Burwell, come down with us. We must
have a deputation to welcome our populace!

[*They go out,* GEORGE, *after standing bewildered for a moment,
is galvanized into sudden action. He hurries the maps and
papers off the table and stuffs them under the bunk; scurries
round the room, shifting chairs and putting them back again,
gathering up various articles that have been lying about the
room—the shirt and socks at the fireplace, towel over a chair,
etc.—and pushes them under the blankets of the bunk; begins
to get cups, plates, etc., from the shelf and set them on the
table. Every now and then he interrupts these preparations
to run and peer out of the window. As he goes to the shelf to
get knives and forks, Burwell comes in, out of breath, his
usually smooth hair ruffled with his exertions.*]

Burwell. Crane! The Colonel says—get his bedroom ready—
for the ladies.

George (*turning abruptly*). Ladies!

Burwell. Yes—two of them.

George. Strike me pink!

Burwell. He says, clean sheets, the best quilt, put away his
clothes—you'd know what to do.

George (*dazed*). Ladies! (*He stares at Burwell, then thrusts
the knives and forks into his hands*). Here, you go on with this
then.

[*He dives into the bedroom, from whence comes a great bustle
of moving furniture, opening and closing of drawers, etc.
BURWELL looks at the cutlery, not quite sure how to proceed;
and is gingerly placing them round the table in what he hopes
is the proper order when GEORGE rushes out with his arms
full of bed-linen and stray garments.*]

George (*on his way to the kitchen*). There's coffee in the tin
on the shelf, Mr. Burwell, sir—(*He disappears.* BURWELL *stares at*

the shelf. GEORGE *comes back*)—and there's water heating in the kettle. You can swing the coffee pot right over the fire.

[*He goes back into the bedroom.* BURWELL *crosses to the shelf, takes down the coffee tin, and peering into it goes with it to the kitchen. More clothes come flying out through the bedroom door. After a second a loud crash is heard in the kitchen.*]

George (*shouting from the bedroom*). What's the matter?

Burwell (*from the kitchen*). I spilt the water.

George.   That handle gets pretty hot. . . .

Burwell.   I've noticed that. (*He comes in, binding a handkerchief round his hand*).

George (*appearing in the bedroom door*). Burn yourself?

Burwell.   A bit.

George.   Butter's a good thing. . . .

[TALBOT'S *voice is heard outside, cheery and encouraging.*]

Talbot.   Here we are, ma'am—just a few steps further, . . . it's a long climb.

[GEORGE *and* BURWELL *hurry to the window.*]

George.   My! Look at the young one!

Burwell.   Black hair, blue eyes . . . Irish, I'll be bound.

George.   Here they come. (*He picks up the scattered garments from the floor, pushes them under the bunk and dashes back into the bedroom*).

Talbot (*outside*). Put your bundles down here, Mr. Pearce— we'll get them later. Come in, come in—

[*He ushers in* JOHN PEARCE *and his wife and daughter.* PEARCE *is a quiet little man, his wife cheerful and buxom;* ISABELLA *their daughter, a lively girl of nineteen or so, full of bounce and vigour and with a very keen pair of eyes. She is, characteristically, the first to enter the room.*]

Isabella.   Pouf! I'm glad to be up that cliff! You do live in a crow's nest, don't you, Colonel?

Mrs. Pearce.   Indeed, it looks wonderfully comfortable, Colonel.

Talbot.   It's a pioneer's house, Mrs. Pearce, so take a good look at it! Let me present Colonel Burwell, Mrs. Pearce, Miss Isabella Pearce—Mr. Pearce, Colonel Burwell.

[*The ladies curtsey,* BURWELL *bows, then shakes hands with* JOHN PEARCE.]

Burwell. I am delighted to welcome you to Port Talbot.

Talbot. Come and see our view, Mrs. Pearce—we're very proud of our scenery. (*Leading her to the window*). This is one of the pleasantest sights on earth to me.

Mrs. Pearce. It's beautiful—isn't it, Bella?

Isabella. It's lovely, lovely! I've never seen such trees . . . what's that big one over there, Colonel Talbot?

Talbot. That's black walnut. We have plenty of them back in the woods.

Isabella. And look at the little white bonnets riding on the waves! Can we have a house on the cliffs, too, father?

Pearce (*smiling*). You'll have to ask Colonel Talbot that!

Talbot. You can have your pick of the countryside, Miss Isabella. Lake or forest, river or valley—they're all here to choose from. We'll give them the first location on the new road, eh Burwell—veterans of the Talbot Settlement!

Mrs. Pearce. Well, I'm sure if we manage anything half as comfortable as this, I'll be well pleased. The others will like this house, won't they, John. You must have worked very hard, Colonel, to have done all this—and by yourself, too!

Talbot. You should have seen our first effort, Mrs. Pearce! We had a three-room shack, and the rain used to drip in on us at nights!

Isabella. Didn't you catch cold?

Talbot. Oh, we got used to it! After a couple of years we built this place, and we've been as snug as nestlings ever since. Try this chair, Mrs. Pearce. Tell me, who are the others you spoke of?

Pearce. Well, you see, we're the forerunners, like, of the party. We came on by boat, to see you, and to spy out the land as you might say; and the rest are following the bush trail with the cattle and the goods.

Talbot. Cattle? You're bringing cattle?

Pearce. We thought we might as well—we'd nought to do with the beasts and we thought they'd be handy. Did we do wrong?

Talbot. Wrong! my dear fellow, it's gloriously right! We've lost nearly all our animals with wolves coming in at night; we must safeguard yours better. How many are coming in your party?

Pearce. Well, there's the Storeys, and the Pattersons, and the Barbers—thirteen souls in all—

Mrs. Pearce. And they've a mint of stuff with them—looms for wool and linen making, and the like—you see, we're used to that work, and the women were all for bringing the things with them. I hope it won't be a burden here.

Talbot. Burden—why it's magnificent! Burwell, d'you hear that? Just to-day the colonel and I were talking of the settlement that's going to grow along these shores—and here it is at our very feet! But I'm talking as usual, and you must be tired and hungry and wanting a wash and a change—we'll have some hot water brought in for you directly. Miss Isabella, how will you like being a pioneer's daughter?

Isabella. I'm going to love every moment of it. Look at this dear little bed! Is this where you sleep, Colonel Talbot?

Talbot (smiling). No, George sleeps there. That's my room over yonder—where you'll sleep tonight.

Isabella. Oh, let me see! (*Running over to look*). Why, it's a real bedroom—Oh!

[*She has discovered* GEORGE, *who appears sheepishly in the doorway of the bedroom.*]

George. Beg pardon, Miss.

Isabella. You made me jump out of my skin! I didn't know there was anyone in there!

Talbot. Why, George! I wondered what had become of you! Don't be afraid, Miss Isabella, he's the mildest fellow in the world —My house-mate and fellow-worker, George Crane—Mr. and Mrs. Pearce—Miss Isabella Pearce—

[GEORGE, *embarrassed, pulls his forelock and mutters something; but* ISABELLA *shakes him firmly by the hand.*]

Isabella. How do you do!

Talbot. I think that we should all celebrate before the ladies go to their room. George, what about that last bottle of English sherry?

George (*glad to escape*). Yes, sir!

Talbot. Sherry all round, George!

Isabella (*gaily*). I'll come and help you, Mr. Crane.

George (*flustered*). There's no need for that, Miss . . . I'll be back in a jiffy.

Isabella. But I'd like to. I've never seen a pioneer kitchen. . . You can show me where everything is. Ah, come on!

[*She grasps the astonished* GEORGE *by the hand and pulls him off to the kitchen. The others laugh.*]

Mrs. Pearce (*apologetically*). Bella gets a bit excited sometimes. It's the journey and all.

Burwell. If you'll excuse me, Colonel, I'll slip down and tie up my boat. I left her pulled up on the beach, and the wind's rising a bit.

Talbot. Be back for the celebration!

Burwell. I'll be sure to do that! (*He goes out*).

Talbot. Well, Mr. Pearce, how does it feel to be on British soil again?

Pearce. Colonel, I don't mind telling you that this is the happiest day I've had in months. We've been living upside down, it seems to me, ever since the war—and we've seen a goodish bit of trouble, one way and another, haven't we, Fanny?

Mrs. Pearce. Indeed we have, John. This just seems like heaven to us, sir—to be quiet and let alone, and some chances of a home again.

Talbot. With all my heart I hope you'll find that home here, Mrs. Pearce. We'll try our best to make up to you for all you've been through. If I could tell what it means to me to see people from the old land again, after all these years! And my own countrymen too—what part of Ireland are you from?

Mrs. Pearce. County Fermanagh, sir—Enniskillen. And you, sir?

Talbot. Dublin—dear, dirty Dublin! Only nine years since I was there . . . but it seems a lifetime.

Mrs. Pearce. It must be a hard struggle, you've had, Colonel.

Talbot. But worth it, ma'am! When I first saw this beautiful country, stretching from Lake Erie to the River La Tranche, I knew that some day I must settle here. I was with Governor Simcoe, and I climbed up to this cliff, and stood looking over the shining Erie waters. "Here will I nest," I cried, "until I make the forests tremble with the wings of the flock I will invite by my warblings round me!" Rather theatrical, wasn't it? but I meant every word of it, and I still do. And—(*looking from* JOHN *to his wife*) here is the vanguard of my flock!

[*There is a peal of laughter from the kitchen, and* ISABELLA's *voice raised merrily.*]

Isabella. Oh, George, you are funny!

George (*outside*). Strike me lucky, Miss Isabella—if you spill that sherry—

Isabella. Silly! I've got it as tight as anything—

[*They enter,* ISABELLA *carrying a wooden tray with two glasses and four pewter mugs on it.*]

Talbot. What, letting the lady do the work, George?

George. She would take it, sir—

Isabella. Of course! This is our very own first celebration, and I'm going to remember it as long as I live (*putting the tray down*). Here they are, Colonel, and they're all exactly the same, because I measured them myself.

Talbot. Splendid! I can't offer you fine Flemish glass, Mrs. Pearce, but I can assure you that the contents are beyond reproach. (*He hands a glass to Mrs. Pearce*) John—(*giving one to Mr. Pearce*)—Miss Isabella, here's yours—

[BURWELL *comes in.*]

Talbot. Burwell, you're just in time!

Isabella (*handing a mug to* BURWELL). Here's yours, Colonel Burwell. Here George, next to me!

Mrs. Pearce. Now, Colonel, you must make a speech.

Pearce. That's it, Colonel—something to remember when we're old homesteaders.

Talbot (standing in the midst of them). I'm just realizing that this is my first speech to my subjects—and I'm feeling a bit nervous. As a matter of fact, I find it difficult to say anything, because when a man sees a dream coming true he feels a pull on his heartstrings that won't let him speak. Ever since I came to this place, on the twenty-first of May, 1803, that dream of mine has been growing; and today, when you set foot on the sands of Port Talbot, I saw it really fulfilled. *(He lifts the mug in his hands).* It is said that once or twice in every man's lifetime there comes to him a magic moment when he looks into the mirror of the future. I think that one of those moments has come to me; for here in this little pewter cup I see the ambitions of youth meeting the fulfilments of mellow age. I know that to-day history is being made; to-day for a magic moment we have touched the garments of posterity. Ladies and gentlemen, I give you—The Talbot Settlement!

All (lifting their glasses). The Talbot Settlement!

[*The glasses and mugs clink gaily against each other as the curtain goes down.*]

KEYS TO ENJOYMENT

In this historical play, Hilda Mary Hooke pictures one incident in the origin of the Talbot Settlement of the Lake Erie region in Ontario. The play takes us back to 1809, six years after Talbot had first arrived to make preparations for the colony which he hoped to found.

1. What evidence is there in the play that the pioneers had to face many dangers? that they had to rely on their own resourcefulness?

2. What important work did Colonel Burwell have to do before the colony could be successfully developed?

3. What important possessions did the Pearces and their party bring to assist them in living in a pioneer colony?

4. What is the significance of the title of the play?

5. Contrast the characters of Talbot, Crane, and Burwell?

6. Successful drama depends upon conflict. What evidence of conflict is present in this play?

ON, ROLL ON MY BALL

FRENCH-CANADIAN FOLK SONG

On, roll on, my ball I roll on, On, roll on my
En rou-lant ma bou-le rou-lant, En rou-lant ma

ball, — on! ball, — on! 1.'Way back at home there
bou - le · bou - le. 1. Der - rièr', chez nous ya -

is a pond, On, roll' on, my ball, on!'Way ball, on! Three
t-un é-tang, En rou-lant ma bou - le, ,Der- bou-le Trois

bon - nie ducks go swim-ming'round, Roll on, my ball, my
beaux ca-nards s'en vont baig-nant, Rou - li rou-lant 'ma

Chorus

ball I roll on.. On, roll on, my ball I roll on,
bou-le. rou-lant. En rou-lant ma bou-le rou-lant,

Stanzas 1-12.   Last Stanza

On, roll on my ball, — on! 2. Three ball on!
En rou-lant ma bou - le. 2. Trois bou - le

En roulant ma boule roulant,
En roulant ma boule.
Derrière, chez nous y a-t-un étang,
En roulant ma boule,

5 Trois beaux canards s'en vont baignant,
Rouli, roulant, ma boule roulant.
En roulant ma boule roulant,
En roulant ma boule.

Trois beaux canards s'en vont baignant,
10 Le fils du roi s'en va chassant.

Le fils du roi s'en va chassant,
Avec son grand fusil d'argent.

Avec son grand fusil d'argent,
Visa le noir, tua le blanc.

15 Visa le noir, tua le blanc,
O fils du roi, tu es méchant!

O fils du roi, tu es méchant
D'avoir tué mon canard blanc!

D'avoir tué mon canard blanc!
20 Par-dessous l'aîle il perd son sang.

Par-dessous l'aîle il perd son sang,
Par les yeux lui sort'nt des diamants.

Par les yeux lui sort'nt des diamants.
Et par le bec, l'or et l'argent.

25 Et par le bec, l'or et l'argent,
Toutes ses plum's s'en vont au vent.

Toutes ses plum's s'en vont au vent,
Trois dam's s'en vont les ramassant.

Trois dam's s'en vont les ramassant,
30 C'est pour en faire un lit de camp.

C'est pour en faire un lit de camp,
Pour y coucher tous les passants.

ON, ROLL ON MY BALL — J. Murray Gibbon

On, roll on, my ball I roll on,
On, roll on my ball, on!
Way back at home there is a pond,
On, roll on, my ball, on!
5   Three bonnie ducks go swimming round,
Roll on, my ball, my ball I roll on.
On, roll on my ball I roll on.
On, roll on my ball on.

Three bonnie ducks go swimming round,
10   The prince goes off a-hunting bound.

The Prince goes off a-hunting bound,
His gun so big with silver crowned.

His gun so big with silver crowned,
The black he saw, the white he downed.

15   The black he saw, the white he downed,
O prince, that was a wicked wound!

O prince, that was a wicked wound,
To kill the white duck I had owned.

To kill the white duck I had owned,
20   Each eye became a diamond.

Each eye became a diamond,
Silver and gold her beak surround.

Silver and gold her beak surround,
Beneath her wings a bloody wound

25   Beneath her wings a bloody wound,
The feathers in the wind fly round.

The feathers in the wind fly round,
Three dames to pick them up are bound.

Three dames to pick them up are bound,
30   They make a camp bed on the ground.

They make a camp bed on the ground,
That passers-by may slumber sound.

KEYS TO ENJOYMENT

The folk songs of French Canada have made an important contribution to our culture. To acquaint us further with their delightful qualities, "En Roulant Ma Boule" is included here. The English version is a close translation of the French, in spirit if not exactly in word. The song is written in cumulative fashion much as was "This is the house that Jack built," one of the favourite stories of children. Sing it with spirit and enjoyment. Several pupils may sing the solo parts and the whole class the refrain. Both the English and the French versions should be sung.

1. In what ways is the song, "En Roulant Ma Boule," similar to a cumulative story like "This is the house that Jack Built"? In what ways is it different?

THE CRADLE 🌾 ADJUTOR RIVARD

FOUR goodly planks of sound wood, stoutly jointed, make the body of the cradle. The corner posts which support the frame are carved at the top in the likeness of a bulrush, and the same rustic skill has given the head-piece an outline of sober grace. The rockers are without a knot and are curved so that the cradle swings easy and smooth as a boat upon the wave.

You have but to fit the bottom board into the notches; to add a tiny mattress and a pillow; furnish sheets, blankets and quilt, on a half-hoop at the head to stretch an awning which shields young eyes from too strong a light; and, let him rock who will, you may be sure that the little lad within will sleep there soundly with closed fists.

The cradle is very old; generations have been rocked in it. In a manner of speaking I could say that our cradle was there from the beginning, for, so many years has it seen, its age is known to none. It was in the house before the chairs with seats of inter-laced horse-hide,—before the dumpy stove which took over the duties of the open fireplace,—before the red kneading-trough that one always remembers in the north-east corner,—before the great blue chest where coverlets have been stored as far back as anyone can recollect. One might risk it that the cradle saw the very house built, room by room, and lay attending the shelter of a roof, for events were just on the edge of need for its services. In truth this bit of furniture is as old as the family itself.

By honoured tradition the cradle passes from generation to generation, a precious family possession; and it is the born right of the eldest daughter to fetch it from her father's roof when she awaits the first visit of the stork. Thus from mother to daughter has the old cradle, affectionately known as the 'blue-box,' descended to us.

And who fashioned it in the far-away past? I like to think of the rugged forefather who brought these four planks together and made of them the cradle of his race, and I seem to see him, remote, standing on the very confines of history.

The colonist has hewn for himself a home in the forest. In the middle of the clearing he has built the house which harbours his love, his joy, his dearest hopes. On the sill of the log-cabin stands his helpmate, and follows her man with her eyes as he departs, axe on shoulder, singing as he goes. The foot-path takes a winding way through the charred stumps, and the sun blazes down on him.

As yet the encircling woods are close at hand, and soon he halts before a lofty maple whose sturdy shaft towers high above the lower growth. With a keen glance he measures the great tree as though pitting himself against it. A sign of the cross, and firmly he plants his feet, the strong back bent, the muscles taut. His good blade swings, burying itself in the green wood; again, and the first chip flies.

"Ahoy there Nicolas! What are you about? This is no time to be clearing your land!"

"True enough. When the season for that comes around the untouched forest shall feel my axe; just now this maple will answer. I chose it from a thousand because it is the strongest. From a thousand I chose it because it is the straightest. See how rough the bark, how sound the heart!" The steel sinks again and again into the living wood and the chips dance in the air.

"Months ago was it that I marked this tree. One evening, the day's work done, at the hour when the fields are misty beneath the setting sun, my young wife sitting by me told me of her hope. With bared head I answered 'Now God be praised!' And from the threshold of our cabin I showed her this maple at the edge of the wood, taller than its fellows:—'That is the very one I shall fell for the cradle'." Swifter the blow and thicker fly the chips.

"And now has come the hour when the tree must fall, for the time is not distant when a cradle will be wanted in my house. A few more days of waiting and you shall see me driving to the village, happy as any prince, and you shall hear the bells ring for the christening. Joy will abound under my roof, and neighbours will be welcome to come through the forest to see the woodman's son, for the table will not be bare." And yet more keenly bites the steel, till the chips rain through the air and strew and whiten the ground.

The wood-cutter smites with all the strength of his rejoicing thews; his axe is at the tree's heart, and still it falls, swings, falls again in the broadening deepening cut. Another blow, and the top shivers against the sky. For the last time the steel flashes . . . the old king bows himself over the wound thus for an instant, shuddering to his uttermost twig, and with a long groan comes crashing to earth.

A good job is done! Now, Nicolas, strip the mighty trunk. Let the neighbours lend a hand. Here! you Johnny Baptistes, stoutly ply the two-handed saw; square the timber skilfully with the shining broad-axe; and now, you sawyers, cut me up this master block. Fine planks they are, and truly sawn! Be at them, Nicolas, with hand-saw, auger and plane. Dove-tail the ends and drill the holes straight. Carve bulrushes on the post heads with your knife. Now, put all together. Here are the pegs, made to fit snugly. Work away with chisel, draw-knife and mallet!

The expected baby may arrive when it likes and the holy water

may flow and the christening bells ring, for here is the cradle
ready!

From mother to daughter the cradle has come down to us—the
cradle of our forefathers, made of the clean straight-grained maple.

In the course of a long life the cradle has known many vicis-
situdes. The pretty slate-blue has dulled to grey. Hard wear has
rounded the corners and made the bulrush heads shiny, and the
touch of many a patient foot has worn away the points of the
rockers. A story of knocks and bangs and bruises and scorchings
is written in the scars it bears.

One night the lightning struck and set the house on fire; first
the baby was saved, then the cradle. The flames were licking the
head-board and the blister is there to see.

In a spring freshet the river overflowed its banks and the water
rose above the floors; people got away as best they could—through
the window in the gable, by canoe; the unhappy cradle battled
about for days in the flood.

Many a wound is there of which I do not know the history,
but the cradle was built to withstand life's onslaughts and is sound
as ever and rocks as smoothly.

When the cradle is not in use it reposes on a beam in the attic;
at the coming of a baby they carry it down again. But the flaxen
heads follow so fast that it is scarcely worth while from year's end
to year's end to stow it away—so unfailing the demand for its good
offices. Nor is there happier sound in the house than the constant
rocking, and the lullabies which keep time to it.

> C'est la poulette grise
> Qu 'a pondu dans l'église . . . [1]

The mother herself it may be, with another child in her arms,
or fingers busy with the knitting, who stirs the cradle with her
foot as she sings. Her voice falls lower and lower as drowsiness
comes, and trails off to silence when baby falls asleep.

---

[1] It is the young grey hen
Who has laid an egg in the church.

> C'esa la poulette caille
> Qu 'a pondu dans la paille . . . [2]

Perhaps the father is there, groping for a softer tone in his hearty voice. His wife is back and forth as she makes the soup; and the ploughman gently swings the tiny cot with the great hand which all day has held the handles of the plough. But the red-cheeked tot does not want to go bye-byes and would rather clutch the beard conveniently in reach of his chubby fist.

> C'est la poulette blanche
> Qu a' pondu dans la grange . . . [3]

Or the eldest girl, not very old at that, has been allowed the treat of putting baby to sleep. Seated on the foot of the cradle, her voice sings out at the pitch of her lungs as though her task were to waken the whole house; and she rocks with such goodwill as to threaten everything with shipwreck!

> C'est la poulette brune
> Qu 'a pondu dans la lune,
> Elle a pondu un beau petit coco
> Pour l'enfant qui va faire dodo.
> Dodiche, dodo!
> Dodiche, dodo! [4]

Though grandmamma's voice quavers and fails, her aid is sought on those evenings when little fits of bad temper possess the occupant of the cradle, for no one has quite the old lady's knack with children—so many a one has she rocked in her day!

[2] It is the young quail hen
Who has laid an egg in the straw.
[3] It is the young white hen
Who has laid an egg in the barn.
[4] It is the young brown hen
Who has laid an egg in the moon.
She has laid a beautiful little egg
For the child who is going to sleep.
Bye, baby, bye;
Bye, baby, bye.

It is when she is beside the cradle that the family loves best to draw near. One is so sure of a smile! Heads bend over curiously; the big people have a word of encouragement, the little folks of amazement:—"Grandma, it has eyes! Look, Grandma, it has a nose!" The small one-before-the-last holds staggeringly to the top of a post and sulks. The tears are not far away, for has she not been turned out of her very own cradle in favour of a little usurping brother! But she is consoled with the promise that she shall have papa's place in the big bed just for to-night.

And when everyone in the house sleeps you might hear the cradle going—fastened to mother's wrist by a string it is rocking in the dark.

O God, do Thou bless the houses where the cradle is held in honour! Bless those hearths where many a birth comes to cheer the ancient cradle and bring it perpetual youth! Bless the families who hold in reverence the virtues of former days, to the glory of our Church and of our Country!

KEYS TO ENJOYMENT

Sometimes we adopt symbols about which to concentrate our ideas and our ideals. The Union Jack is such a symbol. In our present story, the cradle is another. Here it is meant to emphasize the importance of the family and of family possessions and traditions. The birth of children into a family is held to be a natural and an honourable thing, for children are necessary to the Kingdom of God as well as to the progress of our Nation.

The story of the cradle also stresses the importance of careful selection and of efficient workmanship. As in the construction of the cradle here described, so in any work which we have to do, meticulous care and precise craftsmanship are worthy of our attention. A thing worth doing is worth doing well.

1. Outline carefully the steps in the construction of the cradle described by Rivard.

2. In what ways may the cradle as here described be considered a symbol?

3. In what way is a religious emphasis introduced into this story?

4. In what way does this story reveal life among early Canadian pioneer families?

USING WORDS

Match the words in Column B with the corresponding words in Column A.

Column A	Column B
1. recollect	a. change of circumstances
2. thews	b. everlasting
3. mallet	c. attack
4. vicissitude	d. remember
5. onslaught	e. comforted
6. knack	f. take wrongfully
7. usurp	g. muscles
8. consoled	h. trick or device
9. perpetual	i. wooden hammer

THE WAY OF THE WEST 𝕏 NELLIE L. McCLUNG

THOMAS SHOULDICE was displeased, sorely, bitterly displeased; in fact, he was downright mad, and being an Irish Orangeman, this means that he was ready to fight. You can imagine just how bitterly Mr. Shouldice was incensed when you hear that the Fourth of July had been celebrated with flourish of flags and blare of trumpets right under his very nose——in Canada——in British dominions!

The First of July, the day that should have been given up to "doin's," including the race for the greased pig, the three-legged race, and a ploughing match, had passed into obscurity, without so much as a pie-social; and it had rained that day, too, in torrents, just as if Nature herself did not care enough about the First to try to keep it dry.

The Fourth came in a glorious day, all sunshine and blue sky, with birds singing in every poplar bluff, and it was given such a celebration as Thomas had never seen since the "Twelfth" had been held in Souris. The American settlers who had been pouring into the Souris valley had—without so much as asking leave from the Government at Ottawa, the school trustees, or the oldest settler, who was Thomas himself—gone ahead and celebrated. Every American family had brought their own flag-pole, in "joints," with them, and on the Fourth immense banners of stars and stripes spread their folds in triumph on the breeze.

The celebration was held in a large grove just across the road from Thomas Shouldice's little house; and to his inflamed patriotism, every fire-cracker that split the air, every cheer that rent the heavens, every blare of their smashing band music, seemed a direct challenge to King Edward himself, God bless him!

Mr. Shouldice worked all day at his hay-meadow, just to show them! He worked hard, too, never deigning a glance at their "carrin's on," just to let them know that he did not care two cents for their Fourth of July.

His first thought was to feign indifference, but when he saw the Wilsons, the Wrays, the Henrys, Canadian-bred and born, driving over to the enemy's camp, with their Sunday clothes on and big boxes of provisions on the "doggery" of their buckboards, his indifference fled and was replaced by profanity. It comforted him little when he reflected that not an Orangeman had gone. They were loyal sons and true, every one of them. These other ignorant Canadians might forget what they owed to the old flag, but the Orangeman—never.

Thomas's rage against the Yankees was intensified when he saw Father O'Flynn walking across the Plover slough. Then he was sure that the Americans and Catholics were in league against the British.

A mighty thought was conceived that day in the brain of Thomas Shouldice, late Worshipful Master of the Carleton Place Loyal Orange Lodge No. 23. They would celebrate the Twelfth, so they would; he'd like to see who would stop them. Someone would stand up for the flag that had braved a thousand years of battle and the breezes. He blew his nose noisily on his red handkerchief when he thought of this.

They would celebrate the Twelfth! They would "walk." He would gather up "the boys" and get someone to make a speech. They would get a fifer from Brandon. It was the fife that could stir the heart in you! And the fifer would play "The Protestant Boys" and "Rise, Sons of William, Rise!" Anyone that tried to stop him would get a shirt full of sore bones!

Thomas went home full of the plans to get back at the invaders! Rummaging through his trunk, he found, carefully wrapped with chewing tobacco and ground cedar, to keep the moth away, the regalia that he had worn, proudly and defiantly, once in Montreal when the crowd that obstructed the triumphal march of the Orange Young Britons had to be dispersed by the "melitia." It was a glorious day, and one to be remembered with pride, for there had been shots fired and heads smashed.

His man, a guileless young Englishman, came in from mowing, gaily whistling the refrain the Yankee band had been playing at intervals all afternoon. It was "Dixie Land," and at first Thomas did not notice it. Rousing at last to the sinister significance of the tune, he ordered its cessation, in rosy-hued terms, and commended all such Yankee tunes and those that whistled them to that region where popular rumour has it that pots boil with or without watching.

Thomas Shouldice had lived by himself, for a number of years. It was supposed that he had a wife living somewhere in "the States," which term to many Canadians indicates a shadowy region where bad boys, unfaithful wives and absconding embezzlers find refuge and dwell in dim security.

Thomas's devotion to the Orange Order was nothing short of a passion. He believed that but for its institution and perpetuation Protestant blood would flow like water. He always spoke of the "Stuarts" in an undertone, as if he were afraid they might even yet come back and make "rough house" for King Edward.

There were only two Catholic families in the neighbourhood, and peaceable, friendly people they were, too; but Thomas believed they should be intimidated to prevent trouble. "The old spite is in them," he told himself, "and nothing will show them where they stand like a 'walk'."

The next day Thomas left his haying and rounded up the faithful. There were seven members of the order in the community,

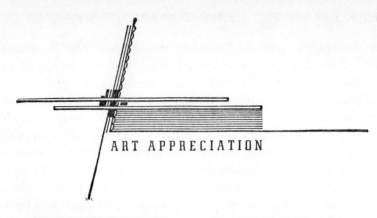

ART APPRECIATION

HABITANT FARM ❧ CORNELIUS KRIEGHOFF

Although Cornelius Krieghoff is considered one of the founders of Canadian painting, his work is of interest today less for its artistic merit than for the light it sheds on French-Canadian life during the middle of the last century. *Habitant Farm* is perfectly typical of the artist's work in its adherence to European traditions of almost photographic realism and attention to detail. This might well be called a "story picture," in that it would be very easy to write a story around the scene here depicted.

HABITANT FARM

Cornelius Krieghoff

CORNELIUS KRIEGHOFF

[1812?-1872]

Like his contemporary, Paul Kane, Cornelius Krieghoff owes his fame not so much to the artistic merits of
his work as to the fidelity with which he portrayed a
particular aspect of the Canadian scene of his day.
Kane's subjects were the Indians of the North-West;
Krieghoff's the French-speaking Canadians of Quebec.
But whereas Kane lived most of his life, from his earliest
boyhood, in Canada, Krieghoff came to this country at
the height of his maturity and spent his declining years
in the United States. Born in Prussia, he spent his early
years in what is now Germany and Holland, where he
studied painting, as well as other subjects. When he
came to the New World, he joined the United States
Army, and eventually reached Quebec by way of Toronto. After marrying a French-Canadian girl and
reaching Montreal in the late 1840's, he fell in love with
the life of the French-Canadian habitant, and devoted
the rest of his artistic life to portraying it with meticulous
accuracy and attention to detail. The same themes run
through his paintings almost like a trade-mark: the outdoor winter scene showing some buildings of French
Canada in the background, some human figures, and in
the foreground a horse hitched to a sleigh, and a dog.

all of whom were ready to stand for their country's honour. There was James Shewfelt, who was a drummer, and could play the tunes without the fife at all. There was John Barker, who did a musical turn in the form of a twenty-three verse ballad beginning:

> When Popery did flourish in
> Dear Ireland o'er the sea,
> There came a man from Amsterdam
> To set ould Ireland free!
> To set ould Ireland free, boys,
> To set ould Ireland free,—
> There came a man from Amsterdam
> To set ould Ireland free!

There was William Breeze, who was a little hard of hearing, but loyal to the core. He had seven boys in his family, so there was still hope for the nation. There was Patrick Mooney, who should have been wearing the other colour if there is anything in a name. But there isn't. There was John Burns, who had been an engineer, but, having lost a foot, had taken to farming. He was the farthest advanced in the order next to Thomas Shouldice, having served a term as District Grand Master, and was well up in the Grand Black Chapter. These would form the nucleus of the procession. The seven little Breezes would be admitted to the ranks if their mother could find suitable decoration for them. Of course, the weather was warm and the subject of clothing was not so serious as it might have been.

Thomas drove nineteen miles to the nearest town to get a speaker and a fifer. The fifer was found, and, quite fortunately, was open for engagement. The speaker was not so easily secured. Thomas went to the Methodist missionary. The missionary was quite a young man and had a reputation of being an orator. He listened gravely while his visitor unfolded his plan.

"I'll tell you what to do, Mr. Shouldice," he said, smiling, when the other had finished the recital of his country's wrongs. "Get Father O'Flynn: he'll make you a speech that will do you all good."

Thomas was too astonished for words. "But he's a Papist!" he sputtered at last.

"Oh, pshaw! Oh, pshaw!, Mr. Shouldice," the young man exclaimed; "there's no division of creed west of Winnipeg. The little priest does all my sick visiting north of the river, and I do his on the south. He's a good preacher, and the finest man at a deathbed I ever saw."

"This is not a deathbed, though, as it happens," Thomas replied, with dignity.

The young minister threw back his head and laughed uproariously. "Can't tell that until it is over—I've been at a few Orange walks down East, you know—took part in one myself once."

"Did you walk?" Thomas asked, brightening.

"No, I ran," the minister said, smiling.

"I thought you said you took part," Thomas snorted, with displeasure.

"So I did, but mine was a minor part. I stood behind the fence and helped the Brennan boys and Patrick Costigan to peg at them!"

"Are ye a Protestant at all?" Thomas roared at him, now thoroughly angry.

"Yes, I am," the minister said, slowly, "and I am something better still; I am a Christian and a Canadian. Are you?"

Thomas beat a hasty retreat.

The Presbyterian minister was away from home, and the English Church minister—who was also a young man lately arrived—said he would go gladly.

The Twelfth of July was a beautiful day, clear, sparkling and cloudless. Little wayward breezes frolicked up and down the banks of Moose Creek and rasped the surface of its placid pools, swollen still from the heavy rains of the "First." In the glittering sunshine the prairie lay a riot of colour; the first wild roses now had faded to a pastel pink, but on every bush there were plenty of new ones, deeply crimson and odorous. Across the creek from Thomas Shouldice's little house, Indian pipes and columbine reddened the edge of the poplar grove, from the lowest branches of which morning-glories, white and pink and purple, hung in graceful profusion.

Before noon a waggon filled with people came thundering down the trail. As they came nearer Thomas was astonished to see that it was an American family from the Chippen Hill district.

"Picnic in these parts, ain't there?" the driver asked.

Thomas was in a genial mood, occasioned by the day and the weather.

"Orange walk and picnic!" he replied, waving his hand toward the bluff, where a few of the faithful were constructing a triumphal arch.

"Something like a cake-walk, is it?" the man asked, looking puzzled.

Mr. Shouldice stared at him increduously.

"Did ye never hear of Orangemen down yer way?" he said.

"Never did, pard," the man answered. "We've peanut men, and apple women, and banana men, but we've never heard much about orange men. But we're right glad to come over and help the show along. Do you want any money for the races?"

"We didn't count on havin' races; we're havin' speeches and some singin'."

The Yankee laughed good-humouredly.

"Well, friend, I pass there; but mother here is a W.C.T.U.-er from away back. She'll knock the spots off the liquor business in fifteen minutes, if you'd like anything in that line."

His wife interposed in her easy, drawling tones: "Now, Abe, you best shet up and drive along. The kids are all hungry and want their dinners."

"We'll see you later, partner," said the man as they drove away.

Thomas Shouldice was mystified. "These Americans are a queer bunch," he thought; "they're ignorant as all get out, but, gosh! they're friendly."

Over the hill to the south came other waggons filled with jolly picnickers, who soon had their pots boiling over quickly-constructed tripods.

Thomas, who went over to welcome them, found that nearly all of them were the very Americans whose unholy zeal for their own national holiday had so embittered his heart eight days before.

They were full of enquiries as to the meaning of an Orange

walk. Thomas tried to explain, but, having only inflamed Twelfth of July oratory for the source of his information, he found himself rather at a loss. But the Americans gathered that it was something he used to do "down East," and they were sympathetic at once.

"That's right, you bet," one grey-haired man with a young face exclaimed, getting rid of a bulky chew of tobacco that had slightly impeded his utterance. "There's nothin' like keepin' up old institootions."

By two o'clock fully one hundred people had gathered.

Thomas was radiant. "Every wan is here now except that old Papist, O'Flynn," he whispered to the drummer. "I hope he'll come, too, so I do. It'll be a bitter pill for him to swallow."

The drummer did not share the wish. He was thinking, uneasily, of the time two years ago—the winter of the deep snow—when he and his family had been quarantined with smallpox, and how Father O'Flynn had come miles out of his way every week on his snowshoes to hand in a roll of newspapers he had gathered up, no one knows where, and a bag of candies for the little ones. He was thinking of how welcome the priest's round face had been to them all those long, tedious six weeks, and how cheery his voice sounded as he shouted, "Are ye needin' anything, Jimmy, avick? All right, I'll be back Thursda', God willin'. Don't be frettin', now, man alive! Everybody has to have smallpox. Sure, you're shaming the Catholics this year, Jimmy, keeping Lent so well." The drummer was decidedly uneasy.

There is an old saying about speaking of angels in which some people still believe. Just at this moment Father O'Flynn came slowly over the hill.

Father O'Flynn was a typical little Irish priest, good-natured, witty, emotional. Nearly every family north of the river had some cause for loving the little man. He was a tireless walker, making the round of his parish every week, no matter what the weather. He had a little house built for him the year before at the Forks of the Assiniboine, where he had planted a garden, set out plants and flowers, and made it a little bower of beauty; but he had lived in it only one summer, for an impecunious English couple, who needed a roof to cover them rather urgently, had taken possession of it during his absence, and the kind-hearted little father could not bring himself to ask them to vacate. When his friends remonstrated with him, he turned the conversation by telling them of another better Man of whom it was written that He "had not where to lay his head."

Father O'Flynn was greeted with delight, by the younger ones especially. The seven little Breezes were very demonstrative, and Thomas Shouldice resolved to warn their father against the priest's malign influence. He recalled a sentence or two from "Maria Monk," which said something like this: "Give us a child until he is ten years old, and let us teach him our doctrine, and he's ours for evermore."

"Oh, they're deep ones, them Jesuits!"

Father O'Flynn was just in time for the "walk."

"Do you know what an Orange walk is, Father?" one of the American women asked, really looking for information.

"Yes, daughter, yes," the little priest answered, a shadow coming over his merry grey eyes. He gave her an evasive reply, and then murmured to himself, as he picked a handful of orange lilies: "It is an institution of the Evil One to sow discord among brothers."

The walk began.

First came the fife and drum, skirling out an Orange tune, at which the priest winced visibly. Then followed Thomas Shouldice, in the guise of King William. He was mounted on his own old, spavined grey mare, that had performed this honourable office many times in her youth. But now she seemed lacking in the pride that befits the part. Thomas was gay with ribbons and a short red coat, whose gilt braid was sadly tarnished. One of the Yankees had kindly loaned a mottled buggy-robe for the saddle-cloth.

Behind Thomas marched the twenty-three verse soloist and the other faithful few, followed by the seven Breeze boys, gay with yellow streamers made from the wrapping of a ham.

The Yankees grouped about were sorry to see so few in the procession. They had brought along three or four of their band instruments to furnish music if it were needed. As the end of the procession passed them, two of the smaller boys swung in behind the last two Breezes.

It was an inspiration. Instantly the whole company stepped into line—two by two, men, women, and children, waving their bunches of lilies!

Thomas, from his point of vantage, could see the whole company following his lead, and his heart swelled with pride. Under the arch the procession swept, stepping to the music, the significance of which most of the company did not even guess at—good-natured, neighbourly, filled with the spirit of the West, that ever seeks to help along.

Everyone, even Father O'Flynn, was happier than James Shewfelt, the drummer.

The fifer paused, preparatory to changing the tune. It was the drummer's opportunity. "Onward, Christian Soldiers," he sang, tapping the rhythm on the drum. The fifer caught the strain. Not a voice was silent, and unconsciously hand clasped hand, and the soft afternoon reverberated with the swelling cadence:

> We are not divided,
> All one body we.

When the verse was done, the fifer led off into another and another. The little priest's face glowed with pleasure. "It is the spirit of the Lord," he whispered to himself, as he marched to the rhythm, his hand closely held by the smallest Breeze boy, whose yellow streamers and profuse decoration of orange lilies were at strange variance with his companion's priestly robes. But on this day nothing was at variance. The spirit of the West was upon them, unifying, mellowing, harmonizing all conflicting emotions—the spirit of the West that calls on men everywhere to be brothers and lend a hand.

The Church of England minister did make a speech, but not the one he had intended. Instead of denominationalism, he spoke of brotherhood; instead of religious intolerance, he spoke of religious liberty; instead of the Prince of Orange, who crossed the Boyne to give religious freedom to Ireland, he told of the Prince of Peace, who died on the cross to save the souls of men of every nation and kindred and tribe.

In the hush that followed Father O'Flynn stepped forward and said he thanked the brother who had planned this meeting; he was glad, he said, for such an opportunity for friends and neighbours to meet; he spoke of the glorious heritage that all had in this great new country, and how all must stand together as brothers. All prejudices of race and creed and doctrine die before the wonderful power of loving service. "The West," he said, "is the home of loving hearts and neighbourly kindness, where all men's good is each man's care. For myself," he went on, "I have but one wish, and that is to be the servant of all, to be the ambassador of Him who went about doing good, and to teach the people to love honour and virtue, and each other." Then, raising his hands, he led the company in that prayer that comes ever to the lips of man when all prayers seem vain—that prayer that we can all fall back on in our sore need:

> Our Father, who art in heaven,
> Hallowed be Thy name,
> Thy kingdom come.

Two hours later a tired but happy and united company sat down to supper on the grass. At the head of the table sat Thomas Shouldice, radiating good-will. A huge white pitcher of steaming golden coffee was in his hand. He poured a cup of it brimming full, and handed it to the little priest, who sat near him.

"Have some coffee, Father?" he said.

Where could such a scene as this be enacted—a Twelfth of July celebration where a Roman Catholic priest was the principal speaker, where the company dispersed with the singing of "God Save the King," led by an American band?

Nowhere but in the Northwest of Canada, the illimitable land, with its great sunlit spaces, where the west wind, bearing on its bosom the spices of millions of flowers, woos the heart of man with a magic spell and makes him kind and neighbourly and brotherly!

UNDERSTANDING THE STORY

In order to appreciate this story, you should read it quickly from beginning to end. Too often misunderstanding among people is caused because their differences are emphasized. In this story Nellie McClung stresses the ideals and points of view which people hold in common because they live in a country with a democratic tradition. The setting of the story is near the forty-ninth parallel in Manitoba. It is not so much a story of the way of the west as one of the way in which intelligent people with common problems and a desire for harmonious living have developed understanding of each other through stress on their likenesses. Basically the people in this story are the same kind of people whether they be Canadian or American, Roman Catholic or Protestant.

1. In what ways does Nellie McClung show us that the problems of the characters in her story have common problems?

2. What important change took place in Thomas Shouldice in this story? Explain how this change was brought about.

3. In what ways had the settlers in this story come to depend upon one another regardless of differences in religion, politics, or nationality?

4. Discuss with your classmates the ways in which it is possible for us to develop greater understanding of people whose race, religion, politics, or nationality is different from our own.

5. Give examples from this story of Nellie McClung's use of humour.

THERE'S A WILD ROSE TANGLED
IN THE PRAIRIE'S WOOL ✻ A. M. STEPHEN

There's a wild rose tangled in the prairie's wool,
Years without number, the tall grass withered,
There were no hands to harvest it.
Now a soft carpet,

1. PRAIRIE'S WOOL—A fanciful name given to the covering of original wild grass that grows on the prairie.

5   decorated with a futuristic design of wild roses,
is spread like a tawny fleece
over the prairie land.

Olaf, the Icelander, has a homestead.
His sod shack is like a fingerprint
10   on a blank page.
Three ponies,
a wall-eyed pinto,
a strawberry roan,
and a sorrel
15   are hitched to his plough.

Sometimes Olaf's eyes are clear
as the hollows of the cup
that rests on the rim of the prairie.
To-day, dreams, like white clouds,
20   fleck the blue of his eyes,

Olaf dreams of a frame house with white curtains—
maybe a fireplace like the one at home,
which threw black and red shadows
when the old bards chanted their stories
25   of the Vikings while the men carded wool
and women spun the yarn.

To-day his plough will card the prairie's wool,
and break the pattern of the wild rose.

His fathers drove through the ocean
30   with pointed beaks of iron.
The white waters churned in their wake.
Their eyes were on far horizons.

Sun-dappled waves of grass curve and flow
before the bright steel of Olaf.

35   The brown sod ripples and falls behind him
     as he steers his sharp prow into the future.
     His eyes are on far horizons.

CLUES TO MEANING

Poetry can be classified as free verse or as conventional poetry. The latter is the type that we are most used to. It is usually arranged in stanzas, each line starts with a capital letter, there is a definite swing or beat to the lines, and the lines have a definite and regular number of syllables. Free verse, on the other hand, often looks and reads more like chopped-up prose, and we wonder if it should be called poetry at all. But whether verse is conventional or free, it deserves to be called poetry only if it has a rhythm or swing, and if it appeals to the feelings or imagination of the audience.

1. Is this selection poetry or prose? Give reasons for your answer.

2. Olaf is an earthbound ploughman, while his Viking ancestors ranged the churning seas. But how are they alike?

3. This poem is rich in similes. A simile is a figure of speech, in which one thing is compared to another. Usually, but not always, the simile is introduced by the word "like" or "as." What similes can you find in this poem? How do they make the poem more vivid?

BOX SOCIAL 🌸 EDWARD A. McCOURT

THE entertainment was announced to begin at eight o'clock. At six-thirty the first buckboard load of guests arrived. It included Mr. and Mrs. Berkslund, their three husky, teen-aged daughters, celebrated throughout the countryside for their phenomenal endur-

ance on the dance floor, and Mrs. Berkslund's mother, aged eighty-
six. Thereafter a steady stream of "rigs" poured down the narrow
trails on either side of the creek—those coming from the north
had to ford the stream in flood—and deposited their loads at the
Stopping House door. From every point of the compass they gathered, from distances up to fifty miles or more, by buckboard, buggy,
wagon, on foot and on horseback. Long before eight o'clock extra
benches had been rushed from the Anglican Mission to the "auditorium" as Miss Libby Peters insisted on calling the Stopping
House waiting-room, and men were standing three deep at the
back. The only untoward incident occurred when Miss Libby's
"Welcome" horseshoe broke from its moorings and knocked out
an unfortunate cowpuncher from the Bar Five ranch. However, he
regained consciousness shortly afterwards, and the disturbance
which the incident had created quickly subsided.

Johnny Bradford and Linda Fraser rode over together from the
Fraser ranch. Matt Fraser was suffering from a knee injury which
he had sustained when a horse, only half-broken, had brushed him
against the rails of the corral. "Anyway," he said, "I'm gettin' too
old to be up all night. Away ye go and enjoy yoursel's."

Johnny carried a large bag containing Linda's party outfit. She
herself carried, in a smaller bag, the carefully prepared and guarded
box of food, which, along with numerous others, would be auctioned
off after the concert, the purchaser of the box enjoying the privilege
of having supper with its owner. It was a convention governing
the institution of the box-social that there should be no marks of
identification on the boxes; the purchaser theoretically did not
know whether he was spending his hard-earned money in order to
eat supper with the maiden of his heart's desire or with some grand-
motherly soul of eighty. In practice, however, either by some subtle
form of telepathy or by downright broad hints, a girl was usually
able to indicate to the man of her choice when to start bidding.

During the ride from the ranch to Pilot Creek, Johnny had made
one or two attempts to secure advance information from Linda, but
had been firmly rebuffed. "I shall take whomsoever the gods send
me," she said. "It might be you, of course, but—"

"And it might be old man Walker or Joe Boggs," growled Johnny. "Honest, Linda, if you still have that maternal feelin' towards me you'll want to see me well fed, won't you?"

Linda chuckled thoughtfully. Then she flashed him a smile. "Well, maybe," she admitted. "We'll see." And with the vague promise of possible relenting, Johnny had to be content.

They stabled their horses in the shed behind the Anglican Mission, where some of the overflow from the livery stable was being accommodated, and went at once to the Stopping House. There they separated, and from then until after the concert Johnny caught only fleeting glimpses of Linda, who was busy helping the Willing Workers. He himself was quickly wedged into a corner, between old man Walker and a puncher from the Lazy U. Old man Walker chewed tobacco continually; every two minutes his head turned with clock-like precision towards the open window behind him. He lived in a constant draught, which may have accounted for the perpetual drop of moisture which shone on the end of his nose.

At eight-fifteen the curtains—several Pilot Creek bedsheets fastened together with safety pins—parted, revealing Judith Sumner's little flock—six small girls and four small boys—shy and uncomfortable in stiffly starched frocks and unnaturally confining collars, arranged in a limp semicircle on a platform constructed of several heavy planks laid along a number of upturned empty molasses kegs. Miss Libby Peters was at the organ—borrowed from the Anglican Mission—and the children, in response to a wheezy chord, burst into the song of welcome which Miss Libby had herself composed:

> "Welcome to our friends so dear,
>   We are glad that you are here;
>   May your worries fade away
>   And all this night be bright and gay."

And so on through twelve stanzas of similar quality and sentiment.

The response of the audience was loud and sincere. Then Mr. Bate, the Anglican Mission student, an earnest young man fresh

from the east, gave the reading. His choice was perhaps unfortunate—a poem by the poet laureate, Alfred Lord Tennyson. This
time the applause, in old man Walker's phrase, was "polite but not
awful enthusiastic." Next Mr. Prothero, resplendent in a loud
check suit across the waistcoat of which shone magnificently a
mighty yardage of gold watch-chain hung with innumerable fobs
and mystic charms, obliged with two vocal numbers, "Nut-Brown
Maiden" and "Rocked in the Cradle of the Deep." The applause
increased ten-fold when, just as Mr. Prothero was taking his bows,
one of the planks slipped and the artist disappeared from view
among the molasses barrels. He was extricated by Mr. Bate and
as many of the audience in the front row as could crowd onto the
platform. As soon as the planks had been replaced, Mr. Prothero
took another bow, and brought down the house with a rendition
of "The Night that Father Fell Downstairs." After he had made
his exit, the juvenile chorus came on again with a number about
the snows of winter being followed by the flowers of spring. Music
by Mendelssohn, words by Miss Libby Peters.

But the *pièce de résistance* [1] was the duet, "The Gypsy's Warning," sung in costume by Miss Libby and Mr. Prothero. They were
called back twice, responding with two selections, "It Was a Lover
and His Lass," and a daring little number entitled "Will You Spark
in the Park After Dark, Pretty Maiden?" during which Mr.
Prothero made terrific play with eyes and moustaches, and Miss
Libby responded with coy excursions and retreats. Afterwards,
flushed and triumphant, she resumed her place at the organ—tem-
porarily relinquished to Judith Sumner—and the entire cast appeared on the platform to lead the audience in the grand finale,
a sing-song.

After "God Save the Queen" had been sung and the rafters had
ceased to rattle, the platform was quickly cleared away and, amid
a rising babble of conversation from all parts of the hall, interrupted by the shrill squeals of a score or more of excited children,
preparations were begun for the auctioning off of the food boxes.
Most of the men in the audience, Johnny included, took advantage
of the break to slip outside for a breath of fresh air or a smoke.

[1] (pyĕs da rĕ zēstäns')—The principal event.

Meanwhile the Willing Workers, under the direction of Mr. Prothero and Mr. Bate, arranged the boxes of food on a table in front of the hall. When all was in readiness, the word was passed among the men, and they surged back into the hall in a body. As he re-entered, Johnny saw Linda, gay in her sky-blue party frock, hurrying up to the table, a swirl of white-lace petticoat showing above her trim ankles. She was carrying a box under her arm, a box ornate with ribbon and tissue-paper, and as she passed she turned and smiled significantly. Johnny grinned back in perfect understanding. There was no possibility of mistaking the box, because of the series of little silver hearts which formed a border all around the top.

As soon as the audience had settled into a semblance of order, Mr. Prothero mounted a small wooden bench that had been placed alongside the table and called for silence. He was rewarded by a mighty roar, followed by an expectant hush. Then he picked up the first box from the top of the great heap and held it high above his head. "What am I hoffered, gents?" he demanded. "Look at it—just look at it! Lovingly fashioned—hadorned with all the graces of its creator—filled to the brim with goodies moulded by 'er own fair 'ands! A lucky man 'e is 'oo gets this treasure—weights ten pounds if it weights an hounce!"

The bidding opened. The box, fashioned by the fair hands of Mrs. Joe Boggs, was finally knocked down to Slim Webber, whose face assumed the expression of a stunned ox when he caught sight of the name written on the little identification ticket attached. Then Mr. Prothero, eye alight, face already damp with sweat, seized another box, swept it aloft, and implored his fellowmen to bid, bid, bid for the love of their wives, daughters, sweethearts, and for the benefit of the Pilot Creek 'ospital. The response was enthusiastic, particularly when Mr. Prothero held up the box, generously proportioned, and artistically fashioned with a gay little sprig of artificial forget-me-nots on top. Two young cowpunchers, one from the Circle K and one from the Bar Diamond, were finally left in possession of the field, Bar Diamond winning out with a bid of twenty-eight dollars, nearly a whole month's salary.

Suddenly Johnny stiffened to attention. The box with the band of silver hearts around it was up for sale. "A bee-ootiful box!" Mr. Prothero crooned ecstatically, "a bee-ootiful box! Wot's the grandeurs that were Greece and the glories that were Rome compared to this gem—this treasure, this product of a pair of bee-ootiful and lovin' hands attached to some fair creature who will nourish the spirit as the contents of the box will nourish the body! Weights ten pounds if it weights an hounce!"

"Five dollars," said Johnny.

There was a ripple of excitement through the crowd. Two dollars was the conventional opening bid. The young bloods pricked up their ears. The Circle K puncher, anxious to redeem himself, challenged Johnny's bid with a two-dollar raise, and the excitement increased until a sort of madness came upon the bidders. When the bids reached thirty dollars, Mr. Prothero interrupted to announce that cheques would be accepted for any sum above that amount. There was a prolonged burst of cheering and a renewed flurry of bids. Amid wild excitement the box was finally knocked down to Johnny for the unheard of price of fifty-seven dollars! But

Linda's warm smile made him feel that the price he had paid was a small one.

The few remaining boxes were quickly disposed of, and the couples scattered into the various rooms at the back, where small tables had been set up around a long central table on which great pots of coffee steamed. Johnny, his box tucked carefully under his arm, emerged from the auditorium to find that Linda had disappeared. He paused in some perplexity. "Guess she must be out in the kitchen," he said to himself, and looked around to find a vacant table where he could wait for her.

"Oh, Mr. Bradford!" It was Miss Libby Peters. There was a dazed, incredulous look on her face, but her eyes were shining.

"Why, hello, Miss Peters," Johnny smiled.

"Mr. Bradford, you were too kind. I have never been so—so—" Miss Libby was close to tears. She turned away her head, and Johnny flipped back the silver heart on the top of the box and looked at the name written underneath.

"Uh, well," he stammered, "it's—uh—"

Miss Libby slipped her arm through his. "Please don't try to explain," she said gently. "I'm really very proud."

Johnny looked down into the little, child-like face under the frame of silver hair. Then he patted Miss Libby's hand. "That makes two satisfied parties, then, Miss Libby," he said. And, suddenly, he knew he meant it.

They found a table in a quiet corner, and for half an hour Miss Libby sat enthralled, while Johnny alternately talked and ate. How it had all come about, Miss Libby had no idea, and she was wise enough not to seek too far for a solution. It was enough that a handsome young man had paid a record price for this privilege of eating supper with her. The experience was a reality of the moment—soon it would be a memory only, but one to be cherished always. And with that assurance, Miss Libby was content.

Once or twice Linda, who was eating supper with the cowpuncher from the Bar Diamond, looked in Johnny's direction. Johnny returned her smile with a grin that extended from ear to ear. He felt no jealousy, and he was enjoying himself because Miss

Libby was so obviously happy. "It's been a lot of fun, Miss Libby," he assured her, as he finished the last mouthful of a huge segment of apple pie. "Any time you want a recommend for cookin' just call on me."

"I'm glad you're enjoying yourself, Mr. Bradford," said Miss Libby gravely. Then, in response to an urgent signal from Mr. Prothero, she stood up reluctantly. "I play the organ for the dancing," she explained, with naïve pride. "I must go now."

"Well, thanks again for everythin'," said Johnny. "Food, company, concert. I'm havin' a swell time."

Miss Libby blushed delightedly. "The concert, I'm afraid, was a little lacking in body. We had hoped to present a little play, but unfortunately it fell through. Last year we did one, with Mr. Conway in the leading role. It was a very great success. But Mr. Conway is away just now—something to do with missions."

"I figger Mr. Conway would put anythin' like that over all right," agreed Johnny.

"Mr. Conway is a truly magnificent thespian,"[2] said Miss Libby. "Mrs. Prothero saw Sir Harry Irving once, in the Old Country. She says that, in comparison to Mr. Conway, he is nothing—simply nothing! Now I really must go. Everyone is waiting." And Miss Libby swept out of the room with a new dignity born of the consciousness that for the past half-hour she had been the envy of almost every feminine heart in the room.

The dance got under way shortly before midnight. Children and babies were put to sleep on sofas and loveseats, for there would be no sitting-out of dances except in the case of cripples and octogenarians. Joe Sawyer, the fiddler from Macleod, provided the music, with Miss Libby chording on the organ. Their places were taken from time to time by the young Harper twins, who played duets on the mouth-organ and guitar. However, as the twins knew only two pieces, they were able to provide only occasional relief.

This was old man Walker's hour of greatness. As caller of the dances, he stood at the front of the room beside a window that was raised sufficiently to enable him to chew in comfort without

[2] Actor.

greater exertion than that occasioned by the clock-like turn of his head towards the window every two minutes. Unlike most callers, he preserved a dignified bodily immobility, except for the periodic turning of the head. But his voice had the power and quality of a fog-horn, and carried to every corner of the room:

> "Birdie hop in,
> Crow hop out,
> Jine all han's,
> 'N' circle about."

This, too, was the great hour for the Berkslund girls. The Berkslunds had come from the States—the lumbering regions of Northern Michigan—where a girl's popularity was traditionally dependent on her endurance and the swirl of her skirts as she wove her way through the intricate figures of the dance. It was whispered that the Berkslund girls descended to unfair tactics in order to win masculine approval—that they actually sewed buckshot in the hems of their calico gowns. Whatever the reason, no skirts whirled quite so triumphantly as theirs, and their popularity attested to a similarity of taste between the Michigan lumber-jack and the Western cowpuncher.

The square-dances, being communal in spirit and movement, made any kind of conversation between partners impossible. Consequently, Johnny waited until Joe Sawyer struck up a waltz before claiming Linda's hand. Booking in advance was unheard of, and Johnny reached the chair in which Linda was sitting just a few inches in the van of a swarm of would-be suppliants. With a cheerful "better luck next time, boys," he led her out onto the floor.

They whirled about the room to the music of the "Skater's Waltz." Linda was an admirable dancer, having a natural, instinctive poise, and sense of rhythm, while Johnny had learned the waltzer's art in many a dance-hall between Pecos and Great Falls. "Mad at me, Johnny?" said Linda. She smiled up at him, but there was the faintest trace of apprehension in her eyes.

"Mad as a hornet," said Johnny calmly.

"Well, the Willing Workers do need money, and, besides, you made Miss Libby awfully happy."

Johnny did not answer.

"And another thing," she said. "You weren't the only one that made sacrifices."

Johnny grinned down at her. "Meanin' that eatin' with young Wilkins was a sacrifice?" he demanded.

"Well, he's awfully nice, but—but—" Suddenly she blushed. "Honestly, Johnny, you know I'd a lot sooner have had supper with you."

"Then why didn't you tip Wilkins off on the wrong box, instead of me?"

"He might not have taken it as well as you—and Miss Libby deserves a good time."

ENJOYING THE STORY

The picture of the box social which Edward McCourt has drawn in this story is faithful to a form of entertainment that was once very popular in rural Canada. With the development of the automobile, good roads, motion pictures, commercialized sports, and other forms of spectator entertainment there are now fewer community enterprises of the type described by McCourt. Besides giving us a picture of a social institution, the author reveals that he has an understanding of people.

1. This story may be divided into four parts: (a) the concert, (b) the auction, (c) the supper, and (d) the dance. Tell how each part contributes to the success of this story.

2. From the story find evidence to suggest when it took place.

3. Why do you think Mr. Bate's choice of a poem by Tennyson was an unfortunate one for the occasion described?

4. What use of dialect is made in this story?

5. Find examples of the misuse of words by one or more of the characters in this story. Why does the author have his characters use words in this way?

6. What evidence is there in the story to suggest the age of Libby Peters?

7. Why did Linda lead Johnny to think that the box he bought was hers? How did Johnny react when he found it was Libby's box? What does this tell us about the kind of person he really was?

8. Why did Linda not give the same misleading cue to "young Wilkins"?

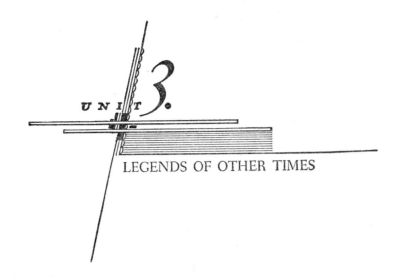

UNIT 13.

LEGENDS OF OTHER TIMES

SHREWD BARGAINING — JUDGE HALIBURTON

"I RAISED a four-year-old colt once, half blood, a perfect pictur' of a horse and a genu*ine* clipper—could gallop like the wind; a rael daisy, perfect doll,—had an eye like a weasel and nostril like Commodore Rodger's speakin' trumpet. Well, I took it down to the races at New York, and father he went along with me; for sais he, 'Sam, you don't know everything, I guess; you ha'n't cut your wisdom teeth yet, and you are goin' among them that's had 'em through their gums this while past.'

"Well, we gets to the races, father he gets colt and puts him in an old waggon with a worn-out Dutch harness and breast band. He looked like Old Nick; that's a fact. Then he fastened a head martingale on and buckled it to the girth twixt his fore legs. Sais I, 'Father, what on airth are you at? I vow I feel ashamed to be seed with such a catamaran as that, and colt looks like Old Saytan himself! no soul would know him.'

" 'I guess I warn't born yesterday,' says he. 'Let me be; I know what I am at. I guess I'll slip it into 'em afore I've done as slick as a whistle. I guess I can see as far into a millstone as the best on 'em.'

235

"Well, father never entered the horse at all but stood by and seed the races; and the winnin' horse was followed about by a matter of two or three thousand people a-praisin' of him and admirin' him. They seemed as if they never had seed a horse afore. The owner of him was all up on eend a-boastin' of him and a-stumpin the course to produce a horse to run agin him for four hundred dollars. Father goes up to him, looking as soft as dough and as meechin' as you please; and sais he, 'Friend, it tante every

one that has four hundred dollars; it's a plaguy sight of money, I tell *you*. Would you run for one hundred dollars and give me a little start? If you would, I'd try my colt out of my old waggon agin you, I vow.'

" 'Let's look at your horse,' says he.

"So away they went and a proper sight of people arter them to look at colt; and when they seed him, they sot up such a larf I felt e'en a'most ready to cry for spite. Sais I to myself, 'What can possess the old man to act arter that fashion? I do believe he has taken leave of his senses.'

" 'You needn't larf,' said father, 'he's smarter than he looks. Our minister's old horse, Captain Jack, is reckoned as quick a beast of his age as any in our location, and that are colt beat him for a lick of a quarter of a mile easy; I seed it myself.' Well they larfed ag'in louder than afore; and sais father, 'If you dispute my word, try me. What odds will you give?'

" 'Two to one,' sais the owner, 'eight hundred to four hundred dollars.'

" 'Well, that's a great deal of money, ain't it?' sais father. 'If I was to lose it, I'd look pretty foolish, wouldn't I? How folks would pass their jokes at me when I went home ag'in. You wouldn't take that are waggon and harness for fifty dollars of it, would you?' sais he.

" 'Well,' sais the other, 'sooner than disappoint you, as you seem to have set your heart on losing your money, I don't care if I do.'

"As soon as it was settled, father drives off to the stables and then returns mounted with a red silk pocket handkerchief tied around his head and colt a-lookin' like himself, as proud as a nabob, chock-full of spring like the wire eend of a bran' new pair of trowsers' galluses.

"One sais, "That's a plaguy nice lookin' colt that are old feller has arter all.'

" 'That horse will show play for it yet,' sais a third.

"And I heerd one feller say, 'I guess that's a rigular Yankee trick, a complete take-in.'

"They had a fair start for it, and off they sot. Father took the lead and kept it, and won the race, tho' it was a pretty tight scratch; for father was too old to ride colt,—he was near about the matter of seventy years old. Well, when the colt was walked round arter the race, there was an amazin' crowd arter him, and several wanted to buy him.

" 'But,' sais father, 'how am I to get home without him, and what shall I do with that are waggon and harness so far as I be from Slickville?' So he kept them in talk till he felt their pulses pretty well; and at last he closed with a Southerner for seven hundred dollars, and we returned, havin' made considerable good spec of colt.

"Sais father to me, 'Sam,' sais he, 'you seed the crowd a-follerin the winnin 'horse when we came there, didn't you?'

"'Yes, sir,' sais I, 'I did.'

"'Well, when colt beat him, no one follered him at all, but come an' crowded about *him*. That's popularity,' sais he, 'soon won, soon lost; cried up sky-high one minit' and desarted the next or run down. Colt will share the same fate. He'll get beat afore long, and then he's done for'."

ENJOYING THE STORY

This story should be read chiefly for the humour of the situation described. It was for this humour that Judge Haliburton, its author, became well known. He combines here an interesting, if dishonest, trick, an illiterate Yankee dialect, and a lesson on popularity.

1. This story is replete with striking expressions such as "I guess I can see as far into a millstone as the best on 'em." Find other expressions of this kind and tell the class what they mean as used here.

2. There are many interesting comparisons used in this story. Find examples of these and tell why you consider them effective.

3. Comment on the language used in this story. Is it appropriate as used here? Why?

HOW SUMMER CAME TO CANADA 🐦

CYRUS MACMILLAN

Once during Glooskap's lifetime and reign in Canada it grew very cold. Everywhere there was snow and ice, and in all the land there was not a flower nor a leaf left alive. The fires that the Indians built could not bring warmth. The food supply was slowly eaten up, and the people were unable to grow more corn because of the hard frozen ground. Great numbers of men and women and children died daily from cold and hunger, and it seemed as if the whole land must soon perish.

Over this extreme cold Glooskap had no power. He tried all his magic, but it was of no avail. For the cold was caused by a powerful giant who came into the land from the Far North, bringing

Famine and Death as his helpers. Even with his breath he could blight and wither the trees so that they brought forth no leaves nor fruit, and he could destroy the corn and kill man and beast. The giant's name was Winter. He was very old and very strong, and he had ruled in the Far North long before the coming of man. Glooskap, being brave and wishing to help his people in their need, went alone to the giant's tent to try to coax or bribe or force him to go away. But even he, with all his magic power, at once fell in love with the giant's home; for in the sunlight it sparkled like crystal and was of many wonderful colours, but in the night under the moonlight it was spotlessly white. From the tent, when Glooskap looked out, the face of the earth was beautiful. The trees had a covering of snow that gave them strange fantastic shapes. The sky was filled by night with flashing quivering lights, and even the stars had a new brightness. The forest, too, was full of mysterious noises. Glooskap soon forgot his people amid his new surroundings. The giant told him tales of olden times when all the land was silent and white and beautiful like his sparkling tent. After a time the giant used his charm of slumber and inaction, until Glooskap fell asleep, for the charm was the charm of the Frost. For six months he slept like a bear. Then he awoke, for he was very strong and Winter could not kill him even in his sleep. But when he arose he was hungry and very tired.

One day soon after he awoke, his tale-bearer, Tatler the Loon, brought him good news. He told of a wonderful Southland, far away, where it was always warm, and where lived a Queen who could easily overcome the giant; indeed she was the only one on earth whose power the giant feared. Loon described carefully the road to the new country. Glooskap, to save his people from Winter and Famine and Death, decided to go to the Southland and find the Queen. So he went to the sea, miles away, and sang the magic song that the whales obeyed. His old friend Blob the Whale came quickly to his call; and getting on her back he sailed away. Now, the whale always had a strange law for travellers. She said to Glooskap: "You must shut your eyes tight while I carry you; to open them is dangerous, for, if you do, I will surely go aground on a reef or a sand bar and cannot get off, and you may then be

drowned." Glooskap promised to keep his eyes shut. Many days the whale swam, and each day the water grew warmer, and the air grew gentler and sweeter, for it came from spicy shores, and the smells were no longer those of the salt sea, but of fruits and flowers and pines. Soon they saw in the sky by night the Southern Cross. They found, too, that they were no longer in the deep sea, but in shallow water flowing warm over yellow sands, and that land lay not far ahead. Blob the whale now swam more cautiously. Down in the sand the clams were singing a song of warning, telling travellers in these strange waters of the treacherous sand bar beneath. "Oh, big whale," they sang, "keep out to sea, for the water here is shallow and you will come to grief if you keep on to shore." But the whale did not understand the language of the little clams. And he said to Glooskap, who understood, "What do they sing?" But Glooskap, wishing to land at once, answered, "They tell you to hurry, for a storm is coming,—to hurry along as fast as you can." Then the whale hurried until she was soon close to the land. Glooskap, wishing the whale to go aground so that he could more easily walk ashore, opened his left eye and peeped, which was contrary to the whale's laws. And at once the whale stuck hard and fast on the beach, so that Glooskap, springing from her head, walked ashore on dry land. The whale, thinking that she could never get off, was very angry, and sang a song of lament and blame. But Glooskap put one end of his strong bow against the whale's jaw, and taking the other end in his hands, he placed his feet against the high bank, and, with a mighty push, he sent old Blob again into the deep water. Then, to keep the whale's friendship, he threw her an old pipe and a bag of Indian tobacco leaves —for Glooskap was a great smoker—and the whale, greatly pleased with the gift, lighted the pipe and smoking it swam far out to sea. Glooskap watched her disappear from view until he could see only clouds of her smoke against the sky. And to this day the whale has Glooskap's old pipe, and sailors often see her rise to the surface to smoke it in peace and to blow rings of tobacco smoke into the air.

When the whale had gone, Glooskap walked with great strides far inland. Soon he found the way of which Loon had told him. It was the Rainbow Road that led to the Wilderness of Flowers. It lay through the land of the Sunrise, beautiful and fresh in the morning light. On each side were sweet magnolias and palms, and all kinds of trees and flowers. The grass was soft and velvety, for by night the dew was always on it, and snow and hail were unknown, and winds never blew coldly, for here the charm of the Frost had no power.

Glooskap went quickly along the flower-lined Rainbow Road, until he came to an orange grove where the air was sweet with the scent of blossoms. Soon he heard sounds of music. He peered through the trees, and saw that the sounds came from an open space not far ahead, where the grass was soft and where tiny streams were flowing and making melody. It was lilac-time in the land, and around the open space all kinds of flowers in the world were blooming. On the trees numberless birds were singing—birds of wonderfully coloured feathers such as Glooskap had never heard or seen before. He knew that he had reached at last the Wilderness of Flowers, of which old Tatler the Loon had spoken. He drew deep breaths of honeysuckle and heliotrope and countless other flowers, until he soon grew strong again after his long voyage.

Then he crept close to the edge of the open space and looked in from behind the trees. On the flower-covered grass within, many fair maidens were singing and dancing, holding in their hands chains of blossoms, like children in a Maypole game. In the centre of the group was one fairer than all the others—the most beautiful creature he had ever seen,—her long brown hair crowned with flowers and her arms filled with blossoms. For some time Glooskap gazed in silence, for he was too surprised to move or to utter speech. Then he saw at his side an old woman,—wrinkled and faded, but still beautiful,—like himself watching the dance. He found his voice and asked, "Who are those beautiful maidens in the Wilderness of Flowers?" And the old woman answered, "The maiden in the centre of the group is the Fairy Queen; her name is Summer; she is the daughter of the rosy Dawn,—the most beautiful ever born; the maidens dancing with her are her children, the Fairies of Light and Sunshine and Flowers."

Glooskap knew that here at last was the Queen who by her charms could melt old Winter's heart and force him to go away, for she was very beautiful and good. With his magic song he lured her from her children into the dark forest; there he seized her and held her fast by a crafty trick. Then, with her as his companion, he began his long return journey north by land. That he might know the way back to the Wilderness of Flowers, he cut a large moose hide, which he always carried, into a long slender cord, and as he ran north with Summer, he let the cord unwind behind him, for he had no time to mark the trail in the usual way. When they had gone, Summer's children mourned greatly for their Queen. For weeks the tears ran down their cheeks like rain on all the land, and for a long time, old Dawn, the Queen's mother, covered herself with dark mourning clouds and refused to be bright.

After many days, still holding Summer in his bosom—for she loved him because of his magic power—Glooskap reached the Northland. He found none of his people, for they were all asleep under the giant's power, and the whole country was cold and lonely. At last he came to the home of old Winter. The giant welcomed him and the beautiful girl, for he hoped to freeze them both and keep them with him always. For some time they talked together in the tent, but, although he tried hard, the giant was unable to put them to sleep. Soon old Winter felt that his power had vanished and that the charm of the Frost was broken. Large drops of sweat ran down his face; then his tent slowly disappeared, and he was left homeless. Summer used her strange power until everything that Winter had put to sleep awoke again. Buds came again upon the trees; the snow ran down the rivers, carrying away the dead leaves, and the grass and the corn sprang up with new life. And old Winter, being sorrowful, wept, for he knew that his reign was ended, and his tears were like cold rain. Summer, the Queen, seeing him mourn and wishing to stop his tears, said: "I have proved that I am more powerful than you; I give you now all the country to the far north for your own, and there I shall never disturb you; you may come back to Glooskap's country six months of every year and reign as of old, but you will be less severe; during the other six months, I myself will come from the south and rule the land." Old Winter could do nothing but accept this offer gracefully, for he feared that if he did not he would melt entirely away. So he built a new home farther north, and there he reigns without interruption. In the late autumn he comes back to Glooskap's country and reigns for six months, but his rule is softer than in olden times. And when he comes, Summer, following Glooskap's moose-hide cord, runs home with her birds to the Wilderness of Flowers. But at the end of six months she always comes back to drive old Winter away to his own land, to awaken the northern world, and to bring it the joys that only she, the Queen, can give. And so, in Glooskap's old country Winter and Summer, the hoary old giant and the beautiful Fairy Queen, divide the rule of the land between them.

ENJOYING THE LEGEND

Many different countries have developed legends in an attempt to explain the cause of the seasons. Of course, none of these is scientifically sound, but they appeal to the imaginative person because of their picturesque quality and their very implausibility. The story of how Glooskap brought the Fairy Queen, Summer, to drive away the giant, Winter, is a Canadian legend to explain the alternation of winter and summer.

1. Name all those who assisted Glooskap in his journey to the Wilderness of Flowers.

2. What is MacMillan's explanation of the whale's spouting of water?

3. Tell the class some other legend that gives an explanation for the alternation of the seasons.

EVANGELINE: A TALE OF ACADIA 🂠

HENRY WADSWORTH LONGFELLOW

PRELUDE

*This is the forest primeval. The murmuring pines and the hem-
   locks,*
*Bearded with moss, and in garments green, indistinct in the twi-
   light,*
Stand like Druids of old, with voices sad and prophetic,
Stand like harpers hoar, with beards that rest on their bosoms.
5 *Loud from its rocky caverns, the deep-voiced neighbouring ocean*
Speaks, and in accents disconsolate answers the wail of the forest.

*This is the forest primeval; but where are the hearts that be-
   neath it*
*Leaped like the roe, when he hears in the woodland the voice of the
   huntsman?*
Where is the thatch-roofed village, the home of Acadian farmers—
10 *Men whose lives glided on like rivers that water the woodlands,*
Darkened by shadows of earth, but reflecting an image of heaven?
Waste are those pleasant farms, and the farmers forever departed!
Scattered like dust and leaves, when the mighty blasts of October
*Seize them, and whirl them aloft, and sprinkle them far o'er the
   ocean.*
15 *Naught but tradition remains of the beautiful village of Grand Pré.*

3. DRUIDS—The old Celtic priests of Britain and Gaul who performed their sacred rites in the forests.
15. GRAND PRÉ (grän prā')—The French words meaning "great meadows."

Ye who believe in affection that hopes, and endures, and is patient,
Ye who believe in the beauty and strength of woman's devotion,
List to the mournful tradition still sung by the pines of the forest;
List to a Tale of Love in Acadie, home of the happy.

PART THE FIRST

I

20   IN THE Acadian land, on the shores of the Basin of Minas,
Distant, secluded, still, the little village of Grand Pré
Lay in the fruitful valley. Vast meadows stretched to the eastward,
Giving the village its name, and pasture to flocks without number.
Dikes, that the hands of the farmers had raised with labour incessant,
25 Shut out the turbulent tides; but at stated seasons the floodgates
Opened, and welcomed the sea to wander at will o'er the meadows.
West and south there were fields of flax, and orchards and cornfields
Spreading afar and unfenced o'er the plain: and away to the northward
Blomidon rose, and the forests old, and aloft on the mountains
30 Sea fogs pitched their tents, and mists from the mighty Atlantic
Looked on the happy valley, but ne'er from their station descended.
There, in the midst of its farms, reposed the Acadian village.
    Strongly built were the houses, with frames of oak and of hemlock,
Such as the peasants of Normandy built in the reign of the Henries.
35 Thatched were the roofs, with dormer windows; and gables projecting

19. ACADIE (ă-kà-dē')—The French spelling for Acadia, which is another name for Nova Scotia.
20. BASIN OF MINAS (mī'nàs)—An inland bay of Nova Scotia, tributary to the Bay of Fundy.
29. BLOMIDON (blŏm'ĭ-dŭn)—A mountainous headland at the entrance of the Basin of Minas.
34. NORMANDY—An ancient province of northern France.
34. HENRIES—A line of early French Kings.

Over the basement below protected and shaded the doorway.
There in the tranquil evenings of summer, when brightly the sunset
Lighted the village street, and gilded the vanes on the chimneys,
Matrons and maidens sat in snow-white caps and kirtles

40 Scarlet and blue and green, with distaffs spinning the golden
Flax for the gossiping looms, whose noisy shuttles within doors
Mingled their sound with the whir of the wheels and the songs of
    the maidens.
Solemnly down the street came the parish priest, and the children
Paused in their play to kiss the hand he extended to bless them.

45 Reverend walked he among them; and up rose matrons and
    maidens
Hailing his slow approach with words of affectionate welcome.

Then came the labourers home from the field, and serenely the
    sun sank
Down to his rest, and twilight prevailed. Anon from the belfry
Softly the Angelus sounded, and over the roofs of the village

50 Columns of pale blue smoke, like clouds of incense ascending,
Rose from a hundred hearths, the homes of peace and contentment.
Thus dwelt together in love these simple Acadian farmers—
Dwelt in the love of God and of man. Alike were they free from
Fear, that reigns with the tyrant, and envy, the vice of republics.

55 Neither locks had they to their doors, nor bars to their windows;
But their dwellings were open as day and the hearts of the owners;
There the richest was poor, and the poorest lived in abundance.

Somewhat apart from the village, and nearer the Basin of Minas,
Benedict Bellefontaine, the wealthiest farmer of Grand Pré,

60 Dwelt on his goodly acres; and with him, directing his household,
Gentle Evangeline lived, his child, and the pride of the village.
Stalwart and stately in form was the man of seventy winters;

39. KIRTLES—Outer petticoats or skirts.

49. ANGELUS—The ringing of the church bell calling to prayer. The custom was
introduced into France in the sixteenth century in commemoration of the visit of
the Angel of the Lord to the Virgin Mary.

59. BENEDICT BELLEFONTAINE (bĕ-lĕ-fŏn-tän')—Benedict comes from Latin,
meaning "blessed."

Hearty and hale was he, an oak that is covered with snowflakes;
White as the snow were his locks, and his cheeks as brown as the
    oak leaves.
65 Fair was she to behold, that maiden of seventeen summers.
Black were her eyes as the berry that grows on the thorn by the
    wayside,
Black, yet how softly they gleamed beneath the brown shade of
    her tresses!
Sweet was her breath as the breath of kine that feed in the
    meadows.
When in the harvest heat she bore to the reapers at noontide
70 Flagons of home-brewed ale, ah! fair in sooth was the maiden.

    Fairer was she when, on Sunday morn, while the bell from its
    turret
Sprinkled with holy sounds the air, as the priest with his hyssop
Sprinkles the congregation, and scatters blessings upon them,

72. HYSSOP (hǐs'ǔp)—An aromatic plant with blue flowers. A brush, made of
the plant, was used by the priest for sprinkling holy water.

Down the long street she passed, with her chaplet of beads and her
    missal,
75 Wearing her Norman cap, and her kirtle of blue, and the earrings,
Brought in the olden time from France, and since, as an heirloom,
Handed down from mother to child, through long generations.
But a celestial brightness—a more ethereal beauty—
Shone on her face and encircled her form, when, after confession,
80 Homeward serenely she walked with God's benediction upon her.
When she had passed, it seemed like the ceasing of exquisite music.

Firmly builded with rafters of oak, the house of the farmer
Stood on the side of a hill commanding the sea; and a shady
Sycamore grew by the door, with a woodbine wreathing around it.
85 Rudely carved was the porch, with seats beneath; and a footpath
Led through an orchard wide, and disappeared in the meadow.
Under the sycamore tree were hives overhung by a penthouse,
Such as the traveller sees in regions remote by the roadside,
Built o'er a box for the poor, or the blessed image of Mary.
90 Farther down, on the slope of the hill, was the well with its moss-
    grown
Bucket, fastened with iron, and near it a trough for the horses.
Shielding the house from storms, on the north, were the barns and
    the farmyard.
There stood the broad-wheeled wains, and the antique ploughs and
    the harrows;
There were the folds for the sheep; and there, in his feathered
    seraglio
95 Strutted the lordly turkey, and crowed the cock, with the selfsame
Voice that in ages of old had startled the penitent Peter.
Bursting with hay were the barns, themselves a village. In each
    one
Far o'er the gable projected a roof of thatch; and a staircase,
Under the sheltering eaves, led up to the odorous corn loft.

74. MISSAL—Prayer book containing the services of the Mass.
94. SERAGLIO (sĕ-räl'yō)—Harem of females.
96. PENITENT PETER—A crowing cock reminded Peter, the Disciple, of sin
which he had committed.

100 There too the dovecot stood, with its meek and innocent inmates
Murmuring ever of love; while above in the variant breezes
Numberless noisy weathercocks rattled and sang of mutation.

Thus, at peace with God and the world, the farmer of Grand Pré
Lived on his sunny farm, and Evangeline governed his household.
105 Many a youth, as he knelt in the church and opened his missal,
Fixed his eyes upon her as the saint of his deepest devotion;
Happy was he who might touch her hand or the hem of her garment.
Many a suitor came to her door, by the darkness befriended,
And, as he knocked and waited to hear the sound of her footsteps,
110 Knew not which beat the louder, his heart or the knocker of iron;
Or at the joyous feast of the Patron Saint of the village,
Bolder grew, and pressed her hand in the dance as he whispered
Hurried words of love, that seemed a part of the music.

But, among all who came, young Gabriel only was welcome;
115 Gabriel Lajeunesse, the son of Basil the blacksmith,
Who was a mighty man in the village, and honoured of all men;
For, since the birth of time, throughout all ages and nations,
Has the craft of the smith been held in repute by the people.
Basil was Benedict's friend. Their children from earliest childhood
120 Grew up together as brother and sister; and Father Felician,
Priest and pedagogue both in the village, had taught them their letters
Out of the selfsame book, with the hymns of the church and the plain-song.
But when the hymn was sung, and the daily lesson completed,
Swiftly they hurried away to the forge of Basil, the blacksmith.
125 There at the door they stood, with wondering eyes to behold him
Take in his leathern lap the hoof of the horse as a plaything,
Nailing the shoe in its place; while near him the tire of the cart wheel

102. MUTATION—Changes, or alterations in the weather or winds.
115. LAJEUNESSE—Pronounced lä-zhō-nā'. BASIL—Pronounced băz'il.

Lay like a fiery snake, coiled round in a circle of cinders.
Oft on autumnal eves, when without in the gathering darkness
130 Bursting with light seemed the smithy, through every cranny and
    crevice,
Warm by the forge within they watched the labouring bellows,
And as its panting ceased, and the sparks expired in the ashes,
Merrily laughed and said they were nuns going into the chapel.
Oft on sledges in winter, as swift as the swoop of the eagle,
135 Down the hillside bounding, they glided away o'er the meadow.
Oft in the barns they climbed to the populous nests on the rafters,
Seeking with eager eyes that wondrous stone, which the swallow
Brings from the shore of the sea to restore the sight of its fledg-
    lings:
Lucky was he who found that stone in the nest of the swallow!

140   Thus passed a few swift years, and they no longer were children.
He was a valiant youth, and his face, like the face of the morning,
Gladdened the earth with its light, and ripened thought into action.
She was a woman now, with the heart and hopes of a woman.

137. WONDROUS STONE—There is an English myth that a mother swallow can
cure blindness in her young by using a small stone from the seashore.

"Sunshine of Saint Eulalie" was she called; for that was the sunshine

145 Which, as the farmers believed, would load their orchards with apples;

She, too, would bring to her husband's house delight and abundance,

Filling it full of love and the ruddy faces of children.

II

Now had the season returned, when the nights grow colder and longer,

And the retreating sun the sign of the Scorpion enters.

150 Birds of passage sailed through the leaden air from the ice-bound,

Desolate northern bays to the shores of tropical islands.

Harvests were gathered in; and wild with the winds of September

Wrestled the trees of the forest, as Jacob of old with the angel.

All the signs foretold a winter long and inclement.

155 Bees, with prophetic instinct of want, had hoarded their honey

Till the hives overflowed; and the Indian hunters asserted

Cold would the winter be, for thick was the fur of the foxes.

Such was the advent of autumn. Then followed that beautiful season,

Called by the pious Acadian peasants the Summer of All-Saints!

160 Filled was the air with a dreamy and magical light; and the landscape

Lay as if new created in all the freshness of childhood.

Peace seemed to reign upon earth, and the restless heart of the ocean

Was for a moment consoled. All sounds were in harmony blended.

144. SUNSHINE OF SAINT EULALIE (û-là-lē')—The name comes from Greek and means "Fair Speech." The people believed that if the sun shone on St. Eulalie's Day, February 12, there would be plenty of apples in the orchards.

149. SCORPION—A constellation of stars which appears during the autumnal months.

153. JACOB—There is an interesting story in the Bible of Jacob's wrestling all night with an angel whom he finally overcame and then from whom at daybreak, he received a blessing.

159. SUMMER OF ALL-SAINTS—The Indian Summer, with its bright warm days, which comes late in the fall and after which winter generally begins.

Voices of children at play, the crowing of cocks in the farmyards,
165 Whir of wings in the drowsy air, and the cooing of pigeons,
All were subdued and low as the murmurs of love, and the great sun
Looked with the eye of love through the golden vapours around him;
While arrayed in its robes of russet and scarlet and yellow,
Bright with the sheen of the dew, each glittering tree of the forest
170 Flashed like the plane tree the Persian adorned with mantles and jewels.

Now recommenced the reign of rest and affection and stillness.
Day with its burden and heat had departed, and twilight descending
Brought back the evening star to the sky, and the herds to the homestead.
Pawing the ground they came, and resting their necks on each other,
175 And with their nostrils distended inhaling the freshness of evening.
Foremost, bearing the bell, Evangeline's beautiful heifer,
Proud of her snow-white hide, and the ribbon that waved from her collar,
Quietly paced and slow, as if conscious of human affection.

Then came the shepherd back with his bleating flocks from the hillside,
180 Where was their favourite pasture. Behind them followed the watchdog,
Patient, full of importance, and grand in the pride of his instinct,
Walking from side to side with a lordly air, and superbly
Waving his bushy tail, and urging forward the stragglers;
Regent of flocks was he when the shepherd slept; their protector,
185 When from the forest at night, through the starry silence, the wolves howled.

170. PLANE TREE—The Persian warrior, Xerxes (zûrk'sēz), was so impressed with the plane tree which he saw in Asia Minor that he decorated it with jewels.
184. REGENT—Ruler.

Late, with the rising moon, returned the wains from the marshes,
Laden with briny hay that filled the air with its odour.

Cheerily neighed the steeds, with dew on their manes and their
    fetlocks,
While aloft on their shoulders the wooden and ponderous saddles,
190 Painted with brilliant dyes, and adorned with tassels of crimson,
Nodded in bright array, like hollyhocks heavy with blossoms.
Patiently stood the cows meanwhile, and yielded their udders
Unto the milkmaid's hand; whilst loud and in regular cadence
Into the sounding pails the foaming streamlets descended.
195 Lowing of cattle and peals of laughter were heard in the farmyard,
Echoed back by the barns. Anon they sank into stillness;
Heavily closed, with a jarring sound, the valves of the barn doors,
Rattled the wooden bars, and all for a season was silent.

Indoors, warm by the wide-mouthed fireplace, idly the farmer
200 Sat in his elbowchair, and watched how the flames and the smoke
    wreaths
Struggled together like foes in a burning city. Behind him,

Nodding and mocking along the wall, with gestures fantastic,
Darted his own huge shadow, and vanished away into darkness.
Faces, clumsily carved in oak, on the back of his armchair
205 Laughed in the flickering light, and the pewter plates on the dresser
Caught and reflected the flame, as shields of armies the sunshine.
Fragments of song the old man sang, the carols of Christmas,
Such as at home, in the olden time, his fathers before him
Sang in their Norman orchards and bright Burgundian vineyards.

210   Close at her father's side was the gentle Evangeline seated,
Spinning flax for the loom, that stood in the corner behind her.
Silent awhile were its treadles, at rest was its diligent shuttle,
While the monotonous drone of the wheel, like the drone of a bag-
        pipe,
Followed the old man's song, and united the fragments together.
215 As in a church, when the chant of the choir at intervals ceases,
Footfalls are heard in the aisles, or words of the priest at the altar,
So, in each pause of the song, with measured motion, the clock
        ticked.

    Thus as they sat, there were footsteps heard, and, suddenly
        lifted,
Sounded the wooden latch, and the door swung back on its hinges.
220 Benedict knew by the hob-nailed shoes it was Basil the blacksmith
And by her beating heart, Evangeline knew who was with him.
"Welcome!" the farmer exclaimed, as their footsteps paused on the
        threshold,
"Welcome, Basil, my friend! Come, take thy place on the settle
Close by the chimney side, which is always empty without thee;
225 Take from the shelf overhead thy pipe and the box of tobacco;
Never so much thyself art thou as when through the curling
Smoke of the pipe or the forge thy friendly and jovial face gleams
Round and red as the harvest moon through the mist of the
        marshes."

    209. BURGUNDIAN—Burgundy is a province in the southeastern part of France
bordering on Switzerland. It has extensive vineyards and is noted for its delicious
wines.

Then, with a smile of content, thus answered Basil the black-
smith,
230 Taking with easy air the accustomed seat by the fireside:
"Benedict Bellefontaine, thou hast ever thy jest and thy ballad!
Ever in cheerfulest mood art thou, when others are filled with
Gloomy forebodings of ill, and see only ruin before them.
Happy art thou, as if every day thou hadst picked up a horseshoe."
235 Pausing a moment to take the pipe that Evangeline brought him,
And with a coal from the embers had lighted—he slowly continued:
"Four days now are passed since the English ships at their anchors
Ride in the Gaspereau's mouth, with their cannon pointed against
us.
What their design may be is unknown; but all are commanded
240 On the morrow to meet in the church, where his Majesty's mandate
Will be proclaimed as law in the land. Alas! in the meantime
Many surmises of evil alarm the hearts of the people."

Then made answer the farmer: "Perhaps some friendlier pur-
pose
Brings these ships to our shores. Perhaps the harvests in England
245 By untimely rains or untimelier heat have been blighted,
And from our bursting barns they would feed their cattle and chil-
dren."
"Not so thinketh the folk in the village," said, warmly, the black-
smith,
Shaking his head, as in doubt; then, heaving a sigh, he continued:
"Louisburg is not forgotten, nor Beau Séjour, nor Port Royal.
250 Many already have fled to the forest, and lurk on its outskirts,
Waiting with anxious hearts the dubious fate of tomorrow.
Arms have been taken from us, and warlike weapons of all kinds;
Nothing is left but the blacksmith's sledge and the scythe of the
mower."

238. GASPEREAU (găs'pĕ-rō)—A river which leads from a lake by the same
name, to Minas Basin, passing through the village of Grand Pré.
249. LOUISBURG (lōō'ĭs-bûrg), BEAU SÉJOUR (bō sā'zhōōr), PORT ROYAL—Ports
which had been captured by the English, recaptured by the French, and captured
by the English a second time, during a series of wars between France and England, which, in America, were called the French and Indian Wars.

Then with a pleasant smile made answer the jovial farmer:
255 "Safer are we unarmed, in the midst of our flocks and our corn-
fields,
Safer within these peaceful dikes, besieged by the ocean,
Than our fathers in forts, besieged by the enemy's cannon.
Fear no evil, my friend, and tonight may no shadow of sorrow
Fall on this house and hearth; for this is the night of the contract.
260 Built are the house and the barn. The merry lads of the village
Strongly have built them and well; and, breaking the glebe round
about them,
Filled the barn with hay, and the house with food for a twelve-
month.
René Leblanc will be here anon, with his papers and inkhorn.
Shall we not then be glad, and rejoice in the joy of our children?"
265 As apart by the window she stood, with her hand in her lover's,
Blushing, Evangeline heard the words that her father had spoken,
And, as they died on his lips the worthy notary entered.

III

Bent like a labouring oar, that toils in the surf of the ocean,
Bent, but not broken, by age was the form of the notary public;
270 Shocks of yellow hair, like the silken floss of the maize, hung
Over his shoulders; his forehead was high; and glasses with horn
bows
Sat astride on his nose, with a look of wisdom supernal.
Father of twenty children was he, and more than a hundred
Children's children rode on his knee, and heard his great watch
tick.
275 Four long years in the times of the war had he languished a cap-
tive,
Suffering much in an old French fort as the friend of the English.

259. CONTRACT—The marriage contract between Evangeline and Gabriel.
261. GLEBE—Earth, plot of land.
262. FOOD FOR A TWELVE-MONTH—It is said to have been a custom in Acadia for
the community to build a house for a young man when he was about to be married, to break up the land about it, and to provide him with necessities of life for
a year.
263. RENÉ LEBLANC—Pronounced rĕ-nä' lĕ-blän'.
276. IN AN OLD FRENCH FORT—In the *Petition of the Acadians to the King* is an
interesting account of the seizure of René Leblanc by the Indians and his four
years' imprisonment in Port Royal.

Now, though warier grown, without all guile or suspicion,
Ripe in wisdom was he, but patient, and simple, and childlike.
He was beloved by all, and most of all by the children;
280 For he told them tales of the Loup-garou in the forest,
And of the goblin that came in the night to water the horses,
And of the white Létiche, the ghost of a child who unchristened
Died, and was doomed to haunt unseen the chambers of children;
And how on Christmas Eve the oxen talked in the stable,
285 And how the fever was cured by a spider shut up in a nutshell,
And of the marvellous powers of four-leaved clover and horseshoes,
With whatsoever else was writ in the lore of the village.

Then up rose from his seat by the fireside Basil the blacksmith,
Knocked from his pipe the ashes, and slowly extending his right
hand,
290 "Father Leblanc," he exclaimed, "thou hast heard the talk in the
village,
And, perchance, canst tell us some news of these ships and their
errand."
Then with modest demeanour made answer the notary public—
"Gossip enough have I heard, in sooth, yet am never the wiser;
And what their errand may be I know not better than others.
295 Yet am I not of those who imagine some evil intention
Brings them here, for we are at peace; and why then molest us?"

"God's name!" shouted the hasty and somewhat irascible black-
smith;
"Must we in all things look for the how, and the why, and the
wherefore?
Daily injustice is done, and might is the right of the strongest!"
300 But, without heeding his warmth, continued the notary public—
"Man is unjust, but God is just; and finally justice
Triumphs: and well I remember a story, that often consoled me
When as a captive I lay in the old French fort at Port Royal."

280. LOUP-GAROU (lōō-gà-rōō')—According to an old myth, a man who could
turn himself into a wolf to devour little children.
282. LÉTICHE—Pronounced lä'tĭ-shä.

This was the old man's favourite tale, and he loved to repeat it
305 When his neighbours complained that any injustice was done them.

"Once in an ancient city, whose name I no longer remember,
Raised aloft on a column, a brazen statue of Justice
Stood in the public square, upholding the scales in its left hand,
And in its right a sword, as an emblem that justice presided
310 Over the laws of the land, and the hearts and homes of the people.
Even the birds had built their nests in the scales of the balance,
Having no fear of the sword that flashed in the sunshine above
them.
But in the course of time the laws of the land were corrupted;
Might took the place of right, and the weak were oppressed, and
the mighty
315 Ruled with an iron rod. Then it chanced in a nobleman's palace
That a necklace of pearls was lost, and ere long a suspicion
Fell on an orphan girl who lived as maid in the household.
She, after form of trial condemned to die on the scaffold,
Patiently met her doom at the foot of the statue of Justice.
320 As to her Father in heaven her innocent spirit ascended,
Lo! o'er the city a tempest rose; and the bolts of the thunder
Smote the statue of bronze, and hurled in wrath from its left hand
Down on the pavement below the clattering scales of the balance,
And in the hollow thereof was found the nest of a magpie,
325 Into whose clay-built walls the necklace of pearls was inwoven."

Silenced, but not convinced, when the story was ended, the
blacksmith
Stood like a man who fain would speak, but findeth no language;
All his thoughts were congealed into lines on his face, as the vapours
Freeze into fantastic shapes on the windowpanes in the winter.

330 Then Evangeline lighted the brazen lamp on the table,
Filled, till it overflowed, the pewter tankard with home-brewed
Nut-brown ale, that was famed for its strength in the village of
Grand Pré;

While from his pocket the notary drew his papers and inkhorn,
Wrote with a steady hand the date and age of the parties,

335 Naming the dower of the bride in flocks of sheep and in cattle.
Orderly all things proceeded, and duly and well were completed,
And the great seal of the law was set like a sun on the margin.
Then from his leathern pouch the farmer threw on the table
Three times the old man's fee in solid pieces of silver;
340 And the notary rising, and blessing the bride and the bridegroom,
Lifted aloft the tankard of ale and drank to their welfare.
Wiping the foam from his lip he solemnly bowed and departed,
While in silence the others sat and mused by the fireside,
Till Evangeline brought the draught-board out of its corner.

345   Soon was the game begun. In friendly contention the old men
Laughed at each lucky hit, or unsuccessful manoeuvre,
Laughed when a man was crowned, or a breach was made in the
    king-row.
Meanwhile, apart, in the twilight gloom of a window's embrasure,
Sat the lovers, and whispered together, beholding the moon rise
350 Over the pallid sea and the silvery mist of the meadows.
Silently, one by one, in the infinite meadows of heaven,
Blossomed the lovely stars, the forget-me-nots of the angels.

    Thus was the evening passed. Anon the bell from the belfry

335. DOWER—The property which a woman brings to her husband at marriage.
344. DRAUGHT (dráft)-BOARD—Checkerboard.

Rang out the hour of nine, the village curfew, and straightway
355 Rose the guests and departed; and silence reigned in the household.
Many a farewell word and a sweet good-night on the doorstep
Lingered long in Evangeline's heart, and filled it with gladness.
Carefully then were covered the embers that glowed on the hearth-
    stone,
And on the oaken stairs resounded the tread of the farmer.
360 Soon with a soundless step the foot of Evangeline followed.

Up the staircase moved a luminous space in the darkness,
Lighted less by the lamp than the shining face of the maiden.
Silent she passed the hall and entered the door of her chamber.

Simple that chamber was, with its curtains of white, and its
    clothespress
365 Ample and high, on whose spacious shelves were carefully folded
Linen and woollen stuffs, by the hand of Evangeline woven.
This was the precious dower she would bring to her husband in
    marriage,

354. CURFEW—A bell rung originally at 8 P.M. as a signal to extinguish all fires
and retire; from the French *couvrefeu* meaning to cover fire.

Better than flocks and herds, being proofs of her skill as a house-
    wife.
Soon she extinguished her lamp, for the mellow and radiant moon-
    light
370 Streamed through the windows, and lighted the room, till the heart
    of the maiden
Swelled and obeyed its power, like the tremulous tides of the ocean.

Ah! she was fair, exceeding fair to behold, as she stood with
Naked snow-white feet on the gleaming floor of her chamber!
Little she dreamed that below, among the trees of the orchard,
375 Waited her lover and watched for the gleam of her lamp and her
    shadow.
Yet were her thoughts of him, and at times a feeling of sadness
Passed o'er her soul, as the sailing shade of clouds in the moonlight
Flitted across the floor and darkened the room for a moment.
And, as she gazed from the window, she saw serenely the moon
    pass
380 Forth from the folds of a cloud, and one star follow her footsteps,
As out of Abraham's tent young Ishmael wandered with Hagar!

IV

Pleasantly rose next morn the sun on the village of Grand Pré.
Pleasantly gleamed in the soft, sweet air the Basin of Minas,
Where the ships, with their wavering shadows, were riding at
    anchor.
385 Life had long been astir in the village, and clamourous labour
Knocked with its hundred hands at the golden gates of the
    morning.
Now from the country around, from the farms and the neighbouring
    hamlets,
Came in their holiday dresses, the blithe Acadian peasants.
Many a glad good-morrow and jocund laugh from the young folk
390 Made the bright air brighter, as up from the numerous meadows,

381. Hagar was Ishmael's mother who was driven out into the wilderness by
Abraham when Ishmael was a very young child.

Where no path could be seen but the track of wheels in the
    greensward,
Group after group appeared, and joined, or passed on the highway.
Long ere noon, in the village, all sounds of labour were silenced.
Thronged were the streets with people; and noisy groups at the
    house doors
395 Sat in cheerful sun, and rejoiced and gossiped together.
Every house was an inn, where all were welcome and feasted;
For with this simple people, who lived like brothers together,
All things were held in common, and what one had was another's.
Yet under Benedict's roof hospitality seemed more abundant:
400 For Evangeline stood among the guests of her father;
Bright was her face with smiles, and words of welcome and glad-
    ness
Fell from her beautiful lips and blessed the cup as she gave it.

    Under the open sky, in the odorous air of the orchard,
Stript of its golden fruit, was spread the feast of betrothal.
405 There in the shade of the porch were the priest and the notary
    seated;
There good Benedict sat, and sturdy Basil, the blacksmith.
Not far withdrawn from these, by the cider press and the beehives,
Michael, the fiddler, was placed, with the gayest of hearts and of
    waistcoats.
Shadow and light from the leaves alternately played on his snow-
    white
410 Hair, as it waved in the wind; and the jolly face of the fiddler
Glowed like a living coal when the ashes are blown from the em-
    bers.
Gaily the old man sang to the vibrant sound of his fiddle,
Tous les Bourgeois de Chartres, and *Le Carillon de Dunkerque*,
And anon with his wooden shoes beat time to the music.

    413. *Tours les Bourgeois de Chartres*—(tōō lä bōōr-zhwäh′ dĕ shär′tr)—"All Citi-
zens of Chartres."
    413. *Le Carillon de Dunkerque*—(lĕ kà-rē′yŏn dĕ dŭn′kûrk)—"The Chimes of
Dunkirk." These songs were taken from a curious collection of French songs in
which the serious canticles are sung to popular airs and dancing tunes.

415 Merrily, merrily whirled the wheels of the dizzying dances
Under the orchard trees and down the path to the meadows;
Old folk and young together, and children mingled among them.
Fairest of all the maids was Evangeline, Benedict's daughter!
Noblest of all the youths was Gabriel, son of the blacksmith!

420 So passed the morning away. And lo! with a summons sonorous
Sounded the bell from its tower, and over the meadows a drum
beat.
Thronged erelong was the church with men. Without in the
churchyard,
Waited the women. They stood by the graves, and hung on the
headstones
Garlands of autumn leaves and evergreens fresh from the forest.
425 Then came the guard from the ships, and marching proudly among
them
Entered the sacred portal. With loud and dissonant clangour
Echoed the sound of their brazen drums from ceiling and case-
ment—
Echoed a moment only, and slowly the ponderous portal
Closed and in silence the crowd awaited the will of the soldiers.

430 Then uprose their commander, and spake from the steps of the
altar,
Holding aloft in his hands, with its seals, the royal commission.
"You are convened this day," he said, "by his Majesty's orders.
Clement and kind has he been; but how you have answered his
kindness
Let your own hearts reply! To my natural make and my tem-
per
435 Painful the task is I do, which to you I know must be grievous.
Yet must I bow and obey, and deliver the will of our monarch;
Namely, that all your lands, and dwellings, and cattle of all kinds
Forfeited be to the crown; and that you yourselves from this
province
Be transported to other lands. God grant you may dwell there

440 Ever as faithful subjects, a happy and peaceable people.
    Prisoners now I declare you; for such is his Majesty's pleasure!"

    As, when the air is serene in the sultry solstice of summer,
    Suddenly gathers a storm, and the deadly sling of the hailstones
    Beats down the farmer's corn in the field and shatters his windows,
445 Hiding the sun, and strewing the ground with thatch from the
        house roofs,
    Bellowing fly the herds, and seek to break their inclosures;
    So on the hearts of the people descended the words of the speaker.
    Silent a moment they stood in speechless wonder, and then rose
    Louder and ever louder a wail of sorrow and anger,
450 And, by one impulse moved, they madly rushed to the doorway.
    Vain was the hope of escape; and cries and fierce imprecations
    Rang through the house of prayer; and high o'er the heads of the
        others
    Rose, with his arms uplifted, the figure of Basil, the blacksmith,
    As, on a stormy sea, a spar is tossed by the billows.
455 Flushed was his face and distorted with passion; and wildly he
        shouted,
    "Down with the tyrants of England; we never have sworn them
        allegiance!
    Death to these foreign soldiers who seize on our homes and our
        harvests!"
    More he fain would have said, but the merciless hand of a soldier
    Smote him upon the mouth, and dragged him down to the pave-
        ment.

460   In the midst of the strife and tumult of angry contention,
    Lo! the door of the chancel opened, and Father Felician
    Entered, with serious mien, and ascended the steps of the altar.
    Raising his reverend hand, with a gesture he awed into silence
    All that clamourous throng; and thus he spake to his people;

---

442. SOLSTICE OF SUMMER—The twenty-first of June when the sun is directly
over the Tropic of Cancer, the northern point at which it turns back southward.
It is the longest day, and at this time storms which may last two or three days are
very frequent.

465 Deep were his tones and solemn; in accents measured and mournful
 Spake he, as, after the tocsin's alarum, distinctly the clock strikes.
 "What is this that ye do, my children? What madness has seized you?
 Forty years of my life have I laboured among you, and taught you,
 Not in word alone, but in deed, to love one another!
470 Is this the fruit of my toils, of my vigils and prayers and privations?
 Have you so soon forgotten all lessons of love and forgiveness?
 This is the house of the Prince of Peace, and would you profane it
 Thus with violent deeds and hearts overflowing with hatred?
 Lo! where the crucified Christ from his cross is gazing upon you!
475 See! in those sorrowful eyes what meekness and holy compassion!
 Hark! how those lips still repeat the prayer, 'O Father, forgive them!'
 Let us repeat that prayer in the hour when the wicked assail us,
 Let us repeat it now, and say, 'O Father, forgive them!'"
 Few were his words of rebuke, but deep in the hearts of his people
480 Sank they, and sobs of contrition succeeded the passionate outbreak,
 While they repeated his prayer, and said, "O Father, forgive them!"

 Then came the evening service. The tapers gleaned from the altar.
 Fervent and deep was the voice of the priest, and the people responded,
 Not with their lips alone, but their hearts; and the *Ave Maria*
485 Sang they, and fell on their knees, and their souls, with devotion translated,
 Rose on the ardour of prayer, like Elijah ascending to heaven.

---

466. TOCSIN—A bell for giving alarms.
484. *Ave Maria* (ä'vä mä-rē'ä)—A prayer to the Virgin Mary.
486. ELIJAH—The reference is to the time when a chariot of fire came down like a whirlwind and snatched Elijah up into heaven.

Meanwhile had spread in the village the tidings of ill, and on all sides

Wandered, wailing, from house to house the women and children.

Long at her father's door Evangeline stood, with her right hand

490 Shielding her eyes from the level rays of the sun, that, descending,

Lighted the village street with mysterious splendour, and roofed each

Peasant's cottage with golden thatch, and emblazoned its windows.

Long within had been spread the snow-white cloth on the table;

There stood the wheaten loaf, and the honey fragrant with wild flowers;

495 There stood the tankard of ale, and the cheese fresh brought from the dairy:

And, at the head of the board the great armchair of the farmer.

Thus did Evangeline wait at her father's door, as the sunset

Threw the long shadows of trees o'er the broad ambrosial meadows.

Ah! on her spirit within a deeper shadow had fallen,

500 And from the fields of her soul a fragrance celestial ascended—

Charity, meekness, love, and hope, and forgiveness, and patience!

Then all forgetful of self, she wandered into the village,

Cheering with looks and words the mournful hearts of the women,

As o'er the darkening fields with lingering steps they departed,

505 Urged by their household cares, and the weary feet of their children.

Down sank the great red sun, and in golden, glimmering vapours

Veiled the light of his face, like the Prophet descending from Sinai.

Sweetly over the village the bell of the Angelus sounded.

Meanwhile, amid the gloom, by the church Evangeline lingered.

510 All was silent within; and in vain at the doors and the windows

Stood she, and listened and looked, till, overcome by emotion,

"Gabriel!" cried she aloud with tremulous voice; but no answer

Came from the graves of the dead, nor the gloomier grave of the living.

507. PROPHET—Moses who came down from the top of Mount Sinai (si'ni) bearing the tablets upon which were written the Ten Commandments.

Slowly at length she returned to the tenantless house of her father.
515 Smouldered the fire on the hearth, on the board was the supper un-
tasted,
Empty and drear was each room, and haunted with phantoms of
terror.
Sadly echoed her step on the stair and the floor of her chamber.
In the dead of night she heard the disconsolate rain fall
Loud on the withered leaves of the sycamore tree by the window.
520 Keenly the lightning flashed; and the voice of the echoing thunder
Told her that God was in heaven, and governed the world He
created!
Then she remembered the tale she had heard of the justice of
Heaven;
Soothed was her troubled soul, and she peacefully slumbered till
morning.

V

Four times the sun had risen and set; and now on the fifth day
525 Cheerily called the cock to the sleeping maids of the farmhouse.
Soon o'er the yellow fields, in silent and mournful procession,
Came from the neighbouring hamlets and farms the Acadian women,
Driving in ponderous wains their household goods to the seashore,
Pausing and looking back to gaze once more on their dwellings,

530 Ere they were shut from sight by the winding road and the woodland.
Close at their sides their children ran, and urged on the oxen,
While in their little hands they clasped some fragments of play-
things.

Thus to the Gaspereau's mouth they hurried; and there on the
sea beach
Piled in confusion lay the household goods of the peasants.
535 All day long between the shore and the ships did the boats ply;
All day long the wains came labouring down from the village.
Late in the afternoon when the sun was near to his setting,
Echoed far o'er the fields came the roll of drums from the church-
yard.
Thither the women and children thronged. On a sudden the church
doors
540 Opened, and forth came the guard, and marching in gloomy proces-
sion
Followed the long imprisoned, but patient, Acadian farmers.
Even as pilgrims, who journey afar from their homes and their
country,
Sing as they go, and in singing forget they are weary and wayworn,
So with songs on their lips the Acadian peasants descended
545 Down from the church to the shore, and their wives and their
daughters.
Foremost the young men came; and, raising together their voices,
Sang with tremulous lips a chant of the Catholic missions:
"Sacred heart of the Saviour! O inexhaustible fountain!
Fill our hearts this day with strength and submission and pa-
tience!"
550 Then the old men, as they marched, and the women that stood by
the wayside
Joined in the sacred psalm, and the birds in the sunshine above
them
Mingled their notes therewith, like voices of spirits departed.
Halfway down to the shore, Evangeline waited in silence,

536. WAINS—Waggons.

Not overcome with grief, but strong in the hour of affliction—
555 Calmly and sadly she waited, until the procession approached
    her,
And she beheld the face of Gabriel pale with emotion.
Tears then filled her eyes, and, eagerly running to meet him,
Clasped she his hands, and laid her head on his shoulder, and
    whispered,
"Gabriel! be of good cheer! for if we love one another
560 Nothing, in truth, can harm us, whatever mischances may happen!"
Smiling she spake these words; then suddenly paused, for her
    father
Saw she slowly advancing.   Alas! how changed was his aspect!
Gone was the glow from his cheek, and the fire from his eyes, and
    his footstep
Heavier seemed with the weight of the heavy heart in his bosom.
565 But with a smile and a sigh, she clasped his neck and embraced
    him,
Speaking words of endearment whose words of comfort availed not.
Thus to the Gaspereau's mouth moved on that mournful proces-
    sion.

    There disorder prevailed, and the tumult and stir of embarking.
Busily plied the freighted boats; and in the confusion
570 Wives were torn from their husbands, and mothers, too late, saw
    their children
Left on the land, extending their arms, with wildest entreaties.
So unto separate ships were Basil and Gabriel carried,
While in despair on the shore Evangeline stood with her father.
Half the task was not done when the sun went down, and the
    twilight
575 Deepened and darkened around; and in haste the refluent ocean
Fled away from the shore, and left the line of the sand-beach
Covered with waifs of the tide, with kelp and the slippery seaweed.
Farther back in the midst of the household goods and the waggons,
Like to a gypsy camp, or a leaguer after a battle,

575. REFLUENT (rĕf'lŏŏ-ĕnt)—Ebbing, flowing back.
579. LEAGUER—The camp of a besieging army.

580 All escape cut off by the sea, and the sentinels near them,
Lay encamped for the night the houseless Acadian farmers.
Back to its nethermost caves retreated the bellowing ocean,
Dragging adown the beach the rattling pebbles, and leaving
Inland and far up the shore the stranded boats of the sailors.
585 Then, as the night descended, the herds returned from their
pastures;
Sweet was the moist air with the odour of milk from their udders;
Lowing they waited, and long, at the well-known bars of the farm-
yard,
Waited and looked in vain for the voice and the hand of the milk-
maid.
Silence reigned in the streets; from the church no Angelus sounded,
590 Rose no smoke from the roofs, and gleamed no lights from the
windows.

But on the shores meanwhile the evening fires had been kindled,
Built of the driftwood thrown on the sands from wrecks in the
tempest.
Round them shapes of gloom and sorrowful faces were gathered,
Voices of women were heard, and of men, and the crying of chil-
dren.
595 Onward from fire to fire, as from hearth to hearth in his parish,
Wandered the faithful priest, consoling and blessing and cheering,
Like unto shipwrecked Paul on Melita's desolate seashore.
Thus he approached the place where Evangeline sat with her
father,
And in the flickering light beheld the face of the old man,
600 Haggard and hollow and wan, and without either thought or
emotion,
E'en as the face of a clock from which the hands have been taken.
Vainly Evangeline strove with words and caresses to cheer him,
Vainly offered him food; yet he moved not, he looked not, he spake
not.

597. PAUL—While Paul was being sent a prisoner to Rome, there arose a terrible tempest on the sea which lasted fourteen days and destroyed the ship. The
crew and the prisoners were cast upon the island of Melita (mĕl'ĭ-tà). Paul went
about healing the sick until they again set sail for Rome.

But with a vacant stare, ever gazed at the flickering firelight.
605 *"Benedicite!"* murmured the priest, in tones of compassion.
More he fain would have said, but his heart was full, and his accents
Faltered and paused on his lips, as the feet of a child on a threshold,
Hushed by the scene he beholds, and the awful presence of sorrow.

Silently, therefore, he laid his hand on the head of the maiden,
610 Raising his tearful eyes to the silent stars that above them
Moved on their way, unperturbed by the wrongs and sorrows of mortals.
Then sat he down at her side and they wept together in silence.

Suddenly rose from the south a light, as in autumn the blood-red
Moon climbs the crystal walls of heaven, and o'er the horizon
615 Titanlike stretches its hundred hands upon mountain and meadows,
Seizing the rocks and the rivers, and piling huge shadows together.
Broader and ever broader it gleamed on the roofs of the village,
Gleamed on the sky and the sea, and the ships that lay in the roadstead.

605. *Benedicite* (bĕn-ê-dīs′ī-tê)—"Bless you."
615. TITANLIKE (tī′tăn-lik)—The Titans were giants of Greek mythology, who waged war on the gods. 618. ROADSTEAD—Bay.

Columns of shining smoke uprose, and flashes of flame were
620 Thrust through their folds and withdrawn, like the quivering hands
of a martyr.
Then as the wind seized the gleeds and the burning thatch, and,
uplifting,
Whirled them aloft through the air, at once from a hundred house-
tops
Started the sheeted smoke with flashes of flame intermingled.
These things beheld in dismay the crowd on the shore and on
shipboard.
625 Speechless at first they stood, then cried aloud in their anguish,
"We shall behold no more our homes in the village of Grand Pré!"
Loud on a sudden the cocks began to crow in the farmyards,
Thinking the day had dawned; and anon the lowing of cattle
Came on the evening breeze, by the barking of dogs interrupted.
630 Then rose a sound of dread, such as startles the sleeping encamp-
ments
Far in the western prairies or forests that skirt the Nebraska,
When the wild horses affrighted sweep by with the speed of the
whirlwind,
Or the loud bellowing herds of buffaloes rush to the river.
Such was the sound that arose on the night as the herds and the
horses
635 Broke through their folds and fences, and madly rushed o'er the
meadows.

Overwhelmed with the sight, yet speechless, the priest and the
maiden
Gazed on the scene of terror that reddened and widened before
them;
And as they turned at length to speak to their silent companion,
Lo! from his seat he had fallen, and stretched abroad on the
seashore

621. GLEEDS—Burning coals.
631. NEBRASKA—Nebraska is the Indian name for flat, broad water and refers to
the Platte River which flows through the state of Nebraska, and is sometimes
called the Nebraska River.

640 Motionless lay his form, from which the soul had departed.
    Slowly the priest uplifted the lifeless head, and the maiden
    Knelt at her father's side, and wailed aloud in her terror.
    Then in a swoon she sank, and lay with her head on his bosom.
    Through the long night she lay in deep, oblivious slumber;
645 And when she woke from the trance, she beheld a multitude near her.
    Faces of friends she beheld, that were mournfully gazing upon her,
    Pallid, with tearful eyes, and looks of saddest compassion.
    Still the blazing of the burning village illumined the landscape,
    Reddened the sky overhead, and gleamed on the faces around her,
650 And like the day of doom it seemed to her wavering senses.
    Then a familiar voice she heard as it said to the people—
    "Let us bury him here by the sea. When a happier season
    Brings us again to our homes from the unknown land of our exile,
    Then shall his sacred dust be piously laid in the churchyard."
655 Such were the words of the priest. And there in haste by the seaside,
    Having the glare of the burning village for funeral torches,
    But without bell or book, they buried the farmer of Grand Pré.
    And as the voice of the priest repeated the service of sorrow,
    Lo! with a mournful sound, like the voice of a vast congregation,
660 Solemnly answered the sea, and mingled its roar with the dirges.
    'Twas the returning tide, that afar from the waste of the ocean,
    With the first dawn of the day, came heaving and hurrying landward.
    Then recommenced once more the stir and noise of embarking;
    And with the ebb of the tide the ships sailed out of the harbour,
665 Leaving behind them the dead on the shore, and the village in ruins.

POSTSCRIPT

Still stands the forest primeval; but under the shade of its branches
Dwells another race, with other customs and language.
Only along the shore of the mournful and misty Atlantic

Linger a few Acadian peasants, whose fathers from exile
670 *Wandered back to their native land to die in its bosom.*
In the fisherman's cot the wheel and the loom are still busy;
Maidens still wear their Norman caps and their kirtles of home-
spun,
And by the evening fire repeat Evangeline's story,
While from its rocky caverns the deep-voiced, neighbouring ocean
675 *Speaks, and in accents disconsolate answers the wail of the forest.*

DISCUSSING THE POEM

The story of "Evangeline" is basically true. The early settlers of Nova Scotia (Acadia) were from France. In later years when the English claim to the land was acknowledged there were some indications that the Acadians would rebel against English rule. To prevent any possible uprising, these descendants of Frenchmen were expelled from the land forever, and in the process of moving a whole people to new lands, many families and friends were separated, never to be reunited. However, one large group did find its way to Louisiana where many of their descendants may be found today.

Henry Wadsworth Longfellow, often called America's best loved poet, earned universal respect in the literary world during his lifetime. He studied in Spain, Germany, France, and Italy, and on his return became one of the first teachers of modern language in an American university. Like "Evangeline," many of his poems were based on real-life happenings, and they reflect his experiences both at home and abroad.

1. Longfellow's poetry is famed for its passages of beautiful description, and "Evangeline" includes some of the finest he wrote. As you go through the poem again, pick out the passages which you think are most helpful in describing the setting. Note especially the descriptions of nature. Begin your search by reading the passages that describe Grand Pré, then give your impression of the community in your own words.

2. Evangeline, Gabriel, Benedict, Basil, and Father Leblanc are principal characters in the tale. Give an account of your first meeting with each of these characters showing what kind of person each one seems to be. Be sure to tell about the making of the contract.

3. Recount the occurrences at the church on the day the plan for exile is announced. How did the Acadians react to the announcement? Describe the scene on the beach as the separations were made. What caused the death of Benedict?

4. The story of the Acadians is a story of displaced persons taken from history. In our own time there have been many examples of large groups of people forcibly evicted from their homes and scattered around the world. Tell about some that you know about personally.

RED RIVER VALLEY 🎵 COWBOY SONG

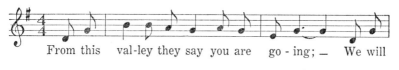

From this val-ley they say you are go - ing; — We will

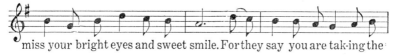

miss your bright eyes and sweet smile. For they say you are tak-ing the

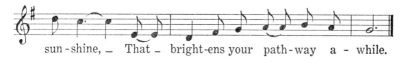

sun - shine, — That — bright-ens your path-way a - while.

5   Won't you think of the valley you're leaving?
    Oh how lonely, how sad it will be.
    Oh think of the fond heart you're breaking,
    And the grief you are causing me to see.

    Come and sit by my side if you love me,
10   Do not hasten to bid me adieu;
    But remember the Red River Valley,
    And the girl that has loved you so true.

KEYS TO ENJOYMENT

The songs of the cowboys, often sung to the accompaniment of the guitar, are characteristic of a romantic way of life that has almost passed from existence. In these days of fenced land, of law and order, and of scientific ranching much of the glamour of the open range is gone. When riding herd at night was a necessity, many a lonely and weary hour was lightened by the singing of rhythmic songs like "Red River Valley." Though much of the environment that inspired them has changed, the songs themselves remain popular. Their chief qualities— rhythm, haunting loneliness, and romantic sentimentality—are to be found in "Red River Valley."

1. What are the chief characteristics of cowboy songs? Name several which you know.

2. What reasons explain the continued popularity of "Red River Valley"?

3. What makes "Red River Valley" a favourite in Canada as well as in the United States?

PEACE RIVER HUMOUR 🐾 ROBERT E. GARD

STANDING in front of the assembled students, Mr. Lloyd Garrison, Principal of the Berwyn High School, gave a delightful rendition of a Peace River tall story. This was in answer to a couple of tales I had told, and I was fast learning that in the Peace River Country the telling of a yarn is taken as a challenge to spin a better one.

"You all know Griffin Creek," the Principal began, "and you all know about the Indians there. (Griffin Creek used to be an Indian reservation.) Well, it was in 1918 and the big "flu" epidemic was in full blast. The Indians were dying so fast it was impossible to keep 'em buried. In fact, there were only a couple of fellows who had any strength; and these two were busy day and night burying folks. They were getting mighty weak themselves, I tell you. Well, cold weather came on as it does up here, and naturally everything froze up solid, including all the deceased Indians. It was a real task trying to dig graves in the frozen ground, so the two fellows who were left just stacked the Indians up like cord-wood, expecting that they'd wait for spring to come and thaw out the ground. But the piles rose so quick and so fast that they saw it wasn't going to do at all. Besides, several of the Indians were in mighty funny positions when they passed out, and one 'specially mean old codger froze in such a twisted position that the two men who were left couldn't get him out of his cabin door. Finally they saw that something had to be done, and done fast, or else the dead Indians would fill up the world. So the men hit on the scheme of scraping the top off a muskeg. They figured that when they got the frozen top scraped off, the soft mud could be just the place to bury all the dead Indians. Well, they did this and started to put the frozen men away. They just put 'em in like fence posts. They were pretty weak, too, remember, and they soon found the only way they could bury the Indians fast enough was to get a big sledge hammer, and just drive 'em down. This worked fine on all the Indians but one. This fellow had frozen with his arm and hand right straight up in the air. They drove all of him into muskeg except this one arm. Try as they might they simply couldn't get that arm under! Now the old-timer who told me this story—and this should prove to you that it's gospel truth—said that for years afterwards, whenever he rode out Griffin Creek way, he used to tie his horse to that Indian's arm!"

There is laughter in the air in the Peace River Country. It is laughter that comes from the land, from the lakes and the rivers, from the courage of the Peace River folk! It is hearty laughter, without malice, and one may hear it in the whistle of the Peace River wind, in the chug of the Northern Alberta Railways Muskeg Limited, in the songs of the birds, or issuing joyfully from the throats of the honest-to-God tale-spinnin'est folks in the West.

There is laughter, too, in the stories old La Boutaille used to tell. He was a trapper of the Lesser Slave Lake region, and he had an eternal struggle to provide for his large family.

"Many years ago," La Boutaille used to say, "I needed food for my family, though I had but little ammunition for my gun, when I started off on what seemed to be a very hopeless chase. At length, I had expended all but one bullet and was prepared to give up in despair. Just then I heard the unmistakable sound of ducks feeding. Looking around some willows, I saw I was on the banks of a small creek, the location of which was strange to me. It was a peculiar stream winding in a series of regular curves across a wooded plain. Examining it, I saw a fat drake feeding just around the first bend. Going farther, I found a still fatter duck in the next bend. The sight encouraged me and exploring, I discovered that nine ducks in all were feeding, one in each bend! I had but one bullet left as I have already told you, and it was a big problem how to use it to the best advantage. Suddenly, I saw the way to feed the hungry family waiting for me far away!

"Quietly dropping to the ground, I carefully surveyed the first bend in the stream, then placing my gun across my knee, I bent it to correspond to its angle. Examining the other bends I bent the gun-barrel this way and that, until at last it was an exact representation of the convolutions of the stream. Then quietly descending to the level of the water, I took steady aim at the first duck. The bullet passed through it and travelling on, its course determined by the kinks in the gun-barrel, it penetrated neatly one after the other, the remaining eight ducks. Turning homeward laden with nine heavy ducks, I reflected that the old proverb about killing two birds was greatly out of date!"

Another La Boutaille tale was one he used to tell about the year of starvation, the year when game had departed from the country around the Slave Lake. "The squaws foraged for berries in vain," related La Boutaille, "and the children, too weak to play, cried themselves into what was perhaps to be their last sleep. I was preparing to join my forefathers beyond the sky's horizon.

"While thinking I was looking on its placid waters for the last time, I saw far away, but approaching me, many birds. They came nearer and I realized I was looking at thousands of geese! But alas, they did not attempt to approach the shore but alighted far out on the waters and commenced to feed. The sight of them kindled a great idea and stirred me into activity. I rushed back to my camp and shouted to everyone to prepare many cords of *babiche*, each with a running noose on one end. While this was being done, I procured a whiplike sapling. The cords were many but light in weight, and I fastened them as well as the stick to my body, rushed toward the lake, and diving in, swam with all my might toward the flock of feeding geese. As I neared them, I sank beneath the unsuspecting birds. I unfastened the cords and with deft fingers slipped a noose around each pair of legs within reach. Moving this way and that, I secured many more until at last, my supply of *babiche* exhausted, I had captured as many geese as would form a feast for half the Indian people of the North.

"Then I popped in the midst of the still feeding birds yelling like one possessed and with my club stirred the startled geese into wildest activity. With a thunderous whirring of wings, they rose clear of the water, each one in doing so tightening the noose around its legs. Up and still up they went, drawing me behind them clear out of the water and into the air.

"With cunning born of many weeks of hunger, I steered the flying birds toward my camp many miles distant. As we approached I gradually hauled in on my lines and as goose after goose came within reach, I could deal it a great whack with my stick, at which it would fall inert to the extent of its cord, thereby acting as a brake on the progress of the remainder. Then, as my lodge surrounded by astonished faces loomed into view, I pulled in desperately on the cords securing the remainder of my winged steeds and smote right and left with my cudgel. Each blow lessened the speed of my flight, and as the supporting geese decreased in number, I gradually descended until with the last few struggling birds, I gently landed on the earth before my tepee."

The Peace River folk are invariably proud of their land and climate. This justifiable pride is imaged in the tales they tell. Campbell Young, a remarkable old-timer who now resides in Edmonton, told me how he once explained the Peace River climate to an Ontario man.

I used to live in Peace River town and before I tell you this story you must remember that the men who pioneered this country had a terrific belief in the land. They also had a flare for impressing strangers with the local wonders. Sometimes our tales were tall, but this was all the better for usually the strangers took the stories in good spirit and went back to the East to relate the wonders of the West.

"One time some members of the Board of Trade in the East were

visiting Peace River. I met one of these immaculately dressed individuals on the street. The fellow wore plus-fours, a bowler hat,
a monocle, and a mustache. He stopped me and said, "How do
you do, sir. Have you lived here long?"

"Several years," I said.

"Then you can surely tell me," said the stranger, "whether or not
this is a healthy climate."

I thought a bit, then I said, "I'll tell you a circumstance. This
will illustrate to you how healthy this climate really is. When the
first settlers came up here they were very lonely. They had nothing
—didn't even have a cemetery. They got to figuring that one of the
things they would need was a cemetery. They, therefore, got together and fixed up a plot, then sat around and waited for somebody to die. Nobody died."

"Remarkable," said the stranger.

"Yes," I said. "So after a while they got discouraged and sent
for all their eldest relatives and friends to come up—knowing that
surely one of these old folks would pass away soon."

"And did they?" asked the stranger.

"Not a single one," I replied. "Not a one of 'em died. In fact,
they all began to get younger. *Nobody* died. Not even a dog."

"What a dreadful situation," breathed the Easterner.

"Yes, and it was even more dreadful because, you see, we'd hired
an undertaker to come up, too—told him what a fine business he'd
have; and that poor fellow was slowly starving. In fact, he got so
weak he crawled over to Saskatchewan where he passed away."

"How did all this turn out?" asked the stranger.

"Why," I replied, "the situation got so desperate that we finally
had to shoot a man to start the cemetery."

Even the young folks love to relate the tall ones. I was talking
one day to the students of the Fairview High School. After I had
finished I asked whether any of them knew any Peace River stories.
One bright young man got up and said he knew about a remarkable event which concerned Spike Drew. I asked who Spike Drew
was, and after being told that he was a man to whom anything in
the world could happen, I sat back and let the yarn take its course.

According to the student, Spike was going across country quite late at night. He was walking along when suddenly he heard a noise behind him. He looked back and saw several pairs of ferocious eyes. He knew they were the eyes of timber wolves, and he began to walk a little faster. The wolves kept right behind him. Spike tried all the old tricks of dropping his gloves, and other articles of apparel and food which he had with him. This didn't do any good, and the wolves began to close in on him. Finally Spike saw a lone tree standing away down ahead, and he made a break for it.

Just as he was shinning up, one of the wolves made a leap for him and snapped the heel of his boot. For a time, however, Spike was safe. He climbed to the top of the tree while the wolves gathered around the trunk in a circle and looked up at him.

Spike sat and waited. So did the wolves. Finally some of the wolves began to get discouraged and drifted away. Eventually they all left except two. These two wolves just kept sitting, looking up at Spike. Soon these two sniffed noses a bit, then went away. Spike thought he was saved. He waited a suitable time then started to crawl down. He'd come about half way down the tree when he saw a terrible sight. The two wolves who had waited so long were coming back, and to his horror Spike saw that they were carrying a beaver between them! Alas, Spike knew he was lost!

CLUES TO THE MEANING

Little stories such as those in this selection are called folk tales. Such tales come, not from celebrated authors, but from the common folk. We neither know nor care who told them first, but enjoy them for their own sake. The same story may take many different forms, be told about different people or different places. Generally, folk tales originate in simple, rural civilizations, such as the agricultural frontiers of Canada and the United States. Thus tales such as these are considered as characteristic of the American and Canadian West.

You will be interested to know that Mr. Garrison, mentioned in the first paragraph, is a very real person who has been teaching in Berwyn since 1932. The story he tells is quite typical of his personality and background. Born in the western United States, he had a varied career as a cowboy, railroader, and farmer, before he became a teacher. Like many American cowboys, he is an expert at rolling Bull Durham cigarettes with one hand.

ENJOYING THE SELECTION

1. One type of "tall tale" is composed by piling one absurdity on another until finally the climax is reached with an incident as absurd as all the others together. Show how the first tale follows this formula.

2. Another type of story is more subtle and indirect. Moreover, you must be brighter to appreciate it, for you must finish it yourself to see the joke. Which story falls into this classification? What is the ending that the author expects us to figure out for ourselves?

3. Actually, "Peace River Humour" is a little collection of four stories. How does Mr. Gard provide his transitions, that is, move smoothly from one story to another?

THE PHANTOM OF PERCE ROCK ⚜

E. C. WOODLEY

Close to the enormous mass of the Percé Rock, which lies off the eastern end of the Gaspé Peninsula, stands another rock of very considerable size, which, viewed from a certain angle, strongly suggests a ship under full sail. Its shape would attract more attention from visitors to the beautiful shores of Gaspé were it not for the very striking appearance of the great Percé Rock near by. Yet it is with the smaller rock that a legend of lost love and lost life will forever be associated.

EARLY in the eighteenth century a young Frenchman of noble birth, Chevalier Raymond de Nerac, became betrothed to a very beautiful girl, Blanche de Beaumont. The Chevalier was an officer in a French regiment and had every reason to anticipate that his life would be spent in the old world and at no time very far from his beloved. But his hopes were suddenly frustrated when an order came that his regiment must go to New France. Already dark clouds were gathering over France's fair western possessions and she was making all too little preparation to avert the catastrophe which, before half a century had passed, was to take them forever from her grasp.

There was a sad parting in the garden of the Chateau de Beaumont when the gallant young officer bade farewell to his beloved and left her with the avowal of undying love still ringing in his ears. There were final adieux at the port of Rochelle when the vessel bearing de Nerac turned her prow westward and sailed out on the dark waters of the broad Atlantic, bound for Quebec, far up the great river St. Lawrence.

The ocean was not kind to the officers and men of de Nerac's regiment, but at length, storm-tossed and weary, they sailed into the quiet waters of the river and, making their way up the mighty stream, at last cast anchor under the fortress of St. Louis, above which waved proudly the lily flag of France. There we must leave the young Chevalier and turn our thoughts to his affianced bride in the distant home-land.

Blanche de Beaumont came of a family whose members had done much for France and who had never failed nor fallen short in time of stress and need. The steadfast spirit which had made their men unyielding fighters on many a battlefield, also made their women great lovers and their love, once given, was never recalled. This was very true of Blanche and, in the peaceful beauty of her French home, her heart was restless. She longed to be with her soldier-lover; she would share his difficulties; she would even rejoice in the trials could they but meet them together. As the days passed her longing became ever greater until, finally, she determined to brave the seas and, at any cost in hardship, join de Nerac at Quebec. She went at once to the same port at which he had embarked and was not long in striking a bargain with the captain of a small vessel who was carrying a cargo and a few passengers to New France.

The voyage was made without incident until the little craft was only one day distant from the shore of the western world. Then dire misfortune suddenly overtook her. It came one beautiful day when the blue waves, tipped here and there with a white edge of foam, seemed to mirror the blue sky with its tiny, fleecy cloudlets.

Far to the south appeared a sail which was seen to belong to a much larger vessel than the French one. Even at a distance there was something unusually forbidding about it and, as it drew nearer, the French captain realized that here was one of the dreaded Spanish pirate vessels which harried the western Atlantic. Flight was impossible for the piratical craft bore down upon them with almost incredible speed and only an hour after she was sighted, she was alongside and had grappled in a death struggle with the French boat.

The pirates swarmed to her decks, meeting with little opposition, and in a short time there were very few Frenchmen left. Then the pirates began to plunder their prize and, as they rushed from one part of the vessel to another, smashing everything which they could not carry away, they discovered a locked cabin. A demand for admission, followed by blows on the door, failed to produce any effect. Thoroughly enraged, they threw their weight against it and the door crashed inward, revealing a girl on her knees in prayer. Even the pirates hesitated before her beauty and innocence, but only for a moment. They seized her roughly and dragged her, half dead with fright, before their captain. As he beheld her beauty, he commanded the men to see that no harm came to her as she was to be his particular prize when the fighting was over.

The struggle went on until not a Frenchman was left alive and the vessel was sacked from prow to stern. Then setting her afire, the Spanish pirate drew off and watched her burn to the water's edge.

When the excitement of the capture had passed, the captain had Blanche de Beaumont brought before him. In no gentle terms she was told her fate and her tears and pleading only incited the Spaniard to more violent threats. In a moment of weakness and appeal she had revealed the purpose of her long journey and of the lover awaiting her in Quebec.

The pirate captain laughed long and harshly. "Forget your brave lieutenant and your dreams of love. You are mine now and never shall you see him again. But no! Just to show you how complete is my power and how little I fear that anyone will ever get you away from me, I will sail up the St. Lawrence until you see the walls of the fort at Quebec and, perchance, even behold your brave lover. But if it should so be, bid him a final farewell for never again will your eyes behold him."

When the captain uttered these heartless words, the vessel was just off the great rock of Percé. For one moment Blanche gazed at her captor with horror-struck eyes. Then, with a wild cry, she darted across the deck and threw herself into the sea. By the time

the captain reached the side of the vessel she was disappearing below the waves and he could just see her arm outstretched and the hand seemingly pointing at him. He turned with a curse on his lips and ordered the men to change the set of the sails.

For a year the pirate captain scoured the seas from the Gulf of Mexico northward, preying on helpless ships, until his name became a terror along the eastern coast of America. Once, caught in a gale, he was driven far out of his intended course and only knew that he was sailing in a northerly direction. When the storm had passed, the vessel was engulfed in a cold, heavy fog. Although he felt that he was not far from land, yet the captain could see nothing. It was exactly a year to a day since the incident of Blanche's drowning, but he had seen so many die since then that he had almost forgotten her.

Suddenly the fog cleared a little, just enough to let him see a great rock towering up, little more than a stone's cast from the ship. With a hurried cry to his sailors to sheer off, he looked up at the dark rock which seemed ready to fall upon the ship's deck. Then, dimly through the mist he saw a figure outlined against the crag. It was a young girl with one arm pointing at him as if indicating him to some unseen power as a fitting object for punishment. He looked at the apparition spellbound as it drew nearer and nearer. A sudden cry rent the air as he recognized the figure of Blanche de Beaumont.

Rushing down the deck he knocked aside the man at the wheel and whirling it widely sought to turn the vessel from its course. But the wheel jammed and he could do nothing. He looked up. The figure of Blanche was still there, the accusing finger pointing at him, but it slowly disappeared as the fog thickened. Darker and darker it became and then a quiver ran through the ship—

When the fog lifted next morning, the few people who dwelt on the neighbouring shore saw a new rock in the waters with which they were so familiar. To them, as to many who have seen it since, it had the form of a large vessel under full sail. If you ask them about the rock, the Gaspé fishermen may tell you the tragic story of Blanche de Beaumont who sought death rather than accept dishonour and whose gentle spirit still haunts the great rock of Percé, near which she perished two centuries ago.

KEYS TO ENJOYMENT

Whenever an imaginative mind sees in nature a resemblance to something with which it is familiar, immediately it begins to weave a romantic story about it by way of explanation. Such stories often persist and are so widely circulated that they become popular legends. So the story of "The Phantom of Percé Rock" presents the legend behind a rock mass off the eastern end of the Gaspé Peninsula. Though the story is itself quite imaginative and romantic, it gives an entertaining explanation to account for one of Nature's visual oddities.

1. What is the importance of the phantom or ghost of Blanche de Beaumont to the success of this legend?

2. Locate on a map of Canada the position of the Gaspé Peninsula. Try to find pictures of the Gaspé country and especially of Percé Rock.

3. Recall similar legends which you have heard or read, and relate these to your classmates.

4. Write a story to account for some unusual formation in your community or in some place you have visited.

HOW HORATIUS KEPT THE BRIDGE ✸

THOMAS BABINGTON MACAULAY

Lars Porsena of Clusium
  By the Nine Gods he swore
That the great house of Tarquin
  Should suffer wrong no more.
5 By the Nine Gods he swore it,
  And named a trysting day,
And bade his messengers ride forth
East and west and south and north,
  To summon his array.

*   *   *   *

10 And now hath every city
  Sent up her tale of men;
The foot are fourscore thousand,
  The horse are thousands ten:
Before the gates of Sutrium
15   Is met the great array.
A proud man was Lars Porsena
  Upon the trysting day.

*   *   *   *

But by the yellow Tiber
  Was tumult and affright:

20 From all the spacious champaign
   To Rome men took their flight.
A mile around the city,
   The throng stopped up the ways;
A fearful sight it was to see
25 Through two long nights and days.

       *   *   *   *

To eastward and to westward
   Have spread the Tuscan bands;
Nor house, nor fence, nor dovecote
   In Crustumerium stands.
30 Verbena down to Ostia
   Hath wasted all the plain;
Astur hath stormed Janiculum,
   And the stout guards are slain.

I wis, in all the Senate,
35   There was no heart so bold,
But sore it ached and fast it beat,
   When that ill news was told.
Forthwith up rose the Consul,
   Up rose the Fathers all;
40 In haste they girded up their gowns,
   And hied them to the wall.

They held a council standing
   Before the River Gate;
Short time was there, ye well may guess,
45   For musing or debate.
Out spake the Consul roundly:
   "The bridge must straight go down;
For, since Janiculum is lost,
   Nought else can save the town."

50 Just then a scout came flying,
   All wild with haste and fear;

"To arms! To arms! Sir Consul:
  Lars Porsena is here."
On the low hills to westward
55   The Consul fixed his eye,
And saw the swarthy storm of dust
  Rise fast along the sky.

And nearer fast and nearer
  Doth the red whirlwind come;
60   And louder still and still more loud
From underneath that rolling cloud
Is heard the trumpet's war-note proud
  The trampling and the hum.
And plainly and more plainly
65   Now through the gloom appears,
Far to left and far to right,
In broken gleams of dark-blue light,
The long array of helmets bright,
  The long array of spears.

70   And plainly and more plainly,
  Above that glimmering line,
Now might ye see the banners
  Of twelve fair cities shine;
But the banner of proud Clusium
75   Was highest of them all,
The terror of the Umbrian,
  The terror of the Gaul.

And plainly and more plainly
  Now might the burghers know,
80   By port and vest, by horse and crest,
  Each warlike Lucumo.
There Cilnius of Arretium
  On his fleet roan was seen:
And Astur of the fourfold shield,

85   Girt with the brand none else may wield,
      Tolumnius with the belt of gold,
   And dark Verbenna from the hold
      By reedy Thrasymene.

   Fast by the royal standard,
90   O'erlooking all the war,
   Lars Porsena of Clusium
      Sat in his ivory car.
   By the right wheel rode Mamilius
      Prince of the Latian name;
95   And by the left false Sextus,
      That wrought the deed of shame.

   But when the face of Sextus
      Was seen among the foes,
   A yell that rent the firmament
100   From all the town arose.
   On the house-tops was no woman
      But spat towards him and hissed,
   No child but screamed out curses,
      And shook his little fist.

105   But the Consul's brow was sad,
      And the Consul's speech was low,
   And darkly looked he at the wall,
      And darkly at the foe.
   "Their van will be upon us
110   Before the bridge goes down;
   And if they once may win the bridge,
      What hope to save the town?"

   Then out spake brave Horatius,
      The Captain of the Gate:
115   "To every man upon this earth
      Death cometh soon or late.

And how can man die better
   Than facing fearful odds,
For the ashes of his fathers,
120   And the temples of his Gods?

*   *   *   *

"Hew down the bridge, Sir Consul,
   With all the speed ye may;
I, with two more to help me,
   Will hold the foe in play.
125 In yon straight path a thousand
   May well be stopped by three.
Now who will stand on either hand,
   And keep the bridge with me?"

Then out spake Spurius Lartius;
130   A Ramnian proud was he;
"Lo, I will stand at thy right hand,
   And keep the bridge with thee."
And out spake strong Herminius;
   Of Titian blood was he;
135 "I will abide on thy left side,
   And keep the bridge with thee."

"Horatius," quoth the Consul,
   "As thou sayest, so let it be."
And straight against that great array
   Forth went the dauntless Three.
140 For Romans in Rome's quarrel
   Spared neither land nor gold,
Nor son nor wife, nor limb nor life,
   In the brave days of old.

Then none was for a party,
145   Then all were for the State:
Then the great man helped the poor,
   And the poor man loved the great,

Then lands were fairly portioned,
  Then spoils were fairly sold;
150 The Romans were like brothers
  In the brave days of old.

Now Roman is to Roman
  More hateful than a foe,
And the Tribunes beard the high,
155   And the Fathers grind the low.
As we wax hot in faction,
  In battle we wax cold:
Wherefore men fight not as they fought
  In the brave days of old.

160 Now while the Three were tightening
  Their harness on their backs
The Consul was the foremost man
  To take in hand an axe:
And Fathers mixed with Commons,
165   Seized hatchet, bar and crow,
And smote upon the planks above,
  And loosed the props below.

Meanwhile the Tuscan army,
  Right glorious to behold,
170 Came flashing back the noonday light,
Rank behind rank, like surges bright
  Of a broad sea of gold.
Four hundred trumpets sounded
  A peal of warlike glee,
175 As that great host, with measured tread,
And spears advanced, and ensigns spread,
Rolled slowly towards the bridge's head,
  Where stood the dauntless Three.

The Three stood calm and silent,

180 And looked upon the foes,
   And a great shout of laughter
    From all the vanguard rose:
   And forth three chiefs came spurring
    Before that deep array;
185 To earth they sprang, their swords they drew,
   And lifted high their shields and flew
    To win the narrow way:

   Aunus from green Tifernum
    Lord of the Hill of Vines;
190 And Seius, whose eight hundred slaves
    Sicken in Ilva's mines;
   And Picus, long to Clusium
    Vassal in peace and war,
   Who led to fight his Umbrian powers
195 From that grey crag where, girt with towers
   The fortress of Nequinum lowers
    O'er the pale waves of Nar.

   Stout Lartius hurled down Aunus
    Into the stream beneath;
200 Herminius struck at Seius
    And clove him to the teeth;
   At Picus brave Horatius
    Darted one fiery thrust;
   And the proud Umbrian's gilded arms
205 Clashed in the bloody dust.

   Then Ocnus of Falerii
    Rushed on the Roman Three;
   And Lausulus of Urgo
    The rover of the sea;
210 And Aruns of Volsinium,
    Who slew the great wild boar,
   The great wild boar that had his den

Amidst the reeds of Cosa's fen,
And wasted fields and slaughtered men
215   Along Albinia's shore.

Herminius smote down Aruns;
    Lartius laid Ocnus low;
Right to the heart of Lausulus
    Horatius sent a blow.
220   "Lie there," he cried, "fell pirate!
    Nor more, aghast and pale,
From Ostia's walls the crowd shall mark
The track of thy destroying bark,
No more Campania's hinds shall fly
225   To woods and caverns when they spy
    Thy thrice accursed sail."

And now no song of laughter
    Was heard among the foes.
A wild and wrathful clamour
230   From all the vanguard rose.
Six spear lengths from the entrance
    Halted that deep array,
And for the space no man came forth
    To win the narrow way.

235   But hark! the cry is Astur;
    And lo! the ranks divide;
And the great Lord of Luna
    Comes with his stately stride.
Upon his ample shoulders
240   Clangs loud the fourfold shield
And in his hand he shakes the brand
    Which none but he can wield.

He smiled on those bold Romans
    A smile serene and high:

245 He eyed the flinching Tuscans
    And scorn was in his eye.
Quoth he, "The she-wolf's litter
    Stand savagely at bay;
But will ye dare to follow
250   If Astur clears the way?"

Then whirling up his broadsword
    With both hands to the height,
He rushed against Horatius
    And smote with all his might.
255 With shield and blade Horatius
    Right deftly turned the blow.
The blow, though turned, came yet too nigh;
It missed his helm, but gashed his thigh;
The Tuscans raised a joyful cry
260   To see the red blood flow.

He reeled, and on Herminius
    He leaned one breathing space;
Then, like a wild cat mad with wounds,
    Sprang right at Astur's face;
265 Through teeth, and skull, and helmet
    So fierce a thrust he sped,
The good sword stood a hand breadth out
Behind the Tuscan's head.

And the great Lord of Luna
270   Fell at that deadly stroke,
As falls on Mount Avernus
    A thunder-smitten oak.
Far o'er the crashing forest
    The giant arms lie spread;
275 And the pale augurs, muttering low,
    Gaze on the blasted head.

On Astur's throat Horatius
   Right firmly pressed his heel,
And thrice and four times tugged amain,
280   Ere he wrenched out the steel.
"And see," he cried, "the welcome
   Fair guests, that waits you here!"
What noble Lucumo comes next
   To taste our Roman cheer?"

285   But at his haughty challenge
    A sullen murmur ran,
Mingled with wrath, and shame, and dread,
   Along that glittering van.
There lacked not men of prowess,
290   Nor men of lordly race;
For all Etruria's noblest
   Were round the fatal place.

But all Etruria's noblest
   Felt their hearts sink to see
295   On earth the bloody corpses,
    In the path the dauntless Three:
And, for the ghastly entrance
   Where those bold Romans stood,
All shrank, like boys who unaware
300   Ranging the woods to start a hare,
Come to the mouth of the dark lair
   Where, growling low, a fierce old bear
    Lies amidst bones and blood.

Was none who would be foremost
305   To lead such dire attack:
But those behind cried "Forward!"
   And those before cried "Back!"
And backward now and forward
   Wavers the deep array;

310   And on the tossing sea of steel,
      To and fro the standards reel;
      And the victorious trumpet-peal
        Dies fitfully away.

315   Yet one man for one moment
        Stood out before the crowd;
      Well known was he to all the Three,
        And they gave him greeting loud,
      "Now welcome, welcome, Sextus!
320   Now welcome to thy home!
      Why dost thou stay, and turn away?
      Here lies the road to Rome."

      Thrice looked he at the city,
        Thrice looked he at the dead;
325   And thrice came on in fury,
        And thrice turned back in dread:
      And, white with fear and hatred,
        Scowled at the narrow way,
      Where, wallowing in the pool of blood,
330   The bravest Tuscans lay.

      But meanwhile axe and lever
        Have manfully been plied;
      And now the bridge hangs tottering
        Above the boiling tide.
335   "Come back, come back, Horatius!"
        Loud cried the Fathers all.
      "Back, Lartius! back, Herminius!
        Back, ere the ruin fall!"

      Back darted Spurius Lartius;
340   Herminius darted back:
      And, as they passed, beneath their feet,
        They felt the timbers crack.

But when they turned their faces,
   And on the farther shore
345 Saw brave Horatius stand alone,
   They would have crossed once more.

But with a crash like thunder
   Fell every loosened beam,
And, like a dam, the mighty wreck
350   Lay right athwart the stream.
And a long shout of triumph
   Rose from the walls of Rome,
As to the highest turret-tops
   Was splashed the yellow foam.

355 And, like a horse unbroken
   When first he feels the rein,
The furious river struggled hard,
   And tossed his tawny mane,
And burst the curb and bounded,
360   Rejoicing to be free,
And whirling down, in fierce career,
Battlement, and plank, and pier,
   Rushed headlong to the sea.

Alone stood brave Horatius,
365   But constant still in mind;
Thrice thirty thousand foes before,
   And the broad flood behind.
"Down with him!" cried false Sextus,
   With a smile on his pale face.
370 "Now yield thee," cried Lars Porsena,
   "Now yield thee to our grace."

Round turned he, as not deigning
   Those craven ranks to see;
Nought spake he to Lars Porsena,
375   To Sextus nought spake he;

But he saw on Palatinus
   The white porch of his home;
And he spake to the noble river
   That rolls by the towers of Rome.

380 "O Tiber! Father Tiber!
   To whom the Romans pray,
A Roman's life, a Roman's arms,
   Take thou in charge today!"
So spake he, and speaking sheathed
385   The good sword by his side,
And with the harness on his back
   Plunged headlong in the tide.

No sound of joy or sorrow
   Was heard from either bank;
390 But friends and foes in dumb surprise
With parted lips and straining eyes,
   Stood gazing where he sank;
And when above the surges
   They saw his crest appear,
395 All Rome sent forth a rapturous cry,
And even the ranks of Tuscany
   Could scarce forbear a cheer.

But fiercely ran the current
   Swollen high with months of rain:
400 And fast his blood was flowing;
   And he was sore in pain.
And heavy with his armour,
   And spent with changing blows;
And oft they thought him sinking,
405   But still again he rose.

Never, I ween, did swimmer,
   In such an evil case,
Struggle through such a raging flood

Safe to the landing-place;
410   But his limbs were borne up bravely
By the brave heart within,
And our good Father Tiber
Bore bravely up his chin.

"Curse on him!" quoth false Sextus;
415   "Will not the villain drown?
But for this stay, ere close of day
We should have sacked the town!"
"Heaven help him!" quoth Lars Porsena,
"And bring him safe to shore;
420   For such a gallant feat of arms
Was never seen before."

And now he feels the bottom,
Now on dry earth he stands;
Now round him throng the Fathers
425   To press his gory hands;
And now, with shouts and clapping,
And noise of weeping loud,
He enters through the River Gate,
Borne by the joyous crowd.

430   They gave him of the corn-land,
That was of public right,
As much as two strong oxen
Could plough from morn to night;
And they made a molten image,
435   And set it up on high,
And there it stands unto this day
To witness if I lie.

It stands in the Comitium,
Plain for all folk to see;
Horatius in his harness,

440   Halting upon one knee:
And underneath is written
In letters all of gold,
How valiantly he kept the bridge
In the brave days of old.

*   *   *   *

445 When the goodman mends his armour,
And trims his helmet's plume;
And when the goodwife's shuttle merrily
Goes flashing through the loom;
With weeping and with laughter
450   Still is the story told,
How well Horatius kept the bridge
In the brave days of old.

ENJOYING THE POEM

One does not need to know much of Roman history or politics to enjoy this poem and to admire the bravery of Horatius and his friends. Actually, the incident of Horatius at the Bridge is supposed to have occurred shortly after the Romans, disgusted with the dishonourable acts of their royal family (of whom "false Sextus" was a member), drove the family into exile and established a republic. Sextus and other members of the family sought aid from enemies of the little Roman state to regain their power, but were ultimately defeated.

At this time the Roman people were divided into to quite definite social and political classes, the common people and the aristocrats. Representatives in the Senate of the common people were the Tribunes; those of the aristocrats were the Fathers. Head of the government was the Consul.

1. The outstanding characteristic of Horatius, as Macaulay portrays him, is his courage, but other qualities of character are also indicated. What are some of these?

2. The characters of two other men, Lars Porsena and Sextus, are also sketched in a few swift pen-strokes. What kind of men were they?

3. The story-teller in this poem is obviously a Roman who lived much later than did Horatius. What contrast does he make between his own time and that of Horatius?

4. Horatius was rewarded for his valorous fight by a grant of public land. Was this his only or most important reward?

5. Peoples' imaginations have always been fired by tales of a few warriors standing off an overwhelming foe. Can you find examples of other comparable battles in ancient or modern history? Who said, "Never in the field of human conflict was so much owed by so many to so few"?

🦋 FOR FURTHER READING: ADVENTURES IN OTHER TIMES

MORRIS BISHOP, *Champlain*
A biography of the famous French Explorer and his attempts to found French colonies in the new world.

MARY JANE CARR, *Young Mac of Fort Vancouver*
A thirteen-year-old Scotch-Indian lad travels down the Columbia River with a company of French fur traders.

WILLA CATHER, *Shadows on the Rock*
The rock is Quebec, and this is the story of a young girl who lived there in the romantic days of Frontenac.

CHARLES CLAY, *Young Voyageur*
The early days of the fur trade—hostile Indians, forest fires, muskeg, and rapids are vividly described.

RALPH CONNOR, *Glengarry School Days*
Spelling bees, oral examinations, shinny, and the old swimming hole are all a part of the school life in the pioneer settlement of Glengarry.

ALLAN DWIGHT, *Drums in the Forest*
Denis de Lornay's encounters with the Indians, coureurs-de-bois and many of his scheming fellow-countrymen.

HERBERT EVANS, *North to the Unknown*
The story of David Thompson, the London charity boy, who became a famous Canadian explorer.

DONALD G. FRENCH, *Famous Canadian Stories*
A veritable treasure house on early inhabitants, discoverers, explorers, settlements, heroic exploits, missions, statesmen, authors, and cities.

GREY OWL, *Men of the Last Frontier*
A picture of the life and privations of the hunters and trappers in the North-West.

John F. Hayes, *Buckskin Colonist*
A Selkirk settler passes from boyhood to manhood in the troubled days of the dispute between the Hudson's Bay Company and the North-West Company.

John F. Hayes, *Treason at York*
"Muddy York" was a dangerous place for an adventurous teen-ager to live during the War of 1812.

E. Pauline Johnson, *Legends of Vancouver*
Legends told to the author by Chief Joe Capilano of Vancouver.

Stephen Leacock, *Sunshine Sketches of a Little Town*
Life, told with humour and irony, in a little Ontario town before the days of World War I.

Kathrene Pinkerton, *Adventure North*
When the Jackman family move to the wilderness of northern Ontario and start a fur farm, there is plenty of work for Ann and Philip.

A. M. Stephen, *Vérendrye*
A stirring narrative poem celebrating the exploits of La Vérendrye, who added the empire of the West to the domain of the king of France.

Virginia C. Watson, *Flags over Quebec*
Two 'teen-age boys who have shared many an adventure are separated and fight under the rivals Wolfe and Montcalm.

CANADIAN HISTORY AND BIOGRAPHY

George W. Brown, Eleanor Harman, and Marsh Jeanneret, *The Story of Canada*

Donalda Dickie, *The Great Adventure*

L. J. Henry, *Canadians: A Book of Biographies*

Richard S. Lambert, *The Adventure of Canadian Painting*

Mary F. Moore, *Canadian Magic*

Mabel Burns McKinley, *Famous Men and Women of Canada*

Frances Allen Ross, *The Land and People of Canada*

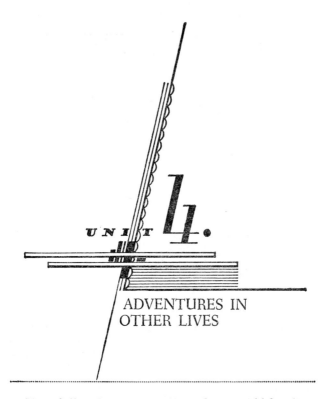

UNIT 4.

ADVENTURES IN
OTHER LIVES

How dull and uninteresting our lives would be if we could not make explorations among other lives. Our ways of living, the things we have that make life pleasant, in fact, our own individual personalities have been fashioned largely out of the adventures and the experiences of others. We depend on the farmers who grow our food, the workers who make our automobiles, the doctors who keep us healthy, the teachers who help us to gain knowledge. And in the past the scientists, the explorers, the statesmen, the writers, and all kinds of persons have helped to set the patterns that we find in ourselves and our times. As we seek new adventures exploring other lives we will find courage, imagination, **and common sense** in every real personality.

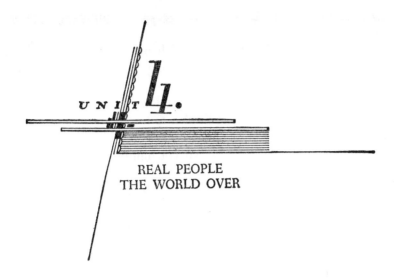

UNIT 4.

REAL PEOPLE
THE WORLD OVER

THE BALLAD OF EAST AND WEST

RUDYARD KIPLING

Oh, East is East, and West is West, and never the twain shall
meet,
Till Earth and Sky stand presently at God's great Judgment
Seat;
But there is neither East nor West, Border, nor Breed, nor Birth,
When two strong men stand face to face, though they come
from the ends of the earth!

5 Kamal is out with twenty men to raise the Border side,
And he has lifted the Colonel's mare that is the Colonel's pride.
He has lifted her out of the stable door between the dawn and
the day,
And turned the calkins upon her feet, and ridden her far away.
Then up and spoke the Colonel's son that led a troop of the
Guides:
10 "Is there never a man of all my men can say where Kamal
hides?"

6. LIFTED—Stolen.
8. CALKINS—Projection on horseshoes to keep the horse from slipping.

Then up and spoke Mohammed Khan, the son of the Ressaldar;
"If ye know the track of the morning mist, ye know where his
    pickets are.
"At dusk he harries the Abazai—at dawn he is unto Bonair,
"But he must go by Fort Bukloh to his own place to fare,
15 "So if ye gallop to Fort Bukloh as fast as a bird can fly,
"By the favour of God ye may cut him off ere he win to the
    Tongue of Jagai.
"But if he be past the Tongue of Jagai, right swiftly turn ye
    then,
"For the length and breadth of that grisly plain is sown with
    Kamal's men.
"There is rock to the left, and rock to the right, and low lean
    thorn between,
20 "And ye may hear a breech-bolt snick where never a man is
    seen."
The Colonel's son has taken a horse, and a raw rough dun
    was he,
With the mouth of a bell and the heart of Hell and the head
    of a gallows-tree.
The Colonel's son to the Fort has won, they bid him stay to
    eat—
Who rides at the tail of a Border thief, he sits not long at his
    meat.
25 He's up and away from Fort Bukloh as fast as he can fly,
Till he was aware of his father's mare in the gut of the Tongue
    of Jagai,
Till he was aware of his father's mare with Kamal upon her
    back,
And when he could spy the white of her eye, he made the
    pistol crack.

'11. MOHAMMED KHAN—*Khan* is a title used in India much as we use "Esquire."
  11. RESSALDAR—The ressaldar was the commander of a troop of native horsemen.
  20. BREECH-BOLT—The breech is that part of a gun immediately behind the
barrel.
  21. DUN—Dull or greyish-brown in colour.
  22. THE MOUTH OF A BELL—With a large mouth.
  26. GUT—A narrow pass.

He has fired once, he has fired twice, but the whistling ball
    went wide.

30 "Ye shoot like a soldier," Kamal said. "Show now if ye can
    ride!"

It's up and over the Tongue of Jagai, as blown dust-devils go,

The dun he fled like a stag of ten, but the mare like a barren
    doe.

The dun he leaned against the bit and slugged his head above,

But the red mare played with the snaffle-bars as a maiden plays
    with a glove.

35 There was rock to the left, and rock to the right, and low lean
    thorn between,

And thrice he heard a breech-bolt snick tho' never a man was
    seen.

They have ridden the low moon out of the sky, their hoofs
    drum up the dawn,

The dun he went like a wounded bull, but the mare like a
    new-roused fawn.

The dun he fell at a water-course—in a woeful heap fell he,

40 And Kamal has turned the red mare back, and pulled the
    rider free.

He has knocked the pistol out of his hand—small room was
    there to strive,

"'Twas only by favour of mine," quoth he, "ye rode so long
    alive:

"There was not a rock for twenty mile, there was not a clump
    of tree,

"But covered a man of my own men with his rifle cocked on his
    knee.

45 "If I had raised my bridle-hand, as I have held it low,

"The little jackals that flee so fast were feasting all in a row;

"If I had bowed my head on my breast, as I have held it high,

"The kite that whistles above us now were gorged till she could
    not fly."

Lightly answered the Colonel's son: "Do good to bird and beast,

34. SNAFFLE-BARS—The bit.

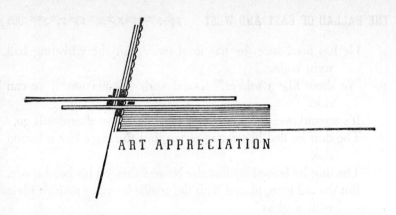

ART APPRECIATION

HEINA ❦ EMILY CARR

Startling and unusual in its subject-matter, this painting follows so many of the principles of artistic composition that it might almost have been painted as an exercise in art appreciation. Note the rhythm in the repetition of the vertical lines of the totem poles, the horizontal lines of the canoes, and the curving lines in the cliffs behind the village. Effective use is also made of contrast, both in the opposition of vertical and horizontal lines, and in the contrast of the brilliant colours of the sand in front of the lodges and the sombre shades of the trees and cliffs. Note also the colour harmonies in the blues, greens, and purples in the foreground, which are repeated in the background. Balance and dominance are also evident in the arrangement of the totem poles which dominate the whole composition.

HEINA

Emily Carr

Courtesy of The National Gallery of Canada, Ottawa

EMILY CARR

[1871-1945]

Emily Carr was a brilliant and eccentric painter and writer who raised dogs and ran a boarding house to make a living, who constantly quarrelled with people but made friends with dogs, a white rat, a peacock, and a monkey, and who died believing that as an artist she was a failure. Yet to-day her paintings have been shown in galleries in the great cities of England, the United States, and Canada, and her fame as a writer is steadily growing. Born in Victoria, B.C., she lived there all her life, with the exception of two trips she made to Europe to study painting and one to San Francisco for the same purpose. Not until she was fifty-six did recognition first come for her canvases, and only four years before her death did her writing receive acclaim, when she won the Governor-General's Award for her first book, KLEE WYCK.

50 "But count who come for the broken meats before thou
      makest a feast.

"If there should follow a thousand swords to carry my bones
      away,

"Belike the price of a jackal's meal were more than a thief could
      pay.

"They will feed their horse on the standing crop, their men
      on the garnered grain,

"The thatch of the byres will serve their fires when all the cattle
      are slain.

55 "But if thou thinkest the price be fair,—thy brethren wait to sup,

"The hound is kin to the jackal-spawn,—howl, dog, and call
      them up!

"And if thou thinkest the price be high, in steer and gear and
      stack,

"Give me my father's mare again, and I'll fight my own way
      back!"

Kamal has gripped him by the hand and set him upon his feet.

60 "No talk shall be of dogs," said he, "when wolf and grey wolf
      meet.

"May I eat dirt if thou has hurt of me in deed or breath;

"What dam of lances brought thee forth to jest at the dawn
      with Death?"

Lightly answered the Colonel's son: "I hold by the blood of
      my clan:

"Take up the mare for my father's gift—by God, she has carried
      a man!"

65 The red mare ran to the Colonel's son, and nuzzled against his
      breast;

"We be two strong men," said Kamal then, "but she loveth
      the younger best.

"So she shall go with a lifter's dower, my turquoise-studded
      rein,

"My 'broidered saddle and saddle-cloth, and silver stirrups
      twain."

54. BYRES—Stables.
62. DAM OF LANCES—A mother of sons who are as sharp and strong as lances.

The Colonel's son a pistol drew and held it muzzle-end,

70 "Ye have taken the one from a foe," said he; "will ye take the
    mate from a friend?"

"A gift for a gift," said Kamal straight; "a limb for the risk of
    a limb.

"Thy father has sent his son to me, I'll send my son to him!"

With that he whistled his only son, that dropped from a moun-
    tain-crest—

He trod the ling like a buck in spring, and he looked like a
    lance in rest.

75 "Now here is thy master," Kamal said, "who leads a troop of
    the Guides,

"And thou must ride at his left side as shield on shoulder rides:

"Till Death or I cut loose the tie, at camp and board and bed,

"Thy life is his—thy fate it is to guard him with thy head.

"So thou must eat the White Queen's meat, and all her foes are
    thine,

80 "And thou must harry thy father's hold for the peace of the
    Borderline,

"And thou must make a trooper tough and hack thy way to
    power—

"Belike they will raise thee to Ressaldar when I am hanged in
    Peshawur."

They have looked each other between the eyes, and there they
    have found no fault,

They have taken the Oath of the Brother-in-Blood on leavened
    bread and salt:

85 They have taken the Oath of the Brother-in-Blood on fire and
    fresh-cut sod,

On the hilt and the haft of the Khyber knife, and the Wond-
    rous Names of God.

The Colonel's son he rides the mare and Kamal's boy the dun,

And two have come back to Fort Bukloh where there went
    forth but one.

79. THE WHITE QUEEN—Queen Victoria.

86. KHYBER—The Kyhber Hills are on the boundary between India and Af-
ghanistan.

And when they drew to the Quarter Guard, full twenty swords
    flew clear—
90 There was not a man but carried his feud with the blood of
    the mountaineer.
"Ha' done! ha' done!" cried the Colonel's son. "Put up the steel
    at your sides!
"Last night ye had struck at a Border thief—to-night 'tis a man
    of the Guides!"

Oh, East is East, and West is West, and never the twain shall
    meet,
Till Earth and Sky stand presently at God's great Judgment
    Seat;
95 But there is neither East nor West, Border, nor Breed, nor Birth,
When two strong men stand face to face, tho' they come from
    the ends of the earth!

89. QUARTER-GUARD—The guard in charge of the soldiers' quarters.

ENJOYING THE POEM

In this poem we have the story of two bold and courageous men to whom fear is unknown. The setting of the story is in India in the days when the control of the British was being challenged by natives who resented the interference of Europeans. Kamal was one of these. His theft of the Colonel's mare was an act of defiance against the authority of the British. The Colonel's son took up the challenge implied in this defiance. This led to the exciting chase described in this narrative. The outcome of the story is not what we should expect, for when Kamal and the Colonel's son recognize the qualities of character possessed by each other, they forget the differences that exist between them and treat each other as equals.

1. What evidence is there to indicate at what period in history this story is supposed to have taken place?

2. What are the chief characteristics possessed by Kamal? by the Colonel's son?

3. Discuss what the poet means when he says:
    "Oh, East is East, and West is West, and never the twain
        shall meet."

4. How did Kamal show his generosity toward the Colonel's son? In what way was it repaid? Tell your classmates of any other example of such generosity that you have seen or read about.

JOHN PHILIP SOUSA* 🎵

KATHERINE LITTLE BAKELESS

WHEN John Philip Sousa[1] was growing up in Washington, the nation's capital, where he was born, he heard a great deal of band music. It was a thrilling time to hear bands, and an unusually thrilling place to hear them, because it was during the Civil War. Band music is always most exciting when patriotic feelings are stirred up, and they are most stirred up in the time of war. Young John Philip was, like all boys, moved in the marrow of his bones by band music. Good or bad, he loved it all.

His own father, Antonio, played trombone in the Marine Band, and since John (or Philip, as his father called him) was exceedingly fond of his father and respected him highly, this fact no doubt had something to do with the lad's preferences. We are all apt to think that what our father does is extra good. Still, there is hardly a boy

---

*Reprinted from *Story-Lives of American Composers* by Katherine Little Bakeless. Copyright 1941 by J. B. Lippincott Company.

[1] SOUSA—Pronounced sōō'zả.

in the whole world, or a girl either, who is not fascinated when a band goes marching up the street. . . .

However, his own music lessons got off to a rather bad start. It came about in this way: An old friend of his father's, also a Spanish gentleman, was in the habit of calling frequently upon the Sousas. One evening, during his visit, Philip persisted in rolling a baseball around the room, disturbing the conversation of the grown-ups. The gentleman, who was a retired orchestra player, said that perhaps a few lessons in solfeggio² might be good for the boy. He knew instrumental music, but alas, he had an atrocious voice for singing. At Philip's first lesson with this gentleman, he could distinguish no difference in the old man's tones. Every tone he tried to sing sounded like every other tone. Philip said the only difference was that "when he was calm he squawked; when excited, he squeaked." At the first lesson, the gentleman wanted Philip to sing the syllables of the scale after him.

"*Do*," squawked the would-be voice teacher.

"*Do*," squawked Philip in imitation.

"No, no, sing *Do*," and this time he squeaked.

"*Do*," squeaked Philip, trying his best to imitate the very sound he had heard.

No wonder lessons like these left the boy worn out. He would have preferred to be out playing baseball.

It was this same gentleman's son who opened a conservatory of music in the neighbourhood where Philip lived. When the boy was seven, he was enrolled among the sixty pupils, and began the study of violin. There were to be more stormy times with this teacher, the son of the old squeaker.

Philip overheard Professor Esputa (the violin teacher) tell Mr. Sousa that even if Philip didn't learn anything it would at least keep him off the streets. Philip was piqued³ by this remark. As a result, he never opened his mouth to volunteer any answers for the first three years he was in Mr. Esputa's classes. The

---

² SOLFEGGIO (sŏl-fĕj'ō)—The arrangement or singing of tones in the scale by the names *do*, *re*, *mi*, and so on.

³ PIQUED (pēkt)—Offended.

teacher could not tell whether the boy was learning anything or not. But all this time, since Philip was very eager to learn music, he was drinking it all in. Finally, at the end of three years the first examinations were held.

Five medals were offered by the school. Imagine everyone's surprise when Philip won not one medal, but all the five medals! Mr. Esputa was in a quandary. He told Mr. Sousa that he could not possibly give all the prizes to his son, for fear of what the other pupils would say. Mr. Sousa, a sensible man, laughed and said he was glad enough to know that his son had won them, but that it would not make him any smarter to *have* them, and the teacher might make better use of the medals if he could. Esputa gave three to Philip and two to other pupils. Though John Philip Sousa was to have many great honours conferred upon him throughout his life, and though medals were awarded to him by kings, he always kept the three little golden lyres given to him by Mr. Esputa. They reminded him always, he said, how he had fooled everyone by his silence, and impressed upon him that "silence is truly golden." . . .

By the time he was thirteen John Philip Sousa had organized his own quadrille band. Except for himself, the players were grown men. He played first violin himself, and the band had a second violin, viola, contra-bass, clarinet, cornet, trombone, and drum. They played for dances, and Philip began to attract notice as a violinist. . . .

It was about that time that Philip heard some music which was an experience he never forgot. He heard a most excellent musician, Theodore Thomas, play "Traumerei" on the violin. It was to him the most beautiful music and the most beautiful playing he had ever heard. For the first time the idea struck him that the most wonderful thing of all would be to write music—music to lull and charm the listener. . . .

After writing a musical comedy and conducting it on tour, there came finally the position in which Sousa made the reputation for which he is known today. He became leader of the Marine Band; leader of the band in which he had played and studied as a boy.

He must then have been thankful that his father interfered and prevented him from running off with the circus.

His first care was to build up the music-library for the Band. There was no new music in it. Everything was out of date and badly arranged for instruments, and he found nothing good about it. The first thing he did was to get good music; then he drilled and rehearsed his men constantly.

The Marine Band is the official band of the President of the United States. When an orchestra is needed at receptions and functions at the White House, the Marine Band is the orchestra. When there are parades, or when concerts are given at the capital, it is the Marine Band which plays. At special functions when ambassadors of foreign countries are present, and courtesy requires a delicate recognition, the Marine Band must be ready with the national airs of the country represented. Sousa was always ready with his special music. He collected the national airs of all lands for their music-library. His published collection includes patriotic and typical airs, not only of the great countries, but also of the small faraway places such as Samoa, Lapland, Abyssinia, and even the songs of many tribes of American Indians. The melodies of the Apache, Cherokee, Chippewa, Dakota, Eskimo, Iowa, Iroquois, and Vancouver tribes appear in Sousa's book of national airs, all harmonized so that the Band could play them. Perhaps the Indians themselves might not recognize their wild tunes tamed to our harmonic rule, but at any rate Sousa went to the trouble of collecting them from ethnologists [4] and people who had lived and travelled among the Indians.

For years, at the White House receptions, when cabinet ministers, ambassadors, generals, and admirals were assembled in the East Room to greet the President, it had been the custom for the band to play "Hail to the Chief" to announce the entrance of the President himself. At one of these affairs, President Arthur left his guests and went out in the corridor for a word with Sousa.

[4] ETHNOLOGISTS (ĕth-nŏl'ô-jĭsts)—Scientists who study the origin and peculiarities of the different races.

"What piece did you play when we went in to dinner?" inquired the President. Sousa replied,

" 'Hail to the Chief,' Mr. President."

"Do you consider it a suitable air?"

"No, sir," answered Sousa, "it was selected long ago on account of its name, and not on account of its character. It is a boat song, and lacks modern military character either for a reception or a parade."

"Then change it!" ordered the President.

Sausa then composed the "Presidential Polonaise"[5] for indoor affairs at the White House, and the "Semper Fidelis[6] March" for outdoor reviews.

Under the auspices of a newspaper, the *Washington Post,* prizes and medals were offered one summer for the best essays written by pupils in the different grades of the public schools. A great day was planned in June, and part of the exercises was to be a programme of music by the Marine Band. One of the proprietors of the newspaper asked Sousa to compose a march for the contest and to play it for the first time on the day the awards were to be made. For this occasion, Sousa composed and played the "Washington Post March," which became so popular that it was played all over the world. On the day when it was first played, all the children of Washington must have been there to hear it. The trees around the bandstand were filled with boys who had climbed up to be near the music. At the first strains of the "Washington Post March," the high school cadets came marching up the street amid cheers of all the assembled children. It was a great day for Washington's children. Later on, Sausa also wrote "High School Cadets March." Once on tour, when he used to receive all kinds of requests to play certain favourites, he was much amused to have a note handed to him asking for the "Ice Cold Cadets!"

As an example of how the "Washington Post March" spread over the world, there is the story about the Army major who, years afterwards, was walking in the jungle of Borneo. Suddenly he

---

[5] Polonaise (pō-lō-nāz')—A stately march.
[6] Semper Fidelis (sĕm'pēr fĭ-dā'lĭs)—Always faithful.

heard sounds of a violin in the forest. It was playing the "Washington Post March." He followed up the sound and came upon a native boy scraping away on his fiddle with a sheet of music pinned up before him on a tree.

Dancing masters seized upon this tune for launching a new dance. It was called the "two-step;" but when Sousa later went to Europe he discovered that in England and in Germany the dance itself was called the "Washington Post."

After John Philip Sousa had drilled the Band into an organization of which he was very proud, and after he was satisfied with its repertoire [7] of good band music, he wanted to take the band on tour so that it might play to people outside of Washington. A patriotic celebration in the town of Fayetteville, North Carolina, commemorated the so-called Mecklenburg Declaration of Independence. The Marine Band was sent to take part in the ceremonies, as the President was unable to be present to deliver a speech. A committee of prominent citizens selected a chairman who discussed with Sousa the musical programme for the occasion. Sousa said:

"Well, we will open with 'The Star-Spangled Banner'."

"Quite right," agred the chairman.

"Then we will play the 'Coronation March' from the opera, *The Prophet,* by Meyerbeer. We will follow with the 'Overture' from *William Tell;* 'On the Blue Danube;' excerpts from *Aida;* and then, 'My Country 'Tis of Thee'."

"That's all very fine," said the Southerner, "but I should like to remind you that there's a tune down here that we love. I don't know whether your band plays it, but we surely would like to hear it."

"What is it?" Sousa's voice sounded rather unconcerned and discouraging.

"It is called 'Dixie'."

"I know the tune," said the bandmaster. Then he added, "I'll think it over, whether we can make use of it or not. You know we are a very artistic organization and must always consider our programmes very seriously."

---

[7] REPERTOIRE (rĕp'ĕr-twär)—A list of pieces, parts, and the like, which a company has thoroughly rehearsed and is prepared to perform.

"Yes, yes," drawled the poor chairman, "but if you can tuck it in, I know the people would love to hear it. Some of them haven't heard it since the Surrender."

Sousa, always keenly aware of the value of a dramatic moment, saw his opportunity. He said no musician would think of going South without "Dixie" in his repertoire.

At the ceremonies people flocked in from the mountains and farms until the town was crowded. They slept in covered waggons, and Sousa even saw some boys asleep in drygoods boxes, under stoops, and on benches. It was a big time in Fayetteville.

The Governor made the first speech, after which Sousa's band stood up and played the national anthem. It was politely and quietly received by a crowd in good behaviour. Then the Chairman made a speech to introduce the Senator who was the "idol of the State." As the Chairman sat down and before the Senator began his speech, Sousa quickly signalled to his men, and they charged right into "Dixie." He said it was like an electric shock. A great yell began in the grandstand and "went booming down the street, through the surging crowd." Hats went flying. Old men cried. Women hugged each other, and for fifteen minutes the ceremonies were held up.

During the week the band was in Fayetteville, their programmes were always something like this: "Overture," *William Tell*; Song, "Dixie;" Waltz, "Blue Danube;" Song, "Dixie;" Airs from *Faust*; Song, "Dixie;" Medley, Favourite Tunes; Song, "Dixie."

"And the encore to every one of those numbers," said Sousa, "was —'Dixie'." Yet "Dixie" had been written by a Northerner, Dan Emmett, and was first sung in a minstrel show in New York during the Civil War. . . .

During a long and busy life, Sousa wrote over a hundred marches, besides waltzes, fantasias, operas, suites, songs, as well as books, including an interesting story of his life, and a story for children called *Pipetown Sandy*. But it is for his marches that he is chiefly remembered, and he seemed to be able to write a march for any occasion. With his famous band, he toured the United States many times. Through these tours he became the most beloved and most popular of American musicians. It was an "event" when Sousa came to town. Sometimes the mayors proclaimed holidays in honour of his visits, and flags were flown. He made several tours of Europe with his band, and once took them around the world.

While in England for the first time, Sousa and the band were asked to play for His Majesty, King Edward VII, the grandfather of King George VI. The King wished it to be a surprise perform-ance for the occasion of the Queen's birthday. It was kept secret even from the men in the band. They had no idea they were to play for royalty until they had taken a train ride to Sandringham, one of the King's homes in the country. On his programme that eve-ning, Sousa played in addition to several of his own marches, his collection and arrangement of hymns of the American churches, and also plantation songs and dances. The King asked for seven encores! Then he presented Sousa with the medal of the Victorian Order.

A little brass-band journal published in England printed an article saying that Sousa was as much entitled to the name of "March King" as Johann Strauss was to the title of "Waltz King."

As the vessel steamed out of the harbour on Sousa's return from his first trip abroad, he paced the deck thinking of all the things he had to attend to when he reached New York. Suddenly inside his brain he felt the rhythmic beat of a band playing. A melody took shape and kept on playing within him during the whole voyage home. He could not get it out of his head, he was completely pos-sessed by it. Upon reaching home he wrote down the imaginary band piece. He never changed a note from the way he had heard it inside his head, day after day, while crossing the ocean. It was the most popular march he ever wrote, "The Stars and Stripes For-ever." It attained the status of a national march. A Frenchwoman once told Sousa that the march "sounded to her like the American eagle shooting arrows into the Aurora Borealis." [8]

By the second time the Sousa band went to England, the leader had written a complimentary march for His Majesty, which he called "Imperial Edward." The band played for the King at Wind-

[8] AURORA BOREALIS (ô-rō′rȧ bō-rē-ā′lĭs)—The Northern Lights.

sor Castle this time, and Sousa was told that when the children heard he was coming, they prepared to play their own concert of Sousa band records on the gramophone in the nursery. They were not permitted to attend the real concert in the great hall in the evening. One of those children is now the King of England.

On that evening Sousa was informed that the King was very anxious to hear the American national anthem at the close of the programme. Therefore Sousa had instructed his men that our anthem was to be played, and that, at the end of it, they were immediately and without a break to go into "God Save the King," beginning very, very softly and make one long, great crescendo to the end. The programme came to a close, and after the applause, there came a fitting silence. Then Sousa brought his men to a standing position. The signal was given. As the soaring phrase of "The Star-Spangled Banner" sounded forth in the great hall of Windsor Castle, the King arose and stood at attention. The audience arose with him. At the end of the phrase . . . "and the home of the brave" the band drew out the long notes, *diminuendo*. Then so quietly that it could scarcely be heard, the very notes changed into the opening of the British anthem, "God Save the King," which is to Americans, "My Country 'Tis of Thee." Sousa was facing the King and saw his countenance change. As the music swelled in volume, it seemed to Sousa that the King was thinking: "These aliens are asking God to protect me and my country." Sousa felt that "in the splendour and solemnity of the moment he seemed to be glorified." Having been the band leader for five presidents of the United States, Sousa felt very sure that a great position glorifies a man, that the grave responsibilities of high office lift a man even above his own average.

The story of another concert given in England shows the ability of the bandsmen. They had given a concert at the Shakespeare Memorial Theatre at Stratford-on-Avon soon after their arrival in the country on one of the tours, and at the last minute the Countess of Warwick asked them to play for her guests at Warwick Castle nearby. But as they were completely booked up she suggested that they give her a midnight concert. It turned out to be a stormy, wild night of wind and rain. Finally the band arrived in its several automobiles, but the car which contained all the music went skidding down a hill completely out of control. The music never arrived until the concert was over. The band had played everything from memory.

Although nearly everyone came to know what Sousa looked like, the famous band leader once went into a bank in Buffalo and was not at first recognized. The band had been playing there for a week, and the band's manager, having received a cheque for several thousand dollars, went with Sousa to the bank to cash the cheque. The cashier said to Sousa: "You'll have to be identified." Thereupon the bandmaster turned his back to the cashier. He raised his arms and started to conduct an invisible band, while whistling "The Stars and Stripes Forever." The clerks burst out laughing and applauding. One of them whispered to the cashier, and the cheque was cashed!

In the spring when he was sixty-two years old, he received word from his friend, John Alden Carpenter, another American composer, that the band at the Naval Station needed help. Would he come? He went, of course. The result was that he joined the Navy as a lieutenant in charge of the music. He formed a band battalion of 350 men with its commander, musical director, and surgeon, and then he organized bands for each regiment at the Naval Station. He was able to send bands to ships or stations whenever and wherever they were wanted. His own band played in Red Cross drives and Liberty Loan drives during World War I and raised millions of dollars.

When he was a young man leading the Marine Band, Sousa already wore a heavy beard. He thought it made him look foreign. American musicians did not have much chance in those days. Americans thought only foreigners could have musical ability, and many American musicians tried to look like foreigners. Sousa really thought his beard had helped his career. As he grew older, judging from his pictures, the beard disappeared altogether. Sousa used to say that his beard won the war. He explained this by adding that when the Kaiser heard that he had shaved off his beard, he quit, declaring that it was useless to fight a people who would make such sacrifices! But the real reason was probably his age. When he joined the Navy at sixty-two, there was a rule that no one over forty-seven could be accepted. But, there was just one Sousa, and the Navy needed him. Perhaps he thought that if he removed his beard, he would look younger than forty-seven!

During his long experience of having his own band, Sousa saw the numbers of American musicians increase more and more. When he assumed the direction of the Marine Band as a young man, there were not more than half a dozen native Americans in the band. Twelve years later, when he organized his own band, he tried to have them all Americans. If the best players of their respective instruments were foreign-born, he used them, but as time went on, most of his bandsmen were Americans. He was very pleased when some of his early bandsmen sent their sons to play under him.

Sousa was very jolly and humorous. He was a genial host and hated more than anything to have to dine alone. His personality was magnetic; people were attracted to him. Though he could be stern and strict when directing, his men were very fond of him. The band had a spirit of comradeship. When the band numbered eighty and sometimes a hundred men, they had their own ball teams and played games for their recreation. . . .

Sousa did not like the violent tone of the Helicon tuba which was at first in use in the Marine Band. It was a large instrument which wound round the player's body. The player had to pull it down over his head. He suggested to an instrument-maker a tuba with a large-sized upright bell, so that the sound would, as he said, "diffuse over the entire band like the frosting on a cake." The instrument was made, and it is still used, and called the Sousaphone. . . .

Sousa did not believe that there is any nationalism in music. He felt that composers who have been called writers of national music were merely interpreting themselves and their own reaction to life. Perhaps he was right. A man in Norway, for instance, would naturally have different feelings about a snowy landscape from the man who lived in a jungle on the equator. These two men would also feel very differently about airplanes. Sousa said, "You cannot bound a melody as you would a country. Music may have many dialects, but its language is universal." In his many travels he found that people's emotional reactions were the same regardless of geography. He said that when he played humorous music, the laughs always came in the same spots, whether he was playing to an audience in Spain or in a town in North Dakota.

He had a happy, busy life, and he wrote happy, busy music. He did not like to play dark, sad music, but if the occasion demanded, he could furnish it. He thought that perhaps his success was due largely to the fact that he and his band "played chiefly sunshine music." For, as Sousa said, "that the world needs always."

DISCUSSING THE SELECTION

When John Philip Sousa began the study of music there were relatively few bands in America. Today, in contrast, there is hardly a community without at least one marching band. Especially in our schools has the band become an activity of interest and importance. And wherever there are bands marching, Sousa's music is being played.

1. Describe Philip's first lessons in music. How did he learn the truth of the saying, "Silence is golden"?

2. Tell why the Marine Band has been called the official band of the President of the United States. On what occasions has it served? How did Sousa improve the Marine Band and make it famous?

3. What two marches did Sousa compose especially for the school children of Washington? Which of them became the basis of a new dance step?

4. Tell about the playing of "Dixie" at a celebration in North Carolina. How did Sousa happen to compose "The Stars and Stripes Forever"?

5. What interesting things happened when Sousa played for the King of England? Explain how he came to be known as the "March King."

6. Sousa said that his success was due to the fact that he and his band played chiefly "sunshine music." Explain how you feel about band music.

RALEGH LOOKS WEST 🏁 ELSIE PARK GOWAN

CHARACTERS

WALTER RALEGH: *Part dreamer, part man of action. In 1583, he was 31.*

HUMPHREY GILBERT: *His brother. Voice softer than Ralegh's. Of a more reflective turn. Older than Ralegh.*

NATHAN STUBBS: *A sea-dog of Devonshire.*

QUEEN ELIZABETH TUDOR:

BESS THROGMORTON: *Afterwards Lady Ralegh.*

FRANCIS CAMPERNOUN: *A young gentleman—Ralegh's cousin.*

KEYMIS: *A sea captain.*

HAYES: *A sea captain.*

OFFICER:

NARRATOR (*Through music*): *Three hundred and fifty years ago, the bravest spirits of England turned their eyes beyond the Atlantic to the New World. No boundaries crossed America then. From Labrador to Cape Horn, the unknown continent called to explorer, fisherman, merchant and buccaneer. There were many who sailed for gold and riches. One man throughout his life followed a broader vision, a nobler plan. He first sent men and women of his own hardy race to make homes in America. The Dominion of Canada today, the Republic of the United States, are built alike upon his dreams.*

This is the story of Walter Ralegh, sailor, poet, and pioneer. It begins in London, on an evening of 1583. Ralegh and his brother Humphrey Gilbert are busy with maps and plans of great enterprise.

Music. Up and out.

Ralegh. Now here's our path . . . from Plymouth to the New Found Land . . .

Gilbert. And when our folk are planted there, we two may sail again, to find a passage by the northwest, to China and the East Indies. . . .

Ralegh. China! I wish there were no talk of China. 'Tis a fool's errand . . . a will o' the wisp, that flies over Irish bogs and tempts men to their death.

Gilbert. But the wealth of the Indies, Wat. The gold!

Ralegh. Aye, the gold! Gold to the fat merchants for their help. Gold to the Queen, for her charter and her royal blessing.

Gilbert. Pray Heaven she grant them both!

Ralegh. Amen to that! Look you now, Humphrey, spread out the map. . . .

Sound. (*Parchment unrolled*).

Ralegh. This New Found Land may be too northerly for English folk. Perhaps here, farther south, we may find good harbour and fine soil. . . .

Sound. (*Heavy door opened quickly*).

Nathan (*coming in breathless*). Master Ralegh . . .

Ralegh. Well, Nathan, what's the matter?

Nathan. A lady and a serving maid, sir, at the river gate. The lady masked, and swore she would come in, and fetched me a great box on the ear when I denied her.

Ralegh (*laughing*). Admit her, Nathan! Admit her with all honour!

Nathan (*going*). Aye, aye, sir . . .

Gilbert (*eagerly*). Elizabeth?

Ralegh. Aye, by her manners, 'tis our gentle queen.

Gilbert. Here is our chance to have the charter signed . . .

Ralegh (*drily*). Wait till we know her humour!

Nathan (*off*). Please you, mistress, come this way.

Elizabeth (*coming in*). Good even, Sir Humphrey.

Gilbert. Your Majesty . . .

Elizabeth. How now, Walter Ralegh. Is this the welcome you promised me to Durham place?

Ralegh. If you come by day, dear Madame, in your own person . . .

Elizabeth. I'll come . . . and go . . . when I will, dear Walter (*calling*) Elizabeth . . . Where is the wench?

Bess (*coming in*). I am here, my lady.

Elizabeth. Come forth, child. Here you have Humphrey Gilbert, a fellow of wild Devon, where boys be nursed on salt water and fed tar with their porridge. The tall rogue is Walter Ralegh. He had the same mother and the devil himself for a father. This Ralegh is the proudest devil in our realm; a vile poet and a faithless lover. Trust him not.

Bess. No, madame.

Elizabeth. Gentlemen . . . Mistress Elizabeth Throgmorton, new come to attend our court.

Ralegh. God save you, lady.

Bess. And you, my lords.

Gilbert. A chair, your majesty.

Elizabeth. I thank you, Gilbert. Now, by your leave, we'll come to business. Now . . . what is this wild scheme to send Englishmen from their native land?

Ralegh. It is no mad scheme, dear madame, if you'll hear us...

Gilbert. We have drawn up a charter . . .

Elizabeth. I need my men at home! The tyranny of Spain will lead to war.

Gilbert. My lady, off the shores of New Found Land there is a great wealth of fish. John Cabot found them in the days of Henry, your grandfather. Push on our fishing trade . . . build ships . . . train men to sail them . . . and we have a navy will drive Spain from the sea.

Ralegh. As I go from London to Devon, I meet on the roads bands of poor fellows, without homes, without work. Yet they're stout lads, who would labour like men to build homes in the New World.

Nathan (*off*). Aye, 'tis the very truth.

Elizabeth. Who spoke there?

Ralegh. It is Nathan Stubbs, madame. A good seaman, in my service.

Elizabeth. Nathan Stubbs, do you answer me? Speak, then.

Nathan. I do say Sir Walter has the right of it. For I have spoke with lusty vagabonds, who swore they would sail beyond the seas and be honest yeomen, if they had land to plough again.

Elizabeth (drily). Is there another will bear witness?

Ralegh. Lady, you see this jewel I wear about my neck?

Elizabeth. A pretty trinket. But it will not bribe me.

Ralegh. This jewel was given me by a great sea captain, on a day Humphrey and I lay on a cliff about Plymouth Hoe, and heard his stories of the Spanish main. He told us of a new Indies where the Spaniard never trod. There, he said, is a multitude of islands, with air sweet as Devon moor, and all manner of fine pastures and orchard lands. In the mountains of the west, the sand of the river is gold, such as you read of in Holy Writ. We two lads swore that when we came to manhood, we would win this land. Then the stranger hung this jewel about my collar.

Gilbert. "And when you win it, what will you do?" he asked my brother. So Walter bowed low, his boy's face red as fire, and he made answer . . . "Then I will give our Gracious Lady the Queen of England, all this fair land, to be her very own".

Elizabeth (moved but speaking harshly). Where is this charter?

Ralegh. Dear Madame, it is here.

Sound. (Parchment unrolled).

Elizabeth. "To the Fellowship for the Discovery of the North West Passage . . . this is tedious long . . .

Gilbert. Lady, it is your order to discover heathen lands not possessed by any Christian prince. To you is reserved one fifth part of all gold and silver ore . . .

Elizabeth (quickly). One *fourth* part.

Gilbert. One fourth part. It then secures to the inhabitants the privileges of English free men.

Elizabeth. Well, I will sign this charter. May God prosper us.

Ralegh. Sweet Lady, thank you . . .

Sound. (Pen on parchment).

Elizabeth.—There! But this venture you have now prepared...
Gilbert.   My voyage to New Found Land . . .
Elizabeth.   You are its admiral?
Gilbert.   Aye, Madame.
Elizabeth.   Then you shall go. But Ralegh shall not.
Ralegh.   But, Madame . . . !
Elizabeth.   I'll not have all my captains from my shores at once.
Let Philip hang you for a trespasser? I'd not be such a fool!
Ralegh.   Dear Lady, let me go. I'll fume and fret at home.
Elizabeth.   We'll keep you busy. You are too precious for a
Spanish bon-fire. Now gentlemen, we'll say good-night. Come,
are you sleeping by the window, there?
Bess (off a little). No, Madame. I watch the boats pass on
the river.
Elizabeth.   Oh to be sweet and twenty, with naught to do but
loon on boats! Sir Humphrey . . . I wish you great good hap, and
safety for your ships.
Gilbert.   I thank your Majesty.

Elizabeth. Come, Nathan Stubbs, my counsellor, lights to our barge! *Good*-night, my Walter . . .

Ralegh. Madame . . . good-night.

Sound. (Footsteps out. Door closed).

Gilbert. I'm sorry, Wat.

Ralegh. There will be other years and other ships. She'll tire of me. Some day we'll sail . . . some day we'll take the road of the sunset together.

Music. Up fast. Out.

Nathan (coming in). Master Ralegh, sir . . . Captain Hayes is come to see you.

Ralegh. Hayes of the Golden Hind? *(calling)* Come in, Hayes, come in! *(To Nathan).* America and back in four months . . . they've made good speed, Nathan. I dreamt of Gilbert last night . . . Welcome home, Captain!

Hayes. My lord Ralegh . . .

Ralegh. And where's my brother? Gone home to Devon, eh?

Hayes. No, my lord. Humphrey Gilbert . . . is gone home . . . to God.

Ralegh. Hayes! *(silence).*

Hayes. We reached the New Found Land, sir, and began plantation there. August 31, we sailed for home, Sir Humphrey on the frigate Squirrel. In a great storm off the Azores, the frigate Squirrel was devoured and swallowed by the sea.

Ralegh. Humphrey . . . that ran with me on the rocks of Devon . . .

Hayes. Last I saw the Admiral, sir, he sat in the stern, a book in his hand. He cried out to us in the Hind "We are as near to heaven by sea as by land".

Ralegh (after a moment's pause). Thank you, Captain. We will talk another time . . .

Hayes. Good-day, my lord.

Sound. (Footsteps out)

Nathan. Master Humphrey was a brave lad, and a good sailor.

332 ♯ᵗ♯ᵗ♯ᵗ♯ᵗ♯ᵗ♯ᵗ♯ᵗ♯ᵗ♯ᵗ♯ᵗ♯ᵗ♯ᵗ

Ralegh. Aye, Nathan, that he was.

Nathan. For me, I've had my bellyful of plantations in America.

Ralegh. Nay . . . Gilbert's life must not be thrown away. Next year we'll try again. We'll try again . . .

Music. Up fast. Held. Out.

Elizabeth. Good morrow, sir Beggar!

Ralegh. Good morrow, Majesty. Dear Lady, I ask your kind thoughts and good offices for English folk in sore distress.

Elizabeth. Where be these folk?

Ralegh. In America, madame, in your colony Virginia.

Elizabeth. *My* colony! Aye, so I thought. A fine scroll of victory you've writ for us these five years. My money wasted there, my ships lost here . . .

Ralegh. Lady, you know that in the spring of last year, our company of one hundred and twenty souls sailed from Plymouth to build a nation in the new world . . . to carry our heritage of freedom beyond the seas . . .

Elizabeth (impatient). Aye, aye, what have they made?

Ralegh. They have built a village, reared a little chapel, planted fields. There has been born there a child of our English race . . . your name child, Madame, Virginia . . . Virginia Dare. This infant's grandfather, Governor John White, has returned to ask for help and supplies, for the growth of colonies is slow. Now in Virginia they watch the sea for ships that bring them food and life. Unless the sails come, says John White, all our folk . . . men, women, children and the babe Virginia, must surely perish. Unless you, dear lady, of your great authority, order that two ships go from England to their help.

Elizabeth. No.

Ralegh. Two small ships will save our empire in the west.

Elizabeth. My empire . . . tsh! Ralegh . . . what year is this?

Ralegh. Year of our Lord, one thousand five, and eighty-eight.

Elizabeth. You were a soldier, friend, before the fever took you. Tell me my duty in this murderous year.

Ralegh. Your duty, Madame, is to govern England.

Elizabeth. Aye, *defend* England! If that man's tyranny should come to England, where then is your heritage of freedom? I must defend this island. This is no time to scatter ships and men to the four winds! Philip's Armada sails in four months.

Ralegh (startled). You know?

Elizabeth. I have my means of knowing. And if invasion comes, there will be death enough for England's people. Quick death by sword, slow anguished death by fire. There will be twenty thousand English children screaming on Spanish steel. I have my dreams, too, Ralegh . . . and they are not pretty. You ask me now to weaken my defense; to send away men, guns, ships . . . I tell you, sir, until that fleet of Spain's is come and gone . . . burnt, beaten, sunk and shattered, not one ship shall leave my realm! My admiral Howard has his orders. Drake has his orders. You, Ralegh, have your orders . . . *not one ship!* You hear me?

Ralegh (quietly). Aye, madame, I have heard.

Elizabeth. My council waits for me . . . I must go in.

Ralegh. Shall I attend you, lady?

Elizabeth. You need not, for I know my way. I've trod it long enough, God knows . . . alone.

Music. Up fast . . . Music of storm and sea. Down and held behind.

Narrator. *Fifteen hundred eighty-eight . . . in that year the great Armada came. In that year the great Armada limped home, burnt, beaten, sunk and shattered, by the winds of heaven and the fury of England's sailors. Years passed . . . the great Queen died. In a new century, under a new king, evil days fell on the old Queen's friends.*

Sixteen hundred and sixteen . . . an old seaman stops a gentleman on the streets of London town . . .

Nathan. Your pardon, sir . . . be you kin to Sir Arthur Campernoun of Budleigh, in Devon?

Francis. I am Francis, son of Arthur Campernoun.

Nathan. Then are ye well met, Master Francis. I am Nathan Stubbs, that served your cousin Ralegh.

Francis. Nathan Stubbs was drowned off Trinidad in '95.

Nathan. Drowned I was not, but prisoner of the Spanish dogs these twenty years. Where be my admiral, sir?

Francis. Ralegh is in the Tower.

Nathan (incredulous). The Tower . . . ?

Francis. He was tried for treason in the first year of the King's reign . . . accused of plotting with Spain against the King.

Nathan. Plotting with Spain? Ralegh that hated Spain as the foul fiend? He that burnt Armadas, and fought like a lion at Cadiz? Who would believe it?

Francis. No honest Englishman, Nathan. But these are bad times, since the great Queen died.

Nathan. Eh, my dear Admiral. He loved the open water as a seabird loves the sky. They keep him behind bars. Come step ye faster, lad. I can no' breathe nor speak till I have ta'en him by the hand.

Music. Faded into Ralegh singing: Or speaking . . .

Ralegh. 'Fear no more the heat o' the sun
    Nor the furious winter's rages
  Thou thy worldly task hast done
    Home art gone and ta'en thy wages.
  Golden lads and girls all must
    As chimney sweepers, come to dust' . . .
Does my verse please you, Bess?

Bess. Did you write it?

Ralegh. It is a catch of Will Shakespeare's, from his new play Cymbeline.

Bess. A melancholy thing.

Ralegh. It suits my humour. Poor Bess . . . a sad life I've given you. . . . First the Queen's fury when she knew us married . . . now these years of prison and disgrace.

Bess. I am the proudest woman in England still.

Ralegh. That's a brave lass! My dear, I chose you and loved you in my best years. What came after, proved I chose aright.

Sound. (*Knocking on heavy door . . . Then bolts drawn back*).

Ralegh. We have a visitor . . .

Sound. (*Door opened*).

Francis. Good day, Cousin Ralegh. I bring you something from the sea.

Ralegh. From the sea . . . ? (*seeing him*). Nathan!

Nathan (*tremulous*). Aye, Master Ralegh . . .

Ralegh. Nathan, my dear old friend . . .

Francis. He's been a prisoner in the Spanish galleys . . .

Nathan. Eh, 'tis a long story, Admiral.

Bess. Welcome home, good Nathan.

Nathan. Your ladyship . . .

Ralegh. Sit down, friends, sit down. Nathan . . . a pipe?

Nathan. Will ye smoke my tobacco, Admiral? 'Tis a proper seaman's twist.

Ralegh. So it is . . . and thank you. Well you see me here, the busiest man in London. I've written a history of the world.

Nathan. Do ye say so!

Ralegh. Then I make my experiments, and on fine days, walk yonder in my rose garden.

Francis. And when he walks, Nathan, great crowds of people gather. A man will hold his child up saying "Look, my son, on a great man that was friend of the Queen and fought Spain."

Ralegh (*smiling*). A harmless old lion with his teeth drawn. Now I am fallen, the people love me as they never did in my proud times.

Nathan. When do they set thee free?

Ralegh. There is hope of that yet, if a plan of mine should please the king. Let us have the maps, Bess.

Bess. I knew we should have maps before long.

Ralegh. Here is the map of the world . . .

Sound. (*Parchment unrolled*).

Ralegh. . . . With the names of my friends writ large on it.

There, off Greenland, Davis Strait. Honest, kindly John. He sailed with me to the Azores in '96.

Nathan. Where be John Davis now?

Francis. Killed by Dutch pirates off Sumatra, ten years past.

Ralegh. There, Frobisher Bay, that Martin hoped might be the north west passage.

Nathan. Have any found the passage?

Francis. None yet. But the French go up this river they call the St. Lawrence. Here, de Champlain has planted a fort he calls Quebec. From it he seeks the western sea.

Ralegh (sadly). And here . . . is Virginia, my lost colony, that I have never seen.

Bess. My mind turns often to that English child, Virginia Dare, to think if she be still alive.

Nathan. There is no word?

Ralegh. One word, our rescue ships found carved upon a tree . . . Croatoan.

Nathan. Croatoan?

Ralegh. That one word . . . but none knew what it meant. (*Sighs*). And here, to the south, is Nombre Dios Bay, where Drake lies twenty fathoms deep.

Nathan. Even in the Spanish galleys, we heard that tale.

Francis. I fear the golden age is gone from England.

Ralegh. Nay, but the golden age shall come again, when we three sail to find Guiana, and the mines of San Thome.

Nathan (eagerly). Guiana, master? El Dorado?

Ralegh. I have a plan before the king, that he should send me out, back to Guiana, and the mines we know of. Look, here's the river, Orinoco . . .

Francis. Dear cousin, don't think of it. James will not let you go.

Ralegh. Had you been there, lad, the vision of Guiana shone in your heart forever, as it does in mine. On both sides of this river we passed the most beautiful country mine eyes ever beheld. The deer came feeding down to the water's edge; the birds towards evening singing in every tree a thousand several tunes. Cranes, and herons, in white, crimson and carnation; the air, fresh, with a gentle wind . . . and every stone that we took up promised us, by its complexion, either silver or gold . . .

Francis. But the mine, Ralegh, is the King of Spain's.

Nathan. The mine is twenty miles from the Spanish town. And when did English captains ask the devil's leave to go exploring?

Francis. Nathan, Elizabeth is dead. We have a king who seeks alliance with England's enemy. Ralegh he hates above all men, for Ralegh is the last great sea-dog that challenged Spain's cruel power beyond the line.

Ralegh. Not the last, Francis. There's my eldest son. We must show my son the Indies, Nathan.

Francis. Ralegh, he will not let you go.

Sound. (*Knocking*).

Ralegh. Another visitor?

Sound. (*Door opened*).

Bess (*off*). Thank you, sir. (*Sound. Door closed*).

Bess (*coming back*). My dear . . . a letter.

Ralegh (*carelessly*). Letters are welcome . . . (*excited*). From Sir Ralph Winwood, Secretary of State!

Francis (*eagerly*). Aye?

Bess. Walter! (*Sound. Letter opened*).

Ralegh. 'Be of good heart, friend Ralegh, for we have persuaded his majesty to your desire. He has come to hope your venture may bring him wealth, and remind Spain we are an ally not to be despised. The Spanish ambassador swears he will have your head if you break the peace in the New World. Look to this. The warrant for your freedom goes forward within the week. The council . . . (*his voice shakes*) . . . he bids you use all good endeavour, that the ships may be ready before the wind shifts in this quarter. Yours, . . . R. Winwood' . . .

Francis. I fear it may be a trap. We cannot trust him.

Ralegh. Trust him or trust him not, I understand of this, one blessed word . . . freedom. Freedom! Nathan, we sail—we sail, again . . . !

Music. Up fast. Faded and held behind.

Narrator. *Ralegh sailed for El Dorado, but it seemed bad luck sailed with him. In the spring, he lay in his Flagship, the Destiny, off the coast of Guiana, waiting for news of Captain Keymis, sent up the Orinoco to find gold.*

Music. Out.

Ralegh (*tired*).   What's the day, Cousin?

Francis.   March third.

Ralegh.   March third. The daffodils are out, in Devon . . . but this fever haunted sea has no breath of coolness.

Francis.   Keymis is gone a month on the river. Surely by this time he has found the mine.

Ralegh.   I should have trusted this venture to no man but myself . . .

Francis.   Dear Ralegh, you were deadly ill. There was no other way, but that we guard the river, while he went.

Nathan (*off, calling*).   Oars off the port bow!

Keymis (*well off*).   What ship is that?

Nathan (*off*).   Destiny, flag ship of the Admiral Ralegh.

Keymis (*off*).   God be thanked. A rope, there, and a lantern.

Sound.   (*Footsteps running on deck*).

Nathan.   Captain Keymis coming aboard, sir!

Ralegh.   Bring him aft, Nathan, bring him aft!

Nathan.   Aye, aye, sir!

Ralegh (*excited*).   Keymis! . . . We spoke of angels, Francis! Order us wine. Plague take this ague in my legs . . .

Francis (*smiling*).   Gently, cousin . . . he'll come to you.

Sound.   (*Footsteps coming in*).

Francis.   Aye, here he is . . .

Ralegh.   Well, Keymis, where's our treasure?

Keymis.   My lord Ralegh . . .

Ralegh.   Nay man, get up. We're sailors here . . . we'll have no kneeling.

Keymis.   My lord . . . forgive me. (*Silence*).

Ralegh (sharply). Where's my son?

Keymis. Your son's in San Thome, by the high altar of the church. He died fighting.

Francis. Then you have broken the peace?

Keymis. We found no peace, my lord, nor gold, nor anything but sickness, treachery and death. My five ships foundered in the Orinoco. Unknown to me, the town of San Thome is moved fifteen miles up the river, and in the darkness, we sailed by its forts. So the Spanish lay between us and the Admiral, and we were driven to fight.

In battle we took San Thome, but there we were shut up wasted by famine and sickness. I've brought back not a basketful of gold to prove our honesty to the King. But I fear he has not been honest with us.

Francis. And why not?

Keymis. I found the plans for this voyage in the Governor's house in San Thome. My lord, I have done my utmost. I had rather laid my bones by young Walter's than have brought this news. Speak to me, sir, I . . .

Francis (very low). Go, Keymis.

Ralegh. I forgive you, Keymis. I cannot hate you . . . for I have no heart in me.

Keymis. My lord, I . . .

Ralegh. Go now. (*Sound. Footsteps out.*)

Francis. No gold, and a fight with Spain. Our case is desperate.

Nathan. Let me up the river, Admiral! I'll find the mine . . .

Francis. We've lost too many men and ships for another trial.

Nathan. There are black looks out there on the deck. These knaves will cut our throats and turn pirate, for the thought of gold was all that held them.

Francis. Ralegh . . . we must take counsel . . .

Ralegh (slowly). There is no need, Francis. I'm going home.

Francis. To England? It's certain death.

Ralegh. To England. I have given my word.

Francis. But why? The world is wide. Steer for a French port, or for Virginia . . .

Nathan. The King will not forgive us this business.

Ralegh. Now I'm come a little to myself . . . I see I have left something in England I must ransom. My good fame. If I fled the land, I failed in my last duty, and God does not prosper a coward.

Nathan. But if they slay you, sir, what will become of your plans? The plantations in America . . .

Ralegh. They will flourish, Nathan, for my blood will water them.

Francis. Ralegh, it's life or death! The king will have your head . . .

Ralegh. If I die, England will think the better of me, and in a hundred years, she will turn to my thoughts and see their truth. Across the seas . . . there lies our destiny. In the New World, where our English freedom may take root and flourish. For this, I must go home.

Music. Up and held behind.

Narrator. *Ralegh returned to England, to a king who would not forgive his failure. In the Palace Yard of Westminster on a frosty morning of October, 1618, Ralegh spoke to England for the last time.*

Sound. (Roll of drums).

Ralegh (speaking in the open air). My lords and good people . . . I thank my God heartily that he has brought me into the light to die, and has not suffered me to die in the darkness of the Tower but in his own sunlight and in this noble company.

Now I must entreat you that you will join with me in prayer to that great God of heaven whom I have so grievously offended, being a man full of vanity. For I have been a sea-faring man, a soldier and a courtier, all of them courses of wickedness. But I trust he will cast away my sin and receive me into everlasting life. I have a long journey to take, and must bid the company farewell.

Officer. My lord . . . if you will turn your face to the east . . .

Ralegh. Friend, all my life, I have turned my face to the west.

How be it, I will do as you say. What matter how the head lie, so the heart be right?
(*Silence*).
Sound. (*Roll of drums*).

Music. Faded into drums. Held. Out.

Nathan. My lady, . . . I have brought ye this jewel the admiral gave me as I stood by him in his last hour.
Bess. I know it well. He called it his charm for El Dorado. Now he is gone there, and has no longer need for a charm . . .
Nathan. Nay, Mistress, grieve not. Those who took his life have done him the best service. There is no honest soul in England but thrills with the shame of it. A spirit is abroad that will breed and multiply and do more than Ralegh did in the cause he loved.
Bess. Think you so, good Nathan?
Nathan. I have been in Virginia, Lady, and seen the noble rivers, and the forests and the plains of deep grass. Some day our people will dwell there, and build a nation. Aye, and wherever on earth there is a free land to be made out of the wilderness, there will they be.
Bess. God has sent me a true consoler, Nathan. I shall weep no more. Rather I shall rejoice that Sir Walter has left to us, and to all the world, an inheritance so princely.

Music. Up to Finale.

CLUES TO MEANING

From the earliest dawn of history, plays have been important in the lives of all civilized peoples. Occasionally even to-day, in London and New York theatres, there are performed plays written over twenty-five hundred years ago. But only during the past quarter-century has the radio play developed as an important literary form. As the radio play is heard only, not seen, it differs in many important respects from the stage play. Thus, action can be indicated only by the sound it makes, such as footsteps, doors opening and closing, knocking, etc. Music is also used much more commonly than with stage plays, and for two important purposes: to provide a transition from one scene to another (since there is no curtain), and to reflect the mood of any particular part of the play. Can you find examples of all these different sound effects in this play?

DISCUSSING THE PLAY

1. Queen Elizabeth is commonly considered to have been stingy, hot-tempered, and jealous. Can you find evidence in this play to indicate she was all of these things? But jealousy, stinginess, and a hot temper would never by themselves have won Elizabeth her reputation of being one of England's greatest monarchs. What qualities of greatness does she exhibit in the play?

2. In contrast to Elizabeth, what is your opinion as to her successor?

3. Ralegh's whole life was dominated by a single idea. How did it originate? What reference did he make to it when he was about to die? Has later history shown that the idea was sound or foolish?

4. From his last expedition Ralegh returned to what he knew would be certain death. Do you admire or condemn him for that? Why? What qualities of character did he show in doing so?

5. Aside from Ralegh and Elizabeth, which character in the play did you find most interesting? Why?

CLARA BARTON [1821–1912] 🦋

ROSEMARY AND STEPHEN VINCENT BENET

G
BRAVE Clara Barton
Stood beside her door,
And watched young soldiers
March away to war.

G1 5 "The flags are very fine," she said,
"The drums and trumpets thrilling.
But what about the wounds
When the guns start killing?"

B   Clara Barton went to work
    10   To help keep men alive,
            And never got a moment's rest
            Till eighteen sixty-five.

G   She washed and she bandaged,
            She shooed away the flies,
    15   She hurried in nurses,
            She begged for supplies.

            She cared for the wounded
            And comforted the dying,
            With no time for sleep
    20   And still less for crying.

B   Clara Barton went abroad
            When the war was ended
            Hoping for a little peace
            Now that things had mended.

G   25   Clara found, as soon
            As her foot touched shore,
            That she'd come just in time
            For the Franco-Prussian War.

All   After that, her life, for her,
    30   Held but little rest,
            With famine in the East
            And earthquakes in the West.

B   Floods, drowning Johnstown,
G   Hurricanes in Texas,
B   35   Fires, out in Michigan,
            Things that fright and vex us.

G   In between the hurry calls,
            Never at a loss,
            She founded and established
    40   The merciful Red Cross.

All   Battle, murder, sudden death,
            Called for Clara Barton.
            No one ever called in vain.
            Clara was a Spartan.

DISCUSSING THE POEM

1. Many people think of the Red Cross as an international organization, but actually there are many independent organizations, such as the Canadian Red Cross, British Red Cross, American Red Cross which work together through an international committee. The movement was started as a result of an unofficial international conference held in Switzerland in 1863. In honour of Switzerland, its flag became the emblem of the movement, but with the colours reversed, that is, a red cross on a white field rather than a white cross on a red field. Clara Barton came to know of the work of the Red Cross in the Franco-Prussian War of 1870, and it was after that date that she was instrumental in organizing the American Red Cross. How do we know that she was the kind of person who saw things to be done and did them?

2. Clara's activities were not limited to the needs of communities in our own country. Tell how she helped in disaster areas abroad.

3. The people of the ancient city of Sparta were famed for their courage and strict personal discipline. They worked without thought for themselves and bore pain unflinchingly. What Spartan characteristics did the poets see in Clara Barton? Do you think the quick rhythmic tone of the poem suits the personality of Miss Barton?

HOW CYRUS LAID THE CABLE ✻

JOHN GODFREY SAXE

B Come, listen all unto my song;
   It is no silly fable;
   'Tis all about the mighty cord
    They call the Atlantic Cable.

  5 Bold Cyrus Field he said, says he,
B1   "I have a pretty notion
   That I can run a telegraph
    Across the Atlantic Ocean."

G Then all the people laughed, and said
  10 They'd like to see him do it;
   He might get half-seas over, but
    He never could go through it.

   To carry out his foolish plan
    He never would be able;
  15 He might as well go hang himself
    With his Atlantic Cable.

B But Cyrus was a valiant man,
    A fellow with decision;
   And heeded not their mocking words,
  20 Their laughter and derision.

    All   Twice did his bravest efforts fail,
                And yet his mind was stable:
                He wa'n't the man to break his heart
                Because he broke his cable.

    B1   25 "Once more, my gallant boys!" he cried;
                "Three times!—you know the fable
                (I'll make it *thirty*," muttered he,
                "But I will lay the cable!").

    B   Once more they tried—hurrah! hurrah!
         30 What means this great commotion?
    All   The Lord be praised! the cable's laid
                Across the Atlantic Ocean!

    G   Loud ring the bells—for, flashing through
                Six hundred leagues of water,
         35 Old Mother England's benison
                Salutes her eldest daughter!

    All   O'er all the land the tidings speed,
                And soon, in every nation,
                They'll hear about the cable with
         40 Profoundest admiration!

    B1   Now, long live President and Queen;
    B2   And long live gallant Cyrus;
    B   And may his courage, faith, and zeal
                With emulation fire us;

    All 45 And may we honour evermore
                The manly, bold, and stable;

35. BENISON—Blessing.

And tell our sons, to make them brave,
How Cyrus laid the cable!

DISCUSSING THE POEM

1. Most of the important inventions and discoveries of our world were once thought the silly ideas of impractical men. Why did people laugh at Cyrus Field's idea of a submarine cable? Why did Cyrus not give up when several attempts failed?

2. Today more than 25 cables span the Atlantic Ocean to serve the world's communication needs. Do you think Cyrus' dream was worth while? Do you know about any other men whose ideas were ridiculed before they were realized? If you do, tell about them.

3. Cyrus Field and his helpers experienced many discouraging difficulties before they found success. The story of their perseverance is a thrilling one. Looking up the history of cables in an encyclopaedia.

KOCH ✣ RUTH FOX

Living, as we are, in an age of tremendous scientific development, it is easy to forget the pioneers who made the wonders of our century possible. Just when the great discoveries began is hard to tell, but in the seventeenth century the Dutchman, Anton van Leeuwenhoek, looked through his home-made microscope one day and saw living things that were too small to see with the natural eyesight. The story of his discovery slowly became known and others began to look through the magnifying glass at these strange living and moving things. Finally the realization came that a whole new world of life, hitherto unknown, was waiting to be investigated.

It was almost a century after the discoveries made by Leeuwenhoek that men like Pasteur, Joseph Lister, and Robert Koch began to suspect that this world of microscopic life was responsible for many things that happened to the world of man. They refused to stand by helpless, as others had for centuries, while thousands of people died of mysterious plagues. Instead they took their problems into the laboratory and began the search that finally revealed the causes of many diseases.

Robert Koch was one of the patient hunters of microbes who laid the foundations upon which the miracles of our century of science are built.

THE theory of Pasteur[1] and the practice of Lister[2] became the obsession of the late nineteenth century. In every university, in every richly endowed laboratory, trained researchers played with the problems which the Frenchman's fermented wines had opened to them. Diseases of wine, Pasteur had said, were caused by some sort of creature not obliging enough to show itself to the naked eye. Lister had drawn his own conclusions about the relation of these microbes to the plagues of hospital life. It was not long before a few unconventional scientists began to discuss the faint possibility that these elusive bits of nothing might have some connection with other diseases, too. But although everyone ranged himself on one side of the argument or the other, no one was prepared to prove either that microbes were a cause of disease or that they were not. As late as 1876 the distinguished Dr. Cohn, Professor of Botany at Breslau,[3] still disposed neatly of bacteria by grouping them all under the title "chaos." Before he would permit them to be called by any other name, someone would have to show him that these creatures really lived, worked, and died, as other plants and animals did, in an orderly, systematic way.

In the small, then Prussian, town of Posen, the wife of the district physician was worrying over a problem which, on the surface, seemed very remote from the academic worries of the mighty scientists. Her husband, Robert Koch, wanted a microscope, which he could not afford. Emmy did not understand what Robert intended to do with so complicated and expensive an instrument. But since he had been known to talk of it from the soup straight through to the apple strudel, she assumed that he had his reason.

Emmy put a covered beer mug on the kitchen shelf and began to drop small coins into it. On her husband's twenty-eighth birthday she gave him his microscope. Almost speechless with excite-

[1]PASTEUR—A French chemist and bacteriologist who developed a method for killing microbes by the use of heat.
[2]LISTER—A British surgeon; the first to use antiseptics in surgery.
[3]BRESLAU—A city in Poland.

ment, Robert carried the precious gift into his office, strung a sheet across the middle of the room, and said: "There! From now on the outside half is the consulting room, and the inside half is the laboratory!"

From the inside half of the district doctor's office emerged the germ theory of disease which had so successfully eluded the grasp of the men who worked in the universities and the highly endowed laboratories.

Robert Koch, from the third year of his life, had wanted to be an explorer. As one of eleven children he had never been overly burdened with parental supervision, and had roamed the fields of his native Hanover at will, playing pirate with himself and dreaming of mighty deeds on the high seas. Since he had also picked up the idea of studying medicine, nobody knew where, he decided to correlate the two ambitions by becoming an army or navy surgeon, or ship's doctor to an exploring expedition.

All through his years of study at Gottingen he had longed for the day which would find him pacing a quarter-deck, discussing problems of navigation with the captain or bargaining for fresh fruit with outlandishly dressed natives on some Caribbean island. And then he had met Emmy Fraatz—Emmy the unromantic, the practical, the phlegmatic.[4]   He told her of all his deeply-rooted dreams and aspirations. She suggested that he stop taking up her time and make room in her father's parlour for other suitors. He asked her to marry him.   She said that under the circumstances marriage was out of the question.

Koch, walking alone by the tall-masted schooners and the squat-funnelled steamships in the harbour, weighed the charms of Emmy Fraatz against the enchantment of the sea and the haunting voices of the boat whistles. The next day he went back to Emmy's house, abjured[5] his madness, and promised to settle down and practise medicine. Emmy, delighted, poured out some elderberry wine and said that he might now call her *Du* instead of *Sie*.[6]

[4] PHLEGMATIC—Unemotional and indifferent.
[5] ABJURED—Renounced.
[6] *Du* . . . *Sie*—The German pronouns are used in different ways. *Du*, meaning *thou*, is a term of intimacy; *sie*, meaning *you*, is a more formal term.

So he would never be an explorer, Robert Koch thought bitterly. Well, that was the price one paid for falling in love. That he would, as a matter of fact, be one of the greatest explorers of all time he had little way of knowing as he fastened the stiff collar which etiquette prescribed for one's wedding day.

The Kochs moved from one village to another, driven by Robert's terrible restlessness and gnawing discontent, settling for a time into a respectable little practice, then packing up and trying out life in some new speck on the map of Prussia.

In 1872, Robert obtained an appointment as district physician to Wollstein, in the province of Posen. Here, Emmy decided, setting her jaw firmly, they would stay. Robert was under the protection of the state now. Some day he might even be drawing a pension. But to take his mind off the fact that he was not happy, she gave him the microscope.

Koch had always had a miraculously logical mind. Now he owned a microscope. The interminable microbe arguments which he followed carefully in the medical journals had stirred him profoundly, and he determined to get into the fight.

His work was cut out for him. Wollstein was farming and grazing country. Sheep and cattle were the main means of livelihood for the inhabitants. Koch, on his evening rounds, was just as likely to find a farmer's wife weeping for a dead sheep as for a sick child; and the mortality rate of the animals of Posen was extremely high.

Most of them died of anthrax—not that anthrax had any prejudice against men. Koch had seen many farmers and sheep-shearers stricken with the terrible disease.

Davaine in France had claimed that anthrax was caused by a microbe. Koch knew that he would have no trouble finding anthrax victims in Posen. The isolation of the anthrax bacillus would be his first step, always assuming that such a thing as an anthrax bacillus really existed.

Since he could not afford to buy even a sick sheep, he settled for a few white mice. Then he took some blood from an anthrax victim which he had found lying in a field, and went to work.

He injected the tainted blood into a mouse. In due course the mouse exhibited anthrax symptoms and died. This was interesting, but hardly conclusive. A second mouse, injected with blood taken from the first mouse, died, as did a third, injected with blood from the second. In thirty days an unbroken chain of thirty mice had passed the disease along to one another and succumbed to it. Here was proof enough even for the unimpressionable Koch that something in the blood stream of anthrax victims was capable of transmitting the disease. Something. But what?

His microscope showed him that anthrax blood swarms with mysterious little rods and sticks and threads. These bodies he could not find in healthy blood, no matter how many specimens he examined. Was this not sufficient proof, then, that the rods and threads were the cause of anthrax, Emmy wanted to know, irritated at her husband's annoying preoccupation.

No, Robert said, not even the beginning of proof. It was entirely possible that these rods and threads were simply disorganized matter which formed as the result of the disease. To prove that they were its cause, and not its effect, he would have to isolate a pure strain of them in a test tube.

Between office hours, between long, exhausting excursions to the outlying farms of Posen, he worked over his dead mice. Emmy began to regret the purchase of the microscope. No woman, she complained bitterly, had ever had so formidable a rival. Three sentences a day was Robert's quota of conversation now. He either growled or was entirely mute at breakfast, as one might expect from a man who slept about four hours a night. He was little better at dinner, after a long day with patients. In the evening he marched grimly back to his laboratory, and that was the last his wife saw of him until the next unpleasant breakfast. Emmy, having neither the brains nor the soul of an Agnes Lister,[7] reaped nothing but unhappiness from her husband's work.

Koch, after many false starts, devised what seemed a logical method of isolating the bacillus. He placed a drop of the clear liquid from an ox's eye on a thin glass slide. Into the liquid he dropped a tiny piece of tissue snipped from one of his dead mice.

[7] AGNES LISTER—The sympathetic wife of the famous British physician.

Then scooping a little well in a thicker slide, he placed it over the thin slide and inverted the two. He now had an air-tight "hanging drop" of liquid. Nothing could get into the culture, and nothing could get out of it. Placing the slide on the stage of his microscope, he waited, his eyes glued to the instrument. Minutes stretched into half an hour. The half-hour dragged into two hours. The little petroleum lamp began to sputter feebly. Then it happened. Before his eyes the rods and threads of the anthrax tissue began to divide and grow and stretch themselves until, within three hours, the slide was covered by a tangled mass of them—more than Koch had ever seen at one time.

His hands shaking, he extracted a drop the size of a pinhead from the slide, and placed in it a second "hanging drop" of ox-eye liquid. The rods and threads, warmed to enthusiasm now, began growing madly, filling every available corner of the drop with their long tendrils. He repeated the process, over and over, until he was convinced that the rods and threads on his eighth slide were only very distant relatives of the original material from the mouse's tissues.

Were these energetic creatures alive? Most definitely so. He had seen them reproduce themselves and grow—the two commonplace activities of living things. There was abundant life on the slide. Of that there was no doubt in his mind. But was this life capable of destroying other life? Here was the critical question.

He took one drop of culture from slide number eight and injected it into a mouse. The next morning the mouse was dead. The germ theory of disease was a theory no longer. It had become a fact overnight.

There was only one loophole; it was a small one, to be sure, but Robert Koch was a man who abhorred loopholes of any kind. The bacilli were delicate little things. They dried up and died after two days, even in the warmth of the laboratory. How could they live in the frozen fields of Posen, winter after winter, returning each spring to infest new herds of sheep and cattle?

Certain of his cultures showed unaccountable little dots, stringing across the slide like black beads. Koch had paid only slight attention to them up to this point, assuming that they were simply broken fragments of the threads. But now he remembered the tiny beads, and remembered also that no one who calls himself a scientist has any right to make assumptions that he cannot prove.

He allowed a culture which showed the black dots to dry up and die. Then he poured some fresh, warm ox-eye fluid onto the slide and watched through his eye-piece while the tiny black dots—spores, he called them—burst open and sprouted into full-grown anthrax bacilli. So that was it! That was why the soil of a field could be polluted with anthrax for year after year—forever, perhaps. The little bacilli were not so delicate after all. In winter they hibernated.[8] In spring they blossomed out again. From spore to full-grown bacillus and back again to spore from the body of a dead sheep to the blood of a living sheep—from that doomed sheep to another living sheep—an endless, immutable[9] cycle of life more destructive than Robert Koch had ever imagined life could be.

On April 22nd, 1876, Herr Professor Cohn of Breslau, who found bacteria so chaotic, received a letter in the morning mail, postmarked Wollstein:

"ESTEEMED HERR PROFESSOR," he read.

"Stimulated by your work on bacteria published in *Contributions to Biology of Plants*, I have for some time been at work on investigations of anthrax contagion. . . . After many vain attempts, I have finally been successful in discovering the process of development of the *bacillus anthracis*. . . . I would therefore respectfully request you to permit me to show you, within a few days, in the Botanical Institute, the essential experiments. . . .

With the highest esteem,

Yours respectfully,

R. KOCH, District Physician."

The process of development of the bacillus . . . R. Koch, District Physician. Cohn smiled to himself. Who was this R. Koch, who claimed to have done something that men like Pasteur and Virchow and—well, why not say it—Ferdinand Cohn had never

---

[8] HIBERNATED (hī'bûr-nāt-ĕd)—Existed in a resting state.
[9] IMMUTABLE—Unchangeable.

managed to do? Since he was a fair-minded man, however, Cohn invited the district doctor to come to town, even provided him with a formidable group of scientists before which to perform: Auerbach, the great physiologist; Cohnheim, the pathologist; Ehrlich, one day to be a medical immortal himself.

The demonstration, given on three successive days, was a theatrical affair during which spores grew, bacilli multiplied, and mice died like seasoned troupers. When at last Koch could peer at the company through his best gold-rimmed spectacles and say "Well, gentlemen, I believe that concludes the demonstration," no one moved for a few moments. Then Cohn rushed out of the room and down the hall to his own laboratory.

"Go at once to Koch!" he shouted to his assistants. "The man's discovery is the greatest ever made with bacteria! He leaves nothing to be proved!"

Eventually the government began to be impressed, for the eyes of the world were soon turned on Robert Koch and, therefore, on Germany. Could such a man be left to rot in a sheep-raising town in Wollstein? Certainly not. Making much of one's men of science was good national publicity. But the government did not like to be rushed and nearly four years passed before Koch was moved to Berlin at the expense of the treasury and established in a large, well-equipped laboratory at the University. He smiled at the memory of the partition in the health office of Posen. In Berlin he was to make the experiments on culture media which established the science of bacteriology. His equipment now in order, he was ready to set out on his greatest voyage of discovery.

With the previous century's conquest of smallpox, another disease had taken its place as the great killer, with one out of every seven people doomed to die of it. Before the ravages of tuberculosis the most skillful doctors in the world were helpless, and acknowledged their helplessness. The tuberculosis field was still split between the disciples of Laënnec, and the disciples of Broussais.[10] The

---

[10] LAËNNEC . . . BROUSSAIS—René Théophile Laënnec (là-â-něk') and François Joseph Broussais (broō-sě')—French physicians; Laënnec believed that tuberculosis was caused by a microbe; Broussais opposed this idea.

present generation of Broussaisites maintained that tuberculosis, far from being caused by a bacillus, was not even contagious. How could irritation be catching? But little René Théophile had always stood firm for his "specific agent." His followers, therefore, sided with Koch; for he too believed in a specific agent.

All that Koch would accept as a fact, however, was the contagiousness of the disease; he had only an instinctive feeling that there was a bacillus involved. No one had ever seen a tuberculosis bacillus, but if one existed he would find it. Early in August of 1881 he began looking. Material with which to work presented no problem at all. Berlin hospitals were full of patients dying of tuberculosis.

Methodical as ever, he outlined a three-point programme for himself. First, he would try to find some type of bacillus that occurred again and again in tuberculous tissue; then he would grow a strain of these bacilli in a test tube; finally, he would inoculate a healthy animal with the new strain, and after its death (if it had the good grace to die), he would look for the bacillus in its body tissue.

The method he had planned was similar to that which he had used in the anthrax experiments. There was, of course, the simple difference that in the anthrax days he had had a bacillus to begin with. This time, for all he knew, he might be looking for something which did not exist.

He was feeling his way through the dark. With no rules to follow, no doctors' dissertations[11] to look up, no teachers to advise him, he had to invent techniques as he went and overcome obstacles as he found them. This was cruel work for him. Pasteur's genius manifested itself by brilliant flashes of imagination which saw into the heart of a problem in split seconds. Koch's genius was less spectacular. He did not work from sudden inspirations that carried him from one step of a problem to another. He simply worked— methodically, without surcease.[12]

His assistant, Gaffky, grew used to arriving at the laboratory in the morning to find Koch just finishing up for the night.

[11] DOCTORS' DISSERTATIONS—Scholarly papers required of those studying for a doctor's degree in a university.   [12] WITHOUT SURCEASE—Without stopping.

The initial words of conversation at such moments soon became standardized.

"Any luck, Herr Doktor?" from Gaffky.

"Confound it, no!" from Koch.

Gaffky, by looking at his employer's hands, could usually tell how many new stains he had tried that night. For Koch's already acid-shrivelled fingers would be far more colourful than a four- or five-shaded rainbow.

"That's the devil of it," he fumed. "I've tried every stain known to me. I've invented more combinations than I thought possible, and still there is nothing—nothing that could begin to pass for a bacillus!"

"You will find it, Herr Doktor. Wait and see."

"Will I?" He laughed. "If it exists, perhaps. But at the moment no one could possibly convince me that it exists. I'm through, Gaffky."

Gaffky had heard that before. He smiled. The doctor would go home to bed now. In the afternoon he would be back, talking to himself about a new stain combination that might bear investigation.

Thus matters stood for some weeks. One morning Koch came in muttering, "There's one thing we haven't tried—I was thinking about it last night—"

He took a fresh tuberculous specimen, made a slide, and stained it with methylene blue. Then he nodded in the direction of the bottle of potassium hydroxide which stood near the test-tube rack. Gaffky handed it to him silently.

When the slide was ready Koch sighed and said, "This is the two hundred and seventy-first."

Then he looked.

Small, and quite slender, and certainly harmless looking were the little rods which he distinguished against the blue background of the slide. They looked without doubt like bacilli, yet not like any specific bacilli that he had ever seen. He stared at them for a few moments and then exclaimed, "Gaffky, look at this!"

Gaffky did. He whistled softly and said, "Do you think they—"

"I don't think anything," Koch snapped nervously. "Not anything."

And he went out for his morning coffee, not permitting himself the obvious conclusion that he, first of all men, had just seen the most destructive creature in the world.

The next day word went round to each hospital in Berlin. Koch at the University wanted a slide from every tuberculosis victim in the wards and in the morgue. Material poured in, all of it subsequently treated by the more elaborate staining system Koch soon adopted, all of it crawling with the little rods he still did not care to name.

"I think," he said late one evening, "that it is safe to suspect some connection between this bacillus whatever-it-is and tuberculosis."

"I think it might be," said Gaffky, flipping through the notebook which bulged with their reports. "But let's not be too hasty."

The sarcasm was entirely lost on Koch, who was too preoccupied with the staining of a slide to be aware that Gaffky had answered him.

"Now," he said cheerfully, some minutes later, "we really start to work."

"What have we been doing up to now?"

"Oh, that staining business wasn't really so bad."

Gaffky laughed, remembering the doctor's almost daily attacks of despair during the search for the bacillus.

Koch was saying, "Now we must make this temperamental creature grow on its own."

Within a few days he was again in despair. The little rods refused to grow in any of the innumerable media he prepared for them.

"Then you see we were wrong. They won't grow. They can't be alive. They aren't bacilli at all. Will I ever learn to stop jumping at conclusions!"

"Herr Doktor," said Gaffky patiently, "I have worked with many researchers before you, and I have never known a man who did less jumping to conclusions than you. Why don't you go home and go to sleep? Frau Koch will be angry if you stay up all night again."

"Yes, I will." But he felt a dull sense of oppression at the thought. The laboratory had a peace of its own that he did not find at home. He was glad when he had an excuse to work for days at a time, snatching a few hours sleep on the couch in his office.

When he came in the next morning, he found Gaffky bent over the microscope examining slides of culture media they had planted a few days before.

"Any luck?" asked Koch.

Gaffky, stifling an impulse to say, "Confound it, no!" shook his head.

Koch began to walk up and down the lab, tugging at his beard thoughtfully.

"Why don't you take off your coat?" Gaffky suggested, peering into the microscope again.

"I was just wondering—" The timid phrase usually portended some startling idea. Gaffky looked up quickly. "—if, since this creature is so sensitive that it will not grow outside the body, we could possibly reproduce the conditions within the body. Perhaps it can be fooled."

"'Reproduce conditions within the body,'" Gaffky repeated thoughtfully. "Yes—of course."

"We might try the serum of cow's blood to begin with . . ."

The cow's blood, carefully centrifuged[18] and purified, was hardened to firm jelly and planted with a tubercle cut from a sick guinea pig's lung. Then the tube was placed in an incubator.

The next morning Koch rushed into the laboratory an hour earlier than usual to look at it. Not a thing was happening in the tube. He put it back in the incubator, muttering, "Perhaps tomorrow."

A week passed . . . "Perhaps tomorrow" . . . Another week passed . . . "Perhaps—no, this is the end. No bacillus in the world would take this long to grow."

"Why, Doktor," said Gaffky softly, "how do you know? Have you personally examined every bacillus in the world? Aren't you really jumping to conclusions now?"

Koch could think of no appropriate answer, so he slung the tube back in the incubator.

The next day he arrived a little later than usual. "Well?" he said shortly to Gaffky, who was sitting at the desk filling out order blanks.

"I haven't looked."

Koch walked across the room casually, as though nothing could be of less interest to him than the contents of the incubator. He pulled out the tube, held it up to the light, then shouted, "Give me a slide—quick!"

Gaffky leaped to his feet, asking, "What is it?" The doctor was staring at the tube fascinated; his eyes behind the thick lenses were bright with greater excitement then Gaffky had ever seen in them.

Koch took the slide which Gaffky handed him and transferred a tiny particle from the tube onto it. Gaffky, peering over his shoulder, could see that the surface of the dried serum in the tube

---

[18] CENTRIFUGED—Separated; the different parts of the blood were separated in a whirling cylinder.

was covered with a faintly discernible growth. Staining the slide was a matter of minutes. Then Koch adjusted the microscope with trembling fingers.

They were there, of course, as he had known in his cautious heart that they must be.

"Yes," he said, "I was really jumping to conclusions."

To Gaffky, who did not remember that he had asked a question on the day before and received no answer, the remark seemed pointless.

"Look," said Koch, "and then get me the healthiest guinea pig in the University, a rabbit, a cat, and—do you think we could find a donkey and a pig?"

". . . These animals were inoculated with culture grown in a medium of dried blood serum," he dictated to Gaffky some days later. "They all exhibited symptoms of tuberculosis and subsequently died. Slides made of tubercles taken from bodies all show the presence of the *bacillus tuberculosis*."

Gaffky looked up. "We have been working with it for six months or more," he observed, "and this is the first time you have ever named it."

Koch smiled. "No, my friend," he said after a few moments, "this is the first time I have ever named it aloud."

The evening of March 24th was cold and rainy, defying Berliners to make *gemütlich*[14] remarks about the return of spring. The meeting of the Berlin Physiological Society was crowded but not congenial. Factions were out in force. So Dr. Koch was going to read a paper, eh? About tuberculosis? Here was something not to be missed. The Laënnecers sat on one side of the room, the sturdy sons of Broussais on the other. Helmholtz and Ehrlich conversed in guarded whispers.

Ehrlich looked around the room. "Virchow is not here," he said.

"Did you expect him to be?" Helmholtz said, smiling.

The mighty Rudolph still regarded Koch as something of an imposter.

Koch said nothing to anybody, but stood making delicate adjust-

[14] *Gemütlich*—German for *cheerful*.

ments on his perfectly focused microscope, wondering how he could possibly speak when his throat was so dry.

When the meeting was called to order, he looked at the audience over the rim of his glasses and then began to read his paper in a shaking voice: "On the Etiology of Tuberculosis."

"That evening remains graven in my mind," Ehrlich wrote later, "as the most majestic scientific event in which I have ever participated."

When Koch sat down and the chairman called for questions or objections, not a man in the room opened his mouth. The paper required no questions and permitted no objections.

The significance of what Koch had done flashed upon the bulk of his audience long before he had finished reading. Tuberculosis was not a degenerative disease which sprang haphazardly from within. It was caused by a real bacillus and spread from victim to victim by the simple process of passing the bacillus along. From this day forward the control of that process would be the supreme social responsibility of every government, every public health department, every obscure district doctor in the world.

DISCUSSING THE SELECTION

1. What were Robert Koch's two ambitions as a young man? How did he plan to combine the two? Tell how his plans were changed.

2. What about Koch's early life as a doctor seemed to indicate that he would have only an ordinary career? What gift from Emmy changed his whole life? Tell about his early work in his home laboratory.

3. Explain how Robert found the cause of anthrax disease. What recognition did this discovery bring him? How was his life changed almost overnight?

4. Much of Koch's success was the result of the extreme care with which he did his experiments. He left nothing to chance and was never satisfied as long as a single question remained unanswered. Give some examples of these characteristics from the selection.

5. Describe the method used to search for the bacillus tuberculosis. What did Koch see on the two hundred and seventy-first slide? What further experiments did he make to check on his discovery?

6. The meeting of the Berlin Physiological Society was a dramatic one. What differences of opinion were represented there? How were the differences erased by Koch's announcment?

7. Robert Koch's methods of research were just as important as his discoveries. Did this selection help you to understand how scientists work? What parts of Koch's method impressed you most? How can we apply the method of science to our own problems?

8. Some of the words below will be familiar to you; some will be new. Discuss the meaning of each word in class, then look up in a dictionary any words which have not been adequately explained.

elusive	culture	chaotic
correlate	assumptions	discernible
obsession	aspirations	factions

AND YET FOOLS SAY 🦋 GEORGE S. HOLMES

HE CAPTURED light and caged it in a glass,
Then harnessed it forever to a wire;
He gave men robots with no backs to tire
In bearing burdens for the toiling mass.

5 He freed the tongue in wood and wax and brass,
Imbued dull images with motions' fire,
Transmuted metal into human choir —
These man-made miracles he brought to pass.

Bulbs banish night along the Great White Way,
10 Thin threads of copper throb with might unseen;
On silver curtains shadow-actors play
That walk and talk from magic-mouthed machine,

While continents converse through skies o'erhead—
And yet fools say that Edison is dead!

3. ROBOTS (rō′bŏts)—Automatic machines that operate with almost human intelligence.

DISCUSSING THE POEM

One of the greatest of modern inventors was Thomas Alva Edison. While he was still young he was known as the "boy wonder of electricity," and before he died he held more than one thousand United States patents. The patents covered developments on the electric light, the storage battery, the stock ticker, the telegraph, the electric generator, the phonograph, and hundreds of other useful things.

1. How many of Edison's inventions can you identify in this poem? Look up a discussion of Edison's life and work in an encyclopaedia and list some other useful things for which he was primarily responsible.

2. "And yet fools say that Edison is dead." Why is it foolish to say this man is dead? What does this tell you about how the things men do live after them?

HE GAVE THEM "WINDOWS" 🐝

J. ALVIN KUGELMASS

THE little French boy, Louis, with the brown, sparkling eyes was playing in his father's pungent-smelling workshop. Suddenly he clutched in his small fist two blue-steeled awls,[1] and triumphantly ran off with them. Then he stumbled. There was a scream. His father, the saddlemaker of the village of Coupvray,[2] hurried to him, but it was of no use. That day three-year-old Louis lost the sight of his left eye, and soon the injury affected the optical nerves of the other eye. Little Louis was totally blinded for life.

His father, in comfortable circumstances as riches were measured in 1812, took him to Paris where he expended the larger part of his savings on physicians. But even the court doctors held out no hope. "When the nerves are mutilated, we can do nothing," they said.

The villagers were kind. "There comes *petit*[3] Louis," they would say when they heard the tapping of his little cane. For him,

---

[1] AWLS—Sharp, pointed tools for piercing holes in leather.
[2] COUPVRAY—Pronounced koo-vra'.
[3] *Petit* (pĕ-tē')—French for *little*.

they scratched out grooves on the road so that he could follow a straight path. His father, a giant of a man, never got over his remorse for the accident, and could not do enough for the little boy. In later years he wrote his son: "It was no accident as such, but my carlessness that blighted your life. I should have kept closer watch over you." Louis never forgot how the big man sobbed while whittling out a cane for him. There were none that small to be bought.

Tap, tap, tap his stick made on the road. So many taps to the big tree where he would sit and rest. So many more to the pond where he could hear the cries of his friends disporting themselves. That many more tappings to the left to his aunt's house. His eyes were at his cane's end, but as he used to explain later, it was the tapping that stayed with him. When finally, after years of torment and struggle, he succeeded in developing his system of reading and writing, Louis Braille called it "frozen taps."

When he was ten years old, Louis was enrolled in the school for the blind at Paris, the *Institution Nationale des Jeunes Aveugles.*[4] It wasn't much of a school, for before 1784, when it was established, no one had given much thought to education for the blind. Under Valentin Hauy, its founder—an unsung pioneer in the teaching of the sightless—Louis learned the alphabet by the "twig" method. From little sticks Hauy had fashioned the twenty-six letters, and along these sticks he guided the fingers of his pupils.

After Louis learned the alphabet he was graduated to the few books created painstakingly by Hauy from letters cut out of cloth and pasted on pages. Each letter was about three inches high and two inches wide. A long word would spread across two to three lines. Thus, only short selections from stories, essays, or poems were available to the young, blind pupil. A fable about Reynard the Fox, for example, filled seven thick books, each weighing about eight pounds.

To little Louis' agile mind, the process of instruction was clumsy, too slow, and clearly limited. Later, when Louis was about 14,

[4] *Institution Nationale des Jeunes Aveugles*—National Institution for the Young Blind.

another pupil noted the ridges on a printed card into which the type had bitten strongly. "Master, master," he came crying to Hauy. The master quickly saw the point and began to turn out embossed letters from movable type set by his pupils. But the letters had to be at least an inch high; a "book" was still a tremendous affair and tantalizingly tedious to read.

It was heart-breaking to the growing boy with the eager intellect. His thought processes were left dangling until his finger caught up with a word, and so "like an idiot," as he told his father, he would gather a phrase, then a sentence. A term's course that way might take as long as five years.

Every few months, Louis would return to his home in Coupvray. As he grew, so grew his impatience with his "ignorance." "Father," he would tell the big man, "the blind are the loneliest people in the world. Here, I can distinguish one bird from another by its call; I can know the entrance to the house by the lintel.[5] But am I never to know what lies beyond the confines of my hearing and my feeling with my hands? Only books can free the blind. But there are no books for the blind that are worth anything."

One day a great thought came to him. He would devise a code for every word in the dictionary—a code that would tell in one symbol an entire phrase, perhaps even a sentence. Thus, the blind could not only have entire books economically abbreviated, but they could perhaps even write. He begged his father for some bits of leather and all through the summer he snipped and cut until his hands were raw. Almost daily he would abandon his quest as hopeless. Then a new idea would strike him, and he would start afresh. He worked with codes based on triangles, squares, and circles, each bearing variations representing different letters. On a circle, for example, he marked out twenty-six positions, one for each letter of the alphabet. But he could work up no easy way for the sightless to determine just what letter was indicated. Nothing evolved that was not too complex, expensive, or cumbersome.

In his early twenties, Braille travelled great distances to uni-

---

[5] LINTEL—A horizontal supporting piece above an opening such as a window or door.

versities and begged professors of history to search for a "for-gotten" key for the blind. He wrote to many foreign countries and met with an even greater indifference than he encountered in France. Except for England, where a school for the blind had been established in 1797, there was little or no interest among pedagogues.

Meanwhile Louis, now a teacher at the *Institution Nationale des Jeunes Aveugles,* had learned of a system of "night writing" de-veloped for military use by a French army captain named Barbier. A message, he was told, could be "written" in dots and dashes to another post; there it could be read by touch without the need for striking a light. He was idling in a Paris café with a friend one evening when the significance of this development suddenly came home to him. He leaped to his feet and began to shout and thump the table.

The proprietor came running. "Monsieur Braille, Monsieur Braille, *pauvre aveugle,*[6] I beg of you, you are disturbing my guests."

Monsieur Braille threw back his head and laughed, then sat down and said humbly: "Forgive me, *messieurs,*[7] I am distraught." And from the blind eyes came hot tears.

"My dear friend," said Braille, "my dear, dear friend. I have solved the impenetrable problem of the blind—the age-long, the death-like trance of the blind. I am grateful. Mine are tears of happiness. I beg of you to forgive me."

He sat quietly for a moment. "I can now give windows to the blind," he said simply. "Why could I not see it before?"

The following day, accompanied by a blind friend, he sought out Captain Charles Barbier, who luckily was in Paris.

"I come to you on an errand of transcendental mercy," he told the captain. "Will you not explain to me, and to my friend who is also blind, your method of 'night writing' if it is not an army secret? The blind for all time to come will honour you."

[6] *Pauvre aveugle* (pōur à-vû'gl)—Poor blind one.
[7] *Messieurs* (mâ-syû')—Gentlemen.

The captain gazed with gentleness at the two men, their faces turned to him beseechingly.

"It is no secret," he said. "How can it be of service to you?"

Braille explained the tedious and awkward teaching methods for the blind. He told how they were shut away from the light that books would give them, from the friendliness that reading would shed in a darkened world.

The captain smote his thigh. "But of course. I had never thought of it." Then he explained how, with an awl, he punched impressions into thick paper so that when it was reversed small protuberances could be felt. A simple army code had been set up: one dot might mean "advance," two dots might mean "retreat," and so on. "As simple as that. I don't quite see how it will help you, my friend, but you are welcome to it." He was silent for a moment. "Of course, you could build a code for the entire language on it. It seems possible."

"It is not only possible," Braille said, "but I know how I can do it. Let me be the first to thank you as the ambassador from the world's blind."

From that day until 1837—when the first book for the blind, using the "Braille system," was published—Braille never rested.

Ironically and fittingly, the system used the very same instrument that had blinded him, the awl. As perfected by him after five years of sustained trial and error, and through a harrowing illness that eventually killed him at the early age of 43, the system used a key of six holes in an oblong. The vertical side of the oblong contained three holes, the horizontal two. Using those six holes, Braille developed sixty-three possible combinations. After the letters of the alphabet were supplied, the remaining symbols were used for punctuation, contractions, and short words such as "and" and "for."

But when Braille offered his gift to the world, it was rejected. In a lecture on his system at the Institute, before his pupils and teachers from many schools and universities, he showed how he could "punch-write" almost as rapidly as someone could read to him. Then he read back what he had written at almost the same pace as a seeing reader. But jealousy kept his method from being instituted. "He has memorized those selections," his colleagues said. He was looked upon as a fanatic.

Soon Braille petitioned the French Academy for a hearing, hoping that the Immortals [8] would approve his system, and that their influence would establish it in the schools for the blind. But his petition was turned down on the ground that the embossing system was the best and that "the blind received sufficient training and education through it."

The blind pupils from the Institute, however, came secretly to Braille and begged to be taught his system. He not only taught them how to read and write rapidly but, through a series of cunningly constructed awls, he punched out mathematical symbols and showed them how equations could be solved. He also worked out a Braille musical code and became a skilled organist.

Not until he was racked by his last illness did he know that he had not failed in gaining acceptance for his system. One of his pupils, a girl, gave a piano recital before a fashionable French audience. At the end of the concert, when she tapped her way to

[8] IMMORTALS—The forty members of the French Academy, so-called because they had attained lasting fame.

the lip of the stage, the listeners rose to their feet and would not stay their clapping. She held up her hand beseechingly.

"*Messieurs et mesdames*[9]—I beg of you, my friends . . . "

The audience seated itself. "The applause you give is not for me. It belongs to a man who is dying."

Then she told how Braille had taught her his method of reading books and music by his punch system. "He has not only given the blind of the world windows, but he has given them music to weep by," she said, herself weeping.

She told how his system was being blocked by jealous persons and by those who held contracts for embossing books for the blind.

The story was caught up by the French press, and in time the heads of the Institute capitulated to public indignation.

Friends came to Braille's bedside and told him what had occurred. "This is the third time in my life I permit myself to weep," he said. "First when I was blinded. Second when I heard about the 'night writing.' And now because I know my life was not a failure. God works in inscrutable ways, and it was fated that I be made sightless." He died soon after.

Braille's system before long swept the civilized world, and toward the end of the nineteenth century most of the nations in Europe and the Western Hemisphere passed laws making education for blind children compulsory. The Braille system became so much a part of the school system that as far back as 1893 the inventor's very name was spelled lower-case in most standard dictionaries to denote a system. Today the system has been adapted even to the Chinese, and a number of magazines around the world (some now printed on powerful, electrically-driven presses) are published in Braille.

A bust erected to Louis Braille outside the saddler's shop at Coupvray is executed with imagination. Most busts appear sightless. This one has the compassionate eyes of a St. Francis of Assisi.[10]

---

[9] *Messieurs et mesdames* (mä-dàm')—Gentlemen and ladies.

[10] ST. FRANCIS OF ASSISI (äs-sē'zè)—The founder of the Franciscan order and famed for his love of all living things.

DISCUSSING THE SELECTION

1. Many things are denied the blind, but they no longer lead the hopeless, unhappy lives they once did. Thanks to Louis Braille's gift of reading and writing, blind children and older persons who become blind may now lead useful, happy lives. How did Braille lose his own sight? What methods for teaching the blind were in use in his childhood? Would you be discouraged if it took you five years to learn a term's work?

2. Braille tried out many ideas before he found a plan for a code that would really work. Explain the system of "night writing" that showed him the way. Describe the basic idea of the Braille system.

3. One would think that any improved method for teaching the handicapped would be eagerly welcomed if only for humanitarian reasons. What selfish interests prevented wide acceptance of Braille's system? How did it finally become known?

4. Braille felt that he had himself been fated to be blind so that he might help others. Do you think it is true that those of us who see cannot appreciate the problems of the blind? Explain how you feel about it.

5. Most encyclopaedias give illustrations of the Braille alphabet. Look it up and note the simplicity of the code. If you should ever lose your sight, do you think you could learn this system?

🌸

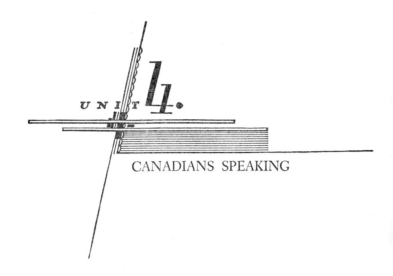

CANADIANS SPEAKING

MY COUNTRY ✒ BRUCE HUTCHISON

NOBODY knows my country, neither the stranger nor its own
sons. My country is hidden in the dark and teeming brain of
youth upon the eve of its manhood. My country has not found
itself nor felt its power nor learned its true place. It is all visions
and doubts and hopes and dreams. It is strength and weakness,
despair and joy, and the wild confusions and restless strivings of
a boy who has passed his boyhood but is not yet a man.

A problem for America, they call us. As well call a young
thoroughbred a problem because he is not yet trained and fully
grown. A backward nation they call us beside our great neighbour
—this though our eleven millons have produced more, earned more,
subdued more, built more than any other eleven millions in the
world. A colony they have thought us though we have rebelled and
fought and bled for the right to our own government and finally
produced the British Commonwealth of equal nations. A timid
race they have called us because we have been slow to change,
because we have not mastered all the achievements nor all the vices
of our neighbours.

They have not known Canada. Who but us can feel our fears and hopes and passions? How can aliens or even blood brothers know our inner doubts, our secret strengths and weaknesses and loves and lusts and shames?

Who can know our loneliness, on the immensity of prairie, in the dark forest and on the windy sea rock? A few lights, a faint glow is our largest city on the vast breath of the night, and all around blackness and emptiness and silence, where no man walks. We flee to little towns for a moment of fellowship and light and

speech, we flee into cities or log cabins, out of the darkness and the loneliness and the creeping silence. All about us lies Canada, forever untouched, unknown, beyond our grasp, breathing deep in the darkness and we hear its breath and are afraid.

No they could not know us, the strangers, for we have not known ourselves.

Long we have been a-growing, but with strong bone and sure muscle—of two bloods, French and British, slow to be reconciled in one body. We have been like a younger boy in the shadow of the two older brothers, and, admiring their powers, watching the pageant of England and the raging energy of America, we have not learned our own proud story nor tested our own strength. But we are no longer children. Now our time is come and if not grasped will be forever lost.

Now we must make our choice. Now must the heaving, fluid stuff of Canada take shape, crystalize, and harden to a purpose. No people of our numbers has ever occupied such a place before in the flood tide of history, for we are of two worlds, the Old and the New, one in each, knowing England, knowing America, joined to each by blood and battle, speech and song. We alone are the hinge between them, and upon us hangs more than we know.

Wondrous and very sweet is our name. Canada! The very word is like a boy's shout in the springtime, is like the clamour of geese going north and the roar of melting rivers and the murmur of early winds.

Can we not hear the sound of Canada? Can we not hear it in the rustle of yellow poplar leaves in October, and in the sudden trout-splash of a silent lake, the whisper of saws in the deep woods, the church bells along the river, the whistle of trains in the narrow passes of the mountains, the gurgle of irrigation ditches in the hot nights, the rustle of ripe grain under the wind, and the bit of steel runners in the snow?

Have we not felt the texture and living stuff of Canada? Have we not felt it in the damp, springy forest floor, in the caress of the new grass upon our face, in the salt spray off Fundy or Juan de Fuca, in the hot sun of the prairies, in the beat of blizzards and the fierce surge of summer growth?

And the colours of Canada, those also have we seen. We have seen them in the harsh sweep of prairie snow, in sunlight and shadow across the heavy-headed wheat, in foaming apple orchards and in maple woods, crimson as blood, and in bleeding sumac of the roadside, and in white sails of schooners out of Lunenberg and in the wrinkled blue face of mountains. And we have smelled the clean, manly smell of Canada, in pine forest and settlers' clearing fires, and alkali lakes and autumn stubble and new sawdust and old stone.

Yes, but we have not grasped it yet, the full substance of it, in our hands, nor glimpsed its size and shape. We have not yet felt the full pulse of its heart, the flex of its muscles, the pattern of its mind. For we are young, my brothers, and full of doubt, and we have listened too long to timid men. But now our time is come and we are ready.

DISCUSSING THE SELECTION

1. In this selection the author tells us many things about Canada and Canadians that we have perhaps never known before. What are some of the characteristics which he ascribes to the Canadian people?

2. What are Bruce Hutchison's own feelings about Canada?

3. Although this selection is written in prose, it reads almost like poetry. Can you find words or expressions that are more characteristic of poetry than prose?

4. Canada is a great country, stretching "A mari usque ad mare"— From sea to sea. How does Hutchison suggest the immense sweep and great variety of our native land?

JUMBO 🌿 D. A. MACMILLAN

IT was fitting that Jumbo should come from a small town in the West.

Kids who grow up in small towns in the West are pretty close to the earth and they have a good sense of values.

In their childhood and youth, living is not a matter of cement sidewalks, and movies, and big brick and steel schoolhouses with organized games and an iron fence around the playground.

They, perhaps, have never seen a street car. They don't know a thing about high buildings, and traffic lights, and elevators, and escalators, and department stores, and taxi cabs and neon lights.

They don't know about the pall of factory smoke, and the smell of the exhausts of thousands and thousands of motor cars.

They don't know about one part of town which is made up of great, ghastly houses, with well-trimmed lawns and hedges and a fancy roof and a glassed-in verandah and a two-car garage.

They don't know about that other part of town which is dirty, and grimy, and sad.

In fact, they are naïve.

They know the incredible blue of the sky, and the vast sweep of the prairie land. They know the soft breath of the spring wind and that indescribably beautiful day when you wake up in the morning to find the sun streaming in the windows, and you know that summer is just around the corner.

They know the smell of fresh-cut hay and the brisk, clear days of Autumn when the air is so clear and sweet you want to take great mouthfuls and run until you're tired.

They know the song of the meadow lark and they've picked crocus blossoms in the spring. They know the crisp, cold nights of winter and the blazing fire in the kitchen stove.

They've spent whole afternoons jumping from the barn to the haystack, and they've gone swimming in the creek and hunting with a .22.

They've walked along and seen the vast distances around them shimmering in the heat. They've walked up a dirt road in their bare feet and had a dog and a pony and a favourite calf.

They didn't grow up, these kids from small towns in the West.

They're young and they haven't peddled papers on the streets and learned about life that way. Nor have they been told that they're somehow a bit different from the boys on the other side of town and that they should make a special effort to become a play-mate of so-and-so because his father has money and influence.

They're just not smart. They accept things as they are, and they don't learn, while they're still very young, that life is a fight and a struggle; that you've got to be smart and shrewd and wise and tough to get ahead.

Jumbo was like that.

Without a doubt, he was the most naïve guy in the whole of Canada.

He was eighteen years old and didn't quite know whether to work for Dad in the general store or take over that quarter-section his uncle wanted to give him.

He talked it over with dad and uncle and decided, maybe he'd take that land. His uncle could help him with the seeding that spring and then, next year, he might be able to work it himself.

It was a very serious choice.

You would have thought it was as involved as the merger of two gigantic trust companies; companies who had engaged the services of a lot of high-priced lawyers to work out some way of cutting down the amount of money they paid to the country.

The same country, of course, which enabled them to make their money in the first place.

Finally it was decided.

Jumbo would take that quarter-section of land and he'd go to work on it himself, right away.

He was only eighteen, but he had worked for quite a few of those years. His big, solid, frame was all muscle and no fat. It was just his general bigness which had earned him the name of Jumbo.

His arms were stocky and hard-muscled. His hands were big and brown and strong. His face was round and good-humoured, and his grey eyes seemed attached to the corners of his mouth.

Every time he grinned, his mouth curled up and his eyes sparkled.

*   *   *   *

Then, news of the war came.

They heard about it on the radio Dad kept going all the time in the store. The townspeople had gathered there to listen to Hitler and hear about Munich in those previous years.

They were gathered together again to learn that they were at war.

Nearly all the soldier-settlers of the district turned out at once.

They were older now. Their hands were rough and gnarled and they showed unmistakable signs of work and worry.

But they were enthusiastic. They would take either the Army or the Home Guard, and they wanted to get in right away.

Uncle joined up too.

He'd been at Vimy in the last war and he had a medal.

Father was a bit older than uncle. He'd been in the last war, too, but he was too old now to take any part in this one.

He was grey and hawk-faced and lean. He was noticeably quiet these days.

Mom and Dad talked it over quietly.

They decided Jumbo was too young to go to war. There was news on the radio that the twenty-one-year-olds would be called up, but that gave Jumbo a couple of years and likely the war would be over by that time anyway.

They talked to Jumbo and he listened.

He was used to taking Dad's advice because Dad was old and wise. Besides, he didn't know anything about wars and things.

*   *   *   *

It was quiet that first winter.

The Canadian Legion held some smokers in the town hall, and quite a few of the men and boys appeared in uniform on Main Street.

There was more talk of conscription, but everybody knew that farmer's sons wouldn't be called up.

Especially, not if they were working land of their own.

They listened every evening to the eight o'clock news on the radio. They heard about Norway, and France, and Denmark, and Dunkirk, and Greece.

Then, one day, there was news of the Canadian boys trapped on Hong Kong.

*   *   *   *

Jumbo talked to Dad one night.

"I've been thinking maybe I should join up, Dad," he said.

He spoke very seriously. It was as though the whole course of the war depended upon his taking a personal hand in it.

That was the way Jumbo did things.

He said it in the same way he might have said. "I think we should put the north corner into summer fallow this year."

Dad said:

"I don't want to advise you, my boy. It's your own choice."

*   *   *   *

The following Monday, Jumbo got up early and put on his good suit. Dad got up and put on his good suit, too. They got the car out of the yard and drove towards the city. It was a long drive, and they talked.

"What's it going to be—the army? I know a bit about the army, but I don't know nothing about that there air force or navy.

Jumbo said:

"I don't know, Dad. I've been thinking maybe I'd try the air force. I'm pretty good with engines and machinery. I got that tractor running, remember? I hear they're looking for men to work on them airplanes."

The sergeant at the recruiting centre smiled when the two of them came to the counter.

Dad walked up to him.

"This boy, here, has come in to find out about joining your air force."

The sergeant looked them over. The old man was tall, gaunt, and shabby. He looked stooped and worn. There were deep lines in his face. His hands were hard and brown.

The kid with him was just another big, husky, farm boy. He

noticed the old-fashioned hat, the ankle shoes and the funny-looking suit which must have been three sizes too small. The trousers stopped two inches above his ankles.

He thought:

Oh well, maybe we can make him a G.D.[1]—if he can pass the intelligence test.

He said:

"Will you have the boy fill out this form, please?"

Dad and Jumbo took a long time to fill out the application form. There were quite a few things on it they didn't understand very well. They had to ask assistance several times.

"All right," the sergeant said. "If you'll sit down and wait, you can see the interviewing officer in a little while."

It seemed a long wait, and Dad and Jumbo felt uncomfortable with all the smart-looking city fellows sitting around too. But they picked out a few boys who, obviously, were from the country. That made them feel a bit more at ease.

Then it was Jumbo's turn for an interview. Dad went in to see the interviewing officer with him. It wasn't the usual thing—the air force preferred that the boys have their interviews on their own —but it didn't really matter, so they let Dad go along.

The interviewing officer was pleasant.

He had a boy of his own in the air force. He knew just about how Dad felt about it.

He said:

"Well, my boy, what can we do for you?"

Dad was sitting a little to one side. He wasn't going to interfere. It was Jumbo's show now.

Jumbo said:

"I thought, mister, that I would join the air force."

The officer smiled.

"Good, and what would you like to do?"

"I thought maybe I could be a mechanic. I've done a lot of work on engines around the farm."

---

[1] G.D.—General Duties classification for airmen who are not trained for a specific air force trade.

"Excellent. We need mechanics. But tell me, have you ever thought of flying?"

Jumbo hadn't.

"You mean:—fly them things?"

That was what the officer meant.

Jumbo looked around at Dad. Dad was interested.

"Flying is by far the best end of the game to be in," the officer said. "If a boy graduates, he gets sergeant's rank immediately. After that, he has a real opportunity for promotion. More than likely he'll get his commission in time. That is, if he makes the grade."

There was some discussion.

Finally Jumbo said.

"Well, Dad, if I'm going into the air force I might as well go in the best part."

The thought of flying had aroused something inside of him. He hadn't thought of it in that way before.

Then, as far as the rest of the day was concerned, Jumbo wasn't quite sure just what happened.

He remembered he had written some kind of examination. It was a long paper full of silly questions and little diagrams you had to pair up together. You only had half-an-hour to do it, too.

He was sure he failed. He couldn't understand what all those silly questions had to do with joining the air force.

But he didn't fail.

In fact, the sergeant who marked the papers looked up in some surprise after he had marked Jumbo's effort.

He thought: You'd never suspect it, but that guy has got something on the ball.

The next thing Jumbo remembered was being told to take his clothes off and stand around with about twenty other men. He'd never been to a Y.M.C.A. It was the first time he'd ever done that.

He stood shyly in a corner and tried to hide himself behind a desk.

The medical officer singled him out.

"All right, Lady Godiva, you're next. Come over here and let's have a look at you."

They classed Jumbo fit for any flying duty except, perhaps, air gunner. He was a bit too stocky to fit comfortably in a gun turret.

Then he was given an address and told to go and get an x-ray of his chest.

The officer said:

"All right, you men. Get your x-rays this afternoon and report here tomorrow. We'll have a chance to check on them by that time."

"But—" Jumbo stammered. "I live—that is, Dad and I—we're about eighty miles out in the country."

"Can't you stay over-night?" the officer asked.

"Well, yes—I guess so."

Jumbo was quite serious. A room would cost three or four dollars.

He and Dad talked it over.

"We'll have to take a room," Dad said. "Maybe we can phone Ma, too, and tell her we're staying over."

Dad wasn't one for staying at one of those new-fangled hotels. He knew of one down on Railway Avenue that was supposed to be clean and not too expensive. He was careful, though, to ask how much it was before they signed the register. He'd heard of those gypping hotels.

He phoned Ma.

Ma was a bit worried, but she thought it would be all right.

"Say, Dad, will you call at one of them city stores and get me a piece of curtain material? I kinda thought it would be nice to get something from the city."

She was a bit bewildered. It was the first night she had spent away from Dad in twenty years.

*   *   *   *

The x-rays were in order, and a new world opened for Jumbo. He felt terribly alone on the trip to the Manning Depot, and he didn't mix with the boys. He'd never been away from home, and he didn't really understand what they were talking about half the time.

He thought maybe he'd made a mistake. He wanted to go back to the farm.

It was a bit better at Manning Depot because he met some boys who were from the farm, too, and were just as frightened as he was. He wrote home and told Dad about it.

They had Jumbo in uniform now and it fitted better than his civilian clothes. He learned too, that he had to keep his buttons and shoes polished.

If that was what you were supposed to do, then Jumbo did it. His buttons and shoes shone to the high heavens. He did well in his classes, too.

He wrote a letter home every day.

Dad wrote back, but he always got the school teacher who roomed with them to put the address on the letter. He didn't want Jumbo's new friends to know that his dad couldn't write very well.

Getting up early in the morning didn't worry Jumbo. And he studied and trained. He was a bit awkward on the drill square, but he learned. He worked hard at his studies, too; he was thorough.

That was the way he did everything.

He also learned many things that weren't on the curriculum. He learned about big cities and street cars. He saw rows of city houses, and factories, and smoke. He saw the department stores and went to movies. He learned the smell of the exhausts of thousands of motor cars. He saw elevators, and escalators, and neon signs, and bright lights. Unconsciously, he saw the greatness and the meanness of the city.

He saw these things, and he learned about them.

But he didn't forget the incredible blue of the sky and the vast sweep of the prairie land. He didn't forget the soft breath of the spring wind and that indescribably beautiful day when you wake up in the morning to find the sun streaming in the window and you know summer is just about here.

He didn't forget the smell of fresh-cut hay and the brisk, clear days of autumn when the air is so sweet and clear you want to take great mouthfuls and run until you're tired.

He didn't forget these, or the meadow larks, and the crocus blossoms in the spring and the blazing fire in the kitchen stove.

Outwardly, he changed.

Inside, he was the same.

He also learned to fly. They made him a pilot, and he flew beautifully.

*   *   *   *

Flying was a serious business to Jumbo. Just like getting the spring ploughing done.

Yes, outwardly, he changed. But, inside, he was the same Jumbo. His hands were still big and brown and strong. His face was still round and good-humoured. His grey eyes still seemed attached to the corners of his mouth. Every time he grinned, his eyes sparkled.

And it was decreed that Jumbo should go to England.

He went on Ops almost at once.

One night, on the way to the target, he was attacked by a fighter. His rear gunner was killed instantly, and one motor was shot out.

Jumbo went on and bombed anyway. That was the way you did things at home on the farm. You took things in your stride; just like dust storms, drought, and early frost.

They gave him a D.F.M.[2] for that effort.

A short time later, he got his commission.

That was Jumbo's first intimate brush with the enemy and he became even more serious than before. He looked like nothing so much as a big, playful, collie pup who had been kicked by a supposed friend.

And it happened that, in the strange way of war, fate smiled on Jumbo. He finished his first tour. He was promoted. He became a Squadron Leader.

He still wrote home every day. He told them he had been promoted.

[2] D.F.M.—Distinguished Flying Medal.

They were very proud.

The papers were full of stories about him, too. One day a man from the city paper came out to see Dad and Ma and ask them questions about their son.

Even the local weekly got Jumbo's picture and printed it.

Ma kept the copy of the weekly paper and the city paper, too.

She cut out the story and the picture and tucked them away in the family Bible.

* * * *

Again, in the strange way of war, Jumbo was made a Wing Commander. He was given a squadron to command in Bomber Group.

As usual, the boys didn't quite know how to take him. They had thought a lot of their previous Wing Commander. They were in a belligerent mood, and they couldn't help looking upon him as an usurper.

They knew that, while Flight Commanders were usually appointed from the same squadron, it was the custom to bring in a Wing Commander from somewhere else. But they were prepared to dislike him.

What's more, he was awkward in the mess and didn't know any off-colour songs and didn't drink.

Only that ribbon on his chest prevented an almost open rebellion.

But Jumbo didn't even know he wasn't wanted.

* * * *

Wing Commanders are not supposed to make more than one trip a month. Jumbo made two in the first three weeks with his new squadron.

The Group Captain from base phoned him. He wanted to know what was going on, and didn't Jumbo know that Wing Commanders were supposed to make one bombing raid a month.

Jumbo mumbled something about wanting to know what the boys were up against these days and that, since the morale on the station wasn't too good, maybe he should fly more to give the boys confidence.

The next time Jumbo flew it was not in his own name. Somebody named "Flight Sergeant Jones" went down in the log book.

The boys in the squadron began to get the idea.

Here was a big, good-natured guy, who was a bit different from anything they'd known before.

Here was a Wing Commander who was fond of taking off his coat and demonstrating to an aero-engine mechanic just how such and such a sparkplug should be cleaned and why.

The squadron spirit picked up. The boys knew that, whenever there was a particularly tough target, Jumbo would be along.

Jumbo got thinking one day and decided his next trip would be as Warrant Officer Brown.

They might get wise at base to what was going on.

Then one day he did get a sarcastic letter from base.

It read:

"Flight Sergeant Jones, Warrant Officer Brown, and Jumbo, are all screened. None of these men will fly until further orders."

*   *   *   *

Jumbo sat tight after that, and the boys carried on. And they had captured his forthright spirit, and the squadron became very famous throughout the length and breadth of the land.

One night, Jumbo announced he was going with them, and that the target would be a bit difficult.

They knew he hadn't flown for some time and suspected he had been saving himself for this particular raid. They knew it would be tough.

It was tough.

Jumbo didn't return.

The next day there were volunteers for a sea search. And they combed the North Sea and they dared the enemy coast and prayed that some of the enemy would come up to challenge them.

None came.

They returned to base, but the station was not quite the same. It was shaken.

But it carried on.

*　　*　　*　　*

It carried on because the spirit that was Jumbo was the solid, earthly, dependable kind that lives.

That was because Jumbo was part of the incredible blue of the sky and the vast sweep of the prairie land. He was the scent of fresh-cut hay, and the crisp, cold nights of winter, and the blazing stove in the kitchen, and the song of the meadow lark and the crocus blossoms in the spring.

He was a lot of solid things that are important: like getting in the wood for the winter, and the spring ploughing done.

He was vast distances shimmering in the heat, and walking up a dirt road in your bare feet, and having a dog, a pony, and a favourite calf.

He was all those things and, because he was, he is part of the tradition of his country.

He made no speeches, he wrote no books, he formed no governments. He just lived and, because he lived, more children are going to be naïve and grow up in the country, and wake up on that indescribably beautiful day when you find the sun streaming in the window and know that summer is just about here.

KEYS TO ENJOYMENT

Jumbo was a naïve young boy who little suspected his own ability and who was never in the least pretentious. From the simple background of his life in a small western town and from the wholesome relationships which existed between himself and his parents he gained that strength of character which he demonstrated as a pilot in the R.C.A.F. Long after he had proved himself to be a capable leader, he continued to accept tasks far beyond the call of duty. This he did simply and sincerely, not because he had to, but because he wanted to.

1. What is the effect of the repetition of the vivid descriptions of Jumbo's prairie surroundings?

2. Point out contrasts between the city atmosphere and the prairie atmosphere as MacMillan pictures them.

3. What are some of the "little things" that enter into the building of sound character?

4. Explain ". . . he is part of the tradition of his country . . ." in such a way as to show the meaning of *tradition*.

5. Write a paragraph using as your topic sentence, "Jumbo's character had many wholesome aspects."

THIS IS CANADA 🌾 MORLEY CALLAGHAN

IN MANY another land I've lain awake thinking of home with pictures of places in my own country sprawling out in my mind. A man dreams of the things he has seen and felt and can't help remembering. There is no one line of thought that ties the pictures together; they all go together as the pieces of a jigsaw puzzle go together to make up the pattern of a man's native land. I remember one night I was out at sea and I lay awake waiting nervously for the sound of the rattle that would mean "action stations" and I was thinking of Halifax and it suddenly seemed to become a warm, home-like, and important place. I could see the longshoremen streaming up the shore from the jetties—the crowded jetties heaped with supplies and with the ships tied up and the sound of the riveters at work. A man reaches out in his mind beyond the harbour—going up the coast maybe past the fishing villages where the fishermen are unloading their catches from the schooners and the sunshine glistens on the teeming fish in the nets. For a few moments the little white churches with their single spires and with their own simple likeness and grace which seems to make them move against the background of the clouds are held there in the mind; or may be it's the sight of the miners streaming in single file down the hills at quitting time to relax for an hour or two on their unpainted stoops with the little picket fence between them and the streets. Some of these sights are not very comforting, yet they are something to remember, something to carry you inland and home—inland down the St. Lawrence where the narrow strips of farmland slope down to the river and where there is always the

spire of a church against the side of a hill. I like Quebec. I like
the way the people seem to be part of the soil, though the houses
with the stairs leading up from the sidewalk don't seem to belong
to this world. I remember that one night out at sea when I seemed
in my thoughts to be hurrying home, I stopped for a long time in
Montreal. It's the city where people like to stop for awhile. It
seemed to be wintertime and on the icy streets a gang of kids were
playing shinny. It was the most beautiful of all the sights I had
seen because the snow was falling just as it might have been falling
all over Canada, and on a thousand ponds and on a thousand
corner rinks across the country I knew the kids were playing
shinny. Or maybe it had taken on the dignity of hockey in places
far removed—like Renfrew, St. Boniface, Smoky Lake, and Trail
out in British Columbia. The snow was falling all over the country
and the kids playing the same game in a thousand different places
seemed to be holding the country together.

Come to think of it, there are other things than hockey or basket-
ball or skiing that seem to be the same all over the country. The
workers in the shops in Montreal are doing the same things as the
workers in the shops in Toronto and Winnipeg are doing. The
workers in the power houses, the insurance buildings, the foundries,
the slaughter houses, the men on ships, on the lake boats going into
Toronto or Collingwood or Midland and the men on ships going

down the St. Lawrence to the sea. And I remember that night I kept on thinking of people doing the same things in all the different towns and cities; girls going into libraries with books under their arms at the same hour in a hundred different cities; little family groups sitting in the living-room listening to the radio. The same jam of logs on the Gatineau as was on the great rivers of northern Ontario. There were great piles of lumber on the Vancouver docks and piles of lumber on other docks in the lake cities. Suddenly I wanted to be off the ship. I wanted to be on the train. No, just watching the train—trains all over the country—skirting the aloofness of the blue Algoma hills or heading straight across the prairies on the endlessly straight tracks gleaming in the sunlight and with the long straight line of telegraph poles beside the track.

But this business of trying to find things that are the same all over the country was a deliberate game I was playing when I could not sleep and the ship was rolling in the heavy sea. Tired and not thinking—too tired even to keep on going home—the bright and mixed-up pictures completely separated—completely different —keep on coming—the pictures a man can't forget—the northland seen from the air, a lake country, patches of water, patches of land looking like jagged holes on a white paper—yet when I was a kid I had always thought of the north country as being a piece of solid rock. How different it is from the wheat lands of Saskatchewan. O shining western star!—shining so early in the prairies with the wind humming in the telegraph wires. The long night, the long silence and the western star always more brightly gleaming. In the morning sunlight in the summertime, the wheatland rises to the blue sky; it looks like a golden bowl and the plain farmhouses seem to be set down there, very small, square objects, in the middle of the golden bowl.

If you feel that you may be in danger out at sea, you try hard to remember beautiful things about home—things like that western star, or the mists that hang over the Saskatchewan river valley around Edmonton in the wintertime; or the time you have spent on the streets of Vancouver looking up at the snow-capped mountain and trying to pick out that peculiar formation in the moonlight which they call the Sleeping Beauty. But then you can't sleep and you know it, and you get up. That night I got up and climbed the ladder to the bridge. It was cold and I looked at the black water and my thoughts were calmer. I seemed to see my own city, Toronto, my own province, Ontario, the rich, fat, farm-lands of Ontario. The wind was bitter cold, yet it was April. For some reason I thought of my father asking me to help him take down the storm windows. All over Canada at that time fathers would be saying to their sons, "How about helping me take down the storm windows tomorrow, son?"

KEYS TO ENJOYMENT

Written as a preface to a volume of photographs entitled **This is Canada,** this passage by Morley Callaghan gives a parade of Canadian sights and activities. Though Canada has many differences in scenery, occupations, and racial background of its people, there are many factors which tend to weld it together because they are common to all parts of the country.

1. What are some of the factors which tend towards Canadian unity?

2. As you think about the things that you associate with life in Canada, which seem most important to you? Make a list of them and then compare yours with that of Morley Callaghan. Account for any differences between the two enumerations.

3. Morley Callaghan has succeeded in revealing something of himself through his writing. What characteristics of Morley Callaghan are so disclosed?

A CANADIAN ABROAD EDWARD WILLIAM THOMPSON

When the croon of a rapid is heard on the breeze,
With the scent of a pine-forest gloom,
Or the edge of the sky is of steeple-top trees,
Set in hazes of blueberry bloom,
5   Or a song-sparrow sudden from quietness trills
His delicate anthem to me,
Then my heart hurries home to the Ottawa hills,
Wherever I happen to be.

When the veils of a shining lake vista unfold,
10 Or the mist towers dim from a fall,
Or a woodland is blazing in crimson and gold,
Or a snow-shroud is covering all,
Or there's honking of geese in the darkening sky,
When the spring sets hepatica free,
15 Then my heart's winging north as they never can fly,
Wherever I happen to be.

When the swallows slant curves of bewildering joy,
As the cool of the twilight descends,
And rosy-cheek maiden and hazel-hue boy
20 Listen grave while the Angelus ends
In a tremulous flow from the bell of a shrine,
Then a far away mountain I see,
And my soul is in Canada's evening shine,
Wherever my body may be.

20. ANGELUS—The call to prayer rung at morning, noon, and evening. It is called the Angelus from the first word of the Annunciation.

ENJOYING THE POEM

When Robert Browning was living in Italy, he wrote a poem entitled "Home Thoughts from Abroad." In it he expressed a wish that he might be in his native England to enjoy the beauty of spring there. Similarly, Thompson writes as a Canadian abroad. Whenever his senses remind him of something that he associates with Canada, he is transported, in memory, to his Canadian homeland.

1. What similarity do you find between "A Canadian Abroad" and "This is Canada"?

2. What are the things that remind the poet of Canada? Which of these make their appeal through the senses? Through which of the senses do they appeal?

3. What are other sights, sounds, or odours that you would remember if you were a Canadian abroad? Why were these not mentioned by Thompson?

ISLAND MAGIC 🌿 JOHN BUCHAN

I AM glad to have at last reached this delectable island. Wherever I go in the Dominion I meet your sons, generally in posts of high importance, and I have always been deeply impressed with their passionate affection for the place of their origin.

What is there about an island that makes its inhabitants regard it with peculiar pride? At the other end of Canada there is also an island, the island of Vancouver, where I have found a like pride and affection. It is the same all over the world. You remember the story of the minister in the little island of Cumbrae in the Firth of Clyde, who used to pray on Sunday for a blessing upon the Great and Little Cumbrae and upon the "adjacent islands of Great Britain and Ireland." That is the proper spirit. We British are an island people and it is to an island that our hearts return.

It has always been so in history from the time of the ancient Greeks, who placed their earthly Paradise not on any mainland, but in what they called the Fortunate Islands, somewhere out in

the western ocean. It was from the island of Delos that the god Apollo sprang, and the little barren island of Ithaca was the home of the great Ulysses. From the tiny island of Iona Christianity came to Scotland. In one of the finest and most poignant songs of exile ever written, the *Canadian Boat Song*, the heart of the wanderer does not turn back to any valley on the Scottish mainland. It is the "lone shieling on the misty island" of which he is thinking. It is the same throughout literature. In the Middle Ages romance centred in the mysterious islands of the western sea. It was on an island that Robinson Crusoe made his home. It was on Robert Louis Stevenson's "Treasure Island" that Jim Hawkins met his adventures.

What is it that gives an island this special charm for the heart of man? I think the main reason is that an island has its clear physical limits, and the mind is able to grasp it and make a picture of it as a whole. Our imagination may be kindled by big things— the far-stretching magnitude of the British Empire, or the vastness of the Dominion of Canada. But it is on little things that our affections lay hold. Cast back your memories to your childhood, and I think you will find that it is some modest-sized place that lingers most in your recollection, the wood where you played, a corner of the sea-shore, the little stream where you caught trout, the field which you regarded as your special property, the bit of the garden at home which was your own special garden. As we grow older our interests are enlarged, but our most idiomatic love is reserved for a village or a parish, what Edmund Burke, in a famous phrase, called "the little platoon in which we were reared." That is the fixed point from which we adjust ourselves to the rest of the world. Let me tell you a story which has the merit of being true. There is a parish in Scotland under the knees of the Grampians, called Rothiemurchus. A friend of mine was visiting some wounded soldiers returned from Mesopotamia and she asked one man where he got his wound. His answer was, "Weel, mem, it was about twa miles on the Rothiemurchus side of Bagdad." For that soldier the world was a simple place, for however far he wandered he could always link it up with his home. There is a profound parable in the saying. No experience will be too novel, and no place too strange if we can link it up with what we already know and love.

I do no think you can exaggerate the value of this local patriotism. The man who has it is at home in the world, for he has his roots deep down in his native soil. But tonight I want to put to you the other side of the matter. If it is essential to have the patriotism of the small unit, it is no less important to have the patriotism of the bigger unit. We begin with a loyalty to little things, a loyalty we should never relinquish—to our village, our parish, our home, our first school. But as we grow older it is important that we should acquire also wider loyalties—our college, our profession, our province, our nation, our fellow men. There is nothing inconsistent between a local patriotism and a patriotism of humanity. Indeed, I think the second is impossible without the first. There is no value in a thin international sentiment which professes an affection for humanity at large and shows no affection for the humanity immediately around us. The wider loyalty can only exist if the smaller loyalty is strong and deep. But there is need of the wider loyalty. Napoleon said very truly that Providence was on the side of the bigger battalions in war, and Providence is on the side, I think, of the bigger social battalions in the world to-day. In our complex modern life a large-scale organization is essential if we are to get the best out of civilization.

You of Prince Edward Island, like all strong peoples, represent a mixture of races. You have among you, I understand, a good many countrymen of my own. Now I am very chary about exaggerating the merits of Scotsmen, for we are only too prone to blow our own trumpet. We have plenty of faults—how many only a Scotsman knows! But we have one quality, I think, which can be praised without qualification. We have a gift of uniting the narrower and the wider patriotisms. We are scattered all over the globe, and wherever we go I think we become good citizens of our new home. Everywhere in the British Commonwealth, and in many lands which are not British, you will find Scotsmen taking a vigorous and loyal part in the national life. But at the same time we never forget the rock whence we were hewn and the pit whence we were digged. I find families of Scottish blood, which have been for generations away from Scotland, still retaining a lively affection for, and a lively interest in, their little country of origin.

That is as it should be, for a man can never have too many loyalties. Therefore I want to see in the citizens of Canada a strong and continuing love of the district to which they belong, but at the same time a strong and continuing interest in the Dominion of which they are a part, the whole Canadian nation.

A Governor-General is in a unique position, for it is his duty to get to know the whole of Canada and all the varieties of her people. This summer I had a trip of more than ten thousand miles, which took me in the tracks of Sir Alexander Mackenzie's journey to the Arctic Ocean, and over all the Northern territories, and also by Mackenzie's trail to the Pacific. In my two years of residence here I have already had the privilege of visiting most parts of the different Provinces. I am filled with admiration for what has already been done, and with wonder and delight at the possibilities of the future! You have a tremendous country, which I believe is destined to be one of the greatest nations in the world.

So I want to make Canadians prouder of Canada—of all Canada. You will only achieve your destiny if, in addition to your strong love of your home, you have also a pride and affection for the whole Dominion, a loyalty to the vast territories which it is your business to shape to the purposes of civilization. I want the older Canada, with its ancient and virile traditions, to realize that these traditions must be not merely proud memories, but an incentive to the shaping of the new Canada, a summons to a high duty and a mighty task. A famous English statesman once talked of calling in the New World to redress the balance of the old. The duty before Canada and the duty before our British Commonwealth of Nations is to use both Old and New to provide for our people an ampler life.

KEYS TO ENJOYMENT

When John Buchan was Governor-General of Canada he was often called upon to make important speeches in his official capacity. Many of these were collected and published in *Canadian Occasions* from which "Island Magic" was taken. In "Island Magic," which Buchan gave as a speech at Charlottetown, Prince Edward Island, in 1937, the author, while stressing the importance of loyalties to local institutions and organizations, points out the necessity of a broader loyalty to our country as a whole. Nationhood, according to Buchan, demands that we contribute our efforts towards building a united Canada with each area contributing whatever its local traditions and talents permit.

1. In praising Prince Edward Island, Buchan attempts to show the importance that islands have had in the history of the world. What are some of the famous islands he mentions? Try to add other famous islands to this list giving the importance of each.

2. What, in the opinion of Buchan, gives an island charm?

3. What are some of the characteristics of Scotsmen as mentioned by Buchan?

4. In what way can your community help to create loyalties broader than those to local institutions? What is the importance of doing so?

5. In what ways does Buchan show that he has read and studied widely?

6. Who was the famous statesman who "once talked of calling in the New World to redress the balance of the old"?

ON BEING CANADIAN ☙ VINCENT MASSEY

WHAT sort of person do we wish our young Canadian to be? What will he be like if he embodies the best in the Canada around him? He will have some reverence for the past, a respect for what has gone before. He will have kept some of the simple virtues of an earlier time which will help him to sort out the real from the counterfeit. He will think for himself, with respect for the views of others. He will work hard and play hard and know how to use his increasing leisure. He will have resources within him to keep him independent of the mechanized pleasure of the age. He will be able to laugh at the absurd and will become angry at the sight of injustice. He will not be ashamed of good manners. He will show an inherited instinct for freedom. He will nurse a personal devotion to the welfare and the safety of his country. He will have a deep and quiet belief in what she is and what she can do.

What might be the credo to express his beliefs? He should be able to say:

I believe in Canada, with pride in her past, belief in her present and faith in her future.

I believe in the quality of Canadian life, and in the character of Canadian institutions.

I believe in the Commonwealth of Nations within whose bounds we have found freedom and outside which our national life would lose its independent being.

I believe in our abiding friendship with our nearest neighbours, an honest friendship without either the subservience or the mimicry which must impair true partnership.

I believe that Canada is one, and that if our minds dwell on those things which its parts have in common, we can find the unity of the whole.

I believe that with sound work, the spirit of the team, and an awareness of ourselves, we can look forward to achievements beyond our imagining.

It will be said that our young Canadian has been given here a formidable list of virtues. But no lesser ideal would be worthy of his country. For no citizen has a nobler inheritance. We are fortunate in Canada beyond our reckoning: in our natural treasure; in our place on the great air highways of the globe and in our neighbourhood in America; in our links with the other British states; above all, fortunate in the skill and character of a people who can rise to any challenge. But there is one thing essential to all these advantages, and that is faith in ourselves. Without it, something will always be missing from the list. We can borrow, if need be, from the faith of others. We can find plenty of it in the early builders, whose speeches still glow in musty pages. We need their vision to carry us on through the years that lie ahead which are not without their perplexities and their dangers. We should remember the advice of the poet, Charles Roberts. What he said to his generation applies no less to ours: "Let thy past convince the future." In the confused and difficult world we see around us, any nation can be pardoned for moments of hesitation. But with all the blessing which Providence has given this land we should have no cause for doubt. If the men of '67 were with us to-day they would call upon us to move forward together with confidence and pride. We can hear them say to their fellow-Canadians, "Let us take the road again."

KEYS TO UNDERSTANDING

The Right Honourable Vincent Massey, after a lifetime spent in the service of his country, tells us here what it means to be a Canadian. The creed which he presents, sets forth the ideals towards which Canadians should strive. To achieve these, says Massey, we must develop a sense of pride in ourselves and in our accomplishments. This can be done only by having faith in ourselves. Such faith is built to a great extent upon a knowledge of our history, for this will develop in us an appreciation of the traditions which we inherit.

1. What are the characteristics which you think a Canadian should have? Does your list include any things that are not in Massey's statement?

2. Why is a knowledge of history so important in developing an appreciation of the meaning of citizenship?

ODE TO NEWFOUNDLAND 🎵 CAVENDISH BOYLE

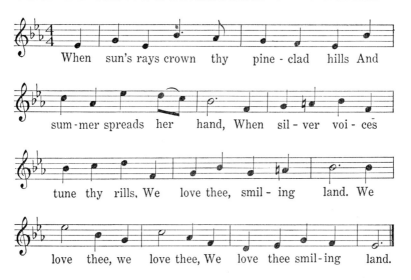

When sun's rays crown thy pine-clad hills And summer spreads her hand, When silver voices tune thy rills, We love thee, smiling land. We love thee, we love thee, We love thee smiling land.

WHEN sun's rays crown thy pine-clad hills
And summer spreads her hand,
When silver voices tune thy rills,
We love thee, smiling land.
5   We love thee, we love thee,
We love thee, smiling land.

When spreads thy cloak of shimmering white,
At winter's stern command,
Through shortened day and starlit night,
10   We love thee, frozen land.
We love thee, we love thee,
We love thee, frozen land.

When blinding storm-gusts fret thy shore,
And wild waves lash thy strand;
15   Though spindrift swirl and tempest roar,

We love thee, wind-swept land.
We love thee, we love thee,
We love thee, wind-swept land.

As loved our fathers, so we love;
20   Where once they stood, we stand;
Their prayer we raise to Heaven above,
God guard thee, Newfoundland.
God guard thee, God guard thee,
God guard thee, Newfoundland.

KEYS TO ENJOYMENT

Canada's newest province is rich in her history, her natural beauty, and her culture, as well as in her pride in herself and the achievement of her people. This pride is expressed in the "Ode to Newfoundland" which has been to Newfoundlanders what "O Canada" has been to other Canadians. Now the Newfoundlanders, while retaining their own ode, join with their fellow Canadians in singing "O Canada." As you sing the "Ode to Newfoundland", try to picture what the words describe.

🕸 FOR FURTHER READING: ADVENTURES IN OTHER LIVES

JOHN BAKELESS, *Fighting Frontiersman*
    A well-written account of Daniel Boone and his fame as an Indian fighter and wilderness explorer.

LAURA BENÉT, *Enchanting Jenny Lind*
    A biography of the singer who became known as the "Swedish Nightingale."

FRANCIS E. BENZ, *Pasteur, Knight of the Laboratory*
    The story of Louis Pasteur, the French scientist, and his struggles to prove his theories in bacteriology.

JOHN BROPHY, *Spearhead*
    An inspiring story of America's fighting men and their supreme courage.

JOHN BUCHAN, *Sir Walter Raleigh*
The colourful life of a gentleman adventurer and buccaneer is told in eleven stories by his followers.

ROGER BURLINGAME, *Inventors Behind the Inventor*
Stories of pioneer inventors whose early work furnished the foundations for others to come.

JOSEPH COTTLER AND HAYM JAFFE, *Heroes of Civilization*
Success stories of thirty-five outstanding people in many fields.

EVE CURIE, *Madame Curie*
The daughter of the famous discoverer of radium tells the story of her mother's struggles and achievements.

JAMES DAUGHERTY, *Poor Richard*
Some experiences of that versatile man Benjamin Franklin.

PAUL DE KRUIF, *The Microbe Hunters*
Biographical sketches of leaders in bacteriology — Leeuwenhoek, Pasteur, and others.

JEANETTE EATON, *David Livingstone, Foe of Darkness*
The story of the explorer, scientist, and great missionary to Africa.

BASSIL FITZGERALD, *Never Surrender*
Ten short biographies of free men in action.

MARION W. FLEXNER, *Drina*
A story of the wayward little girl who was trained to a great sense of duty and who became Queen Victoria.

RUTH FOX, *Great Men of Medicine*
Sketches, like the story of "Koch," of nine outstanding men of science.

ARIADNE GILBERT, *More than Conquerors*
Stories of some of the world's great men—their personalities, struggles, and achievements.

WILLIAM HERMAN, *Hearts Courageous*
A collection of stories about physically handicapped people who found success through remarkable courage.

SALLY KNAPP, *Eleanor Roosevelt*
The biography of one of the famous women of this century.

RICHARD S. LAMBERT, *Franklin of the Arctic*
A biography of one of Canada's great explorers, with emphasis on his search for the North West Passage.

D. A. MACMILLAN, *Only the Stars Know*
Stories of R.C.A.F. bomber air crew who fought in World War II.

ALBERT BIGELOW PAINE, *Girl in White Armour*
A simple and direct telling of Joan of Arc's story.

A. M. PULLEN, *Despite the Colour Bar*
George Washington Carver's story, briefly told.

ANN ROOS, *Man of Malokai*
An interesting account of Father Damien who devoted his life to the lepers on the island of Malokai.

LOWELL JACKSON THOMAS, *Boys' Life of Colonel Lawrence*
The story of the shy young Englishman who led the scattered tribes of Arabia to victory against the Turks.

ELIZABETH WAUGH, *Simon Bolivar, A Story of Courage*
The story of the great liberator of South America is told with sympathy and courage.

L. N. WOOD, *Walter Reed: Doctor in Uniform*
The efforts of a famous bacteriologist to discover the mystery of yellow fever are described in a thrilling account.

EDNA YOST, *Modern Americans in Science and Invention*
Interesting sketches of present-day industrialists and men of science

🐾

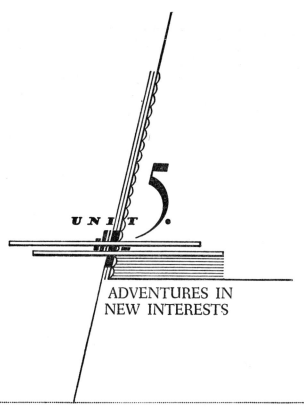

UNIT 5.

ADVENTURES IN NEW INTERESTS

Do you sometimes feel that you are in a rut? Does each day seem much like the one before? Are your daily experiences dull and uninteresting? If so, why not look for some new interests? Surely in the world about you there is something new and exciting waiting for you to find it. Discover for yourself some new interests and you will see that discovery is adventure. So, read on and see how others have kept their eagerness for living. Maybe you will be inspired to ride a dangerous rapid, make a parachute jump, or climb a mountain. But do not forget that sometimes the most interesting ideas are found in a quiet poem, an old song, or a clever romantic story.

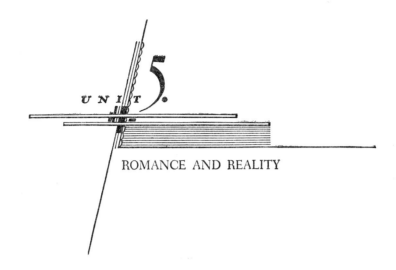

UNIT 5.

ROMANCE AND REALITY

THE LADY OR THE TIGER? ☞ FRANK R. STOCKTON

In the very olden time there lived a semi-barbaric king, whose ideas, though somewhat polished and sharpened by the progressiveness of distant Latin neighbours, were still large, florid, and untrammelled, as became the half of him which was barbaric. He was a man of exuberant fancy, and, withal, of an authority so irresistible that, at his will, he turned his varied fancies into facts. He was greatly given to self-communing, and when he and himself agreed upon anything, the thing was done. When every member of his domestic and political systems moved smoothly in its appointed course, his nature was bland and genial; but whenever there was a little hitch, and some of his orbs got out of their orbits,[1] he was blander and more genial still, for nothing pleased him so much as to make the crooked straight and crush down uneven places.

Among the borrowed notions by which his barbarism had become semi-civilized was that of the public arena, in which, by exhibitions of manly and beastly valour, the minds of his subjects were refined and cultured.

But even here the exuberant and barbaric fancy asserted itself.

[1] ORBS GOT OUT OF THEIR ORBITS—When persons or things deviated from their usual courses.

The arena of the king was built, not to give the people an opportunity of hearing the rhapsodies of dying gladiators nor to enable them to view the inevitable conclusion of a conflict between religious opinions and hungry jaws,[2] but for purposes far better adapted to widen and develop the mental energies of the people. This vast amphitheatre, with its encircling galleries, its mysterious vaults, and its unseen passages, was an agent of poetic justice, in which crime was punished, or virtue rewarded, by the decrees of an impartial and incorruptible chance.

When a subject was accused of a crime of sufficient importance to interest the king, public notice was given that on an appointed day the fate of the accused person would be decided in the king's arena—a structure which well deserved its name; for, although its form and plan were borrowed from afar, its purpose emanated solely from the brain of this man, who, every barley corn a king, knew no tradition to which he owed more allegiance than pleased his fancy, and who ingrafted on every adopted form of human thought and action the rich growth of his barbaric idealism.

When all the people had assembled in the galleries, and the king, surrounded by his court, sat high up on his throne of royal state on one side of the arena, he gave a signal, a door beneath him opened, and the accused subject stepped out into the amphitheatre. Directly opposite him, on the other side of the enclosed space, were two doors, exactly alike and side by side. It was the duty and the privilege of the person on trial to walk directly to these doors and open one of them. He could open either door he pleased. He was subject to no guidance or influence but that of the aforementioned impartial and incorruptible chance. If he opened the one, there came out of it a hungry tiger, the fiercest and most cruel that could be procured, which immediately sprang upon him, and tore him to pieces, as a punishment for his guilt. The moment that the case of the criminal was thus decided, doleful iron bells were clanged, great wails went up from the hired mourners posted on the outer rim of the arena, and the vast audience, with bowed heads and downcast hearts, wended slowly their homeward way, mourning greatly that

[2] CONFLICT BETWEEN RELIGIOUS OPINIONS AND HUNGRY JAWS—Persecuted Christians were thrown into dens of wild animals for punishment.

one so young and fair, or so old and respected, should have merited so dire a fate.

But if the accused person opened the other door, there came forth from it a lady, the most suitable to his years and station that His Majesty could select among his fair subjects; and to this lady he was immediately married, as a reward of his innocence. It mattered not that he might already possess a wife and family, or that his affections might be engaged upon an object of his own selection. The king allowed no such subordinate arrangements to interfere with his great scheme of retribution and reward. The exercises, as in the other instance, took place immediately, and in the arena. Another door opened beneath the king, and a priest, followed by a band of choristers and dancing maidens blowing joyous airs on golden horns and treading in epithalamic[3] measure, advanced to where the pair stood side by side, and the wedding was promptly and cheerily solemnized. Then the gay brass bells rang forth their merry peals, the people shouted glad hurrahs, and the innocent man, preceded by children strewing flowers on his path, led his bride to his home.

This was the king's semi-barbaric method of administering justice. Its perfect fairness is obvious. The criminal could not know out of which door would come the lady. He opened either he pleased, without having the slightest idea whether, in the next instant, he was to be devoured or married. On some occasions the tiger came out of one door, and on some out of the other. The decisions of this tribunal were not only fair—they were positively determinate. The accused person was instantly punished if he found himself guilty, and if innocent he was rewarded on the spot, whether he liked it or not. There was no escape from the judgments of the king's arena.

The institution was a very popular one. When the people gathered together on one of the great trial days, they never knew whether they were to witness a bloody slaughter or a hilarious wedding. This element of uncertainty lent an interest to the occasion which it could not otherwise have attained. Thus the masses

---

[3] EPITHALAMIC (ĕp-ĭ-thá-lăm'ĭk)—In praise of bride and bridegroom.

were entertained and pleased, and the thinking part of the community could bring no charge of unfairness against this plan; for did not the accused person have the whole matter in his own hands?

This semi-barbaric king had a daughter as blooming as his most florid fancies, and with a soul as fervent and imperious as his own. As is usual in such cases, she was the apple of his eye, and was loved by him above all humanity. Among his courtiers was a young man of that fineness of blood and lowness of station common to the conventional heroes of romance who love royal maidens. This royal maiden was well satisfied with her lover, for he was handsome and brave to a degree unsurpassed in all this kingdom, and she loved him with an ardour that had enough of barbarism in it to make it exceedingly warm and strong. This love affair moved on happily for many months, until, one day, the king happened to discover its existence. He did not hesitate nor waver in regard to his duty in the premises. The youth was immediately cast into prison, and a day was appointed for his trial in the king's arena. This, of course, was an especially important occasion, and His Majesty, as well as all the people, was greatly interested in the workings and development of this trial. Never before had such a case occurred—never before had a subject dared to love the daughter of a king. In after years such things became commonplace enough, but then they were, in no slight degree, novel and startling.

The tiger cages of the kingdom were searched for the most savage and relentless beasts, from which the fiercest monster might be selected for the arena, and the ranks of maiden youth and beauty throughout the land were carefully surveyed by competent judges, in order that the young man might have a fitting bride in case fate did not determine for him a different destiny. Of course, everybody knew that the deed with which the accused was charged had been done. He had loved the princess, and neither he, she, nor anyone else thought of denying the fact. But the king would not think of allowing any fact of this kind to interfere with the workings of the tribunal, in which he took such great delight and satisfaction. No matter how the affair turned out, the youth would be disposed of, and the king would take an aesthetic pleasure in watching the course of events which would determine whether or not the young man had done wrong in allowing himself to love the princess.

The appointed day arrived. From far and near the people gathered and thronged the great galleries of the arena, while crowds, unable to gain admittance, massed themselves against its outside walls. The king and his court were in their places, opposite the twin doors—those fearful portals, so terrible in their similarity!

All was ready. The signal was given. A door beneath the royal party opened, and the lover of the princess walked into the arena. Tall, beautiful, fair, his appearance was greeted with a low hum of admiration and anxiety. Half the audience had not known so grand a youth had lived among them. No wonder the princess loved him! What a terrible thing for him to be there!

As the youth advanced into the arena, he turned, as the custom was, to bow to the king. But he did not think at all of that royal personage; his eyes were fixed upon the princess, who sat to the right of her father. Had it not been for the moiety of barbarism[4] in her nature, it is probable that lady would not have been there. But her intense and fervid soul would not allow her to be absent on an occasion in which she was so terribly interested. From the moment that the decree had gone forth that her lover should decide his fate in the king's arena, she had thought of nothing, night or day, but this great event and the various subjects connected with it. Possessed of more power, influence, and force of character than anyone who had ever before been interested in such a case, she had done what no other person had done—she had possessed herself of the secret of the doors. She knew in which of the two rooms behind those doors stood the cage of the tiger, with its open front, and in which waited the lady. Through these thick doors, heavily curtained with skins on the inside, it was impossible than any noise or suggestion should come from within to the person who should approach to raise the latch of one of them. But gold, and the power of a woman's will, had brought the secret to the princess.

[4] MOIETY (moi'ĕ-tǐ) OF BARBARISM—Moiety means half. She was half barbaric.

Not only did she know in which room stood the lady, ready to emerge, all blushing and radiant, should her door be opened, but she knew who the lady was. It was one of the fairest and loveliest of the damsels of the court who had been selected as the reward of the accused youth, should he be proved innocent of the crime of aspiring to one so far above him; and the princess hated her. Often had she seen, or imagined that she had seen, this fair creature throwing glances of admiration upon the person of her lover, and sometimes she thought these glances were perceived and even returned. Now and then she had seen them talking together. It was but for a moment or two, but much can be said in a brief space. It may have been on most unimportant topics, but how could she know that? The girl was lovely, but she had dared to raise her eyes to the loved one of the princess, and, with all the intensity of the savage blood transmitted to her through long lines of wholly barbaric ancestors, she hated the woman who blushed and trembled behind that silent door.

When her lover turned and looked at her, and his eye met hers as she sat there paler and whiter than anyone in the vast ocean of anxious faces about her, he saw, by that power of quick perception which is given to those whose souls are one, that she knew behind which door crouched the tiger, and behind which stood the lady. He had expected her to know it. He understood her nature, and his soul was assured that she would never rest until she had made plain to herself this thing, hidden to all other lookers-on, even to the king. The only hope for the youth in which there was any element of certainty was based upon the success of the princess in discovering this mystery, and the moment he looked upon her, he saw she had succeeded.

Then it was that his quick and anxious glance asked the question, "Which?" It was as plain to her as if he shouted it from where he stood. There was not an instant to be lost. The question was asked in a flash; it must be answered in another.

Her right arm lay on the cushioned parapet before her. She raised her hand, and made a slight, quick movement toward the right. No one but her lover saw her. Every eye but hers was fixed on the man in the arena.

He turned, and with a firm and rapid step he walked across the empty space. Every heart stopped beating, every breath was held, every eye was fixed immovably upon that man. Without the slightest hesitation, he went to the door on the right, and opened it.

Now, the point of the story is this: Did the tiger come out of that door, or did the lady?

The more we reflect upon this question, the harder it is to answer. It involves a study of the human heart which leads us through devious mazes of passion out of which it is difficult to find our way. Think of it, fair reader, not as if the decision of the question depended upon yourself, but upon that hot-blooded, semi-barbaric princess, her soul at a white heat beneath the combined fires of despair and jealousy. She had lost him, but who should have him?

How often, in her waking hours and dreams, had she started in wild horror and covered her face with her hands as she thought of her lover opening the door on the other side of which waited the cruel fangs of the tiger!

But how much oftener had she seen him at the other door! How in her grievous reveries had she gnashed her teeth and torn her hair when she saw his start of rapturous delight as he opened the door of the lady! How her soul had burned in agony when she had seen him rush to meet that woman, with her flushing cheek and sparkling eye of triumph; when she had seen him lead her forth, his whole frame kindled with the joy of recovered life; when she had heard the glad shouts from the multitude, and the wild ringing of the happy bells; when she had seen the priest, with his joyous followers, advance to the couple, and make them man and wife before her very eyes; and when she had seen them walk away together upon their path of flowers, followed by the tremendous shouts of the hilarious multitude, in which her one despairing shriek was lost and drowned!

Would it not be better for him to die at once, and go to wait for her in the blessed regions of semi-barbaric futurity?

And yet, that awful tiger, those shrieks, that blood!

Her decision had been indicated in an instant, but it had been made after days and nights of anguished deliberation. She had known she would be asked, she had decided what she would answer, and, without the slightest hesitation, she had moved her hand to the right.

The question of her decision is one not to be lightly considered, and it is not for me to presume to set up myself as the one person able to answer it. So I leave it with all of you: Which came out of the opened door—the lady or the tiger?

DISCUSSING THE STORY

1. The arena or stadium setting of this story was borrowed from the old Roman times where it was used for all kinds of contests. The monarch, however is a fictitious figure made up of the characteristics of dictators from many ages. What qualities of this monarch stand out in your mind? Who were his advisors? What was his idea of justice?

2. Tell about the romance in the story and how it was broken up.

3. The ending of the story is both a surprise and a problem. The solution depends on how you interpret the character of the princess; and the author has given you all the clues you need. What is your answer to the question on which the story ends? Be prepared to explain your reasoning.

4. Below are some words from the story which may have seemed difficult to you. In each case at least one meaning is given. Study the words and meanings and use each one orally in a sentence. Locating the words in the story may help you to understand them better. If the meanings are still not clear to you, look up the various definitions in a good dictionary.

a. *florid*—highly coloured

b. *untrammelled*—unentangled, free, not restricted by rules, customs, or barriers

c. *exuberant*—superabundant, lavish, more of something than is usually found

d. *rhapsody*—an exaggerated expression of feeling

e. *fervent*—warmth and earnestness of feeling

f. *imperious*—commanding, domineering

g. *aesthetic*—belonging to the appreciation of the beautiful

h. *reveries*—dreamy thoughts

i. *anguish*—acute pain of body or mind

THE GLOVE AND THE LIONS   🖈 LEIGH HUNT

B   KING FRANCIS was a hearty king, and loved a royal sport,
And one day as his lions fought, sat looking on the court;

G   The nobles filled the benches and the ladies in their pride,
And 'mongst them sat the Count de Lorge, with one for whom he sighed;

All   5 And truly 'twas a gallant thing to see that crowning show,
Valour and love, and a king above, and the royal beasts below.

B   Ramped and roared the lions, with horrid laughing jaws;
They bit, they glared, gave blows like beams, a wind went with their paws:
With wallowing might and stifled roar, they rolled on one another,

   10 Till all the pit, with sand and mane, was in a thunderous smother;
The bloody foam above the bars came whisking through the air:

B1   Said Francis, then, "Faith, gentlemen, we're better here than there."

G   De Lorge's love o'erheard the king, a beauteous, lively dame,
With smiling lips, and sharp, bright eyes, which always seemed the same;

G1   15 She thought, "The Count, my lover, is brave as brave can be,
He surely would do wondrous things to show his love for me;
King, ladies, lovers, all look on; the occasion is divine;
I'll drop my glove, to prove his love; great glory will be mine."

G2   She dropped her glove to prove his love, then looked at
        him and smiled,

B2   20 He bowed, and in moment leaped among the lions wild.

B   The leap was quick, return was quick, he has regained his
        place,

        Then threw the glove, but not with love, right in the lady's
        face.

B1   "In faith," cried Francis, "rightly done!" and he rose
        from where he sat;

        "No love," quoth he, "but vanity, sets love a task like that."

DISCUSSING THE POEM

1. In what way does this poem remind you of "The Lady or the
Tiger?" Describe the scene and its spectators.

2. With what challenge did the lady test her lover? How did he answer the challenge?

3. In what way was the lady's act a test of herself? Do you think she
deserved the insult? Define vanity by giving an example from your own
experience.

AU CLAIR DE LA LUNE* ✻ JEAN BAPTISTE LULLY

"Au Clair de la Lune," which means "By the Pale Moonlight," was
written by the French composer, Jean Baptiste Lully, in the latter part
of the eighteenth century. Lully, who was primarily a composer of
operas, was attached to the court of Louis XVI; and this Louis was the
king who was beheaded at the time of the French Revolution. The
song has been very popular in France, and is also sung in many other
countries.

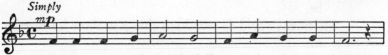

"At thy door I'm knock - ing, By the pale moon - light;

* Words from *The Junior A Cappella Chorus Book,* copyright, 1932, Oliver
Ditson Company. Used by permission.

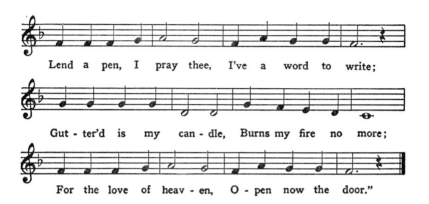

Lend a pen, I pray thee, I've a word to write;

Gut - ter'd is my can - dle, Burns my fire no more;

For the love of heav - en, O - pen now the door."

"At THY door I'm knocking,
By the pale moonlight;
Lend a pen, I pray thee,
I've a word to write;
5   Guttered is my candle,
Burns my fire no more;
For the love of heaven,
Open now the door."

Pierrot cried in answer
10 By the pale moonlight,
"In my bed I'm lying,
Late and chill the night;
Yonder at my neighbour's
Someone is astir;
15 Fire is freshly kindled—
Get a light from her."

To the neighbour's house then,
By the pale moonlight,
Goes our gentle Lubin

19. LUBIN—The name of the singer.

20   To beg a pen to write;
"Who knocks there so softly?"
Calls a voice above;
"Open wide your door now,
'Tis the God of Love."

AU CLAIR DE LA LUNE — Jean Baptiste Lully

"Au clair de la lune,
Mon ami Pierrot,
Prête-moi ta plume,
Pour écrire un mot;
5   Ma chandelle est morte,
Je n'ai plus de feu;
Ouvre-moi ta porte,
Pour l'amour de Dieu."

Au clair de la lune,
10   Pierrot répondit,
"Je n'ai pas de plume,
Je suis dans mon lit.
Va chez la voisine:
Je crois qu'elle y est,
15   Car dans sa cuisine
On bat le briquet."

Dans son lit de plume,
Pierrot se rendort.
Il rêve à la Lune:
20   Son coeur bat bien fort,
Car toujours si bonne
Pour l'enfant tout blanc,
La Lune lui donne
Son croissant d'argent!

THE VIOLIN-MAKER OF CREMONA 🖾

FRANCOIS COPPÉE

In this play by the famous French author, François Coppée, we find ourselves among the Italian musicians and artisans of the eighteenth century. The family of Amati[1] had worked for two centuries in an unbroken line of father to son, as the violin-masters of Cremona. Then Nicolo had been born—Nicolo Amati (1596-1684) in whom two hundred years of skill reached a new perfection.

This great master taught the art to Antonio Stradivari,[2] then a Cremona lad. He, in turn, perfected the work of Amati, and became himself the greatest master of all time. No one has ever equalled his artistry. To-day, a Stradivarius violin is a priceless treasure. Stradivari achieved the perfect pattern for assembling the carefully wrought and complex pieces of mellow wood into precise delicacy of form—using just the right kind and amount of glue, and finishing with a secret varnish which added fullness of tone and a rich amber glow to his beautiful violin. This was in 1700.

When our play opens half a century later, Cremona is still proudly

---

Author—Pronounced frän-swä′ kô-pä′.

[1] AMATI—Pronounced ä-mä′tē.

[2] STRADIVARI—Pronounced strä-dĕ-vä′rē.

carrying on in the glory of his name. Although Stradivari himself has died, taking with him the secret of the famous varnish, his pupil, Taddeo Ferrari,[8] upholds the master's traditions in his own careful workshop. Imbued with the teaching and standards of the greatest violin-maker the world has ever known, Ferrari knows nothing more important than his musical trade of violin-making.

CHARACTERS

TADDEO FERRARI, *master violin-maker*
GIANNINA, *his daughter*
SANDRO, *his pupil*
FILIPPO, *another of his pupils*
GUILD OF VIOLIN-MAKERS *and attendants*

SCENE. *Cremona about the year 1750. A violin workshop of the eighteenth century. At the rear, a workbench and a door, which opens upon the street. Violins, cellos, bass viols, and other musical instruments are scattered around the workshop. At left, there is a counter in full view and a door. At right, a large armchair is placed near a table. As the scene opens,* GIANNINA *stands by* MASTER FERRARI, *seated in the armchair.*

Ferrari. No, Giannina.[4] I have made a vow and I am going to keep it. As surely as my name is Taddeo Ferrari, master violin-maker, patron, and trustee of the people of my trade, whose banner I carry in the processions,[5] you shall be married, and in this way.

Giannina. But Father—

Ferrari. I am proceeding as a reasonable man. Our old mayor, recently dead (may he rest in peace!), wishing that the fame of stringed instruments coming from our old and famous city should continue to be more and more deserved, has just bequeathed his gold chain to the skilled workman that shall make the best violin in the city. The competition is free and will be judged today. I, a simple artisan, inspired by him, have promised to give my house

---

[8] TADDEO FERRARI—Pronounced tä-dä'ō fěr-rä'rē.
[4] GIANNINA—Pronounced jän-nē'nà.
[5] WHOSE BANNER I CARRY IN THE PROCESSIONS—It was the custom for members of a trade to form a kind of association called a guild. These guilds had festival days and processions, and in the procession the banner was carried by the master, or most skilled workman of the group.

and my daughter to the one who by his talent will receive the mayor's golden chain. And, by the saints, it shall be done! It's agreed, concluded, arranged! There's nothing to be excited about!

Giannina. I told you there is someone I prefer.

Ferrari. O, Sandro! [6] You'll forget him.

Giannina. But if this unknown artist should be an evil fellow, not worthy of your house at all?

Ferrari. A skilled workman is always a good man.

Giannina. . . . A lazybones, without a care for the future?

Ferrari. When he is better paid, he can work less.

Giannina. . . . A brute who would beat his wife? There are such men.

Ferrari. If he had not peace at home, I should not blame him.

Giannina. But if he should be so perverse as to refuse my hand? Then—

Ferrari. Such a funny one would certainly be hard to please! No, no, a good match like you, Giannina, is not to be found every day. Your dowry of two thousand crowns is not a trifle—and with my business, favoured pupil as I am of the famous Stradivari—Nay, nay! Besides, I have given my word! So let's say no more about it.

Giannina. But, my father—

Ferrari. That will do!

Giannina. If the victor—I laugh to even think of it—if he should be your small pupil Filippo? [7]

Ferrari. Filippo?

Giannina. Suppose he gets the prize?

Ferrari. Well, I shouldn't be very much surprised, and if he should bring me the mayor's chain, you would marry him the following week.

Giannina. Marry Filippo?

Ferrari. Why not?

Giannina. A hunchback!

Ferrari. If he had two humps like a camel, he should be your husband.

---

[6] SANDRO—Pronounced sän′drō.

[7] FILIPPO—Pronounced fē-lēp′pō.

Giannina. May heaven protect me!

Ferrari. Isn't Filippo one of the best of fellows—good, useful, honest? He looks a little sad, he is hunchback—that's true— but he is a great artist. In the little concert that he gave one day, as I listened he drew from the strings such grief and charm that two great tears dropped from my eyes. And you know, my daughter, that I am a severe judge of music.

Giannina. I esteem Filippo, just as you do, Father. I pity him, and I have done my best, I hope, to make him forget his misery and his deformity which the poor creature endures with such sweetness. He has been as my brother since the day the poor lad stopped at our door to beg for bread. But could I love him— Filippo, the hunchback? Think, Father!

Ferrari. Ta-ra-ta-ta! If you can't offer any more serious objection than that, just leave it there. I am going down cellar to choose our choicest wine for this great day of celebration.

[FERRARI *exits at left.* GIANNINA *drops into the chair with a sigh.* SANDRO *enters from the rear, carrying a black violin case which he places on the counter at the left. When she sees him,* GIANNINA *rises in greeting.*]

Sandro. Well, Giannina?

Giannina (*holding out her hands to him*). Sandro!

Sandro. What's the news? Does the Master still hold to his vow to give you to the best workman in the city?

Giannina. Yes, more firmly than ever.

Sandro. What madness! But does he know how much I love you, and if I cannot wed you, I shall surely die?

Giannina. He said I would forget you.

Sandro. He is cruel!

Giannina (*pointing to the violin case*). Have you finished your masterpiece?

Sandro. If I were as lazy as a snake, I would still be ready; for alas! it is my last hope. Today the experts will decide my lifelong happiness.

Giannina. And are you satisfied with it?

Sandro. Yes and no. I understand my trade, and have made the violin according to the best rules of the art. Its high tones are pure; its low tones, deep. All my time I have devoted to it, with infinite care. I have carefully chosen my wood, my strings, and my varnish. It is an instrument worthy of a master, I am sure.

Giannina (*joyfully*).   The prize will be yours, Sandro!

Sandro.   Perhaps.

Giannina.   But of course you will win the prize! Why do you doubt it? There is no rival you may fear. Is not my father the first artist of Cremona—he from whom you learned your art? Oh, I wish above all that you win the prize!

Sandro.   No rival from another workshop makes me fear.

Giannina.   Well?

Sandro.   But I have one in your own.

Giannina.   What! In our workshop?

Sandro.   Yes, the hunchback! It was an evil day for me when you took him to your house.

Giannina.   I did not know Filippo would compete!

Sandro.   Yesterday he told me so, the little snake-in-the-grass— before your father.

Giannina (*thoughtfully*).   My father, who but now was saying that if he received the prize, I would nevertheless be forced to have him for a husband . . .

Sandro.   Didn't I tell you?

Giannina (*laughing to throw off the thought*).   We shall need the protection of my guardian angel!

Sandro (*still doubtful*).   He thinks you are free—he may hope.

Giannina.   Such a suspicion of the poor fellow does not occur to me. He wants the gold chain and the title of master, and surely we would expect him to be ambitious. But he knows himself too well to claim my hand.

Sandro.   I cannot believe that—and I am sure he will win. In all my life, I have never been so wretched and unhappy, nor so envious.

Giannina.   You envious, Sandro? Oh, no!

Sandro.   Yes, I am, for I know his work; and soon everyone will know it as I do. Listen! The other night I was at my window, enjoying the quiet evening and thinking of you. In the darkness, I heard a nightingale singing, and it seemed his pearly notes mingled with the stars. Suddenly, I heard another song, just as sublime, as touching, as that of the bird. I leaned out and saw the hunchback alone in his attic, seated at his desk, bow in hand. His violin with an accent almost human was pouring out tones of love and sorrow intermingled, equalling in sweetness the voice of the nightingale. For a while I listened entranced, and then so pure was the beauty of his music throbbing out into the evening breeze, twining its melody into the bird's ecstatic song, that I could no longer tell which was the hunchback's magic tone, and which the song of the nightingale.

Giannina. Can the success of a rival make you so sad?

Sandro. It is a feeling unworthy of an artist, I know. But if your father favours him, and he should come out victor . . .

Giannina. It is you whom I love. I will be yours, come what may.

Sandro. You are sure?

Giannina. Yes, I am sure.

Sandro. You are the most precious girl in the world.

Giannina. Here is my hand—to pledge our vow.

Sandro (kissing her hand). So be it. I am more content.

[*Loud noises are heard outside.*]

Giannina. What is that racket?

[FILIPPO *rushes in, and quickly slams the door behind him. He is out of breath and much disturbed.*]

Filippo. Oh, I am here at last. The little ragamuffins! They almost got me.

Giannina. What is it, Filippo? Who was following you?

Filippo. Some little rogues, who tried to knock me down with stones and broken glass. (*He slips into the chair, resting his forehead on his hands. When he takes away his hands, there is blood on his forehead.*)

Sandro. You are bleeding!

Giannina. Water—quick! (*She goes to the sideboard to get a basin, returns and kneels to bathe* FILIPPO's *head.*)

Sandro. Tell us what happened.

Filippo. It is really not very important. Fifteen or twenty rascally schoolboys were throwing stones at a poor sick dog, who was dragging himself along with a broken paw. The miserable creature, backed against the wall, was trying to defend himself with a show of teeth. I who have often been tormented turned sick with sorrow at the sight, and begged them to have pity. They forgot about the dog; grew angry at the hunchback. It was much more fun to chase a running prey. Up and down the alleys I dodged—had they caught me, there would have been no more poor Filippo. But I saved the life of that defenceless dog!

[*He falls exhausted back into the armchair.* GIANNINA *bathes his head with her kerchief, dipped from the basin.*]

Giannina (*with spirit*). Those blackguards! Was there ever such malice? (*To* FILIPPO.) Poor fellow!

Filippo (*aside.*) Her hand on my forehead— Oh, delight!

Giannina. Do you feel better, now?

Filippo (*getting up, and speaking with tremulous voice*). Yes, you are most kind.

Sandro (*aside*). Indeed, that voice speaks more than gratitude. I was not mistaken. He loves her!

[FERRARI *enters, carrying a basket of wine bottles.*]

Giannina. Father . . .

Ferrari. It is you, my Giannina? I was looking for you. Soon, when they have tested the violins, and we know the lucky one you are to marry, I shall entertain the brotherhood at dinner. Come! Help me get ready, that I may look fine in my best wig and blue festal coat. Come!

[*He leaves at right, followed by* GIANNINA.]

Sandro. The eventual moment is fast approaching, Filippo.

Filippo. Yes, comrade.

Sandro. Your violin—is it ready?

Filippo. Yes.

Sandro. You are satisfied with it?

Filippo. Yes, indeed. And you?

Sandro. No, I— No, not quite.

Filippo. I am sorry. In this courteous and friendly competition, my one consolation for failing would be to see you succeed, my comrade at work. Here, give me your hand in friendship before we go forth to the contest.

Sandro (after a silence). No! *(He leaves hastily, at left.)*

Filippo. It is jealousy which torments him—him, with his strength and beauty! Would that a man might rejoice at the bit of merit he finds in a poor friend, who never begrudged him his comeliness. But there—he suffers and I must not blame him. Still it would be good to be friends, as well as rivals. Little does he know your worth, O friendly heart, that yearns for his comradeship. Yet, there is my masterpiece, a solace for all sorrow. Poor, dear violin! how like unto me you are—an exquisite soul in an unshapely case. *(He goes to the cupboard and gets his violin, which is in a red case, and puts it on the table on his right. As he speaks, he lifts it from the case.)*

Come, I wish to see you once again, O my work, dear creation upon which I, the feeble workman, had the strength to spend so many days and nights of effort and of toil. Come, soon there will issue from your deep bosom the chattering scherzo [8] and the weep-

[8] SCHERZO (skĕr'tsō)—A playful, humourous movement.

ing lento[9]—the concert of beauty you can give to the world. I may not again wake the song that sleeps in your heart—only once again would I see myself mirrored in your shining wood—to know that I, the hunchback, am he who have given you your golden voice. Farewell, O dear and noble instrument. I beg that you remember him whose heart speaks to you now, the outcast artist who has breathed into your form the flame of music. (*Puts violin back in red case.*)

How much a child I am! Poor fool, to thus deceive myself! It is not for glory that I bent my fullest effort to this task. It is for her—the sweet, the beautiful Giannina. Of all the world, 'tis she alone whose kindness has reached out to me—cruelly misshapen wretch. When first I wandered to her father's door, a homeless child, she took me in—nor did she laugh at me. Surely so kind, so beautiful a one cannot look upon this cherished love as an offence.

Still, if I win the prize, I shall not ask fulfilment of her father's vow. Only can I hope that when I offer her the golden chain, when she will know that all my genius has been inspired by her, perhaps this daughter of an artist will forget the rest, and think only of my talent. Perhaps—who can tell?—if her heart is still free—for so many reasons, she might indeed . . . Oh, this impossible dream is killing me!

Giannina (*entering*). He is alone. Now I shall find out if Sandro still can hope to win. (*Aloud.*) Filippo!

Filippo (*startled out of his reverie*). It is she!

Giannina. I am disappointed, Filippo, that I alone have not been told what everyone else knows—that you have kept it secret from me, who would have rejoiced to know.

Filippo. What is it that I have kept from you?

Giannina. That you are competing for the prize.

Filippo. It is true, and you above all would have been the first to hear about it. But when I knew about the vow of the master—forgive me, Giannina, then I dared not tell you.

Giannina. I understood—but let's leave that. My old father really loves me too well to thus leave in chance the care of my

[9] LENTO—A slow movement.

happiness. But as for the chain of gold and the master's title—
that is different. Each craftsman in the city has the right to aspire
to that, and you especially from what I have just learned.

Filippo. What is it you have heard?

Giannina. That you have fashioned an exquisite instrument,
a masterpiece . . .

Filippo. Truly I have done my best, but to whom will it matter
whether I succeed or fail?

Giannina. To whom? Will we not all be interested? Are we
not your friends?

Filippo. Forgive me, Giannina. I am afraid. One seems dis-
trustful when one is simply timid, and I owe you half of all my
secrets. When I was wretched, you pitied me, and I know you will
be glad if any honour comes to me. I am indeed sorry. I want to
tell you everything, for I was ungrateful and offended you. Know
then that I am almost sure to succeed. Whether by talent or only
good luck, I do not know, but I have succeeded completely. (*He
shows his violin.*) With all possible care, I built the box of old fir
and the handle of maple—from the start, I wrought with finest art.
But that is nothing—the other violins may be just as good. The
master stroke is that I discovered again, during a sleepless night,
the secret of the amber varnish of former times—the lost secret of
the old masters.

Giannina. What? The famous lustrous varnish of Stradivari
and Amati?

Filippo (*enthusiastically*). I have it! Tomorrow, all shall know
the formula! I have compared my work with their violins—it has
the same sound. Exactly the same sound, I tell you. I am sure of
it!

Giannina (*aside*). Alas, poor Sandro!

Filippo. Since that happy day, I have hidden my secret like a
lover. Whether I get the prize or not, what does it matter to me,
now? My life is a festival.

Giannina (*aside*). Poor, poor Sandro. (*Aloud*). Is it as fine
as that?

Filippo. Listen only to its sound of *la*.

Giannina. Oh, play some song. I would like so much to hear it.

Filippo (aside). Her voice—her plea is almost tender. Does she wish me to succeed? *(Aloud).* Do you really want me to?

Giannina. I truly do. *(Aside).* It is the only way to know whether he flatters himself or speaks the truth.

Filippo. I will play, if you please, the Corelli sonata in *sol*.

Giannina. Anything you wish.

Filippo (behind the counter). Listen to this.

[*Silent scene.* FILIPPO *plays the first measure of a majestic theme on his violin, which has a wonderful richness of tone. The face of* GIANNINA *who is listening attentively is not slow to express a sorrowful admiration. Her head drops into her hands, and she bursts into tears.* FILIPPO *at last sees this, and cries out.*]

What do I see? Giannina, weeping? Is it not consoling and beautiful that this hunchback who has made so many laugh, should with music bring tears to your eyes? I have made you weep—now do I need no other glory—no prize more precious than the dear diamonds that fall from your eyes. Now can I hold up my head in pride, now—

Giannina. Stop! I cannot longer keep my purpose from you. I understand your pride as an artist, and share it as I have shared your grief. But it is not that which makes my tears flow.

Filippo. What is it, then?

Giannina. What I must say will hurt you, but you will pity me, I am sure, when I tell you that among the competitors is one for whom I wished success, one whom I love . . . and all my happiness is now destroyed by what I hear.

Filippo. Ah!

Giannina. Do not be angry with me, Filippo. I did not know of your great talent. In my father's shop, I thought of you still as an unskilled workman. And it was so natural that I should wish success for the man I love. If I had but understood—believe me when I say that it would have been hard for me to have decided between you. How easily I could have accepted the idea of your genius! Then I would not have wept as I did to-day.

Filippo (*pointing to the door from which* SANDRO *left*). You love him?

Giannina (*in a low voice*). Yes.

Filippo. Sandro?

Giannina. I entrust to you freely the secret of my love. He cherished also the hope of winning and it was, I admit, my most ardent wish. But now after what I have just heard, I see that he cannot claim the prize, which would make our dream come true. To lose such a dear hope is cruel, is it not? Yet my sorrow has no bitterness in it—no, because it is my childhood friend, my brother, who deserves this great reward. Still it overwhelmes me— Forgive my helpless tears. (*She weeps freely.*)

Filippo. In truth, I suffer as much as you, and I beg of you . . .

Giannina. I am sorry—this is most unfair. I forget your misfortune, in thinking of my own. I do not remember that you, my poor friend, have only your art to console you. It shall be so—I will weep no more— Love to my dearest Sandro, and glory to you. You are the great artist whom I admire. Indeed, I wish to see you happy. (*She takes both his hands.*) And I shall weep no more. It must be this way—it must! See, I am smiling. (*She bursts out sobbing.*) But it is more than I can bear. (*She goes out.*)

Filippo (*after a moment of sorrowful thought*). What, now, is there left? All is said. She loves another. Another! Yes, that handsome one—my fellow craftsman. And indeed, 'tis right that she should love him! Would it help to protest that she is unjust, and be angry with her? Whom would she naturally choose —she the young maid and fair—between one such dream lover and you—misshapen fellow who makes all to laugh who look upon you!

Miserable cripple, go look at yourself in the mirror! How could she love such as you? Blind! Blind and foolish! To think that I could see nothing of this, nor of her love for this Sandro! You, hunchback, what good will it do you now to win the reward and the prize? I wished to make her happy, and I have only made her sad.

I will not compete! Next in skill after me, in the city, is Sandro. He shall win the prize, and she will be happy again. Come (*Taking his violin.)*—you shall give your life for her happiness—your beautiful song shall be broken, too. (*About to crush violin over his knee, he stops suddenly.*) What an unhappy idea! How fiercely my heart throbs! What if some other workman should win the prize? She would be forced to marry that strange one! (*Looking at the two violin cases on the table.*) I could change— (*His voice full of doubt.*) Ah, no! It is too much. This dear work of my hands I cannot give to him who took my sweeter dream. But, come, it must be done. It was for her this masterpiece was made, and it shall be given for her happiness. A change of cases, and all will be well. Sandro is not so great an artist that he will see the difference between his work and mine when the experts judge them. Courage—let it be done. (*Changes the violins, putting his own in* SANDRO's *case.*) All is finished.

[FERRARI *enters from rear.*]

Ferrari. Come, Sandro, Filippo. 'Tis time to go. Are you not ready yet?

[*Enter* SANDRO *from right.*]

Sandro. I am coming, master.

Filippo. And here are our violins.

Ferrari. My children, I trust that one of you will win and do credit to your master and your workshop. Others may scrape their bows until they burst with music, but the skill which I have taught you should claim the prize. Now from all the town, people are gathering with kerchief and coloured dress to see the judges take their places; the choir master is seated in his armchair; and through the air there breathes a strain of melody. Cremona is pulsing with rhythm, like a quiet hall before a symphony.

Sandro. So, master, it is time to leave?

Ferrari. Yes, let us go.

Sandro. Are you coming with me, Filippo?

Filippo. No, comrade. On so beautiful and musical a day, let the hunchback stay indoors and leave unmarred the gala scene. Would you but do me the kindness to take my violin with yours? 'Tis but a step from here.

Sandro (*taking the hand* FILIPPO *holds out to him*). I will do it. (SANDRO *exits with the two violin cases, at the right.*)

Filippo (*aside*). The sacrifice is made. Even in love, what courage it takes! (*Aloud to* FERRARI.) Are you not going to see his work crowned?

Ferrari. To be sure, to be sure! But the prize is not his, as yet, and you yourself may win the golden chain. Have you less talent, less intelligence than he?

Filippo. You know I have no chance.

Ferrari. 'Tis confidence you're lacking. As straight as a steeple you may not be, but you are a good violin-maker. And if the prize is for you, I tell you you shall be my son-in-law and my successor.

Filippo. But master . . .

Ferrari. Enough! Enough! I must be off. (*Exits.*)

Filippo. Truly, I need all my courage.

[*Enter* GIANNINA.]

What? Does she come again?

Giannina. Filippo, I have just come from the church. I went —forgive me, I was so sad at heart—to pray that Sandro might still be the winner, in spite of everything. But kneeling before our Saint Cecilia, I felt how wrong it was to ask God to do anything unjust. So whatever happens, I have vowed to always be the same toward you. Good-bye . . . (*She crosses the stage, and goes out right.*)

Filippo. Alas! How much she loves him. Had I but been strong and beautiful, how much she would have loved me!

[SANDRO *enters hastily from the right, in great distress.*]

Sandro. Filippo! Filippo!

Filippo. What is this? Tears in your eyes, and your face so pale! What dreadful thing has happened?

Sandro. I have done a shameful deed. I am a wicked scoundrel. Oh, forgive! forgive! forgive!

Filippo. Who? Me pardon you, my friend? For what?

Sandro. You see, I loved her so much. It was too great an anguish that a rival should surpass me in her eyes . . . I am so envious a wretch. The temptation came to me when I held your masterpiece in my hands. Crazy with rage and grief, I yielded. Near here, trembling as a thief in the shadow of a doorway . . . Filippo . . . I changed our violins in their cases!

Filippo (*a little staggered*). You?

Sandro. Then I took them before the judges. The moment the expert opened our two cases, I could not bear the sight. I ran away. Avenge yourself! Before everyone denounce my deed! But for the sake of pity, do not compel me to bear this shame before her. I will write you a confession, then go away and die, for shame is deadly, deadly. (*He falls to his knees.*)

Filippo. No, Sandro. I do not need vengeance. You have brought upon yourself your own punishment.

Sandro. What is it you say?

Filippo. The glory of my masterpiece, I had given to you . . . and you have given it back to me.

Sandro (*perplexed*). I do not understand.

Filippo. Those instruments you changed—I myself had already changed them in their cases.

Sandro. What do I hear? My remorse allows me not to understand. Why did you do it?

Filippo. Because I adore her. And because it is you whom she prefers. If my heart is touched with regret at your deed, it is because your action has taken away what I would have done for her.

Sandro (*rising*). Still is my crime as great, and I must bear punishment. Say but the word, and I will go away. She will forget me—and you are more worthy of her. I must go!

[*Confused noises outside.*]

Filippo. No, stay! Obey me!

[FERRARI *enters from rear door and raises his hand on seeing* FILIPPO. *He is followed by the whole guild of violin-makers, and two pages, decked out in the colours of the city, one carrying the mayor's gold chain on a cushion, and the other* FILIPPO's *violin, decorated with ribbons and flowers.* GIANNINA *appears on the threshold of the door at the right.*]

Ferrari (*to* FILIPPO). Come to my arms, my son! I proclaim you king of the trade, winner of the prize, and Master of the Violin-Makers of Cremona. Here, before the entire brotherhood of our craft, I first keep my promise to the winner, my associate, my son-in-law. Now . . . the gold chain. . . .

Filippo (*taking it from his hands and placing it 'round the neck of* GIANNINA). Gladly I offer it to Giannina, the beautiful, begging her to make it her favourite jewel, when she is the wife of my comrade, Sandro.

Giannina. Dear Filippo!

Sandro (*in a low voice to* FILIPPO). My noble friend! My brother!

Ferrari. Stop! Is it a vow you have taken not to marry that makes you give up your prize like this?

Filippo. No, my good master, no. Tomorrow I shall start out on a journey through the whole of Italy, carrying your fame to every corner of the land. I have had a dream—a mad and foolish dream—from which I am but now awake. All I can wish is that farewell regrets will follow me, as the eye seeks the departing flight of a lone swallow. I ask no faithful memories—only a secret. It is all that my poor life is worth. (*He draws* SANDRO *and* GIANNINA *close to him.*)

And when in the workshop you again take up our labours—you, my comrade at your old place, with her beside you—if perchance a string you stretch upon the wood breaks with a plaintive sound, remember Filippo who felt his poor heart break at this, our last farewell. Nothing you could do would change it—that is true. Still I would like to know that you will not forget that I have loved you dearly.

Ferrari. Ungrateful one! Do you want my house to fall to ruin?

Filippo. You still have Sandro.

Ferrari. Happiness and fortune you throw away! Is there nothing you are keeping?

Filippo (*taking his violin*). This only. (*Aside.*) It will be my comrade and my consolation.

DISCUSSING THE PLAY

It takes a little more imagination to read a play with pleasure than it does to read a short story. The author of a story puts into it more lines of description and explanation than does the playwright. A play, on the other hand, consists mainly of the words to be spoken by the actors. The story of a play is filled out by the actions of the actors and the settings of the stage. It is important, then, that as you read a play you try to visualize the stage, the actors, and the time.

1. Explain Ferrari's plan and tell why he thinks it will bring honour to his daughter. What is Giannina's reaction to the plan?

2. What have you learned about the character of the two pupils of Taddeo Ferrari? In what ways are they alike and in what ways different?

3. What has Filippo discovered that makes him confident of winning the prize? How does Sandro feel about his chances?

4. By what act does Filippo show unselfishness and charity? How does Sandro reverse the decision? How does the contest turn out?

5. Which one of the characters is the hero of this play? Give reasons for your opinion.

6. Each of the following words is accompanied by a word or phrase indicating its meaning. If the meaning of any of the words is not yet clear to you after you have studied the list, look it up in a dictionary. Then use each one of the words correctly in a sentence.

   a. *artisan*—an accomplished workman
   b. *dowry*—a gift which goes with a bride
   c. *medley*—a musical composition of different pieces
   d. *consolation*—comfort

ADVENTURES OF ISABEL OGDEN NASH

Isabel met an enormous bear;
Isabel, Isabel, didn't care.
The bear was hungry, the bear was ravenous,
The bear's big mouth was cruel and cavernous:
5   The bear said, Isabel, glad to meet you,
How do, Isabel, now I'll eat you!
Isabel, Isabel, didn't worry;

Isabel didn't scream or scurry.
She washed her hands and she straightened her hair up,
10 　Then Isabel quietly ate the bear up.

Once on a night as black as pitch
Isabel met a wicked old witch.
The witch's face was cross and wrinkled,
The witch's gums with teeth were sprinkled.
15 　Ho, ho, Isabel! the old witch crowed,
I'll turn you into an ugly toad!
Isabel, Isabel, didn't worry;
Isabel didn't scream or scurry.
She showed no rage and she showed no rancour,
20 　But she turned the witch into milk and drank her.

Isabel met a hideous giant,
Isabel continued self-reliant.
The giant was hairy, the giant was horrid,
He had one eye in the middle of his forehead.
25 　Good morning, Isabel, the giant said,
I'll grind your bones to make my bread.
Isabel, Isabel, didn't worry;
Isabel didn't scream or scurry.
She nibbled the zwieback that she always fed off,
30 　And when it was gone, she cut the giant's head off.

Isabel met a troublesome doctor,
He punched and poked till he really shocked her.
The doctor's talk was of coughs and chills,
And the doctor's satchel bulged with pills.
35 　The doctor said unto Isabel,
Swallow this, it will make you well.
Isabel, Isabel, didn't worry;
Isabel didn't scream or scurry.
She took those pills from the pill-concoctor,
40 　And Isabel calmly cured the doctor.

DISCUSSING THE POEM

Some say that Ogden Nash is a serious poet. Others say that he is a humourist. But everyone enjoys reading his verses, or *Versus* as he has called some of them. After laughing over Isabel's adventures you may want to read more of these witty comments on living, which you will find in the nine volumes that have been published.

1. If you think a little, you will realize that you have met Isabel somewhere before. She is the "mean little kid" who is the hero or heroine of the radio, the puppet show, and the comic strip. Tell about a character of whom you are reminded by Isabel.

2. How did Isabel handle the situations with the bear, the witch, the giant, the doctor? What is it about such situations as these that makes us laugh?

THE REEF* ⚜ SAMUEL SCOVILLE, JR.

LUNE-GREEN and amber, a strip of fading sky glowed across the trail of the vanished sun. Far below, the opal sea paled to mother-of-pearl. Then, over sea and sky, strode the sudden dark of the tropics and in an instant the southern stars flamed and flared through the violet night. A long, tense moment, with sea and sky waiting, and a rim of raw gold thrust itself above the horizon as the full moon of midsummer climbed toward the zenith. Rising, its light made a broad causeway across the sea clear to the dark reef which lurked in the shimmering water.

Suddenly, inked black against the moonpath, showed the lean shape of a canoe. All the way from Carib Island, a day and a night away, Jim Tom, who in his day had been a famous sponge diver, had brought his grandson Jimmy Tom for a first visit to the reef. Both had the cinnamon-red skins of the Red Caribs, who once had ruled mightily the whole Caribbean. Jim Tom's hair was cut to an even edge all the way around his neck; his small, deep-set eyes were

* "The Reef" by Samuel Scoville, Jr., from *St. Nicholas Magazine.* Copyright, 1923, Century Company. Reprinted by permission of the publishers, Appleton-Century-Crofts, Inc.

like glittering crumbs of black glass, and ever since a day when he dived below the twenty-five-fathom mark both of his legs had been paralysed.

Swiftly the little craft neared the reef, and only the splash of the paddles broke the stillness. Then in an instant the molten gold of the water was shattered by a figure like a vast bat, with black wings which measured all of thirty feet from tip to tip, a spiked tail, and long antennae streaming out beyond a huge, hooked mouth. Like a vampire from the pit, it rose into the air, blotting out the moon with its monstrous bulk, and then dropped back with a crash, raising a wave which nearly swamped the canoe. As it disappeared beneath the water, Jimmy Tom turned and looked questioningly at the old man. The latter laughed silently.

"Only a manta ray," [1] he said at last. "They like to fly around in the moonlight and frighten untried young men," he added slyly.

For answer his grandson stretched out his paddle at full length. It showed in the air rigid and motionless as an iron bar. The old man grunted approvingly.

"You may tremble yet before you are through with the reef," was all that he said however, as he steered toward the circle of coral which separated the lagoon from the ocean, which beat against the barrier in a crashing surf. Waiting until several of the great rollers had passed, the paddlers caught the crest of a huge wave and in an instant were swept ten feet in air toward the patch of beach which showed beyond the little lagoon. Just as the wave broke, the canoe tilted and rushed down its long slope like a toboggan, clearing the rim of sharp coral and leaping into the still lagoon beyond.

All the rest of that glorious night, as the moon went westering down the sky, the two slept on the rose-red honey-brown sand, until, without any dawn, the sun suddenly rose above a heliotrope horizon. Then they breakfasted, and Jim Tom became quite talkative —for a Carib.

"We must not waste a moment of this day," he said. "Perhaps before night we may make the hundred dollars you need for that sloop about which you have been bothering me so long. In my

[1] MANTA RAY—A gigantic sea creature better known as the devilfish.

day," he went on severely, "boys were glad enough to have a good canoe."

Jimmy Tom grunted.

"Whoever heard," he said at last, "of making a hundred of dollars in one day?"

"It has been done—and here," returned his grandfather, positively; "but it takes good lungs and—a brave heart."

As they talked, the canoe reached a point where the reef sloped away in a series of terraces to unfathomable depths. There they stopped paddling and started down through the water which lay before them like a thick sheet of plate glass. The great ledge over which they floated was dotted with thickets of coloured corals and purple and gold seafans, among which schools of brilliant fish sped and lazed and drifted like birds in the air. Molten-silver tarpon shot through shoals of chubby cow pilots, all green and gold and indigo, while turquoise-blue parrot fish raced here and there, and crimson cardinal fish crept in and out of crevices in the rocks. There were angel fish with golden fins, orange gills, and vivid blue mouths, while warty purple sea cucumbers showed among clumps of yellow sea anemones.

"This is the treasure ledge of the reef," said Jim Tom suddenly. "Here too," he went on, "death hides and waits," and he paused for a moment.

Jimmy's answer was to slip out of his unbleached cotton shirt and trousers and stand poised like a red-bronze statue of speed with the long, flat muscles rippling over his lithe body and graceful limbs.

"It was here that your father died," said Jim Tom again. "I was lying watching him search among the sponges," he went on after a pause, "when before my very eyes he was gone. My only son," he went on, his voice rising as he harked back over forgotten years, "in the paws of one of those accursed sculpins of the deep water, a *tonu*[2] ten feet long."

"And then?" asked Jimmy Tom, very softly, as the old man stopped.

"And then," went on the old man, fiercely, "everything went red

[2] *Tonu* (tŏn'ŭ)—Large, broad-mouthed, scaleless fish.

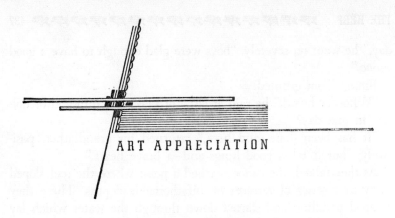

ART APPRECIATION

LUMBERING 🌲 DAVID STONE MARTIN

In pioneer days almost every man was his own lumberjack. With amazing skill he cut down trees and trimmed the logs into beams and planks for his house or barn. Large-scale lumbering began about one hundred and fifty years ago in the woods of the north and east. Men gathered in lumber camps, felled the trees and sledded them to the river banks, and in the spring drove them down the overflowing streams to the sawmills. The lumberjacks were often giants among men, who boasted of the strength and skill they used in their dangerous work. To-day lumbering is a great industry which spreads from the northwest across the Great Lakes area to the northeast and southward through the Appalachians. The work still calls for strong men willing to live rugged lives amid plenty of excitement and danger. The modern lumberjack, however, has the aid of new machinery and equipment. The painting "Lumbering" was inspired by the artist's experiences among these men of the woods while he was painting in the hills and forests of Tennessee. The picture demonstrates how skill and strength are co-operatively applied to a difficult task.

LUMBERING

David Stone Martin

DAVID STONE MARTIN

[1913-   ]

David Stone Martin was born in Chicago, the son of a poor but hard-working minister. David's home was not far from the Art Institute where he began to be interested in painting. His only formal training came in a high-school course taught by an inspiring teacher. This beginning helped him to go on alone with his experimenting and practising. Decorating drug-store windows with crêpe-paper backgrounds was one of his early jobs. Then, during the preparations for the Century of Progress Exposition of 1933 and 1934, he was given the opportunity to do some murals and designs for displays. He did them so well that, at the age of twenty-one, he was appointed supervisor of a mural project employing twenty artists and helpers at the Elgin State Hospital. A year later he went to Tennessee to make a pictorial record of the various developments of the Tennessee Valley Authority. During World War II Martin worked first with the Graphics Division of the Office of War Information, and then, as one of forty-two leading American artists, he visited active war theatres where he made a record of the war in pictures.

around me. I gripped my spike and dove and swam, as I never swam before, down to that lurking, ugly demon. In a second I was on him and stabbed him with all my might—once, twice, three times —until, dying, he went off the ledge into the depths below and I followed him beyond to where no man may dare to swim. There he died. As his hateful mouth gaped I dragged out your father by the arm and brought him back to the top; but when I climbed with him into the canoe he was dead, and I was as you see me now— dead too from the waist down. All the rest of that day and all the night beyond and the next day I paddled and paddled until we came home—my dead son and I. No, no," went on the old man, "let us try the safer side of the reef."

For answer, Jimmy Tom quickly fastened in place the outriggers on either side of the canoe, which made it firm and safe to dive from. Around his neck he slipped the "toa," the wide-mouthed bag with a drawstring into which a sponge-diver thrusts his findings. Around his neck, too, he hung the "spike," a double-pointed stick two feet long of black palmwood, hard and heavy as iron. Then, standing on the bow seat, he filled his great lungs again and again until every air cell was opened. The old man looked at him proudly.

"You are of my blood," he said softly. "Go with God. I will watch above you and be your guard. Forget not to look up at me, and, if I signal, come back to me fast—for I cannot go to you," he finished sadly.

The young man gave a brief nod and, filling his lungs until his chest stood out like a square box, dived high into the air with that jack-knife dive which was invented by sponge-divers and, striking the water clean as the point of a dropped knife, he shot down to- ward the beautiful depths below. Into his lithe body rushed and pulsed the power and energy of the great swinging sea as he swam through the air-clear water toward a thicket of gorgonias, which waved against the white sand like a bed of poppies. In thirty seconds he was twenty fathoms down, where the pressure of sev- enty pounds to the square inch would have numbed and crip- pled an ordinary swimmer, but meant nothing to his steel-strong

body, hardened to the depths by years of deep diving. Even as he reached the gleaming thicket he saw, with a great throb of delight, a soft, golden-brown tuft of silk sponge hidden beneath the living branches. The silk sponge is to spongers in the sea what the silver fox is to trappers on the land, and the whole year's output from all seas is only a few score.

With a quick stroke, Jimmy Tom reached the many-coloured sea-shrub. The moving branches had to be parted carefully with the spike, lest they close and hide, beyond finding, the silky clump growing within their depths. Even as the boy started to slip over his head the cord from which swung the pointed stick, he looked up to see Jim Tom beckoning frantically for him to return. Yet nowhere in the nearby water could he see anything unusual, except a little fish some eight inches long marked with alternate bands of blue and gold, which came close to him and then turned and swam out to sea. Still his grandfather beckoned, his face contorted with earnestness.

The boy hesitated. An arm's length away lay a fortune. It might well be that never again could he find that exact spot if he went back to the surface now. All this passed through his mind in the same second in which he suddenly plunged his bare arm into the centre of the gorgonia clump without waiting to use the spike, as all cautious sponge-divers do. Following the clue of the waving silken end, he grasped a soft mass. Even as he pulled out a silk sponge, worth more than its weight in gold, something sharp as steel and brittle as ice pierced his hand deep, and he felt a score of spines break and rankle in his flesh like splinters of broken glass. By an ill chance he had thrust his hand against one of those chest-nut burs of the ocean, a purple-black sea urchin, whose villainous spines, like those of a porcupine, pierce deep and break off. Setting his teeth against the pain, the boy shifted the silky clump of sponge to his other hand and swam for the canoe with all his might. As he rose he saw his grandfather mouthing the word "Hurry!" every line on his tense face set in an agony of pleading.

Even as the boy shot toward the surface, he caught sight once again of the same brilliant little fish returning from deep water. Close behind it, dim at first, but growing more and more distinct as it came, showed a sinister shape, slate-grey, with yellow-brown stripes, the dreaded tiger shark of deep water, convoyed by the lit-tle jackal of the sea, the pilot fish. It was fortunate for Jimmy Tom that the tiger shark is not among the swiftest of its family and that he was halfway to the surface before the cold deadly eyes of that one caught sight of his ascending body. With a rush like a torpedo boat, the thirty-foot shark shot toward the straining, speeding figure, and reached it just as, with a last desperate effort, Jimmy Tom broke water by the canoe. Only the fact that a shark has to be on its back to bring into play its seven rows of triangular, saw-edged teeth saved the boy's life. The tiny tick of time which the fish took in turning enabled the old man, with a tremendous heave of his powerful arms, to drag Jimmy Tom bodily over the gunwhale just as the fatal jaws snapped shut below him.

For a long minute the sea-tiger circled the canoe with hungry speed. Then, seeing that his prey had escaped, he swam away, guided, as always, by the strange pilot fish, which feeds on the scraps of the feasts which it finds for its companion.

As the shark turned toward deep water, Jimmy Tom sat up from where he had been lying at the bottom of the canoe and grinned cheerfully after his disappearing foe. Then, without a word, he handed Jim Tom the clump of sponge which, throughout his almost dead heat with death, he had held clutched tightly in his left hand. With the same motion, he stretched out his other hand, filled like a pincushion with keen, glassy spines from the sea urchin.

"Not twice in a long lifetime," said his grandfather, "have I seen a finer silk sponge. Already that sloop is half paid for."

Without further words, he drew from his belt a sharp-pointed knife and began the painful process of removing one by one the embedded spines from the boy's right hand before they should begin to fester. He finished this bit of rough-and-ready surgery by washing out each deep puncture with stinging salt water. When he had entirely finished, Jimmy Tom carefully tucked away the sponge in a pocket fastened to the inside of the canoe and, slipping the wide-mouthed bag again over his neck, stood on the thwart ready for another dive.

"Try to remember with your thick head," said his grandfather, severely, "all that I have told you, and if I signal you to come back, you come."

The boy nodded briefly, took several deep breaths, and again shot down through the water, directing his course toward another part of the reef, where the white sand was dotted with shells, all hyaline[3] or clouded with exquisite colours. As he reached the bottom, the boy's swift, supple fingers searched among crystal-white, purple and rose and gold olivellas, dosinias, and tellinas[4] which, in spite of their beauty, had no special value. Just as he was about to return to the surface empty-handed, his eye caught the gleam of several spires of the rare, sky-white coral showing among the waving waterweed. A hasty look aloft showed no signal of danger from his sentinel, and he still had nearly three minutes before water would evact her toll of oxygen from him. A swift stroke brought him to the edge of the weed bed. Just as he was about

---

[3] HYALINE (hī'à-lĭn)—Translucent or clear as glass.

[4] OLIVELLAS, DOSINIAS, AND TELLINAS (ŏl-ĭ-vĕl'ăz, dô-sĭn'ĭ-ăz, tĕ-lĭ'nàz)—Different varieties of bivalve mollusks or shellfish. Some of the shells are thin, delicate, and beautifully coloured.

to reach for the coral, his trained eye caught sight of a gleaming white, beautifully shaped shell nearly as large as the palm of his hand. With a quick motion, he reached under the wavering leaves and, even as his fingers closed on its corrugated surface, realized that he had found at last a perfect specimen of the royal wentle-trap, among the rarest and most beautiful of shells.

In the collections of the world, there are perhaps not six perfect specimens, and sponge-divers and shell-gatherers along a thousand lonely coasts are ever on the lookout for this treasure of the sea. The pure white rounded whorls of this one were set off with wide, frilled varices,[5] each ending in a point above, the whole forming a perfect crown of snow and crystal indescribably airy and beautiful. The sight and feeling of this treasure put every thought out of Jimmy Tom's mind save to reach the surface with it as soon as possible. The coral could wait. For that shell any one of the collectors who called at Carib Island would gladly pay him twice the hundred dollars he needed.

Suddenly, even as he turned toward the surface, from a deep crevice in the coral close to his side, shot a fierce and hideous head, like that of some monstrous snake, ridged with a fin which showed like a crest. Before the boy could move, two long jaws filled with curved teeth snapped shut on his right hand and wrist, and he realized with a dreadful pang of fear and pain that he had been gripped by one of the great conger eels which lurk in the crevices of the reef. Eight feet in length and as large around as a man's leg, they are among the most fearsome of all the seafolk which a diver must brave. For a second, Jimmy Tom tugged with all his strength, but with no result except that the greenish-grey body retreated deeper into its cave. Then it was that he remembered what his grandfather had told him was the only way to escape from the deadly jaws of a conger eel. Relaxing every muscle, he allowed his hand to lie limp in the great fish's teeth. Sooner or later, if he kept quiet, the monster would open its jaws for a better grip.

As the cold, deadly eyes stared implacably into his, the beating

⁵ VARICES—Ridges or ribs.

of his labouring heart sounded in his ears like a drum of doom. If so be that the fierce fish did not relax his grip within the next thirty seconds, the boy knew that his life would go out of him in a long stream of silvery air bubbles. By a tremendous effort of will he strove against the almost irresistible impulse to do something, to pull, to struggle, to slash with his knife at the horrid head. Yet, clinching his teeth grimly, he set himself to that hardest of all tasks—to wait and wait. His eyes, hot and dim with suffused blood, fell on the crowned shell which he held in his free hand, that shell which was to win for him the sloop, and suddenly through the luminous, gleaming water he seemed to see his cabin on far-away Carib Island and his mother's face looking into his.

As the vision faded he felt a slight shifting and loosening of the grim jaws. With a last effort of his will, dimming before the flood of unconsciousness creeping up to his brain, he allowed his body to float limp, and relaxed every straining muscle. Even as he did so, the great jaws gaped apart for an instant and the fierce head thrust itself toward him for a fresh grip. Fighting back the waves of blackness which swept across his eyes, by a quick turn and wrench he freed his imprisoned hand and, with a tremendous scis-sors kick of his powerful legs, shot away just as the curved teeth struck, empty, together.

Up and up and up he sped, swimming as he had never swum before, yet seeming to himself, under the desperate urge of his tortured lungs, to move slow as the hour-hand of a clock. The sunlit surface seemed to move away and away and recede to an immeasurable distance. Just as he felt despairingly that he could no longer resist the uncontrollable desire of his anguished lungs to act, even if they drew in the waters of death, his head shot above the surface. There was a sudden roaring in his ears as the strong arms of Jim Tom pulled him into the canoe. Too weak to speak or move, he lay experiencing the utter happiness there is in breath-ing, which only the half-drowned may know.

All the rest of that day the boy lay in the shade of the towering coral wall, while old Jim Tom dressed his gashed and pierced hand. As the calm weather still held, the old man decided to spend the night in the canoe just outside the sheer wall of the reef, where the water stretched away to unknown depths. Toward evening the boy's strength came back; and after eating and drinking ravenously, he showed but little effect of the strain to which he had been subjected.

"When the moon rises," said his grandfather at length, "we will start for home."

The boy shook his head obstinately.

"Tomorrow, as soon as it is light," he said, "I dive again to bring up such white coral as has not been seen on Carib Island in my day."

"In your day!" exclaimed old Jim Tom, much incensed. "In your minute—for that is all you have lived. Never has any man made a better haul than you. Be satisfied. The reef is not fortunate for the greedy."

"My silk sponge was won from the jaws of a shark and my shell from the conger eel," returned the boy, doggedly. "I ask no favours of the reef."

The old man glanced around apprehensively, while the water seemed to chuckle as it lapped against the coral.

"It is not lucky to talk that way," he said softly. "Sleep now," he went on after a pause. "When morning comes, perhaps there will be a better spirit in you and we will go home."

A little later, while the great moon climbed the sky and the golden sea stretched away unbroken, the two slept. Hours later, Jim Tom awoke with a start. Through his sleep had penetrated the sharp sinister scent of musk, and, even before he opened his eyes, he felt some hostile living presence near him. As he raised his head above the side of the canoe, the still surface of the sea beyond was all a-writhe with what seemed a mass of white sea snakes. Suddenly from out of the livid tangle shot toward the boat two thirty-foot tentacles larger around than a man's body, tapering to a point and covered with round, sucking discs armed with claws of black horn, sharp and curved as those of a tiger. The great white squid, the devilfish of unknown depths, which hardly once or twice in a generation comes to the surface, was before him.

For a moment the old man stared in horror at the twisting, fatal tentacles. Then, with a hoarse cry, he roused Jimmy Tom, who started up, grasping the keen machete which always lay in a sheath at the bottom of the canoe. Even as he unsheathed the curved blade, one of the vast, pale streamers reached the canoe, glowed over its side, and licked around the waist of the old man. On the instant, red stains showed through his thin shirt where the armed discs sank deep into his flesh as the horrid arm dragged his helpless body toward the water. Just in time, the boy swung the machete over his head and severed the clutching streamer, and then, with a return stroke, cut through another that licked out toward him across the boat.

As he returned, the old man stretched his arm out toward the sea with a gasp of horror. Up through the water came a vast cylindrical shape of livid flesh, many times the size of the canoe, from which long tentacles radiated like a wheel. In the middle of the shapless mass was set a head of horror, with a vast parrotlike beak which gnashed over a mouth like a cavern. On either side of the demon jaws glared two lidless eyes, each larger than a barrel, rimmed around with white. Of an inky, unfathomable black, they stared at the boat with a malignancy which no earth-born creature could equal or endure. Unable to sustain their appalling glare, both of the Caribs thrust their arms before their faces, expecting every second to feel the deadly touch of the armed tentacles.

It was the boy who recovered himself first. Setting his teeth grimly, he suddenly raised his head to face again this demon of the lowest depths. At his exclamation of surprise, the old man forced himself to look up. The water stretched before them empty and unbroken. Only the scent of musk and grisly fragments of the death-pale tentacles in the bottom of the canoe were there to prove that the monster had not been a ghastly dream of the night. Without a word, Jimmy Tom shipped the outriggers and, gripping his paddle, took his place in the bow. All the rest of that night and far into the next day they paddled, until at last Carib Island loomed up on the horizon.

From the sale of the wentle trap and the silk sponge Jimmy Tom bought not only his sloop and a new canoe for Jim Tom, but still had the hundred of dollars which makes a man rich on Carib Island. Yet in spite of the fortune he brought back from the reef, he has never returned to it again. When urged by friends or collectors, he only shakes his head and says oracularly, "Enough is plenty."

DISCUSSING THE STORY

Although the adventure of Jimmy Tom and his grandfather is just a story, it is the kind of experience that could have happened to one of the sponge divers of the West Indies. The creatures in the story are just as real and dangerous as they are pictured.

1. Unless you have visited the tropic seas it is difficult to picture the scene of this adventure. However, if you will imagine the brilliant colouring that Samuel Scoville tells about in his description, you will come close to the real thing. Look for words, and word combinations, like these: *lune-green and amber, violet night, rim of raw gold, cinnamon-red skins, heliotrope horizon, purple and gold seafans, turquoise-blue parrot fish.* There are many others. The colour charts found in an encyclopaedia will help you to visualize the brilliant hues and contrasts.

2. Jim Tom had lost the use of his legs in another adventure. Tell about it. Whose life had been lost then?

3. Why was Jimmy so anxious for this expedition to be successful? Do you think he was afraid? How did Jim Tom feel about danger? In what sense did it take courage to dive, even the first time?

4. What valuable item did Jimmy secure during his first dive? How did his disobedience of orders almost result in tragedy? What was the mission of the pilot fish?

5. Tell about the treasure found during the second dive. What rare article did Jimmy leave behind?

6. Explain how Jimmy encountered and escaped from the conger eel. What lesson in the value of self-control does this experience suggest?

7. A third experience in horror came while the two slept. Describe the great white squid. How close were the man and boy to death? What did Jimmy do to protect them?

8. The expedition to the reef ended happily, but Jimmy did not wish to return. Do you think he was wise? Tell, if you can, about an experience when you did not know that "Enough is plenty."

THE LONG JUMP 🎔 WOLFGANG LANGEWIESCHE

Writers find it relatively easy to give factual accounts of adventures, but when they try to write about some inner tenseness, or about a series of emotional explosions from their own experience, they find it a much harder task. For example, only a few have been able to give expression to the "feel" of flying. Fewer, still, have successfully translated the thrilling details of a parachute jump to paper. Wolfgang Langewiesche, however, is an exception to these rules. He planned a delayed jump, remembered how he felt, and was able to put it all down in writing. Even though you know the jump was successful, you will experience some of the chills and thrills of the author as you travel aloft with him, and then plummet to earth.

MY OLD friends, Miller and Johnson, prepared the parachutes. But of my intention to delay the pulling of the rip cord, I did not dare tell them. I was a bit awed by it myself.

Though this was to be my second jump, it came harder than the first one; curiosity was gone, but all the worries were still left. Would I get clear of the ship, or lose my nerve and pull right away, and catch in the tail surface? Would the 'chute, in opening after a long delay, tangle with my feet? Or would the harness tear under the opening shock? I now had much respect for the landing itself; I thought of all the places where I might land: pointed and sharp ones, or perhaps live wires, or the river. Least reasonable worry and yet uppermost: Would the 'chute open properly? And if it didn't, how much time would there be to think, and what would I think?

When I reported on the appointed day, Johnson was out. Miller had my equipment still on the workbench, where he was checking it for the last time.

His assistant was frying hamburgers for lunch. The heat was good, and so was the smell. Outside, it was late autumn. The ceiling was four thousand feet, a solid overcast; the wind was N.E. 12, and it was chilly. Not an inviting day to go falling through the sky.

Was I asking for trouble?

Miller himself had given up jumping years ago. He now spent his life firmly on the ground, servicing other people's parachutes, trading in parachutes, patching and cleaning and folding parachutes; a tailor instead of an airman. Was that his final judgment on parachutes?

"How often, would you guess, can a man jump before it will get him?"

To that type of question most flying men have two answers. One answer is that everything is now under full control, that we have now achieved real mastery of the air. That is the answer you give to cash customers. The other you give to yourself sometimes, and always to the girl you want to impress:

"It is all a chance. When she is ready to hit, she will hit."

But the rigger,[1] wise old bird, had a different point of view, Even parachute jumping, he said, was all right and reasonably safe nowadays, provided you kept your wits about you, and used only good 'chutes packed by reputable riggers like himself—after all, he charged only three dollars for a repacking job—and as long as you observed the law that two 'chutes must be worn on intentional jumps. But the trouble with the parachute-jumping public, as he put it, was that they got used to it and became careless and sloppy. "Then," he added, "it is sure to kill fast."

He snapped and tested one after another the rubber cords that were to tear open the canvas bag and spill out the silk, once the latch was ripped out.

"And don't fool yourself," he said, "that you are an exception and will remain careful, because you won't."

He was right about that in a way. Instead of a straight bailing-out, I wanted to make this a delayed-opening jump. The idea is to let yourself fall, hand on the rip-cord ring, for a thousand feet or so, and only then to rip. It wouldn't have taken much to discourage me, on this cool, grey morning, but I didn't want to be discouraged. So I put it to him gently. I said I had arranged this time to be dumped from a little higher up, because I wanted to hold it a little longer, and that might be easier to do with a little more altitude below.

[1] RIGGER—A worker who assembles and aligns aircraft.

"All right," he said, somewhat to my surprise. As a matter of fact, and quite frankly, last time I had pulled too soon, and it might be wise to learn to hold it a little longer. From below it had looked as if my 'chute had just barely cleared the ship's tail.

I knew that. Last time I had ripped not when it seemed best but when my nerves had ripped—at the exact moment when the fear of tangling in the tail had been overpowered by the horror and confusion of the bottomless drop. This time, I must try for absolute nerve control.

The rigger put the finishing touch to his job. With indelible ink he signed his name and the date on a white cloth label sewn to the pack. This is a licensed rigger's guarantee that a parachute has been opened, inspected, refolded, and repacked within sixty days preceding flight, as the law demands; that it will work. Then he handed it to me for my inspection. I handed it back, and he cracked the standard joke of the occasion:

"If it doesn't work, bring it back and we'll refund your money."

Miller phoned to town for the pilot to come out: this guy was here now and wanted to jump. The mechanics still had considerable fixing to do on the old plane and its World War engine before it would fly. Meanwhile, there was nothing for me to do but to stand around on the field and wait.

Hard on the nerves, because it gives you time to think, and you can't help calculating your chances. The speed of a man falling through the air is one hundred and twenty miles per hour; faster than that he won't fall, because of air resistance, but that is fast enough. It would give me three seconds for every five hundred feet. It would take keen timing not to pancake.

I didn't feel like talking, but a reporter came and questioned me: why jump parachutes?

The real reason, of course, he would not understand, nor would his readers; least of all would the farmer understand it into whose field, in case of mishap, the final mess would burst. The real reason was that a man likes to test his nerve and to get closer and closer and still a little closer to the edge of life.

They were now wheeling the ship out of the hangar. Time to get ready. Word had somehow spread, and cars had come in from the highway. A small crowd was collecting, truck drivers, salesmen, store clerks off for lunch, hoping for a thrill.

The reporter wanted to know if I was married, and whether my mother knew about the jump.

Around and around in my head went a song I had once heard somewhere about "A Little Home in Flatbush." That was what I wanted just then, a little house and a complacent wife and never again any nerve testing. I had had enough of that.

The worst moment of a parachute jump comes when they dress you up and strap the 'chutes on you.

Moriturus: one who is about to die. That was my role as far as the crowd was concerned. They stood and gaped only because they thought that they might see me die. And I felt a little solemn myself. I might die; yet I probably would not die; as a matter of fact I had a date in town for that afternoon. But just now my plans for more than a quarter hour ahead were somehow tentative and strangely uninteresting.

The field manager came to supervise the preparations, and must have seen me shiver in the cool wind. He took off his leather jacket and put it on me. He made me feel better. It kept the wind out, and it also showed that he did not expect to get it back all messed up with dead Langewiesche. The good old Swede.

The rigger and his assistant brought out the 'chutes. They had adjusted the harness. This time it gripped me tight around the legs and around the chest and over the shoulders. It almost hurt, but the feel was good; it pulled you together.

On top of that hung the heavy back pack. Then the chest pack, for emergencies, buckled on in front. Heavy armour. It set you apart from the crowd, and marked you for a strange man off on a strange adventure.

It struck me that nobody wanted to talk to me. The men just stood around, watching. Beyond them, the ship was now noisily warming up its engine.

Again I could feel—by what little signs I could not tell—how some of the crowd were pulling for me but most of them against me. The field manager and the pilots and the flying students were for me, not because they liked me, not because they didn't think I was a fool, doing this without getting paid for it, but because they liked to think that parachutes always work. The rest were against me because they wanted a thrill; the reporter particularly was smelling blood.

The rigger alone was unexcited and workmanlike. He said, putting still another belt around me: "Now don't get mixed up, else you will be down before you know it."

Only the grey-haired little assistant—he who had been with the circuses for forty years—liked me. He reached down and rearranged the leg straps. He spoke some German and he said: "*Mach's gut*,"[2] calling me "thou." He was pulling for me all right.

They put the flying helmet on me and fastened the chin strap, damping out the voices, shutting me off still farther from the crowd. Then the goggles.

Only a few more minutes now. The pilot was climbing into the ship.

One girl was standing there among the men around me, the airport typist, or something like that. She alone now came through to me sharply, body and soul. For a moment I had an experience not given to many men in times of peace, thinking that she might be the last woman I should ever see. She was blonde and good-looking. She was talking to a man while looking at me. But I could not make out whether she was pulling for me or against me.

The ship was ready. There was nothing more to discuss, nothing more to wait for, and I might as well go. It was clumsy walking with all that weight on me, and the rigger had to help me lower myself and my chest pack and my back pack into the front cockpit. Then he said, "O.K.," and stood back. We took off.

At three thousand five hundred feet, ready to take the jump, I stood outboard, on the root of the wing, on the trailing edge, facing the tail. It had been difficult to climb out with all that bulk strapped to me, and now I had to hold on with both hands to the fuselage, not to be blown off.

With the pilot, I was almost face to face as he sat in his cockpit,

[2] "*Mach's gut*" (máks gōōt)—A German expression wishing him well.

looking forward, and I stood beside it, looking rearward. Close enough, but I felt alone. He was busy, scowling at his instruments, at the horizon, at the ground. He was trying to manoeuvre into a position that would land me—maybe—on the flying field. He didn't look at me, he didn't smile. There was no comradeship with him, merely the feeling of a job to be done. The job was to get away from each other smoothly. He hoped I would take a determined jump away from the ship, and that I would not pull prematurely and be blown into the tail and kill both of us. I hoped that he would give a well-timed kick on the rudder, the moment of jumping, to swing the tail out of my way. After that, we would worry each man for himself.

Around me was the empty world of the flier, the grey sky, the sad horizon. From the field, they were now probably watching breathlessly, but the field was small and far away; it was hard to distinguish among the farms. The town was small and far away, too. Word was spread and people were probably watching in the streets, but I was up here alone, shivering in the propeller wash, and all that didn't help me.

Below me was the depth.

Looking down along my fluttering trouser leg I saw the tips of my shoes—good solid shoes for good solid sidewalks—stick out over the void. Far below them, creeping slowly, the farms, a highway, a factory chimney.

There was plenty of time to look down and to face it. Now, I would crash through the roof into a farm wife's soup; now, I would be impaled on a telegraph pole; now, a little wood, much more inviting—the treetops looked soft and bouncy.

Nervously, I went over the top. I wanted to jump. Not much fear was left. My nerves themselves at last remembered again the experience of the first jump; the big fall that had not ended in a catastrophe hit, but in that wild, joyous rip across my chest; the opening shock that had jerked me all over heaven; and, after that, the comfortable sensation as I floated down. Some animal fear of falling might indeed spring up again the moment of actually stepping off, but the thing to do against that was to concentrate on the first few moments of falling, to control myself, and not to pull the rip cord.

The pilot throttled back the engine and went into a glide. He nodded.

It was up to me.

I let go with my hands. Immediately the air stream bowled me over. A cold shock; my right hand gripped frantically all over my left shoulder and chest for the rip cord and couldn't grab it. Balance was already gone, there was no stopping. A quick look, and I found it. Then I kicked myself off, away from the ship.

Down I went in a violent, breathless, silent tumble. The bottom dropped out from under me, from under my brains, my intestines. I couldn't see, I couldn't hear. I only felt I was going to smash.

Now was the time to hold it.

My hand was on the ring, but I must stand this until I could stand it absolutely no longer.

I must hold it still a little longer.

My head cleared, my breath came again, and I saw the ground. It was only a brief glimpse, but it was enough. I had won over the first confusion. I had not ripped, and now the ground was still far away, and there was still plenty of time.

I was falling face downward.

The ground was steady. It was not rushing up to meet me, as water rushes up when you dive off a springboard. It didn't move at all. At this rate, I could keep falling forever.

The fall rolled me over on my side, and then on my back. Between my feet, I could now see the horizon, and against the horizon, the ship. It was flying away from me and doing a curve. Watching it, watching the familiar rhythm of an airplane in flight, gave me back my sense of timing. I got a good long look at it, marvelling all the while that there was so much time, jumping down from the sky. I could see how I was losing height fast; for although the ship's nose was down and it was gliding, it seemed to float upwards rapidly.

A new twist, and I lost sight of it.

I was picking up more speed every instant, and I could feel it in my innards. It was the law of gravitation at work on a falling body, and felt from the inside out. One moment it felt as if I had been merely loafing around. A moment later I seemed to be dropping away like a stone.

Yet, there was still no hurry. I could see the horizon and by it could tell that I was still 'way up.

It may have been three or four seconds after jumping, but it felt more like six or seven, when I first became conscious of the thickness of the air. There was a new sensation. I was no longer dropping through a void.

A bottom was back under things, a soft but firm bottom of air rushing up against me from underneath. I could feel my back lying on it, the calves of my legs, and my arm and hand. It took all the fright out of falling. It was the same thing that holds you up in flying, and that fliers get a feeling for and learn to trust: air plus motion.

The tumbling began again. My head was heavier than the rest of me, and sank faster. I felt myself sliding off my air mattress backwards, headfirst. A glimpse of my own legs, flailing against the clouds. Overhead, which was now below, a flash of green ground. Then the legs fell over in a nasty backwards somersault. It didn't feel safe at all. I almost let her rip.

Somehow I got stabilized again, falling face downward, lying flat on the air stream, lying comfortably, with face, chest, belly, legs, arms, fingers, on a solid transparent nothing; and looking down through it, too. I fell steadily now, not speeding up any more. I had reached terminal velocity, one hundred and twenty miles per hour or thereabouts, and it felt fine. I had worried about it, and about the sharp timing that would be required. But now it wasn't like falling at all, more like flying, and I was quite relaxed. The ground was coming up, but only slowly. I saw a highway, white through the green grassland. I saw the farm I was falling into getting steadily bigger, as if being pulled up by a magnifying lens.

This was comfortable. It took three seconds, perhaps, but it seemed longer.

Then the air stream gave me a new twist. I began to roll over sideways, and my head sank away again. I began to wonder if I hadn't better pull now, while the 'chute could still string out away from my body. I might be all the way down before I would be again in a favourable position. I was still wondering when the farm suddenly took a lunge, blew up, and exploded in my face.

I was THERE.

I managed to pull the rip cord quite slowly, deliberately, with no particular force—so much had the feel of the air stream taken the catastrophe out of falling. I could feel the latch pins snap open; the rip cord, a little farther out, was getting stuck; for safety's sake I gave it another easy pull and got it all the way out.

There was again the ugly split second when you have a piece of slack wire rope in your hand. You can do no more with it, and nothing happens.

Then the big jerk—vicious, quite unelastic. I might as well have lassoed a locomotive. It hurt plenty, but it was all over in a moment. I hung.

I heard excited shouts of children from somewhere. I found I was very low; I hadn't pulled any too soon. There was no time to enjoy the floating down. I was drifting onto a telephone line— or was it high tension? I grabbed two of the shrouds above me and pulled on them, sideslipping the 'chute into an open field. It was dark bare earth, with yesterday's rains still on it in pools. The slip made me swing viciously, pendulum fashion. I was worried about the landing, but there was no time left to steady myself. I was falling through fast. I went limp, and hit.

This time I hit very lightly; it must have been because of the cool, heavy air. I sat down, but only because I was limp. I could have taken it standing up. The canopy was still open and tugged in the wind. I pulled on one shroud until it collapsed. I got up and looked around for someone to come and greet me and help me. I had landed far from the flying field. I was alone except for some cows. The ship was gone from the sky.

I unbuckled the harness and rolled up the silk. Still nobody was in sight, and I loaded my seventy pounds of parachute on my shoulders and started walking, ankle deep in soft black soil.

DISCUSSING THE SELECTION

1. Unless you have personally inspected a parachute and watched a jump, you should look up a discussion of these safety devices in an encyclopaedia. Most such discussions include interesting pictures. Explain the role of the parachute packer and inspector. Why is his job so important? What does this selection tell you about how a parachute works?

2. What are the feelings of the author while waiting for the take-off? What are the attitudes he feels in the others around him? Is there a difference between the attitude of the flier and the nonflier?

3. What feelings did the author have as he climbed out on the wing of the airplane? How do you think the pilot felt? What are the responsibilities of the pilot during a jump?

4. What feelings did you have as you read about the free fall? What caused the differences in falling speed? Why is it necessary to avoid pulling the rip cord too soon?

5. Tell about how the author controlled his fear. Do you think, now, that you would some day like to make a jump? Explain how you feel about jumping.

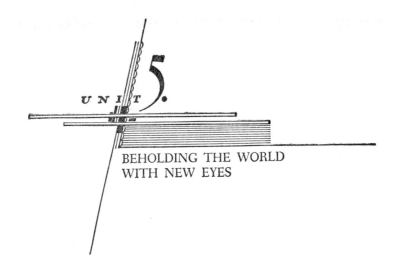

BEHOLDING THE WORLD
WITH NEW EYES

THREE DAYS TO SEE ✤ HELEN KELLER

I HAVE often thought it would be a blessing if each human being were stricken blind and deaf for a few days at some time during his early adult life. Darkness would make him more appreciative of sight; silence would teach him the joys of sound.

Now and then I have tested my seeing friends to discover what they see. Recently I asked a friend, who had just returned from a long walk in the woods, what she had observed. "Nothing in particular," she replied.

How was it possible, I asked myself, to walk for an hour through the woods and see nothing worthy of note? I who cannot see find hundreds of things to interest me through mere touch. I feel the delicate symmetry of a leaf. I pass my hands lovingly about the smooth skin of a silver birch, or the rough, shaggy bark of a pine. In spring I touch the branches of trees hopefully in search of a bud, the first sign of awakening Nature after her winter's sleep. Occasionally, if I am very fortunate, I place my hand gently on a small tree and feel the happy quiver of a bird in full song.

At times my heart cries out with longing to see all these things. If I can get so much pleasure from mere touch, how much more beauty must be revealed by sight. And I have imagined what I should most like to see if I were given the use of my eyes, say, for just three days.

I should divide the period into three parts. On the first day, I should want to see the people whose kindness and companionship have made my life worth living. I do not know what it is to see into the heart of a friend through that "window of the soul," the eye. I can only "see" through my finger tips the outline of a face. I can detect laughter, sorrow, and many other emotions. I know my friends from the feel of their faces.

How much easier, how much more satisfying it is for you who can see to grasp quickly the essential qualities of another person by watching the subtleties of expression, the quiver of a muscle, the flutter of a hand. But does it ever occur to you to use your sight to see into the inner nature of a friend? Do not most of you seeing people grasp casually the outward features of a face and let it go at that?

For instance, can you describe accurately the faces of five good friends? As an experiment, I have questioned husbands about the colour of their wives' eyes, and they often express embarrassed confusion and admit that they do not know.

Oh, the things that I should see if I had the power of sight for just three days!

The first day would be a busy one. I should call to me all my dear friends and look long into their faces, imprinting upon my mind the outward evidences of the beauty that is within them. I should let my eyes rest, too, on the face of a baby, so that I could catch a vision of the eager, innocent beauty which precedes the individual's consciousness of the conflicts which life develops. I should like to see the books which have been read to me, and which have revealed to me the deepest channels of human life. And I should like to look in the loyal, trusting eyes of my dogs, the little Scottie and the stalwart Great Dane.

In the afternoon I should take a long walk in the woods and intoxicate my eyes on the beauties of the world of nature. And I should pray for the glory of a colourful sunset. That night, I think, I should not be able to sleep.

The next day I should arise with the dawn and see the thrilling

miracle by which night is transformed into day. I should behold
with awe the magnificent panorama of light with which the sun
awakens the sleeping earth.

This day I should devote to a hasty glimpse of the world, past
and present. I should want to see the pageant of man's progress,
and so I should go to the museums. There my eyes would see the
condensed history of the earth—animals and the races of men
pictured in their native environment; gigantic carcasses of dino-
saurs and mastodons which roamed the earth before man appeared,
with his tiny stature and powerful brain, to conquer the animal
kingdom.

My next stop would be the Museum of Art. I know well through
my hands the sculptured gods and goddesses of the ancient Nile
land. I have felt copies of Parthenon friezes,[1] and I have sensed
the rhythmic beauty of charging Athenian warriors. The gnarled,
bearded features of Homer[2] are dear to me, for he, too, knew
blindness. So on this, my second day, I should try to probe into
the soul of man through his art. The things I know through touch
I should now see. More splendid still, the whole magnificent world
of painting would be opened to me. I should be able to get only
a superficial impression. Artists tell me that for a deep and true
appreciation of art one must educate the eye. One must learn
through experience to weigh the merits of line, of composition, of
form and colour. If I had my eyes, how happily would I embark
on so fascinating a study!

The evening of my second day I should spend at a theatre or at
the movies. How I should like to see the fascinating figure of
Hamlet, or the gusty Falstaff[3] amid colourful Elizabethan trap-
pings! I cannot enjoy the beauty of rhythmic movement except
in a sphere restricted to the touch of my hands. I can vision only
dimly the grace of a Pavlowa,[4] although I know something of the
delight of rhythm, for often I can sense the beat of music as it
vibrates through the floor. I can well imagine that cadenced motion

---

[1] PARTHENON FRIEZES—Sculptured bands on the Parthenon, a marble building
in Athens.
[2] HOMER—A Greek poet.
[3] HAMLET . . . FALSTAFF—Characters in two plays by Shakespeare.
[4] PAVLOWA (păv'lô-và)—A Russian ballet dancer.

must be one of the most pleasing sights in the world. I have been able to gather something of this by tracing with my fingers the lines in sculptured marble; if this static grace can be so lovely, how much more acute must be the thrill of seeing grace in motion.

The following morning, I should again greet the dawn, anxious to discover new delights, new revelations of beauty. Today, this third day, I shall spend in the workaday world, amid the haunts of men going about the business of life. The city becomes my destination.

First, I stand at a busy corner, merely looking at people, trying by sight of them to understand something of their daily lives. I see smiles, and I am happy. I see serious determination, and I am proud. I see suffering, and I am compassionate.

I stroll down Fifth Avenue. I throw my eyes out of focus, so that I see no particular object but only a seething kaleidoscope [5] of colour. I am certain that the colours of women's dresses moving in a throng must be a gorgeous spectacle of which I should never tire. But perhaps if I had sight I should be like most other women —too interested in styles to give much attention to the splendour of colour in the mass.

From Fifth Avenue I make a tour of the city—to the slums, to factories, to parks where children play. I take a stay-at-home trip abroad by visiting the foreign quarters. Always my eyes are open wide to all the sights of both happiness and misery so that I may probe deep and add to my understanding of how people work and live.

My third day of sight is drawing to an end. Perhaps there are many serious pursuits to which I should devote the few remaining hours, but I am afraid that on the evening of that last day I should again run away to the theatre, to a hilariously funny play, so that I might appreciate the overtones of comedy in the human spirit.

At midnight permanent night would close on me again. Naturally in those three short days I should not have seen all I wanted to see. Only when darkness had again descended upon me should I realize how much I had left unseen.

[5] KALEIDOSCOPE (kȧ-lī′dȯ-skōp)—A variegated, changing scene.

Perhaps this short outline does not agree with the programme you might set for yourself if you knew you were about to be stricken blind. I am, however, sure that if you faced that fate you would use your eyes as never before. Everything you saw would become dear to you. Your eyes would touch and embrace every object that came within your range of vision. Then, at last, you would really see, and a new world of beauty would open itself before you.

I who am blind can give one hint to those who see: Use your eyes as if tomorrow you would be stricken blind. And the same method can be applied to the other senses. Hear the music of voices, the song of a bird, the mighty strains of an orchestra, as if you would be stricken deaf tomorrow. Touch each object as if tomorrow your tactile sense would fail. Smell the perfume of flowers, taste with relish each morsel, as if tomorrow you could never smell and taste again. Make the most of every sense; glory in all the facets of pleasure and beauty which the world reveals to you through the several means of contact which nature provides. But of all the senses, I am sure that sight must be the most delightful.

ABOUT THE AUTHOR

Helen Keller is one of the world's remarkable people. As the result of a severe illness she lost both her sight and hearing, and soon after lost also the power of speech. "Once I knew only darkness and stillness," she has written; "my life was without past or future." But with the aid of a patient, sympathetic teacher, Helen was taught to communicate with others through her hands. She learned to read Braille, to sense sound through vibration, to hear through her sensitive finger tips. She has led a full, almost completely normal life. Her activities, as you might expect, have been devoted to helping other handicapped persons like herself.

DISCUSSING THE SELECTION

1. Miss Keller thinks that the average person fails really to appreciate the gifts of sight and hearing. Do you agree that most people are in many respects unobservant? Think back over your walk or ride to school this morning—what did you see? What did you hear?

2. Trying to imagine the things she would most like to see if she were given her sight for just three days, Miss Keller carefully scheduled her time. Tell how she would spend the first day. Knowing that people rarely look the way we imagine them to look, do you think Miss Keller might be surprised or disappointed in the appearance of her friends?

3. Mention some of the things Miss Keller would like to see and to do on the second and third days. Tell whether or not you think she would be using her time wisely. If you were in her place, would you make the same choices?

4. Reversing the idea in this selection, try to imagine how you would spend the time if you were to be stricken blind and deaf for three days. How would you care for your physical needs? Would you be able to do any work? What would you do for recreation? If, then, you were to regain your sight and hearing, do you think you would have any more appreciation of those senses?

WALKING 🎜 DILYS BENNETT LAING

I walked on a snow-bank that
  squeaked like leather,
Or two wooden spoons that you
  rub together.

I walked on green moss, and
  brown earth, sprouting
With little grass blades on
  their first Spring outing.

5 I walked on blossoms and cool,
    green cresses,
And grass that rustled like
  silken dresses.

I walked on bracken, and dry
  leaves after,
That flamed with colour and
  crackled with laughter.

I walked on the earth as the
seasons came,
10   And under my feet it was never
the same!

ENJOYING THE POEM

1. The sensations experienced from walking depend upon what is under foot. In each of the four seasons of the year these sensations are different. In "Walking", Dilys Laing describes her reactions to walking on crisp snow, on moss and soft earth, on blossoms and grass, and on bracken and leaves. What were the sensations which she associated with each? Relate each to one of the four seasons of the year. To which sense or combination of senses does each appeal?

2. There is interest in variety. What value is there in the changing conditions of the seasons?

SLEIGHT-OF-SPRING 🦋 ETHEL JACOBSON

SPRING is a magic show,
Spring is hocus-pocus:
Now you see a bank of snow,
Now a field of crocus.

5   Nothing's up her sleeve now
But the thousand paper hats
Of daffodils, and a bare bough
Turned to pussy cats!

CLUES TO THE MEANING

In what ways is spring like a magic show? What sleight-of-hand tricks does the poet mention? Can you think of other things that happen as the seasons change that are like magic?

KLOOCHMAN ✻ WILLIAM O. DOUGLAS

KLOOCHMAN ROCK stands on the southern side of the Tieton
Basin in the Cascades.[1] It is an oval-shaped lava rock, running
lengthwise northwest by southeast, a half mile or more. It rises
2000 feet above the basin. The first third of its elevation is gained
through gentle slopes of pine and fir. Next are a few hundred
yards of tumbled rock. Then there is the cliff rising to the sky,
1200 feet or more—straight as the Washington Monument and
over twice as high. . . .

Kloochman is an Indian name for woman. . . . The Indian
legend has it that Kloochman is a woman turned to stone. There
was a chief of the Yakimas known as Meow-wah. He was peaceful
and noted for his wisdom and virtue. He was a bachelor. The
wiles of beautiful Indian maidens were lost on him. His people
decided an effort should be made to have him wed. So they chose
the four loveliest girls from all the tribes and sent them to him
from the north, south, east, and west, bearing gifts. Meow-wah
heard of the plan and consulted Coyote.[2] When the four beauties
came near, Coyote turned them all into stone. The Indian maiden
who came from the south was turned into Kloochman or Woman
Rock.   Coyote, to make the job complete, turned Meow-wah into
the mountain now called Goose Egg.

I climbed Kloochman in the summer of 1948. My climb was a
leisurely one. There are vast rock fields at the base of the towering cliffs—rock fields fringed with willow, Douglas maple, cream-
bush, currant, and serviceberry.   And occasionally the edges of
these fields are decorated with dark green splotches of the prostrate
juniper. I worked my way through these shrubs as I skirted the
base of the rock and finally found on the east an easy incline leading to the top. Almost all the way up I found patches of a dwarf
pentstemon, dark purple and lightly scented. It grew along the

---

[1] CASCADES—Range of mountains extending through Oregon and Washington.
[2] COYOTE (kī'ōt)—The hero and trickster found in many Indian legends.

wall wherever there was a handful of dirt. The delicacy of the flower atoned for the coarse and ragged basalt [8] that in some violent upthrust formed this old sentinel of Tieton Basin. . . .

As I sat on top of Kloochman that afternoon, I relived an earlier ascent of my youth—far from being so leisurely and peaceful.

It was in 1913 when Doug was nineteen and I was not quite fifteen that the two of us made this climb of Kloochman. Walter Kohagen, Doug, and I were camped in the Tieton Basin at a soda spring. The basin was then in large part a vast rich bottomland. We were travelling light, one blanket each. The night, I recall, was so bitter cold that we took turns refueling the campfire so that we could keep our backs warm enough to sleep. We rose at the first show of dawn, and cooked frying-pan bread and trout for breakfast. We had not planned to climb Kloochman, but somehow the challenge came to us as the sun touched her crest.

After breakfast we started circling the rock. There are fairly easy routes up Kloochman, but we shunned them. When we came to the southeast face (the one that never has been conquered, I believe), we chose it. Walter decided not to make the climb, but to wait at the base of the cliff for Doug and me. The July day was warm and cloudless. Doug led. The beginning was easy. For a hundred feet or so we found ledges six to twelve inches wide we could follow to the left or right. Some ledges ran up the rock ten feet or more at a gentle grade. Others were merely steps to another ledge higher up. Thus by hugging the wall we could either ease ourselves upward or hoist ourselves from one ledge to another.

When we were about a hundred feet up the wall, the ledges became narrower and footwork more precarious. Doug suggested we take off our shoes. This we did, tying them behind us on our belts. In stocking feet we wormed up the wall, clinging like flies to the dark rock. The pace was slow. We gingerly tested each toehold and fingerhold for loose rock before putting our weight on it. At times we had to inch along sidewise, our stomachs pressed tightly against the rock, in order to gain a point where we could reach the ledge above us. If we got on a ledge that turned out to be a

---

[8] BASALT (ba-sôlt')—A hard, dark rock containing a number of minerals.

cul-de-sac,[4] the much more dangerous task of going down the rock wall would confront us. Hence we picked our route with care and weighed the advantages of several choices which frequently were given us. At times we could not climb easily from one ledge to another. The one above might be a foot or so high. Then we would have to reach it with one knee, slowly bring the other knee up, and then, delicately balancing on both knees on the upper ledge, come slowly to our feet by pressing close to the wall and getting such purchase[5] with our fingers as the lava rock permitted.

In that tortuous way we made perhaps six hundred feet in two hours. It was late afternoon when we stopped to appraise our situation. We were in serious trouble. We had reached the feared cul-de-sac. The two- or three-inch ledge on which we stood ended. There seemed none above us within Doug's reach. I was longer-legged than Doug; so perhaps I could have reached some ledge with my fingers if I were ahead. But it was impossible to change positions on the wall. Doug was ahead and there he must stay. The problem was to find a way to get him up.

Feeling along the wall, Doug discovered a tiny groove into

---

  [4] CUL-DE-SAC (kŏŏl-dė-săk')—A dead-end passage.
  [5] PURCHASE—Leverage or hold.

which he could press the tips of the fingers of his left hand. It might help him maintain balance as his weight began to shift from the lower ledge to the upper one. But there was within reach not even a lip of rock for his right hand. Just out of reach, however, was a substantial crevice, one that would hold several men. How could Doug reach it? I could not boost him, for my own balance was insecure. Clearly, Doug would have to jump to reach it—and he would have but one jump. Since he was standing on a ledge only a few inches wide, he could not expect to jump for his handhold, miss it, and land safely. A slip meant he would go hurtling down some six hundred feet onto the rocks. After much discussion and indecision, Doug decided to take the chance and go up.

He asked me to do him a favour: if he failed and fell, I might still make it, since I was longer-legged; would I give certain messages to his family in that event? I nodded.

"Then listen carefully. Try to remember my exact words," he told me. "Tell Mother that I love her dearly. Tell her I think she is the most wonderful person in the world. Tell her not to worry—that I did not suffer, that God willed it so. Tell Sister that I have been a mean little devil but I had no malice towards her. Tell her I love her too—that some day I wanted to marry a girl as wholesome and cheery and good as she.

"Tell Dad I was brave and died unafraid. Tell him about our climb in full detail. Tell Dad I have always been very proud of him, that some day I planned to be a doctor too. Tell him I lived a clean life, that I never did anything to make him ashamed. . . . Tell Mother, Sister, and Dad I prayed for them."

Every word burned into me. My heart was sick, my lips quivered. I pressed my face against the rock so Doug could not see. I wept.

All was silent. A pebble fell from the ledge on which I squeezed. I counted seconds before it hit six hundred feet below with a faint, faraway, tinkling sound. Would Doug drop through the same space? Would I follow? When you fall six hundred feet do you die before you hit the bottom? Closing my eyes, I asked God to help Doug up the wall.

In a second Doug said in a cheery voice, "Well, here goes."

A false bravado took hold of us. I said he could do it. He said he would. He wiped first one hand then the other on his trousers. He placed both palms against the wall, bent his knees slowly, paused a split second, and jumped straight up. It was not much of a jump—only six inches or so. But that jump by one pressed against a cliff six hundred feet in the air had daredevil proportions. I held my breath; my heart pounded. The suspense was over.

Doug made the jump, and in a second was hanging by two hands from a strong, wide ledge. There was no toehold; he would have to hoist himself by his arms alone. He did just that. His body went slowly up as if pulled by some unseen winch. Soon he had the weight of his body above the ledge and was resting on the palms of his hands. He then put his left knee on the ledge, rolled over on his side, and chuckled as he said, "Nothing to it."

A greater disappointment followed. Doug's exploration of the ledge showed he was in a final cul-de-sac. There was no way up. There was not even a higher ledge he could reach by jumping. We were now faced with the nightmare of going down the sheer rock wall. We could not go down frontwards because the ledges were too narrow and the wall too steep. We needed our toes, not our heels, on the rock; and we needed to have our stomachs pressed tightly against it. Then we could perhaps feel our way. But as every rock expert knows, descent of a cliff without ropes is often much more difficult than ascent.

That difficulty was impressed on us by the first move. Doug had to leave the ledge he had reached by jumping. He dared not slide blindly to the skimpy ledge he had just left. I must help him. I must move up the wall and stand closer to him. Though I could not possibly hold his weight, I must exert sufficient pressure to slow up his descent and to direct his toe onto the narrow ledge from which he had just jumped.

I was hanging to the rock like a fly, twelve feet or more to Doug's left. I inched my way toward him, first dropping to a lower ledge and then climbing to a higher one, using such toeholds as the rock afforded and edging my way crabwise.

When I reached him I said, "Now I'll help."

Doug lowered himself and hung by his fingers full length. His feet were about six inches above the ledge from which he had jumped. He was now my responsibility. If he dropped without aid or direction he was gone. He could not catch and hold to the scanty ledge. I had little space for manoeuvring. The surface on which I stood was not more than three inches wide. My left hand fortunately found an overhead crevice that gave a solid anchor in case my feet slipped.

I placed my right hand in the small of Doug's back and pressed upward with all my might. "Now you can come," I said.

He let go gently, and the full weight of his body came against my arm. My arm trembled under the tension. My left hand hung onto the crack in the rock like a grappling hook. My stomach pressed against the wall as if to find mucilage in its pores. My toes dug in as I threw in every ounce of strength.

Down Doug came—a full inch. I couldn't help glancing down and seeing the rocks six hundred feet below.

Down Doug moved another inch, then a third. My left hand seemed paralyzed. The muscles of my toes were aching. My right arm shook. I could not hold much longer.

Down came Doug a fourth inch. I thought he was headed for destruction. His feet would miss the only toehold within reach. I could not possibly hold him. He would plunge to his death because my arm was not strong enough to hold him. The messages he had given me for his family raced through my mind. And I saw myself, sick and ashamed, standing before them, testifying to my own inadequacy, repeating his last words.

"Steady, Doug. The ledge is a foot to your right." He pawed the wall with the toes of his foot, searching.

"I can't find it. Don't let go."

The crisis was on us. Even if I had been safely anchored, my cramped position would have kept me from helping him much more. I felt helpless. In a few seconds I would reach the physical breaking point and Doug would go hurtling off the cliff. I did not see how I could keep him from slipping and yet maintain my own balance.

I will never know how I did it. But I tapped some reserve and directed his right foot onto the ledge from which he had earlier jumped. I did it by standing for a moment on my left foot alone and then using my right leg as a rod to guide his right foot to the ledge his swinging feet had missed.

His toes grabbed the ledge as if they were talons of a bird. My right leg swung back to my perch.

"Are you O.K.?" I asked.

"Yes," said Doug. "Good work."

My right arm fell from him, numb and useless. I shook from exhaustion and for the first time noticed that my face was wet with perspiration. We stood against the rock in silence for several minutes, relaxing and regaining our composure.

Doug said, "Let's throw our shoes down. It will be easier going." So we untied them from our belts and dropped them to Walter Kohagen, who was waiting at the rock field below us.

Our descent was painfully slow but uneventful. We went down backwards, weaving a strange pattern across the face of the cliff as we moved from one side to the other. It was perhaps midafternoon when we reached the bottom, retrieved our shoes, and started around the other side of the rock. We left the southeast wall unconquered.

But, being young, we were determined to climb the rock. So once more we started to circle. When we came to the northwest wall, we selected it as our route.

Here, too, is a cliff rising a thousand feet like some unfinished pyramid. But close examination shows numerous toe- and finger-holds that make the start at least fairly easy. So we set out with our shoes on.

Again it was fairly easy going for a hundred feet or so, when Doug, who was ahead, came to a ledge to which he could not step. On later climbs we would send the longer-legged chap ahead. And on other occasions Doug himself has used a rope to traverse this spot. But this day success of the climb depended at this point on Doug's short legs alone. The ledge to which he must move was up to his hips. There were few fingerholds overhead, and none firm enough to carry his whole weight. Only a few tiny cracks were within reach to serve as purchase for him. But Doug would not give up.

He hitched up his trousers, and grasped a tiny groove of rock with the tips of the fingers of his left hand, pressing his right hand flat against the smooth rock wall as if it had magical sticking power. Slowly he shifted his left knee until it was slightly over the ledge above him. To do so he had to stand tiptoe on his right foot. Pulling with his left hand, he brought his right knee up. Doug was now on both knees on the upper ledge. If he could find good purchase overhead for his hands, he was safe. His hands explored the wall above him. He moved them slowly over most of it without finding a hold. Then he reached straight above his head and cried out, "This is our lucky day."

He had found strong rough edges of rock, and on this quickly pulled himself up. His hands were on a ledge a foot wide. He lay down on it on his stomach and grasped my outstretched hand. The pull of his strong arm against the drop of a hundred feet or more was as comforting an experience as any I can recall. In a jiffy I was at his side. We pounded each other on the shoulders and laughed.

My own most serious trouble was yet to come. For a while Doug and I were separated. I worked laterally along a ledge to the south, found easier going, and in a short time was two hundred feet or more up the rock wall. I was above Doug, twenty-five feet or so, and fifty feet to his right. We had been extremely careful to test each toe- and fingerhold before putting our trust in it. Kloochman is full of treacherous rock. We often discovered thin ledges that crumbled under pressure and showered handfuls of rock and dust down below. Perhaps I was careless; but whatever the cause, the thin ledge on which I was standing gave way.

As I felt it slip, I grabbed for a hold above me. The crevasse I seized was solid. But there I was, hanging by my hands two hundred feet in the air, my feet pawing the rock. To make matters worse, my camera had swung between me and the cliff when I slipped. It was a crude and clumsy instrument, a box type that

I carried on a leather strap across my shoulders. Its bulk was actually pushing me from the cliff. I twisted in an endeavour to get rid of it, but it was firmly lodged between me and the wall.

I yelled to Doug for help. He at once started edging toward me. It seemed hours, though it was probably not over a few minutes. He shouted, "Hang on, I'll be there."

Hang on I did. My fingers ached beyond description. They were frozen to the rock. My exertion in pawing with my feet had added to the fatigue. The ache of my fingers extended to my wrists and then along my arms. I stopped thrashing around and hung like a sack, motionless. Every second seemed a minute, every minute an hour. I did not see how I could possibly hold.

I would slip, I thought, slip to sure death. I could not look down because of my position. But in my mind's eye I saw in sharp outline the jagged rocks that seemed to pull me toward them. The camera kept pushing my fingers from the ledge. I felt them move. They began to give way before the pull of a force too great for flesh to resist.

Fright grew in me. The idea of hanging helpless two hundred feet above the abyss brought panic. I cried out to Doug but the words caught in my dry throat. I was like one in a nightmare who struggles to shout—who is then seized with a fear that promises to destroy him.

Then there flashed through my mind a family scene. Mother was sitting in the living room talking to me, telling me what a wonderful man Father was. She told me of his last illness and his death. She told me of his departure from Cleveland, Washington to Portland, Oregon for what proved to be a fatal operation. His last words to her were: "If I die, it will be glory. If I live, it will be grace."

The panic passed. The memory of those words restored reason. Glory to die? I could not understand why it would be glory to die. It would be glory to live. But as Father said, it might take grace to live, grace from One more powerful than either Doug or I.

And so again that day I prayed. I asked God to save my life, to save me from destruction on this rock wall. I asked God to make my fingers strong, to give me strength to hang on. I asked God to give me courage, to make me unafraid. I asked God to give me power to do the impossible.

My fingers were as numb as flesh that is full of novocaine.[6] They seemed detached from me, as if they belonged to someone else. My wrists, my shoulders, cried out for respite from the pain. It would be such welcome relief if they could be released from the weight that was on them.

Hang on? You can't hang on. You are a weakling. The weaklings die in the woods.

Weakling? I'll show you. How long must I hang on? All day? O.K., all day then. I'll hang on, I'll hang on. O God, dear God, help me hang on!

I felt someone pushing my left foot upwards. It was Doug. As if through a dream his voice was saying, "Your feet are eighteen inches below your toehold." Doug found those toeholds for my feet.

I felt my shoes resting in solid cracks. I pulled myself up and leaned on my elbows on the ledge to which my hands had been glued. I flexed my fingers and bent my wrists to bring life back.

Doug came up abreast of me and said, "We're even Stephen now."

"Even Stephen?"

"To-day each of us has saved the other's life."

It was shortly above the point where Doug saved my life that we discovered a classic path up Kloochman. It is a three-sided chimney chute, a few feet wide, that leads almost to the top. There are several such chutes on Kloochman. In later years Cragg Gilbert and Louis Ulrich went up Devil's Chimney on the northeast face in a seven-hour nerve-wracking climb with ropes. Clarence Truitt and many others have gone up the chimney chute that Doug and I discovered. Then as now this chute was filled with loose rock that had to be cleared away. To negotiate the chute we took off our shoes and tied them to our belts. We climbed the chute in stocking feet, pressing our hands and feet against the opposing

_____
[6] NOVOCAINE—A drug used to deaden pain in a small local area.

walls as we kept our backs to the abyss below. This day we went up the chute with ease, stopping every eight feet or so to measure our progress.

The sun was setting when we reached the top. We were gay and buoyant. We talked about the glories of the scene in front of us. We bragged a bit about our skill in rock work—how we must be part mountain goat to have reached the top. We shouted and hallooed to the empty meadows far below us.

On Kloochman Rock that July afternoon both Doug and I valued life more because death had passed so close. It was wonderful to be alive, breathing, using our muscles, shouting, seeing.

We stayed briefly at the top. We went down as we came up, in stocking feet. We raced against darkness, propelled by the thought of spending the night on Kloochman's treacherous wall.

It was deep dusk when we rejoined Walter on the rock fields at the base. We put on our shoes and hurried on. We entered the woods at double-quick time, seeking the trail that led toward the South Fork of the Tieton. We saw the trail from the edge of a clearing as a faint, light streak in a pitch-black night. We had two ways of keeping on it. We had no matches or torch or flashlight. But we could feel the edges with our feet. And we could search out the strip of night sky over the path.

We finally decided that it would take too long to follow the trail to camp in this groping way. We'd take a short cut to Westfall Rocks, whose formless shape we could see against the sky. We took to the brush on our right, and kept our hands out in front to ward off boughs and branches. We crossed a marshy bog where we went in up to our knees. We came to soft earth where we went in up to our hips.

There were animals in the brush. We could hear them in the thickets, disturbed by our approach and going out ahead of us. Thinking they might be bear, we paused to listen. "Cattle," said Doug.

We reached the Tieton River, which we knew could not be forded in many places in that stretch. So we took off our pants, shoes, and shirts and rolled them in bundles which we held on our heads. We waded out into the dark, cold, swift river, Doug in the lead. We had by accident picked one of the few good fords in the Tieton. We were never in water over our waists.

Then we dressed and located the road leading back to camp. As we started along it Doug said: "You know, Bill, there is power in prayer."

That night I prayed again. I knelt on a bed of white fir boughs beside the embers of a campfire and thanked God for saving Doug's life and mine, for giving us the strength to save each other.

ABOUT THE AUTHOR

Some people know William O. Douglas only as a learned justice of the United States Supreme Court. There are others, however, who know Bill Douglas the mountain climber, the adventurer, the lover of nature. It all began when Bill, as a child, almost died of infantile paralysis. The illness left the boy with little strength and with wasted muscles in his legs, and his attempts to rebuild his weakened body included hiking through the hills around his home in Yakima, Washington. Slowly he became strong again, but his explorations into the rugged mountains continued. He realized that he had found a rich life of discovery amid the grandeur of some of the wildest mountain country in the United States.

William O. Douglas, the learned Justice, still spends as much time as he can in this northwestern wilderness. And now he has written a book about his explorations in which he tells how he and his brother first scaled the steep sides of Kloochman Rock in the Cascade Mountains.

DISCUSSING THE SELECTION

1. What does the name Kloochman mean? Tell how the rock got its name.

2. Under what circumstances did William Douglas remember an earlier attempt to climb the mountain? How many were in the party then? Who stayed behind? Tell why the boys chose the route they did.

3. Explain the climbing methods the boys used. What difficulties did they encounter almost from the start? What was their situation after climbing six hundred feet?

4. Tell about Doug's jump and ascent to the ledge and his return. In what ways did both boys exhibit bravery? What was their attitude as they faced possible death? Explain how Doug felt about his family.

5. How did Bill, too, get into serious trouble? Describe his feelings of fright, and then determination, as he hung onto the ledge. In what way was he rescued?

6. How did the two boys feel about their prayers? How did they feel about getting to the top?

7. The story of the climb up Kloochman Rock is a true story. In other years Bill Douglas had many more thrilling adventures in the beautiful and wild mountains of the Pacific Northwest. What do you think makes such a man want to keep going back to the wilds for one adventure after another? What values, important to him as he lives in the cities, do you think he gets from the mountains? Does he think more clearly? understand nature and men better? keep in better health? Is he a braver man because of his experiences? Explain how you feel about these questions.

FOREST FIRE 🦋 EDNA DAVIS ROMIG

G1		WHISPERS of little winds low in the leaves,
B1		Rustle of warm winds through tall green trees,
All		A full resinous fragrance, rich, warm, sweet,
G2		A sharp acrid odour, a hint of heat,
B2	5	Snap, hiss, crackle, a faint blue smoke,
All		A whirl of black swept by tawny flame—
		Deep in the forest the wild wind broke;
		Fast in the wild wake the fire-wind came,
		A soughing of branches swept sudden and strong
	10	Like the rush and crash when the storm winds meet;
G		Crimson streams of fire flowed quickly along
		The tall grey grasses and the spruce needles deep;
B		Red tongues of fire licked the tall pine trees,
		Grey twigs fell as though shrivelled by disease;
All	15	Broad orange streamers floated everywhere
		And bulging puffs of copper smoke filled the molten air.

9. SOUGHING (sŭf'ĭng)—A murmuring sound; a prolonged rustling.

B   A pitiable squeaking came from little furry creatures,
          Chipmunks and marmots as they scurried helter-skelter;
G   Mountain sheep and mountain goats leaping to some
          shelter,
   20   Warned by their instincts—grim, sure teachers—
         And the suffocating stenches from the red relentless
          thing;
G1   Like a plummet dropped a blue jay with a burning
          broken wing;
B1   The eagles screamed in anger from the smoke-be-
          clouded skies;
B   A sudden rush of slender deer, dumb fright in liquid
          eyes . . .
   25   Now burning brands seem missiles sent,
         Projectiles hurled through space,
         Now and then a chuckle, like mirth malevolent,
         A sweeping beauty sinister, a dread and treacherous
          grace;
All   And conflagration with the sound of thunder
   30   Has pulled a thousand tall trees under.
B   But men have come in purpose bent
         To halt the fire's fierce race.
B2   They fell great trees and dig deep lanes,
G2   They smother out small flames;
G   35   With tools and chemicals and wit
         At last they curb, they conquer it.
All   But fire that raged for half a day
         Has burned a hundred years away.

CLUES TO THE MEANING

1. How does the poet describe the slow beginning of the fire? What causes it to develop so quickly?

2. What is the effect of the fire on the animals of the forest? What are the missiles that seem aimed directly at them?

3. Tell how the fire is brought under control. What is meant by the last two lines?

HONEYMOON WITH A HANDICAP ☙

LOUISE BAKER

I BECAME a minor celebrity in my home town at the precocious age of eight. The distinction was not bestowed on me because I was a bright little trick like Joel Kupperman, nor because I could play the piano like a velvet-pantalooned prodigy. I was, to keep the record straight, a decidedly normal and thoroughly untalented child. I wasn't even pretty. My parental grandmother, in fact, often pointed out that I was the plainest girl in three generations of our family, and she had a photograph album full of tintypes to prove it. She hoped that I'd at least be good, but I didn't achieve my fame because of my virtue either. My memorable record in the annals of the town was the result of mere accident.

Completely against parental advice, I took an unauthorized spin on a neighbour boy's bicycle. It was a shiny, red vehicle that I admired inordinately but thoroughly misunderstood. I couldn't even reach the pedals. However, I started a perilous descent of a hill, yelling with giddy excitement. At the bottom, I swung around a corner where I entangled myself and bicycle with an oncoming automobile. As part, apparently, of an ordained pattern, the car was piloted by a woman who was just learning to drive. Her ignorance and mine combined to victimize me.

A crowd gathered. Strong arms lifted me. I had a momentary horrified clarity during which I screamed "Mama!" as I got what proved to be a farewell glimpse of my right leg.

When I regained consciousness ten days later in a white hospital bed, with the blankets propped over me like a canopy, I had one foot in the grave. It was a heavy penalty for my pirated first ride on a bicycle.

However, I was famous. My name, which in the past had excited no stirring sentiments, was mentioned with eulogy in ten county newspapers; five doctors had hovered over me in consultation; twelve churches and one synagogue had offered up prayers for my recovery; and I had been in surgery three times.

The last trip was the fateful one. My old friend Dr. Craig, who had never administered anything more serious than pink pills to me during my brief and healthy span, in final desperation for my life, amputated my right leg above the knee. He then, if there is any truth in local lore, went into his office and had himself a good cry over the whole business.

There were many tears shed over me in the name of my youth. I was, it was mournfully agreed, too young to have such a life-shattering tragedy strike me. Since no one has wept over me in a long time, it is nice to recollect that I once provoked a lot of strong emotion.

However, the emotion bolstered a false theory—the theory that I was too young. I was, I am convinced, precisely the right age. I am not one of those cheerfully smiling brave-hearts who claims to be just too—too happy about a handicap and grateful for the spiritual strength that bearing my burden has bestowed upon me. Spiritual strength bores me—you can't dance on it, and I'm certain it never receives the wholehearted admiration accorded to a well-shaped gam. I'd much rather have two legs, even though a pair of nylon stockings lasts twice as long when you're a uniped. But, granted that Fate has cast an evil designing eye on an appendage, let her make the graceful gesture and snip while the victim is young!

I understand it was a tossup for a while whether my family would have to invest in a tombstone or a pair of crutches for me. But ten weeks of concentrated medical attention combined with my normal healthy resiliency, and I was issued to the world again as damaged goods. Even then, I think I suspected what I *know* now. Fate, for all her worst intentions, was foiled in some fantastic way. She had her pound of flesh, to be sure, but she left me primed for a unique adventure in living that I should never have experienced with the orthodox number of legs.

Perhaps I realized the new turn life had taken when my sister sat by my bedside and sobbed out an ill-made promise that I would never have to help her with the dishes again so long as I lived. Instead of shoving an affidavit at her, I was feeling just sick enough to fancy myself Elsie Dinsmore or her first cousin, Pollyanna. I lightheartedly assured her I'd be back at the pan as soon as I got some crutches. Within a few months we were striking blows at each other over that regrettable exchange of sisterly sentiments.

If I had been a little sharper-witted and had possessed a more pliable pair of parents, I believe I might very well have developed into the most thoroughly spoiled brat the world has ever seen. As it was, I made a close approximation to the pinnacle before I fell under the weight of my own accomplishment.

Even before I left the hospital my sudden power over people was showing itself. First of all, with completely unconscious brilliance, I chose rather inspired subjects to discuss during my five days of post-operative delirium. I rambled on feverishly but with moving feeling about a large doll with real golden hair and blue eyes that opened and closed. I even conveniently mentioned the awesome price and just where such a doll might be purchased, and I sighed over my father's attested poverty which prevented him from buying me this coveted treasure. My delirious words were passed on promptly. The head nurse quoted my pathetic plea to our local telephone operator. The news spread. "That poor little crippled child in the hospital, a breath from death, wants a doll . . ."

Our local toy merchant was no fool. He let ten customers buy identical yellow-haired dolls at $7.98 apiece, even though he knew well enough for what child they were all destined. He also sold seven dark-haired, porcelain-faced beauties when he ran out of blondes. And he did a regular Christmas-bulk business in doll beds, parcheesi games, paper dolls, puzzles, paintboxes and books. People averted their eyes, when they passed the Super Ball-bearing Flyer roller skates that I had also mentioned during my providential spell of wistful delirium. The sight of the roller skates brought a tear to many an eye and usually raised the ante assigned for a present to me by at least a dollar. The merchant decided it might help business to put bicycles in his window.

When I left the hospital it took two cars to transport my loot. I was as well equipped with toys as a princess. Everybody in town, including owners of flower beds on which I had trod and windows which I had broken, suddenly loved me and came bearing gifts. It was a warmhearted, friendly little town. Although it claimed no psychologists or occupational therapists, it was, I believe, the ideal environment for the normal adjustment of a handicapped child.

By putting different coloured ribbons on the ten blonde dolls, I was able to tell them apart and I named them Alice, Virginia, Araminta Ann, Elizabeth, Caroline, Janet, Shirley, Phronsey (after a member of a distinguished fictional family named Pepper), Gwendolyn, and Hortense—a hateful name, but I poked Hortense's eyes out so she didn't deserve anything better. It didn't occur to me to share the dolls with my less lavishly endowed friends. I merely displayed them smugly and let my playmates swallow the water in their mouths.

It took me just ten weeks in the hospital to acquire seventeen new dolls and a very selfish disposition. In time, of course, my parents made me give away the dolls—all except Hortense whose handicap eventually appealed to my better nature, and Araminta Ann who was, for some reason, my favourite. As for my selfishness, that was spanked out of me when my parents finally came to the conclusion that they were going to live with me for a long, long time, and the prospect was anything but cheering.

The first spanking was the hardest—on Father. Later they were much harder on me and easier on him. I'll never forget the shock of that first, firm-handed discipline.

I arrived at the sly conclusion very soon after I came home from the hospital that I didn't really have to be delirious to get what I wanted. Three months before, I was a reasonably well-mannered child who even hesitated to hint for cookies when visiting my own grandmother. Now I was a precocious little gold-digger, and anyone was my fair game. I possessed a magic lamp, a wishing ring—or something just as efficient and much more realistic. I could sit in my wheel chair and watch the normal children playing outdoors. All I had to mumble by way of magic words was, "I'll never be able to run again, will I?" This sad little speech—rhetorically speaking—flung everyone within hearing flat on their faces in abject servitude. The moment was ripe to make almost any demand. As a cousin of mine in reminiscing about our youth once said, "You sure were a little stinker!"

On the particular occasion which was to prove a prologue to the inevitable ripping off of the velvet glove, we had a caller. It was Mrs. Royce, an old friend of the family. She made a great emotional flutter over me. She sniffled into her handkerchief and claimed to have a cold, but she didn't fool me—not for a minute!

"And what shall I bring to this little girlie next time I come?" she cooed at me between her attacks of pseudo-sinusitus.

"Well—" I pondered carefully and commercially. "I can't run or anything any more, you know. I can only sit on the floor and play all by myself." Long sigh. Pause. "I think I'd like to have you bring me an electric train."

I knew well enough the financial magnitude of my aspiration. Electric trains had been discussed frequently in our household. I had about as much chance of getting an electric train from Father as I had of getting fifty-one per cent of the preferred stock in the Atchison, Topeka, and Santa Fe. However, I could see that my speech had worked new havoc on Mrs. Royce's cold, and I was confidently expectant. But although I didn't know it, I had at long last taken the fatal step back to normalcy.

Father cleared his throat noisily and said, "Louise isn't going to have an electric train."

"Oh, now—really!" Kind Mrs. Royce was a childless widow with a solid bank account. "I'd love to give the poor girlie an electric train."

"No," repeated my father, warming to the role that had once been very familiar to him. "We don't want her to have an electric train."

"You see," Mother brought up reinforcements. Obviously, in her own mysterious manner, she was reading Father's mind. "We think electric toys are dangerous. She might get a shock."

"Oh, yes—a shock. She might at that," Mrs. Royce agreed reluctantly. "I'll think of something just as nice and more suitable for a little girlie." (The next day she presented me with a satin-lined sewing basket equipped with coloured thread, blunt scissors,

and a red strawberry in which to embed needles. A splendid thing, that basket, but alas, I wasn't that kind of a girlie.)

Farewells were said and Mrs. Royce departed, after patting my cheek.

"I won't *either* get a shock!" I cried, as soon as the door closed.

"Not from an electric train, you won't!" said Father, and there was a regretful but determined look in his eye. "But you're due for a shock right now."

He headed straight for me. He lifted me gently out of my wheel chair and carefully tilted me over his knee. I saw the tortured expression on Mother's face and heard her gasp. But she didn't make a move to rescue me, even when I screamed, "*Mama!* I'm crippled!" with all the wicked chicanery of my little black heart.

Father spanked me. The honeymoon with my handicap was over.

KEYS TO ENJOYMENT

There are thousands of unfortunate people suffering from one or another handicap. Some of these develop self-pity and become chronic complainers because their deformities prevent them from living as normal people do. Others make the best of the situation, adjusting themselves as well as possible to conditions as they are. Such a person is Louise Baker. With a keen sense of humour and a wholesome outlook on living as close to normalcy as her handicap will permit, she lives a rich and satisfying life.

1. In what way does Louise Baker illustrate that she has a sensible attitude toward her handicap?

2. In what way does she show that, as a handicapped child, she was not so different from most boys and girls in her relationships with others?

3. Discuss the following questions with your classmates:

a. Was Louise justified in trying to make the most profit she could from her affliction?

b. Were Louise's parents wise in their handling of the situation created by the accident to her?

c. What characteristics of Louise made it possible for her to adjust herself to the new situation resulting from her handicap?

d. What part does humour play in the effectiveness of Louise Baker's writing?

OCTOBER SNOW 🐾 LEW SARETT

B	SWIFTLY the blizzard stretched a frozen arm
	From out the hollow night—
G	Stripping the world of all her scarlet pomp,
	And muffling her in white.
B 5	Dead white the hills; dead white the soundless plain;
	Dead white the blizzard's breath—
G	Heavy with hoar that touched each woodland thing
	With a white and silent death.
All	In inky stupor, along the drifted snow,
10	The sluggish river rolled—
	A numb black snake caught lingering in the sun
	By autumn's sudden cold.

CLUES TO THE MEANING

1. How can you tell that Lew Sarett is writing about the first snow of the season? What was the country like before the snow came?

2. What is the sluggish thing that is in contrast with the drifted snow? How is it like a numb black snake? Recall a first snowfall, and let your reading of the poem reflect your remembered feelings.

VELVET SHOES* 🦋 ELINOR WYLIE

G   LET us walk in the white snow
        In a soundless space;
        With footsteps quiet and slow,
        At a tranquil pace,
5   Under veils of white lace.

G1   I shall go shod in silk,
        And you in wool,
        White as a white cow's milk,
        More beautiful
10   Than the breast of a gull.

* Reprinted from *Collected Poems* by Elinor Wylie, by permission of Alfred A. Knopf, Inc. Copyright 1921, 1932 by Alfred A. Knopf, Inc.

G2   We shall wade through the still town
         In a windless peace;
G1   We shall step upon the white down,
         Upon silver fleece,
    15   Upon softer than these.

G3   We shall walk in velvet shoes;
         Wherever we go
G   Silence will fall like dews
         On white silence below.
G3 20   We shall walk in the snow.

CLUES TO THE MEANING

Have you ever thought of trying to write down how you feel about
new snow? Do you think Elinor Wylie has done a good job? What
would you say that is different? Let the girls of the class read the poem
softly and slowly, creating an impression of stillness and magic.

DORCAS WAS DIFFERENT ✿

DOROTHY JEAN CAMPBELL

DORCAS JENNINGS squirmed uncomfortably on the shiny red
leather of the stool in a vain attempt to appear poised before the
superior smile which the pert little waitress was bestowing upon
her—that smile which even the smallest child on her street seemed
to reserve especially for Dorcas. Oh, why hadn't the waitress heard
her the first time? Now the tall gentleman at the far end of the
counter was eyeing her curiously, and the group of junior high
school students in the booth behind her were smiling across at each
other knowingly. Here, then, was the senior they had been told
about; the one who never attended social activities, who ignored
her class mates, girls and boys, as though they did not exist; whose
tongue stumbled painfully before teachers; whose only interest
appeared to be in books; who was, in short, a freak and a misfit
in the pattern of the normal, fun-loving adolescent, a little loud,

a little rude, a little thoughtless, who regards books as unavoidable injuries, and teachers as little better than the modern counterpart of Simon Legree.

Dorcas sank into a sea of warm red as she repeated: "I'd like one coca-cola, please."

The waitress smiled again, this time with exaggerated patience.

"But I've already told you that we're out this afternoon. The truck was supposed to be here an hour ago. Is there anything else you'd like? Coffee, or . . ."

"Yes, yes!" Dorcas agreed hurriedly. Anything to get this over with! She felt all eyes upon her stupidity as the waitress asked:

"Cream and sugar?"

"Please." Dorcas literally trickled into a puddle of relief as the girl turned to attend to her order. The she glanced sideways furtively, to see if anyone else had witnessed her confusion.

"The Prince" was one of four restaurants on the main street of the little prairie town, and the one favoured by the younger set for their after-school rendezvous. Here they discussed grievances suffered at the hands of their crafty opposition, the Strathearn High School staff, and in the conversations, many a conscientious teacher bit the dust. Here, too, the fresh batches of country students, who came in from rural areas to attend the high school, became initiated into the ways of the Kinsiwan teen-age crowd.

Now, as Dorcas nervously surveyed the patrons at "The Prince" for eyes that mocked, or lips that curled in contempt, her glance froze at the doorway where a group of youths were swinging leisurely in. In the group was the shorn head of Cy Roderick, the high school's Apollo and beau ideal of all the feminine students. Dorcas recoiled from meeting any of her fellow-students, as it entailed much agony for her, common and dull as she thought herself, to approach such shining creatures as these cock-o'-the-walk young men. She had been given ample evidence that this opinion of herself was shared by others. Just that morning, as she had quietly entered Room Two, which served as a cloak room for the girls, she had heard Angie Sanford enlightening her bosom friend, Ada Walker, as to the 'latest' on "that Jennings creep."

"Well, you know how gentlemanly Cy is—" Angie was saying

in an unsubdued stage-whisper. "So he opens the door for her, just like he would for any of us. You should've been there! I've never seen anyone get so red!—Did she thank him? She turned and ran like a rabbit up to her home-room and left him standing there holding the door with just the cutest expression on his face—so shocked and everything! Well, you know how Dorcas is. I suppose she can't help it, but really! I mean, Cy Roderick. . . ."

Dorcas hadn't lingered to hear the rest, but the conversation came back to her now, serving to increase her discomfiture as the group approached her on their way to the juke box. Their tones became subdued, almost hushed, as though they were suddenly entering into the presence of an old, respected clergyman, and they hastened by with scattered mutterings of "Hello, Dorcas." She nodded stiffly, aware, as usual, that they had not said "Hi, Jennings!" and slid onto the stools about her to share idle banter, as they would have had she been anyone but "that Jennings creep." Her cold fingers fumbled with her shorthand text as she rose to leave. The book itself was labelled Dorcas. Who else but a 'creep' would spend the precious after-four moments at "The Prince" over homework?

As she turned down her own familiar avenue, Dorcas felt a faint surge of comfort flicker within her. Soon she would be home in her own room with her own books and her own music, with no eyes upon her awkwardness. At this point she heard the sound of a door slamming, and the merry whistling of "Old Rockin' Chair" over the crunch of approaching feet on the frozen walk. She lifted her eyes from their customary concentration on the untravelled ground ahead of her, and recognized Douglas Seigler, a newly returned navy veteran who had about him an air even more confident and carefree than the most assured of the high school youths, and who was adored by all the teen-agers of the town. His apparel, his mannerisms, and his easy-going slang were constantly being aped, and his presence, adult though he was, at their social activities was regarded as a boon rather than a bore. Dorcas shrank inwardly at the thought of any further embarrassing encounters; so she turned swiftly and crossed the street to her own door.

Closing it with a little sigh, she turned to mount the stairway to her sanctuary, but her foot barely rested on the bottom step when her mother burst, voice-first from the kitchen!

"Dorcas! Is that you? For goodness sake, child, where have you been? Here I am, up to my ears in housework. It's Monday, and you know very well I can't manage without you! Now hurry right down again! Your father's coming home for dinner an hour early and I haven't got a thing done. I really can't imagine how you spend your time. It isn't as if you chummed with the other children."

Mrs. Jennings could not understand this chronically red-faced and anti-social mouse who was her daughter. The child was pretty enough, heaven knew, with those big dark eyes and her short curling hair, fair, with auburn glints, so like her own. At least that much had been inherited from her! But the girl was pale and small for her age. Why, when she had been seventeen years old— but there was no comparison! Henry was a good husband, but not a personality like her father. Perhaps, though, if she remained firm with the girl, a change would come!

After the evening meal, Dorcas rose to go to her room, only to be disturbed by her mother's command: "Wait, Dorcas."

"Henry, I do wish you'd speak to that girl! She hasn't been getting enough fresh air or exercise lately. All she does is brood in that room as if she grew there! I can see now that that player was a mistake, but you insist on pampering her. Mrs. Sanford was just telling me this afternoon at bridge how much rosier Angeline's been looking since the rink opened. And look at Dorcas! Why, when I was her age (Dorcas shuddered) I had lots of nice friends to spend an evening with."

"Yeah." put in her brother. "Sometimes I think she's getting queer. You know, in our psychology class . . . "

"There, Joseph! That will do," remonstrated Mr. Jennings. He felt a birds-of-a-feather fondness for his daughter, helpless as they both were under the suffocating cloak of his wife's brisk determination. "Well, now Cassie, why don't you run on down to the rink for an hour or so? It'll do you good. You have been looking a bit peaked lately, you know."

"But, Dad—"

"There's a girl. Have a good time, now," and her father, his duty done, turned hastily to the evening paper.

Dorcas did not have a good time at the rink, for the simple reason that people unnerved her. She dreaded the mortification of a chance fall in front of all that merry crowd, and she felt conspicuous in that she was the only one who never "paired off" but skated in solitary aloofness all night. Once Joe had shown his usual brotherly sympathy by greeting her loudly with "Well, well, if it isn't the Lone Ranger out again to-night!" She was relieved that his freckled face was not among those who were on the ice tonight.

At the end of an hour, filial duty performed, she started for the doorway, but found it blocked by Angie Sanford, whose dark head was bobbing vivaciously against the background of Douglas Seigler's bright plaid shirt. The pair seemed so absorbed in their lively discourse that Dorcas had difficulty in squeezing past them into the snowy darkness outside. As she trudged along the wooded short-cut to Main Street she tried to imagine what it would be like to be a girl like Angie, so popular and happy and contented with herself. For a moment she gave her thoughts full reign and pretty little speeches fluttered through them. "No, no, I couldn't possibly go to the party with you girls to-night. But, why don't you all come over to my house?" or "No, thank you, Cy. I have other arrangements tonight."

An untied boot lace brought her fanciful meanderings to a stop, and as she bent to adjust it, she heard the dull thud of running footsteps on the path behind her. For the second time that day, Dorcas raised her eyes to behold Douglas Seigler's rapidly advancing figure. Only, this time there was no escape. She had braced herself against too great a show of confusion, when to her dismay, Siegler addressed her first in his own mixed-up vernacular.

"Now, see here, Cas. I've had enough of this stand-offishness up with which I will not further put! What's the use of having old friends if the darned things won't even speak to you?"

"But—I . ." faltered Dorcas.

"Now, don't tell me you've forgotten your old Uncle Doug!"

he rambled on. "Why I used to play with you and Joey when you didn't come up to here. (He indicated a navy-serge knee) and my lil' ol' mother used to accuse me of mental cruelty because I didn't pay enough attention to my own family. And now you won't even speak to me! Gad! How callous!"

Dorcas could see nothing familiar about the frank, fun-wrinkled blue eyes, or the stray lock of wheat-coloured hair that flopped persistently on the forehead of the tall, loose-limbed fellow before her, and as for Seigler himself, his memory was not so retentive as he would have had Dorcas believe. He had noted the girl often upon the avenue, always alone, and always with the same hunted-doe expression in the great pensive eyes when they shifted from the ground to survey the passer-by. His curiosity had been aroused when, that afternoon, he had seen her enter the old Jennings house across the street, so, that evening, he had casually asked his mother if the Jennings' still lived there. Only then had he surmised that this wistful-eyed creature and the merry little play-thing of former years were one and the same person. He had felt regret at this change, wondering how it had come about, and now, seeing that his loud largeness had bewildered her, he added smil-ingly.

"At least you know we're neighbours, so we might as well be friends. How's school coming these days?" and he fell in step beside her.

"All right, I guess." faltered Dorcas in reply to the standard question. The warm, red sea had engulfed her as usual. Perhaps, if she walked faster the time would not seem so long.

"Is ol' Miss Greenborough still puttering around the lab?"

When Dorcas, tongue-tied, had nodded assent, he went on. "Why, she used to hammer away at me in chemistry class when I went to school. A-ah, those were the good ol' days! You know, seriously, I liked Miss Greenborough a lot. She's a mighty fine teacher, isn't she?"

And so he continued, volubly reminiscent, until Dorcas realized that her occasional nods sufficed, and that conversation was not expected of her. The tight knot in her throat relaxed as she began to listen more closely.

As they passed the local creamery, Seigler pointed to one of the cans, piled high atop a pyramid of others. The letters stood out in bold black against the bright yellow painted background: R. L. Roderick.

"Their son Cyril's in your class, isn't he? They say he's quite a scholar—good athlete too. How about that? I was talking to his big brother the other day, and it sems he's a pretty fair hand at sketching and the like. Used to sketch myself once, but I gave it up as a bad job. By the way, what do you do with your spare time, Cas?"

"I,—well—I read, and—and then I have my piano lessons." This seemed such a meagre list, that Dorcas flushed painfully, then added vaguely, "but, I'd like to learn to sketch, too." She was instantly grateful when he apparently overlooked this rash statement by saying,

"You would, eh?" and going on agreeably to other remembrances of his own schooldays in an obvious attempt to cover her embarrassment.

They reached Dorcas' doorstep just as her mother was placing the empty milk bottle for the next day's delivery outside the door.

"Well, there you are, child. What kept you? Come on in out of the cold. Hello, Douglas. A lovely night, isn't it? How has your mother been lately? I missed her at choir practice last Thursday."

Her mother's voice faded as Dorcas stumbled up the stairs to her room. How mistaken she had been to envy Angie! She, Dorcas, could never be popular, nor did she wish to be. One blush on the heels of another at her own stupid blunderings! No wonder her mother was disappointed in her! And whatever would Douglas Seigler think of such a queer, stuttering individual! Oh, to be alone! Alone, with no one to embarrass her, or stare or comment or criticize. And so, with self-abnegating thoughts raging within her, Dorcas slipped off to sleep.

On the next day, as Dorcas helped her mother with the Saturday afternoon housecleaning, she heard a knock at the back door.

Pushing her dust cap further back on her head, she steeled herself for an encounter with one of Joe's pals, who she felt sure stood outside. But there stood Douglas Seigler with two sketchbooks tucked under his arm, and an enthusiastic greeting of:

"Hi, Cas! What do you say to a little sketching trip, eh? Dress up warmly, and bring a camera, too, if you've got one. There's . . ."

"Oh, I couldn't!" protested Dorcas, flustered. She felt the familiar warmth creeping up from her neck until her ears glowed. At that point her mother's voice came from behind her.

"Why, hello Douglas. Yes I'm sure Dorcas would love to go on a sketching trip. Run along upstairs, dear, and put on your red parka. It's the warmest. I'll fix a thermos of hot chocolate."

"But, mother, I'd rather . . . " began Dorcas.

"Run along, Dorcas," said Mrs. Jennings in her firmest tone.

"Isn't it rather cold for a sketching trip?" ventured Dorcas timidly as they turned down the avenue towards Main Street.

"Well, no, not if you keep moving, and I always light a bon-fire while I sketch. As a matter of fact, I prefer these winter trips to the summer ones. Now you take a good winter scene—more invigorating! Don't tell me I've got a lily on my hands."

"I was just wondering," Dorcas replied, red-faced.

So they tramped on, past the Dime Store on the corner, past the billiard hall across the street, past the Canadian National Railway Station House, and the sign at the town limits which read: "Visit 'The Prince' for Courtesy and Service."

This was the first of several trips Dorcas and Douglas Seigler made into the gently rolling fields which surrounded the little town. Each time they brought their sketching pads, and a camera. Each time they found some new beauty. Dorcas loved the quiet, lonely fields, and the white silence, unbroken by the querulous, quibbling voices of human beings. Seigler was a patient teacher, cajoling and coaxing. ("That's an excellent sketch, Dorcas, but look here at the annex on your grain elevator. Now look at the real one. See!") Smiling, and encouraging as he was, with his gentle humour and calm persistence, a teacher of human nature, Dorcas slowly began to realize that this kindly fellow, the first adult who

had shown any actual interest in her, was the most understanding person she had ever met. Her cloak of self-consciousness fell away in his presence, "Doug, what would you do here?" or "Guess what Doug, I sketched Miss Greenborough in Chem!"

Spring came, and the ice on the river melted, and Dorcas was happy in anticipation of all the trips she and Doug would be able to make into the browning country-side. The geese flew overhead, their honking barely audible to the pair standing on the crocus-covered hill below. What if she weren't as popular as Angie Sanford! What if she weren't stocking up invitations at the "At Home." She'd rather go sketching with Doug than go to a silly old graduation dance anyway. Not even to herself would Dorcas have admitted just how much the dance did mean to her, for it was her final term at Strathearn High, and for a grad to miss the "At Home," which was the name given to the graduating exercises, was positively unthinkable.

That evening, her mother approached her with "Dorcas, I'm afraid you'll have to see that Joey gets to bed by ten to-night. Your father's taking me to the movies, and there'll be no one here but you."

"Oh. Does father know yet?" Dorcas was so absorbed in her sketching that the words slipped out before she realized it. She blushed furiously, and added vaguely, "I mean—are you sure?"

Her mother's puzzled voice reflected her own shock. "What do you mean 'Does father know yet?' Really, Dorcas! I don't know just what's got into you lately!"

Dorcas didn't know either. Just last week, when she had entered Room Two, again in time to hear Angie Sanford conclude, "And guess who walked her to school this morning? Cy and Bill! Yes, it looks like our little moth is finally coming out of her cocoon," she had remarked in a most un-Dorcas-like fashion,

"Why, Angie, I didn't know you took Biology!"

But the morning that Dorcas officially "arrived", she had been labouring over a Latin exercise, her pencil tracing thought patterns on the edge of her text. She looked up to see Cy Roderick standing beside her desk, fidgeting through his slim length, and studying the blackboard just above her head. His brown eyes held a worried expression, and he seemed at a loss for words to express himself. She had flushed habitually, and then turned to stare, amazed, at what the tall, squirming youth was saying.

"Well, you see—uh . . . Now the way things are—Well—uh—Dorcas would you like to go to the dance with me? (this in a rush). I know it's going to be spiffy, and I'm not much of a dancer, but..."

The pink cloud settled down, and Dorcas had not heard the rest. She recalled, however, that Cy Roderick, swaggering athlete, and crusher of hearts, had blushed and stammered in a manner which would have out-done Dorcas in her prime.

Doug Seigler had shown his pleasure at her success characteristically. "Well, I suppose ol' Uncle Doug will have to take a back seat now, eh Chile? Aah, curse the pain of an aching heart! Fickle, fickle maiden! Go from my sight!" Then, suddenly in a graver mood, he had added "And Cas, there are some kinds of problems that—well, we can only lick 'em by ourselves. Just don't forget, will you, old pal, that problems are solved in life."

Her parents were equally pleased, although Mr. Jennings, at least, was quite frankly puzzled.

"I can't understand it," he murmured. "Dorcas used to be so—well—different! And then, all of a sudden ——?"

"Beats me!" said Joe agreeably.

"Nonsense," stated Mrs. Jennings decisively. "It just goes to show what a little firmness will do in the long run.—Henry! For heavens' sake! Didn't I tell you to go down and turn the water up?"

KEYS TO UNDERSTANDING

Just as there are differences among children and among adults, so there are differences among adolescents. Some are more sensitive or more self-sufficient than others. Some seem to prefer associating with groups of boys and girls of their own age; others prefer more individualistic types of activity. Dorcas was one of these. In fact, she was so much so that she seemed unnatural for one of her age. In this little story we see how a change was brought about in her. It will interest you to know that this story was written by a teen-age girl.

1. In what ways did Dorcas appear to be different from the other boys and girls in her school?

2. Why were Dorcas' parents concerned because she was "different"?

3. What was done to help her develop an interest outside herself? What effect had this upon her relationships with her family? With her classmates?

4. What are some of the questions which adolescents find perplexing? Discuss these with your classmates in order to get as many opinions as possible about answering these questions.

5. How can parents and teachers help adolescents to answer the questions that perplex them? To what extent can their classmates help them? To what extent must they help themselves?

🦋 FOR FURTHER READING: ADVENTURES IN NEW INTERESTS

HELEN DORE BOYLSTON, *Sue Barton, Student Nurse*
Sue's first year as a probationer.

JOHN BUCHAN, *Prester John*
A Young English boy in South Africa is caught in a native uprising which he helps to defeat.

ADELE DE LEEUW, *Clay Fingers*
An exciting new interest leads to a career in ceramics.

RAYMOND L. DITMARS, *Strange Animals I Have Known*
An interest in animals led to many unusual experiences.

ARTHUR CONAN DOYLE, *The Adventures of Sherlock Holmes*
Some amazing adventures of the master detective.

ROGER DUVOISIN, *They Put Out to Sea*
A dramatic story of early explorers whose curiosity about the world
was insatiable.

TOM EADIE, *I Like Diving*
A frank, personal story about the thrills of diving.

JOHN J. FLOHERTY, *Men Without Fear*
Well-written sketches about the men who do the dangerous work
of the world—test pilots, linemen, divers, miners, and others.

MARTIN JOHNSON, *Safari, A Saga of the African Blue*
Adventures in Africa in pursuit of an interesting hobby.

RICHARD S. LAMBERT, *The Adventure of Canadian Painting*
Biographies and paintings of fourteen outstanding Canadian artists.

BURGESS LEONARD, *Victory Pass*
An exciting story of football in a little Southern college.

THOMAS M. LONGSTRETH, *In Scarlet and Plain Clothes*
A young Canadian who joins the Royal Canadian Mounted Police
tells of the training for discipline, endurance, and courage.

CLAIRE PEABODY, *Singing Sails*
An interesting voyage from San Francisco to Hawaii, the South Seas,
and Cape Horn.

TED PETTIT, *Birds in Your Back Yard*
The birds of North America are a fascinating study to those who
know them.

FRANKLIN P. PECK, *Romance of American Transportation*
The whole picture of the development of our transportation system
and its leaders.

MARGARET SCOGGIN, *Lure of Danger*
True accounts of men who like to climb mountains, dive for sunken
treasure, and work amid danger.

DALLAS LORE SHARP, *The Watcher in the Woods*
How to find a whole new world by quiet study of the wild folk of
the woods.

FRANK R. STOCKTON, *The Lady or the Tiger? and Other Stories*
Intriguing short stories showing this author's special skill.

FRANCIS WALLACE, *Big-League Rookie*
Making good in professional baseball requires more than making good on the diamond.

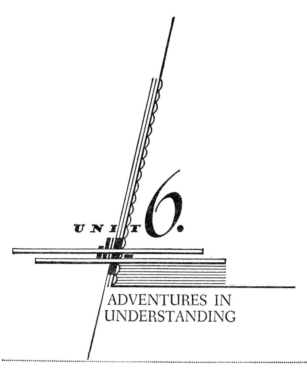

UNIT 6.

ADVENTURES IN UNDERSTANDING

Often the most interesting and exciting adventures are those that are going on within ourselves. A hard problem begins to make sense, and that warm feeling of satisfaction creeps through us. We meet someone new and, gradually, as we come to understand each other, we become friends. We read about some experiences another has had and we get a fuller appreciation of life as he sees it. Possibly the most thrilling adventures in understanding are those that help each one of us to see what we are really like as individuals. If the readings in this unit help us to understand that people are different from each other and have different views of their world, then our adventures will have been worth while. And possibly what we learn about others will help us see ourselves better than ever before.

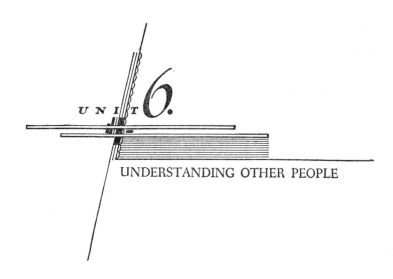

UNIT 6.

UNDERSTANDING OTHER PEOPLE

WITHOUT WORDS ELLIOTT MERRICK

JAN McKENZIE came over a knoll and stopped, head back, his rifle in one mitten, his axe in the other. Below him spread the river, ice-blocked between the hills. A mile across, the birch bluffs were turning blue in the twilight.

He was not given to poetic fancies, for that is not the way of a Scotch-English trapper alone in the middle of Labrador. Nevertheless, it touched him always, coming out to the river after days and nights in the spruces in the east, following brooks and nameless chains of lakes that didn't lead anywhere, ploughing through willow tangles and up and down wooded hills. It gave him a feeling of spaciousness, like stepping out of doors, to see the broad river again, sweeping out of sight between the hills. The river was a known thread that joined him to the nearest trapper fifty miles downstream. The river was the road to home and to his wife, Luce.

It was nine weeks now since the day in September when his canoe and the others from Turner's Harbour had swung off from the wharf and begun the upstream battle. The crowd had waved, and the double-barrelled shotguns split the air in the old-time fare-

503

well, *Boom-boom* . . . and a pause to load . . . *Boom,* saying,
"Good-bye . . . Luck." Then the trappers, floating on the river
in their loaded canoes, raised their guns and fired one answering
shot, "Luck." They picked up their paddles and disappeared
around the point, to be gone five months. Sometimes, even when
they'd passed around the point and the town was lost, they could
still hear the guns, *Boom-boom. . . Boom,* like a last calling. It
gave a fellow something to remember way off where you didn't
hear a thing except your own voice.

It would be pretty near three months yet before he'd be home
with his fur to Luce, he was thinking as he scrambled down the
bank and legged it along the ice for "the house." *This* cabin had
a window and a door with hinges, a good tight roof of birch bark,
and within, such luxuries as a sleeping bag, which his tiny log-tilts [1]
back in the woods had not.

It was nearly dark when he got there, but not too dark to see in
the cove the print of strange snowshoes. And by the point where
the current flowed fast and the ice was thin, somebody had been
chopping a water hole.

"Hello," he called to the cabin.

From the ridge came a mocking "hello," and faintly, seconds
later, a distant hello across the river, the echo of the echo. Jan
crossed the cove bent double, studying the tracks. There were
three of them, a big pair of snowshoes and two smaller pairs. The
small snowshoes had been dragging in a stick of firewood from
along shore—the women.

Jan threw off his bag and hurried into the cabin. Nobody made
snowshoes of that pattern but Mathieu Susaka-shish, the Seven
Islands Indian. Nobody but Mathieu knew this cabin was here.
He and his wife and daughter had come last year and begged a
little tea and sugar. Now they had been here again with their
Indian idea that food belongs to anybody who is hungry. Dirty
dogs! Where three fifty-pound bags of flour had been hanging
only two hung now. They had dripped candle grease onto his
bunk and left his big meat kettle unwashed. He dove under the

[1] LOG-TILTS—Small log houses in which the logs are set upright.

bunk and pulled out his food boxes. They'd made off with some of his split peas and a few of his beans, a handful of candles too. They had sliced a big chunk of salt pork neatly down the middle.

In a frenzy of rage he ripped open his fur-bag. Every skin was there, and in addition, a black and shining otter skin lay crosswise on his bundles of mink and marten, fox and ermine. He held it up and blew the hair and felt its thickness and its length, stroking its blue-black lustre. It was a prize; it would bring sixty dollars, perhaps. But the sight of it made him angrier than before.

"So!" he muttered. "Mathieu thinks one miserable skin of fur pays me for my grub, eh?" He lit a candle, and his hand was trembling with rage. From now on he'd be half-hungry all the time, and hunting meat when he ought to be tending the trap line. He thought of his wife and the blankets, and the windows, and the boats and nets and the new stove they needed at home. This was his whole year's earnings, these five months in the bush. And Mathieu thought he could steal the grub that made it possible, eh? He thought he could come every year and fit himself out, likely.

Jan took his rifle and emptied the magazine. It was only one bag of flour—but still, there were men way off here in the country who'd died for lack of a cupful; yes, a spoonful. Slowly he reloaded with the soft-nosed cartridges he always kept for caribou. Would he tell Luce, would he ever be able to forget that somewhere back in the ridges, by some secret little lake that no one knew, he had shot three Indians and stuffed them through the ice? Didn't the Bible say, an eye for an eye and a tooth for a tooth?

There was bannock bread[2] to bake and fur to be skinned. It was nearly midnight when he stoked up the stove and rolled in on the bunk for the last good sleep he expected to know for a while. At five o'clock in the starlight he was out on the river shore with a candle lantern made out of a baking-powder can, examining tracks. The polished, shallow trench which their two toboggans had left was so plain that a child could have followed it.

Jan studied the track, unconsciously noting every detail. Here

[2] BANNOCK BREAD—Unleavened bread made from oatmeal or barley flour and baked on a griddle.

in this book of the snow he might read Mathieu's thoughts, even a warning of an ambush. Indians were smart in the woods. Did he really think he could out-track an Indian hunter?

"By the Lord Harry, I can have a try," he whispered to himself.

Two mornings ago it was that they passed through here under the firs, across that little brook. Two days was not much start for them. They had sleds and he had none. Mathieu had to break trail, while he had their hard frozen track to walk on. They had all their winter gear, their blankets and kettles, their tin stove and tent, traps, trout nets probably. He had nothing but the game bag on his back, nine cakes of bread, tea and sugar, rifle and axe, a single blanket. The chances were he could travel twice as fast as they.

He passed their first fire, where they had stopped to boil tea and had thrown the tea leaves on the embers. The tea leaves were frozen stiff.

All day he swung on. Once he stopped for ten minutes to sit on a log and munch dry bread, light his pipe, and swing on. It was frosty, and the edges of his fur cap grew white with his breathing.

Before sunset he had long passed their first night's camp. Through the semidarkness of early twilight he pressed on, following the hardness of their track more by touch than by sight. In the starlight he made his fire and boiled tea in a ravine by a brook. Here and there a tree snapped with the frost. The brook murmured under the ice. On the western hill a horn owl was hooting.

Every hour he woke with the cold, threw on more wood, turned over, and slept again. Around three o'clock he woke and could not sleep again. He sat hunched in the blanket, looking into the fire, thinking what a fool he was. He should be on the trap line, not here. He had not come up the river so far away to waste time chasing Indians around the hills. Already he was hungry and wished he had brought more food.

By half past four he had boiled his tea and eaten, and was picking his way along the track again. He should have rested another hour, he knew; it was so slow in the darkness. But he could not rest, though he was tired. He wanted to get it over with.

The Indians were still heading northwest. Likely they were bound for the hundred-mile lake, Panchikamats, not far from the headwaters of streams that flowed into Hudson Bay. Mathieu would feel safe there. It was much farther than Jan could track him, with only three days' grub in the bag.

In the morning he passed their second night's camp. By noontime he had come to the edge of a big, oval marsh that was about six miles wide at its narrowest. On its barren floor there were occasional clumps of dead sticks, juniper and fir, no higher than a man's head, the firs rotten and falling, the junipers gaunt and windcarved. Compared to its bleak, dead savagery the greenwoods borders seemed sociable and friendly and snug. As the merciless northwest wind had stunted and killed the trees, so it could shrivel and kill a man if it caught him out there in a blizzard.

The trail was dim and windscoured. A mile out and there was nothing but the dully shining spots the sleds had polished; two miles out and Mathieu was veering off to the east, deviating now from his northwest course.

The marks petered out entirely, heading, at last, straight east. If Mathieu were really heading northwest, the blue notch at the marsh's far end was the natural way for him. Then why, in the middle of the marsh, did he swing off for the steep ridges to the east?

Jan trotted about in a circle, slapping his mittens together and pounding the toes that were aching in his moccasins. The drifting snow slid by like sand, rising in little eddies as the wind rose.

He stopped and stood with his back to the wind, leaning against it. Mathieu, he figured, wanted to go through the blue notch, but it was too plain. He knew his track could be picked up there first thing. So he cut off in the middle of the marsh, thinking there'd be no mark of it left. Mathieu had just made a little circle-around, and was now right on down the valley.

Jan picked up his game bag and trotted off toward the now-invisible notch. Lord Harry, he was hungry. In the wind he felt like singing; the wind drowned sound, sang a song of its own, saved

a man from feeling that the miles of quiet woods were listening.
He roared in a strong baritone:

"Oh we seen the strangest sights of far-off lands,
And we conquered stormy winds and stinging foam,
But the be-e-est is to see the chee-eery lights of ho-o-ome."

The drifts had obscured the shores now, and he was as though
alone in the middle of a white sea, snow above, below, and on all
sides. But he did not think of it. The wind was compass enough
for him and had been since boyhood.

He clasped his gun and axe in the crook of his elbow, put his
curled mitts up around his mouth, and imitated a mouth organ,
hunching up his shoulders and swinging his body, dancing on his
snowshoes in the gale.

At dusk, miles beyond the blue notch, he picked up the Indians'
tracks again. He glowed with the warmth of a hunter's pride.
They'd never get away now; they were doomed unless it snowed.

A mile farther on they had camped, and there he camped too.
There was still a faint warmth in the depths of their ashes. But
the sight of a bundle lashed in the low branches of a spruce made
him pause. It was a hairy caribou skin, a big trout net, and a heavy-
ish iron Dutch oven. So they were lightening loads, were they?
They knew they were being tracked then. How did they know?

Jan sat on the fir brush of their tent site and thought about it.
They didn't know, couldn't know. Mathieu was just playing
safe, that was all, announcing, if he should be followed, that he
was still a-drivin' 'er for all he was worth, bluffing a pursuer, trying
to say, "I know I am being followed"—just in case he should be
followed. Mathieu would go on for a week, get his women set in
a good camp, then circle back, hunting as he came, and pick up his
stuff again.

That's what you think, Mathieu.

That night he ate another half a bannock, only half when he
could so easily have eaten three whole ones. What a fool he was
to have travelled so light. If, by some mischance, he didn't catch
them now, he'd be stranded off here with nothing to eat.

Rolled in his blanket and their caribou robe, he had the best sleep yet. It was risky. He had his gun beside him. For why couldn't Mathieu come back tonight as well as in a week? All about was the ring of darkness; here was the firelight. What a perfect mark to shoot at. Yes, but Mathieu wouldn't shoot him. Why, Mathieu's father used to camp on the shore at Turner's Harbour in the summertime years ago. Mathieu's cousin used to wrestle with Jan by the hour, and Mathieu himself had been in the foot races they ran on the beach of the blue, cool bay long ago.

He sat and poked at the fire. Mathieu wouldn't shoot you, he was thinking, but you'd shoot Mathieu. Mathieu would steal his grub, but he wouldn't steal Mathieu's grub. Head in hands, he rocked to and fro, bewildered and hating this mental tangle. Oh, if Mathieu only hadn't come along at all; if only Mathieu hadn't taken a whole bag of flour, he would be so glad for Mathieu.

He settled it this way; if Mathieu wants to come along and shoot me to-night, let him, that's good luck for Mathieu; but if Mathieu doesn't, maybe Mathieu will get shot himself to-morrow night.

The stars paled and the east greyed the same as on other mornings. Jan did not set out until there was a little light. It would be so easy for Mathieu to wait hidden by the track.

He walked with his cap on the side, exposing one ear, and when that ear began to freeze he tilted his cap and uncovered the other. Every mile he stopped and listened, mouth open, holding his breath. Late in the afternoon as he stood examining a small valley thick with willows and boulders, he was conscious from the corner of his eye that a tuft of snow was slipping down the face of a grey boulder off to the left. Was somebody behind there? He turned and ran, dodging through the trees. Skirting the end of the willows, he stealthily approached the trail farther on. No, no one had been there. It must have been a willow twig brushing the rock in the breeze. Here were the three prints, just the three prints. Mathieu's almost indistinguishable under the women's and the sleds'. The women had given up hauling tandem.[3] They took turns single, and

---

[3] TANDEM—One behind the other.

when they changed places Mathieu didn't wait for them. They had to run a little to catch up, poor things. Luce could never have hauled like that.

As he stamped, he got to thinking of the otter skin Mathieu had left. It was funny the way Indian hunters would take food. They'd been hunters for so many ages they thought a bag of flour, like a caribou, was anybody's who needed it. But they wouldn't steal fur. Indians! They were like a necessary evil, they were like children. It would be better if they *did* steal fur and left the grub alone. They could pack grub as well as anybody, but they were too lazy. They let the trappers wear themselves to skin and bone struggling up the river in a canoe loaded to the gunwales, risking their lives for it in the white rapids, lugging their loads up The Great Bank, a mile long and steeper than the bridge of Satan's own nose, breaking their backs for it across twelve miles of swamps and brooks and slippery rocks on the Grand Portage where the tumplines [4] pulled their hair out by the roots and they carried till their eyes turned black and their trembling knees sagged under them. And then—the Indians came along and helped themselves as though flour were worth no more up here than down on the bay shore.

They won't help themselves to my grub, Jan thought grimly. Some day I'll come back to the house maybe and find it cleaned right out. And what about me, living on jay's legs and moss till I fall in the snow and die?

The sky was growing deeper grey, darkness coming early. The air was chill with a suspicion of dampness. Come a big batch of snow to cover their tracks and make the walking back heavy, he'd be in a fine fix with no food. He smelled the wind, and it smelled like snow. Before dark it began to fall, and at dark he still had not caught them. Must be getting weak, he thought ruefully. He'd set some rabbit snares tonight. Or maybe he'd get a partridge. And maybe he wouldn't.

He stood on the shore of a little lake and leaned against a tree, uncertain. With the new snow and the dark, there was only the

[4] TUMPLINES—Pack straps.

barest sign of the track now. By morning it would be gone. What was that sharp smell?

He threw back his head and sniffed. Wood smoke! He had caught them. Let the snow pelt down, let it snow six feet in the night; he had caught them and they couldn't get away.

Strange, though, that they should camp before the snow got thick. An hour more and they would have been safe. Well, Mathieu had made his last mistake this time.

Over a knoll in a thick clump of firs Jan built a small fire to boil the kettle. He was ravenous, and weary to the bone. They were camped, they would keep until he got ready for them. And they couldn't smell his smoke with the wind this way.

He ate the last of his bannock, drank four cups of tea, and smoked his pipe to the last dregs. Then he left his bag and axe, took his rifle, and stole out across the dark lake. It was black as ink, and the new snow was like cotton wool to muffle his steps. Just back from the far shore he saw their dome-shaped *meetchwop* glimmering. They were burning a candle in there, one of his own probably.

He crept up closer on his belly, foot by foot. The two sleds were stuck up against a tree; there was the chopping block, the axe, the chips. Snowshoes were hanging from a limb, the two small pairs. But where were the big snowshoes—where was Mathieu? Behind that black tree with his rifle cocked?

He lay silent, scarcely breathing, ears stretched for the slightest sound. There were only the wind and the falling snow and the women's voices and the scraping pan.

He was freezing, he couldn't lie there all night. Inch by inch, he crawled away. Silent as a shadow, he went back across the lake. There was danger everywhere now, every time he moved a muscle. He could feel it all around him, feel a prickling in his scalp and a supernatural certainty that as he was stalking Mathieu, Mathieu was stalking him. Cautiously, with long waits, he approached his camp. The fire was out. His fingers touched the game bag, and drew back. Something was there, something that shouldn't be! *Something was wrong.* Chills went up and down his spine.

There was no sound. Nothing but the soft hiss of the snowflakes drifting down.

Then he smelled it. Bread, new-baked bread, sweet as life to his nostrils. He drew off his mitten and touched the game bag again. His fingers counted them—seven crusty bannock cakes, still warm.

Everything was different now. Noisily he crashed down a big tree for his night's fire. He was sticking up a lean-to by the fireplace, he was chilled by the night's cold, not by the cold horror of that unthinkable job. Lord, he'd rather Mathieu plugged him full of holes than to take a sight on Mathieu. It was like waking up from a nightmare.

I wouldn't forgive Mathieu, he mused, for taking a bag of flour, but he forgives me for trying to kill him. All the time the snow's coming down and he only had to go on a little piece farther to-night to lose me. He knows that, but he takes a chance and sneaks back to feed me, me that's chasing him to kill him. Mathieu don't want I should starve going back to the river. Mathieu—he don't want us to part unfriendly.

Lord, it beat all. If ever he told this to Luce she'd say he was the head liar out of all the liars on the whole river.

He finished one of the fragrant, tender bread cakes and lay down with his back to the fire. It was a long time since he'd felt so happy. Wonderful strange too, how much he and Mathieu had said to each other without words, way off here, never meeting, eating each other's grub.

Toward morning the snow stopped. Just after sunrise the Indian family broke camp and climbed the hill up from the shore. Jan, watching from the opposite hill across the lake, saw them silhouetted, three dark figures on the bare ridge. He pointed his gun at a tree and let go greeting. *Boom-boom . . . Boom.* He saw the two women, startled, duck behind their sled.

But Mathieu stood erect against the brightening sky. He raised his rifle and fired one answering shot.

So they stood for a moment, on opposite hills, with upraised hands. Good-bye, *Luck.*

ABOUT THE AUTHOR

Elliott Merrick is not the kind of writer who sits cozily by his fireside and comes up with an imaginative story of life in the cold bleak climate of northern Labrador. He knows whereof he writes. During the early years of the 1930's he spent some time as a teacher at the Grenfell Mission in Labrador. There he found material for subsequent books—and there he met his wife, an Australian-born nurse whose work furnished material for Elliott's best-seller, *Northern Nurse*. This selection about Jan McKenzie comes from another successful book, *Frost and Fire*.

DISCUSSING THE STORY

1. The men who make their living following the trap lines in the far north need to know many things. They must be far-sighted, alert, quick to meet emergencies. They must know how to prepare for and to adjust to long months of solitary living. Why do you think Jan McKenzie was suited to this kind of life?

2. In such a region, men seldom cross each other's paths. How did Jan know who had visited his camp? Explain why he was so angry at the Indians. Do you think his plan for revenge was justified?

3. To an experienced trapper like Jan the trail of the Indians was quite plain. Why do you think he could not follow the Indians' line of reasoning as well? Why did he still want to kill Mathieu when he knew that Mathieu would not have killed him?

4. As clever as Jan was, the Indians had a surprise for him when he caught up with them. How did Mathieu show that he understood what the really important things of life are? What had Jan and Mathieu said to each other without words? Do you think Jan had more peace of mind than he would have had if he had had his revenge? Tell how you feel about this problem.

ANGUS McGREGOR ✿ LEW SARETT

B   Angus McGregor lies brittle as ice,
With snow tucked up to his jaws,
Somewhere to-night where the hemlocks moan
And crack in the wind like straws.

     5   Angus went cruising the woods last month,
            With a blanket-roll on his back,
            With never an axe, a dirk, or gun,
            Or a compass in his pack.

B1
            "The hills at thirty below have teeth;
    10   McGregor," I said, "you're daft
            To tackle the woods like a simple child."
B2
            But he looked at me and laughed.

            He flashed his teeth in a grin and said:
B3
            "The earth is an open book;
    15   I've followed the woods for forty years,
            I know each cranny and crook.

            "I've battled her weather, her winds, her brutes,
            I've stood with them toe to toe;
            I can beat them back with my naked fist
    20   And answer them blow for blow."

B1
            Angus McGregor sleeps under the stars,
            With an icicle gripped in his hand,
             Somewhere to-night where the grim-lipped peaks
            Brood on a haggard land.

B   25   Oh, the face of the moon is dark to-night,
            And dark the gaunt wind's sigh;
            And the hollow laughter troubles me
            In the wild wolves' cry.

CLUES TO THE MEANING

There are probably too many people who are ready and willing to say, "I told you so," but occasionally it pays to listen. There just might be someone who knows more than we do about something.

1. What sad fate befell Angus? Why did he not heed the warning? Do you know anybody—yourself excepted of course—who is a little like Angus?

2. Read the poem with parts assigned as marked, remembering that strong, clear voices are needed, but that the sound should not become so loud that it will interfere with the thought.

AULD LANG SYNE 🎵 ROBERT BURNS

Robert Burns, who is considered Scotland's greatest poet, has been dead for more than one hundred and fifty years, yet his songs and poems seem as popular as ever. And their popularity has not been any the less because most of them were written in Scotch dialect. "In the Olden Time," as "Auld Lang Syne" may be translated, is really not an original composition of Burns', but is his version of a song that was already old when he was alive. The original has been traced back as far as 1682, but is probably even older.

Should auld ac-quain-tance be for-got, and Nev-er bro't to

mind? Should auld ac - quain - tance be for - got, And

Chorus

days of auld lang syne? For auld lang syne, my dear, For

auld lang syne; We'll tak' a cup o'

kind - ness yet For auld lang syne.

Sʜᴏᴜʟᴅ auld acquaintance be forgot,
And never bro't to mind?
Should auld acquaintance be forgot,
And days of auld lang syne?

5   Chorus: *For auld lang syne, my dear,*
For auld lang syne;
We'll tak' a cup o' kindness yet
For auld lang syne.

And here's a hand, my trusty frien',
10 And gie's a hand o' thine;
We'll tak' a cup o' kindness yet,
For auld lang syne.

EARLY MOWING* 🦋 FRANCES FROST

All   Hɪs knotty hands on the steady snath
He swung through summer's flowery wrath—
Blue vetch for horses, clover for cows,
Butterfly-weed for the winters' mows.

B   5   He never wasted new day in sleeping;
G   In the dark of dawn his lantern, keeping
Time to his strokes, decisive swayed
From the curved scythe handle as he hayed.

GI   He'd mow that farm from north to south
      10 With the cool of the morning wind in his mouth—
BI   When his good breath stopped and he lay dead
Would be time enough to stay in bed.

GI   His lantern, small in the night-end dark,
Woke a startled meadow lark;

* Reprinted by permission of the author and of *The American Girl*, a magazine for all girls published by the Girl Scouts.
1. sɴᴀᴛʜ—The handle of a scythe.

G2 15 Carefully from east to west,
He mowed around her grassy nest.

B   His slow grin puckered to a whistle
As he clipped the head from a corner thistle;
And in an hour the sun blew clear
20 With a redtop stalk behind its ear.

CLUES TO THE MEANING

We may never guess the pleasures a farmer has in his work unless we see him, as the poet has, working in the hour before the sun rises.

1. Describe the mental picture you have of the farmer as he swings lustily on his scythe. Why do you suppose he prefers to mow during the early morning hours?

2. How do you know that he has a spot of tenderness in his character? What do you think his feelings were "as he clipped the head from a corner thistle"?

SEEDING TIME AT McCARTHY'S 𝕏
A. M. STEPHEN

McCarthy, with the blue sky
curving over his shoulder,
steers his caterpillar
across an ocean of brown earth.

5 Behind him, arms of steel
and fingers of iron
do the work of a small army of men.

Gone is the man with the hoe,
Gone is the Sower of Millet!

10 This is the age of machinery.
This is progress.

9. SOWER OF MILLET—Reference is to the celebrated French artist's picture of a man sowing his crop by flinging handfuls of seeds to right and left as he walks across his field.

Seated on a tractor,
man has time to think.

Listen to the profound thoughts
15 of McCarthy:

"There's a knock in the engine, me boy."

*"It's a long way to lunch-time
and the pie that Molly made."*

DISCUSSING THE POEM

1. This poem is one example of a literary form, known as the anti-climax. In developing a climax, a writer goes from one thought to a more important one, until the most important idea is reached at the end of the selection. In an anti-climax, he builds from less to more important ideas, but the final one is usually much less important than any that have gone before it. The device often results in a ludicrous effect, and is often quite humourous. What is the anti-climax here? Do you think it is funny?

2. This poem has three or four metaphors. A metaphor is a figure of speech in which one thing is called something else which may be in some respects similar, but is really quite different. "An ocean of brown earth" is a metaphor, because McCarthy is ploughing not the ocean but the land. How are land and ocean alike? Is the poet's use of the word "caterpillar," a metaphor? Why? What are two other metaphors?

3. How does this little poem differ from the usual type of verse? If you can't tell, look over the notes to A. M. Stephen's "There's a Wild Rose Tangled in the Prairie's Wool" in this book.

OLD GORE ❧ JESSE STUART

"GOOD MORNIN', Shan," Old Gore said as he came through the toolhouse door.

"Good mornin', Gore," I said.

"See you're aputtin' our tools away," he said, watching me put away tools we wouldn't use during the winter.

Old Gore watched me work while the winter wind whipped the

barren treetops unmercifully. I knew on this kind of day he hadn't come to work.

"Shan, I've come to see you about rentin' your house next year," Old Gore said thoughtfully. "This year is about over and I'd like to know what I am agoin' to do."

"I have to keep Uncle Jeff," I said. "He's been with me eleven years. Old Alec's been with me ten years. You've been with me only a year."

"Four years," Old Gore corrected me.

"But I was in the Navy when Pa brought you here," I said. "You've only been here one year with me."

"I'd like to go on with you," Old Gore said. "I know Jeff and Old Alec have been here longer than I have. I thought you'd keep them. And that is right."

"And since I won't have work for you," I said as I watched Old Gore scoot his brogan shoe [1] over a knothole on the toolhouse floor, "I want possession of the house. I want to rent it for cash rent."

Old Gore didn't speak when I asked for possession of the house. His lips trembled like a white-oak leaf in the winter wind. His mind was trying to think of words to say and his trembling lips were trying to shape them. I knew Gore wouldn't want to rent the house for cash rent.

"I hate to lose you, Gore," I said, to break the silence. "You're a good worker and a good neighbour. It's my fault I haven't managed the farm better!"

"That means I'll have to vacate your premises by March 1st?"

"That's right."

"If you need me, let me know."

"All right," I said as he closed the door behind him.

Through the window I watched Old Gore plod up the waggon road where mule tracks and waggon ruts were frozen into the earth. I heard his big brogan shoes whetting against the frozen ground as I stood watching him swinging his big gorilla arms by his side as regular as clock pendulums. His big hands, broader than small fire shovels, were pulling against the icy wind.

---

[1] BROGAN SHOE—A coarse, heavy shoe.

Two weeks after I had told Old Gore I would want my house, I was in Greenwood to get grass seed. While I was in Dawson's Hardware, Willie Felty slapped me on the shoulder.

"Shan, I want to ask you about a man by the name of Chris Gore," Willie said. "He's been up on Cane Creek tryin' to find a house to rent. Wants to work for some farmer by the day. He tried every farmer on Cane Creek. Started at the mouth and went to the head of the creek. He told everybody he lived on your place and he had to get out by March."

"Did he find a house?" I asked.

"No," Willie said.

"Not any empty houses on Cane Creek?"

"Two or three," Willie said.

"Didn't they need any help?" I asked.

"They need help all right," Willie said.

"Then why didn't they rent to Old Gore?"

"See, about everybody on Cane Creek knows you," Willie explained. "They think when you tell a man to go, he's not much good."

"I never thought of that," I said.

"And they didn't like Chris Gore's looks," Willie said.

"He's the kindest man that ever lived on my farm," I said. "He's the best man to a team I've ever known. He never whips a team. You never know he's ploughing in a field unless you see him. You never hear him. The reason he's leavin' my farm is, I have too much help. The men I'm keepin' were with me long before Old Gore came."

"I'll admit I was afraid of 'im when he came to see me," Willie said. "And, I knew if I ever saw you again, I'd ask you about this man. Big shoulders, big arms, legs, and feet, and when he walks he swings his arms like a gorilla. I never saw him smile."

I thought about Old Gore as my car bumped over the frozen dirt road toward home. I knew he would find a house to rent and work to do, if he'd go up some of the hollows in Greenwood County.

It was the middle of January before I saw Old Gore again.

"Thought I'd come down to tell you about a piece of fence that needs fixin', Shan," he said. "It's the dividin' fence betwixt your big pasture and the field where you raise your tobacco!"

"Whats' wrong with that fence?" I said. "We built it only six years ago!"

"But remember you used chestnut posts after the chestnuts had been killed by the blight," he said. "They're all rotted off even with the ground. Quarter of a mile of fence that's alayin' flat on the ground!"

"I thought that fence was perfect," I said. "How'd you come to find it?"

"I was back on the ridge cuttin' stove wood," he said. "Just got a thinkin' that on one side you pastured thirty to fifty head of cattle. On the other side you raised tobacco. I wondered what would happen to a field of green tobacco if fifty head of cattle got into it. They'd destroy it in three hours."

"Now's a good time to fix it," I said. "Get Uncle Jeff and Old Alec and repair it."

Before Uncle Jeff, Old Gore, and Old Alec had finished repairing this fence, I was in Greenwood one day when Hill Porter stopped me.

"Shan, what kind of men do you have workin' for you?" he said.

"Good men," I said. "The very best."

"That fellow Chris Gore went all the way up Maple Branch here a few days ago," he said. "Said he lived on your place and had to move by March. He was tryin' to find a house. Wanted to work for some farmer by the day. Everybody wondered why you's alettin' 'im go since they know people live on your farm until they get ready to leave."

"Lettin' him go because I have too much help," I said. "I'm losin' money on my farm. And the other fellows have been with me longer than Old Gore. That's why I'm lettin' him go!"

"Quit you kiddin', Shan," Hill laughed. "Who'll believe that story?"

"I'm tellin' you the truth," I said.

Hill laughed as he walked away.

Old Gore, Uncle Jeff, and Old Alec found more of the division fence flat on the ground. Frozen ground and a couple of snows delayed their getting the fence repaired until February.

After I paid the men, I didn't see Old Gore again until the middle of February. That was on a bright sunny day when a high wind was blowing and the vegetation on the ground was dry as powder. Old Gore sent a foxhunter, who was looking for a stray hound, to summon all the fire fighters in the neighbourhood to Seaton Ridge. When Uncle Jeff, Old Alec, Pa, and I got there Old Gore, singlehanded, was holding back a line of fire a mile long. He had raked a ring along the ridge and had fired against one of the most dangerous forest fires we had ever had. In one place it had crossed the ridge into my young timber and Gore had stopped it just in time. If he hadn't, it would have ruined five hundred acres of timber and it would have burned two barns and a house.

"Gore, how in the world did you find this fire?" I asked. "How did you know it was comin' up this side of the mountain?"

"When I saw the smoke rise up," he said, "I whiffed the wind and I smelled burnin' leaves! I knew it wasn't smoke from a chimney. I grabbed my rake and come out here just in time to keep it from acomin' over the ridge."

Gore's face was flushed with heat. His eyebrows were singed. His hands were burned. Grey wind-blown ashes had stuck to his sweaty face and pieces of burnt leaves were hanging to his winter beard. He had fought fire and had held the ridge and had done without water to drink. All that afternoon and until midnight we fought fire. We finally stopped it by raking a ring down the mountain to the river and firing against it. Old Gore had saved us.

What a good man Old Gore will make some farmer, I thought, as I walked back home after twelve hours of fighting fire. Then I thought about Old Gore's fighting fire eighteen hours. He had not only fought fire to save my barns, house, and timber, but he had fought fire to save fifteen other homes on our side of the ridge.

On March 1st I walked up the hollow to see if Old Gore had moved from my house. On the road between where we lived, where the creek flowed toward the road, I noticed somebody had dug a channel across a spur of ground that jutted from the opposite hill and had turned the creek to keep it from cutting any more of the roadway. This was a job I had planned to do but had never done. I was glad someone had done it and I wondered if it had been Uncle Jeff, Old Alec, or Old Gore. I didn't have to wonder after I examined the tracks in the soft dirt. The tracks were unmistakably Old Gore's for he wore the largest shoes of anybody that lived on the farm. When I went far enough to see the smoke coming from Old Gore's chimney, I turned back toward home.

When I passed the barn, Old Gore was unhitching my team from the plough.

"Thought I'd better get the barnyard manure turned under on that bottom," he said as he stopped the team. "Lot of cutworms in that ground and I'd better get it turned for we might get another little ground freeze and kill the cutworms. I would have ploughed it long ago but . . ."

Old Gore stopped talking. It was my turn to talk. For I knew Old Gore must have known I'd found out how hard he'd tried to rent a house and find work. And he must know why he couldn't rent a house and find work, I thought, as I looked at the steam rising from the sweaty mules and Old Gore's sweaty clothes.

"Yes, Gore," I said, "plough that bottom. Then plough the next bottom and the next and the next! Freeze the cutworms in all of my bottoms."

Old Gore smiled. First time I'd seen him smile in months. He tapped the mules gently with the lines and spoke to them softly. I watched him drive them through the shadows of dusk toward the big barn.

DISCUSSING THE STORY

1. Like many of the characters in Jesse Stuart's stories, Old Gore was probably a real person, and Shan may have been Jesse himself. Why did Shan feel that he could not employ Old Gore another year? How did he reason that Gore was the one to be let go?

2. Tell about Gore's attempts to find a house and a job. Why was he unsuccessful? Explain the reasoning of Shan's neighbours.

3. In what way, if any, did the prospect of coming unemployment affect Old Gore's attitude toward his job with Shan? Give some examples.

Under what circumstances did Shan discover that Old Gore was an indispensable part of the farm crew of workers? What did Shan do about it?

5. In what way had Shan been unfair without meaning to be so? What lesson did Shan learn about the true meaning of faithfulness?

ELEPHANTS ARE DIFFERENT
TO DIFFERENT PEOPLE 🦋 CARL SANDBURG

WILSON and Pilcer and Snack stood before the zoo elephant.

Wilson said, "What is its name? Is it from Asia or Africa? Who feeds it? Is it a he or a she? How old is it? Do they have twins? How much does it cost to feed? How much does it weigh? If it dies how much will another one cost? If it dies what will they use the bones, the fat, and the hide for? What use is it besides to look at?"

Pilcer didn't have any questions; he was murmuring to himself, "It's a house by itself, walls and windows, the ears came from tall cornfields; the architect of those legs was a workman; he stands like a bridge out across deep water; the face is sad and the eyes are kind; I know elephants are good to babies."

Snack looked up and down and at last said to himself, "He's a tough son-of-a-gun outside and I'll bet he's got a strong heart; I'll bet he's strong as a copper-riveted boiler inside."

They didn't put up any arguments.

They didn't throw anything in each other's faces.

Three men saw the elephant three ways.

And let it go at that.

They didn't spoil a sunny Sunday afternoon;

"Sunday comes only once a week," they told each other.

CLUES TO THE MEANING

1. The three men in Carl Sandburg's bit of poetry writing are just ordinary people, the kind we may meet every day. How do we know that Wilson is the practical business-man type? What kinds of questions would he ask about almost anything he saw?

2. Pilcer seems to be the thinker, or philosopher, of the group. What does he see in the elephant? How do you think he would explain the other things he sees in nature? What kind of occupation do you think Pilcer may have?

3. Snack is probably a factory worker who likes sports and has a little home of his own. As you think about what Snack sees in the elephant, how would you describe him?

4. While all three look at the same object, no one sees what any of the others see. Do you think all three would agree on politics? the United Nations? the Toronto Maple Leafs? the kind of pie they like? or any other subject that might be discussed? Do you think they would argue or fight about their differences?

5. Does this selection suggest to you how many different opinions there might be on any subject? Can you think of anything about which the whole class might agree perfectly?

THE DREAMERS 🌸 THEODOSIA GARRISON

G   The gypsies passed her little gate—
          She stopped her wheel to see—
          A brown-faced pair who walked the road,
            Free as the wind is free;
5   And suddenly her tidy room
            A prison seemed to be.

G1   Her shining plates against the walls,
          Her sunlit, sanded floor,
          The brass-bound wedding chest that held
10   Her linen's snowy store,
          The very wheel whose humming died—
            Seemed only chains she bore.

G   She watched the foot-free gypsies pass;
          She never knew or guessed

15   The wistful dream that drew them close—
        The longing in each breast
        Some day to know a home like hers,
        Wherein their hearts might rest.

CLUES TO THE MEANING

1. Why did the housewife envy the gypsies who passed her door? What were the gypsies thinking as they passed by?
2. Do you think either the housewife or the gypsies would be satisfied to change places permanently? In what sense is this poem another way of saying, "The grass on the other side of the fence is always greener"?

RECIPE FOR PORK 〰 ROBERT H. BLACKBURN

You're new in this part of the country, so maybe you never heard about Nick McGuffin and his wonderful hog-machine. Even some of the young folks that have grown up and married and got farms of their own right around here have never heard much about Nick's machine, and some of us old-timers who know the whole story aren't very fussy about telling it.

Nick McGuffin was a little runt of a man with a big voice. And he had a bush red beard. You could tell him a mile away by his beard, and people used to crack jokes about it, but Nick generally enjoyed the jokes more than anybody. When he got to town Saturday nights, the boys in the poolroom used to tell him he better get his beard shaved off so that he wouldn't get his cue snarled up in it, but he'd laugh and say, "Why, this here beard is what gives me my strength and keeps me from catching cold! I just been reading about a man name of Samson that went all to pieces after he went and got his beard cut off!" Nick was a great reader, and folks used to say he did more reading than farming.

Nick farmed that Hudson Bay quarter, just down the hill from Jacob Akerman's place, where the old windmill is. He never had much of a house on his place, just an old log shack with poles and sods piled on top for a roof. Not even a proper window in it, just a hole in the wall filled with brown and green beer bottles laid one on top of the other. Folks said he cooked all his meals in a white enamel pot with a handle on one side, that he picked up at an auction sale; but I couldn't be sure about that. He had a little shingled barn, and some hogpens, and one or two granaries, and that was all—until he got the windmill.

One night after he got the windmill, somebody in the poolroom says, "Well, this red-bearded Nick friend of ours must of struck gold on his farm, buying a windmill, and all. Next thing you know, he'll be gettin' himself a wife!"

"Not for me," Nick says. "None of the women I ever saw is the kind to appreciate real stain-glass windows like I got in my kitchen. And anyway, the way I figure, that windmill I got can pump more water and give less trouble than any woman on earth."

Of course, stories like that didn't do Nick any good with the women in the neighbourhood, and even Jessie Akerman—that's Jacob Akerman's sister—said that the sight of red beards made her sick to her stomach.

As I was telling you, Nick was a great reader, and folks used to say he wouldn't milk a cow without reading about it in a book first. He always carried a copy of the *Prairie Farmer* in his overalls pocket, and was always sending samples of soil and things up to the University, or asking the district agriculturist for one of his pamphlets. It's no wonder that folks thought he was queer, and didn't pay any attention at first when they heard he had invented a hog-machine. They thought it was just another of his jokes.

It all started one morning when Nick was driving to town with a load of pigs. He stopped to rest his horses at Akerman's gate, and Jacob walked out to say hello. Jacob stepped up on the waggon wheel and looked inside the box. "Nice lot of pigs you got there, Nick," he said. You know the way Jacob talks, quick and excited like.

Nick rubbed the back of one glove along his beard. "Yup. Best pigs in the country." The pigs had been squealing and chuntering and nipping ears, but they stopped dead quiet at the boom of Nick's voice.

RECIPE FOR PORK 𝍌𝍌𝍌𝍌𝍌𝍌𝍌𝍌𝍌𝍌𝍌𝍌𝍌 529

Jacob thought for a while. "Jessie says you been haulin' past here three-four times this last week. You must be raisin' a lotta hogs these days—"

Nick stroked his beard thoughtfully with the back of his glove, until Jacob spoke again: "Been thinkin' I might start raisin' a few hogs myself, if I can find some good sows. You got any sows for sale?"

Nick spat, and wiped his mouth with his glove. "Nope, I don't keep sows any more. Takes too much feed."

"You goin' out of the pig business, then?"

"Nope, I'm just getting started in the pig business. I got a machine that turns out pigs ready for market. I haven't got a pig on my place right now, but to-morrow I'll get my machine going again, and day after to-morrow you'll see me hauling another load just like this one."

Jacob grinned, the way folks do when they don't know what to say, and Nick laughed and drove off to town with his pigs.

Well, at dinner-time Jacob told this story to his sister Jessie, and by mid-afternoon every telephone wire within six miles had buzzed two or three times with it. By Saturday everybody had heard the story, and Saturday night the boys in the poolroom pestered Nick about it until he lost his temper and went home without playing even one game.

Of course everybody still thought that the hog-machine was just another one of Nick's jokes; but every second day Nick would drive to town with a load of pigs, and after two weeks people began to wonder. By the end of the month Nick was hauling pigs to town every day, and folks were thinking that something mighty queer was going on. It got whispered around that Jacob Akerman had gone over to Nick's place one day to borrow a log chain, and had seen a strange machine out beside the windmill, and had seen that Nick's pigpen was empty. But still Nick had hauled pigs to town.

Everybody agreed that Nick's claim that he made pigs in a machine was contrary to nature and could not be true, but many people agreed with Jessie Akerman too, when she said that somebody should report the matter to the police. Reverend Walker preached a long sermon about casting out devils into swine, but folks couldn't quite see what he was driving at, and of course Nick didn't hear the sermon anyway. Then Mr. Nielson, the district agricultural agent, announced that there would be a free public demonstration of McGuffin's new method of hog-raising, and folks came from fifteen miles around to be on hand.

On the day of the demonstration the crowd started to gather before noon, and by two o'clock Nick McGuffin's yard was swarming with farmers and townfolks, men and women and kids and their dogs. At two o'clock Mr. Nielson got up on the first cross-brace of the windmill, right beside Nick's hog-machine, and made a speech about the wonders of scientific agriculture. He said that while he had no claims to make for McGuffin's machine, he knew that everybody present would want to pay careful attention and learn what there was to be learned.

Then it was Nick's turn to speak, and Nick was in his glory. He had prepared a speech too. "Here she is, folks," he started. "Most of you have looked this machine over inside and out, and there ain't no more to it than what you see. Just this big hopper, like a funnel, with buckets of barley and oats and slack-coal and water and salt and other things hung around the top. And under this hopper is the mixing box, big enough to mix up a pig in. See, I got a storage battery hooked up to the box. And under the box, of course, I need this chute down into the waggon. Now I'll make you a pig."

"Wait a minute, Nick!" Mr. Nielson hollered. "The best procedure is to have someone inspect the machine first, just so we can all be certain you haven't got a pig concealed in it before you commence."

Jacob Akerman was the first to volunteer, because he was standing right up front. And then Mr. Nielson himself inspected the machine, inside and out; and after him came six or seven other men to look it over.

"All right," Nick shouted, "Anybody else want to look at her before I start? —All right, here goes! —Now I want you folks to understand that there's nothing very wonderful about this hog-machine. It just turns out full-grown, ready-made, live hogs. You all know that flesh is nothing but a pinch of salt and a bucket of water and bits of this and that; well, all you got to do is to mix the right amounts and you get a pig. All you need is the right recipe. No use starting with a little pig and feeding it for six months when you can mix the recipe and get a full-grown hog in half an hour."

Folks looked at their watches and whispered back and forth uneasily while Nick stood on the ladder and mixed his recipe. His arms were hidden inside the hopper, so that nobody could see what he was doing. After a while he straightened up and stood gazing into the hopper, thoughtful like.

"Is that all? I guess we can go home now, folks," called Jessie Akerman from the edge of the crowd, and there was a snickering of amusement. Nick fumbled for the loop of rope that hung on the side of the ladder; he found it and gave it a jerk. The mixing box turned upside down; the crowd's laughter was cut short by a loud squeal! A full-grown white hog slid out of the box and skidded down the chute, squealing in terror, squirming and struggling for a foothold. But there was no foothold on the slippery boards, and the pig thumped out of sight into the waggon.

Everybody scrambled forward, pushing and pulling so as to get a better look. Mr. Nielson jumped up on the waggon tongue and started to make another speech, but somebody shoved him off backwards and he lost his hat. It looked as though the waggon itself was going to be upset or torn to pieces, but Nick's voice carried above the confusion: "Stand back, you honyocks, stand back there! Think you never saw a hog before in your lives! Stand back and have a little more respect for a man's property. I got something to say to you."

The hubbub simmered down, and then Jacob Akerman shouted, "Nick, what's your recipe?"

Suddenly there was complete silence. "My recipe," Nick said, "calls for water and slack-coal and barley and some of these other things you saw up here in these buckets. At first I didn't use any slack-coal, and I got three or four runts before I figured out what was lacking. I just measure out these things into the box and—"

Mr. Nielson, the agricultural agent, spoke up again. "Ladies and gentlemen, you have just witnessed one of the greatest scientific revelations of this age. Indeed, this may be the beginning of a new age. We can hardly realize what this will mean to the world, being able to produce its food without—"

Jacob Akerman cut in, "Hey, how much water do you use?"

Again there was a silence. Nick spat, and rubbed his beard. "I always have to use just the right amount. I reckon I could make a pig out of that waggon tongue or anything else, if I just knew the right amount of things to mix with it. And now that I did find out how much of these things to mix, I reckon I better not tell everybody else. Inside of a month the whole world would be overrun with pigs and a man couldn't get to sleep at night for the noise."

You see, Nick was trying to turn the question aside with a joke, but the joke didn't take and Jacob came right back. "Look, Nick, if you can make pigs as quick as you like and as often as you like, there won't be any use of the rest of us farmers trying to raise them. And then pretty soon you'll be turning out steers and chickens and —and everything, and nobody else will be able to make a living. You gotta let us know too, or else—"

Nick didn't wait for the threat to be spoken. "Listen, everybody," he called out, "listen. I'm the one that found out how to make pigs, and you came here to see whether I could do it. Now, do you want to see me do it again? Stand back, then; and you boys up on the windmill, you get down on the ground. And you, I don't want you spying on me from the granary roof, either."

This time there was no talking or laughing, for everyone was intent on each move that Nick made, everyone counting silently and trying to guess what was being done. The tension increased, and folks were hardly breathing by the time Nick finished the mixing and looked over the crowd. "This time I'll make you a black one. Jake, hand me up that bag of lamp black."

He added five cupfuls of lampblack to the mix and paused dramatically, peering in triumph from side to side, pointing his red beard at his audience. Then he reached for the loop of rope and yelled, "Here she comes!"

Out slithered a black pig down the chute and into the waggon box.

Only a few people went up to look at the black pig, and nobody said much for a minute or so. Then from the fringe of the crowd, Jessie shouted again, "Now throw in your beard and make us a red one!"

Nick's face looked even redder than usual. "Nope, that's all for to-day, folks. So far I haven't figured out how to make red pigs. Anyway, red is too good a colour for pigs. Black is more fitting." That was in the days when Jessie's hair was still black.

After that, Mr. Nielson got out a tape measure and started measuring the machine and writing in his book, and Jacob Akerman and the stock-buyer from town and three or four other men got talking to Nick very seriously, but they couldn't get him to tell them his recipe for pigs. The rest of the people wandered around and looked at the machine, and studied the two pigs, and finally went home. It was nearly suppertime before Mr. Nielson drove away and Nick was left alone with his pigs and his hog-machine and his recipe.

After dark, Nick lit a lantern and went back out to the machine. He didn't think to look up the windmill, or he might have seen Jacob Akerman perched up there; and if he had looked up to the granary roof he might have seen where Mr. Nielson was hiding. There may have been some others that sneaked back to watch, too, but Jake and Mr. Nielson were the only ones that told about it afterwards.

Nick just climbed the ladder up the side of the hog-machine, set his lantern on the edge of the hopper, and went to work. He reached for the salt bucket first, and carefully measured out eight cupfuls of salt into the mixing box. Then came four cupfuls of some grey powder out of the second bucket. Then, just as he reached for the slack-coal, he must have heard a noise that startled him. He drew back quickly, and in drawing back he tipped the lantern into the hopper. Frantically he reached for the lantern—reached so far that he lost his balance and fell into the hopper himself. He let out a shriek, and then the mixing box turned upside down and the lantern went out.

Mr. Nielson and Jacob climbed down from their hiding places

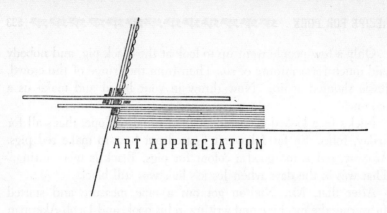

ART APPRECIATION

JOSÉ HERRERA ✥ PETER HURD

José Herrera is a real cowpuncher, not a movie or fiction version. And somehow Peter Hurd has made this real person seem even more glamorous than his fanciful counterpart of film or story. José has strength, determination, and just a hint of a smile written into his weathered features. His clothes, too, are those of a hardworking ranch hand of the sunny southwest. The landscape that provides a frame for the cowboy's portrait is typical of the artist's best work. At first glance the hills seem bare. Then the details and many hues of colour begin to stand out. The more one looks, the more there is to be seen. There is a church steeple, a waggon, a man walking across a field, and of course there are the hundreds of scrubby trees and bushes on the mountain slopes. The particular shades of colour are trade-marks of Peter Hurd's painting —the yellows, browns, greens, blues, and purples.

JOSÉ HERRERA
Peter Hurd

Courtesy of the artist, the University of New Mexico Press, and William Rockhill Nelson Gallery of Art, Kansas City, Missouri

PETER HURD

[1904-   ]

Peter Hurd is a six-foot, blond, good-natured New Mexican who almost became a soldier instead of an artist. Born in Roswell, New Mexico, Hurd attended the New Mexico Military Institute and then continued for two years at the United States Military Academy at West Point before he abandoned his preparation for a military career. Next he attended Haverford College in Pennsylvania where he met N. C. Wyeth, the noted painter and illustrator, who induced Peter to concentrate his efforts on the study of art under his personal direction. This instruction was followed by a period of study at the Pennsylvania Academy of Fine Arts. In 1929 Peter Hurd married Henriette Wyeth, the artist-daughter of his former instructor. In 1942 Hurd became a war artist-correspondent of LIFE magazine and his special assignment was to paint the men and activities of the United States Army Air Force Bomber Command in England. He has said that his assignment gave him the biggest adventure of his life, and the quality and realism of his paintings clearly show that he was indeed inspired by the men and scenes he painted. Peter Hurd now lives in New Mexico, where he keeps busy at his painting and managing his ranch.

as quick as they could in the dark, and ran to help Nick. They climbed up the hopper and struck matches, and looked all around, and called, but they couldn't find him. Even his lantern had disappeared.

Jake ran to the barn for another lantern, and by its light he helped Mr. Nielson search again. They knew before they started

that there was no place for Nick to be, no hidden corner or false floors. But they crawled under and climbed over, calling and looking and flashing their lantern.

There was no sign of Nick. There was nothing but the empty hopper, the buckets, the upturned mixing box, and the slippery chute. There was nothing at all in the waggon except the pigs; one white and one black and one little red runt.

And nobody ever knew what became of Nick McGuffin, and even folks that saw him working his hog-machine that day don't say much about it.

ENJOYING THE STORY

1. Essentially, this is a "tall story," that is, one that is outside the bounds of all possibility, but told with such an air of sincerity that it is

hard to realize that it could not have happened. The quality of seeming to be true, or at least quite possible, is called verisimilitude. It is often obtained by including in the story many little details that do not actually add to the tale but which heighten the sense of reality. What are some of the details making for verisimilitude in this story?

2. An interesting story often has an element of conflict, or struggle, as between two of the characters, or between one character and natural forces. What conflict do you find in this story? Is it necessary to the actual development of the plot?

3. If this story had happened, it could have happened almost any place in English-speaking North America. What details locate it in Western Canada?

4. The final outcome of a story is called the *dénouement*. An American writer, O. Henry, developed a short story form in which the *dénouement* comes as a terrific surprise in almost the last sentence. Show how this story follows the same form.

MY ENCOUNTER WITH A
BUSHMAN 🐟 SELWYN JAMES

WHEN I first saw the aged little Bushman squatting like a bronze image between clumps of green mesquite, I felt a cold dead weight in my stomach. Across his chest he held a small springy bow with sharp, bone-tipped arrows no longer than pencils. He was hardly a reassuring sight, since I happened to be stranded, alone and unarmed, in the middle of the South African nowhere.

As I watched him straighten up on his spindly legs, his knee-caps sticking out like crab apples, I wished that I had taken the advice of my friends back in Johannesburg. "Don't try to cross the Kalahari[1] alone," they had warned. "If your car breaks down you may be there for days before anyone drives by."

Few people drove across the arid bush-covered Kalahari Desert, but I was on my way to Windhoek, Southwest Africa, and this lonely, ill-defined trail would cut my journey by a thousand miles.

[1] KALAHARI—A desert area in southwest Africa of about 350,000 square miles.

Now I was out of luck. A slow leak had emptied the radiator of my coupé, and I was thirty miles from the nearest native kraal.[2]

I had been sitting in the car for an hour, trying to decide whether to pour the last of my drinking water, about two quarts, into the radiator or down my throat. I knew better than to get out and explore. Not that there was danger from wild animals; but the Kalahari, with its sudden dips and rises, is a deceptive place. Turn around a couple of times and you're lost. So I tooted my horn regularly every ten minutes—an SOS in the unlikely event that someone happened to be within earshot.

The sun flared murderously overhead and made an oven of the car. There was no breeze, and to add to the discomfort, swarms of stinging sand flies were beginning to mass on the inside of the windshield. But not until I spotted the Bushman did I feel any real apprehension.

Bushmen have no love for white men, and their emotions, slipping quickly from simple delight to uncontrolled fury, are as crude as their neolithic[3] culture. Moreover, I had heard that Bushmen sometimes stalk white men—a hunter, say, who wanders too far from his camp in pursuit of a wounded kudu[4] and loses himself in the desert. In such circumstances the Bushman wouldn't think of leading him back to camp; instead, he would wait, out of sight, until the hunter dropped from thirst and exhaustion—until the vultures finished him. Then the Bushman would close in—before the jackals did—and pick up the blessings of the white man's civilization: water bottle, boots, belt, and shiny cartridges which, when emptied, made handsome jewellery.

My Bushman had an alert, clever little face, the yellow-brown skin taut over high cheekbones. His tiny berry-bright eyes blinked solemnly under a bulging forehead and tufts of curly black hair. He stood less than four feet, six inches. A tattered animal skin hung from his loins below a round, distended belly.

When he was sure I'd seen him he took a few cautious steps to-

---

[2] KRAAL—Village.
[3] NEOLITHIC—An early stage in man's growth toward civilization.
[4] KUDU (koo'doo)—An African antelope.

ward me. His thick upper lip curled in a patently forced smile which showed a lot of pink gum and a few remarkably white teeth. I didn't respond. It is not by choice that these pygmy-like folk, a dying race, live in the desert wastes. Hounded first by the warlike Kaffir,[5] then by the white colonists, most of them were long ago driven north from their beloved caves and wild-honey grottos and plains teeming with succulent game.

Perhaps this Bushman was one of those who had lately been raiding the Boer [6] farms on the outer edges of the desert. A severe drought had forced them a long way from their hunting grounds in search of meat and water. The farmers regarded them as American ranchers do a marauding coyote. Although it was against the law, shooting parties had been organized to track them down, and during the chase at least one farmer had fallen to a Bushman's poisoned arrow.

He stood motionless in the shimmering waves of heat, watching me, for an hour. When I sounded the horn he croaked gleefully, his fat little stomach quivering. Once, with a flourish, he laid down his bow and arrows and raised his hands high, as if to demonstrate that he came in peace. "Umm," I thought. "I wonder." I waved him away.

Later, as the sun went down, he approached again and started to chatter in his queer tongue-clicking language. He seemed puzzled by my unfriendliness, his brow a mass of plaintive wrinkles. I felt a bit ashamed, but I still couldn't be sure of him. I'd heard too many disturbing tales of Bushman cunning.

Yet at dusk I felt strangely comforted by the little Bushman's presence. Night in the desert is a time of great loneliness, a time when all hope, like the sunlight, has slipped away. With another human nearby, the future didn't loom quite so monstrous. I envied him, too, as he built his fire of dry sticks and mesquite twigs, for night had brought a sudden coolness. He soon had the fire blazing,

---

[5] KAFFIR (kăf'ēr)—One of the most intelligent and powerful of the Bantu races in South Africa. They are among the tallest people in the world and noted for their valour in war.

[6] BOER—South African whites of early Dutch descent.

and curled up so close to it that the sparks must have scorched his calloused skin. Occasionally he turned and waved his hand as if to assure me of his protection during the long night. My fear of him grew less with each passing hour.

Finally I fell asleep, still in my car, and woke just as the dawn spread its glorious pastel shades over heaven and earth, and the thorn-bush insects began their ceaseless day-long humming. My little Bushman was perched cross-legged on the hood, staring at me through the windshield, grinning as usual! I sat up, stiff and cold, and looked about. There was still no sign of help from *my* civilization; and now I had to admit to myself that I might be stuck another day, or even longer, in this stifling wilderness.

I smiled lamely at the Bushman—he looked so harmless. He must have sensed my hopelessness and feeling of utter futility, for suddenly his expression changed, his tongue clicking and snapping like an elastic band on the roof of his mouth. He sounded terribly impatient with me, as though he were a father who had despaired of his witless son.

Then with pounding heart I noticed that attached to his loinskin was the inflated bladder of some small animal. Water! Where did he find it in this desolate country? I had imagined that his thirst, like that of the steinbok [7] he hunted, was satiated [8] by a few licks of the morning dew. My hopes running wild, I stepped out of the car for the first time. He took it as a gesture of faith; he skipped about like a happy child on a spring morning, slapping his thighs and croaking and huffing with pleasure.

In sign language I indicated that I needed water for the car. He understood immediately. "Ah!" he said. "Ahhhhhhhh!" He handed me the bladder he carried, and I poured its contents into the radiator. It was not enough. Then the Bushman trotted off to the smouldering embers of his fire. There he picked up a hollow stick about three feet long and beckoned me with it. A little dubious, I followed a few yards behind him. After five minutes' walk he dropped to his knees and thrust the stick deep in the sandy soil. Fascinated, I watched as he put his lips to the protruding end of

[7] STEINBOK—A small antelope.   [8] SATIATED (sā'shĭ-āt-ĕd)—Satisfied.

the stick; a moment later he spat out a mouthful of water at my feet! He had sucked it from an underground desert stream.

I rushed back to the car for my two-gallon canvas water bag. For a half-hour the Bushman's cheeks moved like a fish's gills, drawing the water into his mouth and transferring it into my carrier. When it was full and he had handed it to me, something like the glow of human brotherhood shone in the face of this little Stone-Age man. His tongue clicked softly, like a whispered prayer. I trudged back, poured the water into the radiator, and then returned to him. But what I saw now was pitiful. He was spitting sand from his mouth. His underground source had run dry. Frantically he darted about, plunging his stick into the earth, drawing on it and bringing up only grit and sand. After some minutes he gave up, smiling ruefully.

We walked back to the car in silence. "I'll drain some water out of the radiator and give it to him," I thought. But I wanted to do something more to show my gratitude. Impulsively I took off my watch and gave it to him. His eyes widened and with tremulous fingers he examined it lovingly. But then he handed it back. Astonished, I shook my head vigorously, trying to explain that I wanted him to keep it as a gift. He wouldn't allow it; his eyes pleaded with me not to press him, nor to force him into such shameful behaviour. "After all," his eyes seemed to say, "you are *my* guest. This is *my* desert, *my* home. I want no reward for my hospitality." I was humbled by those eyes.

He stared, puzzled, as I slid under the car and drained some of the water into the canvas bag. His eyes were moist and his lips trembled a little when, with firm-sounding words, I made him take it. Then we said good-bye; each of us, I am sure, aware of the other's deep feelings. In our brief companionship our hearts had bridged the ages that separated our two worlds. Here was a man who possessed a true unselfish love of his fellow man.

That evening, after pulling up at a comfortable desert hostel, I made a touching discovery. There on the floor of the car, behind the driver's seat, was my water bag. My little Bushman, God keep him, had put it back!

DISCUSSING THE SELECTION

1. If any one of us were to be stranded in the desert with only an African Bushman for company, we would probably feel much the same as this traveller did. Why did he fear to get out of the car? What offers of friendship did the Bushman make?

2. When Mr. James finally indicated his need for water, he found unexpected aid. Tell how the Bushman showed him extraordinary kindness. Why did the little African refuse reward? What further sign of the Bushman's unselfishness did Mr. James find?

3. The author tells this slight incident to show that men are men the world over and that they can understand one another in spite of great differences in their heritage and ways of living. Do you think that these two understood each other better than you do some of your classmates? Tell how you think individuals, even within a small community, can show some of the evidences of human brotherhood shown here.

✂

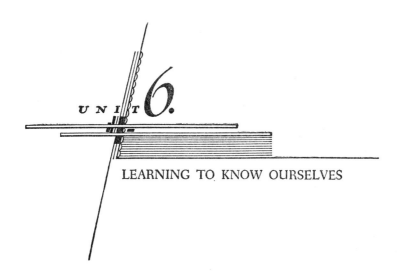

LEARNING TO KNOW OURSELVES

GABILAN ✒ JOHN STEINBECK

AT DAYBREAK Billy Buck emerged from the bunkhouse and stood for a moment on the porch looking up at the sky. He was a broad, bandy-legged little man with a walrus moustache, with square hands, puffed and muscled on the palms. His eyes were a contemplative, watery grey and the hair which protruded from under his Stetson hat was spiky and weathered. Billy was still stuffing his shirt into his blue jeans as he stood on the porch. He unbuckled his belt and tightened it again. The belt showed, by the worn shiny places opposite each hole, the gradual increase of Billy's middle over a period of years. When he had seen to the weather, Billy cleared each nostril by holding its mate closed with his forefinger and blowing fiercely. Then he walked down to the barn, rubbing his hands together. He curried and brushed two saddle horses in the stalls, talking quietly to them all the time; and he had hardly finished when the iron triangle started ringing at the ranch house. Billy stuck the brush and currycomb together and laid them on the rail, and went up to breakfast. His action had been so deliberate and yet so wasteless of time that he came to the house while Mrs. Tiflin was still ringing the triangle. She nodded her grey head to him and withdrew into the kitchen. Billy Buck sat down on the steps, because he was a cow hand, and it wouldn't be fitting that he should go first into the dining room. He heard Mr. Tiflin in the house, stamping his feet into his boots.

The high jangling note of the triangle put the boy Jody in motion. He was only a little boy, ten years old, with hair like dusty yellow grass and with shy polite grey eyes, and with a mouth that worked when he thought. The triangle picked him up out of sleep. It didn't occur to him to disobey the harsh note. He never had; no one he knew ever had. He brushed the tangled hair out of his eyes and skinned his nightgown off. In a moment he was dressed—blue chambray shirt and overalls. It was late in the summer, so of course there were no shoes to bother with. In the kitchen he waited until his mother got from in front of the sink and went back to the stove. Then he washed himself and brushed back his wet hair with his fingers. His mother turned sharply on him as he left the sink. Jody looked shyly away.

"I've got to cut your hair before long," his mother said. "Breakfast's on the table. Go on in, so Billy can come."

Jody sat at the long table which was covered with white oil-cloth washed through to the fabric in some places. The fried eggs lay in rows on their platter. Jody took three eggs on his plate and followed with three thick slices of crisp bacon. . . .

Jody's tall stern father came in then and Jody knew from the noise on the floor that he was wearing boots, but he looked under the table anyway, to make sure. His father turned off the oil lamp over the table, for plenty of morning light now came through the windows.

Jody did not ask where his father and Billy Buck were riding that day, but he wished he might go along. His father was a disciplinarian. Jody obeyed him in everything without questions of any kind. Now, Carl Tifflin sat down and reached for the egg platter.

"Got the cows ready to go, Billy?" he asked.

"In the lower corral," Billy said. "I could just as well take them in alone."

"Sure you could. But a man needs company. Besides your throat gets pretty dry." Carl Tiflin was jovial this morning.

Jody's mother put her head in the door. "What time do you think to be back, Carl?"

"I can't tell. I've got to see some men in Salinas. Might be gone till dark."

The eggs and coffee and big biscuits disappeared rapidly. Jody followed the two men out of the house. He watched them mount their horses and drive six old milk cows out of the corral and start over the hill toward Salinas. They were going to sell the old cows to the butcher.

When they had disappeared over the crown of the ridge Jody walked up the hill in back of the house. The dogs trotted around the house corner hunching their shoulders and grinning horribly with pleasure. Jody patted their heads—Doubletree Mutt with the big thick tail and yellow eyes, and Smasher, the shepherd, who had killed a coyote and lost an ear in doing it. Smasher's one good ear stood up higher than a collie's ear should. Billy Buck said that always happened. After the frenzied greeting the dogs lowered their noses to the ground in a businesslike way and went ahead, looking back now and then to make sure that the boy was coming. They walked up through the chicken yard and saw the quail eating with the chickens. Smasher chased the chickens a little to keep in practice in case there should ever be sheep to herd. Jody continued on through the large vegetable patch where the green corn was higher than his head. The cow-pumpkins were green and small yet. He went on to the sagebrush line where the cold spring ran out of its pipe and fell into a round wooden tub. He leaned over and drank close to the green mossy wood where the water tasted best. Then he turned and looked back on the ranch, on the low, whitewashed house girded with red geraniums, and on the long bunkhouse by the cypress tree where Billy Buck lived alone. Jody could see the great black kettle under the cypress tree. That was where the pigs were scalded. The sun was coming over the ridge now, glaring on the whitewash of the houses and barns, making the wet grass blaze softly. Behind him, in the tall sagebrush, the birds were scampering on the ground, making a great noise among the dry leaves; the squirrels piped shrilly on the sidehills. Jody looked along at the far buildings. He felt an uncertainty in the air, a feeling of change and of loss and of the gain of new and unfamiliar things. Over the hillside two big black buzzards sailed low to the ground and their shadows slipped smoothly and quickly ahead of them. Some animal had died in the vicinity. Jody knew it. It might be a cow or it might be the remains of a rabbit. The buzzards overlooked nothing. Jody hated them as all decent things hate them, but they could not be hurt because they made away with carrion.

After a while the boy sauntered downhill again. The dogs had long ago given him up and gone into the brush to do things in their own way. Back through the vegetable garden he went, and he paused for a moment to smash a green muskmelon with his heel, but he was not happy about it. It was a bad thing to do, he knew perfectly well. He kicked dirt over the ruined melon to conceal it.

Back at the house his mother bent over his rough hands, inspecting his fingers and nails. It did little good to start him clean to school, for too many things could happen on the way. She sighed over the black cracks on his fingers, and then gave him his books and his lunch and started him on the mile walk to school. She noticed that his mouth was working a good deal this morning.

Jody started his journey. He filled his pockets with little pieces of white quartz that lay in the road, and every so often he took a shot at a bird or at some rabbit that had stayed sunning itself in the road too long. At the crossroads over the bridge he met two friends and the three of them walked to school together, making ridiculous strides and being rather silly. School had just opened two weeks before. There was still a spirit of revolt among the pupils.

It was four o'clock in the afternoon when Jody topped the hill and looked down on the ranch again. He looked for the saddle horses, but the corral was empty. His father was not back yet. He went slowly, then, toward the afternoon chores. At the ranch house, he found his mother sitting on the porch, mending socks.

"There's two doughnuts in the kitchen for you," she said. Jody slid to the kitchen, and returned with half of one of the doughnuts already eaten and his mouth full. His mother asked him what he had learned in school that day, but she didn't listen to his dough-nut-muffled answer. She interrupted, "Jody, to-night see you fill the woodbox clear full. Last night you crossed the sticks and it wasn't only half full. Lay the sticks flat to-night. And Jody, some of the hens are hiding eggs, or else the dogs are eating them. Look about in the grass and see if you can find any nests."

Jody, still eating, went out and did his chores. He saw the quail come down to eat with the chickens when he threw out the grain. For some reason his father was proud to have them come. He never allowed any shooting near the house for fear the quail might go away.

When the woodbox was full, Jody took his twenty-two rifle up to the cold spring at the brush line. He drank again and then aimed the gun at all manner of things, at rocks, at birds on the wing, at the big black pig kettle under the cypress tree, but he didn't shoot, for he had no cartridges, and wouldn't have until he was twelve. If his father had seen him aim the rifle in the direction of the house he would have put the cartridges off another year. Jody remembered this and did not point the rifle down the hill again. Two years was enough to wait for cartridges. Nearly all of his father's presents were given with reservations which hampered their value somewhat. It was good discipline.

The supper waited until dark for his father to return, and at last he came in with Billy Buck. After supper, Jody sat by the fireplace and his shy polite eyes sought the room corners, and he waited for his father to tell what it was he contained, for Jody knew he had news of some sort. But he was disappointed. His father pointed a stern finger at him.

"You'd better go to bed, Jody. I'm going to need you in the morning."

That wasn't so bad. Jody liked to do things he had to do as long as they weren't routine things. He looked at the floor and his mouth worked out a question before he spoke it. "What are we going to do in the morning, kill a pig?" he asked softly.

"Never you mind. You better get to bed."

When the door was closed behind him, Jody heard his father and Billy Buck chuckling and he knew it was a joke of some kind. And later, when he lay in bed, trying to make words out of the murmurs in the other room, he heard his father protest, "But, Ruth, I didn't give much for him."

Jody heard the hoot owls hunting mice down by the barn, and he heard a fruit tree limb tap-tapping against the house. A cow was lowing when he went to sleep.

When the triangle sounded in the morning, Jody dressed more quickly than usual. In the kitchen, while he washed his face and combed back his hair, his mother addressed him irritably. "Don't you go out until you get a good breakfast in you."

He went into the dining room and sat at the long white table. He took a steaming hotcake from the platter, arranged two fried eggs on it, covered them with another hotcake, and squashed the whole thing with his fork.

His father and Billy Buck came in. Jody knew from the sound on the floor that both of them were wearing flat-heeled shoes, but he peered under the table to make sure. His father turned off the oil lamp, for the day had arrived, and he looked stern and disciplinary, but Billy Buck didn't look at Jody at all. He avoided the shy questioning eyes of the boy and soaked a whole piece of toast in his coffee.

Carl Tiflin said crossly, "You come with us after breakfast!"

Jody had trouble with his food then, for he felt a kind of doom in the air. After Billy had tilted his saucer and drained the coffee which had slopped into it, and had wiped his hands on his jeans, the two men stood up from the table and went out into the morning light together, and Jody respectfully followed a little behind them. He tried to keep his mind from running ahead, tried to keep it absolutely motionless.

His mother called, "Carl! Don't you let it keep him from school."

They marched past the cypress, where a singletree hung from

a limb to butcher the pigs on, and past the black iron kettle, so it was not a pig killing. The sun shone over the hill and threw long, dark shadows of the trees and buildings. They crossed a stubble field to shortcut to the barn. Jody's father unhooked the door and they went in. They had been walking toward the sun on the way down. The barn was black as night in contrast and warm from the hay and from the beasts. Jody's father moved over toward the one box stall. "Come here!" he ordered. Jody could begin to see things now. He looked into the box stall and then stepped back quickly.

A red pony colt was looking at him out of the stall. Its tense ears were forward and a light of disobedience was in its eyes. Its coat was rough and thick as an Airedale's fur and its mane was long and tangled. Jody's throat collapsed in on itself and cut his breath short.

"He needs a good currying," his father said, "and if I ever hear of you not feeding him or leaving his stall dirty, I'll send him off in a minute."

Jody couldn't bear to look at the pony's eyes any more. He

gazed down at his hands for a moment, and he asked very shyly, "Mine?" No one answered him. He put his hand out toward the pony. Its grey nose came close, sniffling loudly, and then the lips drew back and the strong teeth closed on Jody's fingers. The pony shook its head up and down and seemed to laugh with amusement. Jody regarded his bruised fingers. "Well," he said with pride— "Well, I guess he can bite all right." The two men laughed, some-what in relief. Carl Tiflin went out of the barn and walked up a sidehill to be by himself, for he was embarrassed, but Billy Buck stayed. It was easier to talk to Billy Buck. Jody asked again —"Mine?"

Billy became professional in tone. "Sure! That is, if you look out for him and break him right. I'll show you how. He's just a colt. You can't ride him for some time."

Jody put out his bruised hand again, and this time the red pony let his nose be rubbed. "I ought to have a carrot," Jody said. "Where'd we get him, Billy?"

"Bought him at a sheriff's auction," Billy explained. "A show went broke in Salinas and had debts. The sheriff was selling off their stuff."

The pony stretched out his nose and shook the forelock from his wild eyes. Jody stroked the nose a little. He said softly, "There isn't a—saddle?"

Billy Buck laughed. "I'd forgot. Come along."

In the harness room he lifted down a little saddle of red morocco leather. "It's just a show saddle," Billy Buck said disparagingly. "It isn't practical for the brush, but it was cheap at the sale."

Jody couldn't trust himself to look at the saddle either, and he couldn't speak at all. He brushed the shining red leather with his finger tips, and after a long time he said, "It'll look pretty on him though." He thought of the grandest and prettiest things he knew. "If he hasn't a name already, I think I'll call him Gabilan Moun-tains," he said.

Billy Buck knew how he felt. "'It's a pretty long name. Why don't you just call him Gabilan? That means hawk. That would be a fine name for him." Billy felt glad. "If you will collect tail

GABILAN 551

hair, I might be able to make a hair rope for you sometime. You could use it for a hackamore."[1]

Jody wanted to go back to the box stall. "Could I lead him to school, do you think—to show the kids?"

But Billy shook his head. "He's not even halterbroke yet. We had a time getting him here. Had to almost drag him. You better be starting for school though."

"I'll bring the kids to see him here this afternoon," Jody said.

Six boys came over the hill half an hour early that afternoon, running hard, their heads down, their forearms working, their breath whistling. They swept by the house and cut across the stubble field to the barn. And then they stood self-consciously before the pony, and then they looked at Jody with eyes in which there was a new admiration and a new respect. Before to-day Jody had been a boy, dressed in overalls and a blue shirt—quieter than most, even suspected of being a little cowardly. And now he was different. Out of a thousand centuries they drew the ancient admiration of the footman for the horseman. They knew instinctively that a man on a horse is spiritually, as well as physically, bigger than a man on foot. They knew that Jody had been miraculously lifted out of equality with them, and had been placed over them. Gabilan put his head out of the stall and sniffed them.

"Why'n't you ride him?" the boys cried. "Why'n't you braid his tail with ribbons like in the fair?" "When you going to ride him?"

Jody's courage was up. He too felt the superiority of the horseman. "He's not old enough. Nobody can ride him for a long time. I'm going to train him on the long halter. Billy Buck is going to show me how."

"Well, can't we even lead him around a little?"

"He isn't even halterbroke," Jody said. He wanted to be completely alone when he took the pony out the first time. "Come and see the saddle."

[1] HACKAMORE—A halter of horsehair usually made with a loop that may be tightened around a horse's mouth for the purpose of breaking him.

They were speechless at the red morocco saddle, completely shocked out of comment. "It isn't much use in the brush," Jody explained. "It'll look pretty on him though. Maybe I'll ride bareback when I go into brush."

"How you going to rope a cow without a saddle horn?"

"Maybe I'll get another saddle for every day. My father might want me to help him with the stock." He let them feel the red saddle, and showed them the brass chain throat-latch on the bridle and the big brass buttons at each temple where the headstall and brow band crossed. The whole thing was too wonderful. They had to go away after a little while, and each boy, in his mind, searched among his possessions for a bribe worthy of offering in return for a ride on the red pony when the time should come.

Jody was glad when they had gone. He took brush and currycomb from the wall, took down the barrier of the box stall, and stepped cautiously in. The pony's eyes glittered, and he edged around into kicking position. But Jody touched him on the shoulder and rubbed his high arched neck as he had always seen Billy Buck do, and he crooned, "So-o-o Boy," in a deep voice. The pony gradually relaxed his tenseness. Jody curried and brushed until a pile of dead hair lay in the stall and until the pony's coat had taken on a deep red shine. Each time he finished he thought it might have been done better. He braided the mane into a dozen little pigtails, and he braided the forelock, and then he undid them and brushed the hair out straight again.

Jody did not hear his mother enter the barn. She was angry when she came, but when she looked in at the pony and at Jody working over him, she felt a curious pride rise up in her. "Have you forgot the woodbox?" she asked gently. "It's not far off from dark and there's not a stick of wood in the house, and the chickens aren't fed."

Jody quickly put up his tools. "I forgot, ma'am."

"Well, after this do your chores first. Then you won't forget. I expect you'll forget lots of things now if I don't keep an eye on you."

"Can I have carrots from the garden for him, ma'am?"

She had to think about that. "Oh—I guess so, if you only take the big tough ones."

"Carrots keep the coat good," he said, and again she felt the curious rush of pride.

Jody never waited for the triangle to get him out of bed after the coming of the pony. It became his habit to creep out of bed even before his mother was awake, to slip into his clothes, and to go quietly down to the barn to see Gabilan. In the grey quiet mornings when the land and the brush and the houses and the trees were silver-grey and black like a photograph negative, he stole toward the barn, past the sleeping stones and the sleeping cypress tree. The turkeys, roosting in the tree out of coyotes' reach, clicked drowsily. The fields glowed with a grey frostlike light and in the dew the tracks of rabbits and of field mice stood out sharply. The good dogs came stiffly out of their little houses, hackles up and deep growls in their throats. Then they caught Jody's scent, and their stiff tails rose up and waved a greeting—Doubletree Mutt with the big thick tail, and Smasher, the incipient shepherd—then went lazily back to their warm beds.

It was a strange time and a mysterious journey, to Jody—an extension of a dream. When he first had the pony he liked to torture himself during the trip by thinking Gabilan would not be in his stall, and worse, would never have been there. And he had other delicious little self-induced pains. He thought how the rats had gnawed ragged holes in the red saddle, and how the mice had nibbled Gabilan's tail until it was stringy and thin. He usually ran the last little way to the barn. He unlatched the rusty hasp of the barn door and stepped in, and no matter how quietly he opened the door, Gabilan was always looking at him over the barrier of the box stall and Gabilan whinnied softly and stamped his front foot, and his eyes had big sparks of red fire in them like oakwood embers.

Sometimes, if the work horses were to be used that day, Jody found Billy Buck in the barn harnessing and currying. Billy stood with him and looked at Gabilan and he told Jody a great many things about horses. He explained that they were terribly afraid for their feet, so that one must make a practice of lifting the legs and patting the hoofs and ankles to remove their terror. He told Jody how horses love conversation. He must talk to the pony all the time, and tell him the reasons for everything. Billy wasn't sure a horse could understand everything that was said to him, but it was impossible to say how much was understood. A horse never kicked up a fuss if someone he liked explained things to him. Billy could give examples, too. He had known, for instance, a horse nearly dead beat with fatigue to perk up when told it was only a little farther to his destination. And he had known a horse paralysed with fright to come out of it when his rider told him what it was that was frightening him. While he talked in the mornings, Billy Buck cut twenty or thirty straws into neat three-inch lengths and stuck them into his hatband. Then during the whole day, if he wanted to pick his teeth or merely to chew on something, he had only to reach up for one of them.

Jody listened carefully, for he knew and the whole country knew that Billy Buck was a fine hand with horses. Billy's own horse was a stringy cayuse [2] with a hammer head, but he nearly always won the first prizes at the stock trials. Billy could rope a steer, take a double half-hitch about the horn with his riata, [3] and dismount, and his horse would play the steer as an angler plays a fish, keeping a tight rope until the steer was down or beaten.

Every morning after Jody had curried and brushed the pony, he let down the barrier of the stall, and Gabilan thrust past him and raced down the barn and into the corral. Around and around he galloped, and sometimes he jumped forward and landed on stiff legs. He stood quivering, stiff ears forward, eyes rolling so that the whites showed, pretending to be frightened. At last he walked snorting to the water trough and buried his nose in the water up to the nostrils. Jody was proud then, for he knew that was the way to judge a horse. Poor horses only touched their lips to the water, but a fine spirited beast put his whole nose and mouth under, and only left room to breathe.

[2] CAYUSE (kī-ūs')—An Indian pony.
[3] RIATA (rė-ä'tà)—A lariat.

Then Jody stood and watched the pony, and he saw things he had never noticed about any other horse, the sleek, sliding flank muscles and the cords of the buttocks, which flexed like a closing fist, and the shine the sun put on the red coat. Having seen horses all his life, Jody had never looked at them very closely before. But now he noticed the moving ears which gave expression and even inflection of expression to the face. The pony talked with his ears. You could tell exactly how he felt about everything by the way his ears pointed. Sometimes they were stiff and upright and sometimes lax and sagging. They went back when he was angry or fearful, and forward when he was anxious and curious and pleased; and their exact position indicated which emotion he had.

Billy Buck kept his word. In the early fall the training began. First there was the halterbreaking, and that was the hardest because it was the first thing. Jody held a carrot and coaxed and promised and pulled on the rope. The pony set his feet like a burro when he felt the strain. But before long he learned. Jody walked all over the ranch leading him. Gradually he took to dropping the rope until the pony followed him unled wherever he went.

And then came the training on the long halter. That was slower work. Jody stood in the middle of a circle, holding the long halter. He clucked with his tongue and the pony started to walk in a big circle, held in by the long rope. He clucked again to make the pony trot, and again to make him gallop. Around and around Gabilan went thundering and enjoying it immensely. Then he called, "Whoa," and the pony stopped. It was not long until Gabilan was perfect at it. But in many ways he was a bad pony. He bit Jody in the pants and stomped on Jody's feet. Now and then his ears went back and he aimed a tremendous kick at the boy. Every time he did one of these bad things, Gabilan settled back and seemed to laugh to himself.

Billy Buck worked at the hair rope in the evenings before the fireplace. Jody collected tail hair in a bag, and he sat and watched Billy slowly constructing the rope, twisting a few hairs to make a string and rolling two strings together for a cord, and then braiding a number of cords to make the rope. Billy rolled the finished rope on the floor under his foot to make it round and hard.

The long halter work rapidly approached perfection. Jody's father, watching the pony stop and start and trot and gallop, was a little bothered by it.

"He's getting to be almost a trick pony," he complained. "I don't like trick horses. It takes all the—dignity out of a horse to make him do tricks. Why, a trick horse is kind of like an actor—no dignity, no character of his own." And his father said, "I guess you better be getting him used to the saddle pretty soon."

Jody rushed for the harness room. For some time he had been riding the saddle on a sawhorse. He changed the stirrup length over and over, and could never get it just right. Sometimes, mounted on the sawhorse in the harness room, with collars and hames and tugs hung all about him, Jody rode beyond the room. He carried his rifle across the pommel. He saw fields go flying by; and he heard the beat of the galloping hoofs.

It was a ticklish job, saddling the pony the first time. Gabilan hunched and reared and threw the saddle off before the cinch could be tightened. It had to be replaced again and again until at last the pony let it stay. And the cinching was difficult, too. Day by day Jody tightened the girth a little more until at last the pony didn't mind the saddle at all.

Then there was the bridle. Billy explained how to use a stick of licorice for a bit until Gabilan was used to having something in his mouth. Billy explained, "Of course we could force-break him to everything, but he wouldn't be as good a horse if we did. He'd always be a little bit afraid, and he wouldn't mind because he wanted to."

The first time the pony wore the bridle he whipped his head about and worked his tongue against the bit until the blood oozed from the corners of his mouth. He tried to rub the headstall off on the manger. His ears pivoted about and his eyes turned red with fear and with general rambunctiousness. Jody rejoiced, for he knew that only a mean-souled horse does not resent training.

And Jody trembled when he thought of the time when he would first sit in the saddle. The pony would probably throw him off. There was no disgrace in that. The disgrace would come if he did not get right up and mount again. Sometimes he dreamed that he lay in the dirt and cried and couldn't make himself mount again. The shame of the dream lasted until the middle of the day.

Gabilan was growing fast. Already he had lost the long-leggedness of the colt; his mane was getting longer and blacker. Under the constant currying and brushing his coat lay as smooth and gleaming as orange-red lacquer. Jody oiled the hoofs and kept them carefully trimmed so they would not crack.

The hair rope was nearly finished. Jody's father gave him an old pair of spurs and bent in the side bars and cut down the strap and took up the chainlets until they fitted. And then one day Carl Tiflin said:

"The pony's growing faster than I thought. I guess you can ride him by Thanksgiving. Think you can stick on?"

"I don't know," Jody said shyly. Thanksgiving was only three weeks off. He hoped it wouldn't rain, for rain would spot the red saddle.

Gabilan knew and liked Jody by now. He nickered when Jody came across the stubble field, and in the pasture he came running when his master whistled for him. There was always a carrot for him every time.

Billy Buck gave him riding instructions over and over. "Now when you get up there, just grab tight with your knees and keep your hands away from the saddle, and if you get throwed, don't let that stop you. No matter how good a man is, there's always some horse can pitch him. You just climb up again before he gets to feeling smart about it. Pretty soon, he won't throw you no more, and pretty soon he *can't* throw you no more. That's the way to do it."

"I hope it don't rain before," Jody said.

"Why not? Don't want to get throwed in the mud?"

That was partly it, and also he was afraid that in the flurry of bucking, Gabilan might slip and fall on him and break his leg or his hip. He had seen that happen to men before, had seen how they writhed on the ground like squashed bugs, and he was afraid of it.

He practised on the sawhorse how he would hold the reins in his left hand and a hat in his right hand. If he kept his hands thus busy, he couldn't grab the horn if he felt himself going off. He didn't like to think of what would happen if he did grab the horn. Perhaps his father and Billy Buck would never speak to him again, they would be so ashamed. The news would get about and his mother would be ashamed too. And in the schoolyard—it was too awful to contemplate.

He began putting his weight in a stirrup when Gabilan was saddled, but he didn't throw his leg over the pony's back. That was forbidden until Thanksgiving.

Every afternoon he put the red saddle on the pony and cinched it tight. The pony was learning already to fill his stomach out unnaturally large while the cinching was going on, and then to let it down when the straps were fixed. Sometimes Jody led him up to the brush line and let him drink from the round green tub, and sometimes he led him up through the stubble field to the hilltop from which it was possible to see the white town of Salinas and the geometric fields of the great valley, and the oak trees clipped by the sheep. Now and then they broke through the brush and came 'o little cleared circles so hedged in that the world was gone and only the sky and the circle of brush were left from the old life. Gabilan liked these trips and showed it by keeping his head very high and by quivering his nostrils with interest. When the two came back from an expedition they smelled of the sweet sage they had forced through.

Time dragged on toward Thanksgiving, but winter came fast. The clouds swept down and hung all day over the land and brushed the hilltops, and the winds blew shrilly at night. All day the dry oak leaves drifted down from the trees until they covered the ground, and yet the trees were unchanged.

Jody had wished it might not rain before Thanksgiving, but it did. The brown earth turned dark and the trees glistened. The cut ends of the stubble turned black with mildew; the haystacks greyed from exposure to the damp, and on the roofs the moss, which had been all summer as grey as lizards, turned a brilliant yellow-green. During the week of rain, Jody kept the pony in the box stall out of the dampness, except for a little time after school when he took him out for exercise and to drink at the water trough in the upper corral. Not once did Gabilan get wet.

The wet weather continued until little new grass appeared. Jody walked to school dressed in a slicker and short rubber boots. At length one morning the sun came out brightly. Jody, at his work in the box stall, said to Billy Buck, "Maybe I'll leave Gabilan in the corral when I go to school to-day."

"Be good for him to be out in the sun," Billy assured him. "No animal likes to be cooped up too long. Your father and me are going back on the hill to clean the leaves out of the spring." Billy nodded and picked his teeth with one of his little straws.

"If the rain comes, though—" Jody suggested.

"Not likely to rain to-day. She's rained herself out." Billy pulled up his sleeves and snapped his arm bands. "If it comes on to rain—why a little rain don't hurt a horse."

"Well, if it does come on to rain, you put him in, will you, Billy? I'm scared he might get cold so I couldn't ride him when the time comes."

"Oh, sure! I'll watch out for him if we get back in time. But it won't rain to-day."

And so Jody, when he went to school, left Gabilan standing out in the corral.

Billy Buck wasn't wrong about many things. He couldn't be. But he was wrong about the weather that day, for a little after noon the clouds pushed over the hills and the rain began to pour down. Jody heard it start on the schoolhouse roof. He considered holding up one finger for permission to go to the outhouse and, once outside, running for home to put the pony in. Punishment would be prompt both at school and at home. He gave it up and took ease from Billy's assurance that rain couldn't hurt a horse.

When school was finally out, he hurried home through the dark rain. The banks at the sides of the road spouted little jets of muddy water. The rain slanted and swirled under a cold and gusty wind. Jody dog-trotted home, slopping through the gravelly mud of the road.

From the top of the ridge he could see Gabilan standing miserably in the corral. The red coat was almost black, and streaked with water. He stood head down with his rump to the rain and wind. Jody arrived running and threw open the barn door and led the wet pony in by his forelock. Then he found a gunny sack and rubbed the soaked hair and rubbed the legs and ankles. Gabilan stood patiently, but he trembled in gusts like the wind.

When he had dried the pony as well as he could, Jody went up to the house and brought hot water down to the barn and soaked the grain in it. Gabilan was not very hungry. He nibbled at the hot mash, but he was not very much interested in it, and he still shivered now and then. A little steam rose from his damp back.

It was almost dark when Billy Buck and Carl Tiflin came home.

"When the rain started we put up at Ben Herche's place, and the rain never let up all afternoon," Carl Tiflin explained. Jody looked reproachfully at Billy Buck and Billy felt guilty.

"You said it wouldn't rain," Jody accused him.

Billy looked away. "It's hard to tell, this time of year," he said, but his excuse was lame. He had no right to be fallible,[4] and he knew it.

"The pony got wet, got soaked through."

"Did you dry him off?"

"I rubbed him with a sack and I gave him hot grain."

Billy nodded in agreement.

"Do you think he'll take cold, Billy?"

"A little rain never hurt anything," Billy assured him.

Jody's father joined the conversation then and lectured the boy a little. "A horse," he said, "isn't any lap-dog kind of thing." Carl Tiflin hated weakness and sickness, and he held a violent contempt for helplessness.

---

[4] FALLIBLE (făl'ĭ-b'l)—Liable to be mistaken.

Jody's mother put a platter of steaks on the table and boiled potatoes and boiled squash, which clouded the room with their steam. They sat down to eat. Carl Tiflin still grumbled about weakness put into animals and men by too much coddling.

Billy Buck felt bad about his mistake. "Did you blanket him?" he asked.

"No. I couldn't find any blanket. I laid some sacks over his back."

"We'll go down and cover him up after we eat, then." Billy felt better about it then. When Jody's father had gone in to the fire and his mother was washing dishes, Billy found and lighted a lantern. He and Jody walked through the mud to the barn. The barn was dark and warm and sweet. The horses still munched their evening hay. "You hold the lantern!" Billy ordered. And he felt the pony's legs and tested the heat of the flanks. He put his cheek against the pony's muzzle and then he rolled up the eyelids to look at the eyeballs and he lifted the lips to see the gums, and he put his fingers inside the ears. "He don't seem so chipper," Billy said. "I'll give him a rubdown."

Then Billy found a sack and rubbed the pony's legs violently and he rubbed the chest and the withers. Gabilan was strangely spiritless. He submitted patiently to the rubbing. At last Billy brought an old cotton comforter from the saddle room, and threw it over the pony's back and tied it at neck and chest with string.

"Now he'll be all right in the morning," Billy said.

Jody's mother looked up when he got back to the house. "You're late up from bed," she said. She held his chin in her hand and brushed the tangled hair out of his eyes and she said, "Don't worry about the pony. He'll be all right. Billy's as good as any horse doctor in the country."

Jody hadn't known she could see his worry. He pulled gently away from her and knelt down in front of the fireplace until it burned his stomach. He scorched himself through and then went in to bed, but it was a hard thing to go to sleep. He awakened after what seemed a long time. The room was dark but there was a greyness in the window like that which precedes the dawn. He got up and found his overalls and searched for the legs, and then the clock in the other room struck two. He laid his clothes down and got back into bed. It was broad daylight when he awakened again. For the first time he had slept through the ringing of the triangle. He leaped up, flung on his clothes, and went out of the door still buttoning his shirt. His mother looked after him for a moment and then went quietly back to her work. Her eyes were brooding and kind. Now and then her mouth smiled a little but without changing her eyes at all.

Jody ran on toward the barn. Halfway there he heard the sound he dreaded, the hollow rasping cough of a horse. He broke into a sprint then. In the barn he found Billy Buck with the pony. Billy was rubbing its legs with his strong thick hands. He looked up and smiled gaily. "He just took a little cold," Billy said. "We'll have him out of it in a couple of days."

Jody looked at the pony's face. The eyes were half closed and the lids thick and dry. In the eye corners a crust of hard mucus stuck. Gabilan's ears hung loosely sideways and his head was low. Jody put out his hand, but the pony did not move close to it. He coughed again and his whole body constricted with the effort. A little stream of fluid ran from his nostrils.

Jody looked back at Billy Buck. "He's awful sick, Billy."

"Just a little cold, like I said," Billy insisted. "You go get some breakfast and then go back to school. I'll take care of him."

"But you might have to do something else. You might leave him."

"No, I won't. I won't leave him at all. Tomorrow's Saturday. Then you can stay with him all day." Billy had failed again, and he felt bad about it. He had to cure the pony now.

Jody walked up to the house and took his place listlessly at the table. The eggs and bacon were cold and greasy, but he didn't notice it. He ate his usual amount. He didn't even ask to stay home from school. His mother pushed his hair back when she took his plate. "Billy'll take care of the pony," she assured him.

He moped through the whole day at school. He couldn't answer any questions nor read any words. He couldn't even tell anyone the pony was sick, for that might make him sicker. And when school was finally out he started home in dread. He walked slowly and let the other boys leave him. He wished he might continue walking and never arrive at the ranch.

Billy was in the barn, as he had promised, and the pony was worse. His eyes were almost closed now, and his breath whistled shrilly past an obstruction in his nose. A film covered that part of the eyes that was visible at all. It was doubtful whether the pony could see any more. Now and then he snorted to clear his nose, and by the action seemed to plug it tighter. Jody looked dispiritedly at the pony's coat. The hair lay rough and unkempt and seemed to have lost all of its old lustre. Billy stood quietly beside the stall. Jody hated to ask, but he had to know.

"Billy, is he—is he going to get well?"

Billy put his fingers between the bars under the pony's jaws and felt about. "Feel here," he said and he guided Jody's fingers to a large lump under the jaw. "When that gets bigger, I'll open it up and then he'll get better."

Jody looked quickly away, for he had heard about that lump. "What is the matter with him?"

Billy didn't want to answer, but he had to. He couldn't be wrong three times. "Strangles," he said shortly, "but don't you worry about that. I'll pull him out of it. I've seen them get well when they were worse than Gabilan is. I'm going to steam him now. You can help."

"Yes," Jody said miserably. He followed Billy into the grain room and watched him make the steaming bag ready. It was a long canvas nose bag with straps to go over a horse's ears. Billy filled it one-third full of bran and then he added a couple of handfuls of dried hops. On top of the dry substance he poured a little carbolic acid and a little turpentine. "I'll be mixing it all up while you run to the house for a kettle of boiling water," Billy said.

When Jody came back with the steaming kettle, Billy buckled the straps over Gabilan's head and fitted the bag tightly around his nose. Then through a little hole in the side of the bag he poured the boiling water on the mixture. The pony started away as a cloud of strong steam rose up, but then the soothing fumes crept through his nose and into his lungs, and the sharp steam began to clear out the nasal passages. He breathed loudly. His legs trembled in an ague,[5] and his eyes closed against the biting cloud. Billy poured in more water and kept the steam rising for fifteen minutes. At last he set down the kettle and took the bag from Gabilan's nose. The pony looked better. He breathed freely, and his eyes were open wider than they had been.

"See how good it makes him feel," Billy said. "Now we'll wrap him up in the blanket again. Maybe he'll be nearly well by morning."

"I'll stay with him to-night," Jody suggested.

"No. Don't you do it. I'll bring my blankets down here and put them in the hay. You can stay tomorrow and steam him if he needs it."

The evening was falling when they went to the house for their supper. Jody didn't even realize that someone else had fed the chickens and filled the woodbox. He walked up past the house to the dark brush line and took a drink of water from the tub. The spring water was so cold that it stung his mouth and drove a shiver through him. The sky above the hills was still light. He saw a hawk flying so high that it caught the sun on its breast and shone like a spark. Two blackbirds were driving him down the sky, glittering as they attacked their enemy. In the west, the clouds were moving in to rain again.

Jody's father didn't speak at all while the family ate supper, but after Billy Buck had taken his blankets and gone to sleep in the barn, Carl Tiflin built a high fire in the fireplace and told stories. He told about the wild man who ran naked through the country and had a tail and ears like a horse, and he told about the rabbit-cats of Moro Cojo that hopped into the trees for birds. He revived the famous Maxwell brothers who found a vein of gold and hid the traces of it so carefully that they could never find it again.

Jody sat with his chin in his hands; his mouth worked nervously and his father gradually became aware that he wasn't listening very carefully. "Isn't that funny?" he asked.

[5] AGUE (ā′gū)—A chill.

Jody laughed politely and said, "Yes, sir." His father was angry and hurt, then. He didn't tell any more stories. After a while, Jody took a lantern and went down to the barn. Billy Buck was asleep in the hay, and, except that his breath rasped a little in his lungs, the pony seemed to be much better. Jody stayed a little while, running his fingers over the red rough coat, and then he took up the lantern and went back to the house. When he was in bed, his mother came into the room.

"Have you enough covers on? It's getting winter."

"Yes, ma'am."

"Well, get some rest to-night." She hesitated to go out, stood uncertainly. "The pony will be all right," she said.

Jody was tired. He went to sleep quickly and didn't awaken until dawn. The triangle sounded, and Billy Buck came up from the barn before Jody could get out of the house.

"How is he?" Jody demanded.

Billy always wolfed his breakfast. "Pretty good. I'm going to open that lump this morning. Then he'll be better maybe."

After breakfast, Billy got out his best knife, one with a needle point. He whetted the shining blade a long time on a little carborundum stone. He tried the point and the blade again and again on his calloused thumb-nail, and at last he tried it on his upper lip.

On the way to the barn, Jody noticed how the young grass was up and how the stubble was melting day by day into the new green crop of volunteer. It was a cold sunny morning.

As soon as he saw the pony, Jody knew he was worse. His eyes were closed and sealed shut with dried mucus. His head hung so low that his nose almost touched the straw of his bed. There was a little groan in each breath, a deep-seated, patient groan.

Billy lifted the weak head and made a quick slash with the knife. Jody saw the yellow pus run out. He held up the head while Billy swabbed out the wound with weak carbolic acid salve.

"Now he'll feel better," Billy assured him. "That yellow poison is what makes him sick."

Jody looked unbelieving at Billy Buck. "He's awful sick."

Billy thought a long time what to say. He nearly tossed off a careless assurance, but he saved himself in time. "Yes, he's pretty sick," he said at last. "I've seen worse ones get well. If he doesn't get pneumonia, we'll pull him through. You stay with him. If he gets worse, you can come and get me."

For a long time after Billy went away, Jody stood beside the pony, stroking him behind the ears. The pony didn't flip his head the way he had done when he was well. The groaning in his breathing was becoming more hollow.

Doubletree Mutt looked into the barn, his big tail waving provocatively, and Jody was so incensed at his health that he found a hard black clod on the floor and deliberately threw it. Doubletree Mutt went yelping away to nurse a bruised paw.

In the middle of the morning, Billy Buck came back and made another steam bag. Jody watched to see whether the pony improved this time as he had before. His breathing eased a little, but he did not raise his head.

The Saturday dragged on. Late in the afternoon Jody went to the house and brought his bedding down and made up a place to sleep in the hay. He didn't ask permission. He knew from the way his mother looked at him that she would let him do almost anything. That night he left a lantern burning on a wire over the box stall. Billy had told him to rub the pony's legs every little while.

At nine o'clock the wind sprang up and howled around the barn. And in spite of his worry, Jody grew sleepy. He got into his blankets and went to sleep, but the breathy groans of the pony sounded in his dreams. And in his sleep he heard a crashing noise which went on and on until it awakened him. The wind was rushing through the barn. He sprang up and looked down the lane of stalls. The barn door had blown open, and the pony was gone.

He caught the lantern and ran outside into the gale, and he saw Gabilan weakly shambling away into the darkness, head down, legs working slowly and mechanically. When Jody ran up and caught him by the forelock, he allowed himself to be led back and put into his stall. His groans were louder, and a fierce whistling came from his nose. Jody didn't sleep any more then. The hissing of the pony's breath grew louder and sharper.

He was glad when Billy Buck came in at dawn. Billy looked for a time at the pony as though he had never seen him before. He felt the ears and flanks. "Jody," he said, "I've got to do something you won't want to see. You run up to the house for a while."

Jody grabbed him fiercely by the forearm. "You're not going to shoot him?"

Billy patted his hand. "No. I'm going to open a little hole in his windpipe so he can breathe. His nose is filled up. When he gets well, we'll put a little brass button in the hole for him to breathe through."

Jody couldn't have gone away if he had wanted to. It was awful to see the red hide cut, but infinitely more terrible to know it was being cut and not to see it. "I'll stay right here," he said bitterly. "You sure you got to?"

"Yes. I'm sure. If you stay, you can hold his head. If it doesn't make you sick, that is."

The fine knife came out again and was whetted again just as carefully as it had been the first time. Jody held the pony's head up and the throat taut, while Billy felt up and down for the right place. Jody sobbed once as the bright knife point disappeared into the throat. The pony plunged weakly away and then stood still, trembling violently. The blood ran thickly out and up the knife and across Billy's hand and into his shirtsleeve. The sure square hand sawed out a round hole in the flesh, and the breath came bursting out of the hole, throwing a fine spray of blood. With the rush of oxygen, the pony took a sudden strength. He lashed out with his hind feet and tried to rear, but Jody held his head down while Billy mopped the new wound with carbolic salve. It was a good job. The blood stopped flowing and the air puffed out the hole and sucked it in regularly with a little bubbling noise.

The rain brought in by the night wind began to fall on the barn roof. Then the triangle rang for breakfast. "You go up and eat while I wait," Billy said. "We've got to keep this hole from plugging up."

Jody walked slowly out of the barn. He was too dispirited to tell Billy how the barn door had blown open and let the pony out. He emerged into the wet grey morning and sloshed up to the house, taking a perverse pleasure in splashing through all the puddles. His mother fed him and put dry clothes on. She didn't question him. She seemed to know he couldn't answer questions. But when he was ready to go back to the barn she brought him a pan of steaming meal. "Give him this," she said.

But Jody did not take the pan. He said, "He won't eat anything," and ran out of the house. At the barn, Billy showed him how to fix a ball of cotton on a stick, with which to swab out the breathing hole when it became clogged with mucus.

Jody's father walked into the barn and stood with them in front of the stall. At length he turned to the boy. "Hadn't you better come with me? I'm going to drive over the hill." Jody shook his head. "You better come on, out of this," his father insisted.

Billy turned on him angrily. "Let him alone. It's his pony, isn't it?"

Carl Tiflin walked away without saying another word. His feelings were badly hurt.

All morning Jody kept the wound open and the air passing in and out freely. At noon the pony lay wearily down on his side and stretched his nose out.

Billy came back. "If you're going to stay with him to-night, you better take a little nap," he said. Jody went absently out of the barn. The sky had cleared to a hard thin blue. Everywhere the birds were busy with worms that had come to the damp surface of the ground.

Jody walked to the brush line and sat on the edge of the mossy tub. He looked down at the house and at the old bunkhouse and at the dark cypress tree. The place was familiar, but curiously changed. It wasn't itself any more, but a frame for things that were happening. A cold wind blew out of the east now, signifying that the rain was over for a little while. At his feet Jody could see the little arms of new weeds spreading out over the ground. In the mud about the spring were thousands of quail tracks.

Doubletree Mutt came sideways and embarrassed up through the vegetable patch, and Jody, remembering how he had thrown the clod, put his arm about the dog's neck and kissed him on his wide black nose. Doubletree Mutt sat still, as though he knew some solemn thing was happening. His big tail slapped the ground gravely. Jody pulled a swollen tick out of Mutt's neck and popped it dead between his thumbnails. It was a nasty thing. He washed his hands in the cold spring water.

Except for the steady swish of the wind, the farm was very quiet. Jody knew his mother wouldn't mind if he didn't go in to eat his lunch. After a little while he went slowly back to the barn. Mutt crept into his own little house and whined softly to himself for a long time.

Billy Buck stood up from the box and surrendered the cotton swab. The pony still lay on his side and the wound in his throat bellowsed in and out. When Jody saw how dry and dead the hair looked, he knew at last that there was no hope for the pony. He had seen the dead hair before on dogs and cows, and it was a sure sign. He sat heavily on the box and let down the barrier of the box stall. For a long time he kept his eyes on the moving wound, and at last he dozed, and the afternoon passed quickly. Just before dark his mother brought a deep dish of stew and left it for him and went away. Jody ate a little of it, and, when it was dark, he set the

lantern on the floor by the pony's head so he could watch the
wound and keep it open. And he dozed again until the night chill
awakened him. The wind was blowing fiercely, bringing the north
cold with it. Jody brought a blanket from his bed in the hay and
wrapped himself in it. Gabilan's breathing was quiet at last; the
hole in his throat moved gently. The owls flew through the hayloft,
shrieking and looking for mice. Jody put his hands down on his
head and slept. In his sleep he was aware that the wind had increased. He heard it slamming about the barn.

It was daylight when he awakened. The barn door had swung
open. The pony was gone. He sprang up and ran out into the
morning light.

The pony's tracks were plain enough, dragging through the
frostlike dew on the young grass, tired tracks with little lines
between them where the hoofs had dragged. They headed for the
brush line halfway up the ridge. Jody broke into a run and followed them. The sun shone on the sharp white quartz that stuck
through the ground here and there. As he followed the plain trail,
a shadow cut across in front of him. He looked up and saw a high
circle of black buzzards, and the slowly revolving circle dropped
lower and lower. The solemn birds soon disappeared over the
ridge. Jody ran faster then, forced on by panic and rage. The
trail entered the brush at last and followed a winding route among
the tall sage bushes.

At the top of the ridge Jody was winded. He paused, puffing
noisily. The blood pounded in his ears. Then he saw what he was
looking for. Below, in one of the little clearings in the brush, lay
the red pony. In the distance, Jody could see the legs moving
slowly and convulsively. And in a circle around him stood the
buzzards, waiting for the moment of death they knew so well.

Jody leaped forward and plunged down the hill. The wet ground
muffled his steps and the brush hid him. When he arrived, it was
all over. The first buzzard sat on the pony's head and its beak had
just risen dripping with dark eye fluid. Jody plunged into the
circle like a cat. The black brotherhood arose in a cloud, but the
big one on the pony's head was too late. As it hopped along to take

off, Jody caught its wing tip and pulled it down. It was nearly as big as he was. The free wing crashed into his face with the force of a club, but he hung on. The claws fastened on his leg and the wing elbows battered his head on either side. Jody groped blindly with his free hand. His fingers found the neck of the struggling bird. The red eyes looked into his face, calm and fearless and fierce; the naked head turned from side to side. Then the beak opened and vomited a stream of putrefied fluid. Jody brought up his knee and fell on the great bird. He held the neck to the ground with one hand while his other found a piece of sharp white quartz. The first blow broke the beak sideways and black blood spurted from the twisted, leathery mouth corners. He struck again and missed. The red fearless eyes still looked at him, impersonal and unafraid and detached. He struck again and again, until the buzzard lay dead, until its head was a red pulp. He was still beating the dead bird when Billy Buck pulled him off and held him tightly to calm his shaking.

Carl Tiflin wiped the blood from the boy's face with a red bandanna. Jody was limp and quiet now. His father moved the buzzard with his toe. "Jody," he explained, "the buzzard didn't kill the pony. Don't you know that?"

"I know it," Jody said wearily.

It was Billy Buck who was angry. He had lifted Jody in his arms, and had turned to carry him home. But he turned back on Carl Tiflin. " 'Course he knows it," Billy said furiously. "Man, can't you see how he'd feel about it?"

DISCUSSING THE STORY

Jody was serious, and a little shy, as a boy living in the country is likely to be. But even when he was on the ranch he was not lonely. He had friends, and he played games that were as exciting as any enjoyed by the boys in town. Then came the Red Pony, and life was suddenly overflowing with wonderful experiences.

1. What was Jody's life like on the ranch? Tell about the daily schedule, the meals, the two dogs, the walks up the hill, the chores.

2. Carl Tiflin was a disciplinarian. What does this tell you about the kind of man Jody's father was? What was Jody's attitude towards his

father? Explain why you think Carl was or was not a good father to
Jody.

3. Billy Buck was certainly a good friend to Jody. Why was Billy a
valuable man to have around the ranch? What things that he knew
about were especially interesting to Jody?

4. Tell about Jody's reactions when he first saw the Red Pony. How
did the pony react toward the boy? Explain why Jody was looked upon
with new respect by the friends from school after their visit to the ranch.

5. Having a horse of one's own involves the acceptance of responsibility for its care and training. What tasks were added to Jody's routine
after the arrival of the pony? Tell about the pony's training, indicating
the several steps of the procedure.

6. As you probably know from your own experience, many pleas-
urable experiences are accompanied by some things that are not so
pleasant. Tell about the illness of the pony. Do you think that Billy
Buck did his best to bring about a cure? How did the illness and
death affect Jody?

7. John Steinbeck has written more about the adventures of Jody on
the ranch. Of course he gets a new horse of his own. In what ways do
you think he will be better prepared to care for his second horse after
his experiences with the Red Pony? Do you think he will always feel
a little bitter about his loss? Explain how you feel about this.

8. Are you satisfied with the way this story ends? Can you suggest
another ending that would be more suitable? In what ways do you
think this story is like real life?

THE OXEN ✺ THOMAS HARDY

CHRISTMAS Eve, and twelve of the clock,
'Now they are all on their knees,'
An elder said as we sat in a flock
By the embers in hearthside ease.

5   We pictured the meek mild creatures where
They dwelt in their strawy pen,
Nor did it occur to one of us there
To doubt they were kneeling then.

THE PRIZE CAT 573

So fair a fancy few would weave
10 In these years! Yet, I feel
If someone said on Christmas Eve,
'Come; see the oxen kneel

'In the lonely barten by yonder coomb
Our childhood used to know,'
15 I should go with him in the gloom,
Hoping it might be so.

DISCUSSING THE POEM

1. Through the ages, since the first Christmas, many beautiful stories and legends have been told about Christmas. One of these relates that at midnight on Christmas Eve domestic animals such as those that surrounded the newborn Christ in the manger are given the power of speech, and that they kneel to worship the Son of God. To-day, belief in such miraculous happenings, although perhaps strong in children, is usually replaced by scepticism and doubt in adults.

Hardy wishes that he might again believe that the oxen kneeled in their stalls on Christmas Eve. But what much more important belief does belief in such a miracle represent?

2. What other legends do you know that are associated with Christmas? Do you think that people once sincerely believed them?

THE PRIZE CAT E. J. PRATT

Pure blood domestic, guaranteed,
Soft-mannered, musical of purr,
The ribbon had declared the breed,
Gentility was in the fur.

5 Such feline culture in the gads,
No anger ever arched her back—
What distance since those velvet pads
Departed from the leopard's track!

And when I mused how Time had thinned
10 The jungle strains within the cells,
How human hands had disciplined
Those prowling optic parallels;

I saw the generations pass
Along the reflex of a spring,
15 A bird had rustled in the grass,
The tab had caught it on the wing:

Behind the leap so furtive-wild
Was such ignition in the gleam,
I thought an Abyssinian child
20 Had cried out in the whitethroat's scream.

UNDERSTANDING THE POEM

E. J. Pratt suggests in this poem that, though environment has done much to influence and refine the cat, its primitive characteristics are never destroyed. When conditions arise that appeal to these basic characteristics, they assert themselves.

1. Discuss the question, "Does the influence of environment completely overcome basic characteristics of animals?"

2. Discuss the question, "To what extent has civilization succeeded in leading man away from his primitive and savage characteristics?"

3. Pratt uses both figurative language and expressive vocabulary to draw the pictures he presents in this poem. Find examples of both. What are some of the unusual expressions which he uses? Why are they effective?

TALL GRASS 🌾 MAUREEN DALY

OUR house is just on the edge of town. Beyond, across a gravel road, stretch several blocks of undeveloped real-estate property which gradually blend into the landing field of the county airport and further on into straight-rowed cornfields. By the middle of

June, the white stakes marking off the lots are hidden in clover and the boundary lines are obscured in the thick, waving grass. This whole stretch of land is commonly called the Field, and when we were younger it was our favourite place to play.

One day stands out in my mind. My mother and father had gone out of town, and my sister Kathleen and I were home alone for the day. We packed a lunch and started down the grass road that led through the field to the creek. It was the end of July, and the air shimmered with summer heat. We walked slowly, stopping often to pick violets and rest in the tall grass. For a short while we played house, each beating down a flat space in the tall clover with a connecting path between. Here we lay on our backs, squinting at the bright sky. Sometimes a bobolink would fly low with its peculiar call that sounded like shiny bubbles bursting, and then circle higher and higher till it melted into the blueness of the sky. Small black-and-yellow wasps with sharp, striped bodies zigzagged between clover heads, and occasional pink blossoms were weighted down with fat, droning bumblebees. After a while we roused ourselves from the sunny stupor and went on down the road.

One part of the field is marshy, and here coarse, dark-green swamp grass growing in tufts replaces the meadow grass, and here wild iris with thin-petaled purple blossoms grow on hummocks. Kathleen and I picked a bunch, and the smooth stems made a skreaking sound as they slipped out between the green leaves. The soft ground squished beneath our weight and oozed around our shoes. It was almost noon before we reached the creek.

Kathleen, because she was older, spread out the lunch. She was hot and dirty by this time and edged herself carefully down the crumbling clay bank to wash in the creek first. I remember noticing then the brooch she had borrowed from my mother's dressing table to fasten her dress at the neck, glinting in the sun. It was a small, gold swallow with wings outstretched, each feather carefully outlined in the metal.

We had brought a clean white dishtowel for a tablecloth, and Kathleen spread it carefully on the grass. We had bread-and-butter sandwiches, hard-boiled eggs, cookies, milk, and small round tomatoes from the garden, so ripe that their skins seemed tight. The milk we had carried in two canning jars, and it was warm and flecked with cream. We set the jars down in the shallow edges of the running creek to cool off, and slowly ate the rest of our lunch.

It was almost three o'clock before we shook the crumbs from our skirts, folded up the dishtowel tablecloth, and started for home.

This time we didn't take the straight road but wandered aimlessly through the tall grass. Sometimes green grasshoppers jumped against our bare legs or clung for a moment to our skirts. Farther from the creek and nearer home the long grass was drier, already turned brown from the sun. Every year the real-estate dealer set fire to these dry lots to thin out the grass for the next spring. Because of the hot summer we had had, it was almost time then for the burning.

We were almost at the gravel road when Kathleen noticed her dress was open at the neck. The swallow pin was gone! Somewhere between the creek and the gravel road! Instantly the futility of searching struck us, and yet at the same moment our steps turned back toward the field. We looked in silence, little shivers of fear around our hearts. Step by step we retraced our way to the creek. Carefully we sought out the place where Kathleen's footsteps had crumbled the banks and left prints in the soft clay along the shore. Back we went, searching for the bush on which the meadow lark had sung, following our faint trail through the waving grass, refinding the places where the violets were thickest. Neither of us spoke. In one spot we ran across a bunch of wilted iris we had laid down and forgotten. Down we went on our hands and knees, pushing aside the slim, cool grass with edges that sometimes cut our fingers. Frantically, we stamped among the tall clover, and the broken stems and bruised leaves sent up a pungent, earthy odour. Swiftly we searched, swiftly and silently, our breath coming in short sobs. It must be found to-night. It was getting darker. Perhaps to-morrow the real estate men might set fire to the dry grass. It must be found to-night.

Later, much later, we turned for home—much later, when the crickets had begun the steady chant of evening and a paper-thin moon was pasted high in the sky. White-winged night moths fluttered close to the grass, and our feet were heavy as we crossed the gravel road. "We will tell her just as soon as she gets in the door."

So we sat in our nightgowns, waiting. Our hair was brushed and our faces clean and our legs and knees were nipping from small grass-cuts washed over with soap. Shortly we saw them coming, the headlights of the car sweeping the lawn as the car turned in the drive. "We will tell her right away. We will tell her as soon as she gets in the door," Kathleen said again.

In a moment my mother was there looking at us, so clean in our nightgowns, standing, smiling with a small, brown bag of candy in her hand, and Kathleen suddenly blurted, "I lost it. Your gold-swallow pin—somewhere out in the field. Somewhere!"

Then no one said a word. My mother took off her hat and set the candy bag on the table. My father had come in and stood by the door, and she looked at him and said quietly, "You remember —my mother gave it to me in Glasgow station. Just before the train pulled out for Liverpool and the boat. My gold-swallow pin." She said it very softly with a sadness in her voice.

There was nothing to do then, so we tiptoed upstairs, Kathleen and I, and cried in our beds. Outside it was very quiet, and the sky was darker around the moon, and the crickets' chant was lonely, and in the field soft night winds whispered in the tall grass.

DISCUSSING THE STORY

1. What is it that makes some experiences stand out sharply in our memories while others fade and are soon forgotten? Perhaps we cannot explain why—but we all know that the sight of a familiar place, a sudden odour, a snatch of song may recall to us a vividly remembered experience. Tell briefly about the single, keenly felt experience that the sight of "The Field" brings back to Maureen Daly.

2. The story Miss Daly tells is not exciting. The simple picnic was probably like many other picnics. The lost brooch was probably not worth a great deal of money. Why was every small detail of the day burned into the minds of the two girls?

3. Have you ever had an experience enough like this one that you can understand how the girls felt? Perhaps you may want to tell about it. Have you ever, like the mother, lost something dear to you for very personal reasons? If so, you will understand how she felt. Tell how you think we may use such experiences to deepen our understanding of the people we meet every day.

MIRACLES 🌸 WALT WHITMAN

WHY! who makes much of a miracle?
As to me, I know of nothing else but miracles,
Whether I walk the streets of Manhattan,
Or dart my sight over the roofs of houses toward the sky,
5 Or wade with naked feet along the beach, just in the edge of
    the water,
Or stand under trees in the woods,
Or talk by day with anyone I love—or sleep in the bed at night
    with anyone I love,
Or sit at table at dinner with my mother,
Or look at strangers opposite me riding in the car,
10 Or watch honeybees busy around the hive, of a summer fore-
    noon,
Or animals feeding in the fields,
Or birds—or the wonderfulness of insects in the air,

Or the wonderfulness of the sundown—or of stars shining so
    quiet and bright,
Or the exquisite, delicate, thin curve of the new moon in
    spring;
15 Or whether I go among those I like best, and that like me
    best—mechanics, boatmen, farmers,
Or among the savants—or to the soirée—or to the opera,
Or stand a long while looking at the movements of machinery,
Or behold children at their sports,
Or the admirable sight of the perfect old man, or the perfect
    old woman,
20 Or the sick in hospitals, or the dead carried to burial,
Or my own eyes and figure in the glass;
These, with the rest, one and all, are to me miracles,
The whole referring—yet each distinct, and in its place.

To me, every hour of the light and dark is a miracle,
25 Every cubic inch of space is a miracle,
Every square yard of the surface of the earth is spread with
    the same,
Every foot of the interior swarms with the same;
Every spear of grass—the frames, limbs, organs, of men and
    women, and all that concerns them,
All these to me are unspeakably perfect miracles.

30 To me the sea is a continual miracle;
The fishes that swim—the rocks—the motion of the waves—
    the ships, with men in them,
What stranger miracles are there?

16. SAVANTS—Men of learning.
16. SOIREE (swä-rā')—A social gathering.

CLUES TO THE MEANING

Even though Walt Whitman had very little formal education, he became one of the most important poets in the history of America. In
between his writing of poetic pieces, he did a great many other things

including teaching school, writing for newspapers, and serving as a nurse in the army hospitals during the American Civil War. After read-ing this selection, you may agree that he also learned how to recognize a miracle when he saw one.

1. A miracle is a wonderful thing that cannot be explained fully in any human or natural way. Do you agree that all the things Walt Whitman mentions in this poem are miracles? Which ones, if any, would you except?

2. Do you agree that the world is filled with miracles? What miracles, not mentioned in this poem, have you seen? Can you name some things that you see around you that can be fully explained, and thus not be miracles? How can a poem like "Miracles" help you to understand yourself and your world better?

TWO RIVERS ✣ WALLACE STEGNER

His father's voice awakened him. Stretching his back, arching against the mattress, he looked over at his parents' end of the sleeping porch. His mother was up too, though he could tell from the flatness of the light outside that it was still early. He lay on his back quietly, letting complete wakefulness come on, watching a spider that dangled on a golden, shining thread from the rolled canvas of the blinds. The spider came down in tiny jerks, his legs wriggling, then went up again in the beam of sun. From the other room the father's voice rose loud and cheerful:

> "Oh I'd give every man in the army a quarter
> If they'd all take a shot at my mother-in-law."

The boy slid his legs out of bed and yanked the nightshirt over his head. He didn't want his father's face poking around the door, saying, "I plough deep while sluggards sleep." He didn't want to be joked with. Yesterday was too sore a spot in his mind. He had been avoiding his father ever since the morning before, and he was not yet ready to accept any joking or attempts to make up. No-body had a right hitting a person for nothing, and you bet they weren't going to be friends. Let him whistle and sing out there, pretending nothing was the matter. The whole business yesterday was the matter, the Ford that wouldn't start was the matter, the whole lost Fourth of July was the matter, the missed parade, the missed ball game in Chinook were the matter. The cuff on the ear his father had given him when he got so mad at the Ford he had to have something to hit was the matter.

In the other room, as he pulled on his overalls, the bacon was snapping in the pan, and he smelled its good morning smell. His father whistled, sang.

The boy pulled the overall straps over his shoulders and went into the main room. His father stopped singing and looked at him. "Hello, Cheerful," he said. "You look like you'd bit into a wormy apple."

The boy mumbled something and went outside to wash at the bench. It wasn't any fun waking up today. You kept thinking about yesterday, and how much fun it had been waking then, when you were going to do something special and exciting, drive fifty miles to Chinook and spend the whole day just having fun. Now there wasn't anything but the same old thing to do you did every day. Run the trap line, put out some poison for the gophers, read the mail-order catalogue.

At breakfast he was glum, and his father joked him. Even his mother smiled, as if she had forgotten already how much wrong had been done the day before. "You look as if you'd been sent for and couldn't come," she said. "Cheer up."

"I don't want to cheer up."

They just smiled at each other, and he hated them both.

After breakfast his father said, "You help your Ma with the dishes, now. See how useful you can make yourself around here."

Unwillingly, wanting to get out of the house and away from them, he got the towel and swabbed off the plates. He was rubbing a glass when he heard the Ford sputter and race and roar and then calm down into a steady mutter. His mouth opened, and he looked at his mother. Her eyes were crinkled with smiling.

"It goes!" he said.

"Sure it goes." She pulled both his ears, rocking his head. "Know what we're going to do?"

"What?"

"We're going to the mountains anyway. Not to Chinook—there wouldn't be anything doing to-day. But to the mountains, for a picnic. Pa got the car going yesterday afternoon, when you were down in the field, so we decided to go to-day. If you want to, of course."

"Yay!" he said. "Shall I dress up?"

"Put on your shoes, you'd better. We might climb a mountain."

The boy was out into the porch in three steps. With one shoe on and the other in his hand he hopped to the door. "When?" he said.

"Soon as you can get ready."

He was trying to run and tie his shoelaces at the same time as he went out of the house. There in the Ford, smoking his pipe, with one leg over the door and his weight on the back of his neck, his father sat. "What detained you?" he said. "I've been waiting a half hour. You must not want to go very bad."

"Aw!" the boy said. He looked inside the Ford. There was the lunch all packed, the fat wet canvas waterbag, even Spot with his tongue out and his ears up. Looking at his father, all his sullenness gone now, the boy said, "When did you get all this ready?"

His father grinned. "While you slept like a sluggard we worked like a buggard," he said. Then the boy knew that everything was perfect, nothing could go wrong. When his father started rhyming things he was in his very best mood, and not even breakdowns and flat tires could make him do more than puff and blow and play-act.

He clambered into the front seat and felt the motor shaking under the floorboards. "Hey, Ma!" he yelled. "Hurry up! We're all ready to go!"

Their own road was a barely marked trail that wiggled out over the burnouts along the east side of the wheat field. At the line it ran into another coming down from the homesteads to the east, and at Cree, a mile inside the Montana boundary, they hit the straight sectionline road to Chinook. On that road they passed a trotting team pulling an empty waggon, and the boy waved and yelled, feeling superior, feeling as if he were charioted on pure speed and all the rest of the world were earth-footed.

"Let's see how fast this old boat will go," the father said. He nursed it down through a coulee[1] and onto the flat. His fingers pulled the gas lever down, and the motor roared. Looking back with the wind-stung tears in his eyes, the boy saw his mother hanging on to her hat, and the artificial cherries on the hat bouncing. The Ford leaped and bucked, the picnic box tipped over, the dog leaned out and the wind blew his eyes shut and his ears straight back. Turning around, the boy saw the blue sparks leaping from the magneto box and heard his father wahoo. He hung onto the side and leaned out to let the wind tear at him, tried to count the fence posts going by, but they were ahead of him before he got to ten.

The road roughened, and they slowed down. "Good land!" his mother said from the back seat. "We want to get to the Bearpaws, not wind up in a ditch."

"How fast were we going, Pa?"

"Forty or so, I guess. If we'd been going any faster you'd have hollered 'nuff. You were looking pretty peaked."

"I was not."

"Looked pretty scared to me. I guess Ma was hopping around back there like corn in a popper. How'd you like it, Ma?"

"I liked it all right," she said, "but don't do it again."

They passed a farm, and the boy waved at three open-mouthed kids in the yard. It was pretty good to be going somewhere, all right. The mountains were plainer now in the south. He could see dark canyons cutting into the slopes, and there was snow on the upper peaks.

"How soon'll we get there, Pa?"

His father tapped the pipe out and put it away and laughed. Without bothering to answer, he began to sing:

> "Oh, I dug Snoqualmie River,
>   And Lake Samamish too,

---

[1] COULEE (kōō'lǐ)—A steep-walled valley.

And paddled down to Kirklan
In a little birch canoe.

"I built the Rocky Mountains,
And placed them where they are. . . ."

It was then, with the empty flat country wheeling by like a great turntable, the wheat fields and the fences and the far red peaks of barns rotating slowly as if in a dignified dance, wheeling and slipping behind and gone, and his father singing, that the strangeness first came over the boy. Somewhere, sometime . . . and there were mountains in it, and a stream, and a swing that he had fallen out of and cried, and he had mashed ripe blackberries in his hand and his mother had wiped him off, straightening his stiff finger and wiping hard.

. . . His mind caught on that memory from a time before there was any memory, he rubbed his finger tips against his palm and slid a little down in the seat.

His father tramped on both pedals hard and leaned out of the car, looking. He swung to stare at the boy as a startled idiot might have looked, and in a voice heavy with German gutturals he said, "Vot it iss in de crass?"

"What?"

"Is in de crass somedings. Besser you bleiben right here."

He climbed out, and the boy climbed out after him. The dog jumped over the side and rushed, and in the grass by the side of the road the boy saw the biggest snake he had ever seen, long and fat and sleepy. When it pulled itself in and faced the still-legged dog he saw that the hind legs and tail of a gopher stuck out of the stretched mouth.

"What is it?" the mother said from the car, and the boy yelled back, "A snake, a great big snake, and he's got a whole gopher in his mouth!"

The father chased the pup away, found a rock, and with one careful throw crushed the big flat head. The body, as big around as the boy's ankle, tightened into a rigid convulsion of muscles, and the tail whipped back and forth.

The father lifted the snake by the tail and held it up. "Look," he said. "He's no longer than I am." But the mother made a face and turned her head while he fastened it in the forked top of a fence post. It trailed almost two feet on the ground. The tail still twitched.

"He'll twitch till the sun goes down," the father said. He climbed into the car again, and the boy followed.

"What was it, Pa?"

"Milk snake. They come into barns sometimes and milk the cows dry. You saw what he did to that gopher. Milk a cow dry as powder in ten minutes."

"Gee," the boy said. He sat back and thought about how long and slick the gopher had been, and how the snake's mouth was all stretched, and it was a good feeling to have been along and to have shared something like that with his father. It was a trophy, a thing you would remember all your life, and you could tell about it. And while he was thinking that already, even before they got to the mountains at all, he had something to remember about the trip, he remembered that just before they saw the snake he had been remembering something else, and he puckered his eyes in the sun, thinking. He had been right on the edge of it, it was right on the tip of his tongue, and then his father had tramped on the pedals. But it was something a long time ago, and there was a strangeness about it, something bothersome and a little scary, and it hurt his head the way it hurt his head sometimes to do arithmetical sums without pencil and paper. When you did them in your head something went round and round, and you had to keep looking inside to make sure you didn't lose sight of the figures that were pasted up there somewhere, and if you did it very long at a time you got a sick headache out of it. It was something like that when he had almost remembered just a while ago, only he hadn't quite been able to see what he knew was there. . . .

By ten o'clock they had left the graded road and were chugging up a winding trail with toothed rocks embedded in the ruts. Ahead of them the mountains looked low and disappointing, treeless, brown. The trail ducked into a narrow gulch and the sides rose up around them, reddish gravel covered with bunch grass and sage.

"Gee whiz," the boy said. "These don't look like mountains."

"What'd you expect?" his father said. "Expect to step out onto a glacier or something?"

"But there aren't any trees," the boy said. "Gee whiz, there isn't even any water."

He stood up to look ahead. His father's foot went down on the low pedal, and the Ford growled at the grade. "Come on, Lena," his father said. He hitched himself back and forward in the seat, helping the car over the hill, and then, as they barely pulled over the hump and the sides of the gully fell away, there were the real mountains, high as heaven, the high slopes spiked and tufted with trees, and directly ahead of them a magnificent V-shaped door with the sun touching grey cliffs far back in, and a straight-edged violet shadow streaming down from the eastern peak clear to the canyon floor.

"Well?" the father's voice said. "I guess if you don't like it we can drop you off here and pick you up on the way back."

The boy turned to his mother. She was sitting far forward on the edge of the seat. "I guess we want to come along all right," she said, and laughed as if she might cry. "Anything as beautiful as that! Don't we, sonny?"

"You bet," he said. He remained standing all the way up over the gentle slope of the alluvial fan[2] that aproned out from the canyon's mouth, and when they passed under the violet shadow, not violet any more but cool grey, he tipped his head back and looked up miles and miles to the broken rock above.

The road got rougher. "Sit down," his father said. "First thing you know you'll fall out on your head and sprain both your ankles."

He was in his very best mood. He said funny things to the car, coaxing it over steep pitches. He talked to it like a horse, patted it on the dashboard, promised it an apple when they got there. Above them the canyon walls opened out and back, went up steeply

---

[2] ALLUVIAL (ă-lū'vĭ-ăl) FAN—The sand or gravel deposit of a stream as it emerges from a gorge upon an open plain.

high and high and high, beyond the first walls that the boy had thought so terrific, away beyond those, piling peak on peak, and the sun touched and missed and touched again.

"Yay!" the boy said. He was standing up, watching the deep insides of the earth appear behind the angled rock, and his mind was soaring again, up into the heights where a hawk or eagle circled like a toy bird on a string.

"How do you like it?" his mother shouted at him. He turned around and nodded his head, and she smiled at him, wrinkling her eyes. She looked excited herself. Her face had colour in it, and the varnished cherries bouncing on her hat gave her a reckless, girlish look.

"Hi, Ma," he said, and grinned.

"Hi yourself," she said, and grinned right back. He lifted his face and yelled for the very pressure of happiness inside him.

They lay on a ledge high up on the sunny east slope and looked out to the north through the notch cut as sharply as a wedge out of a pie. Far below them the golden plain spread level, golden-tawny grass and golden-green wheat checker-boarded in a pattern as wide as the world. Back of them the spring they had followed up the slope welled out of the ledge, spread out in a small swampy spot, and trickled off down the hill. There were trees, a thick cluster of spruce against the bulge of the wall above them, a clump of twinkling, sunny aspen down the slope, and in the canyon bottom below them a dense forest of soft maple. The mother had a bouquet of leaves in her hand, a little bunch of pine cones on the ground beside her. The three lay quietly, looking down over the steeply dropping wall to the V-shaped door, and beyond that to the interminable plain.

The boy wriggled his back against the rock, put his hand down to shift himself, brought it up again prickled with brown spruce needles. He picked them off, still staring out over the canyon gateway. They were far above the world he knew. The air was cleaner, thinner. There was cold water running from the rock, and all around there were trees. And over the whole canyon, like a haze in the clear air, was that other thing, that memory or ghost of a memory, a swing he had fallen out of, a feel of his hands sticky with crushy blackberries, his skin drinking cool shade, and his father's anger—the reflection of ecstasy and the shadow of tears.

"I never knew till this minute," his mother said, "how much I've missed the trees."

Nobody answered. They were all stuffed with lunch, pleasantly tired after the climb. The father lay staring off down the canyon, and the sour smell of his pipe, in that air, was pleasant and clean. The boy saw his mother put the stem of a maple leaf in her mouth and make a half-pleased face at the bitter taste.

The father rose and dug a tin cup from the picnic box, walked to the spring, and dipped himself a drink. He made a breathy sound of satisfaction. "So cold it hurts your teeth," he said. He brought the mother a cup, and she drank.

"Brucie?" she said, motioning with the cup.

He started to get up, but his father filled the cup and brought it, making believe he was going to pour it on him. The boy ducked and reached for the cup. With his eyes on his father over the cup's rim, he drank, testing the icy water to see if it really did hurt the teeth. The water was cold and silvery in his mouth, and when he swallowed he felt it cold clear down to his stomach.

"It doesn't either hurt your teeth," he said. He poured a little of it on his arm, and something jumped in his skin. It was his skin that remembered. Something numbingly cold, and then warm. He felt it now, the way you waded in it.

"Mom," he said.

"What?"

"Was it in Washington we went on a picnic like this and picked blackberries and I fell out of a swing and there were big trees, and we found a river that was half cold and half warm?"

His father was relighting his pipe. "What do you know about Washington?" he said. "You were only knee-high to a grasshopper when we lived there."

"Well, I remember," the boy said. "I've been remembering it all day long, ever since you sang that song about building the Rocky Mountains. You sang it that day, too. Don't you remember, Mom?"

"I don't know," she said doubtfully. "We went on picnics in Washington."

"What's this about a river with hot and cold running water?" his father said. "You must remember some time you had a bath in a bathtub."

"I do not," the boy said. "I got blackberries mashed all over my hands and Mom scrubbed me off, and then we found that river and we waded in it and half was hot and half was cold."

"Oh-h-h," his mother said. "I believe I do. . . . Harry, you remember once up in the Cascades, when we went out with the Curtises? And little Bill Curtis fell off the dock into the lake." She turned to the boy. "Was there a summer cottage there, a brown shingled house?"

"I don't know," the boy said. "I don't remember any Curtises. But I remember blackberries and that river and a swing."

"Your head is full of blackberries," his father said. "If it was the time we went out with the Curtises there weren't any blackberries. That was in the spring."

"No," the mother said. "It was in the fall. It was just before we moved to Redmond. And I think there was a place where one river from the mountains ran into another one from the valley, and they ran alongside each other in the same channel. The mountain one was a lot colder. Don't you remember that trip with the Curtises, Harry?"

"Sure I remember it," the father said. "We hired a buckboard and saw a black bear and I won six bits from Joe Curtis pitching horseshoes."

"That's right," the mother said. "You remember the bear, Brucie."

The boy shook his head. There wasn't any bear in what he remembered. Just feelings, and things that made his skin prickle.

His mother was looking at him, a little puzzled wrinkle between her eyes. "It's funny you should remember such different things than we remember," she said. "Everything means something different to everybody, I guess." She laughed, and the boy thought her eyes looked very odd and bright. "It makes me feel as if I didn't know you at all," she said. She brushed her face with the handful of leaves and looked at the father, gathering up odds and ends and putting them in the picnic box. "I wonder what each of us will remember about to-day?"

"I wouldn't worry about it," the father said. "You can depend on Bub here to remember a lot of things that didn't happen."

"I don't think he does," she said. "He's got a good memory."

The father picked up the box. "It takes a good memory to remember things that never happened," he said. "I remember once a garter snake crawled into my cradle and I used it for a belt to keep my breechclout on. They took it away from me and I bawled the crib so full of tears I had to swim for shore. I drifted in three days later on a checkerboard raft with a didie for a sail."

The boy stood up and brushed off his pants. "You do too remember that river," he said.

His father grinned at him. "Sure. Only it wasn't quite as hot and cold as you make it out."

It was evening in the canyon, but when they reached the mouth again they emerged into full afternoon, with two hours of sun left them. The father stopped the car before they dipped into the gravelly wash between the foothills, purpling in the shadows, the rock glowing golden-red far back on the faces of the inner peaks. The mother still held her bouquet of maple leaves in her hand.

"Well, there go the Mountains of the Moon," she said. The moment was almost solemn. In the front seat the boy stood looking back. He felt the sun strong against the side of his face, and the mountains sheering up before him were very real.

In a little while, as they went forth, they would begin to melt together, and the patches of snow would appear far up on the northern slopes. His eyes went curiously out of focus, and he saw the mountains as they would appear from the homestead on a hot day, a ghostly line on the horizon.

He felt his father twist to look at him, but the trance was so strong on him that he didn't look down for a minute. When he did he caught his mother and father looking at each other, the look they had sometimes when he had pleased them and made them proud of him.

"Okay," his father said, and stabbed him in the ribs with a hard thumb. "Wipe the black bears out of your eyes."

He started the car again, and as they bounced down the rocky trail toward the road he sang at the top of his voice, bellowing into the still, hot afternoon—

> "I had a kid and his name was Brucie,
> Squeezed black bears and found them juicy,
> Washed them off in a hot-cold river,
> Now you boil and now you shiver,
> Caught his pants so full of trout
> He couldn't sit down till he got them out.
> Trout were boiled from the hot-side river,
> Trout from the cold side raw as liver,
> Ate the boiled ones, ate the raw,
> And then went howling home to Maw."

The boy looked up at his father, his laughter bubbling up, everything wonderful, the day a swell day, his mother clapping hands in time to his father's fool singing.

"Aw, for gosh sakes," he said, and ducked when his father pretended he was going to swat him one.

DISCUSSING THE STORY

1. Most families now and then enjoy the kind of outing told about in this story. Why was this particular picnic such an eventful day for this family? Do you think they often took such trips?

2. Nothing exciting or extraordinary happened on this picnic, but it was a happy day. What slight incidents on the way to the mountains did the whole family enjoy?

3. What early childhood experience did this day recall for the boy? Have you ever had a similar experience of trying to recall the details of a dimly remembered incident? What kind of details usually stand out in our memories? Do you think age and experience have anything to do with the kind of things we remember?

4. How did the boy's parents contribute to the fun of this outing? Tell about a day of fun you have enjoyed with your own family.

PRAYERS OF STEEL ✴ CARL SANDBURG

LAY me on an anvil, O God.
Beat me and hammer me into a crowbar.
Let me pry loose old walls;
Let me lift and loosen old foundations.

5 Lay me on an anvil, O God.
Beat me and hammer me into a steel spike.
Drive me into the girders that hold a skyscraper together.
Take red-hot rivets and fasten me into the central girders.
Let me be the great nail holding a skyscraper through blue
   nights into white stars.

CLUES TO THE MEANING

1. In "Prayers of Steel" Carl Sandburg prays that he may become a part of the progress of Western civilization. In what sense might an individual be like a crowbar and help to tear down things that are old?

Do you think he means to tear down only buildings, or does he mean to destroy old ideas and ways, too? Can you think of any old things that need to be destroyed and replaced by new ones?

2. What is the purpose of rivets and spikes? How can a person be somewhat like a rivet or spike? Does this idea suggest to you that even such a detail as a single spike in a building is of great importance?

IF — ✣ RUDYARD KIPLING

B1	IF you can keep your head when all about you
	Are losing theirs and blaming it on you;
B2	If you can trust yourself when all men doubt you,
	And make allowance for their doubting too;
All 5	If you can wait and not be tired by waiting,
	Or being lied about don't deal in lies,
	Or being hated don't give way to hating,
	And yet don't look too good nor talk too wise:

G1	If you can dream—and not make dreams your master;
G2 10	If you can think—and not make thoughts your aim;
G	If you can meet with Triumph and Disaster
	And treat these two imposters just the same;
B	If you can bear to hear the truth you've spoken
	Twisted by knaves to make a trap for fools,
15	Or watch the things you gave your life to, broken,
	And stoop and build 'em up with worn-out tools:

All	If you can make one heap of all your winnings
	And risk it on one turn of pitch-and-toss,
	And lose, and start again at your beginnings
20	And never breathe a word about your loss;
G	If you can force your heart and nerve and sinew
	To serve your turn long after they are gone,
	And so hold on when there is nothing in you
	Except the Will which says to them: "Hold on!"

B 25 If you can talk with crowds and keep your virtue,
    Or walk with kings—nor lose the common touch,
   If neither foes nor loving friends can hurt you,
    If all men count with you, but none too much;
All   If you can fill the unforgiving minute
 30 With sixty seconds' worth of distance run,
   Yours is the Earth and everything that's in it,
    And—what is more—you'll be a Man, my son!

CLUES TO THE MEANING

It has often been said that it is easier to give advice than to be guided by it. However, when the advice comes from a man who made a great name for himself, and who found through experience what makes people worth while, his words are worth thinking about.

1. Why is it so hard to keep yourself under control when you are being blamed for something you did not do? Can you explain why it is better to keep a level head than to allow yourself to explode at such a time?

2. Why is it important to dream? What happens if there is too much dreaming without action? Explain what you think your attitude should be whether you win or lose.

3. What does Mr. Kipling say about having a swelled head about something you have done? about the wise use of all your time? Which, in your opinion, is the hardest "If"?

YOUTH* 🦋 LANGSTON HUGHES

All WE HAVE tomorrow
   Bright before us
   Like a flame.

   Yesterday
 5 A night-gone thing,
   A sun-down name.

And dawn-today
Broad arch above the road we came.

We march!

CLUES TO THE MEANING

In "Youth" the poet is asking us to think about the hope and opportunity that is available to us in every to-morrow. Explain what you think our attitude should be toward the days that are to come. How should we feel about the day that is gone? Explain whether you think remembering the things you have done or thinking of things to be done is of more importance.

"TO YOU IS BORN" ⚜ DORIS J. BERRY

ANNOUNCER. *It is dusk in Bethlehem, the town of David. The low-roofed white-walled houses squat close to the darkening ground. In the narrow streets noisy throngs of men and women hurry by. On the outskirts of the town the yellow light of an oil lamp flickers into unsteady life in the window of a one-roomed hut. This is the home of Judah the shepherd and his wife Rachel. (Judah is forty years old).*

Judah (irritated). Must you always be late with the evening meal when I start for the fields at night?
Rachel. Listen to him! Always be late indeed! As if a woman had nothing else to do but guard the fire and prepare the meals.
Judah. Why were you so late getting back from the well?
Rachel. I had to stand in line three times as long as usual waiting to get water. The town is simply bursting with people of the line of David.
Judah. Rome never thinks of all the trouble and commotion she causes when she issues a decree. "Go to the town of your forefathers that you may be taxed"—and straightway the roads are filled with poor devils and their goods.

Rachel. And because Bethlehem is David's town, we must suffer the inconvenience of these crowds of his descendants. I talked to a woman from Galilee. There were others in their party —a man and woman from Nazareth, I think she said. I feel sorry for the woman. Her time is due with child and she's had all that weary travel . . . (*rattling on*). You know, that star is brighter still to-night, Judah. It was as though the moon was up when I came through the streets. The star was straight above me and so low.

Judah. Don't chatter so, Rachel. I want my meal.

Rachel. It's ready now. Must you be so impatient? One would think you liked your work you are so impatient to be off.

Judah. It is a thankless business guarding silly sheep. If one but runs away they all follow in a flood even though they would break their necks on the rocks. And then the poor shepherd must after them to head them off.

Rachel. Can you not call them?

Judah. Not I. They pay no heed to me. Reuben says it is because I do not love them. (*Laughs*). As if one could love a silly sheep! Ah, well, I'll not be a shepherd all my days.

Rachel. Judah, why will you never be content? It is always this way . . . a few months at a task and you can stand it no longer. You are always complaining, always moving on. Why do you not think of me a little and what it means to be the wife of a man who cannot keep his work?

Judah (*flaring*). So busy tongues are wagging about what concerns them not! Who says I cannot keep my work?

Rachel. Never mind who says it. It is true. You know it.

Judah. It is not true. Can I help it if Ben Ezra had not enough work in the carpenter shop to keep another busy too?

Rachel. He has hired another helper since you left. You know he told you to go because of your sharp tongue. You drove the trade from his shop.

Judah. Bar Benjamin wanted his nephew to share his profits in the inn.

Rachel. That was the way he chose to get you from his doors. And if you are not careful Nathan will tell you soon that his father wants a shepherd from his brother's sons, and you will have to go again.

Judah. Pah! That will not. . . .

Rachel (pleading). Do you not see, Judah, it is your own fault that you must change from work to work? (*Self pity*). Do you not care for the disgrace you bring upon your wife? I am ashamed to go to the well. The other women talk and laugh together but they fall silent when I draw near. I see their glances of pity.

Judah. Have done! A woman has no right to speak thus to her husband! I will hear no more! Bring me my cloak.

Rachel But your food is untouched.

Judah. Bring me my cloak!

Rachel (exasperated). Here. But it is the truth I speak, Judah. Why will you not learn?

Sound of heavy door slamming. Dead air. Then fade in sounds of lowing sheep. Establish and hold behind.

Reuben (quiet). There's something in the air to-night, Nathan. The sheep are restless. As if we're all waiting for something. (*Reuben is sixty years old*).

Nathan (laughs). Waiting for Judah to come. He should have been here just after sundown. (*Nathan is eighteen years old*).

Reuben. I don't mean that. This is something big. I've been a shepherd on these hills for thirty years. I know the weather before it comes by the whisperings of the wind on the hillside, and I know the moods of the sheep as I know the knots in my shepherd's crook. This is no ordinary night. The hillsides are holding their breath. Waiting.

Nathan. I feel it too. Do you suppose it has anything to do with the star, Reuben? It's brighter than ever to-night.

Reuben. And closer. Every night it has drawn nearer and now it has stopped. Right over Bethlehem, behind the hills.

Nathan. What do you suppose it means?

Sound of sheep during pause.

Reuben. Listen! (*Pause.*)

Nathan. It's Judah at last. (*Raising his voice*). Why are you so late, Judah?

Reuben. Nathan and I have been guarding the sheep alone these last hours.

Judah (*irritated*). Could Machir not have stayed until I came?

Reuben. He had to be off to his cousin's wedding feast.

Nathan. Besides, you know you should have been here at sundown. My father wants shepherds he can trust.

Judah (*exploding*). Stop nagging, will you? I know I'm late! My wife was late with the evening meal. (*Awkward pause*).

Nathan (*to break the ice*). Are . . . are the crowds still growing in Bethlehem?

Judah. One can hardly walk through the streets for the jostling.

Reuben. I'm afraid some people will not find lodging. The inn must be full long before this.

Judah. Curse these Romans girding us down with their laws and their taxes. When will they be overthrown?

Nathan (*without bitterness*). Surely the time must come soon for our people to be released. The Lord cannot shut His eyes much longer to our sufferings.

Reuben. Suffering teaches much, lad. Perhaps Israel has learned the lessons the Lord has set her and the time is coming when He will visit and redeem His people. These last few weeks my heart has been stirring with a great hope . . . that the scriptures will be fulfilled.

Nathan. The Messiah?

Reuben. Yes.

Nathan. Do you think the star . . . ?

Reuben. I do not know. But these last nights the spirit of the Lord has walked upon these hills of Bethlehem.

Nathan (*eager*). Won't it be splendid when He comes! He will sweep down from heaven in rolling clouds of blackness and will stretch forth His hand, and the Romans will be scattered into the ocean and the people of Israel will be free!

Judah. Nonsense!

Reuben. Leave the boy be, Judah. Older heads than his have dreamed such dreams.

Nathan. If I could only go to the Messiah when He comes and help Him. . . . Sometimes at night, Reuben, when you think I'm asleep by the fire, I'm really off serving the Messiah . . . being His cupbearer, or His messenger. There's nothing I would rather do than lay my life at His feet!

Judah. It's little need the Messiah would have for the likes of you.

Reuben. Lay that thorn bush on the fire, Judah. It's burning down.

Nathan. Look! Look at the light!

Judah. It's the sparks from the fire!

Nathan. No, it isn't! Over there in the sky above Bethlehem!

Reuben. The sky is ablaze around the star!

Judah (stark fear). Lord save us from our sins!

Sound of mixed voices singing, fades up.

Nathan. The whole sky is on fire!

Reuben. This is holy ground! Let us to our knees!

Judah (terrified). Oh Lord, strike not Thy people! Depart from us! Let not this thing come nigh unto us, Oh Lord!

Wordless chorus swells up in triumphant ecstasy then ceases abruptly for:

Heavenly Voice. Fear not! . . . For behold, I bring you good tidings of great joy which shall be to all people. For unto you is born this day in the city of David a Saviour, which is Christ the Lord. And this shall be a sign unto you; ye shall find the babe wrapped in swaddling clothes, lying in a manger.

Chorus in (strongly). Glory to God in the highest, and on earth peace, good will toward men.

Chorus changes to wordless strain which dies away.

Dead Air.

Nathan (dazed). The light is gone!
Reuben (in awe). "For unto us a child is born, unto us a son is given. . . ."
Nathan. The angels spoke to us!
Judah. They said "Fear not!" . . . The angel of the Lord told us not to be afraid.
Reuben. In Bethlehem, the city of David . . . the Messiah has come!
Nathan. I want to see the baby. The angel said we would find him in a manger. Let us go to Bethlehem.
Judah. I shall stay here.
Reuben. The sheep will be safe, Judah. This is no ordinary night.
Judah. You say truly! I would not dare to leave my duty now. *(Sotto voce).* That awful light!
Nathan. Come with us, Judah. We shall see the babe.
Judah (emphatic). No.
Reuben. As you will, then. Come, Nathan.

Sound of lowing sheep for several seconds.

Judah (sotto voce). Let them go . . . but what if that light should come again? . . . will Nathan make me lose this work? What would Rachel say? I could not face her this time and say, "I am no more a shepherd." . . . What would I do? . . . The angel said, "Fear *not.*" Others do not fear as I. It was my voice that cried out in fear just now—not theirs. . . . I've always been afraid—that's why I lashed out at Nathan when he said that I was late. . . . I was afraid he'd make me lose my work. . . . I *(sudden flash).* But they nag me so! How can a man work when—*(honest).* But I always lost my temper when Ben Ezra scolded me about my work. . . . I was afraid of what Rachel would say if she knew . . . and then he let me go and that was worse. . . . And with Asa it was the same. . . . Water carrier, carpenter . . . stable boy, shepherd. . . . I've been them all . . . it's always been the same. *(Beaten).* And Rachel knows.

Sound of sheep in pause.

(*Puzzled*). Why do I say these things? What has happened inside my mind since I heard the angel speak? . . . But the angel said "Fear *not*" . . . He spoke to *me*. . . . But if I do not fear, what do I trust? . . . Oh God, what do I trust? . . . He said, "Good tidings of great joy." In Bethlehem. There must be something more. I must go and see.

Music with decision, fading into sound of footsteps on cobbles, walking purposefully. Stops.

Judah. Reuben!
Reuben (*off, coming up*). Judah, is that you? So you came after all.
Judah. I had to come.
Reuben. I know. There's something very strange about this, Judah. Nathan and I came to the inn, thinking the keeper would know all the news of the town. We asked him where the child is to be found, and he stared and said, "What child?"
Nathan. And then we said, "Did you not see the light and hear the angels?" And he looked at us and laughed.
Judah. The streets were empty as I came along. There was not a single light.
Nathan. Except that one over there.
Judah. That's just the stable of the inn.
Reuben. But the angel said, "Lying in a manger." Come quickly.

Sound of heavy door opening slowly.

Nathan. Oh!
Reuben. The child!
Joseph (*warm and quiet*). Come in, my friends, we have been expecting you.
Reuben. To-night we were keeping watch over our flocks on

the hills and a great light shone 'round us. Angels told us of the child.

Mary (off). Come and see Him.

Nathan. He is so little!

Reuben. How peacefully He sleeps!

Mary. His name is Jesus.

Joseph. It was the Lord who named Him so.

Mary. He told me I should bring forth a son, and call His name Jesus, for He shall save the people from their sins.

Reuben. You have come here to be taxed?

Joseph. Yes. Mary and I are from Nazareth.

Reuben. Are you of David's line, even as the prophet said?

Joseph. Even so.

Mary. The angel said the Lord would give unto the child the throne of David.

Nathan. Is He to be a King?

Mary. We know only what the angel told us. He said the kingdom would last forever.

Judah (indignant). A king should not be born in a stable. You should have insisted that the inn keeper give you a room.

Joseph. He had no room. The town is crowded so that every bed was taken long before we came.

Mary. We are comfortable here. Joseph asked that hide from the village carpenter, and nailed it so that draughts do not reach me and the babe.

Judah. How you must hate Rome! To make you travel at a time like this! I too have felt her cruelty. One day upon the highway a Roman soldier. . . .

Joseph (interrupting). You misunderstand us, friend. We do not hate Rome. We feel that in our coming here to Bethlehem the will of God has been fulfilled. This child of David's line has been born in David's town and we rejoice that it is so.

Reuben. There have been others here to see the child?

Mary. No one. You are the first.

Reuben. The first? Poor shepherds in the fields, and we were chosen by the Lord to be the first to see the King. We are not worthy.

Mary. I felt as you when the angel said I would be the mother of the Son of God. But the Lord looks not on rank and wealth. He looks upon men's hearts. He knows that yours are good.

Judah (desperate). Not mine! There is no good in me!

Joseph. That is not so, or you would not be here to-night. *(Gently).* Why did you come?

Judah (confused). I . . . the angel said, "Fear not" . . . I've always been afraid . . . and I thought . . . I know not what I thought . . . but I was compelled to come.

Joseph. I know. Sometimes I am afraid too. This journey with Mary. . . . At first I was afraid—for her. But God assured me He would watch over us, and we travelled with complete trust in His care.

Judah (wistful). I wish I had your faith.

Joseph. You can have faith. God honours trust.

Mary. He always takes away our fears. I was afraid for my son when God said He would be a king. Sometimes the world is not kind to Kings. There must be heartache and danger ahead for Him. But now I know that the Lord will show the way.

Nathan (eager). Do you think . . . could I help Him with His kingdom? I would give my life!

Joseph. He is but a baby, lad. But the Lord sent you here to-night. He must have had a reason. Keep your heart to His will and you will know.

Reuben. Are you going to stay here with the child?

Joseph. We do not know. But God will show us in His good time.

Reuben. This night the Lord has laid His hand upon us all. We do not yet know His mighty purpose; we only know that we are privileged beyond the rank of kings. Sir, may we pay homage to the child before we go? In prayer and thankfulness.

Joseph. Come nearer and kneel here.

Pause.

Reuben. The Lord be with the three of you.

Sound of door opening and closing.
Sound of three sets of footsteps walking slowly.

Nathan (excited). Where are we going now? Who shall we tell first?

Reuben (in a daze). What did you say?

Nathan. Whom shall we tell about the Messiah?

Judah. No one.

Nathan (ignoring him). It will be wonderful to tell that we were the first to see the King. Where shall we go? I want to tell my father.

Judah. We're going back to the sheep.

Nathan. Oh, be quiet, Judah. You're always against everything. Reuben, who shall we go to first?

Reuben. Judah's right, Nathan. We should go back to the sheep.

Nathan. But why? All Israel is waiting for this news. . . . You do believe that the baby is the Messiah, don't you, Reuben?

Reuben. With my whole heart. But that is why we must go back to our work. The angel did not tell us to spread the news abroad. Nor has God shown the mother and father what they shall do next. We, too, must wait for His leading.

Nathan. I did not think of that. *(humbly)*: I have much to learn. It seems I was just a child when I babbled about how the Messiah would come with rolling clouds of blackness and great splendour. . . . And now I've seen Him and He's just a baby born in a stable. When I was kneeling there beside the manger I felt so close to the Lord, and I wanted to serve Him more than ever I did when I dreamed beside the fire. And yet when I come away the first thing I think of doing is all wrong. How will I ever learn?

Reuben. God loves an eager heart, lad. You're young, yet He chose you to hear His message. It's just as Joseph said, keep your heart close to the will of the Lord, and He will direct you. Perhaps what He wants now is for you to be faithful in your work. That is where He spoke to you first.

Nathan. That's not as exciting as being a cupbearer to a King!

Judah (beaten). That's fine for Nathan, but what about me? I'm different. God can speak to you. You're good, you're kind. But everybody knows what I am like. A coward, full of hate and meanness. . . . Even my fears are different. They said they knew what fear was like but their fears were not as mine. His were for his wife, and the mother's for her son . . . but mine, mine were for myself, my work, what people think of me. . . . I wish it were not so!

Nathan. He said God honours trust. I wonder what he meant.

Judah (hopeless). How can you trust what you do not know? God never has been real to me.

Reuben. Was He not real to-night?

Nathan. Nor to me, Judah. That's why I talked the way I did about clouds and cupbearers and all that show. But now I want to know the Lord the way that Mary and Joseph do . . . though I don't understand how.

Judah. Joseph said there must be good in me, but how can I be sure?

Reuben. Do you not feel some good thing stirring, in your hearts? Act on it.

Judah. I'm so confused. . . . I wonder what Rachel would say to what I'm thinking now.

Troubled music up.

Rachel (still on edge). You say a light shone 'round you in the fields? There was no light in Bethlehem.

Judah (quiet, no irritation). I know. The streets were dark and empty when we reached the town. But we found the manger, and the baby just as the angel said. And something happened to me there, Rachel. I saw things I had never seen before.

Rachel. What was the baby like?

Judah. He slept. So little and so calm. But that is not what I mean. The things I saw here about me . . . and us.

Rachel. How was the mother?

Judah. Her face shone. And so did Joseph's. But that was not what mattered. It was what was in the air.

Rachel. More angels?

Judah. No. The love. The love they bore each other and their love of God. I envied them their happiness, Rachel. They were so sure, so satisfied. And I thought of us when we were married. Then you looked at me the way that Mary looked at Joseph.

Rachel. It's plain they have not been married long.

Judah. I blamed you for having changed. . . . Sometimes I'm afraid you hate me now. . . . But suddenly I saw myself as I really am.

Rachel. I've tried to tell you all these years.

Judah. I know. But I never understood before. I remembered how much you have done without because I could not keep my work. And how angry I was last week when you said the fault was mine. I know now you were right.

Rachel. Well! At last.

Judah. You make this very hard for me, Rachel.

Rachel. I'm sure I don't know why. As you've just said yourself, I've known this all along, and tried to tell you but you would not listen. Still, I must admit that something has made you different.

Judah. It was the angel who spoke to me, and seeing the baby, and the parents in the stable. I saw God for the first time. I think He put His hand on me that night. . . . These last days when I've been with the sheep, I've thought of nothing else . . . Rachel, I do want to be different, to try again to have a happy home as we had once.

Rachel. Hmm. You say that they are still in town? It must be hard for them to manage, with her first baby, and in the stable too. I dare say they could use some of this bread I baked today. I wonder if she would like some linen for the child. (*Fading*). I'll take it right away.

Walking music fading into sound of (knock) on heavy door.

Mary. Come in.

Sound of door opening.

Mary. Do come in.

Rachel (off). You are Mary, with the babe?

Mary. Yes.

Rachel (coming up). I'm Rachel. . . . The wife of Judah the shepherd who was here the night the child was born.

Mary. I'm glad you came. Do sit on this bench. Or would you like to see Jesus first. He's over here. I'll pick Him up.

Rachel. How peacefully He sleeps. . . . He's very beautiful.

Mary. Yes, He is.

Rachel. This morning was my baking day. I thought you might be able to use some loaves since you are in this—since you have no oven.

Mary. Why, thank you, my dear. How kind you are.

Rachel. No, not kind. I wanted to see you and your husband, and the baby too. Forgive me for my blunt tongue, but I must tell the truth.

Mary. Of course.

Rachel. I wanted to see a woman and a man who in one short visit could tell my husband all his faults, and have him listen. I've been trying all these years.

Mary. We said nothing about his faults. He talked to us.

Rachel. You must have cast a spell on him.

Mary. Say rather that the Lord laid His hand on him.

Rachel. Judah said that too! What do you mean?

Mary. Sometimes God has a special task for us to do. He has one for me. And one for Joseph. He wants us to bring this child up as His own son. And we will do in all things as He directs us. The other night He spoke to shepherds keeping watch over their flocks and told them of our child. He spoke to them, and to no others here in Bethlehem. There must have been a purpose.

Rachel (puzzled). It seems as though there were, when I hear you say it. But why would the Lord want Judah? *(Working up).* He has a bad temper. He cannot hold his work. He . . . .

Mary. It is not for us to judge if one is worthy. God decides that. We must look to our own hearts.

Rachel. Do you mean . . . there might be something wrong with me?

Pause.

Rachel (*defensive*). But I wait on him hand and foot. I prepare his meals and fetch his cloak. And he's always so ungrateful!

Mary. How do you do these things?

Rachel. I do not understand.

Mary. Do you do them out of love for your husband?

Rachel. Why of course . . . at least I used to. . . . I think I've forgotten that the last few years. (*softening*). Strange, I remember how I used to have the meals ready and wait so eagerly for his coming. He used to enjoy them so. . . (*irritated*). Now he never has a good word for anything I cook.

Mary. Perhaps the meals are different now.

Rachel (*surprised*). Yes. They are. . . . It doesn't seem to matter any more. . . . They're cold . . . or late . . . they're often late now . . . Oh!

Mary. Yes?

Rachel. I never thought of it before, but when Ben Ezra asked Joseph to leave the carpenter shop one of the reasons was that Judah was so often late. (*A difficult admission*). And it was my fault many times.

Mary. We women can do much to help our husbands.

Rachel. I've tried to help. I've told him where he's wrong. But he never listens.

Mary. How do you tell him?

Rachel. You do ask the strangest questions. . . . I think I see why Judah has been different since he was here. How do I tell him? (*thoughtful*). I suppose you mean, do I tell him in love? . . . I certainly tell him what he should hear . . . but . . . maybe my voice is not as gentle as a dove's . . . and I . . . well, to put it plainly, I suppose I nag at him. . . . (*touchingly*). It doesn't seem to help.

Mary (*smile in voice*). It never does.

Rachel. You truly believe that? You must, for it shines in your face. . . You give out love. And so, in some strange way, does that child in your arms. I can feel it in the room . . . (*breaking*). Oh,

Mary, I am not happy. You have such peace and joy. . . . I had almost forgotten what love is like . . . but when we were married, Judah was very different.

Mary. And you know why.

Rachel (*sobbing*). Yes. I see that now. This morning Judah said he'd blamed me for having changed. He thinks I hate him now.

Mary. And do you?

Rachel. Oh no! But my heart has grown hard with his failures and I tried to drive him toward success. . . (*pathetic*). Where do you get your patience, Mary?

Mary. In prayer.

Rachel. Yes. That, too, I had forgotten. I used to know.

Mary. It always is the way.

Rachel. I shall remember. . . . I must go now. (*eagerly*). I must not be late with the meal this evening. There is so much to say to Judah before he returns to the fields. . . . Good-bye, Mary

Mary. Good-bye, my dear.

Rachel. I . . . it is so little to say "thank you". . . . God bless you, Mary!

Music happy and intense, up to quiet pastoral fading into sound of lowing sheep.

Nathan (*happy*). Do I look any different, Reuben?

Reuben (*amused*). I don't know, Nathan.

Nathan. This morning I had an idea and I must look different since then because I feel so different.

Reuben. Why?

Judah (*calling off*). Hello-oh!

Nathan. Good, there's Judah back already.

Reuben. He's early. (*semi-call*). Is anything wrong, Judah?

Judah (*up cheerfully*). I'm ahead of time. We had an early supper.

Reuben. You make that sound important.

Judah. It is. There's something new in the household of Rachel and Judah.

Nathan. What is it?

Judah. Happiness.

Nathan. So you found it too?

Judah. Too? Nathan, what has happened to you? Your face is shining, just like Mary's and Joseph's.

Nathan. I know. It happened this morning. . . . Ever since that night that Reuben said the Lord might want me to stay here with the sheep there's been resentment in my heart. I was sure that because God had spoken to me He must want me to do something great—though I had no idea what it might be. But Joseph's words kept ringing in my mind.

Reuben. About keeping close to the will of the Lord?

Nathan. Yes. I could not understand it very well but this morning when I woke, suddenly I knew. It's the same thing as the prophet said, "What does the Lord require of you but to do justly . . ." and I stopped right there. Because I don't do justly. . . (*sincere*). I have not been just to you, Judah. I've criticized you . . . almost hated you at times. I'm sorry now. Can we be better friends?

Judah. You hated me because I was hateful, Nathan. I'm sorry too. I'd like to be your friend.

Nathan. And I see now that I don't have to wait till the Messiah grows up to serve the Lord. I can do it now. Right here.

Judah. I've learned that, too, Nathan.

Nathan. How wonderful are the ways of the Lord! The angel told the mother Mary to call the child Jesus for He shall save the people from their sins. The babe is only a few days old yet already His spirit has transformed our lives.

Nathan. He has brought purpose to my life.

Judah. And happiness and trust to mine.

Reuben. And to my soul a great peace and a certain knowledge that the Lord is with His people.

Instrumental music: "Joy to the World, the Lord hath Come."

DISCUSSING THE PLAY

This play illustrates how the spirit of the true meaning of Christmas resulted in happiness for a group of shepherds and how it changed their relationships among themselves and with others. As you read the play, try to imagine the action that is taking place. Better still, have some of the members of your class present it as if they were a company of radio players producing the play for a broadcast. It was actually written and produced as part of a Christmas programme of the Canadian Broadcasting Corporation.

1. What important characteristic of the real spirit of Christmas is illustrated in this play?

2. As the play begins, what impression do you form of Judah? of Rachel?

3. In what ways do the shepherds show that they are interested in their work? in religious matters?

4. What do the rest of the shepherds think of Judah?

5. You might read the Bible story of the nativity and compare it with the story presented here. In what ways is it much the same? What added purpose did the writer of this play have that was not part of the Bible story? Give possible reasons for introducing this.

6. What was Judah's first reaction to the scene he saw at the manger in Bethlehem? Why did he react in this way?

7. What was the ultimate effect which this scene had upon Judah and upon the rest of the shepherds?

8. Discuss the reasons which prompted Rachel to visit Mary and the Child. What was the result of this visit?

9. Tell the class about other incidents in which the spirit of Christmas has had a similar effect in influencing the lives of people whom you know or have read about.

10. Examine the way in which the writer has arranged the scenes of this play to lead up to an important and interesting conclusion. Discuss with your classmates the purpose of each scene to the success of the whole play.

11. In a radio play, there can be no curtain. How did the writer of this play indicate changes of scene? Suggest other ways in which a writer of radio drama might show such changes.

✣ FOR FURTHER READING: ADVENTURES
IN UNDERSTANDING

Louisa May Alcott, *Little Women*
  A story of family life beloved by generations of readers.
Margery Bianco, *Other People's Houses*
  Present-day problems often experienced by unskilled workers.
Betty Cavanna, *Spurs for Suzanna*
  The story of a girl who had a lot to learn about growing up.
Joseph Gollomb, *Windows on the World*
  A story of decision—a choice between personal ambitions and the
  welfare of others.
Douglas Gorsline, *Farm Boy*
  A "problem boy" learns a great deal about farming—and about him-
  self.
Janet Lambert, *Miss Tippy*
  Present-day problems of a teen-ager.
Lois Lenski, *Cotton in My Sack* and *Strawberry Girl*
  Regional stories of Arkansas and Florida.
C. R. Mansell, *The Rag-Tail Patrol*
  Under wise leadership the tarnished reputation of an English Girl
  Guide group is refurbished.
Francis F. Neilson, *Bruce Benson*
  A story of deep-sea diving, kidnapping, and learning how to get along
  with others.
Ella W. Porter, *The Wind's in the West*
  How can a girl make friends with people who do not want to be
  friendly?
Leland Silliman, *The Purple Tide*
  A sports story which includes many aspects of school life.
Elsie Singmaster, *Isle of Que*
  The story of a flood and a boy's victory over personal fears.
Hildegarde Swift, *North Star Shining*
  Pictorial glimpses of Negro friends.
John R. Tunis, *All-American*
  A football story with thrills, suspense, and understanding of school
  life.
Regina Llewellyn Woody, *Boarding School*
  After many mistakes, a young girl finds poise and happiness in
  adjustment to her surroundings.

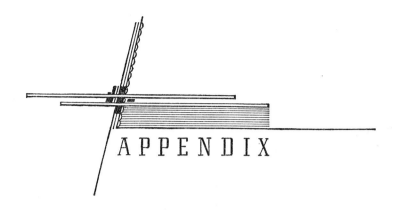

APPENDIX

SOME OF THE AUTHORS IN THIS BOOK

SHERWOOD ANDERSON [1876–1941]

Sherwood Anderson was born in Camden, Ohio, and very early began to earn his own way in the world. He had little time for education after the age of fourteen, but he was an eager reader and gave all his after-work hours to reading and writing. For a time he worked in a factory in Chicago, then found some interesting experiences in the advertising business, and for a short time managed a paint factory in Elyria, Ohio. His longing to write, however, was so great that in the midst of dictating a letter one day, he suddenly rose and walked out of the factory and never returned. From the first, his writing was realistic and concerned with accurate pictures of life as he saw it. His varied experiences had given him understanding of people, and he drew heavily on his own boyhood and youth for material for his stories. In "Stolen Day" he has recorded a personal experience which might have happened to anyone.

ROSEMARY CARR BENÉT [1898–   ]

Rosemary Carr was working for Chicago *Tribune* in Paris, France, when she met Stephen Vincent Benét, who was there on a fellowship for study and writing. Sharing common interests they were married and began to work together on writing projects. They collaborated in writing portraits of other writers for a book review magazine, and together they wrote *A Book of Americans*. Since the death of her husband Mrs. Benét has been associated with the *Saturday Review of Literature*.

STEPHEN VINCENT BENÉT [1898–1943]

🐟 From the time he was a small boy Stephen Benét was thrilled by stories of America's history and growth. The son of an army officer, he had access to many old military records, and he liked nothing better than to re-create in his own stories and poems the historical incidents that excited him most. One of his best works is *John Brown's Body*, a long poem based on an interesting figure of the Civil War period. Another long poem, *Western Star*, celebrates the westward movement and the American pioneer. With his wife, Rosemary Carr Benét, whom he met as a young student in Paris, he wrote *A Book of Americans*, the clever, witty rhymes that make many American heroes real and very human.

ARTHUR CHRISTOPHER BENSON [1862–1925]

🐟 A. C. Benson was an English scholar, essayist, and poet. Educated at Eton and Cambridge, he spent most of his life as a teacher and writer. As a poet he is best known for the lyric "Land of Hope and Glory" written to Elgar's "Pomp and Circumstance." His novels were not particularly effective. It is for his essays, usually literary and philosophical, that he will be remembered longest.

DORIS J. BERRY [1915–   ]

🐟 Doris J. Berry, the daughter of a clergyman, was born and educated in Alberta. During her University work she specialized in French and German, graduating with B.A. Honours in Modern Languages. To follow a family teaching tradition of several generations, she took her Bachelor of Education degree and taught for several years before going into school broadcast work with the Department of Education. Further specialized training followed at the University of Wisconsin where she studied script-writing and school broadcast teaching techniques. As Co-ordinator of School Broadcasts for Alberta she has had wide experience in aural education and has written many outstanding radio scripts. One of these, *Paul at Philippi*, was presented on the *Way of the Spirit* series, produced by the Canadian Broadcasting Corporation.

JEAN BLEWETT [1862–1934]

🐟 Jean McKishnie was born in Kent County, Ontario, and was educated at the St. Thomas Collegiate Institute. She served for many years on the staff of the Toronto *Globe*. In 1915 she retired from active journalism. Besides the novel *Out of the Depths*, she published several volumes of poems *Heart Songs* (1897), *The Cornflower and Other Poems* (1906), and *Poems* (1922).

ROBERT H. BLACKBURN   [1919–   ]

Bob Blackburn is a native Albertan who has, contrary to a well-established Canadian custom, migrated eastwards to become Assistant Librarian at the Toronto University Library. He specialized in English at the University of Alberta, and after graduating, joined the R.C.A.F. to train as a navigator. After graduating at the top of his class from Air Observer School, he was commissioned and appointed navigation instructor. After leaving the air force, he returned to university, studying library science at the University of Toronto. He has had numerous stories and poems published in such magazines as the *Atlantic Monthly*.

JOHN BUCHAN, LORD TWEEDSMUIR   [1875–1940]

John Buchan was educated in Scotland and England. At both Glasgow and Oxford Universities he had a distinguished record before he entered upon his legal training. This won him a post on Lord Milner's staff in 1901. After his return to England in 1903 he wrote the series of novels and biographies for which he is best known. He served in many important journalistic, clerical, and diplomatic offices, and, for his successful career in all of them, received many important awards. He is best known to Canadians as the Governor-General of Canada from 1935-1940.

PEARL BUCK   [1892–   ]

Born in Hillsboro, West Virginia, Pearl Buck was taken to China with her missionary parents when she was only four years old. As might be expected, her childhood was lonely, but there were many bright hours spent with her Chinese *amah* or nurse, who told her stories of the wars, floods, and famines that happen so frequently in China. Her education was supervised almost entirely by her mother, who showed her the singular beauty of Chinese art, music, and literature. It was her mother, too, who encouraged her to write about the Chinese life about her. At seventeen she returned to America and entered Randolph-Macon Woman's College, where, although she was a leader in many activities, she did not feel at home. Returning to China, she taught at the University of Nanking and began to do serious writing. She is probably most famous for her novel, *The Good Earth*, which won the Pulitzer Prize in 1932. Later books also have been concerned with the Chinese people whom she loves and understands. In 1938 she was the third American to receive the Nobel Prize for literature "for rich and genuine epic portrayals of Chinese peasant-life, and for masterpieces of biography."

ROBERT BURNS [1759–1796]

🌑 Robert Burns had few of the early advantages which one might think necessary for the rearing of a great poet. He was born in a humble two-room cottage near Ayr in Scotland and had only a few months' formal schooling. The son of a gardener, he had to do the largest part of the farm work on the "poorest land in Ayrshire" at the age when an average Canadian boy of to-day is entering high school. However, Burns' mother fed his hungry imagination from her rich store of Scottish legends and ballads. Conversations with his kind father taught him many things, and his family encouraged his keen appetite for good reading. He liked to memorize good poetry and to try his hand at imitating what he read. Throughout Burns' poetry, we find his devotion to his native land, Bonnie Scotland. He is known as one of the greatest of the Scottish bards.

MORLEY CALLAGHAN [1903–   ]

🌑 Both Canadians and Americans enjoy the writings of the Canadian author, Morley Callaghan. His works are well known in Canadian and American periodicals. For nine consecutive years he was represented in O'Brien's collections, *The Best Short Stories*. A graduate of St. Michael's College of the University of Toronto, he has been writing since he was twenty-three. At twenty-six he went abroad and there met and was influenced by the American writer, Ernest Hemingway. He has been to many places and seen many people; but he likes best to write about the little problems in human relationships—little problems on which so much of our daily happiness depends. Without preaching, he tries to have his stories point out the causes of misunderstandings and so to suggest how to heal or avoid them.

ELIZABETH COATSWORTH [1893–   ]

🌑 Elizabeth Coatsworth was born in Buffalo, New York, but much of her childhood was spent travelling with her parents. She attended Vassar College and Columbia University. Always interested in books, she began her own career of writing for children when she wrote *The Cat and the Captain* in answer to a friendly argument that had come up between herself and a companion. Since then she has written many books, notably *Alice-All-by-Herself*, *Away Goes Sally*, *Five-Bushel Farm*, *The Fair American*, *The White Horse*, *Trudy and the Tree House*, *Sword of the Wilderness*, and *The Cat Who Went to Heaven*, which won the Newberry Medal as a distinctive piece of writing. Her husband, Henry Beston, is a writer, too, and together they enjoy living on their farm near Damariscotta Lake in Maine.

PADRAIC COLUM [1881—   ]

❧ Padraic Colum is a native of Ireland, but he has lived in America for many years. That is not to say he has forgotten his homeland, for his entire literary success is a product of his Irish heritage. From his grandmother he heard countless stories of the "little people" and fairy folk the Irish love so well, and through his own study of the Irish language and traditional folklore he has become one of Ireland's most famous storytellers. Some years ago, at the invitation of the Hawaiian government, Mr. Colum made a survey of Polynesian folklore and published some of his findings in two books of legends. A more recent book called *Legends of Hawaii* is interesting to young readers. Other popular books by Mr. Colum are *The Children of Odin, The Legend of Saint Colomba, The Adventures of Odysseus,* and *The Tale of Troy.*

FRANCOIS COPPEE [1842—1908]

❧ François Coppée was a French poet and novelist famed for his writings about the problems, joys, and sorrows of the common people. As a young man he worked as a clerk in government service. Much of his spare time was spent reading and studying in the Paris library or wandering about the streets and countryside. He learned to know the simple, humble workers of the cities and the villages, and described their lives with real insight and understanding.

MAUREEN DALY [1921—   ]

❧ The name of Maureen Patricia Daly suggests an Irish ancestry, which is quite correct, for Maureen was born in Castlecanfield, County Tyrone, in Ireland. When she was two years old, her family came to America and settled in Fond du Lac, Wisconsin. She describes her childhood as "pretty routine," and her mother as a strict disciplinarian. After an experience of waiting for a phone call which never came, an experience which most teen-agers understand, Miss Daly wrote the short story "Sixteen," mainly, as she says, "to relieve the tense, hurt feelings inside of me." The story was an immediate success and started her on a career of writing and editing. Following advice to continue writing about what she knew best, she wrote the novel, *Seventeenth Summer.* She is now on the staff of the *Ladies' Home Journal,* where she writes a regular column for teen-age girls.

EMILY DICKINSON [1830—1886]

❧ Emily Dickinson spent most of her life in the quiet home town of Amherst, Massachusetts. Her family was cultured and well-to-do, and

Emily was educated at the South Hadley Female Seminary, now Mount Holyoke College. She had a quick wit and, even as a child, a startling way of expressing herself. Early in life she became somewhat of a recluse and withdrew more and more into a world of her own. Secure within the privacy of her room and garden, she wrote hundreds of the charming little verses that seem to say so much in so few words. Miss Dickinson never intended her work to be published, but after her death more than a thousand poems were found in a bureau drawer. Recognizing their worth, her family arranged for their publication. To-day many of the poems are frequently quoted and some are set to music for choral groups.

WILLIAM O. DOUGLAS [1898–   ]

🏵 William O. Douglas is not primarily a writer, but his recent book, *Of Men and Mountains,* is only further evidence of the brilliant mind and zestful spirit of the learned lawyer and Justice of the United States Supreme Court. Born in Maine, Minnesota, he was brought up in Yakima, Washington—a fortunate locale for a child who was lamed by infantile paralysis and who found the rugged mountains of the Pacific Northwest a means of restoring health and strength. Although handicapped by lack of funds, he worked in ingenious ways to earn money to attend Whitman College at Walla Walla, Washington, and Columbia University Law School. After some years he became a professor of law at Yale and entered the service of the government under Herbert Hoover. President Roosevelt appointed him to the Supreme Court in 1939. The secret of Douglas' success lies perhaps in the spirit with which he has attacked every problem of life. "I learned early that the richness of life is found in adventure," he says. "It develops self-reliance and independence. Life then teems with excitement. There is stagnation only in security. This book [*Of Men and Mountains*] may help others to use the mountains to prepare for adventure."

WILLIAM HENRY DRUMMOND [1854–1907]

🏵 Although William Henry Drummond was born in Ireland, he came to Canada when still a boy. He attended high school and university in Montreal, then trained as a doctor at University of Bishop's College, Lennoxville, Quebec, where in later years he became a professor. Through his fondness for sports and his practice of medicine he developed an insight into the lives of the French-speaking Canadian *habitants* seldom equalled in one of Anglo-Saxon parentage. His sympathy for these people flowered in his poems which have become a permanent part of Canadian literature.

CHARLES J. FINGER [1871—1941]

🐾 Born in Willesden, England, on Christmas Day in 1871, Charles Finger came to America at the age of sixteen. It was not until he was fifty, however, that he began to write the stories of his adventures as a traveller and collector of folklore. As a youth he had attended King's College in London, studied music in Germany, and then travelled over Alaska, Canada, Mexico, and South America. For a time he settled in Texas where he was interested in railroads, but after fourteen years he moved to Arkansas and took up farming. This venture proved unsuccessful, and for more congenial work Finger turned to writing. One of his most popular books is *Tales From Silver Lands,* which is a collection of legends gathered from the Indians of Brazil. *Tales Worth Telling* is a group of fairy stories from Mexico, North Africa, Norway, Ireland, and other countries. Another favourite with young readers is *Courageous Companions,* which tells the story of a boy who sailed with Magellan and represents some of the author's personal experiences.

FRANCES FROST [1905—   ]

🐾 Born near St. Albans, Vermont, Frances Frost attended the local schools and Middlebury College where she was a student until her marriage in 1926. She has taught and done journalistic work. She wrote several volumes of poetry including, *Hemlock Wall, Blue Harvest, These Acres, Pool in the Meadow,* and *Woman of This Earth.* Her first novel, *Innocent Summer,* has been followed by several others. In all her writing the New England scene is an important factor.

ROBERT FROST [1875—   ]

🐾 Robert Frost is considered by many to be America's greatest living poet. Certainly he is one of New England's most famous spokesmen. Born in San Francisco, California, he was taken to his grandfather's home in Lawrence, Massachusetts, when he was ten years old. All his life he hated formal methods of education, although he attended Dartmouth College and Harvard University. For twelve years he tried to make a living by farming but had to supplement his income by teaching. Meanwhile he had published some poems which had created little interest. When the opportunity to sell his farm came, Mr. Frost took his family and went to England. His work was recognized there, and when he returned to America he found that his fame had preceded him. Since then he has taught at various colleges and has continued to produce slim volumes of verse at regular intervals. His poems are filled with the everyday things of New England life and with pictures of the New England countryside. Some of them are deceptively simple—easy to read, yet packed with meaning.

ROBERT E. GARD

🦋 Robert Gard, who incorporated so much of Alberta folklore into his book *Johnny Chinook,* is not an Albertan, but was born and educated in Kansas. After teaching drama and literature at Cornell University, he joined the staff of the University of Alberta to conduct the Alberta Folklore and Local History Project for the Rockefeller Foundation. Although Robert Gard has now left Alberta for Wisconsin, his creation of the character *Johnny Chinook* remains as a memorial of his stay in Western Canada.

THEODOSIA GARRISON [1874–1944]

🦋 Theodosia Garrison was born in Newark, New Jersey. She had a private school education and as a young woman began contributing verse and stories to magazines. Her work as a writer kept her busy for the major part of her life. She was a member of the Author's League and of the Poetry Society of America.

ELSIE PARK GOWAN

🦋 From her native Scotland Elsie Park came to Edmonton with her parents in time to begin her elementary school education. After completing her high school training in Edmonton, she attended the Camrose Normal School and taught for four years in one-room schools before coming up to the University of Alberta. From this university she graduated in 1930 with a B.A. degree with First Class Honours in History. This was followed by three years as a teacher of history in the Lacombe High School. In 1933 she married E. H. Gowan, now Professor of Physics at the University of Alberta. In 1935 Elsie Park Gowan won the Carnegie Award for playwriting with her one-act play, *The Royal Touch.* Encouraged by Miss Sheila Marryat, Mrs. Gowan directed her talents to the writing of historical drama, first in collaboration with Gwen Pharis in *New Lamps for Old* and later by herself. In 1938 the C.B.C. national network carried twenty plays of her series *The Building of Canada.* Since then, Elsie Park Gowan has contributed constantly to the C.B.C. as a free-lance dramatist. In addition, she has contributed talks to the C.B.C. International Service and has taught radio writing at the Banff School of Fine Arts and at Queen's

Summer Radio Institute. *The Royal Touch* is included in *Canadian Plays for Schools* (Ryerson Press); the broadcast on the *Group of Seven* is included in *Proud Procession* (J. M. Dent and Sons (Canada) Limited).

THOMAS CHANDLER HALIBURTON [1796—1865]

🐦 Judge Haliburton was a Canadian historian and humorist born at Windsor, Nova Scotia. After practising law in Halifax, he was elevated to the bench in 1829. In 1841 he became a Judge of the Supreme Court of Nova Scotia. From this position he resigned in 1856 to spend his later years in England where he served as a member of parliament in 1859 and the years following. Besides his *Historical and Statistical Account of Nova Scotia* (1829), Haliburton wrote several series of humorous sketches centred about Sam Slick of Slickville. The "Sam Slick" stories are chiefly important because through them Haliburton developed an indigenous school of Canadian humour making use of American dialect as a medium of expression.

NANCY HALE [1908—]

🐦 Born in Boston, Massachusetts, Nancy Hale counted among her distinguished ancestors Nathan Hale, the famous patriot, Edward Everett Hale, author of "The Man Without a Country;" Lucretia Hale, creator of the well-known family in *The Peterkin Papers;* and great-aunt Harriet Beecher Stowe, who wrote the widely-read *Uncle Tom's Cabin.* It is not surprising, then, that Nancy Hale should turn to writing, although she first studied at the Boston Museum of Fine Arts with the intention of becoming an artist like her parents. She began by writing short stories for magazines, then published several books. She continues to write for current periodicals, frequently describing memories of her youth as she does in the story, "Between the Dark and the Daylight."

THOMAS HARDY [1840—1928]

🐦 Although Thomas Hardy was trained as an architect after he had studied at King's College, London, he left that profession to begin a writing career that was to earn him an enduring place in the history of English literature. Although Hardy is best known as a novelist, his stories never reached the "best seller" class because of their melancholy atmosphere and often tragic themes. Hardy's underlying doubt and sadness are also often evident in his poems.

HILDA MARY HOOKE

Hilda Mary Hooke was born in London, Ontario, and has spent most of her life there. She has written poetry, plays and prose works. With her husband, Richard Smith, she has taken an active part in the producing and directing of plays. Her best-known work is probably *Thunder in the Mountains*. She has also written a volume of plays based on Canadian history. Most of these deal with the beginning of the Talbot settlement north of Lake Erie.

LANGSTON HUGHES [1902—   ]

Langston Hughes was born in Joplin, Missouri, the descendant of Negroes freed before the Civil War. His father was a lawyer and the family lived in many different cities during Langston's boyhood. He began to write poetry as a high-school student in Cleveland, Ohio, but actually did little with it for some years. He gained experience by working in New York, serving as a doorman and cook in Paris, and travelling through Italy and Spain. Working as a bus boy in a hotel, he had an opportunity to show some of his work to the poet, Vachel Lindsay, who encouraged him and helped to get his first poems published. Since then he has written several volumes of verse which picture the lives, thoughts, and feelings of the Negro people. Many of his poems have the rhythm of Negro folk-music; some are rollicking songs, and some are examples of the popular Negro "blues" songs.

(JAMES HENRY) LEIGH HUNT [1784—1859]

Leigh Hunt was born in England in 1784. He early developed a liking for books and especially poetry. He attended Christ's Church 1791-1799. After spending 1803-1805 in his brother's law office and the three following years in the office of the Secretary of War, he became editor of *The Examiner*, a political journal. As a result of critical articles, Hunt and his brother were jailed for some time. An unfortunate venture in Italy in 1821-1825 was followed by Hunt's return to England where he devoted his life to editing and writing. He is noted as a poet, essayist, journalist, critic, and translator.

WILLIAM BRUCE HUTCHISON [1901—   ]

Shortly after his birth at Prescott, Ontario, Bruce Hutchison moved with his parents to British Columbia near the city of Victoria. There he received his public and high school education. An interest in lacrosse in particular and in sports in general led to his becoming a sports writer. In 1925, however, he turned to political reporting with an assignment to the Press Gallery in Ottawa. Since then he has had many important reporting duties both at home and abroad. In 1946 he was associate editor of the *Winnipeg Free Press*. From the variety of his experiences and a keen interest in Canada and her people have come many of his short stories. These have been published in such magazines as the *Saturday Evening Post* and *Cosmopolitan*. *The Unknown Country*, a full-length book, received the Governor-General's Award for non-fiction in 1934. *Hollow Men*, a novel, and *The Fraser*, a contribution in the series of the rivers of America, have added to his importance as a writer.

E. PAULINE JOHNSON (TEKAHIONWAKE) [1862–1913]

🪶 Pauline Johnson was the youngest child of G. H. M. Johnson, head chief of the Six Nations Indians and of a noble Mohawk line. Her mother was of English parentage. She was born on her father's estate, near Brant, Ontario. Pauline Johnson had little formal schooling, but was an avid reader and maker of verses from her earliest childhood. After she grew up, she made many tours across Canada and England, reciting her own poetry. Her self-chosen task in life seems to have been to interpret the Indian to the white man. Although she was very popular in her life-time, with the exception of a few poems her work is now little read.

OSA JOHNSON [1904–   ]

🪶 Osa Johnson's life is as full of excitement as the breath-taking stories she writes. Born in Chanute, Kansas, she met her husband, Martin Johnson, when he was a struggling young photographer travelling about the country. When he decided to make his hobby into a life work, he and Osa spent many years exploring the jungles and wilds of Australia, Borneo, and Africa. Mrs. Johnson and her notebook were inseparable, and each adventure was recorded in detail. Moving-picture films caught many of the thrilling episodes of the jungle, and the Johnsons were able to show stay-at-home Americans some of the amazing habits and customs of wild animals. The airplane made travelling easier for them, and they flew more than 50,000 miles over parts of Africa and Australia.

Martin Johnson's death in 1937 left Osa to carry on the work he had been doing, and she continues their study of wild life in Africa.

HELEN KELLER [1880—   ]

⚜ Helen Keller has often been called a great woman—not for her literary achievements, nor for any artistic contributions, but for her victory over tremendous physical handicaps. Born at Tuscumbia, Alabama, Miss Keller suffered a severe illness when she was little more than a year old, which left her unable to see, hear, or speak. For six years she lived in a world of darkness and silence—unable to communicate in any way with anyone. But her parents did not despair, and soon they were able to find the perfect teacher for Helen—Miss Anne Sullivan, who taught her to "hear" through her finger tips, to read Braille, to type, to sense sound through vibration, even to speak in an almost normal way. For nearly fifty years they were constant companions. Even a college education was not denied Miss Keller, for her textbooks were in Braille and the lectures were spelled into her hand by her willing teacher. Her greatest desire has been to help other handicapped persons. In 1931 she raised a fund of one million dollars for the American Foundation for the Blind, and after World War II she visited wounded veterans in hospitals all over the country. In recent years she has lectured in England, France, Italy, and Greece on behalf of the handicapped. To understand Miss Keller's long struggle and achievements one has only to read the absorbing records of her life—*The Story of My Life, Out of the Dark, Midstream: My Later Life,* and *The World I Live In.*

RUDYARD KIPLING [1865—1936]

⚜ Rudyard Kipling had the good fortune to be born of English parents in Bombay, India. As a small child he learned the native language from his *ayah* or Indian nurse, and many hours were spent listening in wide-eyed enchantment to native tales about the jungle animals. When he was six years old, the boy was sent to England to be educated, and there he spent some of the most miserable and some of the most happy years of his life. Returning to India at seventeen, he began to work as a reporter and soon developed a lively imagination and a flair for writing his own poems and stories. In a search for interesting material to write about, Mr. Kipling travelled widely, visiting China, Japan, and the United States. Later he married an American girl and lived for a short time in Brattleboro, Vermont. There, for the enjoyment of his own children, he wrote the *Jungle Books* and the *Just So Stories,* those delightful tales that relate how the elephant got his trunk and how Mowgli learned the laws of the jungle. Kipling's zest for writing and his popularity with readers continued throughout a long life. Among his books still enjoyed to-day are *Captains Courageous, All the Mowgli Stories, Kim, The Complete Stalky,* and *Songs for Youth,* a small collection of poetry.

SELMA LAGERLÖF [1858–1940]

🙣 Selma Lagerlöf was an obscure teacher in a school for girls in Landskrona, Sweden, when she unexpectedly won a prize for a story submitted to a magazine. From that time on, she gave up all other work and devoted herself to writing. Born on a large estate called Marbacka, she had been lame as a child and had found her chief entertainment in listening to the tales told by the servants and in reading the many books in her father's home. After the publication of her first book, the Swedish school authorities asked Miss Lagerlöf to write a book for children which would keep alive the traditions and well-loved folk tales of Sweden. For this assignment she created the boy who rode all over Sweden on the back of a wild goose and thus learned of the geography, industries, wildlife, and folklore of his country. This book, *The Wonderful Adventures of Nils,* and its sequel, *The Further Adventures of Nils,* won for Miss Lagerlöf the Nobel Prize for literature. She continued to write the fairy tales her lively imagination conjured up, and to-day most of her books have been translated into English for other readers to enjoy.

CHARLES LAMB [1775–1834]

🙣 Charles Lamb lived and wrote more than a hundred years ago, but he still holds an outstanding place among English writers. Born in London, he attended a charity school until he was fourteen. At seventeen he took a job as a clerk in the offices of the trading company known as India House, and there he remained for thirty-three years. He was not unhappy, however, although his life was shadowed by personal tragedy. A strain of insanity ran through the family, and to care for his sister Mary, who suffered from periods of violent depression, Lamb gave up all thought of personal ambition. When Mary was well, they enjoyed working together, and their home became a famous meeting place of the brilliant writers and conversationalists of the day. Lamb's best works are his charming essays on trivial subjects such as "A Chapter on Ears" and "Dissertation on Roast Pig."

WOLFGANG LANGEWIESCHE [1907–   ]

🙣 Wolfgang Langewiesche is well known as a contributor of aviation and scientific articles to current magazines. He is a licensed pilot of gliders, land planes, and sea planes, and during World War II served as a teacher of young military pilots. Besides his skill in flying, he seems to have equal skill in writing on such technical subjects as aerodynamics, weather forecasting, and instrument flying. Perhaps he is able to write clearly and simply because his articles are based on thorough knowledge and personal experience. He never uses background information as a substitute for first-hand investigation. One of his most interesting books is *I'll Take the High Road*. He has also written *Light Plane Flying* and *A Student's Odyssey*.

HENRY WADSWORTH LONGFELLOW   [1807–1882]

℣ Henry Wadsworth Longfellow is one of America's best-loved poets. He was born in the seaport town of Portland, Maine, and received an excellent early education. To please his father he studied law, but his real interest was in literature. Upon his graduation from Bowdoin College, Longfellow studied in Europe for several years and came back to teach languages and literature at Harvard University. He began then to write the long narrative poems for which he is most famous—"The Song of Hiawatha," "The Courtship of Miles Standish," and "Evangeline." Many of his short poems have great appeal to children, and because he was so generally loved by the children of Cambridge, he became known as "the children's poet." His work, more than that of any other early poet, helped to spread the love of poetry in America.

JEAN BAPTISTE LULLY   [1633–1687]

℣ Born at Florence, Italy, Lully went to Paris at the age of fourteen. Through his musical ability he soon won recognition at the French court, becoming court composer by 1653 and royal music superintendent by 1672. He became most famous for his operas, *Alceste* (1674), *Theseé* (1675), *Atys* (1676), *Phaeton* (1683), *Roland* (1635), and *Armide* (1686). His work added a distinctive character to French opera of the latter part of the eighteenth century.

CYRUS MACMILLAN   [1882–   ]

℣ The Honourable Cyrus MacMillan was born at Wood Island, P.E.I.   He received his education at Prince of Wales College, Charlottetown, at McGill University, and at Harvard University. Except for a period of service during the First World War and a short parliamentary career in which he served as a minister in the Federal Cabinet in 1930, Cyrus MacMillan devoted his life to education. After 1924 he was a Professor of English and Chairman of the English Department at McGill University. His writings include *Canadian Fairy Tales, The Folk-Songs of Canada, Tales the Woodsman Told, McGill and Its Story, Canadian Wonder Tales,* and *Canadian Hero Stories.*

NELLIE L. MCCLUNG

🦋 Nellie McClung was born in Chatsworth, Ontario, but received her education in Manitoba where she lived until she moved to Alberta in 1914. In recent years she has been resident in Victoria, B.C. She took an active part in the social, religious, and political life of the communities in which she lived. For a time she was a member of parliament in Alberta. She is chiefly noted for her novels and short stories which deal largely with the Western Canadian scene, much of it with a Manitoba background. From 1936-1942 she served on the Board of Governors of the Canadian Broadcasting Corporation.

THOMAS BABINGTON MACAULAY [1800—1859]

🦋 Even at the early age of seven years, Thomas Babington Macaulay gave some indications of his future genius by writing history and poetry. This remarkable child learned to read at the age of three, and all his life he was interested in literature. After attending a private school, he attended Cambridge University. Although he later studied law, he soon left the legal profession to devote his life to writing, in which field he became an outstanding essayist, poet, and historian. In 1830 he entered Parliament, becoming an outstanding and eloquent debater and exerted his influence to effect badly needed political reforms. In 1842 he published his *Lays of Ancient Rome,* from which "How Horatius Kept the Bridge" is taken. In 1857 Queen Victoria created him Baron Macaulay of Rothley.

EDWARD ALEXANDER MCCOURT [1907—   ]

🦋 Though born in Ireland, Edward McCourt received his elementary and high school education in Alberta schools. He graduated from the University of Alberta with a B.A. degree in 1932. A Rhodes Scholarship took him to Oxford where he received the B.A. and M.A. degrees. Since his return to Canada he has taught at Ridley College, Upper Canada College, Queen's University and the University of Saskatchewan where he is now an Associate Professor of English. His literary output includes several critical articles, a number of short stories, and two books, *The Flaming Hour* and *Music at the Close.* "Box Social" is an excerpt from *The Flaming Hour.*

D. A. MACMILLAN

🎋 Don MacMillan grew up in Regina, Saskatchewan, where he early became keenly interested in hockey. Unable to make the grade as a professional hockey player himself, he became a sports writer, in which field he is still active. He has also written fiction and articles, and worked in the radio industry. During World War II he enlisted in the R.C.A.F. Found unfit for flying duties, he was transferred to the Public Relations branch of the service. As a result of his experience in this work he wrote *Only the Stars Know*, from which "Jumbo" is taken. Since the war he has also written a novel called *Rink Rat*.

JOHN MASEFIELD [1878–]

🎋 John Masefield was born in England and early showed a dislike for school and a love for the sea. At fourteen he was apprenticed to a sea captain and began the first of the voyages which gave him the experiences that have furnished material for so much of his writing. When he was seventeen he decided to settle down in America for a while and worked at various jobs to earn his living—in a bakery, a livery stable, a carpet factory. Afternoons and evenings were spent with his favourite form of entertainment—reading. It was while reading a book of poems that he suddenly decided to try his hand at writing—and he began then to train himself for the career of a poet. Besides his *Salt Water Ballads*, he has written many adventure stories and other types of prose. *Jim Davis* and *Mainsail Haul* are especially exciting reading for boys. In 1930, Masefield succeeded Bridges as Poet Laureate and was awarded the O.M. in 1935.

VINCENT MASSEY [1887–]

🎋 Vincent Massey was born and educated in Toronto where he graduated from the University of Toronto with the B.A. degree. After receiving his M.A. degree from Oxford University, he returned to the University of Toronto as a lecturer in modern history. Since then he has had a distinguished career as a soldier, statesman, administrator, and author. From 1935-46 he was the Canadian High Commissioner for Canada in the United Kingdom. Among the many honours which he now holds is that of Chancellor of the University of Toronto. He was recently head of a Royal Commission investigating the cultural phases of Canadian life. The honours he has received are a worthy tribute to his life of service to Canadians, and in 1952 he became the first Canadian to be appointed Governor-General of Canada.

ELLIOTT MERRICK [1905–   ]

🐦 Elliott Merrick was born in 1905 and has lived most of his life on the farm. In 1948 he wrote *Green Mountain Farm.*

OGDEN NASH [1902–   ]

🐦 Ogden Nash, born in Rye, New York, comes from an old Southern family, one of whom gave his name to the city of Nashville, Tennessee. He attended Harvard for a year but gave up school for business in New York. For a time he served as a manuscript reader for a publishing house where, he says, he found other people's manuscripts so poor he was inspired to write his own. Nash's chief claim to fame is his light verse in which he "treads gently on all toes." He likes to poke fun at women's hats, salads, strenuous athletics, and infants. He has an original style and an ingenious system of making words rhyme. His work appears frequently in the *New Yorker* and the *Saturday Evening Post.*

ALFRED NOYES [1880–   ]

🐦 Born in Staffordshire, England, Alfred Noyes enjoyed a childhood rich with books. In college at Oxford, he continued to read enormously and thus prepared himself for his own writing career. Almost immediately following his graduation, he wrote successful poems and knew little of the hardships some writers experience in getting started. His poetry was especially popular in America and for some years he taught at Princeton University. During World War I he served on a British trawler on mine-destroying duty in the Baltic Sea. In the Second World War his home on the Isle of Wight was taken over by the British government, and Noyes moved to Santa Barbara, California, where he is a member of the faculty of the University of California.

EDWIN J. PRATT [1883–   ]

🐦 Born the son of a Methodist minister at Western Bay, Newfoundland, E. J. Pratt was educated at St. John's, and at Victoria College, Toronto. Though he had intended to enter the ministry, he became first a lecturer in psychology in the University of Toronto and later, through the interest of Pelham Edgar, a professor of English in Victoria College. His poetic work has shown great variety in subject and treatment. His shorter lyrics show "wit, fancy, and a capacity for irony." His narratives of the sea, of which "The Cachalot" is typical, are full of vitality and action. They show man in his ever-constant struggle with primitive nature His long poem, "Brébeuf and his Brethren," is a study in appreciation of the character of the Jesuits who ministered to the Indians and French during the early period of Canadian history. As editor of the *Canadian Poetry Magazine,* Professor Pratt for many years gave encouragement to many young Canadian poets. E. K. Brown places Pratt among the central figures in Canadian poetry.

MARJORIE KINNAN RAWLINGS   [1896—   ]

🙞 As early as the age of eleven, Marjorie Kinnan Rawlings had begun to write stories and had decided that she would become a writer. She was born in Washington, D. C., and after graduating from Wisconsin University she did newspaper work in Louisville, New York City, and Rochester. She cared little for this type of writing, however, because it always had to be done in a hurry. It was during a visit to Florida that she found the quiet surroundings and peacefulness she had been looking for, and with money from the sale of her father's farm she purchased a large orange plantation in Cross Creek, Florida. Here she wrote *The Yearling,* the poignant story of Jody Baxter which seems destined to become a classic. The countryside near her home has become known as "the Yearling country," and Mrs. Rawlings' work continues to deal with material "round her own back door."

ADJUTOR RIVARD   [1868—1945]

🙞 Born at St. Grégoire, Quebec, Rivard attended Le Petit Seminary from which he graduated with the M.A. degree in 1900. He received the D. Litt. degree from Laval University, Quebec, in 1902. In 1918 he was given the LL. D. degree. In 1921 Rivard became a Justice of the Court of Appeal, P. Q. Prior to this he had practised law and had served as a professor at Laval University, first on the faculty of arts and later on the faculty of law. He wrote widely both in the field of law and the field of literature. Many awards were made to him for his professional and literary contribution. *Chez Nous,* from which the excerpt in this text is taken, was written in 1914. The translation here is from that of Hume Blake made in 1924.

SIR CHARLES G. D. ROBERTS   [1860—1943]

🙞 Roberts comes of a writing family, for his brothers and his cousin, Bliss Carman, were also contributors to Canadian literature. Born near Fredericton, New Brunswick, Roberts was educated at the University of New Brunswick where he received a sound classical education. From 1896-1907 he lived in New York. During the First World War he was in the active force, serving later with Lord Beaverbrook in the writing of the official account of Canada's participation in that war. He has won for himself a reputation as a narrator of animal and nature stories and as a writer of Canadian nature poetry. Though his work shows a strong influence of Wordsworth, it is individual in its sensitivity to the Canadian scene. Roberts expressed through his verse an intimate understanding of the Canadian landscape in its many dresses.

ARCHIBALD RUTLEDGE [1883–]

🙰 Archibald Rutledge grew up on a great plantation in South Carolina where he learned to know its swamps and snakes and every form of wildlife that inhabited its acres. When he was twenty-four, he began to write about what he had learned. Since then a steady stream of poetry and prose has come from his pen. One of his most popular books is *Wild Life of the South,* and many of his stories and articles appear in current magazines. He is known as a champion of wild creatures and writes of them with the sympathy and understanding that are expressed in his essay, "Dilemmas of the Wild." He still lives on Hampton Plantation in McClellanville, South Carolina.

CARL SANDBURG [1878–]

🙰 Carl Sandburg was born in Galesburg, Illinois, the son of Swedish immigrants. As a boy he worked at all kinds of jobs to help his family and to educate himself. At Lombard College in Galesburg he discovered his inclination for writing, but for several years after graduation he was interested in politics and worked on various newspapers. Then he began to write poetry seriously and to travel about the country lecturing and reading his own work. On his travels he collected a huge assortment of ballads and folk songs directly from the people, and one of his chief delights is to read from *The American Songbag.* His poetry is extremely varied, ranging from descriptions of city noise and confusion to quiet nature lyrics and shrewd analyses of people and nations. His prose, too, is varied and includes both fiction and nonfiction. Among his best books for young people are the biography, *Abe Lincoln Grows Up,* and his collections of poems, *Early Moon* and *Smoke and Steel.*

LEW SARETT [1888–]

🙰 Lew Sarett is a foremost American poet and teacher. As a child he spent a good bit of his time roaming the North Woods near Lake Superior where he learned to know and understand the wildlife around him. He had many friends among the Indians and was adopted in a tribal ceremony by the Chippewa Indians of the region. For the most part Mr. Sarett worked his own way through school by acting as guide and ranger during the summer months. Although he studied law, teaching is his real interest. At present he is on the faculty of Northwestern University.

RUTH SAWYER [1880–   ]

❧ Born in Boston, Massachusetts, Ruth Sawyer was educated in private schools in New York and at Columbia University. During her childhood she spent hour upon hour listening to old Irish folk tales told by her nurse, and when the opportunity to go to Ireland presented itself, she began to make a fascinating collection of stories and bits of folklore. She also studied Spanish and collected Spanish folk tales, and soon was known as one of the few really great story-tellers in the United States. In private life she is Mrs. Albert C. Durand, and lives in Ithaca, New York. Among her best books is *Roller Skates,* which tells of her life as a child in New York City and which won the Newberry Medal for distinguished literature in 1937. *The Year of Jubilee* is also a delightful book.

DUNCAN CAMPBELL SCOTT [1862–1947]

❧ Born in Ottawa, Duncan Campbell Scott was educated in the public school there and at Stanstead College, Quebec. He entered the Department of Indian Affairs of the Federal Government of Canada and continued his service there until his retirement. For many years he was head of that department. His avocational interests included both music and poetry. His poetry has a wide variety of style and of subject matter and is marked by precision of diction, beauty of word music, and power of imagery.

SAMUEL SCOVILLE, JR. [1872–1950]

❧ Samuel Scoville, Jr. was born in Norwich, New York. His father was a minister and his mother was the daughter of the famous preacher, Henry Ward Beecher. His interest in writing began while he was a student at Yale, but he chose law as his profession and used writing as an avocation. He especially enjoyed nature study and liked to write about his observations. Among his early books are *Wild Folk, Lords of the Wild,* and *Man and Beast.* Nature stories written especially for young readers are *Boy Scouts in the Wilderness, The Blue Pearl, The Inca Emerald,* and *The Out-of-Doors Club.*

ARMSTRONG SPERRY [1897–]

🜚 Armstrong Sperry was born in New Canaan, Connecticut, and in-herited a passion for sea adventure. As a boy he listened to his great-grandfather's stories of the China Seas, of islands rich in pearls and inhabited by cannibals. Armstrong was sure that some day he must find these islands. Years later his early ambition was kindled afresh by the reading of Frederick O'Brien's story, *White Shadows in the South Seas.* Day and night the tale haunted him. Yielding at last, he went to Tahiti and from there to the island of Bora Bora.

Eager for adventure, Mr. Sperry found more than excitement and thrilling experiences. He found friendship and respect for the strange people of the islands. He saw their islands swept by hurricanes, their homes and crops destroyed. He watched them patiently rebuild those homes and replace the vanilla bean vines, the main source of their liveli-hood. He saw them meet disaster with supreme courage. It is this cour-age that is the theme of many of Mr. Sperry's books. Whether he writes of storm at sea or of pioneer days in the West, Mr. Sperry reveals the quiet heroism with which simple people face unexpected misfortune. Among his most interesting books are *Call It Courage, All Sail Set,* and *Storm Canvas.*

JOHN STEINBECK [1902–]

🜚 John Steinbeck was born in Salinas, California, where his father was a local county official and where his mother had taught in the tiny red schoolhouse of the Big Sur country. When he began to write, it was this locale that provided the setting for much of his work. For a time he studied at Stanford University, taking only such courses as interested him. In the years that followed he travelled about the country and worked at a number of miscellaneous jobs. He was a reporter on a New York paper, a bricklayer, a chemist, and a caretaker. In the meantime he had begun to write, but it was not until his fourth book was published that he really found success. Most of his books are concerned with human problems, and he writes in the realistic fashion of "Gabi-lan." As he shows in that story, he sees the beauty and joy of life as well as its pain and cruelty.

WALLACE STEGNER [1909–]

🜚 Wallace Stegner was born in Lake Mills, Iowa, but his family moved about so much that he calls himself the "original homeless and footloose American." He has lived in North Dakota, Washington, Sas-katchewan, Montana, Utah, Nevada, California, and Vermont. Working as a salesman, part-time teacher, or at other odd jobs, he studied at the University of Utah and Iowa University. When his novelette, *Remembering Laughter,* won a $2500 prize, he settled down to serious writing. For a time he taught at the University of Wisconsin and now holds a post at Harvard. His writings are filled with stories of his own childhood, and he resolutely refuses to have "a battery of card files and secretaries" to prevent inaccuracies in his work. He prefers to make a personal search for his material and to rely on his memories.

ALEXANDER MAITLAND STEPHEN [1882–1942]

Alexander Maitland Stephen was born in Grey County, Ontario, but upon graduating from high school moved to Kamloops, B. C. Eventually he became a school teacher, but worked at many different occupations—on the stage, in logging camps, on cattle ranches, and the like. His published works include four books of verse, two novels, a book of historical plays for classroom use, and two school anthologies. Mr. Stephen also gained renown as a contributor to literary journals and as a lecturer, making several cross-country trips for this purpose. As a result of military service during World War I, he lost the use of his right arm, but learned not only to write but also to type with his left hand.

FRANK R. STOCKTON [1834–1902]

Boys and girls everywhere enjoy the stories of Frank R. Stockton, who inherited a love of writing from his father. Born in Philadelphia, Stockton ended his formal studies when he graduated from high school. He immediately found a job as an engraver, but while he worked, he planned fairy tales full of giants, gnomes, dragons, and magic of all kinds. When the day's work was done, he rushed home to write the stories which were waiting impatiently to be put into words. Stockton liked to amuse readers by writing surprise stories with puzzling and unsolved endings. Perhaps his most entertaining and perplexing story is "The Lady or the Tiger?" which he wrote to read to a group of club members. So many listeners enjoyed it that it has since been translated into many different languages. Other humorous books which are still enjoyed are *Rudder Grange* and *The Casting Away of Mrs. Lecks and Mrs. Aleshine.*

JESSE STUART [1907–   ]

Jesse Stuart is naturally proud of the recognition he has won as a poet, short story writer, and novelist, but he is even more proud of his family and his Kentucky heritage. Indeed, it is to the hill people of his native state that he owes his success, for they have provided the characters and material for his stories and longer books. Convinced that the most sincere writing is that which comes out of one's first-hand experience, he has written of the mountain people with sympathetic insight and understanding. He knows their problems, their struggles, their joys, and hopes, and has made them real to his readers. His stories have appeared in many magazines such as *Harper's*, the *Atlantic Monthly*, and the *Saturday Evening Post*. Because he genuinely likes farm people everywhere he also frequently has stories published in *Household Magazine* and other publications directed to a rural audience. Since his service in World War II he has returned to his farm in Kentucky where he continues to be interested in education and regional projects for the well being of his people. Among his more recent publications are *Taps for Private Tussy*, 1943, *Album of Destiny*, 1944, (poems), *Foretaste of Glory*, 1946, (novel), *Tales from the Plum Grove Hills*, 1946, (stories), and *The Thread That Runs So True*, 1949.

EDWARD WILLIAM THOMPSON [1849–1924]

✻ Edward William Thompson was born and brought up in Ontario. He served with a cavalry regiment during the Civil War in the United States and with the Queen's Own Rifles in the Fenian Raid. He was for many years editorial writer for the Toronto *Globe* and later edited the *Youth's Companion*. For several years he lived in Ottawa as the correspondent of the *Boston Transcript*. He is best known for his short stories, especially for *Old Man Savarin*.

WALT WHITMAN [1819–1892]

✻ Walt Whitman was born in West Hills, Long Island. He had little formal schooling, but learned much from his boyhood experiences roaming around New York, Brooklyn, and the shores of Long Island. All his life he was greatly interested in people and made many friends among all kinds. As a young man he took a trip to New Orleans which gave him a new understanding of the country and developed his friendly spirit of brotherhood. During the Civil War he became a nurse and served the wounded with amazing devotion. When he began to write, he put all his love for people into his poetry, writing on friendship, love, the brotherhood of man, and the meaning of democracy. He wrote in "free verse," discarding the usual patterns of rhythm and rhyme. It was no wonder that his poetry was not well received at first—it was too different from the poetry that people knew. But in the last years of his life, while he suffered from the effects of a paralytic stroke, his genius was recognized and people flocked to his home in Camden, New Jersey, to visit him. He is still one of America's greatest spokesmen for democracy.

EDWARD CARRUTHERS WOODLEY [1878–   ]

❧ E. C. Woodley was born in Montreal where he received his high school education and later graduated from McGill University. He had an outstanding career as a teacher both in India and Canada. Of late years he has served the Quebec Department of Education as a special officer. Many honours have been accorded him, not least of which was his election as a Fellow of the Royal Historical Society. His published works include historical treatises on India and Canada, legends of French Canada, and numerous literature and history texts. He makes his home in Montreal.

ELINOR WYLIE [1885–1928]

❧ Elinor Wylie, born in Somerville, New Jersey, came from an important and wealthy family in Pennsylvania. She was educated in private schools in Philadelphia and Washington, and for a long time wavered between her interest in literature and her desire to paint. She finally found herself in writing delicate poems filled with emotional feeling and vivid imagery. With her husband, William Rose Benét, she established a kind of literary colony in New York and became a recognized leader among writers. Much of her work is for adults, but young people like the pictures she creates in such poems as "Velvet Shoes."

❧

CHORAL READING

When people tap their feet to music, or sing softly while an orchestra plays, or join in group singing, they are saying, "We want to take part." That desire of everyone to take part, rather than to sit and watch or listen to someone else perform, is one of the reasons choral reading has come to be a popular activity. Hearing one person read aloud can be an enjoyable experience, but if that person goes on for hours, his voice becomes monotonous to us. This cannot happen in choral speaking, for in group participation there can be a great variety of voice combinations. Choral reading is new in name, but it is old in the customs of people. New ways of reading have been devised, but the activity itself is related to group singing, group praying, and even to the massed cheering heard at athletic contests. More and more groups are finding it a delightful form of reading.

Everyone recognizes the fact that speaking voices are different from each other. If you are at a distance from two people who are talking together, you may be able to hear the sound of their voices but not what they are saying. The difference between their voices is in something called *timbre*. All voices can be identified according to their timbre and can be separated into three groups known as *light*, *medium*, and *dark* voices. Singing groups are usually divided into basses, tenors, altos, and sopranos in this same way.

Most classes, of course, read aloud together frequently. That is called "unison" reading. Choral reading, however, goes further than unison reading by making some very pleasing sound effects through different combinations of grouped voices. Sometimes all of the boys read together—especially material which represents a man's view or activity. Sometimes the girls will read. Occasionally there will be a "solo" part, as in music, when a single voice is used to represent the words or thoughts of an individual person. Sometimes, too, the whole group will read together—the combined dark, medium, and light voices being used effectively to bring out the desired meaning of the poem or other material being read.

Poetry is the written material that sounds best when read chorally. One of the reasons for this is that poetry has a natural rhythm that keeps the group together. Another reason is that poetry is usually written to be read aloud—certain sounds and word combinations being conceived by the poet to create the picture or emotion he desires to effect in his reader.

The first thing that must be done before any poem can be read chorally is to classify the voices of the group. Once this is done, the classifications can remain for all poems in which this activity is used. To make this classification, the group may read a poem in unison, while the teacher listens to individual voices and classifies them. All pupils with dark voices will sit together as a group; all with medium voices as another group; and all light voices as still another. When all the voices of each classification read together, any misplaced voice will stand out from the group and can be reclassified. The groups are then ready to read according to the marginal directions for the poem or according to any other plan of reading they may desire. Many varied combinations may be worked out and there can be fun in experimentation, but the meaning of the poem should be thoroughly understood before choral reading is attempted.

❦

ACKNOWLEDGMENTS

Appleton-Century-Crofts, Inc.: "El Poniente" from *Narratives in Verse* by Ruth Comfort Mitchell, copyright, 1923, D. Appleton & Company; "The Reef" by Samuel Scoville, Jr., from *St. Nicholas Magazine,* copyright, 1923, Century Company; both reprinted by permission of the publishers, Appleton-Century-Crofts, Inc.

Doris J. Berry: "To You is Born."

Robt. H. Blackburn: "Recipe for Pork". First published in *Atlantic Monthly,* 1947.

Brandt & Brandt: "Two Rivers" by Wallace Stegner, copyright, 1942, by Wallace Stegner; "Clara Barton" from *A Book of Americans* published by Rinehart & Company, Inc., copyright, 1933, by Rosemary and Stephen Vincent Benét.

Christian Herald Magazine: "He Gave Them Windows" by J. Alvin Kugelmass.

B. J. Chute and *Boys' Life Magazine:* "Ski High."

Coward-McCann, Inc.: "The Navajo" from *Compass Rose* by Elizabeth Coatsworth, copyright, 1929, by Coward-McCann, Inc.

J. M. Dent & Sons (Canada) Limited: "Jumbo" from *Only the Stars Know* by D. A. MacMillan; "On Being Canadian" from *On Being Canadian* by Vincent Massey; "En Roulant Ma Boule" from *Canadian Folk Songs Old and New,* edited by J. Murray Gibbon.

Dorrance & Company, Inc.: "And Yet Fools Say" from *Yes, This is Washington* by George Sanford Holmes, reprinted by permission of the author; "Forest Fire" from *Blue Hills* by Edna Davis Romig.

Doubleday & Company, Inc.: "The Dreamers" from *The Dreamers and Other Poems* by Theodosia Garrison, copyright, 1917, by Doubleday & Company, Inc.; "Three Days to See" from *Three Days to See* by Helen Keller, copyright, 1933, reprinted by permission of Doubleday & Company, Inc.; "The Rat Trap" from *Harvest* by Selma Lagerloff, copyright, 1934, 1935, by Doubleday & Company, Inc.

Executive Council of the Provincial Government of Newfoundland: "Ode to Newfoundland" by Cavendish Boyle.

Frances Frost: "Early Mowing."

W. J. Gage and Company Limited, Toronto: "A Canadian Abroad" by Edward W. Thompson, from *An Introduction to Literature.*

George Allen & Unwin Ltd., London: "The South" by Wang Chien from *More Poems from the Chinese,* translated by Arthur Waley.

Ginn and Company, Toronto: Words and Music for "Red River Valley" from *On Wings of Song* by Marguerite V. Hood, Glenn Gildersleeve, and Helen S. Leavitt.

Mark Hager and *Collier's Magazine*: "The Magic Cane."

Harcourt, Brace and Company, Inc.: "The Long Jump" from *I'll Take the High Road* by Wolfgang Langewiesche, copyright, 1939, by Wolfgang Langewiesche, reprinted by permission of Harcourt, Brace and Company, Inc.; "Elephants are Different to Different People" from *Home Front Memo* by Carl Sandburg, copyright, 1943, by Carl Sandburg, reprinted by permission of Harcourt, Brace and Company, Inc.

Harper & Brothers: "Kloochman" from *Of Men and Mountains* by William O. Douglas, copyright, 1950, by William O. Douglas.

Henry Holt and Company, Inc.: "Prayers of Steel" from *Cornhuskers* by Carl Sandburg, copyright, 1918, by Henry Holt and Company, Inc., copyright, 1943, by Carl Sandburg; "The Last Word of a Bluebird" from *Complete Poems of Robert Frost*. Copyright, 1930, 1949, by Henry Holt and Company, Inc.; "October Snow" and "Angus McGregor" from *The Collected Poems of Lew Sarett*, copyright, 1922, 1931, 1941, by Henry Holt and Company, Inc. All used by permission of the publishers.

Houghton Mifflin Company: "How Cyrus Laid the Cable" by John Godfrey Saxe.

Ethel Jacobson and *The Saturday Review of Literature*: "Sleight-of-Spring."

Selwyn James and *The Readers' Digest*: "My Encounter with a Bushman."

Alfred A. Knopf, Inc.: "Youth from *The Dream Keeper* by Langston Hughes, by permission of Alfred A. Knopf, Inc., copyright, 1932, by Alfred A. Knopf, Inc.; "Velvet Shoes" from *Collected Poems* by Elinor Wylie, by permission of Alfred A. Knopf, Inc., copyright, 1921, 1932, by Alfred A. Knopf, Inc.

John Lane The Bodley Head Limited: "The Hawk" by A. C. Benson from *Twentieth Century Poetry*.

J. B. Lippincott Company: "John Philip Sousa" from *Story-Lives of American Composers* by Katherine Little Bakeless, copyright, 1941, by J. B. Lippincott Company; "The Lady and the Elephants" from *I Married Adventure*, by Osa Johnson, by permission of the publishers, J. B. Lippincott Company; "The Highwayman" by Alfred Noyes, from *Collected Poems in One Volume*, copyright, 1906, 1934, 1947, by Alfred Noyes, reprinted by permission of J. B. Lippincott Company.

Little, Brown & Company: "The Snake" from *The Poems of Emily Dickinson*, edited by Martha Dickinson and Alfred Leete Hampson, reprinted by permission of the publishers; "Adventures of Isabel" by Ogden Nash, copyright, 1936, by Ogden Nash.

by Elsie Park Gowan, by permission of the author, Lady Tweedsmuir, and Thomas Nelson & Sons Limited, Edinburgh.

Harold Ober Associates: "Stolen Day" by Sherwood Anderson, copyright, 1941, by Eleanor Anderson, reprinted by permission of Harold Ober Associates.

Theodore Presser Co.: Words for "Au Clair de la Lune" from *The Junior A Cappella Chorus Book,* copyright, 1932, Oliver Ditson Company. Reprinted by permission of Theodore Presser Co.

Random House, Inc.: "Koch" from *Great Men of Medicine* by Ruth Fox, reprinted by permission of Random House, Inc., copyright, 1947, by Random House, Inc.

Archibald Rutledge: "Dilemmas of the Wild."

The Ryerson Press, Toronto: "The Fishers of the Air" from *Wisdom of the Wilderness* by Sir Charles G. D. Roberts; "Ottawa Before Dawn" by Duncan Campbell Scott, by permission of the Estate of Duncan Campbell Scott and The Ryerson Press; "This is Canada" by Morley Callaghan from *This is Canada;* "Box Social" from *The Flaming Hour* by Edward McCourt, by permission of the author and The Ryerson Press.

Charles Scribner's Sons: "Between the Dark and the Daylight" from *Between the Dark and the Daylight* by Nancy Hale, copyright, 1936, 1943, by Nancy Hale; "Without Words" from *Frost and Fire* by Elliott Merrick, copyright, 1939, by Elliott Merrick; "This is Jody's Fawn" from *The Yearling* by Marjorie Kinnan Rawlings, copyright, 1938, by Marjorie Kinnan Rawlings; "The Lady or the Tiger?" by Frank R. Stockton; all used by permission of the publishers, Charles Scribner's Sons.

Simon and Schuster, Inc.: Melody notes for "Au Clair de la Lune" from *Fireside Book of Folk Songs.*

The L. W. Singer Company, Inc.: "The Violin-Maker of Cremona" by François Coppée, translated by Mary J. Nelson.

The Estate of A. M. Stephen: For "There's a Wild Rose Tangled in the Prairie's Wool" and "Seeding Time at McCarthy's" from the volume *Brown Earth and Bunch Grass.*

Jesse Stuart: "Old Gore."

The Viking Press, Inc.: "The Magic Box" from *The Way of the Storyteller* by Ruth Sawyer, copyright, 1942, by Ruth Sawyer; "Gabilan," a selection from *The Red Pony* by John Steinbeck, copyright, 1937, by John Steinbeck; reprinted by permission of The Viking Press, Inc., New York.

A. P. Watt & Son, London: "If" from *Rewards and Fairies* by Rudyard Kipling, copyright, 1910, by Rudyard Kipling, reprinted by permission of Mrs. George Bambridge and the Macmillan Company of Canada Limited.

The John C. Winston Company: "The Tale of Anahuac" from *Golden Tales From Faraway* by Charles J. Finger.

E. C. Woodley: "The Phantom of Percé Rock".

Yale University Press: "The Woman from Lalo-Hana" from *Legends of Hawaii* by Padraic Colum.

Whilst every effort has been made to trace the owners of copyrights, in a few cases this has proved impossible and we take this opportunity of tending our apologies to any owners whose rights may have been unwittingly infringed.

🌿

INDEX OF TITLES

✿

INDEX OF AUTHORS